## University of Plymouth Library

Subject to status this item may be renewed
via your Voyager account

**http://voyager.plymouth.ac.uk**

Exeter  tel: (01392) 475049
Exmouth  tel: (01395) 255331
Plymouth  tel: (01752) 232323

The Major International
Treaties since 1945

# The Major International Treaties Since 1945
## A *history and guide with texts*

J.A.S. Grenville and
Bernard Wasserstein

Methuen

London and New York

First published in 1987 by
Methuen & Co. Ltd
11 New Fetter Lane, London EC4P 4EE

Published in the USA by
Methuen & Co.
in association with Methuen, Inc.
29 West 35th Street, New York NY 10001

Printed in Great Britain by T.J. Press (Padstow) Ltd
Padstow, Cornwall

**British Library Cataloguing in Publication Data**
Grenville, J.A.S.
  The major treaties since 1945: a history
  and guide with texts.
  1. Treaties – Collections
  I. Title    II. Wasserstein, Bernard
  341'.026    JX171

  ISBN 0-416-38080-8

**Library of Congress Cataloging in Publication Data**
Grenville, J.A.S. (John Ashley Soames), 1928–
  The major international treaties since 1945.

  Includes index.
  1. Treaties – Collections.    2. World politics –
20th century.  I. Wasserstein, Bernard.  II. Title.
JX171.C745  1987    341'.026    87-11250
ISBN 0-416-38080-8

# Contents

# Preface

The purpose of this book is to provide the texts of the major international treaties since the Second World War, together with the necessary historical background and analysis. This is not meant to be a diplomatic history; it is intended for use with such histories. The introductory sections in each chapter have accordingly been limited to the minimum necessary to render the treaty texts and their context intelligible to the reader.

An earlier version of this book was published in 1974 as *The Major International Treaties 1914–1973*, edited by J.A.S. Grenville. The present volume incorporates much from the earlier edition, covering the years 1945 to 1973. But changes in international diplomacy since 1974 have been so great that the entire text has had to be revised thoroughly for the period 1945 to 1973. In addition a large number of treaties have been added for the period 1974–86. Almost one-third of the book is now concerned with the later period, reflecting in particular the large production of treaties in the period 1974–9 when détente was still alive and when Middle East peace efforts were at their height.

The most authoritative source for treaty texts in the post-war period is the *United Nations Treaty Series*. By 1985 this series had reached volume 1093. Unfortunately the U.N. series suffers from a number of defects. Article 102 of the United Nations Charter requires that 'every treaty and every international agreement entered into by any Member of the United Nations after the present Charter comes into force shall as soon as possible be registered with the Secretariat and published by it'. Most treaties are so registered, but not all (secret agreements, of course, are neither registered nor published), and many States delay before registering treaties. Even in the case of treaties that are registered, a further long delay generally ensues before publication by the U.N. In 1985 the U.N. series was still engaged in publishing the volumes for the year 1978 (many of these treaties, registered in 1978, had been concluded in 1977, 1976, or even earlier). The non-membership of some States in the U.N. has further limited registration of treaties, and consequently the usefulness of the U.N. series. For all these reasons the U.N. series, although the best starting point for the collection of treaty texts, is incomplete, and in the case of treaties for the past decade almost useless.

Treaty texts in this book have generally been drawn from the U.N. series or (in the case of more recent treaties which have not yet been reached by the United Nations series) from the facsimile reproductions in the periodical, *International Legal Materials*. Many treaties are printed in full. But others are so long that they have had to be edited. In all cases where excisions have been made these have been indicated by an ellipse mark (. . .). In general, the parts omitted have been the more technical sections of treaties or those containing purely formal material. To have included the entire texts of treaties discussed or mentioned in this book would have required at least twenty volumes and would have defeated our purpose which is to highlight the significant and to bring the operative sections of the major treaties within one manageable volume.

The choice of treaties has been difficult and inevitably subjective. The second edition of Peter H. Rohn's *World Treaty Index* (Santa Barbara, 1984), covering the period 1920 to 1980, includes some 44,000 treaties. The *United Nations Treaty Series* gives the texts of more than sixteen thousand treaties for the period from 1945 to the late 1970s. Clearly, therefore, we have had to be ruthless in our selectivity. Our basic criterion has been the long-term political and diplomatic importance of treaties. We have thus excluded those dealing with purely technical, legal, military, or financial matters. Treaties dealing with economic relations or aid issues (more than half of all those listed by Rohn) have in general been left out; the only exceptions have been economic treaties which have had enduring political significance (such as the *Treaty of Rome, 1957*, which established the European Economic Community). This book gives the text of 111 international agreements, and it also analyses many more of which the texts are not given. A few of those we include seemed of little importance when they were concluded, but have acquired a retrospective significance because of later events (an example is the *Anglo-Argentine Agreement of 1971 concerning the Falkland Islands*). No doubt others which seem important now will fade into insignificance with the passing of years.

Specialists on particular areas or themes will no doubt wish to consult more narrowly defined collections (two models of their kind are J.C. Hurewitz's *The Middle East and North Africa in World Politics: A Documentary Record*, New Haven, 1975, and *SALT Handbook: Key Documents and Issues 1972–1979*, edited by Roger P. Labrie, Washington, D.C., 1979). But for the reader who seeks a general grasp of contemporary diplomacy we hope that this volume will provide the necessary documentary basis.

Many of the treaties printed here deal with sensitive territorial issues. In general we have used geographical designations most familiar to English-speaking readers (thus Persian rather than Arabian Gulf, Falkland Islands rather than Malvinas and so on); needless to say, such usages should not be taken to imply any particular political view. In their original forms treaties dealing with territorial issues often include large-scale maps; it is not practicable to include these here. Unfortunately most historical atlases currently on the market do not show in sufficient detail the large numbers of frontier changes effected by treaties over the past four decades. The reader is therefore advised to study a good modern atlas, comparing recent with earlier editions (the various editions of *The Times Atlas of the World*, first published in 1895, fulfil this purpose admirably).

The present edition carries treaty texts up to September 1986, but has been amended at proof stage to reflect developments up to July 1987.

We plan to revise the contemporary treaties and bring them up to date at regular intervals of time, and hope this work will continue to prove useful, both to the students of international relations and a wider enquiring public wishing to be well-informed on the crucial issues of our times.

We wish to thank the staffs of the various libraries and archives in which we have worked, as well as our publishers and Bruce Hunter of David Higham Associates. Valuable research assistance was provided by Paul Salstrom and David Soule. Broadly speaking, work on the pre-1973 period was done by John Grenville and on the more recent period by Bernard Wasserstein; but we take joint responsibility for the work as a whole. For encouragement and patience beyond the call of duty we thank our wives.

*July 1987*

John A.S. Grenville
*Birmingham University*

Bernard Wasserstein
*Brandeis University*

# Introduction: International treaties

## The role of treaties

*Pacta sunt servanda* ('agreements must be kept') – this precept of Roman law has been recognized as the fundamental principle of modern international law. The Latin tag heads article 26 of the *Vienna Convention on the Law of Treaties, 22 May 1969*, which declares: 'Every treaty in force is binding upon the parties to it and must be performed by them in good faith.' Yet international treaties have frequently turned out to be no stronger than the paper on which they are written.

How then does one explain the fact that during the four decades since the end of the Second World War more treaties have been signed than during the whole of the previous four centuries? The inflation in the sheer number of the treaties has been accompanied in the twentieth century by an expansion in their length and complexity. Some post-war treaties, such as the *Treaty of Rome, 1957*, establishing the European Economic Community, run to hundreds of articles and fill a single volume; others occupy several volumes; and still others, with accompanying amendments, for example the *General Agreement on Tariffs and Trade*, signed at Geneva in 1947, fill several shelves.

There are some obvious explanations for the increase in the number and length of treaties. There exist now more sovereign nations than ever before; there has also been a spectacular growth of international organizations which sign treaties in the same way as single States; treaties since 1919 have moreover been increasingly concerned with economic and social questions. The one explanation that cannot be seriously advanced is that mutual faith in the honourable behaviour of countries party to a

treaty has been noticeably strengthened over the years. The solemn undertakings and promises, the general intentions of friendship and cooperation embedded in the language of the treaties, do not by themselves carry
more conviction now than they did in times past; they are no guarantee
of observance. Nor has there developed any effective way of bringing to
justice a treaty violator by an international tribunal backed by effective
international sanction, especially when the offending nation is a powerful
one. That morality as the basis of international dealings has not been
strengthened in the twentieth century even the least cynical observer has
to admit.

International lawyers have not had an easy time attempting to reconcile
the realities of policy with the notion of the rule of law in international
affairs. Ultimately there has to be some moral foundation to law and this is
difficult to demonstrate as a fundamental consideration in the formation of
national policies the world over. There has indeed been an interesting shift
in the way in which international lawyers and diplomats have looked upon
treaties during this century. A standard work on diplomatic practice was
compiled by Sir Ernest Satow in 1917 (*A Guide to Diplomatic Practice*, 2
vols., London, 1917). The chapters dealing with treaties in the edition of
1922 were based on the principle of the absolute sanctity of treaties once
signed; they could not be altered or abandoned by one party to them
without the agreement of the others, national necessities notwithstanding.
This Satow was able to assume. By the time a new 1957 edition was prepared by Sir Nevile Bland, who had served in the Treaty Department of
the British Foreign Office, the whole question of whether or not treaties
could be unilaterally terminated without violating the normal practice of
international law required lengthy discussion. The world meantime had
witnessed the disregard of treaty obligations by Hitler, Stalin, Mussolini
and the Japanese in the 1930s. Certain questions now had to be posed even
if they could not be answered satisfactorily. Is a country bound by the
provisions of a treaty even when the conditions prevailing when the treaty
was made have greatly changed? Can there ever be permanent treaties in a
rapidly changing world? One distinguished international lawyer replied a
little obscurely with a double negative: 'There is nothing juridically
impossible in the existence of a treaty creating obligations which are
incapable of termination except by agreement of all parties...[there is
thus a] general presumption against unilateral termination.' Another
authority on international law concluded that a commercial treaty could
'always be dissolved after notice, although such notice be not expressly
provided for', and he extended this possibility to alliance treaties. There is

in fact no agreement among international lawyers. The late Professor Hersch Lauterpacht, one of the most distinguished lawyers, used to ask his students whether international law was law properly so called. International law is 'incomplete' and in a 'state of transition' he concluded. Although a body of customary international law is developing, international law among nations in our own time remains far removed from the rule of law as generally recognized and practised by civilized communities within their own borders.

There are international judicial institutions such as the International Court of Justice of the United Nations, the successor of the Permanent Court of International Justice set up after the First World War. All members of the United Nations (and also some non-members, such as Switzerland) are parties to the *Statute of the International Court of Justice, 1945* (see chapter XIV of the *United Nations Charter*, p. 75). Under article 36 of the Statute, States 'may at any time declare that they recognize as compulsory...the jurisdiction of the Court'. But by 1 January 1986 only forty-seven States had accepted compulsory jurisdiction. These included Britain, the United States and India, but not the U.S.S.R., France or China. Moreover, most States accepting compulsory jurisdiction did so only with reservations or conditions. Some States that had earlier accepted compulsory jurisdiction later withdrew their acceptance when confronted with decisions (or the prospect of decisions) that they disliked. For example, Israel gave notice on 19 November 1985 of termination of her acceptance of such jurisdiction effective 21 November 1986; and the United States gave similar notice on 7 October 1985, effective 7 April 1986. In these circumstances the power of the International Court or of international arbitration tribunals to reach enforceable decisions in serious political disputes is obviously limited. The possibility of international sanctions based on a legal judgment is thus unlikely to prove a serious deterrent to the prospective treaty-breaker.

Nor is time on the side of treaty observance. The longer a treaty is intended to last the more chance is there that it will cease to correspond to national interests and international conditions. On this the most diverse of men who have guided national policies in the twentieth century are agreed. This was one of Lord Salisbury's objections to the prosposal to conclude an Anglo-German alliance at the turn of the century: 'the British Government cannot undertake to declare war, for any purpose, unless it is a purpose of which the electors of this country would approve...I do not see how, in conscious honesty, we could invite other nations to rely upon our aids in a struggle, which must be formidable and probably supreme, when we have no means whatsoever of knowing what may be the humour of our people in circumstances which cannot be foreseen.' He concluded that national honour as well as good principles of policy required that future decisions should not be mortgaged by treaty obligations. By way of contrast, Hitler regarded morality, good faith and principles of international law, as decadent democratic weaknesses. He wrote in *Mein Kampf*: 'No consideration of foreign policy can proceed from any other criterion than this: Does it benefit our nationality now or in the future, or will it be injurious to it? . . . Partisan, religious, humanitarian and all other criteria in general are completely irrelevant.' The conclusion and violation of treaties were decisions of policy, and other States could be, and were, misled by Hitler's repeatedly proclaimed readiness to conclude and abide by the agreements he signed; for he broke them without the slightest scruple.

During the inter-war period apologists for treaty-breakers sometimes invoked the Roman law principle under which every contract carried with it the implication *rebus sic stantibus* (provided the situation remains the same). National Socialist Germany invoked this doctrine, that an international agreement is binding only so long as the state of affairs present at the time of its signature continues to exist, in order to justify its remilitarization of the Rhineland in 1936. Meanwhile in the Soviet Union the doctrine was reformulated to signify that every international agreement was the expression of the established social order and must be observed only so long as that order endured. The Vienna Convention on the Law of Treaties expressly excludes (in article 62) the *rebus sic stantibus* doctrine as a basis for unilateral termination of treaties, declaring: 'A fundamental change of circumstances may not be invoked as a ground for terminating or withdrawing from a treaty.' (Only very limited exceptions are allowed.) Nevertheless it is still sometimes argued (for example, by Athanassios Vamvoukos, *The Termination of Treaties in International Law*, Oxford, 1985, p. 216) that 'the rule of *rebus sic stantibus* is neither an exception to, nor in conflict with, the rule of *pacta sunt servanda*'.

After the Second World War, Dean Acheson, the American Secretary of State, grappled with the dilemma of whether treaty obligations could be relied on when the passage of time had changed international circumstances. When negotiating the North Atlantic Treaty Organization Acheson asked himself, 'What was this sovereign – the United States of America – and how could it insure faith in promised future conduct?' Acheson recognized, as Salisbury had done half a century earlier, that the fundamental problem did not affect only a Government dependent on representative institutions. 'In reality,' wrote Acheson, 'the problem was general and insoluble, lying in inescapable change of circumstances and of national leadership and in the weakness of words to bind, especially when the juice of continued purpose is squeezed out of them and their husks analyzed to a dryly logical extreme.'

Important treaties have been and still are signed with much ceremony, with film and television cameras ensuring some public involvement. Such displays of cooperation may make a temporary impression on public opinion but are discounted by the professional diplomat. The trappings are forgotten long before a violation may occur. With the archives of the Foreign Office in London, of the Ministry of Foreign Affairs in Moscow, of the State Department in Washington and every other capital full of broken treaties, how can treaties be viewed other than in a cynical and negative way? If the behaviour of the policy-makers is rational – even if, according to the opinion of historians, sometimes misguided – why are scores of new treaties negotiated and signed every year?

For this there are good reasons too. In the first place, notwithstanding the many well-publicized instances of broken treaties, the fact remains that most treaties (particularly the large number dealing with financial or technical matters) are in fact observed – just as most debts are paid. Nobody would expect a banker to put up his shutters merely because of the existence of a minority of bad debtors; the prudent banker will instead make adequate provision for bad debts. Similarly the prudent diplomat makes provision (as adequate as the circumstances may allow) for the faithless treaty-maker – or for the change in circumstances which might lead to the breaking of a treaty obligation. One example of such 'provision' is the device of the 'treaty of guarantee' whereby one or more powers pledge to ensure that treaty obligations will be honoured. The *Cyprus Guarantee Treaty, 16 August 1960* (p. 394) is an instance of such a treaty – although subsequent history also demonstrated the limited effectiveness of such arrangements. Another device is the additional side-arrangement whereby a major treaty (for example the *Israel–Egypt Peace Treaty, 26 March 1979*, p. 381) is accompanied by one or more subsidiary agreements, sometimes with third parties (in the case of the Israel–Egypt Peace Treaty there were several such agreements involving the United States, some trilateral, some bilateral), designed to secure the better observance of the main treaty.

Even when there is no expectation that a country will remain faithful to its treaty obligations in perpetuity, calculations of national self-interest may make it probable that treaty provisions will be kept for a foreseeable future period of time. At least one of the parties has to believe that, whatever the secret plans of the other, or no agreement would be reached. Should there be a presumption that treaty obligations might be broken then there still has to be the possibility in the mind of one of the signatories that they will not be. The claim has been made for Chamberlain's foreign policy that he signed the Munich Agreement with Hitler on 29 September 1938 to test Hitler's good faith; but even so, Chamberlain must have thought that there was a worthwhile chance that Hitler would keep the undertakings of Munich. An open breach of treaty, such as Hitler's violation of this settlement, can (and did) still serve one important purpose in helping to rally public opinion and reluctant allies.

Not many treaties are as cynically or immediately broken as the Munich Agreement. An international treaty can be viewed as a bargain or contract. There are three inducements for keeping treaty provisions which are generally more important than any other: firstly, the positive one that a treaty contains a balance of advantages and the country which violates a treaty must expect to lose its advantages. At the simplest level, for example, when one country expels a foreign diplomat a reciprocal expulsion often follows. More important is the fact that a serious violation of a treaty may end it. Sometimes a violation is not easy to establish. Treaties on arms limitations are for this reason especially difficult to negotiate; control of armaments has not proved easy to reconcile with national sovereignty. The second inducement for keeping a treaty is the deterrent element it may contain. Before acting, political leaders have to decide whether the violation of a treaty is worth the risk of the possible counter-measures taken by the aggrieved State or States. A third inducement is that a Government has to consider its international credibility; failure to fulfil a treaty may well weaken the defaulting country's international position as other States calculate whether treaties still in force with it will be honoured, and whether new agreements can any longer usefully be concluded.

Treaties are landmarks which guide nations in their relations with each other. They express intentions, promises and normally appear to contain reciprocal advantages. Treaties represent attempts to reduce the measure of uncertainty inherent in the conduct of international affairs. In a world of growing interdependence, economic, political and strategic, where relations have become exceedingly complex and where no nation can prosper and feel secure in complete isolation from all its neighbours, the endeavour to reach agreements is an attempt to safeguard at least some vital interests.

It must be remembered that the signing of the actual treaty is only the starting point of the relationship it purports to establish. Cooperation and further detailed agreements based on the principles of the original treaty, as for instance is the case with the European Economic Community, may strengthen it. On the other hand a treaty may be drained of its effectiveness by disuse or mutual suspicions long before it is actually broken or abandoned. (An example of this is the SEATO treaty, p. 120.) Despite appearances the treaty does not 'freeze' relationships; they remain fluid, and the treaty may become more meaningful or just a form of words. No one would judge the strength of a marriage by the form of vows exchanged at a ceremony. So it is with treaties; they may prosper and encompass an increasingly wide range of agreements as time passes or they may end in disillusionment. The contents of the treaty may indeed be less important than the relationship that is established as the result of agreement.

Some political scientists have spoken of the 'treaty trap' – the false hope of basing foreign policy on the expectation that the legal requirements of a treaty will be fulfilled. When measured against historical evidence this reliance is seen to be a 'trap'. Such a trap exists, however, only for those who divorce the signing of a treaty from the necessary continuous vigilance over the relations that develop after its signature. Careful assessment has to be made of how 'national interests' are viewed by the leaders of other countries, the personalities of the leaders and future leaders, and all the likely influences including public opinion which can affect their policies, because it is against this 'total' policy background that the continuing strength of a treaty, once signed, has to be judged. When this is neglected, or when serious miscalculations are made, then one party is taken totally by surprise by the other's breach of a treaty, as was Stalin when, in spite of the Nazi – Soviet Pact of 1939, Hitler invaded the Soviet Union in 1941. No practising diplomat can sensibly view a treaty merely from a juridical point of view, in a kind of legal vacuum separated from all those influences which actually shape the conduct of foreign policies. The treaty may be one of the very important influences on that policy; it can never be the sole consideration.

The alternative to imperfect agreements is either anarchy or complete uncertainty. Treaties do not by themselves assure peace and security, but far more often than not they have contributed to stability for a measurable and worthwhile period of years. The spectacular instances where they have become instruments of aggression should therefore not blind us to the utility of treaties in general.

## The form and structure of treaties

The technical and legal aspects of treaties have over the years received much scholarly attention. Here it may be useful to summarize those points which are especially important to the historian of international relations. There are no hard-and-fast rules, although the *Vienna Convention on the Law of Treaties* establishes the closest to a generally agreed framework for treaty-making. This convention, concluded on *22 May 1969*, was to come into force (under its penultimate article, number 84) only when thirty-five States had deposited instruments of accession or ratification. Although thirty-two States signed immediately, not all of these ratified it. More than a decade passed before the convention finally entered into force on 27 January 1980 (following the accession of Togo). By 1986, forty-seven States were parties (including Britain and Japan, but not China, France, the U.S.A. or U.S.S.R.). The U.S. State Department, while declining to accede, nevertheless declared that the convention 'although not yet in force...is already generally recognized as the authoritative guide to current treaty law and practice'. The convention therefore carries considerable international authority in spite of the fact that most States are not yet parties to it.

### DEFINITION

International treaties are concluded between sovereign States and presuppose their existence. There have been a few exceptions to this simple working definition: States under the suzerainty of another State have sometimes concluded international treaties; the degree of a State's sovereignty may be in dispute, as for instance in the case of the two Boer Republics, the Transvaal and the Orange Free State, which in 1899 went to war with Britain to assert their complete independence. There are other exceptions, but the overwhelming number of treaties are concluded between sovereign States; in the twentieth century they are also concluded between an organization of States such as the European Community and another State. Here the organization of States acts in a collective capacity as one party to a treaty.

The major treaties discussed and printed in this book are those which are intended to create legal rights and obligations between the countries which are party to them. Whether there can be 'treaties' properly so called which do not create such rights and obligations depends on definition. The *Atlantic Charter of 14 August 1941* was a 'Joint Declaration' by Roosevelt and Churchill setting out certain agreed principles of policy; no legal obligations were incurred by Britain and the United States, though Churchill's signature as Prime Minister had been approved by the War Cabinet. Was it a genuine treaty or a press communiqué? The point need not be laboured. Not all diplomatic agreements of importance need be 'treaties' in the conventional sense: it has been established in international law that even oral undertakings may be enforceable as international agreements – even where such validity is contested by one of the parties.

In the nineteenth century and earlier, treaties were always concluded between the Heads of State, whether Monarchs or Presidents. This still remains true for many treaties. But equally important treaties may be concluded between Governments rather than Heads of State, as was the North Atlantic Treaty of 4 April 1949 and the Peace Treaty with Italy of 10 February 1947.

It is generally accepted that unless there are contrary provisions laid down by the signatories of a treaty not inconsistent with overriding principles of international law, all questions concerning the interpretation and execution of treaties, their validity and how they may be ended, are governed by international custom and where appropriate by general principles of law recognized by civilized nations.

## FORM

What's in a name? Less when it comes to a treaty than in almost anything else. The Vienna Convention defines a 'treaty' as 'an international agreement concluded between States in written form and governed by international law, whether embodied in a single instrument or in two or more related instruments and whatever its particular designation'.

What a treaty is called may be a matter of chance or design but it is not significant by itself. The obligations and rights have to be studied in each case with equal care: for example, an 'alliance' may not create the relationship and obligations which the common meaning of the word would lead one to expect. The Alliance for Progress of 1961 was not, in fact, an 'alliance' in the conventional meaning of the word. On the other hand, not all alliance treaties are so named. It is therefore not possible to distinguish treaties, or the rights or obligations arising from them, or their relative importance, by their particular form or heading. One has to work from the other end and disentangle from the contents of the treaty the precise obligations and rights. This is a point of great importance in the understanding of international relations. The historian, for instance, will be especially concerned to discover whether a treaty contains commitments to go to war, or merely promises support in more general terms avoiding any automatic commitment to go to war in conditions specified by the treaty. Whether the treaty is called an 'Alliance Treaty' or a 'Declaration' makes no difference. Treaties have been called by many other names and each type of treaty is usually cast in its own conventional form. Some of the more common types of treaties are headed Convention, *Acte Final*, Pact, Agreement, Protocol, Exchange of Notes, *Modus Vivendi*, or Understanding, as well as Treaty, with some prefix such as alliance, boundary, etc.; and this list is not comprehensive. It also has to be noted that until the actual contents of a document are examined it cannot be assumed that any legal rights or obligations do in fact arise, and so the document may not be a treaty at all despite appearances. The historian thus has to exercise extreme caution in distinguishing between the 'content' and the 'form' or 'packaging' of diplomatic agreements.

## LANGUAGE

The language of treaties varies. Until the seventeenth century most treaties (at any rate, most treaties involving European states) were in Latin. Thereafter French became the major language of diplomacy and of treaties. Hence the frequency of Latin and French expressions in the vocabulary even of current diplomacy and treaty-making. In the twentieth century English has emerged as the dominant language in treaty-making. Nationalistic considerations have often (particularly since 1945) dictated the use of a particular language as the 'authentic' text of a treaty. The Vienna Convention specifies that 'when a treaty has been authenticated in two or more languages, the text is equally authoritative in each language, unless the treaty provides or the parties agree that, in case of divergence, a particular text shall prevail'. A case in point of such agreement was the Israel–Egypt Peace Treaty of 1979 which was written 'in triplicate in the English, Arabic, and Hebrew languages, each text being equally authentic' – with the added proviso that 'in case of any divergence of interpretation, the English text shall prevail'. All the treaties in this book are, of course, printed in English. It should therefore be borne in mind by the reader that, in cases where the 'authentic' text is not English, the version given here is not legally binding – even where it is an 'official' translation.

## THE VALIDITY OF TREATIES AND THEIR RATIFICATION

There is a wide range of choice as to the means by which a country may assume treaty obligations. There is no one answer to the question of what needs to be done before a treaty becomes binding and precisely when this moment occurs. If the treaty is in the form of an exchange of notes it usually comes into force as soon as the documents have been signed, and only rarely is additional ratification provided for. The number of treaty agreements under this heading has become large. Such treaties are not necessarily confined to questions of a technical nature or of minor importance. Exchanges of notes may deal with questions of major importance or with delicate issues which the parties may prefer not to magnify by the conclusion of a 'treaty'. An example of the latter was the *Anglo-Argentine agreement on the Falklands in 1971* (p. 433).

It is not necessary that States have diplomatic relations with each other in order to conclude treaties (although it helps). This book contains a number of agreements concluded between States which had no diplomatic relations at the time of signature. The *Cuba–United States agreement on hijacking of 15 February 1973* (p. 420) is a case in point. An interesting example of such an agreement was the arrangement between Iran and the United States for settlement of the hostage crisis in January 1981 (p. 403). Here relations between the two parties were so strained that the agreement took the form of a declaration by a third party (Algeria). It was none the less regarded as legally binding on the U.S.A. and Iran.

Most treaties do not come into force immediately upon signature but require ratification. In some cases (normally emergency situations), however, treaties may be concluded which expressly stipulate that they come into force at the moment of signature and require no ratification. This can sometimes be the case even in States whose normal constitutional practices require ratification by a legislative body.

A Government in practice has to choose how it will assume treaty obligations. Even where a country has a written constitution which requires the submission and consent of a representative assembly to a treaty, as is the case in the United States where Senate is required to approve treaties by a two-thirds majority, means may be found to circumvent the powers of such assemblies. Senator William Fulbright, the former Chairman of the Senate Foreign Relations Committee, once observed that since 1940, 'the beginning of this age of crisis...the Senate's constitutional powers of advice and consent have atrophied into what is widely regarded as, though never asserted to be, a duty to give prompt consent with a minimum of advice'. Presidents have resorted to 'executive agreements' at times when the consent of Senate to a treaty appeared doubtful. The important Anglo-American Agreement embodying the destroyers/bases deal of September 1940 was concluded in this form.

A treaty is concluded when signed, but where ratification is necessary becomes binding only when ratified. Traditionally ratification signified the consent of the Sovereign to a treaty negotiated by the Sovereign's plenipotentiary, who might have no means of consulting the Sovereign when negotiating in distant countries. In modern times speed of communication has made it possible to submit the actual text of a treaty to the Government before it is signed. The practical importance of ratification now lies in the need to secure the consent of a Parliament or other elected assembly before the Government is ready to advise ratification of a treaty. In Britain, though treaty-making powers are vested in the Sovereign, the real decision lies with the Government and, where legislation is required to adapt British law to bring it into line with that required by the treaty, also with Parliament, for the necessary enabling legislation must first be passed by Parliament before the treaty can be ratified 'by the Sovereign' on the advice of the Government. The legislative and treaty-making process of Britain's adhesion to the European Economic Community provides a good example. It is the practice in Britain for the texts of all treaties requiring ratification to lie on the table of the House of Commons for twenty-one days before ratification by the Sovereign. In France, the 1946 constitution, though vesting treaty-making power in the President, required that a wide range of treaties did not become valid unless embodied in a law passed by the French Parliament. The precise powers of representative assemblies differ widely and the constitution and practice of each country have to be considered separately.

Non-ratification need not necessarily destroy the political effectiveness of a treaty (although it prevents it having any legal enforceability). The *SALT II Agreement, 18 June 1979* (p. 471) was never ratified by the U.S. Senate, but the United States nevertheless undertook voluntarily to comply with its provisions (until 1986). The ratification process may, on the other hand, introduce significant modifications into treaties (though these are not binding on other parties except by agreement). The reservations attached by the U.S. Senate to its acceptance of the *Panama Canal Treaties of 1977* (p. 414) are a case in point.

Ratification is therefore not always a formality; important treaties may have to be submitted to the approval of elected assemblies before the Government of the State concerned is able to give its consent to the treaty becoming binding. This may be due to constitutional custom or constitutional requirement, or to a Government's desire to retain the support of a majority of the elected representatives in order to continue in power.

## The drafting of treaties

By this stage it will have become clear that there are no rules as to how a treaty has to be drawn up. This is a question on which the participants have free choice. But it is possible to speak of some widely adopted conventions which tend to give treaties certain common forms. Many diplomats in the world's various Foreign Ministries are employed in treaty drafting: their task is to put the intentions of the parties to a treaty in acceptable professional legal phraseology, which can at times strike the reader as rather stylized and even archaic. By way of example, a common form of treaty is here considered.

Such a treaty commences with a *descriptive title*, as for instance the 'Treaty of Mutual Cooperation and Security between the United States of America and Japan'. Then follows the *preamble*, beginning with the names or description of the High Contracting Parties as 'The United States of America and Japan'; next the general purpose is set out, 'Desiring to strengthen the bonds of peace and friendship traditionally existing between them etc. . . . Having resolved to conclude a treaty of mutual cooperation and security, therefore agree as follows. . . .' The preamble often includes also, though not in the particular treaty here cited, the names and designation of the plenipotentiaries who have produced their full powers, which have been found in good order, and have agreed as follows. . . . Next follow the substantive articles each with a numeral, I, II, III, etc. which constitute the objectives, the obligations and the rights of the signatories; these articles are frequently arranged beginning with the more general and leading to the more specific. Where appropriate, an article follows which sets out the provisions for other States which may wish to accede to the treaty. Next follows an article (or articles) concerning ratification where this is provided for, the duration of the treaty and provisions for its renewal. Finally a clause is added stating 'in witness whereof' the undersigned plenipotentiaries have signed this treaty; the place where the treaty is signed is given, together with a statement as to the authentic languages of the treaty texts; and last the date is written in, followed by the seals and the signatures of the plenipotentiaries.

*Conventions, Protocols* and other types of treaties each have their own customary form.

## The vocabulary of treaties

Some terms used in treaty-making – a few of them in French and Latin – have special meanings.

*Accession* or *adhesion*: these terms are used interchangeably to describe the practice where a State which is not a party to a treaty later on joins such a treaty. No State has a right to accede to a treaty; the possibility and method of accession are often contained in a clause of the treaty as signed by the original parties to it.

*Aggression*: the common meaning of the term is an unjustified attack, and efforts have been made to define aggression by means of treaties. For example, a convention was signed in July 1933 by Russia, Afghanistan, Estonia, Latvia, Persia, Poland, Rumania and Turkey which defined aggression as having been committed by the State which first (*a*) declares war on another State, or (*b*) invades another State with its armed forces, or (*c*) attacks with its armed forces the territory, naval vessels or aircraft of another State, or (*d*) initiates a naval blockade of coasts or ports of another State; or (*e*), most interestingly of all, renders 'aid to armed bands formed on the territory of a State and invading the territory of another State, or refuses, despite demands on the part of the State subjected to attack, to take all possible measures on its own territory to deprive said bands of any aid and protection'. On 14 December 1974 the U.N. General Assembly adopted a resolution which defined aggression as 'the use of armed force by a State against the sovereignty, territorial integrity or political independence of another State, or in any other manner inconsistent with the Charter of the United Nations'. The definition went on to specify invasion, bombardment, blockade, or the sending into another state of 'armed bands, groups, irregulars or mercenaries' as examples of aggression. But it specified that the list was not exhaustive and that 'the Security Council may determine that other acts constitute aggression under the provisions of the Charter'. Despite the existence of such declarations, however, in the last resort each State or international tribunal has to judge on the merits of the facts before it whether particular actions constitute aggression or not.

*Bilateral* treaties are those between two States; *multilateral* treaties are concluded between three or more States.

*Casus foederis* is literally the case contemplated by the treaty, usually one of alliance; it is the event which when it occurs imposes the duty on one or more of the allies to render the assistance promised in the treaty to the other; *casus belli* has a different meaning frequently confused with *casus foederis; casus belli* is the provocative action by one State which in the opinion of the injured State justifies it in declaring war.

*Compromis* in diplomacy has a meaning different from the everyday modern meaning of 'compromise'. Deriving from the Latin word *compromissum*, meaning 'mutual promise', a *compromis* in diplomacy is an agreement to abide by an arbitrator's award.

*Delimitation* and *demarcation* of boundaries: boundaries of State territories are the lines drawn to divide the sovereignties of adjoining States. They form the frontiers of each country. Concern for frontiers is the basis of the majority of political treaties and the cause of many conflicts and wars. When a boundary can be drawn on a map and is accepted by the States which are divided by it, even though the boundary has not been physically marked out on the ground by frontier posts, then it is said to have been *delimited*. The frontier is also *demarcated* when it has been physically set out on the ground and not just marked on a map. The distinction between delimitation and demarcation is an important one. European frontiers have all been both delimited and demarcated. The same is not true of all boundary lines in the world, especially in difficult and unpopulated regions. There are no settled principles of demarcation, though there are certain common practices, such as to draw boundary lines through the middle of land-locked seas and rivers where they lie between two States. Estuaries and mountain ranges, however, cause more difficulty. In the absence of specific agreements the demarcation of an actual frontier based on a general boundary treaty signed much earlier – quite possibly when the state of geographical knowledge was imperfect – can become a matter of serious dispute. To avoid such disputes countries sometimes sign treaties setting out how a boundary is to be demarcated; an example is the boundary treaty between Great Britain and the United States of 11 April 1908 respecting the demarcation of the boundary between Canada and the United States. In other cases of dispute the two nations may resort to arbitration by a third party; or a commission of two States or an international commission may have the power to demarcate boundaries. There are still boundaries which have been neither delimited nor demarcated; instead there is a *de facto* line. This is true of many stretches of boundaries in Asia. Sometimes boundaries have been arbitrarily drawn by cartographers over country so difficult that it has not been surveyed and mapped with complete accuracy.

*Demilitarization* is an agreement between two or more States by treaty not to fortify or station troops in a particular zone of territory; such zones are known as *demilitarized zones*.

*Denunciation* is the giving of notice by a State of its intention to terminate a treaty. Some treaties provide for termination by one of the parties on giving of a certain period of notice. Others contain no such provision but are nevertheless denounced. Denunciation of treaties is a common occurrence after revolutionary changes in government, where the incoming régime adopts a different diplomatic stance from its predecessor. But international law recognizes no automatic right to such unilateral denunciation.

*Internationalization* refers to the placing under multilateral control of land or sea areas. Rivers (such as the Danube) have also often been the subject of such agreements.

*Modus vivendi* usually refers to a temporary or provisional agreement which it is intended shall later be replaced by a more permanent and detailed treaty.

*Most-favoured-nation clause*: many commercial treaties between countries contain this clause, the effect of which is that any commercial advantages either State has granted in the past to other nations, or may grant in the future, have to be granted also to the signatories of a treaty which contains a most-favoured-nation clause. The intent is therefore that the commercial advantages of two States which have signed a treaty with this provision shall never be less than those of any third State which is not a signatory. The United States has not recognized quite so unconditional an operation of this clause.

*Procès-verbal* is the official record or minutes of the daily proceedings of a conference and of any conclusions arrived at, and is frequently signed by the participants; a *Protocol* is sometimes used in the same sense but more accurately is a document which constitutes an international agreement.

*Reservation* is defined in the Vienna Convention as meaning 'a unilateral statement, however phrased or named, made by a State, when signing, ratifying, accepting, approving or acceding to a treaty, whereby it purports to exclude or to modify the legal effect of certain provisions of the treaty in their application to that State'. The International Court of Justice, in an advisory opinion in 1951 concerning reservations to the Genocide Convention (see p. 493), declared that 'no reservation was valid unless it was accepted by all the contracting parties'. The Vienna Convention does provide for reservations, and lays down rules (articles 19–23) concerning their formulation, acceptance, legal effects, withdrawal, and procedure.

*Revision* of treaties (save where the treaty itself specifically provides for subsequent changes) is generally permissible only by agreement of the parties.

*Sine qua non* describes a condition or conditions that have to be accepted by another party to a proposed agreement; it implies that without such acceptance the agreement cannot be proceeded with.

*Status quo*: the common meaning is the state of affairs existing, but an agreement can refer specifically to a previous state of affairs as for instance in the phrase *status quo ante bellum* which means the state existing before the war began, for example as relating to frontiers.

*Succession* has been the subject of a further *Vienna Convention* on the *Succession of States in Respect of Treaties*, which was opened for signature on *23 August 1978*. This states that ' "succession of states" means the replacement of one State by another in the responsibility for the international relations of territory'.

## Treaties imposed by force

How can any system of law admit that right is based on might? This is what is involved if in the relations between States international law accepts that the stronger nation may impose its terms on the weaker nation by war or by threat of force.

Before 1914, war and the use of force were accepted as legitimate means of securing national interests when diplomacy failed to achieve the desired objects. Two Great Powers of Europe, Germany and Italy, owed their very unity and existence to war. Indeed, the 1914 frontiers of the continental States of Europe were based on treaties concluded by the victorious Powers. The colonial empires of Britain and other Powers, moreover, had all been acquired mainly by conquest. Might was right in the sense that the mighty rarely admit to wrongdoing.

The League of Nations was to usher in a new era of international relations, based on the acceptance of the League Covenant which limited the right to go to war. Henceforth there would be two kinds of war, illegal wars waged in breach of the League Covenant and 'legal' wars which were not in breach of treaty engagements. The Pact of Paris of 1928 and the United Nations Charter extended the limitations of the signatories to threaten or to use force. International lawyers since then have wrestled with the problem of whether treaties imposed by countries which have used force in breach of their treaty engagements are valid. In the 1930s there evolved the principle of 'non-recognition' whereby States refused to recognize rights derived from the illegal use of force. But as one distinguished international lawyer put it, the attitude of other States 'may, after a prolonged period of time, be adjusted to the requirements of international peace and stability'. The Vienna Convention on the Law of Treaties in 1969 declared that 'A treaty is void if its conclusion has been procured by the threat of force in violation of the principles of international law embodied in the Charter of the United Nations' (Article 52). An amendment proposed during the drafting of the Convention, which would have defined force to include 'economic or political pressure', was withdrawn. Article 75 of the Convention appears to mean that an aggressor State cannot claim protection under Article 52 if other States acting in conformity with the Charter use force against the aggressor and then impose a treaty related to the aggression.

As long as individual States or international organizations of States apply and interpret the law, political considerations will remain a strong, even a predominant influence. Progress in the codification of international law is made. Yet today we are far from a position where general agreement on how to apply it regulates international conduct on issues where nations wish to use force. Important national interests will induce States to recognize many rights 'illegally' secured, and this will remain true so long as it is believed that legal and moral precepts alone cannot determine foreign policy.

# I · The foundations of post-war diplomacy

## The war-time conferences

The basic structure of international diplomacy after the Second World War originated in the discussions at the series of inter-Allied conferences convened between 1943 and 1945. At these meetings plans were drawn up not only for military cooperation to defeat the Axis powers but also for the political disposition of the post-war world. The agreements arrived at ranged from detailed blueprints to the vaguest of understandings. Behind these sometimes tortured formulations lurked a mutual suspicion between the Soviet Union and the Western Allies which was soon to burst into the open with the onset of the 'cold war'.

So long as the war against Germany and Japan continued, however, the overriding common objective of military victory prevented Allied differences from developing into major rifts. At the Yalta Conference of February 1945 the 'Great Power' interests of Britain, the United States and the Soviet Union largely determined the post-war settlements not only of defeated enemies but also of the smaller Allies. At Yalta, the Big Three displayed at least an outward show of unanimity of purpose and wartime comradeship. By the time of the Potsdam Conference a few months later the Allied differences which developed into the 'cold war' were already strongly in evidence.

The thirteen major Allied conferences of this period fall into two divisions: (1) predominantly Anglo-American, and (2) Three Power conferences of Russia, Britain and the United States, sometimes with other countries present. The table on pages 20–1 summarizes their sequence.

The first two important conferences of 1943 endeavoured to coordinate

The major war-time conferences

| Date | Place | Participants | Subjects discussed |
|---|---|---|---|
| 14–25 January 1943 | Casablanca | Britain, U.S. | Reconciling rival French leaders on the allied side; 'unconditional surrender' call; Far Eastern and European strategy. |
| 19–24 August 1943 | Quebec | Britain, U.S., Canada | Atomic research and use of atomic bomb; 'second front' in Europe; Far Eastern strategy; Italian surrender. |
| 18–30 October 1943 | Moscow | Britain, U.S., U.S.S.R. (Foreign Ministers) | U.N.; Austria; surrender terms; war criminals. |
| 22–6 November 1943 | Cairo | Britain, U.S., China | Japanese surrender terms; Far Eastern settlement; Far Eastern military strategy. |
| 28 November–1 December 1943 | Teheran | Britain, U.S., U.S.S.R. | European and Far Eastern strategy; Russia and Japan; U.N.; Turkey; Italy; Russia's frontiers; Poland; Germany's eastern frontier. |
| 21 August–7 October 1944 | Dumbarton Oaks | Britain, U.S., U.S.S.R., China (China participated 29 September–7 October) | U.N. |
| 11–19 September 1944 | Quebec | Britain, U.S., Canada | Germany; military strategy in Europe and in war against Japan. |

| Date | Location | Participants | Topics |
| --- | --- | --- | --- |
| 9–20 October 1944 | Moscow | Britain, U.S.S.R. (with U.S. observer) | Balkan 'spheres of influence'; Poland; Soviet entry into war against Japan. |
| 30 January– 3 February 1945 | Malta | Britain, U.S. | Military strategy; occupation zones in Germany; Italy; China. |
| 4–11 February 1945 | Yalta | Britain, U.S., U.S.S.R. | Post-war policies: Germany, U.N., Poland, liberated Europe, Russia, Japan and China. |
| 25 April–26 June 1945 | San Francisco | 50 countries | U.N. |
| 1–22 July 1945 | Bretton Woods | 28 countries | International finance and trade. |
| 17 July– 2 August 1945 | Potsdam | Britain, U.S., U.S.S.R. | Draft peace treaties; Germany; Poland; Japan. |

British and United States diplomacy and did not involve the Russians. From a political point of view the *Conference of Casablanca* (the British Prime Minister, Churchill, the U.S. President, Roosevelt, and the Combined Chiefs of Staff), *14–25 January 1943* was notable for the attempt made to bring together the Free French General de Gaulle and his rival, General Giraud, who assumed command of the French forces in north Africa; also for the 'unconditional surrender' call as the only terms the Allies would offer their enemies. The phrase 'unconditional surrender' had been under discussion, but was omitted from the final communiqué, though publicly announced in a press conference given by President Roosevelt.

Research which was to lead to the making of the atomic bomb was the subject of a secret Anglo-American agreement at the *Quebec Conference of August 1943*, not disclosed until 1954. The exclusive possession of the bomb with its secrets, and the unknown possible applications of atomic energy after the war, made these secrets one of the most prized assets of power in the war and in the post-war world. These secrets were not shared with the Soviet Union. *The Agreement on Anglo-American–Canadian collaboration in development of atomic research* was signed on *19 August 1943* by Churchill and Roosevelt. It set out the policy of pooling in the United States the scientists (many of them émigrés from Nazi Europe) and resources to speed the project. The two countries undertook not to use the atomic bomb against each other; they also agreed not to use it against another country without each other's consent; they agreed not to communicate any information to another country without their mutual consent. Britain disclaimed any 'post-war advantages of an industrial or commercial character' beyond what the President of the United States considered fair and just and for the welfare of the world. Allocation of materials, all policy, and interchange of information was to be the function of a Combined Policy Committee of three American, one Canadian and two British officials. Information about large-scale plants was to become the subject of later agreements. The first atomic bomb was dropped by an American plane on Hiroshima on 6 August 1945 and the second on Nagasaki on 9 August 1945. The post-war operation of this secret executive agreement caused Anglo-American differences of opinion in 1945 and 1946 after Roosevelt's death; its existence was unknown to Congress. The American desire to preserve secrecy and military nuclear monopoly led to the passing of the McMahon Act in 1946 which rendered the wartime agreement inoperative (p. 437).

At the *Conference of Foreign Ministers at Moscow 18–30 October 1943,* agreement was reached on a *Four-Power Declaration of General Security* whereby the United States, Great Britain, the Soviet Union and China agreed to help establish a general international organization for the maintenance of peace and security, and to continue their collaboration in peace as in war. The conference also agreed to set up a *European Advisory Commission* with headquarters in London to consider all specific questions concerning the surrender terms and their execution; the commission was empowered to make recommendations but could exercise no mandatory authority. An *Advisory Council for Italy* was also established but exercised little influence. The Foreign Ministers agreed that Austria should be reestablished as an independent State after the war. A decision on cooperating in the punishment of individuals responsible for atrocities was also reached. At the end of the conference an official communiqué was issued together with four *Declarations on General Security, Italy, Austria, and German Atrocities, 30 October 1943*.

The *Cairo Conference took place on 22–6 November 1943* (Roosevelt, Churchill, Chiang Kai-shek). The Russians would not attend since they were not at war with Japan. Besides military strategy in the Far East, the post-war settlement there was discussed. The final communiqué outlined the territorial peace terms the three Allies would impose on Japan, and promised Korea independence in due course.

Roosevelt and Churchill next flew to Persia to participate with the Russians in the *Teheran Conference* (Churchill, Roosevelt, Stalin, Combined Chiefs of Staff), *28 November–1 December 1943*. The military situation in Europe and the Far East was discussed. Stalin declared Russia would join in the war against Japan after victory over Germany. There were exploratory discussions concerning the future of France, Germany and Poland. Roosevelt initiated a discussion on the establishment of a post-war international organization to preserve peace and security. It was agreed that 'Overlord', the Anglo-American invasion of northern France, would take place on 1 May 1944. Turkey and Italy were also discussed. No formal written agreement was reached on Russia's and Poland's western frontiers, though Churchill agreed to the Curzon line as a basis. Originally a British proposal of 1920, this excluded from Poland a broad slice of territory inhabited largely by Ukrainians and other non-Poles. By way of compensation for Poland, Churchill further agreed to the Polish acquisition of German territory east of the Oder river. A declaration promised to Iran independence and territorial integrity. A communiqué on the results of the conference was published on 6 December 1943.

More than a year elapsed after the conclusion of the Teheran Conference before Churchill, Roosevelt and Stalin met again at Yalta in February 1945. Meantime, Roosevelt and Churchill and the Combined Chiefs of Staff had met at *Quebec, 11–19 September 1944* to discuss future policy towards Germany. Churchill flew to *Moscow* to discuss post-war spheres of influence, the Balkans and Poland, with Stalin; Averell Harriman attended as an American observer, *9–20 October 1944.* Shortly before Yalta, British and American military and political representatives (not including Roosevelt) met at *Malta, 30 January–3 February 1945*, to examine military strategy and the Anglo-American zones of occupation, and other issues.

The 'Big Three' meeting at *Yalta* (Churchill, Roosevelt, Stalin, and their military and political advisers) *4–11 February 1945* (p. 27) was the most crucial of the war in moulding the reconstruction of the post-war world. Roosevelt was anxious to secure a firm Russian undertaking to join in the war against Japan. He acceded to Stalin's condition that Russia should resume her old rights in China, lost as a result of the Russo-Japanese war of 1904–5.

Despite the difficulties of China's rights, *a secret tripartite agreement was signed concerning Russia's participation in the war against Japan on 11 February 1945* (p. 31); this agreement was only published a year after its signature. Allied policy towards Germany led to discussions and agreements at Yalta. The European Advisory Commission had reached agreed recommendations which formed the basis of the awards at Yalta on the zones of occupation, on Berlin and on the form of Allied control. At Yalta agreement was also reached to allow the French a zone of occupation and to admit France as an equal member of the Allied Control Commission for Germany. A decision on reparations was referred to a Reparations Commission to be set up in Moscow. The decisions concerning Allied treatment of Germany reached at Yalta lacked precision and were vague, since practical details were not worked out. They were summarized in Protocols III, IV, V and VI of the Proceedings of the Conference. Protocol I set out the agreement on the setting up of a world organization of the United Nations, and more especially on the voting formula for the Security Council; it was agreed to call a United Nations Conference at San Francisco on 25 April 1945 (p. 58).

The future of Poland was a most contentious and difficult issue at Yalta, and no precise conclusions were reached on post-war Polish boundaries (though the Curzon line with some small digressions in Poland's favour was referred to as Poland's eastern frontier). Nor was there agreement over the 'reconstruction' of the Polish Government. The ambiguous Declaration on Poland was embodied in Protocol VII. A number of other important post-war problems were set out in Protocols IX to XIV. Finally, the Declaration on Liberated Europe, Protocol II, is noteworthy as an attempt, on American initiative, to commit Russia to the restoration of democratic national self-government to the States occupied by the Russian armies at the close of the war.

By the time of the next Big Three meeting at Potsdam in July 1945 the war in Europe was over. Admiral Dönitz, who had succeeded Hitler as German leader, authorized Germany's unconditional surrender, and the instrument of surrender was signed at General Eisenhower's headquarters in Rheims on 7 May 1945; Stalin insisted on a second capitulation at Marshal Zhukov's headquarters in Berlin on 9 May 1945, a day after the fighting had ended. Before the Potsdam meeting the agreements reached at Yalta were being differently interpreted by the Allies. Russian pressure for the establishment of a communist Government in Poland was regarded by the Western Allies as in breach of the Declaration on Liberated Europe. On 10 March 1945, Stalin assigned to Rumania the part of Transylvania which Hitler had awarded to Hungary in 1940. Allied disputes over the future Polish Government continued. On 12 April 1945 Roosevelt died and Harry Truman was sworn in as President of the United States. Serious Allied differences over the control of Austria, deep suspicion of Russian intentions in Poland, problems in occupied Germany, hard-won agreement over the establishment of an international organization and the reparations question were all part of the diplomatic confrontation during the immediate aftermath of the war in Europe. Some differences were patched up. The Charter of the United Nations was signed on 26 June 1945 (p. 64). The British and American Governments recognized a reorganized Soviet-sponsored Polish Provisional Government of National Unity on 5 July 1945. The machinery of Allied control over Germany was established, and the zones of occupation brought under the respective military controls of the U.S.S.R., France, Britain and the United States. The Polish western frontier had not been finally settled at Yalta; the Russians handed over German territory as far as the rivers Oder and the western Neisse to Polish administration. The Potsdam Conference was to settle future Allied policies, to lay the foundation for definitive peace settlements and to reach agreed policies on the treatment of Germany.

*The Potsdam Conference, 17 July–2 August 1945* (p. 32) was attended by Churchill (Prime Minister until 26 July when the General Election brought Clement Attlee and the Labour Party to power), Stalin and Truman. The French were not invited. The talks appeared to get off to a good start with an agreement on an American proposal that a Council of

Foreign Ministers should be set up to prepare drafts of peace treaties with the ex-enemy States in Europe and Asia (this body replaced the European Advisory Commission); London was chosen as the permanent seat of the council. The French had not been invited to Potsdam but were to be represented on the Council of Foreign Ministers. Germany's frontiers were not established with finality, though it was agreed that the frontiers of 1937 should be taken as the basis for discussion, excluding Austria, the territory taken from Czechoslovakia by Germany at the Munich Conference in 1938, as well as German-occupied Poland. The Polish question led to acrimonious debate, particularly over the extent of Polish expansion eastward at Germany's expense, the Russians and Britain and the United States differing later as to what had been settled. The agreement left under Polish administration the territory assigned to them by the Russians, adding that it was 'considered as part of the Soviet zone of occupation of Germany'; while the final delimitation of Poland's western frontier was reserved until the conclusion of a German peace treaty. Russian claims to about half of East Prussia including Königsberg were accepted by Britain and the United States which undertook to support Russia when a peace conference assembled. Agreement was reached on the treatment of Austria. But Soviet insistence that immediate recognition be granted to the Soviet-sponsored Armistice Governments of Hungary, Bulgaria and Rumania proved unacceptable to the Western Powers; Western insistence on supervised genuinely free elections was dismissed by Stalin who said that such an attitude made agreement impossible. In practice these three countries were left in Soviet control. The Western interpretation of the Yalta Declaration on Liberated Europe could not be realized. Many questions remained unsettled, such as the Turkish Straits and the Italian colonies. On the central problem of the treatment of Germany, agreements were reached which reflected paper compromises. The idea of partitioning Germany into a number of States was dropped. Supreme authority in Germany was to be exercised by the Commanders-in-Chief of the British, French, American and Russian armed forces in their respective zones, whilst for Germany as a whole they were to act jointly as members of the Control Council. Principles governing the treatment of the whole of Germany leading to disarmament, de-Nazification and demilitarization were agreed. But policies in practice differed widely between the Russian and Western zones of occupation. Similarly, it was agreed that Germany was to be treated as a single economic unit with a living standard for the German people not exceeding the average of other Europeans, but again control of German industry was exercised differently in each zone, as was the collection of reparations despite agreement on general principles. The differing views of the Russians and Western Powers on reparations and the German frontiers proved among the most intractable problems of the conference. The decisions concerning Germany in practice undermined the general principle of treating occupied Germany as a whole, and confirmed the divisions of Germany especially as between the Russian and Western zones. A major problem was the settlement of German refugees, several million of whom were either fleeing or being expelled from Polish-occupied Germany, from the Czech Sudetenland, East Prussia and Hungary. Their expulsion was accepted at Potsdam as necessary but it was to be carried out in an 'orderly and humane manner'.

## Report of the Crimea Conference (Yalta Conference), 11 February 1945

For the past eight days Winston S. Churchill, Prime Minister of Great Britain, Franklin D. Roosevelt, President of the United States of America, and Marshal J.V. Stalin, Chairman of the Council of People's Commissars of the Union of Soviet Socialist Republics, have met with the Foreign Secretaries, Chiefs of Staff and other advisers in the Crimea.

The following statement is made by the Prime Minister of Great Britain, the President of the United States of America, and the Chairman of the Council of People's Commissars of the Union of Soviet Socialist Republics, on the results of the Crimea Conference.

### I · THE DEFEAT OF GERMANY

We have considered and determined the military plans of the three Allied Powers for the final defeat of the common enemy. The military staffs of the three Allied nations have met in daily meetings throughout the Conference. These meetings have been most satisfactory from every point of view and have resulted in closer coordination of the military effort of the three Allies than ever before. The fullest information has been interchanged. The timing, scope and coordination of new and even more powerful blows to be launched by our armies and air forces into the heart of Germany from the East, West, North and South have been fully agreed and planned in detail.

Our combined military plans will be made known only as we execute them, but we believe that the very close working partnership among the three staffs attained at this Conference will result in shortening the war. Meetings of the three staffs will be continued in the future whenever the need arises.

Nazi Germany is doomed. The German people will only make the cost of their defeat heavier to themselves by attempting to continue a hopeless resistance.

### II · THE OCCUPATION AND CONTROL OF GERMANY

We have agreed on common policies and plans for enforcing the unconditional surrender terms which we shall impose together on Nazi Germany after German armed resistance has been finally crushed. These terms will not be made known until the final defeat of Germany has been accomplished. Under the agreed plan, the forces of the Three Powers will each occupy a separate zone of Germany. Coordinated administration and control has been provided for under the plan through a central Control Commission consisting of the Supreme Commanders of the Three Powers with headquarters in Berlin. It has been agreed that France should be invited by the Three Powers, if she should so desire, to take over a zone of occupation, and to participate as a fourth member of the Control Commission. The limits of the French zone will be agreed by the four Governments concerned through their representatives on the European Advisory Commission.

It is our inflexible purpose to destroy German militarism and Nazism and to ensure that Germany will never again be able to disturb the peace of the world. We are determined to disarm and disband all German armed forces; break up for all time the German General Staff that has repeatedly contrived the resurgence of German militarism; remove or destroy all German military equipment; eliminate or control all German industry that could be used for military production; bring all war criminals to just and swift punishment and exact reparation in kind for the destruction wrought by the Germans; wipe out the Nazi party, Nazi laws, organizations and institutions, remove all Nazi and militarist influences from public office and from the cultural and economic life of the German people; and take in harmony such other measures in Germany as may be necessary to the future peace and safety of the world. It is not our purpose to destroy the people of Germany, but only when Nazism and militarism have been extirpated, will there be hope for a decent life for Germans, and a place for them in the comity of nations.

III · Reparation by Germany

We have considered the question of the damage caused by Germany to the Allied nations in this war and recognized it as just that Germany be obliged to make compensation for this damage in kind to the greatest extent possible. A Commission for the Compensation of Damage will be established. The Commission will be instructed to consider the question of the extent and methods for compensating damage caused by Germany to the Allied countries. The Commission will work in Moscow.

IV · United Nations Conference

We are resolved upon the earliest possible establishment with our Allies of a general international organization to maintain peace and security. We believe that this is essential, both to prevent aggression and to remove the political, economic and social causes of war through the close and continuing collaboration of all peace-loving peoples.

The foundations were laid at Dumbarton Oaks. On the important question of voting procedure, however, agreement was not there reached. The present Conference has been able to resolve this difficulty.

We have agreed that a Conference of United Nations should be called to meet at San Francisco in the United States on the 25th April 1945, to prepare the charter of such an organization, along the lines proposed in the informal conversations at Dumbarton Oaks.

The Government of China and the Provisional Government of France will be immediately consulted and invited to sponsor invitations to the Conference jointly with the Governments of the United States, Great Britain and the Union of Soviet Socialist Republics. As soon as the consultation with China and France has been completed, the text of the proposals on voting procedure will be made public.

V · Declaration on Liberated Europe

We have drawn up and subscribed to a Declaration on Liberated Europe. This Declaration provides for concerting the policies of the Three Powers and for joint action by them in meeting the political and economic problems of liberated Europe in accordance with democratic principles. The text of the Declaration is as follows:

The Premier of the Union of Soviet Socialist Republics, the Prime Minister of the United Kingdom, and the President of the United States of America have consulted with each other in the common interests of the peoples of their countries and those of liberated Europe. They jointly declare their mutual agreement to concert during the temporary period of instability in liberated Europe the policies of their three Governments in assisting the peoples liberated from the domination of Nazi Germany and the peoples of the former Axis satellite States of Europe to solve by democratic means their pressing political and economic problems.

The establishment of order in Europe and the rebuilding of national economic life must be achieved by processes which will enable the liberated peoples to destroy the last vestiges of Nazism and Fascism and to create democratic institutions of their own choice. This is a principle of the Atlantic Charter — the right of all peoples to choose the form of government under which they will live — the restoration of sovereign rights and self-government to those peoples who have been forcibly deprived of them by the aggressor nations.

To foster the conditions in which the liberated peoples may exercise those rights, the three Governments will jointly assist the people in any European liberated State or former Axis satellite State in Europe where in their judgement conditions require: (a) to establish conditions of internal peace; (b) to carry out emergency measures for the relief of distressed peoples; (c) to form interim governmental authorities broadly representative of all democratic elements in the population and pledged to the earliest possible establishment through free elections of Governments responsive to the will of the people; and (d) to facilitate where necessary the holding of such elections.

The three Governments will consult the other United Nations and provisional authorities or other Governments in Europe when matters of direct interest to them are under consideration.

When, in the opinion of the three Governments, conditions in any European liberated State or any former Axis satellite State in Europe make such action necessary, they will immediately consult together on the measures necessary to discharge the joint responsibilities set forth in this Declaration.

By this Declaration we reaffirm our faith in the principles of the Atlantic Charter, our pledge in the Declaration by the United Nations, and our determination to build in cooperation with other peace-loving nations a world order under law, dedicated to peace, security, freedom and the general well-being of all mankind.

In issuing this Declaration, the Three Powers express the hope that the Provisional Government of the French Republic may be associated with them in the procedure suggested.

## VI · POLAND

We came to the Crimea Conference resolved to settle our differences about Poland. We discussed fully all aspects of the question. We reaffirm our common desire to see established a strong, free, independent and democratic Poland. As a result of our discussions we have agreed on the conditions in which a new Polish Provisional Government of National Unity may be formed in such a manner as to command recognition by the three major Powers.

The agreement reached is as follows:

A new situation has been created in Poland as a result of her complete liberation by the Red Army. This calls for the establishment of a Polish Provisional Government which can be more broadly based than was possible before the recent liberation of western Poland. The Provisional Government which is now functioning in Poland should therefore be reorganized on a broader democratic basis with the inclusion of democratic leaders from Poland itself and from Poles abroad. This new Government should then be called the Polish Provisional Government of National Unity.

M. Molotov, Mr Harriman and Sir A. Clark Kerr are authorized as a Commission to consult in the first instance in Moscow with members of the present Provisional Government and with other Polish democratic leaders from within Poland and from abroad, with a view to the reorganization of the present Government along the above lines. This Polish Provisional Government of National Unity shall be pledged to the holding of free and unfettered elections as soon as possible on the basis of universal suffrage and secret ballot. In these elections all democratic and anti-Nazi parties shall have the right to take part and to put forward candidates.

When a Polish Provisional Government of National Unity has been properly formed in conformity with the above, the Government of the Union of Soviet Socialist Republics, which now maintains diplomatic relations with the present Provisional Government of Poland, and the Government of the United Kingdom and the Government of the United States will establish diplomatic relations with the new Polish Government of National Unity, and will exchange Ambassadors by whose reports the respective Governments will be kept informed about the situation in Poland.

The three Heads of Government consider that the eastern frontier of Poland should follow the Curzon line with digressions from it in some regions of 5 to 8 kilometres in favour of Poland. They recognize that Poland must receive substantial accessions of territory in the north and west. They feel that the opinion of the new Polish Provisional Government of National Unity should be sought in due course on the extent of these accessions and that the final delimitation of the western frontier of Poland should thereafter await the Peace Conference.

## VII · YUGOSLAVIA

We have agreed to recommend to Marshal Tito and Dr Subasić that the Agreement between them should be put into effect immediately, and that a new Government should be formed on the basis of that Agreement.

We also recommend that as soon as the new Government has been formed it should declare that:

(i) The Anti-Fascist Assembly of National Liberation (Avnoj) should be extended to include members of the last Yugoslav Parliament (Skupshtina) who have not compromised themselves by collaboration with the enemy, thus forming a body to be known as a temporary Parliament; and

(ii) Legislative acts passed by the Assembly of National Liberation will be subject to subsequent ratification by a Constituent Assembly.

There was also a general review of other Balkan questions.

## VIII · MEETINGS OF FOREIGN SECRETARIES

Throughout the Conference, besides the daily meetings of the Heads of Governments, and the Foreign Secretaries, separate meetings of the three Foreign Secretaries, and their advisers, have also been held daily.

These meetings have proved of the utmost value and the Conference agreed that permanent machinery should be set up for regular consultation between the three Foreign Secretaries. They will, therefore, meet as often as may be necessary, probably about every three or four months. These meetings will be held in rotation in the three capitals, the first meeting being held in London, after the United Nations Conference on World Organization.

## IX · UNITY FOR PEACE AS FOR WAR

Our meeting here in the Crimea has reaffirmed our common determination to maintain and strengthen in the peace to come that unity of purpose and of action which has made victory possible and certain for the United Nations in this war. We believe that this is a sacred obligation which our Governments owe to our peoples and to all the peoples of the world.

Only with continuing and growing co-operation and understanding among our three countries, and among all the peace-loving nations, can the highest aspiration of humanity be realized – a secure and lasting peace which will, in the words of the Atlantic Charter 'Afford assurance that all the men in all the lands may live out their lives in freedom from fear and want'.

Victory in this war and establishment of the proposed international organization will provide the greatest opportunity in all history to create in the years to come the essential conditions of such a peace. (Signed)

WINSTON S. CHURCHILL
FRANKLIN D. ROOSEVELT
J.V. STALIN
*11th February 1945*

## Yalta Agreement on the Kuriles and entry of the Soviet Union in the war against Japan, 11 February 1945

The leaders of the three Great Powers – the Soviet Union, the United States of America and Great Britain – have agreed that in two or three months after Germany has surrendered and the war in Europe has terminated the Soviet Union shall enter into the war against Japan on the side of the Allies on condition that:

1. The *status quo* in Outer Mongolia (The Mongolian People's Republic) shall be preserved;
2. The former rights of Russia violated by the treacherous attack of Japan in 1904 shall be restored, viz:

(a) the southern part of Sakhalin as well as all the islands adjacent to it shall be returned to the Soviet Union,

(b) the commercial port of Dairen shall be internationalized, the pre-eminent interests of the Soviet Union in this port being safeguarded and the lease of Port Arthur as a naval base of the U.S.S.R. restored,

(c) the Chinese-Eastern Railroad and the South-Manchurian Railroad which provides an outlet to Dairen shall be jointly operated by the establishment of a joint Soviet–Chinese Company, it being understood that the pre-eminent interests of the Soviet Union shall be safeguarded and that China shall retain full sovereignty in Manchuria;

3. The Kuril islands shall be handed over to the Soviet Union.

It is understood that the agreement concerning Outer Mongolia and the ports and railroads referred to above will require concurrence of Generalissimo Chiang Kai-shek. The President will take measures in order to obtain this concurrence on advice from Marshal Stalin.

The Heads of the three Great Powers have agreed that these claims of the Soviet Union shall be unquestionably fulfilled after Japan has been defeated.

For its part the Soviet Union expresses its readiness to conclude with the National Government of China a pact of friendship and alliance between the U.S.S.R. and China in order to render assistance to China with its armed forces for the purpose of liberating China from the Japanese yoke.

*February 11, 1945*
J. STALIN
FRANKLIN D. ROOSEVELT
WINSTON S. CHURCHILL

[The agreement was made public on 11 February 1946.]

# Potsdam Conference Protocol, 2 August 1945

The Berlin Conference of the three Heads of Government of the U.S.S.R., U.S.A., and U.K., which took place from July 17 to August 2, 1945, came to the following conclusions:

## I · Establishment of a Council of Foreign Ministers

A. The Conference reached the following agreement for the establishment of a Council of Foreign Ministers to do the necessary preparatory work for the peace settlements:

1. There shall be established a Council composed of the Foreign Ministers of the United Kingdom, the Union of Soviet Socialist Republics, China, France, and the United States.

2. (i) The Council shall normally meet in London which shall be the permanent seat of the joint Secretariat which the Council will form. . . .

3. (i) As its immediate important task, the Council shall be authorized to draw up, with a view to their submission to the United Nations, treaties of peace with Italy, Rumania, Bulgaria, Hungary and Finland, and to propose settlements of territorial questions outstanding on the termination of the war in Europe. The Council shall be utilized for the preparation of a peace settlement for Germany to be accepted by the Government of Germany when a Government adequate for the purpose is established.

(ii) For the discharge of each of these tasks the Council will be composed of the Members representing those States which were signatory to the terms of surrender imposed upon the enemy State concerned. For the purposes of the peace settlement for Italy, France shall be regarded as a signatory to the terms of surrender for Italy. Other Members will be invited to participate when matters directly concerning them are under discussion.

(iii) Other matters may from time to time be referred to the Council by agree-ment between the Member Governments.

4. (i) Whenever the Council is con-sidering a question of direct interest to a State not represented thereon, such State should be invited to send representatives to participate in the discussion and study of that question.

(ii) The Council may adapt its proce-dure to the particular problems under consideration. In some cases it may hold its own preliminary discussions prior to the participation of other interested States. In other cases, the Council may convoke a formal conference of the States chiefly interested in seeking a solution of the particular problem.

B. It was agreed that the three Govern-ments should each address an identical invitation to the Governments of China and France to adopt this text and to join in establishing the Council. . . .

[It was agreed to recommend that the European Advisory Commission be dis-solved.]

## II · The principles to govern the treatment of Germany in the initial control period

### A · POLITICAL PRINCIPLES

1. In accordance with the Agreement on Control Machinery in Germany, supreme authority in Germany is exercised, on instructions from their respective Govern-ments, by the Commanders-in-Chief of the armed forces of the United States of America, the United Kingdom, the Union of Soviet Socialist Republics, and the French Republic, each in his own zone of occupation, and also jointly, in matters affecting Germany as a whole, in their capacity as members of the Control Council.

2. So far as is practicable, there shall be uniformity of treatment of the German population throughout Germany.

3. The purposes of the occupation of

Germany by which the Control Council shall be guided are:

(i) The complete disarmament and demilitarization of Germany and the elimination or control of all German industry that could be used for military production. . . .

(ii) To convince the German people that they have suffered a total military defeat and that they cannot escape responsibility for what they have brought upon themselves, since their own ruthless warfare and the fanatical Nazi resistance have destroyed German economy and made chaos and suffering inevitable.

(iii) To destroy the National Socialist Party and its affiliated and supervised organizations, to dissolve all Nazi institutions, to ensure that they are not revived in any form, and to prevent all Nazi and militarist activity or propaganda.

(iv) To prepare for the eventual reconstruction of German political life on a democratic basis and for eventual peaceful cooperation in international life by Germany.

4. All Nazi laws which provided the basis of the Hitler régime or established discriminations on grounds of race, creed, or political opinion shall be abolished. No such discriminations, whether legal, administrative or otherwise, shall be tolerated.

5. War criminals and those who have participated in planning or carrying out Nazi enterprises involving or resulting in atrocities or war crimes shall be arrested and brought to judgement. Nazi leaders, influential Nazi supporters and high officials of Nazi organizations and institutions and any other persons dangerous to the occupation or its objectives shall be arrested and interned.

6. All members of the Nazi Party who have been more than nominal participants in its activities and all other persons hostile to Allied purposes shall be removed from public and semi-public office, and from positions of responsibility in important private undertakings. Such persons shall be replaced by persons who, by their political and moral qualities, are deemed capable of assisting in developing genuine democratic institutions in Germany.

7. German education shall be so controlled as completely to eliminate Nazi and militarist doctrines and to make possible the successful development of democratic ideas.

8. The judicial system will be reorganized in accordance with the principles of democracy, of justice under law, and of equal rights for all citizens without distinction of race, nationality or religion.

9. The administration in Germany should be directed towards the decentralization of the political structure and the development of local responsibility. To this end:

(i) local self-government shall be restored throughout Germany on democratic principles and in particular through elective councils as rapidly as is consistent with military security and the purposes of military occupation;

(ii) all democratic political parties with rights of assembly and of public discussion shall be allowed and encouraged throughout Germany;

(iii) representative and elective principles shall be introduced into regional, provincial and State (*Land*) administration as rapidly as may be justified by the successful application of these principles in local self-government;

(iv) for the time being, no central German Government shall be established. Notwithstanding this, however, certain essential central German administrative departments, headed by State Secretaries, shall be established, particularly in the fields of finance, transport, communications, foreign trade and industry. Such departments will act under the direction of the Control Council.

10. Subject to the necessity for maintaining military security, freedom of speech, press and religion shall be permitted, and religious institutions shall be respected. Subject likewise to the maintenance of military security, the formation of free trade unions shall be permitted.

B · Economic principles

11. In order to eliminate Germany's war potential, the production of arms, ammunition and implements of war as well as all types of aircraft and sea-going ships shall be prohibited and prevented. Production of metals, chemicals, machinery and other items that are directly necessary to a war economy shall be rigidly controlled and restricted to Germany's approved post-war peacetime needs to meet the objectives stated in paragraph 15. Productive capacity not needed for permitted production shall be removed in accordance with the reparations plan recommended by the Allied Commission on Reparations and approved by the Governments concerned or if not removed shall be destroyed.

12. At the earliest practicable date, the German economy shall be decentralized for the purpose of eliminating the present excessive concentration of economic power as exemplified in particular by cartels, syndicates, trusts and other monopolistic arrangements.

13. In organizing the German economy, primary emphasis shall be given to the development of agriculture and peaceful domestic industries.

14. During the period of occupation Germany shall be treated as a single economic unit. To this end common policies shall be established in regard to:

(a) mining and industrial production and its allocation;

(b) agriculture, forestry and fishing;

(c) wages, prices and rationing;

(d) import and export programmes for Germany as a whole;

(e) currency and banking, central taxation and customs;

(f) reparation and removal of industrial war potential;

(g) transportation and communications.

In applying these policies account shall be taken, where appropriate, of varying local conditions.

15. Allied controls shall be imposed upon the German economy but only to the extent necessary....

16. In the imposition and maintenance of economic controls established by the Control Council, German administrative machinery shall be created and the German authorities shall be required to the fullest extent practicable to proclaim and assume administration of such controls....

17. Measures shall be promptly taken:

(a) to effect essential repair of transport;

(b) to enlarge coal production;

(c) to maximize agricultural output; and

(d) to effect emergency repair of housing and essential utilities.

18. Appropriate steps shall be taken by the Control Council to exercise control and the power of disposition over German-owned external assets not already under the control of United Nations which have taken part in the war against Germany.

19. Payment of reparations should leave enough resources to enable the German people to subsist without external assistance. In working out the economic balance of Germany the necessary means must be provided to pay for imports approved by the Control Council in Germany. The proceeds of exports from current production and stocks shall be available in the first place for payment for such imports....

## III · Reparations from Germany

1. Reparation claims of the U.S.S.R. shall be met by removals from the zone of Germany occupied by the U.S.S.R., and from appropriate German external assets.

2. The U.S.S.R. undertakes to settle the reparation claims of Poland from its own share of reparations.

3. The reparation claims of the United States, the United Kingdom and other countries entitled to reparations shall be met from the Western zones and from appropriate German external assets.

4. In addition to the reparations to be taken by the U.S.S.R. from its own zone of occupation, the U.S.S.R. shall receive

additionally from the Western zones:

(a) Fifteen per cent of such usable and complete industrial capital equipment, in the first place from the metallurgical, chemical and machine manufacturing industries as is unnecessary for the German peace economy and should be removed from the Western zones of Germany, in exchange for an equivalent value of food, coal, potash, zinc, timber, clay products, petroleum products, and such other commodities as may be agreed upon.

(b) Ten per cent of such industrial capital equipment as is unnecessary for the German peace economy and should be removed from the Western zones, to be transferred to the Soviet Government on reparations account without payment or exchange of any kind in return.

Removals of equipment as provided in (a) and (b) above shall be made simultaneously....

8. The Soviet Government renounces all claims in respect of reparations to shares of German enterprises which are located in the Western zones of Germany as well as to German foreign assets in all countries except those specified in paragraph 9 below.

9. The Governments of the U.K. and U.S.A. renounce all claims in respect of reparations to shares of German enterprises which are located in the Eastern zone of occupation in Germany, as well as to German foreign assets in Bulgaria, Finland, Hungary, Rumania and Eastern Austria....

## IV · Disposal of the German Navy and Merchant Marine

A. The following principles for the distribution of the German Navy were agreed:

1. The total strength of the German Surface Navy, excluding ships sunk and those taken over from Allied Nations, but including ships under construction or repair, shall be divided equally among the U.S.S.R., U.K., and U.S.A....

The German Merchant Marine, surrendered to the Three Powers and wherever located, shall be divided equally among the U.S.S.R., the U.K., and the U.S.A.

## V · City of Koenigsberg and the adjacent area

The Conference examined a proposal by the Soviet Government to the effect that pending the final determination of territorial questions at the peace settlement, the section of the western frontier of the Union of Soviet Socialist Republics which is adjacent to the Baltic Sea should pass from a point on the eastern shore of the Bay of Danzig to the east, north of Braunsberg-Goldap, to the meeting point of the frontiers of Lithuania, the Polish Republic and East Prussia.

The Conference has agreed in principle to the proposal of the Soviet Government concerning the ultimate transfer to the Soviet Union of the City of Koenigsberg and the area adjacent to it as described above subject to expert examination of the actual frontier.

The President of the United States and the British Prime Minister have declared that they will support the proposal of the Conference at the forthcoming peace settlement.

## VI · War criminals

[Trials to begin at earliest possible date.]

. . .

## VII · Austria

The Conference examined a proposal by the Soviet Government on the extension of the authority of the Austrian Provisional Government to all of Austria.

The three Governments agreed that they were prepared to examine this question after the entry of the British and American forces into the city of Vienna.

It was agreed that reparations should not be exacted from Austria.

## VIII · Poland

### A · DECLARATION

We have taken note with pleasure of the agreement reached among representative Poles from Poland and abroad which has made possible the formation, in accordance with the decisions reached at the Crimea Conference, of a Polish Provisional Government of National Unity recognized by the Three Powers. The establishment by the British and United States Governments of diplomatic relations with the Polish Provisional Government of National Unity has resulted in the withdrawal of their recognition from the former Polish Government in London, which no longer exists.

The British and United States Governments have taken measures to protect the interest of the Polish Provisional Government of National Unity as the recognized Government of the Polish State in the property belonging to the Polish State located in their territories and under their control, whatever the form of this property may be. They have further taken measures to prevent alienation to third parties of such property. All proper facilities will be given to the Polish Provisional Government of National Unity for the exercise of the ordinary legal remedies for the recovery of any property belonging to the Polish State which may have been wrongfully alienated.

The Three Powers are anxious to assist the Polish Provisional Government of National Unity in facilitating the return to Poland as soon as practicable of all Poles abroad who wish to go, including members of the Polish armed forces and the Merchant Marine. They expect that those Poles who return home shall be accorded personal and property rights on the same basis as all Polish citizens.

The Three Powers note that the Polish Provisional Government of National Unity, in accordance with the decisions of the Crimea Conference, has agreed to the holding of free and unfettered elections as soon as possible on the basis of universal suffrage and secret ballot in which all democratic and anti-Nazi parties shall have the right to take part and to put forward candidates, and that representatives of the Allied press shall enjoy full freedom to report to the world upon developments in Poland before and during the elections.

### B · WESTERN FRONTIER OF POLAND

In conformity with the agreement on Poland reached at the Crimea Conference the three Heads of Government have sought the opinion of the Polish Provisional Government of National Unity in regard to the accession of territory in the north and west which Poland should receive. The President of the National Council of Poland and members of the Polish Provisional Government of National Unity have been received at the Conference and have fully presented their views. The three Heads of Government reaffirm their opinion that the final delimitation of the western frontier of Poland should await the peace settlement.

The three Heads of Government agree that, pending the final determination of Poland's western frontier, the former German territories east of a line running from the Baltic Sea immediately west of Swinamunde, and thence along the Oder river to the confluence of the western Neisse river and along the western Neisse to the Czechoslovak frontier, including that portion of East Prussia not placed under the administration of the Union of Soviet Socialist Republics in accordance with the understanding reached at this Conference and including the area of the former Free City of Danzig, shall be under the administration of the Polish State and for such purposes should not be considered as part of the Soviet zone of occupation in Germany.

## IX · Conclusion of peace treaties and admission to the United Nations Organization

The three Governments consider it desirable that the present anomalous position of Italy, Bulgaria, Finland, Hungary and Rumania should be terminated by the conclusion of peace treaties. They trust that the other interested Allied Governments will share these views....

As regards the admission of other States into the United Nations Organization, Article 4 of the Charter of the United Nations declares that:

1. Membership in the United Nations is open to all other peace-loving States who accept the obligations contained in the present Charter and, in the judgement of the Organization, are able and willing to carry out these obligations.

2. The admission of any such State to membership in the United Nations will be effected by a decision of the General Assembly upon the recommendation of the Security Council.

The three Governments, so far as they are concerned, will support applications for membership from those States which have remained neutral during the war and which fulfil the qualifications set out above.

The three Governments feel bound however to make it clear that they for their part would not favour any application for membership put forward by the present Spanish Government, which having been founded with the support of the Axis Powers, does not, in view of its origins, its nature, its record and its close association with the aggressor States, possess the qualifications necessary to justify such membership.

## X · Territorial trusteeship

The Conference examined a proposal by the Soviet Government on the question of trusteeship territories as defined in the decision of the Crimea Conference and in the Charter of the United Nations Organization.

After an exchange of views on this question it was decided that the disposition of any former Italian colonial territories was one to be decided in connection with the preparation of a peace treaty for Italy and that the question of Italian colonial territory would be considered by the September Council of Ministers of Foreign Affairs.

## XI · Revised Allied Control Commission procedure in Rumania, Bulgaria and Hungary

[Revision of procedures to be undertaken.]

. . .

## XII · Orderly transfer of German populations

The three Governments, having considered the question in all its aspects, recognize that the transfer to Germany of German populations, or elements thereof, remaining in Poland, Czechoslovakia and Hungary, will have to be undertaken. They agree that any transfers that take place should be effected in an orderly and humane manner....

## XIII · Oil equipment in Rumania

[Commission of experts to investigate.]

. . .

## XIV · Iran

It was agreed that Allied troops should be withdrawn immediately from Teheran, and that further stages of the withdrawal of troops from Iran should be considered at the meeting of the Council of Foreign Ministers to be held in London in September 1945.

## XV · International zone of Tangier

[Agreement to be reached.]

. . .

## XVI · The Black Sea Straits

The three Governments recognized that the Convention concluded at Montreux should be revised as failing to meet present-day conditions.

It was agreed that as the next step the matter should be the subject of direct conversations between each of the three Governments and the Turkish Government.

. . .

[Signed] Stalin, Truman, Attlee.

## Peacemaking in Europe

Peace treaties among some of the belligerents of the Second World War were signed, after much wrangling, within a few years after the end of the war, but the attempt to arrive at a final peace treaty and comprehensive settlement with Germany was, after much argument, tacitly abandoned (see Chapter 4).

The Potsdam Conference laid down the procedures to be followed to arrive at peace settlements and charged the Council of Foreign Ministers to draft peace treaties immediately with Italy, Rumania, Bulgaria, Hungary and Finland. A peace settlement for Germany was expected to take longer to conclude since in 1945 the time seemed distant and uncertain when a German Government could be re-established that could accept and sign a peace treaty with the Allies. Not all members of the Council of Foreign Ministers were to participate in the drafting of peace terms but only those representing States signatory to the terms of surrender of the enemy State concerned. China thus had a voice only in the Far Eastern settlements. France was entitled to participate in the Italian treaty and, it was understood, would participate in any eventual treaty with Germany. The United States would play no part in the treaty with Finland. The Great Powers would draft the treaties and then submit them to the other Allies for approval. The special position of the Great Powers in their peacemaking role was thus emphasized as it had been at the earlier peace conferences at Vienna in 1814–15 and at Paris in 1919.

During the eighteen months after the end of the war there were six major rounds of Allied negotiations: the Council of Foreign Ministers in London (September–October 1945), the Foreign Ministers Meeting of the U.S.S.R., U.S.A. and Great Britain in Moscow (December 1945), the Council of Foreign Ministers Meetings in Paris (April–May 1946 and June–July 1946), followed by the Paris Peace Conference of twenty-one nations (29 July–15 October 1946) and a final Council of Foreign Ministers Meeting in New York (4 November–12 December 1946). From these negotiations there emerged the drafts of peace treaties with Italy, Rumania, Bulgaria, Hungary and Finland. Peace treaties with these States were formally concluded in February 1947.

## THE ITALIAN PEACE TREATY, 10 FEBRUARY 1947 (p. 42)

Eleven headings and seventeen annexes made up the treaty between Italy on the one hand and the Allied and Associated Powers on the other. The preamble acknowledged that the Fascist régime was overthrown not only in consequence of Allied victory but also 'with the assistance of the democratic elements of the Italian people'. Territorially Italy was re-established in its frontiers of 1 January 1938 with a number of important exceptions. The Fascist conquests of Albania and Ethiopia were annulled, the Dodecanese were ceded to Greece and some Italian islands in the Adriatic were transferred to Greece and to Yugoslavia. There were also territorial adjustments involving Italian cessions along the boundary between Italy and France.

It was the eastern frontier of Italy that caused the greatest diplomatic difficulties. The larger part of the Venezia Giulia peninsula including Fiume was ceded to Yugoslavia by the peace treaty. Trieste with a small hinterland, formerly Italian, was set up as the Free Territory of Trieste under the guarantee of the Security Council of the U.N. The Free Territory was divided into Zone A, comprising mainly the city of Trieste, to be administered by Britain and the United States, and a Zone B under Yugoslav administration. Britain and the United States after 1948 gradually handed their Trieste zone over to the Italians. By October 1954 a settlement was reached between the Four Powers (U.S.S.R., U.S., Great Britain and France), Yugoslavia and Italy whereby nearly all of Zone A reverted to Italy while Zone B, with a small addition, was ceded to Yugoslavia; Trieste retained its status as a free port and the rights of ethnic minorities were safeguarded.

The Italians retained the south Tyrolean region of Bolzano which led to disturbances among some of its German-speaking population and to differences with Austria. A comprehensive Italian–Austrian settlement of these differences in principle was reached on 30 November 1969 after long negotiations.

The future of the Italian African colonies of Libya, Eritrea and Somaliland was not settled by the peace treaty. The treaty provided that if the Four Powers failed to reach agreement within one year of the coming into force of the peace treaty, then the matter was to be referred to the General Assembly of the United Nations. Under the auspices of the U.N., Libya became independent in December 1951, an autonomous Eritrea was federated to Ethiopia in 1952, and in 1950 Somaliland became a U.N. trust territory under Italian administration, leading to the independence of Somalia in 1960 formed by unifying previously British and Italian administered Somalilands.

The Italian navy, army and air force were limited until modified 'by agreement between the Allied and Associated Powers and Italy or, after Italy becomes a member of the United Nations, by agreement between the Security Council and Italy'.

The political clauses of the Italian peace treaty included provisions for human rights and fundamental freedoms, and specifically an obligation that Fascist and other anti-democratic organizations would not be permitted to revive. The treaty also provided for the trial of war criminals. Military clauses limited Italian armaments so that Italy would not again be able to wage aggressive war, but it was foreseen that the military clauses might later be relaxed 'in whole or in part by agreement between the Allied and Associated Powers and Italy...' (Article 46), or secondly if an agreement were reached between Italy and the Security Council once Italy had been admitted to membership of the U.N. Allied troops were to be withdrawn from Italy by December 1947. Reparations were exacted and the Soviet Union was to receive some 100 million dollars over a period of seven years; other reparation payments were to be paid to Yugoslavia (125 million dollars), Greece (105 million dollars), Ethiopia (25 million dollars) and Albania (5 million dollars). France, Britain and the U.S. agreed to forgo their reparations claims.

## THE PEACE TREATIES WITH RUMANIA, HUNGARY, BULGARIA AND FINLAND, 10 FEBRUARY 1947

These were all concluded at the same time as the Italian treaty, on 10 February 1947, and followed it in their form and structure. The political clauses of these treaties guaranteed human rights and the elimination of Fascist organizations. In 1949 Great Britain and the United States complained that the peoples of Rumania, Hungary and Bulgaria were not enjoying the fundamental freedoms so guaranteed. The military clauses placed limitations on the armed forces of the defeated States. Reparations were paid as follows: Rumania and Finland to pay 300 million dollars each to the Soviet Union; Hungary to pay 200 million dollars to the Soviet Union, and 100 million dollars each to Czechoslovakia and Yugoslavia; Bulgaria to pay 45 million dollars to Greece and 25 million dollars to Yugoslavia. The re-establishment of international control over, and freedom of, navigation along the Danube was not finally settled in the peace treaties but became a matter of serious dispute between the Soviet

Union and the Western Powers. On 18 August 1948 the Soviet Union took the lead in establishing a *Danube Commission* comprising Bulgaria, Czechoslovakia, Hungary, Rumania, the Ukraine, the U.S.S.R. and Yugoslavia, but excluding Austria and the Western Powers. The United States, Great Britain and France refused to recognize this commission for it deprived Greece, Britain, France, Italy and Belgium of their rights under earlier treaties. Austria joined the Commission in 1959 and West Germany followed in 1963.

The peace treaties brought about a number of territorial changes. *Bulgaria* was recognized within its frontiers of 1 January 1941; by this settlement Bulgaria retained the southern Dobruja acquired by an earlier Axis treaty from Rumania in September 1940. But Bulgaria returned Serbian territory to Yugoslavia and western Thrace to Greece.

*Hungary* was required to return northern Transylvania, acquired in August 1940, to Rumania. Hungary had to return to Czechoslovakia southern Slovakia, which had been secured after the Munich Conference in 1938, and also to cede additional Hungarian territory across the Danube opposite Bratislava to Czechoslovakia.

*Rumania*: the cession of Bessarabia and northern Bukovina to the U.S.S.R., first occupied by Russia in June 1940, was confirmed in 1947. The Soviet Union retained a special right in 1947 to maintain enough troops in Rumania and Hungary to safeguard its communications with the Red Army in the Soviet zone of Austria until the conclusion of a treaty with Austria.

*Finland* confirmed the cession of three territories originally ceded to the Soviet Union in 1940: the province of Petsamo, an area along the central portion of the Soviet–Finnish frontier, and the province of the Karelian isthmus in south-eastern Finland. The Soviet Union renounced its right to the lease of the Hango Peninsula, but secured instead a fifty-year lease of the Porkkala–Udd area as a naval base to protect the entrance to the Gulf of Finland; this lease was terminated by Russia in 1955.

By 1947 the first phase of peacemaking in Europe was complete. The next such treaty, the Austrian State Treaty, was not signed until 1955 (see p. 189).

# Peace Treaty between the Allies and Italy, 10 February 1947

## Part I · Territorial clauses

SECTION I · FRONTIERS

*Article 1.* The frontiers of Italy shall, subject to the modifications set out in Articles 2, 3, 4, 11 and 22, be those which existed on January 1, 1938. These frontiers are traced on the maps attached to the present Treaty (Annex I). In case of a discrepancy between the textual description of the frontiers and the maps, the text shall be deemed to be authentic.

*Article 2.* The frontier between Italy and France, as it existed on January 1, 1938, shall be modified as follows:

1. *Little St Bernard Pass...*
2. *Mont Cenis Plateau...*
3. *Mont Thabor-Chaberton...*
4. *Upper Valleys of the Tinée, Vesubie and Roya...*

*Article 3.* The frontier between Italy and Yugoslavia shall be fixed as follows...

SECTION V. GREECE (special clause)

*Article 14.* 1. Italy hereby cedes to Greece in full sovereignty the Dodecanese Islands indicated hereafter, namely Stampalia (Astropalia), Rhodes (Rhodos), Calki (Kharki), Scarpanto, Casos (Casso), Piscopis (Tilos), Misiros (Nisyros), Calimnos (Kalymnos), Leros, Patmos, Lipsos (Lipso), Simi (Symi), Cos (Kos) and Castellorizo, as well as the adjacent islets.

2. These islands shall be and shall remain demilitarized....

## Part II · Political clauses

SECTION I · GENERAL CLAUSES

Article 15. Italy shall take all measures necessary to secure to all persons under Italian jurisdiction, without distinction as to race, sex, language or religion, the enjoyment of human rights and of the fundamental freedoms, including freedom of expression, of press and publication, of religious worship, of political opinion and of public meeting.

*Article 16.* Italy shall not prosecute or molest Italian nationals, including members of the armed forces, solely on the ground that during the period from June 10, 1940, to the coming into force of the present Treaty, they expressed sympathy with or took action in support of the cause of the Allied and Associated Powers.

*Article 17.* Italy, which, in accordance with Article 30 of the Armistice Agreement, has taken measures to dissolve the Fascist organizations in Italy, shall not permit the resurgence on Italian territory of such organizations, whether political, military or semi-military, whose purpose it is to deprive the people of their democratic rights.

*Article 18.* Italy undertakes to recognize the full force of the Treaties of Peace with Roumania, Bulgaria, Hungary and Finland and other agreements or arrangements which have been or will be reached by the Allied and Associated Powers in respect of Austria, Germany and Japan for the restoration of peace.

...

SECTION III · FREE TERRITORY OF TRIESTE

*Article 21.* 1. There is hereby constituted the Free Territory of Trieste, consisting of the area lying between the Adriatic Sea and the boundaries defined in Articles 4 and 22 of the present Treaty. The Free Territory of Trieste is recognized by the Allied and Associated Powers and by Italy, which agree that its integrity and independence shall be assured by the Security Council of the United Nations.

2. Italian sovereignty over the area constituting the Free Territory of Trieste, as above defined, shall be terminated upon the coming into force of the present Treaty.

3. On the termination of Italian sovereignty, the Free Territory of Trieste shall be governed in accordance with an instrument for a provisional régime drafted by the Council of Foreign Ministers and approved by the Security Council. This Instrument shall remain in force until such date as the Security Council shall fix for the coming into force of the Permanent Statute which shall have been approved by it. The Free Territory shall thenceforth be governed by the provisions of such Permanent Statute. The texts of the Permanent Statute and of the Instrument for the Provisional Régime are contained in Annexes VI and VII.

4. The Free Territory of Trieste shall not be considered as ceded territory within the meaning of Article 19 and Annex XIV of the present Treaty.

5. Italy and Yugoslavia undertake to give to the Free Territory of Trieste the guarantees set out in Annex IX.

*Article 22.* The frontier between Yugoslavia and the Free Territory of Trieste shall be fixed as follows...

SECTION IV · ITALIAN COLONIES

*Article 23.* 1. Italy renounces all right and title to the Italian territorial possessions in Africa, i.e. Libya, Eritrea and Italian Somaliland.

2. Pending their final disposal, the said possessions shall continue under their present administration.

3. The final disposal of these possessions shall be determined jointly by the Governments of the Soviet Union, of the United Kingdom, of the United States of America, and of France within one year from the coming into force of the present Treaty, in the manner laid down in the joint declaration of February 10, 1947, issued by the said Governments, which is reproduced in Annex XI.

SECTION V · SPECIAL INTERESTS OF CHINA

*Article 24.* Italy renounces in favour of China all benefits and privileges resulting from the provisions of the final Protocol signed at Pekin on September 7, 1901, and all annexes, notes and documents supplementary thereto...

SECTION VI · ALBANIA

*Article 27.* Italy recognizes and undertakes to respect the sovereignty and independence of the State of Albania.

*Article 28.* Italy recognizes that the Island of Saseno is part of the territory of Albania and renounces all claims thereto.

SECTION VII · ETHIOPIA

*Article 33.* Italy recognizes and undertakes to respect the sovereignty and independence of the State of Ethiopia.

*Article 34.* Italy formally renounces in favour of Ethiopia all property (apart from normal diplomatic or consular premises), rights, interests and advantages of all kinds acquired at any time in Ethiopia by the Italian State, as well as all para-statal property as defined in paragraph 1 of Annex XIV of the present Treaty.

Italy also renounces all claims to special interests or influence in Ethiopia.

*Article 35.* Italy recognizes the legality of all measures which the Government of Ethiopia has taken or may hereafter take in order to annul Italian measures respecting Ethiopia taken after October 3, 1935, and the effects of such measures.

*Article 36.* Italian nationals in Ethiopia will enjoy the same juridical status as other foreign nationals, but Italy recognizes the legality of all measures of the Ethiopian Government annulling or modifying concessions or special rights granted to Italian nationals, provided such measures are taken within a year from the coming into force of the present Treaty.

*Article 37.* Within eighteen months from the coming into force of the present Treaty, Italy shall restore all works of art, religious objects, archives and objects of historical value belonging to Ethiopia or its nationals and removed from Ethiopia to Italy since October 3, 1935.

*Article 38.* The date from which the

provisions of the present Treaty shall become applicable as regards all measures and acts of any kind whatsoever entailing the responsibility of Italy or of Italian nationals towards Ethiopia, shall be held to be October 3, 1935.

SECTION VIII · INTERNATIONAL AGREEMENTS

*Article 39.* Italy undertakes to accept any arrangements which have been or may be agreed for the liquidation of the League of Nations, the Permanent Court of International Justice and also the International Financial Commission in Greece.

*Article 40.* Italy hereby renounces all rights, titles and claims deriving from the mandate system or from any undertakings given in connection therewith, and all special rights of the Italian State in respect of any mandated territory.

*Article 41.* Italy recognizes the provisions of the Final Act of August 31, 1945, and of the Franco-British Agreement of the same date on the Statute of Tangier, as well as all provisions which may be adopted by the Signatory Powers for carrying out these instruments.

*Article 42.* Italy shall accept and recognize any arrangements which may by made by the Allied and Associated Powers concerned for the modification of the Congo Basin Treaties with a view to bringing them into accord with the Charter of the United Nations.

*Article 43.* Italy hereby renounces any rights and interests she may possess by virtue of Article 16 of the Treaty of Lausanne signed on July 24, 1923.

SECTION IX · BILATERAL TREATIES

*Article 44.* 1. Each Allied or Associated Power will notify Italy, within a period of six months from the coming into force of the present Treaty, which of its pre-war bilateral treaties with Italy it desires to keep in force or revive. Any provisions not in conformity with the present Treaty shall, however, be deleted from the above-mentioned treaties.

2. All such treaties so notified shall be registered with the Secretariat of the United Nations in accordance with Article 102 of the Charter of the United Nations.

3. All such treaties not so notified shall be regarded as abrogated.

Part III · War criminals

*Article 45.* 1. Italy shall take all necessary steps to ensure the apprehension and surrender for trial of:

(a) Persons accused of having committed, ordered or abetted war crimes and crimes against peace or humanity;

(b) Nationals of any Allied or Associated Power accused of having violated their national law by treason or collaboration with the enemy during the war.

2. At the request of the United Nations Government concerned, Italy shall likewise make available as witnesses persons within its jurisdiction, whose evidence is required for the trial of the persons referred to in paragraph 1 of this Article.

3. Any disagreement concerning the application of the provisions of paragraphs 1 and 2 of this Article shall be referred by any of the Governments concerned to the Ambassadors in Rome of the Soviet Union, of the United Kingdom, of the United States of America, and of France, who will reach agreement with regard to the difficulty.

Part IV · Naval, military and air clauses

SECTION I · DURATION OF APPLICATION

*Article 46.* Each of the military, naval and air clauses of the present Treaty shall remain in force until modified in whole or in part by agreement between the Allied and Associated Powers and Italy or, after Italy becomes a member of the United Nations, by agreement between the Security Council and Italy.

SECTION II · GENERAL LIMITATIONS

*Article 47.* 1. (a) The system of permanent Italian fortifications and military installations along the Franco-Italian frontier, and their armaments, shall be destroyed or removed...

*Article 48.* 1. (a) Any permanent Italian fortifications and military installations along the Italo-Yugoslav frontier, and their armaments, shall be destroyed or removed...

SECTION III · LIMITATION OF THE ITALIAN NAVY

*Article 59.* 3. The total standard displacement of the war vessels, other than battleships, of the Italian Navy, including vessels under construction after the date of launching, shall not exceed 67,500 tons.

4. Any replacement of war vessels by Italy shall be effected within the limit of tonnage given in paragraph 3. There shall be no restriction on the replacement of auxiliary vessels.

5. Italy undertakes not to acquire or lay down any war vessels before January 1, 1950, except as necessary to replace any vessel, other than a battleship, accidentally lost, in which case the displacement of the new vessel is not to exceed by more than 10 per cent the displacement of the vessel lost.

6. The terms used in this Article are, for the purposes of the present Treaty, defined in Annex XIII A.

*Article 60.* 1. The total personnel of the Italian Navy, excluding any naval air personnel, shall not exceed 25,000 officers and men....

SECTION IV · LIMITATION OF THE ITALIAN ARMY

*Article 61.* The Italian Army, including the Frontier Guards, shall be limited to a force of 185,000 combat, service and overhead personnel and 65,000...

SECTION V · LIMITATION OF THE ITALIAN AIR FORCE

*Article 64.* 1. The Italian Air Force, including any naval air arm, shall be limited to a force of 200 fighter and reconnaissance aircraft and 150 transport, air-sea rescue, training (school type) and liaison aircraft. These totals include reserve aircraft. All aircraft except for fighter and reconnaissance aircraft shall be unarmed. The organization and armament of the Italian Air Force as well as their deployment throughout Italy shall be designed to meet only tasks of an internal character, local defence of Italian frontiers and defence against air attack.

2. Italy shall not possess or acquire any aircraft designed primarily as bombers with internal bomb-carrying facilities.

*Article 65.* 1. The personnel of the Italian Air Force, including any naval air personnel, shall be limited to a total of 25,000 effectives, which shall include combat, service and overhead personnel.

. . .

SECTION VII · PREVENTION OF GERMAN AND JAPANESE REARMAMENT

*Article 68.* Italy undertakes to cooperate fully with the Allied and Associated Powers with a view to ensuring that Germany and Japan are unable to take steps outside German and Japanese territories towards rearmament.

. . .

## Part V · Withdrawal of Allied forces

*Article 73.* 1. All armed forces of the Allied and Associated Powers shall be withdrawn from Italy as soon as possible and in any case not later than ninety days from the coming into force of the present Treaty.

2. All Italian goods for which compensation has not been made and which are in possession of the armed forces of the Allied and Associated Powers in Italy at the coming into force of the present Treaty shall be returned to the Italian Government within the same period of ninety days or due compensation shall be made.

3. All bank and cash balances in the hands of the forces of the Allied and Associated Powers at the coming into force of the present Treaty which have

been supplied free of cost by the Italian Government shall similarly be returned or a corresponding credit given to the Italian Government.

## Part VI · Claims arising out of the war

### SECTION I · REPARATION

*Article 74.* A. *Reparation for the Union of Soviet Socialist Republics* 1. Italy shall pay the Soviet Union reparation in the amount of $100,000,000 during a period of seven years from the coming into force of the present Treaty. Deliveries from current industrial production shall not be made during the first two years.

2. Reparation shall be made from the following sources:

(a) A share of the Italian factory and tool equipment designed for the manufacture of war material, which is not required by the permitted military establishments, which is not readily susceptible of conversion to civilian purposes and which will be removed from Italy pursuant to Article 67 of the present Treaty;

(b) Italian assets in Roumania, Bulgaria and Hungary, subject to the exceptions specified in paragraph 6 of Article 79;

(c) Italian current industrial production, including production by extractive industries.

3. The quantities and types of goods to be delivered shall be the subject of agreements between the Governments of the Soviet Union and of Italy, and shall be selected and deliveries shall be scheduled in such a way as to avoid interference with the economic reconstruction of Italy and the imposition of additional liabilities on other Allied or Associated Powers. Agreements concluded under this paragraph shall be communicated to the Ambassadors in Rome of the Soviet Union, of the United Kingdom, of the United States of America, and of France.

4. The Soviet Union shall furnish to Italy on commercial terms the materials which are normally imported into Italy and which are needed for the production of these goods. Payments for these materials shall be made by deducting the value of the materials furnished from the value of the goods delivered to the Soviet Union.

5. The four Ambassadors shall determine the value of the Italian assets to be transferred to the Soviet Union.

6. The basis of calculation for the settlement provided in this Article will be the United States dollar at its gold parity on July 1, 1946, i.e. $35 for one ounce of gold.

B. *Reparation for Albania, Ethiopia, Greece and Yugoslavia.* 1. Italy shall pay reparation to the following States:

| | |
|---|---|
| Albania in the amount of | $5,000,000 |
| Ethiopia in the amount of | $25,000,000 |
| Greece in the amount of | $105,000,000 |
| Yugoslavia in the amount of | $125,000,000 |

These payments shall be made during a period of seven years from the coming into force of the present Treaty. Deliveries from current industrial production shall not be made during the first two years.

2. Reparation shall be made from the following sources:

(a) A share of the Italian factory and tool equipment designed for the manufacture of war material, which is not required by the permitted military establishments, which is not readily susceptible of conversion to civilian purposes and which will be removed from Italy pursuant to Article 67 of the present Treaty;

(b) Italian current industrial production, including production by extractive industries;

(c) All other categories of capital goods or services, excluding Italian assets which, under Article 79 of the present Treaty, are subject to the jurisdiction of the States mentioned in paragraph 1 above. Deliveries under this paragraph shall include either or both of the passenger vessels *Saturnia* and *Vulcania*, if, after their value has been determined by the four Ambassadors, they are claimed within ninety days by one of the States mentioned in paragraph 1 above. Such deliveries may also include seeds.

3. The quantities and types of goods and services to be delivered shall be the subject of agreements between the Governments entitled to receive reparation and the Italian Government, and shall be selected and deliveries shall be scheduled in such a way as to avoid interference with the economic reconstruction of Italy and the imposition of additional liabilities on other Allied or Associated Powers.

4. The States entitled to receive reparation from current industrial production shall furnish to Italy on commercial terms the materials which are normally imported into Italy and which are needed for the production of these goods. Payment for these materials shall be made by deducting the value of the materials furnished from the value of the goods delivered.

5. The basis of calculation for the settlement provided in this Article will be the United States dollar at its gold parity on July 1, 1946, i.e. $35 for one ounce of gold.

6. Claims of the States mentioned in paragraph 1 of part B of this Article, in excess of the amounts of reparation specified in that paragraph, shall be satisfied out of the Italian assets subject to their respective jurisdictions under Article 79 of the present Treaty.

. . .

D. *Reparation for other States.* 1. Claims of the other Allied and Associated Powers shall be satisfied out of the Italian assets subject to their respective jurisdictions under Article 79 of the present Treaty.

2. The claims of any State which is receiving territories under the present Treaty and which is not mentioned in part B of this Article shall also be satisfied by the transfer to the said State, without payment, of the industrial installations and equipment situated in the ceded territories and employed in the distribution of water, and the production and distribution of gas and electricity, owned by any Italian company whose *siège social* is in Italy or is transferred to Italy, as well as by the transfer of all other assets of such companies in ceded territories.

3. Responsibility for the financial obligations secured by mortgages, *liens* and other charges on such property shall be assumed by the Italian Government.

E. *Compensation for property taken for reparation purposes.* The Italian Government undertakes to compensate all natural or juridical persons whose property is taken for reparation purposes under this Article.

SECTION II · RESTITUTION BY ITALY

*Article 75.* 1. Italy accepts the principles of the United Nations Declaration of January 5, 1943, and shall return, in the shortest possible time, property removed from the territory of any of the United Nations.

2. The obligation to make restitution applies to all identifiable property at present in Italy which was removed by force or duress by any of the Axis Powers from the territory of any of the United Nations, irrespective of any subsequent transactions by which the present holder of any such property has secured possession.

3. The Italian Government shall return the property referred to in this Article in good order and, in this connection, shall bear all costs in Italy relating to labour, materials and transport.

# Peacemaking in the Far East

The British and American delegations at Potsdam agreed, on behalf of the nations at war with Japan, on a declaration calling upon Japan to submit to surrender 'unconditionally', and published the *Potsdam Declaration on 26 July 1945*. In effect this declaration outlined surrender conditions. On 6 and 9 August 1945 atomic bombs were dropped on Hiroshima and Nagasaki. On 8 August 1945 the Soviet Union declared war on Japan, to take effect the following day when the Russian armies began occupying Manchuria. On 10 August the Japanese acceptance of the conditions of the Potsdam Declaration was received by the Americans, but Japan's acceptance was conditional on the Allies agreeing that the prerogatives of the Emperor as a sovereign ruler were not prejudiced. The Americans replied on 11 August 1945 that the Emperor would be subject to the Supreme Commander and that the 'ultimate form of government of Japan shall, in accordance with the Potsdam Declaration, be established by the freely expressed will of the Japanese people'. On these conditions the Japanese surrendered on 14 August 1945. The formal instrument of surrender was signed on 2 September 1945 in Tokyo Bay. Japanese armies throughout Asia surrendered to the military Commander-in-Chief in each region. The Japanese armies in Manchuria, Korea north of the 38th parallel, the Kuriles and Sakhalin surrendered to the Russians. The Soviet Union regularized the hasty Russian invasion of Manchuria by concluding the *Sino-Soviet Treaty of Friendship on 14 August 1945* (p. 51).

After Japan's surrender to the Allies, General Douglas MacArthur as Supreme Allied Commander headed the (predominantly American) occupation forces of Japan. The Emperor, a Japanese Government and Diet, under the overall authority and supervision of the Supreme Commander, governed the country. The seven Allied Powers which had been at war with Japan were represented on the *Far Eastern Commission* in Washington, which came into being in the spring of 1946 together with an Allied Council in Tokyo. In practice the United States, represented by General MacArthur, maintained its predominant influence in carrying through the occupation policies of the Allies with the broad objectives of democratizing and demilitarizing Japan. In 1946 a new constitution was promulgated for Japan. Its preamble pledged the people to maintain the high ideals of the democratic constitution, dedicated to peaceful cooperation among nations and the blessings of liberty. The Emperor's powers were limited to those of a constitutional monarch; henceforth he became only 'the symbol of the state of the unity of all the people' and his position derived 'from the will of the people with whom resides sovereign power'. In Article 9 of the constitution war was renounced and no armed forces were to be maintained. 'Aspiring sincerely to an international peace based on justice and order, the Japanese people forever renounce war as a sovereign right of the nation and the threat or use of force as means of settling territorial disputes. In order to accomplish the aim of the preceding paragraph, land, sea, and air forces, as well as other war potential, will never be maintained. The right of belligerency of the State will not be recognized.'

The surrender limited Japanese sovereignty from north to south, to the island of Honshu, Hokkaido, Kyushu and Shikoku, together with some minor islands. The Kurile islands and southern Sakhalin were administered by the Soviet Union. In Korea, Japanese forces north of latitude 38° surrendered to the Russians and south of the line to the Americans, thus creating two military zones. Soviet forces withdrew from North Korea in October 1948 after the establishment of a communist North Korean Government; the United States withdrew from South Korea in June 1949 where a Government was also established under U.N. auspices. Formosa and the Pescadores were handed over to China; the Ryukyu Islands including Okinawa were placed under U.S. administration, and the Japanese trusteeship of Germany's former Pacific islands became a United Nations trust territory under American administration.

In preparing a peace treaty for Japan, the Soviet Union and the Western Powers were soon in dispute. A breach occurred over the rejection in January 1950 of the Soviet demand that the Nationalist Chinese representative on the Far Eastern Commission be replaced by the representative of the People's Republic of China, and the consequent Soviet withdrawal from the Far Eastern Commission. The years 1949 and 1950 brought about far-reaching changes in Eastern Asia and fundamental reappraisals of Great Power diplomacy. In 1949 the Communist Chinese defeated the Nationalist Chinese, who withdrew to Taiwan (Formosa). On 25 June 1950 the Korean War began, involving the North Koreans and eventually Chinese 'volunteers' on the one side, and the South Koreans and the United States and U.N. allies, who came to the defence of South Korea, on the other. For the United States these events led to basic policy decisions to maintain a line of defence including Taiwan, Japan and South Korea. In the midst of the Korean War, the United States resolved to conclude a peace treaty with Japan even if Soviet approval could not be won, and to convert a defeated enemy into a willing ally. President Harry Truman sent Ambassador John Foster Dulles to America's principal allies to work out an agreed draft peace treaty. Then, on the basis of an Anglo-American draft, the United States and Britain invited fifty allied nations which had declared war on Japan to a Peace Conference at San Francisco to meet in September 1951. The Soviet Union was included in the invitation, but neither Nationalist nor Communist China (the three associated States of Indo-China on the other hand received an invitation). India,

Burma and Yugoslavia declined the invitation. The Soviet Union attended, but refused to sign the treaty.

*The Japanese Peace Treaty of 8 September 1951* (p. 55), negotiated substantially in advance before the San Francisco conference opened, was thus signed by the majority of nations at war with Japan but not by the U.S.S.R. nor either of the Chinas. The territorial terms corresponded to the dispositions at the end of the war, and Japan renounced its rights to all territories surrendered by the armistice of 2 September 1945, and all special privileges in China. But no title of possession over former Japanese territories, the Kuriles and southern Sakhalin was granted to the U.S.S.R. or over Taiwan to China. The peace treaty established that in principle Japan should pay reparations, but left amounts to later bilateral negotiations. Japan agreed to follow the principles of the U.N. Charter as well as internationally accepted fair practices in trade and commerce. Sovereignty and independence were restored to Japan, and the occupation régime was to end ninety days after the treaty became effective; but the treaty did not prevent the stationing of foreign troops in consequence of a treaty made by Japan with one or more Allied Powers. Comparing the Japanese peace treaty with the European peace treaties already negotiated, there is one marked feature of difference in the absence from the Japanese treaty of military clauses restricting the military forces of Japan. As has been noted earlier, the Japanese constitution of 1946 forbade the maintenance of any Japanese armed forces. Article 5 of the peace treaty promised Japanese assistance in action taken in accordance with the U.N. Charter (the Korean War), and the Allied Powers who were signatories confirmed Japan's 'inherent right of individual or collective self-defence' referred to in Article 51 of the Charter of the United Nations, which permitted Japan to enter voluntarily into collective security arrangements.

The result of these arrangements was the transformation of Japan from an occupied vassal of the United States into a valued American ally in the Western Powers' confrontation with the Soviet Union and Communist China. On the same day as the Japanese Peace Treaty was signed, *the United States signed a Security Treaty with Japan* (see pp. 118–19). The constitutional bar on the maintenance of armed forces was circumvented after 1950 by the formation of a 'Self-Defence Force'.

The *Nationalist Chinese (Taiwan) signed a Peace Treaty with Japan on 28 April 1952*, but (in large measure as a consequence) no agreement between Japan and Communist China was reached until the 1970s (see Chapter 6). Although the Soviet Union resumed diplomatic relations with Japan in 1956, no peace treaty between the two powers was ever signed. Soviet retention after 1945 of the formerly Japanese-governed southern Kurile islands as well as the southern half of Sakhalin island (gained by Japan from Russia in 1905) developed in the 1970s into a minor but persistent irritant in Soviet–Japanese relations.

# Treaty of Friendship and Alliance between China and the Soviet Union, Moscow, 14 August 1945

## I · Treaty of Friendship and Alliance

The President of the National Government of the Republic of China and the Praesidium of the Supreme Soviet of the Union of Soviet Socialist Republics,

Being desirous of strengthening the friendly relations which have always prevailed between the Republic of China and the Soviet Union, by means of an alliance and by good neighbourly post-war collaboration;

Determined to assist each other in the struggle against aggression on the part of the enemies of the United Nations in this World War and to collaborate in the common war against Japan until that country's unconditional surrender;

Expressing their unswerving resolve to collaborate in maintaining peace and security for the benefit of the peoples of both countries and of all peace-loving nations . . . have agreed as follows:

*Article 1.* The High Contracting Parties undertake jointly with the other United Nations to prosecute the war against Japan until final victory is achieved. The High Contracting Parties mutually undertake to afford one another all necessary military and other assistance and support in this war.

*Article 2.* The High Contracting Parties undertake not to enter into separate negotiations with Japan or conclude, except by mutual consent, any armistice or peace treaty either with the present Japanese Government or any other Government or authority set up in Japan that does not clearly renounce all aggressive intentions.

*Article 3.* On the conclusion of the war against Japan, the High Contracting Parties undertake to carry out jointly all the measures in their power to render impossible a repetition of aggression and violation of the peace by Japan.

Should either of the High Contracting Parties become involved in hostilities with Japan in consequence of an attack by the latter against that party, the other High Contracting Party will at once render to the High Contracting Party so involved in hostility all the military and other support and assistance in its power.

This Article shall remain in force until such time as, at the request of both High Contracting Parties, responsibility for the prevention of further aggression by Japan is placed upon the 'United Nations' Organization.

*Article 4.* Each High Contracting Party undertakes not to conclude any alliance and not to take part in any coalition directed against the other Contracting Party.

*Article 5.* The High Contracting Parties, having regard to the interests of the security and economic development of each of them, agree to work together in close and friendly collaboration after the re-establishment of peace and to act in accordance with the principles of mutual respect for each other's sovereignty and territorial integrity and non-intervention in each other's internal affairs.

*Article 6.* The High Contracting Parties agree to afford one another all possible economic assistance in the post-war period in order to facilitate and expedite the rehabilitation of both countries and to make their contribution to the prosperity of the world.

*Article 7.* Nothing in this Treaty should be interpreted in such a way as to prejudice the rights and duties of the High Contracting Parties as Members of the Organization of the 'United Nations'.

*Article 8.* The present Treaty is subject to ratification in the shortest possible time. The instruments of ratification shall be exchanged in Chungking as soon as possible.

The Treaty comes into force immediately upon ratification, and shall remain in force for thirty years. Should neither of the High Contracting Parties make, one year before the date of the Treaty's expiry, a statement of its desire to denounce it, the Treaty will remain in force for an unlimited period, provided that each High Contracting Party may invalidate it by announcing its intention to do so to the other Contracting Party one year in advance.

. . .

## Exchange of Notes

### No. 1

In connection with the signing on this date of the Treaty of Friendship and Alliance between China and the Union of Soviet Socialist Republics, I have the honour to place on record that the following provisions are understood by both Contracting Parties as follows:

1. In accordance with the spirit of the above-mentioned Treaty and to implement its general idea and its purposes, the Soviet Government agrees to render China moral support and assist her with military supplies and other material resources, it being understood that this support and assistance will go exclusively to the National Government as the Central Government of China.

2. During the negotiations on the ports of Dairen and Port Arthur and on the joint operation of the Chinese Changchun Railway, the Soviet Government regarded the Three Eastern Provinces as part of China and again affirmed its respect for the complete sovereignty of China over the Three Eastern Provinces and recognition of their territorial and administrative integrity.

3. With regard to recent events in Sinkiang, the Soviet Government confirms that, as stated in Article 5 of the Treaty of Friendship and Alliance, it has no intention of interfering in the internal affairs of China.

. . .

### No. 3

In view of the frequently manifested desire for independence of the people of Outer Mongolia, the Chinese Government states that, after the defeat of Japan, if this desire is confirmed by a plebiscite of the people of Outer Mongolia, the Chinese Government will recognize the independence of Outer Mongolia within her existing frontiers. . . .

## II · Agreement between the Chinese Republic and the Union of Soviet Socialist Republics on the Chinese Changchun Railway, signed at Moscow on 14 August 1945

The President of the National Government of the Republic of China and the Praesidium of the Supreme Soviet of the U.S.S.R. being desirous of strengthening, on the basis of complete regard for the rights and interests of each of the two parties, friendly relations and economic ties between the two countries, have agreed as follows:

*Article 1.* After the expulsion of the

Japanese armed forces from the Three Eastern Provinces of China, the main trunk lines of the Chinese Eastern Railway and the South Manchurian Railway leading from the station of Manchouli to the station of Pogranichnaya and from Harbin to Dairen and Port Arthur, shall be combined to form a single railway system to be known as 'Chinese Changchun Railway', and shall become the joint property of the U.S.S.R. and the Chinese Republic and be jointly exploited by them. Only such lands and branch lines shall become joint property and be jointly exploited as were constructed by the Chinese Eastern Railway while it was under Russian and joint Soviet-Chinese management, and by the South Manchurian Railway while under Russian management, and which are intended to serve the direct needs of those railways. Ancillary undertakings directly serving the needs of those railways and constructed during the above-mentioned periods shall also be included. All other railway branch lines, ancillary undertakings and lands will be the exclusive property of the Chinese Government. The joint exploitation of the above-mentioned railways shall be effected by a single administration under Chinese sovereignty as a purely commercial transport undertaking.

[*Articles 2–18.* Details of administration.]

. . .

### III · Agreement on the Port of Dairen, signed at Moscow on 14 August 1945

Whereas a Treaty of Friendship and Alliance has been concluded between the Chinese Republic and the Union of Soviet Socialist Republics, and whereas the U.S.S.R. has guaranteed to respect the sovereignty of China over the Three Eastern Provinces as an inalienable part of China, the Chinese Republic, in order to protect the interests of the Union of Soviet Socialist Republics in Dairen as a port for

the import and export of goods, hereby agrees:

1. To proclaim Dairen a free port, open to the trade and shipping of all countries.

2. The Chinese Government agrees to allocate docks and warehouse accommodation in the said free port to be leased to the U.S.S.R. under a separate agreement.

### Protocol

1. The Government of China when requested to do so by the Soviet Union shall grant the Soviet Union, freely and without consideration, a thirty years' lease of one-half of all harbour installations and equipment, the other half of the harbour installations and equipment remaining the property of China.

. . .

### IV · Agreement on Port Arthur, signed at Moscow on 14 August 1945

In accordance with the Sino-Soviet Treaty of Friendship and Alliance and as an addition thereto, both Contracting Parties have agreed on the following:

1. In order to strengthen the security of China and the U.S.S.R. and prevent a repetition of aggression on the part of Japan, the Government of the Chinese Republic agrees to the joint use by both Contracting Parties of Port Arthur as a naval base . . . .

### V · Agreement on relations between the Soviet Commander-in-Chief and the Chinese administration following the entry of Soviet forces into the territory of the three Eastern Provinces of China in connection with the present joint war against Japan, signed at Moscow on 14 August 1945

The President of the National Government of the Chinese Republic and the Praesidium of the Supreme Soviet of the Union of Soviet Socialist Republics, being desirous that after the entry of Soviet forces into the territory of the Three Eastern Provinces of China in connection with the present joint war of China and the U.S.S.R. against Japan, relations between the Soviet Commander-in-Chief and the Chinese administration conform with the spirit of friendship and alliance existing between both countries, have agreed on the following:

1. After the entry, as a result of military operations, of Soviet troops into the territory of the Three Eastern Provinces of China, the supreme authority and responsibility in the zone of military activity in all matters relating to the conduct of the war shall, during the period necessary for conducting such operations, be vested in the Commander-in-Chief of the Soviet Armed Forces.

2. A representative of the National Government of the Chinese Republic and a staff shall be appointed in any recaptured territory, who shall:

(a) Organize and control, in accordance with the laws of China, the administration on the territory freed from the enemy;

(b) Assist in establishing cooperation in restored territories between the Chinese armed forces, whether regular or irregular, and the Soviet armed forces;

(c) Ensure the active collaboration of the Chinese administration with the Soviet Commander-in-Chief and, in particular, issue corresponding instructions to the local authorities, being guided by the requirements and desires of the Soviet Commander-in-Chief.

3. A Chinese Military Mission shall be appointed to the Headquarters of the Soviet Commander-in-Chief for the purpose of maintaining contact between the Soviet Commander-in-Chief and the representative of the National Government of the Chinese Republic.

4. In zones that are under the supreme authority of the Soviet Commander-in-Chief, the administration of the National Government of the Chinese Republic for restored territories shall maintain contact with the Soviet Commander-in-Chief through a representative of the National Government of the Chinese Republic.

5. As soon as part of a recaptured territory ceases to be a zone of direct military operations, the National Government of the Chinese Republic shall assume complete power in respect of civil affairs and shall render the Soviet Commander-in-Chief all assistance and support through its civil and military organs.

6. All members of the Soviet armed forces on Chinese territory shall be under the jurisdiction of the Soviet Commander-in-Chief. All Chinese citizens whether civil or military, shall be under Chinese jurisdiction...

## Minutes

At the fifth meeting between Generalissimo Stalin and Mr T.V. Soong, President of the Executive Yuan, which took place on 11 July 1945, the question of the evacuation of Soviet forces from Chinese territory after participation of the U.S.S.R. in the war against Japan was discussed. Generalissimo Stalin declined to include in the Agreement on the Entry of Soviet Forces into the Territory of the Three Eastern Provinces any provision for the evacuation of Soviet troops within three months following the defeat of Japan. Generalissimo Stalin stated, however, that the Soviet forces would begin to be withdrawn within three weeks after the capitulation of Japan.

Mr T.V. Soong asked how much time would be required to complete the evacuation. Generalissimo Stalin stated that in his opinion the evacuation of troops could be completed within a period of not exceeding two months. Mr. T.V. Soong again asked whether the evacuation would really be completed within three months. Generalissimo Stalin stated that three months would be a maximum period sufficient for the completion of the withdrawal of troops.

# Treaty of Peace with Japan, San Francisco, 8 September 1951

Whereas the Allied Powers and Japan are resolved that henceforth their relations shall be those of nations which, as sovereign equals, cooperate in friendly association to promote their common welfare and to maintain international peace and security, and are therefore desirous of concluding a Treaty of Peace which will settle questions still outstanding as a result of the existence of a state of war between them;

Whereas Japan for its part declares its intention to apply for membership in the United Nations and in all circumstances to conform to the principles of the Charter of the United Nations; to strive to realize the objectives of the Universal Declaration of Human Rights; to seek to create within Japan conditions of stability and well-being as defined in Articles 55 and 56 of the Charter of the United Nations and already initiated by post-surrender Japanese legislation; and in public and private trade and commerce to conform to internationally accepted fair practices;

Whereas the Allied Powers welcome the intentions of Japan set out in the foregoing paragraph;

The Allied Powers and Japan have therefore determined to conclude the present Treaty of Peace, and have accordingly appointed the undersigned plenipotentiaries, who, after presentation of their full powers, found in good and due form, have agreed on the following provisions:

## Chapter I: Peace

*Article 1.* (a) The state of war between Japan and each of the Allied Powers is terminated as from the date on which the present Treaty comes into force between Japan and the Allied Power concerned as provided for in Article 23.

(b) The Allied Powers recognize the full sovereignty of the Japanese people over Japan and its territorial waters.

## Chapter II: Territory

*Article 2.* (a) Japan, recognizing the independence of Korea, renounces all right, title and claim to Korea, including the islands of Quelpart, Port Hamilton and Dagelet.

(b) Japan renounces all right, title and claim to Formosa and the Pescadores.

(c) Japan renounces all rights, title and claim to the Kurile islands, and to that portion of Sakhalin and the islands adjacent to it over which Japan acquired sovereignty as a consequence of the Treaty of Portsmouth of September 5, 1905.

(d) Japan renounces all right, title and claim in connection with the League of Nations Mandate System, and accepts the action of the United Nations Security Council of April 2, 1947, extending the trusteeship system to the Pacific islands formerly under mandate to Japan.

(e) Japan renounces all claim to any right or title to or interest in connection with any part of the Antarctic area, whether deriving from the activities of Japanese nationals or otherwise.

(f) Japan renounces all right, title and claim to the Spratly islands and to the Paracel islands.

. . .

## Chapter III: Security

*Article 5.* (a) Japan accepts the obligations set forth in Article 2 of the Charter of the United Nations, and in particular the obligations

(i) to settle its international disputes by peaceful means in such a manner that international peace and security, and justice, are not endangered;

(ii) to refrain in its international relations from the threat or use of force against the territorial integrity or political independence of any State or in any other manner inconsistent with the Purposes of the United Nations;

(iii) to give the United Nations every assistance in any action it takes in accordance with the Charter and to refrain from giving assistance to any State against which the United Nations may take preventive or enforcement action.

(b) The Allied Powers confirm that they will be guided by the principles of Article 2 of the Charter of the United Nations in their relations with Japan.

(c) The Allied Powers for their part recognize that Japan as a sovereign nation possesses the inherent right of individual or collective self-defense referred to in Article 51 of the Charter of the United Nations and that Japan may voluntarily enter into collective security arrangements.

*Article 6.* (a) All occupation forces of the Allied Powers shall be withdrawn from Japan as soon as possible after the coming into force of the present Treaty, and in any case not later than ninety days thereafter. Nothing in this provision shall, however, prevent the stationing or retention of foreign armed forces in Japanese territory under or in consequence of any bilateral or multilateral agreements which have been or may be made between one or more of the Allied Powers, on the one hand, and Japan on the other.

(b) The provisions of Article 9 of the Potsdam Proclamation of July 26, 1945, dealing with the return of Japanese military forces to their homes, to the extent not already completed, will be carried out.

. . .

*Chapter IV: Political and economic clauses*

. . .

*Article 10.* Japan renounces all special rights and interests in China, including all benefits and privileges resulting from the provisions of the final Protocol signed at Peking on September 7, 1901, and all annexes, notes and documents supplementary thereto, and agrees to the abrogation in respect to Japan of the said Protocol, annexes, notes and documents.

*Article 11.* Japan accepts the judgements of the International Military Tribunal for the Far East and of other Allied War Crimes Courts both within and outside Japan, and will carry out the sentences imposed thereby upon Japanese nationals imprisoned in Japan. The power to grant clemency, to reduce sentences and to parole with respect to such prisoners may not be exercised except on the decision of the Government or Governments which imposed the sentence in each instance, and on the recommendation of Japan. In the case of persons sentenced by the International Military Tribunal for the Far East, such power may not be exercised except on the decision of a majority of the Governments represented on the Tribunal, and on the recommendation of Japan.

*Article 12.* [Trade arrangements]. . .(c) In respect to any matter, however, Japan shall be obliged to accord to an Allied Power national treatment, or most-favored-nation treatment, only to the extent that the Allied Power concerned accords Japan national treatment or most-favored-nation treatment, as the case may be, in respect of the same matter.

. . .

*Chapter V: Claims and property*

*Article 14.* (a) It is recognized that Japan should pay reparations to the Allied Powers for the damage and suffering caused by it during the war. Nevertheless it is also recognized that the resources of Japan are not presently sufficient, if it is to maintain a viable economy, to make complete reparation for all such damage and suffering and at the same time meet its other obligations.

Therefore,

(i) Japan will promptly enter into negotiations with Allied Powers so desiring, whose present territories were occupied by Japanese forces and damaged by Japan, with a view to assisting to compensate those countries for the cost of repairing the damage done, by making available the services of the Japanese people in production, salvaging and other work for the Allied Powers in question. Such arrangements shall avoid the imposition of additional liabilities on other Allied Powers, and, where the manufacturing of raw materials is called for, they shall be supplied by the Allied Powers in question, so as not to throw any foreign exchange burden upon Japan. . . .

(b) Except as otherwise provided in the present Treaty, the Allied Powers waive all reparations claims of the Allied Powers, other claims of the Allied Powers and their nationals arising out of any actions taken by Japan and its nationals in the course of the prosecution of the war, and claims of the Allied Powers for direct military costs of occupation.

. . .

*Article 16.* As an expression of its desire to indemnify those members of the armed forces of the Allied Powers who suffered undue hardships while prisoners of war of Japan, Japan will transfer its assets and those of its nationals in countries which were neutral during the war, or which were at war with any of the Allied Powers, or, at its option, the equivalent of such assets, to the International Committee of the Red Cross which shall liquidate such assets and distribute the resultant fund to appropriate national agencies, for the benefit of former prisoners of war and

their families on such basis as it may determine to be equitable. . . .

*Chapter VII: Final clauses*

*Article 23.* (a) The present Treaty shall be ratified by the States which sign it, including Japan, and will come into force for all the States which have then ratified it, when instruments of ratification have been deposited by Japan and by a majority, including the United States of America as the principal occupying Power. . . .

*Article 26.* Japan will be prepared to conclude with any State which signed or adhered to the United Nations Declaration of January 1, 1942, and which is at war with Japan, or with any State which previously formed a part of the territory of a State named in Article 23, which is not a signatory of the present Treaty, a bilateral treaty of peace on the same or substantially the same terms as are provided for in the present Treaty, but this obligation on the part of Japan will expire three years after the first coming into force of the present Treaty. Should Japan make a peace settlement or war claims settlement with any State granting that State greater advantages than those provided by the present Treaty, those same advantages shall be extended to the parties to the present Treaty.

## The United Nations

As early as 1941, with the Axis powers seemingly at the height of their power, inter-Allied discussions began on the formation of a new world organization to replace the defunct League of Nations. Following Anglo-American talks in Washington, and after consultation with the USSR, the three major allies (together with twenty-three minor allies who were invited to sign 'on a take-it-or-leave-it basis') issued the *United Nations Declaration of 1 January 1942.* This pledged the signatories to continue to fight together until the final defeat of the Axis powers; although the declaration made no mention of an international organization, the use of the term 'United Nations' maked the first embryonic stage of development of the wartime alliance into a universal body. The name appears to have been devised by President Roosevelt.

At the Allied meetings at Moscow and Teheran in the autumn of 1943 support was declared for the establishment of an international organization for the maintenance of peace and international security. Britain, the United States, Russia and China agreed to work out the functions and powers of an international world organization at a meeting in Washington to be held in two parts, with the Soviet Union, not then at war with Japan, leaving the conference to make way for a second stage where China would participate. Accordingly the *Dumbarton Oaks Conference* took place in two phases *from 21 August to 28 September 1944 and from 29 September to 7 October 1944.* The communiqué after the conference on 9 October 1944 published 'Proposals for the Establishment of a General International Organization', which outlined the main structure of the United Nations; but on the crucial question of whether one of the Great Powers holding a permanent seat on the Security Council could exercise a veto on a dispute involving itself, no final agreement was reached. (It was, however, agreed that a permanent member of the Security Council could exercise a veto on issues in which his country was not directly involved.) The proposals left open to later agreement three contentious issues: the voting procedures of the Security Council, the membership of the organization and the question of trusteeship and colonial territories. At the Yalta Conference in February 1945 the Big Three reached agreement on an American proposal for the voting procedure on the Security Council whereby the veto would not apply to every issue before it; procedural questions or the peaceful adjustments of disputes would not be subject to the veto; but the unanimity of all the permanent members would be required in all decisions involving enforcement measures. Nevertheless the wording of this agreement proved too imprecise to prevent later dispute. On the question of U.N. membership it was agreed that three Russian States would be admitted, including the Ukraine and Byelorussia. All the States that had declared war on the Axis by 1 March 1945 were also to be founder members. It was further agreed that a Drafting Conference should convene at San Francisco on 25 April 1945 and that China and France should be invited together with the Big Three.

*The San Francisco Conference of 25 April–26 June 1945* was attended by the Foreign Ministers of the Great Powers and their delegations, as well as by delegations of countries at war with Germany. But the Polish Government did not attend, as the Russian-sponsored Polish Government was not recognized by the Western Powers. The Soviet Union, for its part, objected unsuccessfully to the participation of Argentina.

The most bitter dispute of the conference, which even threatened the founding of an international organization, concerned the voting procedure of the proposed Security Council. This procedure was complicated by the distinction drawn between the different types of decisions the Security Council would be asked to reach.

1. It was accepted by the delegates at San Francisco that each of the permanent members, that is, the 'Five', Britain, France, China, Russia and the United States, whether a party to a dispute or not, would have to concur if any sanctions including military action were decided on to restore peace or to meet aggression. Each of the 'Big Five' thus held a veto against action involving enforcement.

2. Questions merely of 'procedure' in the event of a dispute being brought before the Security Council could be decided by a majority of any seven members out of eleven (after 1965, nine out of the increased membership of fifteen).

3. The third category would arise when the Security Council discussed a dispute, and reached and recorded conclusions about it intended to facilitate a peaceful settlement but not involving enforcement action. Such decisions or resolutions are called 'substantive' and it was agreed that they would require the unanimity of all the permanent members of the Security Council, but that any permanent members themselves involved in the dispute could not vote. In other words, a permanent member in these circumstances could exercise a veto only if his country was not involved in the dispute. The trouble was, and remains, one of defining 'procedural', 'substantive', and what constitutes precisely 'enforcement action'. The widest interpretation of the veto held by the Soviet Union in 1945 was not in the end accepted by the conference, but the freedom of the Security Council to work for the *peaceful resolution* of disputes was also curtailed. The temporary absence of the Soviet Union, in protest at the presence of Nationalist China on the Security Council, created an exceptional circumstance which enabled the council to *recommend* in June 1950 that Member States furnish military help to South Korea in order to repel invasion from the north, though the absent permanent member, Russia, backed North Korea.

The standing military force to be placed at the disposal of the Security Council, as envisaged in Article 43 of the Charter, does not exist for this article has never been implemented. Consequently the Security Council cannot enforce military sanctions as was apparently intended, but can only *recommend* that Member States furnish troops to ad hoc forces to preserve peace or to resist aggression. Economic sanctions can be invoked by the Security Council, and were for the first time in December 1966 against the régime of Southern Rhodesia.

The San Francisco Conference safeguarded the rights of nations to defend themselves singly or in alliance with others in the event that (as occurred) the Security Council through lack of agreement should find itself unable to act. This right is embodied in Article 51.

The Charter was unanimously adopted on 26 June 1945. By 24 October 1945, the 'Big Five' (Britain, China, France, the Soviet Union and the United States) and a majority of other signatory States had ratified it and it was brought into effect. It established the United Nations Organization whose members are sovereign states. By 1986 membership had grown from the original 51 member states to a total of 159, primarily as a result of the adhesion of former colonial states. The two German states became members in 1973. In 1971 the People's Republic of China finally took over the Chinese seat from the nationalist Republic of China (Taiwan), the latter subsequently finding itself excluded from the organization. Membership of the United Nations by sovereign states became nearly universal by the 1980s. In 1965 Indonesia withdrew and sought to organize a rival body; this failed and Indonesia soon returned. Among important states only the two Koreas and Switzerland remained non-members (though all three have observer status); yet, curiously, the former headquarters of the League of Nations, the Palais des Nations in Geneva, became, with the consent of the Swiss Federal Government, the European offices of the U.N. (whose main headquarters were located in New York). The success of the U.N. in achieving virtual universality of membership contrasted strikingly with the limited membership of the League of Nations between the wars. Even such disparate entities as the Holy See (the Vatican) and the Palestine Liberation Organization were granted observer status. With the exception of Taiwan no state has been excluded from membership of the organization, although South Africa (one of the original members) has been effectively prevented from participating in the General Assembly in recent years.

The United Nations consists of four main organs: the General Assembly to which all members belong; the Security Council built around the nucleus of the five Powers thereby defined (in the event unrealistically) as the Great Powers and a number of lesser Powers elected to the Security Council; the Secretariat under an elected Secretary-General; and an International Court of Justice. In contrast to the League of Nations, unanimity is not required in the Assembly or the Security Council of the U.N. The complex voting procedure of the Security Council has been discussed; in the Assembly 'important questions' are decided by a two-thirds majority. Under the Charter, the Security Council has special authority in all questions of peace and security. The General Assembly enjoys exclusive and ultimate authority in other fields.

The failure of the Security Council to enforce peace in cases of disagreement led to attempts to bypass the Security Council. Under the 'Uniting for Peace' Resolution of 2 November 1950 the General Assembly was empowered to meet within twenty-four hours if the Security Council failed in its responsibilities to maintain peace and security, and could take a number of steps *recommending* Member States to furnish armed forces for use as a U.N. unit. The Secretary-General too under Article 99 can take the initiative to bring problems to the attention of the Security Council and secure powers to maintain peace. Peacekeeping forces responsible to the Security Council were set up in the Middle East (the United Nations Truce Supervision Organization, UNTSO) to maintain the 1949 armistice between Israel and her Arab neighbours. In the conflict between India and Pakistan over Kashmir, a United Nations Military Observer Group for India and Pakistan (UNMOGIP) was set up in 1949. In Korea the United Nations Military Command was set up in July 1950, and since July 1953 it has supervised the armistice line between South and North Korea. United Nations forces were sent to Egypt during the Suez crisis of 1956 and in 1960 to the Congo. A United Nations Peace-Keeping Force in Cyprus (UNFICYP) was set up in March 1964 to help prevent communal strife between the Greeks and the Turks on the island.

While the success of the United Nations in its peacekeeping function has been limited, a wide variety of organs and agencies forming part of the U.N. or working with the U.N. have contributed to international cooperation in the fields of education, social welfare, human rights, health, regional economic development and international trade. Among United Nations activities, or activities of international organizations related to the United Nations, the following may be especially noted:

*The Economic and Social Council* is assigned the tasks of acting as a link between independent special agencies and promoting study in aspects not covered by these agencies in order to fulfil the U.N. Charter's purpose in the social and economic fields, including 'human rights'. In a complex structure sub-commissions, regional commissions and specialized agencies are responsible to ECOSOC, among them the United Nations Development Programme and the United Nations High Commission for Refugees.

*The United Nations Educational, Scientific and Cultural Organization* (UNESCO) has since 1946 promoted many international educational and cultural projects, including a campaign against illiteracy and the saving of the Abu Simbel temple sculptures. Nearly all states joined UNESCO; South Africa withdrew in 1956. In 1984 the United States, the largest financial contributor, withdrew complaining of the politicization of the organization's activities. Britain and Singapore withdrew in 1985. In 1986 there were 155 members.

*The World Health Organization* is a specialized agency to combat disease on a global scale. In 1986 there were 165 members.

*The United Nations Children's Fund* (UNICEF) was founded in 1946 to aid mothers and children in need as a result of war or from other causes, especially in developing countries. It is financed by voluntary contributions.

*The International Labour Organization* (ILO) was originally established in 1919. By 1986 membership had grown to 149. It is concerned internationally with establishing agreed conditions of labour and is also concerned with social security, economic planning and full employment.

*The United Nations Relief and Rehabilitation Administration* (UNRRA) was established in November 1943 and ceased operations in March 1949. Its main purpose was to provide relief, especially food, to parts of Europe and China devastated by war, and to stave off famine and collapse. Financed mainly by the United States during the early years, UNRRA personnel and foreign aid were despatched to Italy, Greece, Poland and Yugoslavia. Foreign aid was granted to Eastern Europe including the Ukraine and Byelorussia. UNRRA had provided help for several million refugees before ceasing its operations; this work was taken over by the International Refugee Organization until 1951, and then by the High Commissioner for Refugees.

*The United Nations Relief and Works Agency*, established in 1949, has been responsible for the housing, education, feeding and medical care of Palestinian Arab refugees.

*The International Atomic Energy Agency* (IAEA) was set up in 1957 to promote the use of atomic energy for peace, health and prosperity, and to ensure that help under the programme is not misused for military purposes.

*The Food and Agriculture Organization* (FAO) established in 1945 was set up to raise living standards by improving production and distribution of agricultural produce. In 1986 membership stood at 152 States.

International cooperation in world trade and finance developed from the *United Nations Monetary Conference at Bretton Woods in New Hampshire, 1–22 July 1944*, which recommended the establishment of two institutions. *The International Bank for Reconstruction and Development* or World Bank (p. 78) was set up in December 1945 to promote the economic development of Member States by encouraging and making investments. In 1986 there were 141 members; these included most non-Communist States as well as the People's Republic of China. The U.S.S.R. is not a member; nor is Switzerland. Two organizations affiliated to the International Bank for Reconstruction and Development are, firstly, the *International Development Association* to help economic development in the less developed areas of the world, and secondly, *the International Finance Corporation*, set up in 1956 to stimulate private enterprise in less developed countries.

*The International Monetary Fund* (p. 79) exists to promote international cooperation in trade and finance and to help promote stability in currency exchanges, which was regarded as an essential condition of expanding trade. Membership by 1986 had reached 141. The U.S.S.R. and Switzerland did not join; the People's Republic of China did.

In 1947 a multilateral tariff treaty known as GATT (*General Agreement on Tariffs and Trade*) was negotiated to remove barriers to the growth of world trade, raise standards of living and promote the economic growth of its signatories. After 1955 it was turned into an organization by the creation of a permanent Secretariat. In 1986 there were 92 members, including Poland, Czechoslovakia, Rumania and Switzerland, but not the U.S.S.R. One purpose of all these organizations is to ensure the liberalization of trade. This purpose has only been fulfilled imperfectly. Between 1947 and 1979 seven lengthy 'rounds' of GATT negotiations, designed to eliminate or reduce tariff barriers, had taken place (Geneva 1947, Annecy 1949, Torquay 1950–1, Geneva II 1955–6, the 'Dillon round' 1961–2, 'Kennedy round' 1963–7, and 'Tokyo round' 1973–9). An eighth round of talks began at Punta del Este in Uruguay in September 1986.

Though the Charter makes disarmament and the regulating of armaments one of the principal concerns of the organization, and the United Nations has set up a series of commissions and committees on the subject since 1946, negotiations directly conducted under the aegis of the United Nations have largely been fruitless. Real advances have been negotiated by the Powers concerned at conferences set up especially for the purpose.

With the increase in membership of the U.N., effective power within the organization passed from the Western allies (whose voice was predominant in the early years) to the Afro-Asian bloc. Although the U.N. remained important as a forum for debate and propaganda, it did not play a central role in efforts to resolve international crises or disputes after the 1960s. Although its organs spawned large numbers of multilateral conventions and agreements these tended to be either of a narrow technical nature or mere declaratory pronouncements empty of enforcement provisions. There were a few exceptions, such as the *Law of the Sea Treaty* of 1982 (see p. 498), but increasingly the real centre of gravity of international diplomacy shifted from the U.N. to the relationship between the two 'superpowers' that emerged from the débris of the Second World War – the United States and the Soviet Union.

## Charter of the United Nations, San Francisco, 26 June 1945

[The text as given here includes subsequent amendments made to Articles 23, 27, 61 and 109.]

*We the Peoples of the United Nations determined*

to save succeeding generations from the scourge of war, which twice in our lifetime has brought untold sorrow to mankind, and

to reaffirm faith in fundamental human rights, in the dignity and worth of the human person, in the equal rights of men and women and of nations large and small, and

to establish conditions under which justice and respect for the obligations arising from treaties and other sources of international law can be maintained, and

to promote social progress and better standards of life in larger freedom,

*and for these ends*

to practise tolerance and live together in peace with one another as good neighbours, and

to unite our strength to maintain international peace and security, and

to ensure, by the acceptance of principles and the institution of methods, that armed force shall not be used, save in the common interest, and

to employ international machinery for the promotion of the economic and social advancement of all peoples,

*have resolved to combine our efforts to accomplish these aims.*

Accordingly, our respective Governments, through representatives assembled in the city of San Francisco, who have exhibited their full powers found to be in good and due form, have agreed to the present Charter of the United Nations and do hereby establish an international organization to be known as the United Nations.

*Chapter I: Purposes and Principles*

*Article 1.* The Purposes of the United Nations are:

1. To maintain international peace and security and to that end: to take effective collective measures for the prevention and removal of threats to the peace, and for the suppression of acts of aggression or other breaches of the peace, and to bring about by peaceful means, and in conformity with the principles of justice and international law, adjustment or settlement of international disputes or situations which might lead to a breach of the peace;

2. To develop friendly relations among nations based on respect for the principle of equal rights and self-determination of peoples, and to take other appropriate measures to strengthen universal peace;

3. To achieve international cooperation in solving international problems of an economic, social, cultural, or humanitarian character, and in promoting and encouraging respect for human rights and

for fundamental freedoms for all without distinction as to race, sex, language, or religion; and

4. To be a centre of harmonizing the actions of nations in the attainment of these common ends.

*Article 2.* The Organization and its Members, in pursuit of the Purposes stated in Article 1, shall act in accordance with the following Principles.

1. The Organization is based on the principle of the sovereign equality of all its Members.

2. All Members, in order to ensure to all of them the rights and benefits resulting from membership, shall fulfil in good faith the obligations assumed by them in accordance with the present Charter.

3. All Members shall settle their international disputes by peaceful means in such a manner that international peace and security, and justice, are not endangered.

4. All Members shall refrain in their international relations from the threat or use of force against the territorial integrity or political independence of any State, or in any other manner inconsistent with the Purposes of the United Nations.

5. All Members shall give the United Nations every assistance in any action it takes in accordance with the present Charter, and shall refrain from giving assistance to any State against which the United Nations is taking preventive or enforcement action.

6. The Organization shall ensure that States which are not Members of the United Nations act in accordance with these Principles so far as may be necessary for the maintenance of international peace and security.

7. Nothing contained in the present Charter shall authorize the United Nations to intervene in matters which are essentially within the domestic jurisdiction of any State or shall require the Members to submit such matters to settlement under the present Charter; but this principle shall not prejudice the applica-

tion of enforcement measures under Chapter VII.

*Chapter II: Membership*

*Article 3.* The original Members of the United Nations shall be the States which, having participated in the United Nations Conference on International Organization at San Francisco, or having previously signed the Declaration by United Nations of January 1, 1942, sign the present Charter and ratify it in accordance with Article 110.

*Article 4.* 1. Membership in the United Nations is open to all other peace-loving States which accept the obligations contained in the present Charter and, in the judgement of the Organization, are able and willing to carry out these obligations.

2. The admission of any such State to membership in the United Nations will be effected by a decision of the General Assembly upon the recommendation of the Security Council.

*Article 5.* A Member of the United Nations against which preventive or enforcement action has been taken by the Security Council may be suspended from the exercise of the rights and privileges of membership by the General Assembly upon the recommendation of the Security Council. The exercise of these rights and privileges may be restored by the Security Council.

*Article 6.* A Member of the United Nations which has persistently violated the Principles contained in the present Charter may be expelled from the Organization by the General Assembly upon the recommendation of the Security Council.

*Chapter III: Organs*

*Article 7.* 1. There are established as the principal organs of the United Nations: a General Assembly, a Security Council, an Economic and Social Council, a Trusteeship Council, an International Court of Justice, and a Secretariat.

2. Such subsidiary organs as may be

found necessary may be established in accordance with the present Charter.

*Article 8.* The United Nations shall place no restrictions on the eligibility of men and women to participate in any capacity and under conditions of equality in its principal and subsidiary organs.

*Chapter IV: The General Assembly*

COMPOSITION

*Article 9.* 1. The General Assembly shall consist of all the Members of the United Nations.

2. Each Member shall have not more than five representatives in the General Assembly.

FUNCTIONS AND POWERS

*Article 10.* The General Assembly may discuss any questions or any matter within the scope of the present Charter or relating to the powers and functions of any organs provided for in the present Charter, and, except as provided in Article 12, may make recommendations to the Members of the United Nations or to the Security Council or to both on any such questions or matters.

*Article 11.* 1. The General Assembly may consider the general principles of co-operation in the maintenance of international peace and security, including the principles governing disarmament and the regulation of armaments, and may make recommendations with regard to such principles to the Members or to the Security Council or to both.

2. The General Assembly may discuss any questions relating to the maintenance of international peace and security brought before it by any Member of the United Nations, or by the Security Council, or by a State which is not a Member of the United Nations in accordance with Article 35, paragraph 2, and, except as provided in Article 12, may make recommendations with regard to any such question to the State or States concerned or to the Security Council or to both. Any such question on which action is necessary shall be referred to the Security Council by the General Assembly either before or after discussion.

3. The General Assembly may call the attention of the Security Council to situations which are likely to endanger international peace and security.

4. The powers of the General Assembly set forth in this Article shall not limit the general scope of Article 10.

*Article 12.* 1. While the Security Council is exercising in respect of any dispute or situation the functions assigned to it in the present Charter, the General Assembly shall not make any recommendations with regard to that dispute or situation unless the Security Council so requests.

2. The Secretary-General, with the consent of the Security Council, shall notify the General Assembly at each session of any matters relative to the maintenance of international peace and security which are being dealt with by the Security Council and shall similarly notify the General Assembly, or the Members of the United Nations if the General Assembly is not in session, immediately the Security Council ceases to deal with such matters.

*Article 13.* 1. The General Assembly shall initiate studies and make recommendations for the purpose of:

(a) promoting international cooperation in the political field and encouraging the progressive development of international law and its codification;

(b) promoting international cooperation in the economic, social, cultural, educational, and health fields, and assisting in the realization of human rights and fundamental freedoms for all without distinction as to race, sex, language, or religion.

2. The further responsibilities, functions, and powers of the General Assembly with respect to matters mentioned in paragraph 1 (b) above are set forth in Chapters IX and X.

*Article 14.* Subject to the provisions of Article 12, the General Assembly may recommend measures for the peaceful adjustment of any situation, regardless of origin, which it deems likely to impair the general welfare or friendly relations among nations, including situations resulting from a violation of the provisions of the present Charter setting forth the Purposes and Principles of the United Nations.

*Article 15.* 1. The General Assembly shall receive and consider annual and special reports from the Security Council; these reports shall include an account of the measures that the Security Council has decided upon or taken to maintain international peace and security.

2. The General Assembly shall receive and consider reports from the other organs of the United Nations.

*Article 16.* The General Assembly shall perform such functions with respect to the international trusteeship system as are assigned to it under Chapters XII and XIII, including the approval of the trusteeship agreements for areas not designated as strategic.

*Article 17.* 1. The General Assembly shall consider and approve the budget of the Organization.

2. The expenses of the Organization shall be borne by the Members as apportioned by the General Assembly.

3. The General Assembly shall consider and approve any financial and budgetary arrangements with specialized agencies referred to in Article 57 and shall examine the administrative budgets of such specialized agencies with a view to making recommendations to the agencies concerned.

VOTING

*Article 18.* 1. Each member of the General Assembly shall have one vote.

2. Decisions of the General Assembly on important questions shall be made by a two-thirds majority of the members present and voting. These questions shall include: recommendations with respect to the maintenance of international peace and security, the election of the non-permanent members of the Security Council, the election of the members of

the Economic and Social Council, the election of members of the Trusteeship Council in accordance with paragraph 1 (c) of Article 86, the admission of new Members to the United Nations, the suspension of the rights and privileges of membership, the expulsion of Members, questions relating to the operation of the trusteeship system, and budgetary questions.

3. Decisions on other questions, including the determination of additional categories of questions to be decided by a two-thirds majority, shall be made by a majority of the members present and voting.

*Article 19.* A Member of the United Nations which is in arrears in the payment of its financial contributions to the Organization shall have no vote in the General Assembly if the amount of its arrears equals or exceeds the amount of the contributions due from it for the preceding two full years. The General Assembly may, nevertheless, permit such a Member to vote if it is satisfied that the failure to pay is due to conditions beyond the control of the Member.

PROCEDURE

*Article 20.* The General Assembly shall meet in regular annual sessions and in such special sessions as occasion may require. Special sessions shall be convoked by the Secretary-General at the request of the Security Council or of a majority of the Members of the United Nations.

*Article 21.* The General Assembly shall adopt its own rules of procedure. It shall elect its President for each session.

*Article 22.* The General Assembly may establish such subsidiary organs as it deems necessary for the performance of its functions.

*Chapter V: The Security Council*

COMPOSITION

*Article 23.* 1. The Security Council shall consist of fifteen Members of the United Nations. The Republic of China, France, the Union of Soviet Socialist Republics, the United Kingdom of Great Britain and Northern Ireland, and the United States of America shall be permanent members of the Security Council. The General Assembly shall elect ten other Members of the United Nations to be non-permanent members of the Security Council, due regard being specially paid, in the first instance to the contribution of Members of the United Nations to the maintenance of international peace and security and to the other purposes of the Organization, and also to equitable geographical distribution.

2. The non-permanent members of the Security Council shall be elected for a term of two years. In the first election of the non-permanent members after the increase of the membership of the Security Council from eleven to fifteen, two of the four additional members shall be chosen for a term of one year. A retiring member shall not be eligible for immediate re-election.

3. Each member of the Security Council shall have one representative.

FUNCTIONS AND POWERS

*Article 24.* 1. In order to ensure prompt and effective action by the United Nations, its Members confer on the Security Council primary responsibility for the maintenance of international peace and security, and agree that in carrying out its duties under this responsibility the Security Council acts on their behalf.

2. In discharging these duties the Security Council shall act in accordance with the Purposes and Principles of the United Nations. The specific powers granted to the Security Council for the discharge of these duties are laid down in Chapters VI, VII, VIII, and XII.

3. The Security Council shall submit annual and, when necessary, special reports to the General Assembly for its consideration.

*Article 25.* The Members of the United Nations agree to accept and carry out the decisions of the Security Council in accordance with the present Charter.

*Article 26.* In order to promote the establishment and maintenance of international peace and security with the least diversion for armaments of the world's human and economic resources, the Security Council shall be responsible for formulating, with the assistance of the Military Staff Committee referred to in Article 47, plans to be submitted to the Members of the United Nations for the establishment of a system for the regulation of armaments.

VOTING

*Article 27.* 1. Each member of the Security Council shall have one vote.

2. Decisions of the Security Council on procedural matters shall be made by an affirmative vote of nine members.

3. Decisions of the Security Council on all other matters shall be made by an affirmative vote of nine members including the concurring votes of the permanent members; provided that, in decisions under Chapter VI, and under paragraph 3 of Article 52, a party to a dispute shall abstain from voting.

PROCEDURE

*Article 28.* 1. The Security Council shall be so organized as to be able to function continuously. Each member of the Security Council shall for this purpose be represented at all times at the seat of the Organization.

2. The Security Council shall hold periodic meetings at which each of its members may, if it so desires, be represented by a member of the Government or by some other specially designated representative.

3. The Security Council may hold meetings at such places other than the seat of the Organization as in its judgement will best facilitate its work.

*Article 29.* The Security Council may establish such subsidiary organs as it deems necessary for the performance of its functions.

*Article 30.* The Security Council shall adopt its own rules of procedure, including the method of selecting its President.

*Article 31.* Any Member of the United Nations which is not a member of the Security Council may participate, without vote, in the discussion of any question brought before the Security Council whenever the latter considers that the interests of that Member are specially affected.

*Article 32.* Any Member of the United Nations which is not a member of the Security Council or any State which is not a Member of the United Nations, if it is a party to a dispute under consideration by the Security Council, shall be invited to participate, without vote, in the discussion relating to the dispute. The Security Council shall lay down such conditions as it deems just for the participation of a State which is not a Member of the United Nations.

*Chapter VI: Pacific settlement of disputes*

*Article 33.* 1. The parties to any dispute, the continuance of which is likely to endanger the maintenance of international peace and security, shall, first of all, seek a solution by negotiation, enquiry, mediation, conciliation, arbitration, judicial settlement, resort to regional agencies or arrangements, or other peaceful means of their own choice.

2. The Security Council shall, when it deems necessary, call upon the parties to settle their dispute by such means.

*Article 34.* The Security Council may investigate any dispute, or any situation which might lead to international friction or give rise to a dispute, in order to determine whether the continuance of the dispute or situation is likely to endanger the maintenance of international peace and security.

*Article 35.* 1. Any Member of the United Nations may bring any dispute, or any situation of the nature referred to in Article 34, to the attention of the Security Council or of the General Assembly.

2. A State which is not a Member of the United Nations may bring to the atten-

tion of the Security Council or of the General Assembly any dispute to which it is a party if it accepts in advance, for the purposes of the dispute, the obligations of pacific settlement provided in the present Charter.

3. The proceedings of the General Assembly in respect of matters brought to its attention under this Article will be subject to the provisions of Articles 11 and 12.

*Article 36.* 1. The Security Council may, at any stage of a dispute of the nature referred to in Article 33 or of a situation of like nature, recommend appropriate procedures or methods of adjustment.

2. The Security Council should take into consideration any procedures for the settlement of the dispute which have already been adopted by the parties.

3. In making recommendations under this Article the Security Council should also take into consideration that legal disputes should as a general rule be referred by the parties to the International Court of Justice in accordance with the provisions of the Statute of the Court.

*Article 37.* 1. Should the parties to a dispute of the nature referred to in Article 33 fail to settle it by the means indicated in that Article, they shall refer it to the Security Council.

2. If the Security Council deems that the continuance of the dispute is in fact likely to endanger the maintenance of international peace and security, it shall decide whether to take action under Article 36 or to recommend such terms of settlement as it may consider appropriate.

*Article 38.* Without prejudice to the provisions of Articles 33 to 37, the Security Council may, if all the parties to any dispute so request, make recommendations to the parties with a view to a pacific settlement of the dispute.

*Chapter VII: Action with respect to threats to the peace, breaches of the peace, and acts of aggression*

*Article 39.* The Security Council shall

determine the existence of any threat to the peace, breach of the peace, or act of aggression and shall make recommendations, or decide what measures shall be taken in accordance with Articles 41 and 42, to maintain or restore international peace and security.

*Article 40.* In order to prevent an aggravation of the situation, the Security Council may, before making the recommendations or deciding upon the measures provided for in Article 39, call upon the parties concerned to comply with such provisional measures as it deems necessary or desirable. Such provisional measures shall be without prejudice to the rights, claims, or position of the parties concerned. The Security Council shall duly take account of failure to comply with such provisional measures.

*Article 41.* The Security Council may decide what measures not involving the use of armed force are to be employed to give effect to its decisions, and it may call upon the Members of the United Nations to apply such measures. These may include complete or partial interruption of economic relations and of rail, sea, air, postal, telegraphic, radio, and other means of communication, and the severance of diplomatic relations.

*Article 42.* Should the Security Council consider that measures provided for in Article 41 would be inadequate or have proved to be inadequate, it may take such action by air, sea, or land forces as may be necessary to maintain or restore international peace and security. Such action may include demonstrations, blockade, and other operations by air, sea, or land forces of Members of the United Nations.

*Article 43.* 1. All Members of the United Nations, in order to contribute to the maintenance of international peace and security, undertake to make available to the Security Council, on its call and in accordance with a special agreement or agreements, armed forces, assistance, and facilities, including rights of passage, necessary for the purpose of maintaining international peace and security.

2. Such agreement or agreements shall govern the numbers and types of forces, their degree of readiness and general location, and the nature of the facilities and assistance to be provided.

3. The agreement or agreements shall be negotiated as soon as possible on the initiative of the Security Council. They shall be concluded between the Security Council and Members or between the Security Council and groups of Members and shall be subject to ratification by the signatory States in accordance with their respective constitutional processes.

*Article 44.* When the Security Council has decided to use force it shall, before calling upon a Member not represented on it to provide armed forces in fulfilment of the obligations assumed under Article 43, invite that Member, if the Member so desires, to participate in the decisions of the Security Council concerning the employment of contingents of that Member's armed forces.

*Article 45.* In order to enable the United Nations to take urgent military measures, Members shall hold immediately available national airforce contingents for combined international enforcement action. The strength and degree of readiness of these contingents and plans for their combined action shall be determined, within the limits laid down in the special agreement or agreements referred to in Article 43, by the Security Council with the assistance of the Military Staff Committee.

*Article 46.* Plans for the application of armed force shall be made by the Security Council with the assistance of the Military Staff Committee.

*Article 47.* 1. There shall be established a Military Staff Committee to advise and assist the Security Council on all questions relating to the Security Council's military requirements for the maintenance of international peace and security, the employment and command of forces placed at its disposal, the regulation of armaments, and possible disarmament.

2. The Military Staff Committee shall consist of the Chiefs of Staff of the permanent members of the Security Council or their representatives. Any Member of the United Nations not permanently represented on the Committee shall be invited by the Committee to be associated with it when the efficient discharge of the Committee's responsibilities requires the participation of that Member in its work.

3. The Military Staff Committee shall be responsible under the Security Council for the strategic direction of any armed forces placed at the disposal of the Security Council. Questions relating to the command of such forces shall be worked out subsequently.

4. The Military Staff Committee, with the authorization of the Security Council and after consultation with appropriate regional agencies, may establish regional sub-committees.

*Article 48.* 1. The action required to carry out the decisions of the Security Council for the maintenance of international peace and security shall be taken by all the Members of the United Nations or by some of them, as the Security Council may determine.

2. Such decisions shall be carried out by the Members of the United Nations directly and through their action in the appropriate international agencies of which they are members.

*Article 49.* The Members of the United Nations shall join in affording mutual assistance in carrying out the measures decided upon by the Security Council.

*Article 50.* If preventive or enforcement measures against any State are taken by the Security Council, any other State, whether a Member of the United Nations or not, which finds itself confronted with special economic problems arising from the carrying out of those measures shall have the right to consult the Security Council with regard to a solution of those problems.

*Article 51.* Nothing in the present Charter shall impair the inherent right of individual or collective self-defence if an armed attack occurs against a Member of the United Nations, until the Security Council has taken measures necessary to maintain international peace and security. Measures taken by Members in the exercise of this right of self-defence shall be immediately reported to the Security Council and shall not in any way affect the authority and responsibility of the Security Council under the present Charter to take at any time such action as it deems necessary in order to maintain or restore international peace and security.

*Chapter VIII: Regional arrangements*

*Article 52.* 1. Nothing in the present Charter precludes the existence of regional arrangements or agencies for dealing with such matters relating to the maintenance of international peace and security as are appropriate for regional action, provided that such arrangements or agencies and their activities are consistent with the Purposes and Principles of the United Nations.

2. The Members of the United Nations entering into such arrangements or constituting such agencies shall make every effort to achieve pacific settlement of local disputes through such regional arrangements or by such regional agencies before referring them to the Security Council.

3. The Security Council shall encourage the development of pacific settlement of local disputes through such regional arrangements or by such regional agencies either on the initiative of the States concerned or by reference from the Security Council.

4. This Article in no way impairs the application of Articles 34 and 35.

*Article 53.* 1. The Security Council shall, where appropriate, utilize such regional arrangements or agencies for enforcement action under its authority. But no enforcement action shall be taken under regional arrangements or by regional agencies without the authorization of the Security Council, with the exception of measures against any Enemy State, as defined in paragraph 2 of this Article, provided for pursuant to Article 107 or in regional arrangements directed against renewal of aggressive policy on the part of any such State, until such time as the Organization may, on request of the Governments concerned, be charged with the responsibility for preventing further aggression by such a State.

2. The term Enemy State as used in paragraph 1 of this Article applies to any State which during the Second World War has been an enemy of any signatory of the present Charter.

*Article 54.* The Security Council shall at all times be kept fully informed of activities undertaken or in contemplation under regional arrangements or by regional agencies for the maintenance of international peace and security.

*Chapter IX: International economic and social cooperation*

*Article 55.* With a view to the creation of conditions of stability and well-being which are necessary for peaceful and friendly relations among nations based on respect for the principle of equal rights and self-determination of peoples, the United Nations shall promote:

(a) higher standards of living, full employment, and conditions of economic and social progress and development;

(b) solutions of international economic, social, health, and related problems; and international cultural and educational cooperation; and

(c) universal respect for, and observance of, human rights and fundamental freedoms for all without distinction as to race, sex, language, or religion.

*Article 56.* All Members pledge themselves to take joint and separate action in cooperation with the Organization for the achievement of the purposes set forth in Article 55.

*Article 57.* 1. The various specialized agencies, established by intergovernmental agreement and having wide international responsibilities, as defined in their basic instruments, in economic, social, cultural, educational, health, and related fields, shall be brought into relationship with the United Nations in accordance with the provisions of Article 63.

2. Such agencies thus brought into relationship with the United Nations are hereinafter referred to as specialized agencies.

*Article 58.* The Organization shall make recommendations for the coordination of the policies and activities of the specialized agencies.

*Article 59.* The Organization shall, where appropriate, initiate negotiations among the States concerned for the creation of any new specialized agencies required for the accomplishment of the purposes set forth in Article 55.

*Article 60.* Responsibility for the discharge of the functions of the Organization set forth in this Chapter shall be vested in the General Assembly and, under the authority of the General Assembly, in the Economic and Social Council, which shall have for this purpose the powers set forth in Chapter X.

*Chapter X: The Economic and Social Council*

COMPOSITION

*Article 61.* 1. The Economic and Social Council shall consist of fifty-four Members of the United Nations elected by the General Assembly. . . .

FUNCTIONS AND POWERS

*Article 62.* 1. The Economic and Social Council may make or initiate studies and reports with respect to international economic, social, cultural, educational, health, and related matters and may make recommendations with respect to any such matters to the General Assembly, to the Members of the United Nations, and to the specialized agencies concerned. . . .

[*Articles 62–6* set out in detail these functions and powers.]

VOTING

*Article 67.* 1. Each member of the Economic and Social Council shall have one vote.

2. Decisions of the Economic and Social Council shall be made by a majority of the members present and voting.

[*Articles 68–72* set out in detail the procedure to be followed.]

*Chapter XI: Declaration regarding non-self-governing territories*

*Article 73.* Members of the United Nations which have or assume responsibilities for the administration of territories whose peoples have not yet attained a full measure of self-government recognize the principle that the interests of the inhabitants of these territories are paramount, and accept as a sacred trust the obligation to promote to the utmost, within the system of international peace and security established by the present Charter, the well-being of the inhabitants of these territories, and, to this end:

(a) to ensure, with due respect for the culture of the peoples concerned, their political, economic, social, and educational advancement, their just treatment, and their protection against abuses;

(b) to develop self-government, to take due account of the political aspirations of the peoples, and to assist them in the progressive development of their free political institutions, according to the particular circumstances of each territory and its peoples and their varying stages of advancement;

(c) to further international peace and security;

(d) to promote constructive measures of development, to encourage research, and to cooperate with one another and, when and where appropriate, with specialized international bodies with a view to the practical achievement of the social, economic, and scientific purposes set forth in this Article; and

(e) to transmit regularly to the Secretary-General for information purposes, subject to such limitation as security and constitutional considerations may require, statistical and other information of a technical nature relating to economic, social, and educational conditions in the territories for which they are respectively responsible other than those territories to which Chapters XII and XIII apply.

*Article 74.* Members of the United Nations also agree that their policy in respect of the territories to which this Chapter applies, no less than in respect of their metropolitan areas, must be based on the general principle of good-neighbourliness, due account being taken of the interests and well-being of the rest of the world, in social, economic, and commercial matters.

*Chapter XII: International trusteeship system*

*Article 75.* The United Nations shall establish under its authority an international trusteeship system for the administration and supervision of such territories as may be placed thereunder by subsequent individual agreements. These territories are hereinafter referred to as trust territories.

*Article 76.* The basic objectives of the trusteeship system, in accordance with the Purposes of the United Nations laid down in Article 1 of the present Charter, shall be:

(a) to further international peace and security;

(b) to promote the political, economic, social, and educational advancement of the inhabitants of the trust territories, and their progressive development towards self-government or independence as may be appropriate to the particular circumstances of each territory and its peoples and the freely expressed wishes of the peoples concerned, and as may be provided by the terms of each trusteeship agreement;

(c) to encourage respect for human rights and for fundamental freedoms for all without distinction as to race, sex, language, or religion, and to encourage recognition of the interdependence of the peoples of the world; and

(d) to ensure equal treatment in social, economic, and commercial matters for all Members of the United Nations and their nationals, and also equal treatment for the latter in the administration of justice, without prejudice to the attainment of the foregoing objectives and subject to the provisions of Article 80.

*Article 77.* 1. The trusteeship system shall apply to such territories in the following categories as may be placed thereunder by means of trusteeship agreements:

(a) territories now held under mandate;

(b) territories which may be detached from Enemy States as a result of the Second World War; and

(c) territories voluntarily placed under the system by States responsible for their administration.

2. It will be a matter for subsequent agreement as to which territories in the foregoing categories will be brought under the trusteeship system and upon what terms.

*Article 78.* The trusteeship system shall not apply to territories which have become Members of the United Nations, relationship among which shall be based on respect for the principle of sovereign equality.

*Article 79.* The terms of trusteeship for each territory to be placed under the trusteeship system, including any alteration or amendment, shall be agreed upon by the States directly concerned, including the mandatory power in the case of territories held under mandate by a Member of the United Nations, and shall be approved as provided for in Articles 83 and 85.

*Article 80.* 1. Except as may be agreed upon in individual trusteeship agreements, made under Articles 77, 79, and 81, placing each territory under the trusteeship system, and until such agreements have been concluded, nothing in this

Chapter shall be construed in or of itself to alter in any manner the rights whatsoever of any States or any peoples or the terms of existing international instruments to which Members of the United Nations may respectively be parties.

2. Paragraph 1 of this Article shall not be interpreted as giving grounds for delay or postponement of the negotiation and conclusion of agreements for placing mandated and other territories under the trusteeship system as provided for in Article 77.

*Article 81.* The trusteeship agreement shall in each case include the terms under which the trust territory will be administered and designate the authority which will exercise the administration of the trust territory. Such authority, hereinafter called the administering authority, may be one or more States or the Organization itself.

*Article 82.* There may be designated, in any trusteeship agreement, a strategic area or areas which may include part or all of the trust territory to which the agreement applies, without prejudice to any special agreement or agreements made under Article 43.

*Article 83.* 1. All functions of the United Nations relating to strategic areas, including the approval of the terms of trusteeship agreements and of their alteration or amendment, shall be exercised by the Security Council.

2. The basic objectives set forth in Article 76 shall be applicable to the people of each strategic area.

3. The Security Council shall, subject to the provisions of the trusteeship agreements and without prejudice to security considerations, avail itself of the assistance of the Trusteeship Council to perform those functions of the United Nations under the trusteeship system relating to political, economic, social, and educational matters in the strategic areas.

*Article 84.* It shall be the duty of the administering authority to ensure that the trust territory shall play its part in the maintenance of international peace and security. To this end the administering authority may make use of volunteer forces, facilities, and assistance from the trust territory in carrying out the obligations towards the Security Council undertaken in this regard by the administering authority, as well as for local defence and the maintenance of law and order within the trust territory.

*Article 85.* 1. The functions of the United Nations with regard to trusteeship agreements for all areas not designated as strategic, including the approval of the terms of the trusteeship agreements and of their alteration or amendment, shall be exercised by the General Assembly.

2. The Trusteeship Council, operating under the authority of the General Assembly, shall assist the General Assembly in carrying out these functions.

*Chapter XIII: The Trusteeship Council*

COMPOSITION

*Article 86.* 1. The Trusteeship Council shall consist of the following Members of the United Nations:

(a) those Members administering trust territories;

(b) such of those Members mentioned by name in Article 23 as are not administering trust territories; and

(c) as many other Members elected for three-year terms by the General Assembly as may be necessary to ensure that the total number of members of the Trusteeship Council is equally divided between those Members of the United Nations which administer trust territories and those which do not.

2. Each member of the Trusteeship Council shall designate one specially qualified person to represent it therein.

FUNCTIONS AND POWERS

*Article 87.* The General Assembly and, under its authority, the Trusteeship Council, in carrying out their functions, may:

(a) consider reports submitted by the administering authority;

(b) accept petitions and examine them in consultation with the administering authority;

(c) provide for periodic visits to the respective trust territories at times agreed upon with the administering authority; and

(d) take these and other actions in conformity with the terms of the trusteeship agreements.

*Article 88.* The Trusteeship Council shall formulate a questionnaire on the political, economic, social, and educational advancement of the inhabitants of each trust territory, and the administering authority for each trust territory within the competence of the General Assembly shall make an annual report to the General Assembly upon the basis of such questionnaire.

VOTING

*Article 89.* 1. Each member of the Trusteeship Council shall have one vote.

2. Decisions of the Trusteeship Council shall be made by a majority of the members present and voting.

PROCEDURE

*Article 90.* 1. The Trusteeship Council shall adopt its own rules of procedure, including the method of selecting its President....

*Chapter XIV: The International Court of Justice*

*Article 92.* The International Court of Justice shall be the principal judicial organ of the United Nations. It shall function in accordance with the annexed Statute, which is based upon the Statute of the Permanent Court of International Justice and forms an integral part of the present Charter.

*Article 93.* 1. All Members of the United Nations are *ipso facto* parties to the Statute of the International Court of Justice.

2. A State which is not a Member of the United Nations may become a party to the Statute of the International Court of Justice on conditions to be determined in

each case by the General Assembly upon the recommendation of the Security Council.

*Article 94.* 1. Each Member of the United Nations undertakes to comply with the decision of the International Court of Justice in any case to which it is a party.

2. If any party to a case fails to perform the obligations incumbent upon it under a judgement rendered by the Court, the other party may have recourse to the Security Council, which may, if it deems necessary, make recommendations or decide upon measures to be taken to give effect to the judgement.

*Article 95.* Nothing in the present Charter shall prevent Members of the United Nations from entrusting the solution of their differences to other tribunals by virtue of agreements already in existence or which may be concluded in the future.

*Article 96.* 1. The General Assembly or the Security Council may request the International Court of Justice to give an advisory opinion on any legal question.

2. Other organs of the United Nations and specialized agencies, which may at any time be so authorized by the General Assembly, may also request advisory opinions of the Court on legal questions arising within the scope of their activities.

*Chapter XV: The Secretariat*

*Article 97.* The Secretariat shall comprise a Secretary-General and such staff as the Organization may require. The Secretary-General shall be appointed by the General Assembly upon the recommendation of the Security Council. He shall be the chief administrative officer of the Organization.

*Article 98.* The Secretary-General shall act in that capacity in all meetings of the General Assembly, of the Security Council, of the Economic and Social Council, and of the Trusteeship Council, and shall perform such other functions as are entrusted to him by these organs. The Secretary-General shall make an annual report to the General Assembly on the work of the Organization.

*Article 99.* The Secretary-General may bring to the attention of the Security Council any matter which in his opinion may threaten the maintenance of international peace and security.

*Article 100.* 1. In the performance of their duties the Secretary-General and the staff shall not seek or receive instructions from any Government or from any other authority external to the Organization. They shall refrain from any action which might reflect on their position as international officials responsible only to the Organization.

2. Each Member of the United Nations undertakes to respect the exclusively international character of the responsibilities of the Secretary-General and the staff and not to seek to influence them in the discharge of their responsibilities.

*Article 101.* 1. The staff shall be appointed by the Secretary-General under regulations established by the General Assembly. . . .

*Chapter XVI: Miscellaneous provisions*

*Article 102.* 1. Every treaty and every international agreement entered into by any Member of the United Nations after the present Charter comes into force shall as soon as possible be registered with the Secretariat and published by it.

2. No party to any such treaty or international agreement which has not been registered in accordance with the provisions of paragraph 1 of this Article may invoke that treaty or agreement before any organ of the United Nations.

*Article 103.* In the event of a conflict between the obligations of the Members of the United Nations under the present Charter and their obligations under any other international agreement, their obligations under the present Charter shall prevail.

[*Articles 104–5.* Legal privileges of the Organization and its representatives in member countries.]

## Chapter XVII: Transitional security arrangements

Article 106. Pending the coming into force of such special agreements referred to in Article 43 as in the opinion of the Security Council enable it to begin the exercise of its responsibilities under Article 42, the parties to the Four Nation Declaration, signed at Moscow, October 30, 1943, and France, shall, in accordance with the provisions of paragraph 5 of that Declaration, consult with one another and as occasion requires with other Members of the United Nations with a view to such joint action on behalf of the Organization as may be necessary for the purpose of maintaining international peace and security.

Article 107. Nothing in the present Charter shall invalidate or preclude action, in relation to any State which during the Second World War has been an enemy of any signatory to the present Charter, taken or authorized as a result of that war by the Governments having responsibility for such action.

## Chapter XVIII: Amendments

Article 108. Amendments to the present Charter shall come into force for all Members of the United Nations when they have been adopted by a vote of two-thirds of the members of the General Assembly and ratified in accordance with their respective constitutional processes by two-thirds of the Members of the United Nations, including all the permanent members of the Security Council,

Article 109. 1. A General Conference of the Members of the United Nations for the purpose of reviewing the present Charter may be held at a date and place to be fixed by a two-thirds vote of the members of the General Assembly and by a vote of any nine members of the Security Council. Each Member of the United Nations shall have one vote in the conference.

2. Any alteration of the present Charter recommended by a two-thirds vote of the conference shall take effect when ratified in accordance with their respective constitutional processes by two-thirds of the Members of the United Nations including all the permanent members of the Security Council.

3. If such a conference has not been held before the tenth annual session of the General Assembly following the coming into force of the present Charter, the proposal to call such a conference shall be placed on the agenda of that session of the General Assembly, and the conference shall be held if so decided by a majority vote of the members of the General Assembly and by a vote of any seven members of the Security Council.

## Chapter XIX: Ratification and signature

Article 110. 1. The present Charter shall be ratified by the signatory States in accordance with their respective constitutional processes.

2. The ratifications shall be deposited with the Government of the United States of America, which shall notify all the signatory States of each deposit as well as the Secretary-General of the Organization when he has been appointed.

3. The present Charter shall come into force upon the deposit of ratifications by the Republic of China, France, the Union of Soviet Socialist Republics, the United Kingdom of Great Britain and Northern Ireland, and the United States of America, and by a majority of the other signatory States. A Protocol of the ratifications deposited shall thereupon be drawn up by the Government of the United States of America which shall communicate copies thereof to all the signatory States.

4. The States signatory to the present Charter which ratify it after it has come into force will become original Members of the United Nations on the date of the deposit of their respective ratifications.

Article 111. The present Charter, of which the Chinese, French, Russian, English and Spanish texts are equally authentic, shall remain deposited in the archives of the Government of the United States of America. Duly certified copies thereof shall be transmitted by that Government to the Governments of the other signatory States.

IN FAITH WHEREOF the representatives of the Governments of the United Nations have signed the present Charter.

DONE at the city of San Francisco the twenty-sixth day of June, one thousand nine hundred and forty-five.

## Articles of Agreement of the International Bank for Reconstruction and Development (World Bank), 27 December 1945

The Governments on whose behalf the present Agreement is signed agree as follows:

*Introductory Article.* The International Bank for Reconstruction and Development is established and shall operate in accordance with the following provisions:

*Article I: Purposes.* The purposes of the Bank are:

(I) To assist in the reconstruction and development of territories of members by facilitating the investment of capital for productive purposes, including the restoration of economies destroyed or disrupted by war, the reconversion of productive facilities to peacetime needs and the encouragement of the development of productive facilities and resources in less developed countries.

(II) To promote private foreign investment by means of guarantees or participations in loans and other investments made by private investors; and when private capital is not available on reasonable terms, to supplement private investment by providing, on suitable conditions, finance for productive purposes out of its own capital, funds raised by it and its other resources.

(III) To promote the long-range balanced growth of international trade and the maintenance of equilibrium in balances of payments by encouraging international investment for the development of the productive resources of members, thereby assisting in raising productivity, the standard of living and conditions of labour in their territories.

(IV) To arrange the loans made or guaranteed by it in relation to international loans through other channels so that the more useful and urgent projects, large and small alike, will be dealt with first.

(V) To conduct its operations with due regard to the effect of international investment on business conditions in the territories of members and, in the immediate post-war years, to assist in bringing about a smooth transition from a war-time to a peacetime economy.

The Bank shall be guided in all its decisions by the purposes set forth above.

. . .

# Articles of Agreement of the International Monetary Fund, Washington, 27 December 1945

The Governments on whose behalf the present Agreement is signed agree as follows:

*Introductory Article.* The International Monetary Fund is established and shall operate in accordance with the following provisions:

*Article 1: Purposes.* The purposes of the International Monetary Fund are:

(I) To promote international monetary cooperation through a permanent institution which provides the machinery for consultation and collaboration on international monetary problems.

(II) To facilitate the expansion and balanced growth of international trade, and to contribute thereby to the promotion and maintenance of high levels of employment and real income and to the development of the productive resources of all members as primary objectives of economic policy.

(III) To promote exchange stability, to maintain orderly exchange arrangements among members, and to avoid competitive exchange depreciation.

(IV) To assist in the establishment of a multilateral system of payments in respect of current transactions between members and in the elimination of foreign exchange restrictions which hamper the growth of world trade.

(V) To give confidence to members by making the Fund's resources available to them under adequate safeguards, thus providing them with opportunity to correct maladjustments in their balance of payments without resorting to measures destructive of national or international prosperity.

(VI) In accordance with the above, to shorten the duration and lessen the degree of disequilibrium in the international balances of payments of members.

The Fund shall be guided in all its decisions by the purposes set forth in this Article.

. . .

# II · The United States treaty system

When the war came to an end the United States alone among the victorious Great Powers faced the future without alliance commitments to any single power or separate group of powers. Even during the course of the war Roosevelt had concluded no formal alliances but signed executive agreements not requiring a two-thirds majority of the Senate for approval. Thus the United States, for instance, was bound to its allies by only an executive agreement as one of the signatories of the *Declaration by the United Nations, 1 January 1942* (p. 57), whose obligations ceased with the end of the war. In 1945 the United States administration tried to return to its 'normal' peacetime diplomacy, rejecting exclusive alliances which, it was feared, would once again divide the world into hostile groupings. In the place of alliances, the U.S. had become a principal advocate and founder of the United Nations. But the objectives of American policy in 1945 remained global, based on the expectation of continued cooperation among the 'Big Three', Britain, the Soviet Union and the United States.

## The United States and the Americas

At the same time as adopting the global approach to foreign policy, the United States maintained its tradition of claiming special rights and responsibilities in the Western hemisphere as embodied in the Monroe Doctrine (1823). In practice this has meant that the United States, whilst recognizing how varied the Latin American Republics are, and how much of the time their interests have conflicted with each other, has also claimed that they form part of an American system. American Presidents have claimed the right to intervene unilaterally, if need be, if the vital interests of the United States were held to be endangered – vital interests which were declared to be equally in the interests of the American Republics as a whole. This might happen if a Latin American Republic developed close ties with a State potentially hostile to the United States and especially, as in Cuba, where foreign military bases or weapons were involved. Geographically, U.S. intervention has been confined in the main to the strategically vital Caribbean region; the United States possesses Guantanamo naval base in Cuba and controls the Panama Canal. Until Franklin D. Roosevelt proclaimed the Good Neighbor policy in 1933, United States armed intervention had been frequent, especially in Cuba, Panama, Nicaragua, Mexico, Haiti and the Dominican Republic, despite the attempts of inter-American conferences to prevent United States military action.

Eight international conferences of the American States met before the end of the Second World War: the first took place in Washington during 1889 and 1890, and since then numerous other special inter-American conferences have also been convened. They have produced many treaties, declarations and enunciations of principles, but the gap between these aspirations and practical achievements has been a wide one. Fervent expressions of faith in the principles of democracy have rung especially hollow when subscribed to by dictatorships in some of the Latin American Republics. Nor have the political, economic and international objectives of the Governments of the Latin American Republics always coincided with those of the much more powerful United States; the Republics are also divided on many issues among each other.

The International American Conferences have been concerned with four basic aspects of inter-American relations: (i) establishing the independence and sovereignty of each State, thus ensuring non-intervention by any other State especially by the United States; (ii) hemispheric security; (iii) inter-American cooperation in many fields, economic and social, which frequently entails attempting to secure favourable trading conditions and economic aid from the United States; (iv) establishing effective machinery for settling inter-American disputes peacefully.

Inter-American solidarity was not prominently in evidence during the First World War. After the war, *the Fifth International Conference of American States, meeting in Santiago, 25 March–3 May 1923*, was notable for the conclusion of a *Treaty to Avoid or Prevent Conflicts*, generally known as the *Gondra Treaty*; this provided for a commission to investigate disputes and a six-months cooling-off period. At a special conference of

American States, held in Washington, *10 December 1928–5 January 1929*, two treaties were adopted, the *General Convention of Inter-American Conciliation* and the *General Treaty of Inter-American Arbitration*; but the weakness of the latter treaty was that both parties to a dispute would have to agree to setting up arbitration machinery. A special commission of American jurists, appointed after the Sixth International Conference at Havana (1928), drew up a *Convention Defining the Rights and Duties of States* which was adopted by the *Seventh International Conference of American States at Montevideo, 3–26 December 1933*; according to Article 8 of this convention, no State had the right to intervene in the internal or external affairs of another. The United States ratified the convention in June 1934, but President Roosevelt in practice interpreted Article 8 as referring only to armed intervention. On 29 May 1934 Roosevelt abrogated the *Platt Amendment* under which the United States enjoyed special rights in Cuba.

A large number of resolutions and conventions were agreed and signed at a special *Inter-American Conference for the Maintenance of Peace, held in Buenos Aires, December 1936*. This conference also led to the conclusion in treaty form of acceptance of the principle of non-intervention in the *Non-Intervention Additional Protocol between the United States and Other American Republics, 23 December 1936*. Two years later, at the *Eighth International Conference of American States at Lima, December 1938*, one of many declarations (no. 109) provided for periodic consultations of the Foreign Ministers of the American Republics and affirmed the continental solidarity of the American Republics in case the peace, security or territorial integrity of any one of them was threatened. But despite the many treaties and convention resolutions from 1890 to 1938 the actual degree of inter-American cooperation and solidarity remained limited, and the machinery for settling disputes in the Americas peacefully was far from effective. The twenty Republics had not succeeded in achieving complete security from undue United States influence in their affairs, although Roosevelt's Good Neighbor policy brought about a great improvement in their relationship. Nor had the United States secured complete security through the establishment of the kind of inter-American cooperation that would have induced all the Latin American Republics to give priority to relations with America as against relations with European States.

With the outbreak of war in Europe in September 1939, inter-American cooperation was strengthened. The first meeting of the Foreign Ministers of the Republics took place in *Panama, 23 September–3 October 1939*. This conference adopted the *Act of Panama*, a multilateral executive agreement, which included a general declaration of neutrality; an agreement on the setting-up of a committee of experts for the duration of the war to study and make recommendations on problems of neutrality; a declaration that a neutral zone was established on the high seas 300 miles from the shores of the Republics; and, most important of all, a resolution that if any region in the Americas belonging to a European State should change sovereignties, thereby endangering the security of the Americas, a consultative meeting should be called urgently. The German conquests of the Netherlands and of France brought about a danger of the kind contemplated at Panama, and the Foreign Ministers therefore met again in *Havana, 21–30 July 1940*, and adopted the *Act of Havana*. It stated that should a change of sovereignty be threatened in the case of the European colonies, then the American Republics would create a committee to administer them; but should the emergency arise before a committee could act, then one State could take action alone, which in practice meant the United States. Another resolution declared that aggression against one of the Republics would be regarded as aggression against all, though in that event they were bound only to consult on measures of common defence. The United States concluded many bilateral agreements with individual American States during the Second World War, providing credit, purchasing raw materials and securing bases.

When, shortly after Pearl Harbor, the *third consultative meeting of American Foreign Ministers took place in Rio de Janeiro, 15–28 January 1942*, nine Central American and Caribbean States had declared war on the Axis and eleven Latin American States either broke off diplomatic relations or declared non-belligerency. But inter-American military co-operation remained far from wholehearted, with the Argentine being sympathetic to the Axis, and only by the time war was drawing to a close in 1945 had all the American Republics declared war on Germany and Japan. The future relations of the American Republics and inter-American cooperation in the post-war world formed the principal subject of the *Inter-American Conference on Problems of War and Peace, in Mexico City, 21 February–8 March 1945*. The conference was more concerned with post-war problems, and especially with the United Nations organization, than with problems of wartime alliance. The *Dumbarton Oaks* proposals (p. 58) were generally endorsed, but resolutions were also passed urging adequate representation for Latin American States on the proposed Security Council; in general the Latin American Republics wished to reduce the dominant role of the Great Powers. Agreement was reached on the *Act of Chapultepec* (Resolution 8) which provided for sanctions and appropriate regional action in the event of an American or non-American State committing aggression against another American State, but with the additional proviso that such action would need to be consistent with the purpose of the world international organization when established. The Act of Chapultepec remained in force only so long as the war continued; it was intended that a new treaty should replace it later in time of peace. Other resolutions called upon the next American conference to agree on measures to strengthen inter-American collaboration in the economic and other fields. At the *San Francisco Conference* establishing the United Nations (p. 58), the United States and the Latin American States secured an important modification of the Dumbarton Oaks proposals. It emerged as Article 51 of the Charter, which permitted groups of States to make treaties for collective self-defence to meet an armed attack. But this right is limited to the point of time when the Security Council takes what action it deems appropriate. It is nevertheless an important safeguard where the Security Council is deadlocked or where one of the permanent members uses its veto against any enforcement action (p. 59). Article 51 is further limited by Articles 53 to 54, which state that whilst the Security Council may authorize some regional action for 'enforcement action', no such action may be taken without the authorization of the Security Council; the Security Council also has to be kept fully informed of any action in contemplation. Thus Article 51 confers a right only of self-defence in case of armed attack, not of enforcement against a State that is more vaguely accused of aggression or aggressive intent before an armed attack has occurred.

The *Ninth Inter-American Conference for the Maintenance of Continental Peace and Security met near Rio de Janeiro, 15 August–2 September 1947*, under the shadow of the 'cold war'; the deliberations concluded with the signature of the *Inter-American Treaty of Reciprocal Assistance, 2 September 1947* (p. 88), also known as the *Pact of Rio*, which became effective after ratification by two-thirds of the signatories on 3 December 1948. It was signed by all the American States except Canada, Nicaragua and Ecuador. In March 1960 Cuba withdrew from the treaty. The Pact of Rio established an inter-American alliance of collective defence against armed attack as permitted by Article 51 of the U.N. Charter; it was also a regional agreement laying down the procedures to be followed in the event of any other act, or threat of aggression. Although Canada was not a party to the treaty, Article 4 defined the region covered as all of North and South America, and included Canada and Greenland and a part of Antarctica. The treaty left it to each signatory to act immediately as it considered necessary after an armed attack had taken place, until by a two-thirds majority the members of the pact decided on what future action was required. But if 'indirect aggression' was claimed to have taken place, such as the support of revolution in one State by another (many Latin American Republics shared United States fears of communist subversion), then no automatic right of intervention was allowed to any one State or a group of States; in such an event members of the treaty would meet to decide on what joint measures to take. According to Article 53 of the U.N. Charter, any 'enforcement action' then decided on would require the Security Council's authorization. The Rio treaty made hemispheric defence the joint responsibility of the American Republics, but did not supersede the Monroe Doctrine or the claim of the United States to act unilaterally in defence of its own vital interests. The Rio treaty was significant in another respect, for it provided the model for other regional treaties to which the United States was a party, especially the North Atlantic Treaty (p. 106).

The second treaty, complementing the Rio pact, which reorganized the inter-American system in the post-Second-World-War years, was the *Charter of the Organization of American States, 30 April 1948* (p. 91), signed by all twenty-one American Republics. Trinidad joined in February 1967, and other former colonies followed after attaining independence. Cuba was expelled in February 1962. By 1984 there were thirty-two members. This treaty emerged from the negotiations at the *Ninth International Conference of American States at Bogotá, 30 March–2 May 1948*. The Charter of the Organization of American States (O.A.S.) comprised 112 articles. It placed the inter-American system on a permanent treaty basis within the U.N. framework. Articles 32 to 101 defined the structure and functions of the O.A.S. The supreme organ of the O.A.S. was the Inter-American Conference, which in ordinary session met every five years, though at the request of two-thirds of the members a special conference might be convened. The old Pan-American Union at Washington became the permanent central organ and general secretariat of the O.A.S. Its council was composed of a representative from each Member State. The council acted as a consultative body in the event of an act of aggression; it also decided by majority to call a consultative meeting of Foreign Ministers when requested by one member. The council worked through three organs: the Inter-American Economic and Social Council, the Inter-American Council of Jurists and the Inter-American Cultural Council. In addition, some twelve specialized organizations, commissions and agencies operated within the framework of the O.A.S. The charter set out the purpose, principles, duties and rights of the O.A.S.; the purpose of the organization was to facilitate the pacific settlements of disputes, to strengthen inter-

American solidarity and to raise economic, social and cultural standards.

The third treaty on which post-war inter-American relations were to be based was the *American Treaty on Pacific Settlement, 30 April 1948*, known as the *Pact of Bogotá* (p. 93). Its purpose was to coordinate treaties signed at earlier conferences to ensure that disputes between American States would be settled by peaceful means. Although the treaty provided for compulsory arbitration (Article 46) and for the compulsory jurisdiction of the International Court (Article 32), reservations made to the pact at the time of signature by seven American Republics, including the United States, made these compulsory procedures, wherein the main strength of the pact lies, inoperative in practice.

It is a characteristic of all these treaties that no State is automatically bound to offer armed assistance to any other signatory; also important is the fact that the United States is not prevented from acting in accordance with the treaty, if it decides to do so, by the possible opposition of one or more of the Latin American Republics.

The United States administration endeavoured to draw the attention of the Latin American States to the dangers of international communism during the early 1950s, but without much response. The election of President Arbenz in Guatemala in 1950 alarmed the administration, which regarded him as sympathetic to communist policies. At the *Tenth International Conference of American States at Caracas, 1–28 March 1954*, Secretary of State John Foster Dulles secured the passage of a resolution directed against the control of the political institutions of any American State by the 'international communist movement'; but no resolution specifically allowed for any joint intervention in the affairs of an American State. In June 1954 Guatemala was invaded from Honduras, and Arbenz was overthrown. It was widely believed that the United States was chiefly responsible and that the Central Intelligence Agency was involved in the invasion. Latin American fears of a return by the United States to a policy of intervention, and dissatisfaction with the economic policies of the United States, made the 1950s a bleak decade in relations between the United States and its South American neighbours. The decade ended with Fidel Castro's successful Cuban Revolution. The United States broke off diplomatic relations with Castro in 1961. Cuba's communist alignment represented a major challenge to United States leadership in the Americas. An attempt to bring about Castro's fall by aiding Cuban exiles to land in the Bay of Pigs and to raise a revolt ended in a fiasco in April 1961. This setback to inter-American relations was counterbalanced by President Kennedy's initiative in launching the 'Alliance for Progress'.

A special meeting of the *Inter-American Economic and Social Council held in Punta del Este, Uruguay, 5–17 August 1961, adopted the Charter of Punta del Este, establishing an Alliance for Progress* (p. 98). The United States undertook to provide 20 billion dollars, mainly from public funds, over a period of ten years. But these vast funds were not to be applied in the normal way of foreign aid. They were to be utilized to transform society in Latin America. Latin American Governments pledged themselves to carry through far-reaching social reforms 'to permit a fair distribution of the fruits of economic and social progress'. These provisional reforms ranged from better use of land, housing, and education, to the elimination of corruption and to economic collaboration. The results in Latin America were disappointing during the 1960s in terms of the objectives set out in the Alliance for Progress.

The United States continued to show itself ready to act unilaterally when it believed its vital interests were threatened. When Russian missiles were being erected in Cuba, Kennedy secured their removal in his confrontation with Khrushchev during the thirteen days of the *Cuban Missile Crisis of 16–28 October 1962*. But the United States also received a measure of support from the American States when the O.A.S. adopted a resolution on 23 October which sanctioned the use of armed force if necessary against Cuba under the terms of the Rio treaty. Three years later, in April 1965, President Johnson intervened in the Dominican Republic where a revolution threatened to establish a Government judged by his administration to be controlled by communists. The United States again acted unilaterally in the Caribbean since it believed its most vital interests threatened by a hostile Government which, as in Cuba, might have linked itself with the Soviet Union. This intervention was motivated by fears of another Castro-type régime developing in the Caribbean.

Similar fears by President Reagan's administration two decades later led to United States military intervention on the Caribbean island of Grenada in 1983, and to so-called 'covert' American support for the 'contra' rebels operating from Honduras against the left-wing 'Sandinista' Government of Nicaragua after 1979. 'Covert' political support was also given by the United States to the military revolt in Chile in 1973 which overthrew the leftist Government of President Salvador Allende.

In spite of the defects of the Latin American treaty system established by the U.S.A. in the late 1940s (and notwithstanding the extent to which several States, most notably the U.S.A., ignored the underlying principle of non-intervention in the internal affairs of fellow-signatories) the formal structure remained largely intact in the 1980s. The most important new security treaty affecting the region signed by the United States in the intervening period was the *Panama Canal Treaty of 7 September 1977* (see Chapter 9).

By contrast with the frequently troubled relations between the United States and its southern neighbours, American–Canadian relations throughout the post-war period were relatively smooth. Occasional spasms of anti-American nationalism in Canada did not seriously impair the relationship; nor did the emergence for a while in the 1970s of a movement (ultimately unproductive) calling for an independent Francophone Quebec. The close interlocking of the two countries' economies, and the gradual shedding by English-speaking Canadians of their residual sentimental allegiance to Great Britain, brought Canada and the United States into intimate cooperation. A Permanent Joint Board of Defense had been established between the two countries in 1940, and in 1947 they agreed to continue it indefinitely. In 1951 and 1955 agreements were signed establishing radar warning systems across Canada linking the western Alaskan islands to the eastern Canadian shore. Canada was a founding member of NATO, and after 1958 the air defences of North America were coordinated in a joint command (NORAD). In 1959 agreement was reached for establishing a ballistic missile early warning system. Numerous other agreements on questions of joint defence were reached. But Canada pursued a notably independent foreign policy, both on the world stage and in the western hemisphere. Initially because of her membership of the Commonwealth, later more because of a desire to avoid embroilment in conflicts between the U.S.A. and its southern neighbours, Canada held aloof from Pan-American organizations.

## Inter-American Treaty of Reciprocal Assistance, Rio de Janeiro, 2 September 1947

In the name of their Peoples, the Governments represented at the Inter-American Conference for the Maintenance of Continental Peace and Security, desirous of consolidating and strengthening their relations of friendship and good neighborliness, and

Considering...

That the High Contracting Parties reiterate their will to remain united in an Inter-American System consistent with the purposes and principles of the United Nations, and reaffirm the existence of the agreement which they have concluded concerning those matters relating to the maintenance of international peace and security which are appropriate for regional action;

That the High Contracting Parties reaffirm their adherence to the principles of inter-American solidarity and cooperation, and especially to those set forth in the preamble and declarations of the Act of Chapultepec, all of which should be understood to be accepted as standards of their mutual relations and as the juridical basis of the Inter-American System...

That the obligation of mutual assistance and common defense of the American Republics is essentially related to their democratic ideals and to their will to cooperate permanently in the fulfillment of the principles and purposes of a policy of peace...

Have resolved, in conformity with the objectives stated above, to conclude the following Treaty, in order to assure peace, through adequate means, to provide for effective reciprocal assistance to meet armed attacks against any American State, and in order to deal with threats of aggression against any of them:

*Article 1.* The High Contracting Parties formally condemn war and undertake in their international relations not to resort to the threat or the use of force in any manner inconsistent with the provisions of the Charter of the United Nations or of this Treaty.

*Article 2.* As a consequence of the principle set forth in the preceding Article, the High Contracting Parties undertake to submit every controversy which may arise between them to methods of peaceful settlement and to endeavour to settle any such controversy among themselves by means of the procedures in force in the Inter-American System before referring it to the General Assembly or the Security Council of the United Nations.

*Article 3.* 1. The High Contracting Parties agree that an armed attack by any State against an American State shall be considered as an attack against all the American States and, consequently, each one of the said Contracting Parties undertakes to assist in meeting the attack in the exercise of the inherent right of individual

or collective self-defense recognized by Article 51 of the Charter of the United Nations.

2. On the request of the State or States directly attacked and until the decision of the Organ of Consultation of the Inter-American System, each one of the Contracting Parties may determine the immediate measures which it may individually take in fulfillment of the obligation contained in the preceding paragraph and in accordance with the principle of continental solidarity. The Organ of Consultation shall meet without delay for the purpose of examining those measures and agreeing upon the measures of a collective character that should be taken.

3. The provisions of this Article shall be applied in case of any armed attack which takes place within the region described in Article 4 or within the territory of an American State. When the attack takes place outside of the said areas, the provisions of Article 6 shall be applied.

4. Measures of self-defense provided for under this Article may be taken until the Security Council of the United Nations has taken the measures necessary to maintain international peace and security.

*Article 4.* The regions to which this Treaty refers are the North and South American continents and Greenland and an area of Antarctica.

*Article 5.* The High Contracting Parties shall immediately send to the Security Council of the United Nations, in conformity with Articles 51 and 54 of the Charter of the United Nations, complete information concerning the activities undertaken or in contemplation in the exercise of the right of self-defense or for the purpose of maintaining inter-American peace and security.

*Article 6.* If the inviolability or the integrity of the territory or the sovereignty or political independence of any American State should be affected by an aggression which is not an armed attack or by an extra-continental or intracontinental conflict, or by any other fact or situation that might endanger the peace of America, the Organ of Consultation shall meet immediately in order to agree on the measures which must be taken in case of aggression to assist the victim of the aggression or, in any case, the measures which should be taken for the common defense and for the maintenance of the peace and security of the continent.

*Article 7.* In the case of a conflict between two or more American States, without prejudice to the right of self-defense in conformity with Article 51 of the Charter of the United Nations, the High Contracting Parties meeting in consultation shall call upon the contending States to suspend hostilities and restore matters to the *status quo ante bellum*, and shall take in addition all other necessary measures to re-establish or maintain inter-American peace and security and for the solution of the conflict by peaceful means. The rejection of the pacifying action will be considered in the determination of the aggressor and in the application of the measures which the consultative meeting may agree upon.

. . .

[*Article 8.* Sanctions ranged from breaking off diplomatic relations, to economic sanctions, to the use of armed force.]

*Article 9.* In addition to other acts which the Organ of Consultation may characterize as aggression, the following shall be considered as such:

(a) Unprovoked armed attack by a State against the territory, the people, or the land, sea or air forces of another State;

(b) Invasion, by the armed forces of a State, of the territory of an American State, through the trespassing of boundaries demarcated in accordance with a treaty, judicial decision, or arbitral award, or, in the absence of frontiers thus demarcated, invasion affecting a region which is under the effective jurisdiction of another State.

*Article 10.* None of the provisions of this Treaty shall be construed as impairing the rights and obligations of the High Contracting Parties under the Charter of the United Nations.

*Article 11.* The consultations to which this Treaty refers shall be carried out by means of the Meetings of Ministers of Foreign Affairs of the American Republics which have ratified the Treaty, or in the manner or by the organ which in the future may be agreed upon.

*Article 12.* The Governing Board of the Pan-American Union may act provisionally as an organ of consultation until the meeting of the Organ of Consultation referred to in the preceding Article takes place.

*Article 13.* The consultations shall be initiated at the request addressed to the Governing Board of the Pan-American Union by any of the signatory States which has ratified the Treaty.

*Article 14.* In the voting referred to in this Treaty only the representatives of the signatory States which have ratified the Treaty may take part.

*Article 15.* The Governing Board of the Pan-American Union shall act in all matters concerning this Treaty as an organ of liaison among the signatory States which have ratified this Treaty and between these States and the United Nations.

*Article 16.* The decisions of the Governing Board of the Pan-American Union referred to in Articles 13 and 15 above shall be taken by an absolute majority of the members entitled to vote.

*Article 17.* The Organ of Consultation shall take its decisions by a vote of two-thirds of the signatory States which have ratified the Treaty.

*Article 18.* In the case of a situation or dispute between American States, the parties directly interested shall be excluded from the voting referred to in two preceding Articles.

*Article 19.* To constitute a quorum in all

the meetings referred to in the previous Articles, it shall be necessary that the number of States represented shall be at least equal to the number of votes necessary for the taking of the decision.

*Article 20*. Decisions which require the application of the measures specified in Article 8 shall be binding upon all the signatory States which have ratified this Treaty, with the sole exception that no State shall be required to use armed force without its consent.

*Article 21*. The measures agreed upon by the Organ of Consultation shall be executed through the procedures and agencies now existing or those which may in the future be established.

. . .

[*Articles 22–4*. Ratification and Registration. Ratification by two-thirds of signatories necessary.]

*Article 25*. This Treaty shall remain in force indefinitely, but may be denounced by any High Contracting Party by a notification in writing to the Pan-American Union, which shall inform all the other High Contracting Parties of each notification of denunciation received.

After the expiration of two years from the date of the receipt by the Pan-American Union of a notification of denunciation by any High Contracting Party, the present Treaty shall cease to be in force and with respect to such State, but shall remain in full force and effect with respect to all the other High Contracting Parties.

*Article 26*. The principles and fundamental provisions of this Treaty shall be incorporated in the Organic Pact of the Inter-American System.

RESERVATION OF HONDURAS

[Concerning Honduras–Nicaraguan boundary.]

## *Charter of the Organization of American States, Bogotá, 30 April 1948*

IN THE NAME OF THEIR PEOPLES, THE STATES REPRESENTED AT THE NINTH INTERNATIONAL CONFERENCE OF AMERICAN STATES,

Convinced that the historic mission of America is to offer to man a land of liberty, and a favorable environment for the development of his personality and the realization of his just aspirations;

Conscious that that mission has already inspired numerous agreements, whose essential value lies in the desire of the American peoples to live together in peace, and, through their mutual understanding and respect for the sovereignty of each one, to provide for the betterment of all, in independence, in equality and under law;

Confident that the true significance of American solidarity and good neighborliness can only mean the consolidation on this continent, within the framework of democratic institutions, of a system of individual liberty and social justice based on respect for the essential rights of man;

Persuaded that their welfare and their contribution to the progress and the civilization of the world will increasingly require intensive continental cooperation;

Resolved to persevere in the noble undertaking that humanity has conferred upon the United Nations, whose principles and purposes they solemnly reaffirm;

Convinced that juridical organization is a necessary condition for security and peace founded on moral order and on justice; and

In accordance with Resolution IX of the Inter-American Conference on Problems of War and Peace, held at Mexico City,

Have agreed upon the following CHARTER OF THE ORGANIZATION OF AMERICAN STATES

## Part One

*Chapter I: Nature and purposes*

*Article 1.* The American States establish by this Charter the international organization that they have developed to achieve an order of peace and justice, to promote their solidarity, to strengthen their collaboration, and to defend their sovereignty, their territorial integrity and their independence. Within the United Nations, the Organization of American States is a regional agency.

. . .

*Article 4.* The Organization of American States, in order to put into practice the principles on which it is founded and to fulfill its regional obligations under the Charter of the United Nations, proclaims the following essential purposes:

(a) To strengthen the peace and security of the continent;

(b) To prevent possible causes of difficulties and to ensure the pacific settlement of disputes that may arise among the Member States;

(c) To provide for common action on the part of those States in the event of aggression;

(d) To seek the solution of political, juridical and economic problems that may arise among them; and

(e) to promote, by cooperative action, their economic, social and cultural development.

*Chapter II: Principles*

[*Article 5.* These affirm good faith, condemn aggression, aspire to social justice and economic cooperation.]

. . .

*Chapter III: Fundamental rights and duties of States*

*Article 6.* States are juridically equal, enjoy equal rights and equal capacity to exercise these rights, and have equal duties. The rights of each State depend not upon its power to ensure the exercise thereof, but upon the mere fact of its existence as a person under international law.

[*Articles 7–14.* Set out the rights and duties.]

. . .

*Article 15.* No State or group of States has the right to intervene, directly or indirectly, for any reason whatever, in the internal or external affairs of any other State. The foregoing principle prohibits not only armed force but also any other form of interference or attempted threat against the personality of the State or against its political, economic and cultural elements.

*Article 16.* No State may use or encourage the use of coercive measures of an economic or political character in order to force the sovereign will of another State and obtain from it advantages of any kind.

*Article 17.* The territory of a State is inviolable; it may not be the object, even temporarily, of military occupation or of other measures of force taken by another State, directly or indirectly, on any grounds whatever. No territorial acquisitions or special advantages obtained either by force or by other means of coercion shall be recognized.

*Article 18.* The American States bind themselves in their international relations not to have recourse to the use of force, except in the case of self-defense in accordance with existing treaties or in fulfillment thereof.

*Article 19.* Measures adopted for the maintenance of peace and security in accordance with existing treaties do not constitute a violation of the principles set forth in Articles 15 and 17.

*Chapter IV: Pacific settlement of disputes*

*Article 20.* All international disputes that may arise between American States shall be submitted to the peaceful procedures set forth in this Charter, before being referred to the Security Council of the United Nations.

[*Articles 21–3.* Briefly set out the peaceful procedures.]

. . .

*Chapter V: Collective security*

*Article 24.* Every act of aggression by a State against the territorial integrity or the inviolability of the territory or against the sovereignty or political independence of an American State shall be considered an act of aggression against the other American States.

*Article 25.* If the inviolability or the integrity of the territory or the sovereignty or political independence of any American State should be affected by an armed attack or by an act of aggression that is not an armed attack, or by an extra-continental conflict, or by a conflict between two or more American States, or by any other fact or situation that might endanger the peace of America, the American States, in furtherance of the principles of continental solidarity or collective self-defense, shall apply the measures and procedures established in the special treaties on the subject.

. . .

*Chapter VI: Economic standards*

[*Articles 26–7.*]

*Chapter VII: Social standards*

[*Articles 28–9.*]

*Chapter VIII: Cultural standards*

[*Articles 30–1.*]

# American Treaty on Pacific Settlement (Pact of Bogotá), Bogotá, 30 April 1948

In the name of their peoples, the Governments represented at the Ninth International Conference of American States have resolved, in fulfillment of Article XXIII of the Charter of the Organization of American States, to conclude the following Treaty:

*Chapter One: General obligation to settle disputes by pacific means*

*Article I.* The High Contracting Parties, solemnly reaffirming their commitments made in earlier international conventions and declarations, as well as in the Charter of the United Nations, agree to refrain from the threat or the use of force, or from any other means of coercion for the settlement of their controversies, and to have recourse at all times to pacific procedures.

*Article II.* The High Contracting Parties recognize the obligation to settle international controversies by regional pacific procedures before referring them to the Security Council of the United Nations.

Consequently, in the event that a controversy arises between two or more signatory States which, in the opinion of the parties, cannot be settled by direct negotiations through the usual diplomatic channels, the parties bind themselves to use the procedures established in the present Treaty, in the manner and under the conditions provided for in the following Articles, or, alternatively, such special procedures as, in their opinion, will permit them to arrive at a solution.

*Article III.* The order of the pacific procedures established in the present Treaty does not signify that the parties may not have recourse to the procedure which they consider most appropriate in each case, or that they should use all these procedures, or that any of them have preference over others except as expressly provided.

*Article IV.* Once any pacific procedure has been initiated, whether by agreement between the parties or in fulfillment of the present Treaty or a previous pact, no other procedure may be commenced until that procedure is concluded.

*Article V.* The aforesaid procedures may not be applied to matters which, by their nature, are within the domestic jurisdiction of the State. If the parties are not in agreement as to whether the controversy concerns a matter of domestic jurisdiction, this preliminary question shall be submitted to decision by the International Court of Justice, at the request of any of the parties.

*Article VI.* The aforesaid procedures, furthermore, may not be applied to matters already settled by arrangement between the parties, or by arbitral award or by decision of an international court, or which are governed by agreements or treaties in force on the date of the conclusion of the present Treaty.

*Article VII.* The High Contracting Parties bind themselves not to make diplomatic representations in order to protect their nationals, or to refer a controversy to a court of international jurisdiction for that purpose, when the said nationals have had available the means to place their case before competent domestic courts of the respective State.

*Article VIII.* Neither recourse to pacific means for the solution of controversies, nor the recommendation of their use, shall, in the case of an armed attack, be ground for delaying the exercise of the right of individual or collective self-defense, as provided for in the Charter of the United Nations.

*Chapter Two: Procedures of good offices and mediation*

*Article IX.* The procedure of good offices consists in the attempt by one or more American Governments not parties to the controversy, or by one or more eminent citizens of any American State which is not a party to the controversy, to bring the parties together, so as to make it possible for them to reach an adequate solution between themselves. [Procedures detailed in Articles X–XIV.]

. . .

*Chapter Three: Procedure of investigation and conciliation*

*Article XV.* The procedure of investigation and conciliation consists in the submission of the controversy to a Commission of Investigation and Conciliation, which shall be established in accordance with the provisions established in subsequent Articles of the present Treaty, and which shall function within the limitations prescribed therein.

. . .

*Article XVIII.* Without prejudice to the provisions of the foregoing Article, the Pan-American Union shall draw up a permanent panel of American conciliators, to be made up as follows:

(a) Each of the High Contracting Parties shall appoint, for three-year periods, two of their nationals who enjoy the highest reputation for fairness, competence and integrity;

(b) The Pan-American Union shall request of the candidates notice of their formal acceptance, and it shall place on the panel of conciliators the names of the persons who so notify it;

(c) The Governments may, at any time, fill vacancies occurring among their appointees; and they may reappoint their members.

*Article XIX.* In the event that a controversy should arise between two or more American States that have not appointed the Commission referred to in Article

XVII, the following procedure shall be observed:

(a) Each party shall designate two members from the permanent panel of American conciliators, who are not of the same nationality as the appointing party;

(b) These four members shall in turn choose a fifth member, from the permanent panel, not of the nationality of either party;

(c) If, within a period of thirty days following the notification of their selection, the four members are unable to agree upon a fifth member, they shall each separately list the conciliators composing the permanent panel, in order of their preference, and upon comparison of the lists so prepared, the one who first receives a majority of votes shall be declared elected. The person so elected shall perform the duties of chairman of the Commission.

*Article XX.* In convening the Commission of Investigation and Conciliation, the Council of the Organization of American States shall determine the place where the Commission shall meet. . . .

[*Articles XX–XXVI.* Procedure of Commission.]

*Article XXVII.* If an agreement is reached by conciliation, the final report of the Commission shall be limited to the text of the agreement and shall be published after its transmittal to the parties, unless the parties decide otherwise. If no agreement is reached, the final report shall contain a summary of the work of the Commission; it shall be delivered to the parties, and shall be published after the expiration of six months unless the parties decide otherwise. In both cases, the final report shall be adopted by a majority vote.

*Article XXVIII.* The reports and conclusions of the Commission of Investigation and Conciliation shall not be binding upon the parties, either with respect to the statement of facts or in regard to questions of law, and they shall have no other character than that of recommenda-

tions submitted for the consideration of the parties in order to facilitate a friendly settlement of the controversy.

. . .

*Chapter Four: Judicial procedure*

*Article XXXI.* In conformity with Article 36, paragraph 2, of the Statute of the International Court of Justice, the High Contracting Parties declare that they recognize in relation to any other American State, the jurisdiction of the Court as compulsory *ipso facto*, without the necessity of any special agreement so long as the present Treaty is in force, in all disputes of a juridical nature that arise among them concerning:

(a) The interpretation of a treaty;

(b) Any question of international law;

(c) The existence of any fact which, if established, would constitute the breach of an international obligation;

(d) The nature or extent of the reparation to be made for the breach of an international obligation.

*Article XXXII.* When the conciliation procedure previously established in the present Treaty or by agreement of the parties does not lead to a solution, and the said parties have not agreed upon an arbitral procedure, either of them shall be entitled to have recourse to the International Court of Justice in the manner prescribed in Article 40 of the Statute thereof. The Court shall have compulsory jurisdiction in accordance with Article 36, paragraph 1, of the said Statute.

*Article XXXIII.* If the parties fail to agree as to whether the Court has jurisdiction over the controversy, the Court itself shall first decide that question.

*Article XXXIV.* If the Court, for the reasons set forth in Articles V, VI and VII of this Treaty, declares itself to be without jurisdiction to hear the controversy, such controversy shall be declared ended.

*Article XXXV.* If the Court for any other reason declares itself to be without jurisdiction to hear and adjudge the controversy, the High Contracting Parties obligate themselves to submit it to arbitration, in accordance with the provisions of Chapter Five of this Treaty.

. . .

*Chapter Five: Procedure of arbitration*

*Article XXXVIII.* Notwithstanding the provisions of Chapter Four of this Treaty, the High Contracting Parties may, if they so agree, submit to arbitration differences of any kind, whether juridical or not, that have arisen or may arise in the future between them.

. . .

[*Articles XXXIX—XLV.* Details of procedure of selecting arbiters or arbiter either by the Council of the Organization from nominations of parties in dispute, or by the parties who may by mutual agreement establish the Arbitration Tribunal in the manner they deem most appropriate.]

*Article XLVI.* The award shall be accompanied by a supporting opinion, shall be adopted by a majority vote, and shall be published after notification thereof has been given to the parties. The dissenting arbiter or arbiters shall have the right to state the grounds for their dissent.

The award, once it is duly handed down and made known to the parties, shall settle the controversy definitively, shall not be subject to appeal, and shall be carried out immediately.

*Article XLVII.* Any differences that arise in regard to the interpretation or execution of the award shall be submitted to the decision of the Arbitral Tribunal that rendered the award.

. . .

*Chapter Six: Fulfillment of decisions*

*Article L.* If one of the High Contracting Parties should fail to carry out the obligations imposed upon it by a decision of the International Court of Justice or by an arbitral award, the other party or parties concerned shall, before resorting to the Security Council of the United Nations, propose a Meeting of Consultation of Ministers of Foreign Affairs to agree upon appropriate measures to ensure the fulfillment of the judicial decision or arbitral award.

*Chapter Seven: Advisory opinions*

*Article LI.* The parties concerned in the solution of a controversy may, by agreement, petition the General Assembly or the Security Council of the United Nations to request an advisory opinion of the International Court of Justice on any juridical question.

The petition shall be made through the Council of the Organization of American States.

. . .

*Article LVI.* The present Treaty shall remain in force indefinitely, but may be denounced upon one year's notice, at the end of which period it shall cease to be in force with respect to the State denouncing it, but shall continue in force for the remaining signatories. The denunciation shall be addressed to the Pan-American Union, which shall transmit it to the other Contracting Parties.

The denunciation shall have no effect with respect to pending procedures initiated prior to the transmission of the particular notification.

. . .

RESERVATIONS

*Argentina.* The Delegation of the Argentine Republic, on signing the American Treaty on Pacific Settlement (Pact of Bogotá), makes reservations in regard to the following Articles, to which it does not adhere:

1. VII, concerning the protection of aliens;
2. Chapter Four (Articles XXXI to XXXVII), Judicial procedure;
3. Chapter Five (Articles XXXVIII to XLIX), Procedure of arbitration;

4. Chapter Six (Article L), Fulfillment of decisions.

Arbitration and judicial procedure have, as institutions, the firm adherence of the Argentine Republic, but the Delegation cannot accept the form in which the procedures for their application have been regulated, since, in its opinion, they should have been established only for controversies arising in the future and not originating in or having any relation to causes, situations or facts existing before the signing of this instrument. The compulsory execution of arbitral or judicial decisions and the limitation which prevents the States from judging for themselves in regard to matters that pertain to their domestic jurisdiction in accordance with Article V are contrary to Argentine tradition. The protection of aliens, who in the Argentine Republic are protected by its Supreme Law to the same extent as the nationals, is also contrary to that tradition.

*Bolivia*. The Delegation of Bolivia makes a reservation with regard to Article VI, inasmuch as it considers that pacific procedures may also be applied to controversies arising from matters settled by arrangement between the parties, when the said arrangement affects the vital interests of a State.

*Ecuador*. The Delegation of Ecuador, upon signing this Pact, makes an express reservation with regard to Article VI and also every provision that contradicts or is not in harmony with the principles proclaimed by or the stipulations contained in the Charter of the United Nations, the Charter of the Organization of American States, or the Constitution of the Republic of Ecuador.

*United States of America*. 1. The United States does not undertake as the complainant State to submit to the International Court of Justice any controversy which is not considered to be properly within the jurisdiction of the Court.

2. The submission on the part of the United States of any controversy to arbi-

tration, as distinguished from judicial settlement, shall be dependent upon the conclusion of a special agreement between the parties to the case.

3. The acceptance by the United States of the jurisdiction of the International Court of Justice as compulsory *ipso facto* and without special agreement, as provided in this Treaty, is limited by any jurisdictional or other limitations contained in any Declaration deposited by the United States under Article 36, paragraph 4, of the Statute of the Court, and in force at the time of the submission of any case.

4. The Government of the United States cannot accept Article VII relating to diplomatic protection and the exhaustion of remedies. For its part, the Government of the United States maintains the rules of diplomatic protection, including the rule of exhaustion of local remedies by aliens, as provided by international law.

*Paraguay*. The Delegation of Paraguay makes the following reservation:

Paraguay stipulates the prior agreement of the parties as a prerequisite to the arbitration procedure established in this Treaty for every question of a non-juridical nature affecting national sovereignty and not specifically agreed upon in treaties now in force.

*Peru*. The Delegation of Peru makes the following reservations:

1. Reservation with regard to the second part of Article V, because it considers that domestic jurisdiction should be defined by the State itself.

2. Reservation with regard to Article XXXIII and the pertinent part of Article XXXIV, inasmuch as it considers that the exceptions of *res judicata*, resolved by settlement between the parties or governed by agreements and treaties in force, determine, in virtue of their objective and peremptory nature, the exclusion of these cases from the application of every procedure.

3. Reservation with regard to Article XXXV, in the sense that, before arbitra-

tion is resorted to, there may be, at the request of one of the parties, a meeting of the Organ of Consultation, as established in the Charter of the Organization of American States.

4. Reservation with regard to Article XLV, because it believes that arbitration set up without the participation of one of the parties is in contradiction with its constitutional provisions.

*Nicaragua.* The Nicaraguan Delegation, on giving its approval to the American Treaty on Pacific Settlement (Pact of Bogotá) wishes to record expressly that no provisions contained in the said Treaty may prejudice any position assumed by the Government of Nicaragua with respect to arbitral decisions the validity of which it has contested on the basis of the principles of international law, which clearly permit arbitral decisions to be attacked when they are adjudged to be null or invalidated. Consequently, the signature of the Nicaraguan Delegation to the Treaty in question cannot be alleged as an acceptance of any arbitral decisions that Nicaragua has contested and the validity of which is not certain.

Hence the Nicaraguan Delegation reiterates the statement made on the 28th of the current month on approving the text of the above-mentioned Treaty in Committee III.

# The Charter of Punta Del Este establishing an Alliance for Progress, 17 August 1961

## Declaration to the Peoples of America

Assembled in Punta del Este, inspired by the principles consecrated in the Charter of the Organization of American States, in Operation Pan-America and in the Act of Bogotá, the representatives of the American Republics hereby agree to establish an Alliance for Progress: a vast effort to bring a better life to all the peoples of the continent.

This Alliance is established on the basic principle that free men working through the institution of representative democracy can best satisfy man's aspirations, including those for work, home and land, health and schools. No system can guarantee true progress unless it affirms the dignity of the individual which is the foundation of our civilization.

Therefore the countries signing this Declaration in the exercise of their sovereignty have agreed to work toward the following goals during the coming years:

To improve and strengthen democratic institutions through application of the principle of self-determination by the people.

To accelerate economic and social development, thus rapidly bringing about a substantial and steady increase in the average income in order to narrow the gap between the standard of living in Latin American countries and that enjoyed in the industrialized countries.

To carry out urban and rural housing programs to provide decent homes for all our people.

To encourage, in accordance with the characteristics of each country, programs of comprehensive agrarian reform, leading to the effective transformation, where required, of unjust structures and systems of land tenure and use; with a view to replacing *latifundia* and dwarf holdings by an equitable system of property so that, supplemented by timely and adequate credit, technical assistance and improved marketing arrangements, the land will become for the man who works it the basis of his economic stability, the foundation of his increasing welfare, and the guarantee of his freedom and dignity.

To assure fair wages and satisfactory working conditions to all our workers; to establish effective systems of labor-management relations and procedures for consultation and cooperation among government authorities, employers' associations, and trade unions in the interests of social and economic development.

To wipe out illiteracy; to extend, as quickly as possible, the benefits of primary education to all Latin Americans; and to provide broader facilities, on a vast scale, for secondary and technical training and for higher education.

To press forward with programs of health and sanitation in order to prevent sickness, combat contagious disease, and strengthen our human potential.

To reform tax laws, demanding more from those who have most, to punish tax evasion severely, and to redistribute the national income in order to benefit those who are most in need, while, at the same time, promoting savings and investment and reinvestment of capital.

To maintain monetary and fiscal policies which, while avoiding the disastrous effects of inflation or deflation, will protect the purchasing power of the many, guarantee the greatest possible price stability, and form an adequate basis for economic development.

To stimulate private enterprise in order to encourage the development of Latin American countries at a rate which will help them to provide jobs for their growing populations, to eliminate unemployment, and to take their place among the modern industrialized nations of the world.

To find a quick and lasting solution to the grave problem created by excessive price fluctuations in the basic exports of Latin American countries on which their prosperity so heavily depends.

To accelerate the integration of Latin America so as to stimulate the economic and social development of the continent. This process has already begun through the General Treaty of Economic Integration of Central America and, in other countries, through the Latin American Free Trade Association.

This Declaration expresses the conviction of the nations of Latin America that these profound economic, social, and cultural changes can come about only through the self-help efforts of each country. Nonetheless, in order to achieve the goals which have been established with the necessary speed, domestic efforts must be reinforced by essential contributions of external assistance.

The United States, for its part, pledges its efforts to supply financial and technical cooperation in order to achieve the aims of the Alliance for Progress. To this end, the United States will provide a major part of the minimum of twenty billion dollars, principally in public funds, which Latin America will require over the next ten years from all external sources in order to supplement its own efforts.

The United States will provide from public funds, as an immediate contribution to the economic and social progress of Latin America, more than one billion dollars during the twelve months which began on March 13, 1961, when the Alliance for Progress was announced.

The United States intends to furnish development loans on a long-term basis, where appropriate running up to fifty years and in general at very low or zero rates of interest.

For their part, the countries of Latin America agree to devote a steadily increasing share of their own resources to economic and social development, and to make the reforms necessary to assure that all share fully in the fruits of the Alliance for Progress.

Further, as a contribution to the Alliance for Progress, each of the countries of Latin America will formulate a comprehensive and well-conceived national program for the development of its own economy.

Independent and highly qualified experts will be made available to Latin American countries in order to assist in formulating and examining national development plans.

Conscious of the overriding importance of this Declaration, the signatory countries declare that the inter-American community is now beginning a new era when it will supplement its institutional, legal, cultural and social accomplishments with immediate and concrete actions to secure a better life, under freedom and democracy, for the present and future generations.

## The Charter of Punta del Este

*Establishing an Alliance for Progress within the framework of Operation Pan-America*

*Preamble.* We, the American Republics, hereby proclaim our decision to unite in a common effort to bring our people accelerated economic progress and broader social justice within the framework of personal dignity and political liberty.

Almost two hundred years ago we began in this hemisphere the long struggle for freedom which now inspires people in all parts of the world. Today, in ancient lands, men moved to hope by the revolutions of our young nations search for liberty. Now we must give a new meaning to that revolutionary heritage. For America stands at a turning point in history. The men and women of our hemisphere are reaching for the better life which today's skills have placed within their grasp. They are determined for themselves and their children to have decent and ever more abundant lives, to gain access to knowledge and equal opportunity for all, to end those conditions which benefit the few at the expense of the needs and dignity of the many. It is our inescapable task to fulfill these just desires – to demonstrate to the poor and forsaken of our countries, and of all lands, that the creative powers of free men hold the key to their progress and to the progress of future generations. And our certainty of ultimate success rests not alone on our faith in ourselves and in our nations but on the indomitable spirit of free man which has been the heritage of American civilization.

Inspired by these principles, and by the principles of Operation Pan-America and the Act of Bogotá, the American Republics hereby resolve to adopt the following program of action to establish and carry forward an Alliance for Progress.

. . .

[TITLE I. The Treaty sets out the objectives of the alliance in conformity with the Declaration to the Peoples of America.]

[TITLE II. Economic and social development: requirements, National Development Programs, immediate and short-term measures.]

. . .

*Chapter IV: External assistance in support of National Development Programs*

1. The economic and social development of Latin America will require a large amount of additional public and private financial assistance on the part of capital-exporting countries, including the members of the Development Assistance Group and international lending agencies. The measures provided for in the Act of Bogotá and the new measures provided for in this Charter, are designed to create a framework within which such additional assistance can be provided and effectively utilized.

2. The United States will assist those participating countries whose development programs establish self-help measures and economic and social policies and programs consistent with the principles of this Charter. To supplement the domestic efforts of such countries, the United States is prepared to allocate resources which, along with those anticipated from other external sources, will be of a scope and magnitude adequate to realize the goals envisaged in this Charter. Such assistance will be allocated to both social and economic development and, where appropriate, will take the form of grants or loans on flexible terms and conditions. The participating countries will request the support of other capital-exporting countries and appropriate institutions so that

they may provide assistance for the attainment of these objectives.

3. The United States will help in the financing of technical assistance projects proposed by a participating country or by the General Secretariat of the Organization of American States for the purpose of:

(a) Providing experts contracted in agreement with the Governments to work under their direction and to assist them in the preparation of specific investment projects and the strengthening of national mechanisms for preparing projects, using specialized engineering firms where appropriate;

(b) Carrying out, pursuant to existing agreements for cooperation among the General Secretariat of the Organization of American States, the Economic Commission for Latin America, and the Inter-American Development Bank, field investigations and studies, including those relating to development problems, the organization of national agencies for the preparation of development programs, agrarian reform and rural development, health, cooperatives, housing, education and professional training, and taxation and tax administration; and

(c) Convening meetings of experts and officials on development and related problems.

The Governments or above-mentioned organizations should, when appropriate, seek the cooperation of the United Nations and its specialized agencies in the execution of these activities.

4. The participating Latin American countries recognize that each has in varying degree a capacity to assist fellow Republics by providing technical and financial assistance. They recognize that this capacity will increase as their economies grow. They therefore affirm their intention to assist fellow Republics increasingly as their individual circumstances permit.

*Chapter V: Organization and procedures*

1. In order to provide technical assistance for the formulation of development programs, as may be requested by participating nations, the Organization of American States, the Economic Commission for Latin America, and the Inter-American Development Bank will continue and strengthen their agreements for coordination in this field, in order to have available a group of programming experts whose service can be used to facilitate the implementation of this Charter. The participating countries will also seek an intensification of technical assistance from the specialized agencies of the United Nations for the same purpose.

2. The Inter-American Economic and Social Council, on the joint nomination of the Secretary-General of the Organization of American States, the President of the Inter-American Development Bank, and the Executive Secretary of the United Nations Economic Commission for Latin America, will appoint a panel of nine high-level experts, exclusively on the basis of their experience, technical ability, and competence in the various aspects of economic and social development. The experts may be of any nationality, though if of Latin American origin an appropriate geographical distribution will be sought. They will be attached to the Inter-American Economic and Social Council, but will nevertheless enjoy complete autonomy in the performance of their duties. They may not hold any other remunerative position. The appointment of these experts will be for a period of three years, and may be renewed.

3. Each Government, if it so wishes, may present its program for economic and social development for consideration by an *Ad hoc* Committee, composed of no more than three members drawn from the panel of experts referred to in the preceding paragraph together with an equal number of experts not on the panel. The experts who compose the *Ad hoc* Committee will be appointed by the Secretary-General of the Organization of American States at the request of the interested Government and with its consent.

4. The Committee will study the development program, exchange opinions with the interested Government as to pos-

sible modifications and, with the consent of the Government, report its conclusions to the Inter-American Development Bank and to other Governments and institutions that may be prepared to extend external financial and technical assistance in connection with the execution of the program.

. . .

[7. A Government whose program has been approved by the *Ad hoc* Committee with respect to external financial re-

quirements may submit the program to the Inter-American Development Bank so that the Bank may negotiate the finance.

8. The Inter-American Economic and Social Council will review progress of development programs and submit recommendations to the Council of the O.A.S.]

[TITLE III. Dealt with economic integration of Latin America.]

[TITLE IV. Basic export commodities.]

## The Atlantic Alliance

As has already been noted, the wartime alliance commitments of the United States ceased with the end of the war in 1945. But the American determination before 1947 to avoid new exclusive alliance commitments outside the Americas in peacetime, other than the general obligations of the United Nations Charter, was replaced by a search for reliable allies after 1947 in the new era of East–West relations that became known as the 'cold war'. It is not possible to date the origin of this 'cold war' in the same way as the origins of a shooting war. In a sense it goes back to the Bolshevik Revolution, for the mutual suspicions then aroused were never overcome, not even during the years of alliance in the Second World War. At the end of that war Soviet influence and military power had tremendously increased in Europe, and Stalin treated the region of Central and Eastern Europe as belonging to the Soviet sphere of influence. This attitude precluded the restoration of Poland and the Balkan States to their pre-war independence; and it also introduced to these countries, to some gradually and to others immediately, the suppression of individual political freedom, the secret police, imprisonment without trial and the 'purge'. In 1946 Churchill characterized the Soviet-imposed isolation of communist-dominated Europe as an 'iron curtain'. Genuine Allied cooperation in the government of Germany as a whole proved a pipedream. In Germany, and in the United Nations, the Soviet Union clashed with the policies of the Western Powers.

There was no sharing of the secrets of the atomic bomb; faced with a huge preponderance of Soviet armies in Europe, the West had retained sole possession of the atomic bomb. Many believed that this alone could restore the balance and deter Stalin from further expansion. That this was his intention Britain and the United States deduced from Soviet pressure on Turkey and from the Soviet Union's unwillingness to with-draw from northern Iran in accordance with wartime agreements; after U.S. protests, the Soviet Union in March 1946 did announce its with-drawal from Iran. Truman saw communist revolt in Greece (which, in fact, received little help from Stalin) as part of a general Soviet strategy to spread communist power under the direction of the Soviet Union, and responded with an address to Congress, broadcast to the nation, which contained the passage that became known as the *Truman Doctrine, 12 March 1947*.

The immediate need to help Greece was placed by Truman in the wider context of helping free peoples everywhere to maintain their institutions and their national integrity against aggressive movements that attempted to impose on them totalitarian government. He warned that such direct or indirect aggression, if successful, would undermine the foundations of international peace. American help, Truman advised, should be extended primarily through economic and financial aid. Greece and Turkey received American help. This was only a beginning. A few months later the *Marshall Plan*, originally proposed by the Secretary of State on *5 June 1947*, provided massive economic support to the countries of Western Europe (p. 203).

Until the spring of 1948 the United States continued to rely mainly on granting economic support and on diplomacy to prevent the extension of Soviet influence and power. But communist successes and pressures in 1948 and 1949 led to a reappraisal of American policies. In Europe the Czech Communists gained complete control of Czechoslovakia in February 1948. Soon after, in April 1948, the divergence of Soviet and Western policies over Germany impelled Stalin to put pressure on the Western Powers by impeding Western land and water communications with Berlin. By 1 July 1948 the Russians had imposed a complete land and sea blockade in breach of Allied agreements, but they desisted from interfering with the air corridors.

The Western Powers responded to events in Czechoslovakia and to Soviet hostility in Germany with a military alliance, the *Brussels Treaty*, and later pursued a policy which would lead to the creation of a rehabi-litated, sovereign and rearmed West German State (p. 207). In Washing-ton, the *Vandenberg Resolution*, adopted by the Senate on *11 June 1948*, gave bi-partisan Congressional support for an American alliance policy within the U.N. framework to meet any military communist threat; the resolution did not actually use the word 'alliance', but instead referred to 'collective arrangements'. It stated that the United States Government should pursue 'regional and other collective arrangements for individual and collective self-defense', and sanctioned the 'association of the United States by constitutional process' with such arrangements as affected American security. By 'constitutional process' was meant the necessary consent of the Senate to any alliance treaty as required by the constitution. The resolution also required that any treaty engagements entered into should be mutual in their application, i.e. if the United States undertook to aid another country to meet aggression, that country would be bound to aid the United States in similar conditions.

The Vandenberg Resolution made possible the association of the United States (and Canada) with the West European States in an Atlantic military alliance, the *North Atlantic Treaty, 4 April 1949* (p. 106). This treaty involved no automatic commitment on the part of the United States to go to war. The key article is no. 5; it stipulated that an armed attack against one or more signatories would be regarded as an attack on all, but only required the other signatories to assist the victim of an attack by such action as each deemed necessary. Article 6 defined the area covered by the treaty, which included the territory of the Federal Republic of Germany and West Berlin since the troops of the signatories were stationed there. The practical expectation that an attack on one signatory would in fact entail war with all was brought much closer eighteen months after signature when, in accordance with Article 3 (which required the signatories to develop their collective capacity to resist), agreement was reached that NATO would establish an integrated defence force. An integrated command structure with a Supreme Commander was developed. The supreme command has always been held by an American general.

Of great importance in the development of NATO has been the question of nuclear capacity and its control. From 1957 to 1960 the United States signed agreements concerning 'cooperation' in atomic weapons with Britain, Canada, France, the German Federal Republic, Greece, the Netherlands and Italy. NATO since 1957 has had nuclear capacity, but its actual use is subject to the consent of the President of the United States. A Nuclear Planning Committee is intended to provide for consultation. Britain, a NATO signatory, has independent nuclear capacity and so has France, but these independent nuclear forces are small compared to the capacity of the United States. Under an agreement with the United States signed in December 1962, Britain received from the United States Polaris missiles. Only the stock of American atomic weapons and missiles, however, is capable of matching the capacity for nuclear attack of the Soviet Union.

A significant article of the NATO treaty from the American, or more precisely the Senate's point of view, is Article 11, which required that the treaty be ratified by each country according to its own 'constitutional processes'. This meant that ratification would be required by a two-thirds majority of the Senate. The NATO treaty was duly ratified by the Senate on 21 July 1949. There existed at that time an understanding between leaders of Congress on the one hand, and the President and his administration on the other, that treaties involving military collaboration against communism should contain a clause requiring ratification by 'constitutional process', that is by the Senate.

Supplementing the United States participation with Western Europe, Congress passed the *Mutual Defense Act, 6 October 1949*, which permitted the administration to sign bilateral treaties to aid and rearm countries for broad political reasons, or for the sake of the security of the United States. Huge sums were expended in such aid. Bilateral treaties were concluded with each of the European NATO allies on 27 January 1950.

In spite of internal differences within the alliance NATO remained the core of the American alliance system and of Western security planning. Differences did sometimes develop into serious threats to alliance cohesion, as at the time of the Anglo-French invasion of Egypt in 1956, and as a result of French withdrawal from the integrated military command structure in 1966. In the early 1980s opposition (mainly from the left) in several European countries to the stationing of American missiles on their territories, and rifts (particularly after an American bombing raid on Libya in 1986) over the most effective response to international terrorism seemed to betoken increased strains within the alliance. But its inherent strength, and the centrality of the NATO connection in American strategic thinking, emerged clearly in 1982 when war broke out between two American allies, Argentina and Great Britain (the Falklands war, p. 431): the U.S.A. decided, with little compunction, to support its NATO ally rather than its hemispheric partner.

The original members of NATO were Belgium, Canada, Denmark, France, Iceland, Italy, Luxemburg, the Netherlands, Norway, Portugal, Britain, and the United States. These were later joined by Greece (1952), Turkey (1952), and West Germany (1955).

Greece withdrew from military cooperation in NATO after the Turkish invasion of Cyprus in 1974; she resumed participation in the alliance in October 1980, but in August 1984 further disputes with Turkey led Greece to announce she would not participate in NATO joint exercises. The left-wing Greek Government of Andreas Papandreou, elected in

1981, although committed to the ejection of American bases, neverthe-less signed a five-year *United States–Greece agreement on defense and economic cooperation in September 1983*. This provided for the continuation of the four existing American bases in Greece and for the payment of $500 million in U.S. military aid to Greece.

Spain, ruled by the last surviving Fascist dictator, Generalissimo Francisco Franco, until his death in 1975, was not admitted to NATO for more than three decades. But the *United States and Spain concluded a Defense Agreement on 26 September 1953* providing for the establishment of American naval and air bases in Spain and for military and economic aid by the U.S.A. to Spain. This was not a treaty but an executive agreement, and was therefore not subject to ratification by the U.S. Senate. Only after the death of Franco and movement towards the restoration of democracy in Spain did the two countries sign the *Treaty of Friendship and Coopera-tion between Spain and the United States, 24 January 1976*. A new *United States–Spain Defense Agreement was signed in 1982*. This provided for con-tinued use by the U.S.A. of bases in Spain for a further five years. In May 1982 Spain entered NATO. Some left-wing opposition to membership of the alliance was voiced, but on 11 March 1986 a national referendum on the question approved Spanish membership by a wide margin of votes. (On NATO see also p. 211.)

# North Atlantic Treaty between Belgium, Canada, Denmark, France, Iceland, Italy, Luxemburg, the Netherlands, Norway, Portugal, Britain and the United States, Washington, 4 April 1949

The parties to this Treaty reaffirm their faith in the purposes and principles of the Charter of the United Nations and their desire to live in peace with all peoples and all Governments.

They are determined to safeguard the freedom, common heritage and civiliza-tion of their peoples, founded on the prin-ciples of democracy, individual liberty and the rule of law.

They seek to promote stability and well-being in the North Atlantic area.

They are resolved to unite their efforts for collective defence and for the preserva-tion of peace and security.

They therefore agree to this North Atlantic Treaty:

*Article 1.* The parties undertake, as set forth in the Charter of the United Nations, to settle any international dis-putes in which they may be involved by peaceful means in such a manner that international peace and security and justice are not endangered, and to refrain in their international relations from the threat or use of force in any manner inconsistent with the purposes of the United Nations.

*Article 2.* The parties will contribute toward the further development of peaceful and friendly international relations by strengthening their free institutions, by bringing about a better understanding of the principles upon which these institutions are founded, and by promoting conditions of stability and well-being. They will seek to eliminate conflict in their international economic policies and will encourage economic collaboration between any or all of them.

*Article 3.* In order more effectively to achieve the objectives of this Treaty, the parties, separately and jointly, by means of continuous and effective self-help and mutual aid, will maintain and develop their individual and collective capacity to resist armed attack.

*Article 4.* The parties will consult together whenever, in the opinion of any of them, the territorial integrity, political independence or security of any of the parties is threatened.

*Article 5.* The parties agree that an armed attack against one or more of them in Europe or North America shall be considered an attack against them all; and consequently they agree that, if such an armed attack occurs, each of them in exercise of the right of individual or collective self-defence recognized by Article 51 of the Charter of the United Nations, will assist the party or parties so attacked by taking forthwith, individually and in concert with the other parties, such action as it deems necessary, including the use of armed force, to restore and maintain the security of the North Atlantic area.

Any such armed attack and all measures taken as a result thereof shall immediately be reported to the Security Council. Such measures shall be terminated when the Security Council has taken the measures necessary to restore and maintain international peace and security.

*Article 6.* For the purpose of Article 5 an armed attack on one or more of the parties is deemed to include an armed attack on the territory of any of the parties in Europe or North America, on the Algerian Departments of France, on the occupation forces of any party in Europe, on the islands under the jurisdiction of any party in the North Atlantic area north of the Tropic of Cancer, or on the vessels or aircraft in this area of any of the parties.

*Article 7.* This Treaty does not affect, and shall not be interpreted as affecting, in any way the rights and obligations under the Charter of the parties which are members of the United Nations, or the primary responsibility of the Security Council for the maintenance of international peace and security.

*Article 8.* Each party declares that none of the international engagements now in force between it and any other of the parties or any third State is in conflict with the provisions of this Treaty, and undertakes not to enter into any international engagement in conflict with this Treaty.

*Article 9.* The parties hereby establish a Council, on which each of them shall be represented, to consider matters concerning the implementation of this Treaty. The Council shall be so organized as to be able to meet promptly at any time. The Council shall set up such subsidiary bodies as may be necessary; in particular it shall establish immediately a Defence Committee which shall recommend measures for the implementation of Articles 3 and 5.

*Article 10.* The parties may, by unanimous agreement, invite any other European State in a position to further the principles of this Treaty and to contribute to the security of the North Atlantic area to accede to this Treaty. Any State so invited may become a party to the Treaty by depositing its instrument of accession with the Government of the United States of

America. The Government of the United States of America will inform each of the parties of the deposit of each such instrument of accession.

*Article 11.* This Treaty shall be ratified and its provisions carried out by the parties in accordance with their respective constitutional processes. The instruments of ratification shall be deposited as soon as possible with the Government of the United States of America, which will notify all the other signatories of each deposit. The Treaty shall enter into force between the States which have ratified it as soon as the ratifications of the majority of the signatories, including the ratifications of Belgium, Canada, France, Luxembourg, the Netherlands, the United Kingdom and the United States, have been deposited, and shall come into effect with respect to other States on the date of the deposit of their ratifications.

*Article 12.* After the Treaty has been in force for ten years, or at any time thereafter, the parties shall, if any of them so requests, consult together for the purpose of reviewing the Treaty, having regard for the factors then affecting peace and security in the North Atlantic area, including the development of universal as well as regional arrangements under the Charter of the United Nations for the maintenance of international peace and security.

*Article 13.* After the Treaty has been in force for twenty years, any party may cease to be a party one year after its notice of denunciation has been given to the Government of the United States of America, which will inform the Governments of the other parties of the deposit of each notice of denunciation.

*Article 14.* This Treaty, of which the English and French texts are equally authentic, shall be deposited in the archives of the Government of the United States of America. Duly certified copies thereof will be transmitted by that Government to the Governments of the other signatories.

## United States treaty relations in the Far East

On the same day the peace treaty with Japan was signed (p. 55), a *Japanese–United States Security Treaty, 8 September 1951* (p. 118) was concluded. This treaty allowed the United States to maintain armed forces 'in and about Japan', and at the request of the Japanese Government to use U.S. forces to put down large-scale internal riots in Japan caused by the instigation or intervention of an outside power. Japan undertook not to grant to any other country either bases or garrisons without the prior assent of the United States.

The 1951 treaty was replaced on *19 January 1960* by a *Treaty of Mutual Cooperation and Security between the United States and Japan*. This treaty, signed on the above date, entered into force on 23 June 1960. During the 1950s revision of the 1951 treaty had developed into a passionate issue in Japanese internal politics. As victims of the first nuclear bombs, the Japanese evinced acute sensitivity on all nuclear-weapon-related issues. The basic Japanese desire was for security with minimal military involvement. As Japan entered a period of rapid economic growth and social transformation, the United States became more ready to acquiesce in Japanese demands. American troops stationed in Japan were greatly reduced in number. The treaty of 1960 contained important revisions: it removed all derogations of sovereignty, and acknowledged that Japanese forces could be used only in self-defence. The United States (Article 6), for the purpose of contributing to the security of Japan and the maintenance of international peace and security in the Far East, was granted the continued use of bases in Japan for its land, air and naval forces. The use of these facilities was governed by a separate exchange of notes whereby the United States agreed on prior consultation with the Japanese Government before increasing U.S. forces in Japan, making any essential change of arming its forces (nuclear weapons), or using any bases under Japanese rule outside the treaty area. On 22 June 1970 the Japanese Government announced its intention to continue the Security Treaty of 1960, which would remain in force indefinitely unless either country gave one year's notice to terminate it. Negotiations for the return of the Ryukyu Islands and Okinawa were concluded by a *Japanese–United States Treaty signed on 17 June 1971*: the islands were to revert to Japan and they were returned in the spring of 1972; the Mutual Security Treaty became fully applicable to them and Japan granted continued use of bases to America on the same conditions as agreed under the Security Treaty of 1960.

The communist victory in China in 1949, the conclusion of the Sino-Soviet Treaty in February 1950 (p. 165), and American awareness that the Soviet Union also had exploded an atomic bomb in September 1949 – all these events had helped produce the end of the American occupation in Japan, and the U.S. decision to seek to transform a defeated and occupied enemy into an ally. The United States, in pursuing this course, was following a similar policy vis-à-vis Japan to that adopted in Europe vis-à-vis Germany. Both policies were to be crowned with considerable success. Meanwhile, alarmed by the communist successes in the Chinese civil war, the United States had already begun to shore up its defences in east Asia by building a network of security treaties in the region. In the Philippines the United States had secured bases by the *Philippine–United States Treaty, 14 March 1947*.

South Korea, although ruled by a pro-American régime, was not an American ally in the formal sense prior to the outbreak of the Korean War with the North Korean invasion of the south on 25 June 1950 (p. 296). The *Agreement between the United States and Korea to establish a Military Advisory Group, 26 January 1950* (p. 116) merely provided for the presence of 500 American military advisers in South Korea. The outbreak of the

Korean War both confirmed the existing objectives of American foreign policy in the region and led to new commitments and policies.

The new elements of American policy after the outbreak of war in Korea were, firstly, the decision to commit American naval and air forces to fight on the Asian mainland in South Korea; and secondly, the decision to interpose the Seventh Fleet between the Chinese mainland and Taiwan (Formosa), thus intervening in the Chinese Civil War. This latter decision was reached by Truman on 26 June 1950, and meant that each side was forbidden to attack the other, though clearly the danger was seen to arise from a communist attack on Taiwan; Truman declared that in the new circumstances this 'would be a direct threat to the Pacific area and to the United States forces performing their lawful and necessary functions there'. (It should be noted that before the outbreak of the conflict Truman had stated in January 1950 that the United States would not 'pursue a course which will lead to involvement in the civil conflict in China'.) On 29 and 30 June 1950 Truman committed U.S. ground forces in South Korea as well.

The Korean War, with its varying military fortunes, and especially with Communist Chinese intervention in late October 1950, changed the emphasis of America's China policy. During the months preceding the Korean War, the United States had refused to recognize Mao Tse-tung's proclaimed People's Republic of China (1 October 1949) as the Government of China. After the outbreak of the Korean War, the United States gradually decided to give full support to Chiang Kai-shek's Republic of China established in Taiwan. The possibility of a more flexible policy towards mainland China was abandoned for some years.

During the period from 1950 to 1954 the United States administration concluded that the threat to stability and peace arising from the possibility of communist direct attack or subversion was increasing and could be met only by throwing the military weight of America behind Asian and European allies willing to resist aggression. The objective was deterrence. The cohesion of the European NATO alliance was accordingly strengthened with substantial American and German military contributions. In Asia a search for new allies was intensified in 1950. But in Asia there was no continuous ring of developed nations that could be formed among China's neighbours. Running from north to south, Japan, South Korea, Taiwan, and the Philippines formed an unbroken flank, but in the South China Sea, Malaysia and Indonesia kept aloof; south of Indonesia and far removed from China were Australia and New Zealand; these two joined the United States alliance groupings. On the mainland of Asia,

Thailand and South Vietnam were associated in alliances; Cambodia and Laos were never securely brought in; Burma, India and Ceylon refused to join an anti-communist alliance, but Pakistan in 1954 did so; the American arc of defensive alliances against the Soviet Union continued unbroken thereafter through Iran to Turkey and Greece.

Two further important points need to be noted: firstly, the European anti-Soviet grouping of NATO was a separate alliance system not directly linked to the alliances of Asia. The only link was provided by the United States as a member of all these alliances in both Asia and Europe; Britain and (nominally) France were also involved in one Asian alliance, SEATO, as well as in NATO. Secondly, the Asian allies did not undertake to defend each other collectively; their commitment was limited to the particular treaty which they signed. Only the United States was committed to all as the signatory of all the treaties.

The Asian alliances which the United States negotiated were of necessity a patchwork rather than a unified system, since each Asian ally was often at least as concerned with its own regional problems and conflicts as with general opposition to communist expansion. Australia and New Zealand desired assurances of American support against any renewal of a threat from a revived Japan. The Philippines were involved in disputes with Indonesia and Malaysia; Chiang Kai-shek proclaimed intentions of reconquering the Chinese mainland; Pakistan periodically remained in conflict with India especially over Kashmir; and the South Koreans refused to abandon hopes of unification. The key to American policy in the western Pacific was Japan.

To overcome the obstacles to a Japanese peace treaty and to strengthen the defences of southern Asia, *the United States concluded a Security Treaty with Australia and New Zealand, 1 September 1951 (ANZUS)* (p. 117), and also at the same time the *Philippine–American Security Treaty, 30 August 1951*. Both treaties had the same joint defence clause which bound each signatory to act against any armed attack on either signatory in the Pacific; such action would be taken in accordance with each country's 'constitutional processes'. The signatories undertook by self-help and mutual aid to develop their collective capacity to resist armed attack. In the case of the Philippine treaty no joint consultative machinery was established (until the Philippine Mutual Defense Board in 1958), but American forces continued to be stationed in the Philippines as provided for in the treaty of 1947. The ANZUS treaty established a Consultative Council of Foreign Ministers, which undertook coordinating work. Neither treaty involved any automatic commitment to go to war though their language certainly implied a moral commitment. The ANZUS treaty was significant of one great shift in the relative balance of power: Britain (which was not a party, although expressing a desire to join) was no longer seen by Australia or New Zealand as the primary guarantor of their security. Events in the Far East since 1941 dictated that the defence and foreign policies of these Dominions would henceforth be orientated primarily towards Washington rather than London.

The treaty remains in force, although the cohesion of the alliance was threatened after 1985 by the anti-nuclear policies of the Labour Government in New Zealand headed by David Lange. The refusal of the New Zealand Government to permit U.S. ships capable of carrying nuclear weapons to visit New Zealand ports evoked a complaint by the United States that New Zealand had decided 'to renege on an essential element of its ANZUS participation'. The United States therefore declared in August 1986 that it was 'suspending its security obligations to New Zealand'. Trilateral exchange of intelligence information was halted, and New Zealand was in effect expelled from the alliance which henceforth became a bilateral one between Australia and the U.S.A.

The next United States security treaty in the region followed the signature of the *Korean Armistice, 27 July 1953* (p. 302). *The Mutual Defense Treaty between Korea and the United States, 10 October 1953* (p. 119), reassured South Korea and was the price paid by America for South Korean acceptance of the armistice, and especially for abandoning a policy of re-unification by force. This treaty permitted the stationing of American troops in and about Korea; it took effect on 17 November 1954, the Senate in a reservation underscoring that the United States was committed to come to the aid of South Korea only 'in case of an external armed attack . . . against territory which has been recognized by the United States as lawfully brought under the administrative control of the Republic of Korea'.

During the year following the Korean armistice, in 1954, the Chinese Communists launched a bombardment of two small islands, Quemoy and Matsu, close to the mainland of China but held by nationalist garrisons. The United States committed itself to the defence of nationalist-held Taiwan (Formosa) and the Pescadores islands, but allowed itself latitude whether or not to defend Quemoy and Matsu. A *Mutual Defense Treaty between the United States and China, 2 December 1954* (p. 123), was concluded on terms similar to the other American defence treaties in Asia. It involved a promise to act to meet armed attack in accordance with each State's constitutional processes. But in approving the treaty the United States Senate added three understandings of importance: the ultimate legal

THE UNITED STATES TREATY SYSTEM    113

title to Formosa and the Pescadores was not affected by the treaty, thus the United States was not committed ultimately to the claims of sovereignty of either side in the Chinese Civil War; secondly, the United States would act only if the nationalists were forced to fight in self-defence; finally, there was to be no extension territorially of the U.S. commitment without the prior consent of the Senate.

Mao Tse-tung's victory had brought Communist China to the borders of Indo-China in 1949. The opportunity for spreading communism throughout Indo-China seemed favourable. Ho Chi Minh, leader of the Vietnamese communists, and his supporters had been fighting the French army since December 1946 after abortive negotiations with the French Fourth Republic for the independence of Vietnam. Subsequently, in 1949, France recognized the independence of Vietnam, Laos and Cambodia, but within the French Union and in practice under leadership acceptable to the French, i.e. ready to oppose Ho Chi Minh and the communists. Ho Chi Minh continued to fight. Strengthened by Chinese help, the Vietminh (communist) army began to strike at French garrisons in October 1950. The United States by then had become involved in granting aid and supplies to the French-led armies, a consequence of a decision taken by Truman the previous May. Truman acted on the conviction that there was a threat of communism spreading throughout south-east Asia and that the loss of this whole region, coming after the loss of mainland China, would undermine the global defences of the West. The outbreak of the Korean War intensified this sense of threat, and American aid to the French-led armies in Vietnam was increased. Despite this aid the French were losing the struggle, and on 6 May 1954, when the Vietminh overran the French defences at Dien Bien Phu, a conference at Geneva had already been convened to work out an armistice and a settlement of the Indo-Chinese conflicts. The French Government had lost heart in the struggle and at the *Geneva Conference, 26 April–21 July 1954* (p. 268) agreed to a settlement in Indo-China which restricted their influence to South Vietnam, with the possibility of losing even that if elections to be held in 1956 should favour Ho Chi Minh.

Although the French had received massive economic support from the United States, and the Eisenhower administration in the spring of 1954 had even considered supporting the French with ground forces (provided this was a joint action with allies such as Britain, France and Australia and, if possible, Thailand and the Philippines), the French Government preferred to end the first phase of the Indo-Chinese war on the terms of the Geneva settlement.

John Foster Dulles, Secretary of State in the Eisenhower administration, disapproved of the Geneva settlement; the United States would not sign it but in a declaration promised not to upset these arrangements. Dulles continued to strengthen opposition to the spread of communism in southern Asia in the face of the French military disaster. He conducted negotiations for an alliance of collective defence among the major powers interested in this region, Britain, France, Australia and New Zealand, together with such Asian States as would join in the grouping. The new treaty would thus extend and complement ANZUS.

The outcome of the negotiations was the *South-East Asia Collective Defense Treaty (SEATO), signed in Manila on 8 September 1954* (p. 120), together with a *Pacific Charter* (p. 122) of principles. The eight signatories were the United States, Britain, France, Australia, New Zealand, and the three Asian States, Pakistan, Thailand and the Philippines. It followed the general structure of other United States defence treaties in that the signatories bound themselves separately and jointly by self-help and mutual aid to develop their individual and collective capacity to resist armed attack or subversion (Article 2); an armed attack on one signatory was recognized as constituting a danger to all, and each signatory agreed to 'act to meet the common danger in accordance with its own constitutional processes'; the signatories further would consult together if the integrity or independence of a signatory, or of any State designated in the treaty, were threatened by other than armed attack or 'by any fact or situation which might endanger the peace of the area'. A number of provisions, however, rendered the treaty rather vague or flexible in its possible application. The treaty area as geographically defined in Article 8 excluded Hong Kong and Taiwan. An additional Protocol designated Cambodia, Laos, and the 'free territory under the jurisdiction of the State of Vietnam' as falling within the treaty area for the purposes of Article 4. Cambodia rejected the protection of SEATO in 1956.

From 1954 to 1961 SEATO's capacity for providing effective aid in Laos and Vietnam was not tested; but renewal of conflict in South Vietnam by the Vietcong and North Vietnamese in 1960, and in Laos by the Pathet Lao forces, raised the question at SEATO's ministerial council which met in Bangkok in March 1961. In the event neither France nor Britain would support military action in Laos. Laos was neutralized in 1962 (p. 271). During the Laos crisis of 1962, the United States, principally with British, New Zealand and Australian support, moved forces and established bases in north-eastern Thailand to reassure Thailand. The United States provided unilateral support for the neutralist régime in Laos after 1962. SEATO was further weakened in the 1960s by Pakistan's concern over its conflict with India. A specific American and Australian reservation had excluded the application of the treaty to such a conflict. Pakistan drew closer to China; the United States and Britain rushed arms to India during and after the Indian–Chinese border conflict of 1962 (p. 261), which also strengthened India against Pakistan and caused bitter resentment in Pakistan, a SEATO ally. France became increasingly opposed to United States involvement in Vietnam during the 1960s and withdrew from military cooperation in SEATO in 1967. In the Vietnamese conflict, Britain refused active military cooperation, and after 1968 ran down its bases east of Suez. Of the SEATO Powers only Australia and the Philippines contributed small forces to fight in South Vietnam. SEATO had been conceived as providing United States, British and French 'Big Power' support to the Asian States willing to contain the threat of communism and Chinese expansion, i.e. Thailand, Pakistan, New Zealand, Australia, the Philippines and the three Indo-Chinese States, by providing military and economic assistance.

The weaknesses resulting from a lack of British and French support, from Pakistan's virtual withdrawal and the changing policies of the United States in south-east Asia spelt the doom of the arrangement. In November 1972 Pakistan withdrew completely from the alliance. France suspended membership payments from January 1974. By this time SEATO had virtually ceased to exist although the organization was not formally wound up until 1977.

The collapse of the pro-American Government in South Vietnam and the communist takeovers there and in Laos and Cambodia, as well as the beginnings of the American rapprochement with mainland China, had by that time rendered SEATO obsolete. Thenceforth American security policy in the region was based not on a multilateral organization but on bilateral arrangements. The experience of Vietnam had rendered the United States wary of entering into far-reaching commitments which might entail military involvement. U.S. forces, stationed in Thailand since 1962, began to be withdrawn in 1973. Between 1977 and 1979 some reductions were made in American troop strengths in South Korea. Meanwhile the United States reduced the numbers of its troops in Taiwan, and ultimately, with the abrogation of the 1954 treaty (see p. 299), withdrew its forces altogether from the island.

After the American withdrawal from Vietnam in 1973 the United States thus abandoned any significant presence on the east Asian mainland. The most important U.S. military bases in the region (the largest outside the United States) were thenceforth the longstanding Subic Bay

Naval Station and Clark Air Base on the Philippines. These bases, used by the United States since the turn of the century, were secured to the U.S.A. under the terms of the 1947 Philippine–United States Treaty for a period of ninety-nine years. The treaty was revised in 1965 and again in 1979. The latter revision confirmed Philippine sovereignty over the base areas and provided for five-yearly reviews. The first such review in 1983 produced a promise from the United States of $900 million in military and economic assistance to the Philippines. Following the revolution of 25 February 1986, in which President Ferdinand Marcos was replaced by Corazón Aquino, some internal pressure was manifested for the removal of U.S. bases. But the Aquino Administration, no less pro-American than its predecessor, adopted a policy of permitting the bases to remain at least until the expiration of the existing agreement in 1991.

## Agreement between the United States and Korea to establish a Military Advisory Group, Seoul, 26 January 1950

*Preamble*. In conformity with the request of the Government of the Republic of Korea to the Government of the United States, the President of the United States has authorized the establishment of the United States Military Advisory Group to the Republic of Korea (hereinafter referred to as the Group), under the terms and conditions specified below:

*Article I*. The purpose of the Group will be to develop the Security Forces of the Republic of Korea within the limitations of the Korean economy by advising and assisting the Government of the Republic of Korea in the organization, administration and training of such forces. [U.S. advisers not to exceed 500.]

*Article II*. This Agreement may be terminated at any time:
1. By either Government, provided that six months' written notice is given to the other Government;

2. By recall of the Group when either Government deems such recall to be in its public interest and shall have so notified the other Government without necessity of compliance with provision (1) of this Article. However, termination of this Agreement by recall does not relieve the Government of the Republic of Korea from its obligations arising under this Agreement during such time, not exceeding three months, reasonably necessary to permit the Group to terminate its functions and physically depart from Korea.

*Article III*. The functions of the Group shall be to provide such advice and assistance to the Government of the Republic of Korea on military and related matters as may be necessary to accomplish the purposes set forth in Article I of this Agreement. . . .

# Security Treaty between Australia, New Zealand and the United States (ANZUS), San Francisco, 1 September 1951

The parties to this Treaty,

Reaffirming their faith in the purposes and principles of the Charter of the United Nations and their desire to live in peace with all peoples and all Governments, and desiring to strengthen the fabric of peace in the Pacific area,

Noting that the United States already has arrangements pursuant to which its armed forces are stationed in the Philippines, and has armed forces and administrative responsibilities in the Ryukyus, and upon the coming into force of the Japanese Peace Treaty may also station armed forces in and about Japan to assist in the preservation of peace and security in the Japan area,

Recognizing that Australia and New Zealand as members of the British Commonwealth of Nations have military obligations outside as well as within the Pacific area,

Desiring to declare publicly and formally their sense of unity, so that no potential aggressor could be under the illusion that any of them stand alone in the Pacific area, and

Desiring further to coordinate their efforts for collective defense for the preservation of peace and security pending the development of a more comprehensive system of regional security in the Pacific area,

Therefore declare and agree as follows:

*Article I.* The parties undertake, as set forth in the Charter of the United Nations, to settle any international disputes in which they may be involved by peaceful means in such a manner that international peace and security and justice are not endangered and to refrain in their international relations from the threat or use of force in any manner inconsistent with the purposes of the United Nations.

*Article II.* In order more effectively to achieve the objective of this Treaty the parties separately and jointly by means of continuous and effective self-help and mutual aid will maintain and develop their individual and collective capacity to resist armed attack.

*Article III.* The parties will consult together whenever in the opinion of any of them the territorial integrity, political independence or security of any of the parties is threatened in the Pacific.

*Article IV.* Each party recognizes that an armed attack in the Pacific area on any of the parties would be dangerous to its own peace and safety and declares that it would act to meet the common danger in accordance with its constitutional processes.

Any such armed attack and all measures taken as a result thereof shall be immediately reported to the Security Council of the United Nations. Such measures shall be terminated when the Security Council has taken the measures necessary to restore and maintain international peace and security.

*Article V.* For the purpose of Article IV, an armed attack on any of the parties is deemed to include an armed attack on the metropolitan territory of any of the parties, or on the island territories under its jurisdiction in the Pacific or on its armed forces, public vessels or aircraft in the Pacific.

*Article VI.* This Treaty does not affect and shall not be interpreted as affecting in any way the rights and obligations of the parties under the Charter of the United Nations or the responsibility of the United Nations for the maintenance of international peace and security.

*Article VII.* The parties hereby establish a Council, consisting of their Foreign Ministers or their Deputies, to consider matters concerning the implementation of this Treaty. The Council should be so organized as to be able to meet at any time.

*Article VIII.* Pending the development of a more comprehensive system of regional security in the Pacific area and the development by the United Nations of more effective means to maintain international peace and security, the Council, established by Article VII, is authorized to maintain a consultative relationship with States, Regional Organizations, Associations of States or other authorities in the Pacific area in a position to further the

purposes of this Treaty and to contribute to the security of that area.

*Article IX.* This Treaty shall be ratified by the parties in accordance with their respective constitutional processes. . . .

*Article X.* This Treaty shall remain in force indefinitely. Any party may cease to be a member of the Council established by Article VII one year after notice has been given to the Government of Australia, which will inform the Governments of the other parties of the deposit of such notice.

[*Article XI.* Certified copies and deposit.]

## Security Treaty between the United States and Japan, 8 September 1951

Japan has this day signed a Treaty of Peace with the Allied Powers. On the coming into force of that Treaty, Japan will not have the effective means to exercise its inherent right of self-defense because it has been disarmed.

There is danger to Japan in this situation because irresponsible militarism has not yet been driven from the world. Therefore Japan desires a Security Treaty with the United States of America to come into force simultaneously with the Treaty of Peace between the United States of America and Japan.

The Treaty of Peace recognizes that Japan as a sovereign nation has the right to enter into collective security arrangements, and further, the Charter of the United Nations recognizes that all nations possess an inherent right of individual and collective self-defense.

In exercise of these rights, Japan desires, as a provisional arrangement for its defense, that the United States of America should maintain armed forces of its own in and about Japan so as to deter armed attack upon Japan.

The United States of America, in the interest of peace and security, is presently willing to maintain certain of its armed forces in and about Japan, in the expectation, however, that Japan will itself increasingly assume responsibility for its own defense against direct and indirect aggression, always avoiding any armament which could be an offensive threat or serve other than to promote peace and security in accordance with the purposes and principles of the United Nations Charter.

Accordingly, the two countries have agreed as follows:

*Article I.* Japan grants, and the United States of America accepts, the right, upon the coming into force of the Treaty of Peace and of this Treaty, to dispose United States land, air and sea forces in and about Japan. Such forces may be utilized to contribute to the maintenance of international peace and security in the Far East and to the security of Japan against armed attack from without, including assistance given at the express request of the Japanese Government to put down large-scale internal riots and disturbances in Japan, caused through instigation or intervention by an outside Power or Powers.

*Article II.* During the exercise of the right referred to in Article I, Japan will not grant, without the prior consent of the United States of America, any bases or any rights, powers or authority whatsoever, in or relating to bases or the right of garrison or of maneuver or transit of ground, air or naval forces to any third Power.

*Article III.* The conditions which shall govern the disposition of armed forces of the United States of America in and about Japan shall be determined by administrative agreements between the two Governments.

*Article IV.* This Treaty shall expire whenever in the opinion of the Governments of the United States of America and Japan there shall have come into force such United Nations arrangements or such alternative individual or collective security dispositions as will satisfactorily provide for the maintenance by the United Nations or otherwise of international peace and security in the Japan area.

*Article V.* This Treaty shall be ratified by the United States of America and Japan and will come into force when instruments of ratification thereof have been exchanged by them at Washington.

. . .

## Note: The Japanese Constitution
*Chapter II: Renunciation of war*

*Article 9.* Aspiring sincerely to an international peace based on justice and order, the Japanese people forever renounce war as a sovereign right of the nation and the threat or use of force as means of settling international disputes.

In order to accomplish the aim of the preceding paragraph, land, sea, and air forces, as well as other war potential, will never be maintained. The right of belligerency of the State will not be recognized.

# Mutual Defense Treaty between the United States and Korea (South), Washington, 10 October 1953

The parties to this Treaty . . . have agreed as follows:

*Article I.* The parties undertake to settle any international disputes in which they may be involved by peaceful means . . .

*Article II.* The parties will consult together whenever, in the opinion of either of them, the political independence or security of either of the parties is threatened by external armed attack. Separately and jointly, by self-help and mutual aid, the parties will maintain and develop appropriate means to deter armed attack and will take suitable measures in consultation and agreement to implement this Treaty and to further its purposes.

*Article III.* Each party recognizes that an armed attack in the Pacific area on either of the parties in territories now under their respective administrative control, or hereafter recognized by one of the parties as lawfully brought under the administrative control of the other, would be dangerous to its own peace and safety and declares that it would act to meet the common danger in accordance with its constitutional processes.

*Article IV.* The Republic of Korea grants,

and the United States of America accepts, the right to dispose United States land, air and sea forces in and about the territory of the Republic of Korea as determined by mutual agreement.

*Article V.* This Treaty shall be ratified by the United States of America and the Republic of Korea in accordance with their respective constitutional processes...

*Article VI.* This Treaty shall remain in force indefinitely. Either party may terminate it one year after notice has been given to the other party.

[The United States ratified the Treaty on 17 November 1954 subject to the following understanding:

It is the understanding of the United States that neither party is obligated, under Article III of the above Treaty, to come to the aid of the other except in case of an external armed attack against such party; nor shall anything in the present Treaty be construed as requiring the United States to give assistance to Korea except in the event of an armed attack against territory which has been recognized by the United States as lawfully brought under the administrative control of the Republic of Korea.]

# South-East Asia Collective Defense Treaty (SEATO), Manila, 8 September 1954

The parties to this Treaty,

Recognizing the sovereign equality of all the parties,

Reiterating their faith in the purposes and principles set forth in the Charter of the United Nations and their desire to live in peace with all peoples and all Governments,

Reaffirming that, in accordance with the Charter of the United Nations, they uphold the principle of equal rights and self-determination of peoples, and declaring that they will earnestly strive by every peaceful means to promote self-government and to secure the independence of all countries whose peoples desire it and are able to undertake its responsibilities,

Desiring to strengthen the fabric of peace and freedom and to uphold the principles of democracy, individual liberty and the rule of law, and to promote the economic well-being and development of all peoples in the treaty area,

Intending to declare publicly and formally their sense of unity, so that any potential aggressor will appreciate that the parties stand together in the area, and

Desiring further to coordinate their efforts for collective defense for the preservation of peace and security,

Therefore agree as follows:

*Article I.* The parties undertake, as set forth in the Charter of the United Nations, to settle any international disputes in which they may be involved by peaceful means in such a manner that international peace and security and justice are not endangered, and to refrain in their international relations from the threat or use of force in any manner inconsistent with the purposes of the United Nations.

*Article II.* In order more effectively to achieve the objectives of this Treaty, the parties, separately and jointly, by means of continuous and effective self-help and mutual aid will maintain and develop their individual and collective capacity to resist armed attack and to prevent and counter subversive activities directed from without against their territorial integrity and political stability.

*Article III.* The parties undertake to strengthen their free institutions and to cooperate with one another in the further development of economic measures, including technical assistance, designed both to promote economic progress and social well-being and to further the individual and collective efforts of Governments toward these ends.

*Article IV.* 1. Each party recognizes that aggression by means of armed attack in the treaty area against any of the parties or against any State or territory which the parties by unanimous agreement may hereafter designate, would endanger its own peace and safety, and agrees that it will in that event act to meet the common danger in accordance with its constitutional processes. Measures taken under this paragraph shall be immediately reported to the Security Council of the United Nations.

2. If, in the opinion of any of the parties, the inviolability or the integrity of the territory or the sovereignty or political independence of any party in the treaty area or of any other State or territory to which the provisions of paragraph 1 of this Article from time to time apply is threatened in any way other than by armed attack or is affected or threatened by any fact or situation which might endanger the peace of the area, the parties shall consult immediately in order to agree on the measures which should be taken for the common defense.

3. It is understood that no action on the territory of any State designated by unanimous agreement under paragraph 1 of this Article or on any territory so designated shall be taken except at the invitation or with the consent of the Government concerned.

*Article V.* The parties hereby establish a Council, on which each of them shall be represented, to consider matters concerning the implementation of this Treaty. The Council shall provide for consultation with regard to military and any other planning as the situation obtaining in the treaty area may from time to time require. The Council shall be so organized as to be able to meet at any time.

*Article VI.* This Treaty does not affect and shall not be interpreted as affecting in any way the rights and obligations of any of the parties under the Charter of the United Nations or the responsibility of the United Nations for the maintenance of international peace and security. Each party declares that none of the international engagements now in force between it and any other of the parties or any third party is in conflict with the provisions of this Treaty, and undertakes not to enter into any international engagement in conflict with this Treaty.

*Article VII.* Any other State in a position to further the objectives of this Treaty and to contribute to the security of the area may, by unanimous agreement of the parties, be invited to accede to this Treaty. . . .

*Article VIII.* As used in this Treaty, the 'treaty area' is the general area of southeast Asia, including also the entire territories of the Asian parties, and the general area of the south-west Pacific not including the Pacific area north of 21 degrees 30 minutes north latitude. The parties may, by unanimous agreement, amend this Article to include within the treaty area the territory of any State acceding to this Treaty in accordance with Article VII or otherwise to change the treaty area.

*Article IX.* . . . The Treaty shall be ratified and its provisions carried out by the parties in accordance with their respective constitutional processes. . .

*Article X.* This Treaty shall remain in force indefinitely, but any party may cease to be a party one year after notice of denunciation has been given. . .

[*Article XI.* Languages of authentic texts.]

UNDERSTANDING OF THE UNITED
STATES OF AMERICA

The United States of America in executing the present Treaty does so with the understanding that its recognition of the effect of aggression and armed attack and its agreement with reference thereto in Article IV, paragraph 1, apply only to communist aggression but affirms that in the event of other aggression or armed attack it will consult under the provisions of Article IV, paragraph 2.

### Protocol to the South-East Asia Collective Defense Treaty signed at Manila on 8 September 1954

DESIGNATION OF STATES AND TERRITORY AS TO WHICH PROVISIONS OF ARTICLE IV AND ARTICLE III ARE TO BE APPLICABLE

The parties to the South-east Asia Collective Defense Treaty unanimously designate for the purposes of Article IV of the Treaty the States of Cambodia and Laos and the free territory under the jurisdiction of the State of Vietnam.

The parties further agree that the above-mentioned States and territory shall be eligible in respect of the economic measures contemplated by Article III.

This Protocol shall enter into force simultaneously with the coming into force of the Treaty.

In witness whereof, the undersigned plenipotentiaries have signed this Protocol to the South-east Asia Collective Defense Treaty.

Done at Manila, this eighth day of September, 1954.

## Pacific Charter, Manila, 8 September 1954

The Delegates of Australia, France, New Zealand, Pakistan, the Republic of the Philippines, the Kingdom of Thailand, the United Kingdom of Great Britain and Northern Ireland, and the United States of America,

Desiring to establish a firm basis for common action to maintain peace and security in south-east Asia and the south-west Pacific,

Convinced that common action to this end, in order to be worthy and effective, must be inspired by the highest principles of justice and liberty,

Do hereby proclaim:

First, in accordance with the provisions of the United Nations Charter, they uphold the principle of equal rights and self-determination of peoples and they will earnestly strive by every peaceful means to promote self-government and to secure the independence of all countries whose peoples desire it and are able to undertake its responsibilities;

Second, they are each prepared to continue taking effective practical measures to ensure conditions favorable to the orderly achievement of the foregoing purposes in accordance with their constitutional processes;

Third, they will continue to cooperate in the economic, social and cultural fields in order to promote higher living standards, economic progress and social well-being in this region;

Fourth, as declared in the South-east Asia Collective Defense Treaty, they are determined to prevent or counter by appropriate means any attempt in the treaty area to subvert their freedom or to destroy their sovereignty or territorial integrity.

# Mutual Defense Treaty between the United States and the Republic of China (Taiwan), Washington, 2 December 1954

The parties to this Treaty,

Reaffirming their faith in the purposes and principles of the Charter of the United Nations and their desire to live in peace with all peoples and all Governments, and desiring to strengthen the fabric of peace in the West Pacific area,

Recalling with mutual pride the relationship which brought their two peoples together in a common bond of sympathy and mutual ideals to fight side by side against imperialist aggression during the last war,

Desiring to declare publicly and formally their sense of unity and their common determination to defend themselves against external armed attack, so that no potential aggressor could be under the illusion that either of them stands alone in the West Pacific area, and

Desiring further to strengthen their present efforts for collective defense for the preservation of peace and security pending the development of a more comprehensive system of regional security in the West Pacific area,

Have agreed as follows:

*Article I.* The parties undertake, as set forth in the Charter of the United Nations, to settle any international dispute in which they may be involved by peaceful means in such a manner that international peace, security and justice are not endangered and to refrain in their international relations from the threat or use of force in any manner inconsistent with the purposes of the United Nations.

*Article II.* In order more effectively to achieve the objective of this Treaty, the parties separately and jointly by self-help and mutual aid will maintain and develop their individual and collective capacity to resist armed attack and communist subversive activities directed from without against their territorial integrity and political stability.

*Article III.* The parties undertake to strengthen their free institutions and to cooperate with each other in the development of economic progress and social well-being and to further their individual and collective efforts toward these ends.

*Article IV.* The parties, through their Foreign Ministers or their deputies, will consult together from time to time regarding the implementation of this Treaty.

*Article V.* Each party recognizes that an armed attack in the West Pacific area directed against the territories of either of the parties would be dangerous to its own peace and safety and declares that it would act to meet the common danger in accordance with its constitutional processes.

Any such armed attack and all measures taken as a result thereof shall be immediately reported to the Security Council of the United Nations. Such measures shall be terminated when the Security Council has taken the measures necessary to restore and maintain international peace and security.

*Article VI.* For the purposes of Articles II and V, the terms 'territorial' and 'territories' shall mean in respect of the Republic of China, Taiwan and the Pescadores; and in respect of the United States of America, the island territories in the West Pacific under its jurisdiction. The provisions of Articles II and V will be applicable to such other territories as may be determined by mutual agreement.

*Article VII.* The Government of the Republic of China grants, and the Government of the United States of America accepts, the right to dispose such United States land, air and sea forces in and about Taiwan and the Pescadores as may be required for their defense, as determined by mutual agreement.

*Article VIII.* This Treaty does not affect and shall not be interpreted as affecting in any way the rights and obligations of the parties under the Charter of the United Nations or the responsibility of the United Nations for the maintenance of international peace and security.

*Article IX.* This Treaty shall be ratified by the United States of America and the Republic of China in accordance with their respective constitutional processes...

*Article X.* This Treaty shall remain in force indefinitely. Either party may terminate it one year after notice has been given to the other party...

# Treaty of Mutual Cooperation and Security between the United States and Japan, 19 January 1960

...

*Article I.* The parties undertake, as set forth in the Charter of the United Nations, to settle any international disputes in which they may be involved by peaceful means in such a manner that international peace and security and justice are not endangered and to refrain in their international relations from the threat or use of force against the territorial integrity or political independence of any State, or in any other manner inconsistent with the purposes of the United Nations.

The parties will endeavor in concert with other peace-loving countries to strengthen the United Nations so that its mission of maintaining international peace and security may be discharged more effectively.

*Article II.* The parties will contribute toward the further development of peaceful and friendly international relations by strengthening their free institutions, by bringing about a better understanding of the principles upon which these institutions are founded, and by promoting conditions of stability and well-being. They will seek to eliminate conflict in their international economic policies and will encourage economic collaboration between them.

*Article III.* The parties, individually and in cooperation with each other, by means of continuous and effective self-help and mutual aid, will maintain and develop, subject to their constitutional provisions, their capacities to resist armed attack.

*Article IV.* The parties will consult together from time to time regarding the implementation of this Treaty, and, at the request of either party, whenever the security of Japan or international peace and security in the Far East is threatened.

*Article V.* Each party recognizes that an armed attack against either party in the territories under the administration of Japan would be dangerous to its own peace and safety and declares that it would act to meet the common danger in accordance with its constitutional provisions and processes.

Any such armed attack and all measures taken as a result thereof shall be immediately reported to the Security Council of the United Nations in accordance with the provisions of Article 51 of the Charter. Such measures shall be terminated when the Security Council has taken the measures necessary to restore and maintain international peace and security.

*Article VI.* For the purpose of contributing to the security of Japan and the maintenance of international peace and security in the Far East, the United States of America is granted the use by its land, air and naval forces of facilities and areas in Japan.

The use of these facilities and areas as well as the status of United States armed forces in Japan shall be governed by a separate agreement, replacing the Administrative Agreement under Article III of the Security Treaty between the United States of America and Japan, signed at Tokyo on February 28, 1952, as amended, and by such other arrangements as may be agreed upon.

*Article VII.* This Treaty does not affect and shall not be interpreted as affecting in any way the rights and obligations of the parties under the Charter of the United Nations or the responsibility of the United Nations for the maintenance of international peace and security.

*Article VIII.* This Treaty shall be ratified by the United States of America and Japan in accordance with their respective constitutional processes....

*Article IX.* The Security Treaty between the United States of America and Japan signed at the city of San Francisco on September 8, 1951 shall expire upon the entering into force of this Treaty.

*Article X.* This Treaty shall remain in force until in the opinion of the Governments of the United States of America and Japan there shall have come into force such United Nations arrangements as will satisfactorily provide for the maintenance of international peace and security in the Japan area.

However, after the Treaty has been in force for ten years, either party may give notice to the other party of its intention to terminate the Treaty, in which case the Treaty shall terminate one year after such notice has been given....

## Agreed Minute to the Treaty of Mutual Cooperation and Security

*Japanese plenipotentiary:*

While the question of the status of the islands administered by the United States under Article 3 of the Treaty of Peace with Japan has not been made a subject of discussion in the course of treaty negotiations, I would like to emphasize the strong concern of the Government and people of Japan for the safety of the people of these islands since Japan possesses residual sovereignty over these islands. If an armed attack occurs or is threatened against these islands, the two countries will of course consult together closely under Article IV of the Treaty of Mutual Cooperation and Security. In the event of an armed attack, it is the intention of the Government of Japan to explore with the United States measures which it might be able to take for the welfare of the islanders.

*United States plenipotentiary:*

In the event of an armed attack against these islands, the United States Government will consult at once with the Government of Japan and intends to take the necessary measures for the defense of these islands, and to do its utmost to secure the welfare of the islanders.

## Exchanges of Notes between Japan and the United States

WASHINGTON, *January 19, 1960*
EXCELLENCY:

I have the honour to refer to the Treaty of Mutual Cooperation and Security between Japan and the United States of America signed today, and to inform Your Excellency that the following is the understanding of the Government of Japan concerning the implementation of Article VI thereof:

Major changes in the deployment into Japan of United States armed forces, major changes in their equipment, and the use of facilities and areas in Japan as bases for military combat operations to be undertaken from Japan other than those conducted under Article V of the said Treaty, shall be the subjects of prior consultation with the Government of Japan.

I should be appreciative if Your Excellency would confirm on behalf of your Government that this is also the understanding of the Government of the United States of America.

I avail myself of this opportunity to renew to Your Excellency the assurance of my highest consideration.

**Agreement under Article VI**

*Article 2.* ...2. At the request of either Government, the Governments of the United States and Japan shall review such arrangements and may agree that such facilities and areas shall be returned to Japan or that additional facilities and areas may be provided.

3. The facilities and areas used by the United States armed forces shall be returned to Japan whenever they are no longer needed for purposes of this Agreement, and the United States agrees to keep the needs for facilities and areas under continual observation with a view toward such return. . . .

## United States treaty relations in the Middle East

Two unrelated conflicts involved the United States in the Middle East: firstly, the tension between the Soviet Union on the one hand and its Middle Eastern neighbours, Turkey and Iran, on the other; and secondly, the foundation of Israel and the continuing conflict between Israel and the Arab States. United States policy sought both to strengthen anti-Soviet and anti-communist alignments, and to give support to the State of Israel sufficient to ensure its survival among the hostile Arab States. Beginning in about 1955 these two separate strands, the 'cold war' and 'Arab–Israeli' conflicts, began to intertwine and cause much perplexity to American policy-makers.

The first post-war involvement of the United States in the region was to provide economic, diplomatic and military aid to Iran, Turkey and Greece to withstand the Soviet Union and communist expansion (Truman Doctrine, p. 103). Aid to these three countries continued throughout the 1950s on a growing scale based on the Mutual Defense Program begun in 1949.

When Israel was proclaimed on 14 May 1948, the United States under the Truman administration expressed its moral support by recognizing the Provisional Government on the same day. The armistice agreements with Egypt, Lebanon, Jordan, and Syria, signed in 1949 (p. 360), established temporary boundaries for the State of Israel, which the Arabs refused to accept as permanent; indeed, the Arab States would not accept a State of Israel as permanent. But the United States joined with Britain and France in the *Tripartite Declaration, 25 May 1950* (p. 366), which expressed their opposition to an arms race between Israel and the Arab States and declared that if any of the States should prepare to violate the armistice lines or the frontier, they would in these circumstances immediately take action. This declaration in effect supported Israel's right to exist within the frontiers established by force of arms pending a peace treaty. The United States signed a Mutual Defense Assistance Agreement with Israel in July 1952 and has provided economic aid and military equipment to Israel since that year.

The second phase of the Middle Eastern crisis developed in 1956. Again two strands of conflict intermingled: Britain and France versus Egypt, especially over the issue of President Nasser's nationalization of the Suez Canal (July 1956); and rising tensions between Israel on the one hand and Egypt, whose leaders called for a united Arab effort to destroy Israel, on the other. The military moves of Israeli, French and British forces were secretly coordinated. On 29 September Israel launched the attack on Egypt (p. 350). On 31 October 1956 Britain and France began their attack on Egypt – first by bombing airfields and then on 5 November by landing troops on the western end of the Suez Canal. The United States, not informed in advance of the Anglo-French attack, worked for a cease-fire and for an Israeli, French and British withdrawal. The ceasefire went into force on 6 November and Britain and France withdrew in December 1956. The Soviet Union (which had supplied Egypt with arms) supported Egypt, and gained much credit in Arab eyes (see also p. 350).

The growing influence of the Soviet Union in Egypt and Syria, and a possible spread of communist influence after Suez and the 1956 war, alarmed the American administration and led to a Joint Resolution of Congress, signed by the President, which became known as the *Eisenhower Doctrine, 5 January 1957*. It pledged American support for the inde-pendence and integrity of Middle Eastern States as a vital American interest; American armed support was promised to resist armed aggression 'from any country controlled by international communism', provided the President regarded it as necessary, and provided such armed support was requested. In accordance with this resolution the United States supported Jordan in April 1957 and sent increased arms to Lebanon, Turkey and Iraq. When in July 1958 the pro-Western Government of Iraq was over-thrown and King Faisal was murdered, Jordan and Lebanon requested American help. American marines were landed in the Lebanon immedi-ately (British troops went to the assistance of Jordan). *On 28 July 1958, by executive agreements with Britain, Turkey, Iran and Pakistan, the United States* (p. 352) linked herself to these States of the *Baghdad Pact*. The pact was renamed the *Central Treaty Organization, CENTO*, after the formal withdrawal of Iraq in 1959.

CENTO never established itself as a cohesive alliance on the model of NATO. It was more or less moribund long before March 1979 when both Iran and Pakistan withdrew. CENTO was formally dissolved on 26 September 1979.

After the 'Six-Day War' of June 1967 between Israel on the one hand and Egypt, Jordan, and Syria on the other, the United States found itself drawn much more deeply into involvement in the Arab–Israeli conflict. Israel henceforth came to rely ever more heavily on American arms supplies, economic aid, and diplomatic support. The Israeli setbacks in the initial phases of the October 1973 war against Egypt and Syria emphasized Israel's increasing dependence on the American connection and provided the background to the imaginative diplomatic successes of the U.S. Secretary of State, Dr Henry Kissinger, in the Middle East in the period from 1973 to 1975 (see Chapter 8).

During this period Egypt undertook a dramatic shift in foreign policy orientation, scrapping its previous alignment with the Soviet Union in favour of a much closer relationship to the United States. The *Agreement between Egypt and the United States, 14 June 1974* (p. 130), signed on the occasion of President Nixon's visit to Cairo, heralded the new friendship. Although one of the most publicized sections of the agreement (Article III, concerning the provision to Egypt by the U.S.A. of nuclear technology) was not put into effect, the ensuing decade was marked by continuing close relations between the two countries, with the United States providing massive economic aid to Egypt after 1979 and also instituting a substantial programme of military supplies and cooperation with Egypt.

At the same time the U.S.A. maintained and even extended its relations with Israel. One fruit of this triangular relationship was the signature of the *Camp David Agreements, 17 September 1978* (p. 374). The six years of negotiation after 1973 tied Israel firmly to the United States; indeed, during that period of Arab resurgence based on the power of the 'oil weapon', the United States was Israel's only important ally. Yet the two countries did not sign a formal alliance treaty. Several of the agreements between Israel and her neighbours in the 1970s did, however, include attached documents in which the United States entered into various diplomatic, economic, and arms supply commitments towards Israel. The 'intelligence communities' of the U.S.A. and Israel developed close contacts at the same time. But it was only in 1981 that the two countries signed something approaching an alliance agreement: the *Israel–United States Memorandum of Understanding on Strategic Cooperation, 30 November 1981* (p. 133) marked a new stage in Israel–American relations. Although it was 'suspended' by the United States only a few weeks after its signature (because of Israel's annexation of the Golan Heights), strategic cooperation between the two countries was later quietly resumed.

By the 1980s, therefore, the U.S.A. had succeeded in forging both Egypt and Israel into linchpins of its alliance structure in the Middle East. This was all the more opportune for the United States because of complications in relations with its two other major allies in the region – Turkey and Iran.

In the case of Turkey, the United States faced the embarrassing problem of balancing the claims of two NATO allies after the Turkish attack on Cyprus in 1974 (p. 392). But the decision was never seriously in doubt: although the Greek ethnic lobby in the U.S.A. was vocal, the United States administration recognized that Turkey, militarily much stronger and strategically more important than Greece, was crucial to American interests, and the U.S.A. in effect sided with Turkey.

The problems with Iran were much more serious. As one of the 'hawks' in the oil price 'war' after 1973, the Shah of Iran, although accused of being an agent of American imperialism, in fact showed little sympathy towards Western economies battered by the massive increases in oil prices after 1973. Yet the United States continued to give diplomatic support to the Shah and to help supply his grandiose projects for modernization and for the build-up of a vast arsenal of advanced weaponry. The Shah had signed several agreements with the Soviet Union, but he owed his throne to the United States (C.I.A. agents had helped engineer his return to power in Iran in 1953) and the *Agreement of Cooperation between Iran and the United States, 5 March 1959* (p. 130) remained the cornerstone of his policy. The fall of the Shah in 1979 and the installation of a vehemently anti-American régime (p. 398) destroyed virtually all American influence in Iran, and marked a major setback for United States interests in the region. The Soviet Union was not slow to take advantage of the opportunity thus offered: in December 1979 Soviet troops occupied Afghanistan, the first significant military movement of Soviet forces outside the generally recognized Soviet sphere of influence since the Russian withdrawal from northern Iran in early 1946.

## Agreement of Cooperation between Iran and the United States, 5 March 1959

...

[Similar treaties were concluded between the United States and Pakistan, and Turkey.]

*Article I.* The Imperial Government of Iran is determined to resist aggression. In case of aggression against Iran, the Government of the United States of America, in accordance with the Constitution of the United States of America, will take such appropriate action, including the use of armed forces, as may be mutually agreed upon and as is envisaged in the Joint Resolution to Promote Peace and Stability in the Middle East, in order to assist the Government of Iran at its request.

*Article II.* The Government of the United States of America, in accordance with the Mutual Security Act of 1954, as amended, and related laws of the United States of America, and with applicable agreements heretofore or hereafter entered into between the Government of the United States of America and the Government of Iran, reaffirms that it will continue to furnish the Government of Iran such military and economic assistance as may be mutually agreed upon between the Government of the United States of America and the Government of Iran, in order to assist the Government of Iran in the preservation of its national independence and integrity and in the effective promotion of its economic development.

*Article III.* The Imperial Government of Iran undertakes to utilize such military and economic assistance as may be provided by the Government of the United States of America in a manner consonant with the aims and purposes set forth by the Governments associated in the Declaration signed at London on July 28, 1958, and for the purpose of effectively promoting the economic development of Iran and of preserving its national independence and integrity.

*Article IV.* The Government of the United States of America and the Government of Iran will cooperate with the other Governments associated in the Declaration signed at London on July 28, 1958, in order to prepare and participate in such defensive arrangements as may be mutually agreed to be desirable, subject to the other applicable provisions of this Agreement.

*Article V.* The provisions of the present Agreement do not affect the cooperation between the two Governments as envisaged in other international agreements or arrangements.

*Article VI.* This Agreement shall enter into force upon the date of its signature and shall continue in force until one year after the receipt by either Government of written notice of the intention of the other Government to terminate the Agreement.

## Agreement between Egypt and the United States on Principles of Relations and Cooperation, Cairo, 14 June 1974

The President of the United States of America, Richard Nixon, and the President of the Arab Republic of Egypt, Muhammed Anwar el-Sadat,

Having held wide-ranging discussions on matters of mutual interest to their two countries,

Being acutely aware of the continuing

need to build a structure of peace in the world and to that end and to promote a just and durable peace in the Middle East, and,

Being guided by a desire to seize the historic opportunity before them to strengthen relations between their countries on the broadest basis in ways that will contribute to the well-being of the area as a whole and will not be directed against any of its states or peoples or against any other state,

Have agreed that the following principles should govern relations between the United States and Egypt.

## I. General principles of bilateral relations

Relations between nations, whatever their economic or political systems, should be based on the purposes and principles of the United Nations Charter, including the right of each state to existence, independence and sovereignty; the right of each state freely to choose and develop its political, social, economic and cultural system; non-intervention in each other's internal affairs; and respect for territorial integrity and political independence.

Nations should approach each other in the spirit of equality respecting their national life and the pursuit of happiness.

The United States and Egypt consider that their relationship reflects these convictions.

Peace and progress in the Middle East are essential if global peace is to be assured. A just and durable peace based on full implementation of United Nations Security Council Resolution 242 of November 22, 1967, should take into due account the legitimate interests of all of the peoples in the Middle East, including the Palestinian people, and the right to existence of all states in the area. Peace can be achieved only through a process of continuing negotiations as called for by United Nations Security Council Resolution 338 of October 22, 1973, within the framework of the Geneva Middle East Peace Conference.

In recognition of these principles, the Governments of the United States of America and the Arab Republic of Egypt set themselves to these tasks:

They will intensify consultations at all levels, including further consultations between their Presidents, and they will strengthen their bilateral cooperation whenever a common or parallel effort will enhance the cause of peace in the world.

They will continue their active cooperation and their energetic pursuit of peace in the Middle East.

They will encourage increased contacts between members of all branches of their two Governments — executive, legislative and judicial — for the purpose of promoting better mutual understanding of each other's institutions, purposes and objectives.

They are determined to develop their bilateral relations in a spirit of esteem, respect and mutual advantage. In the past year, they have moved from estrangement to a constructive working relationship. This year, from that base, they are moving to a relationship of friendship and broad cooperation.

They view economic development and commercial relations as an essential element in the strengthening of their bilateral relations and will actively promote them. To this end, they will facilitate cooperative and joint ventures among appropriate governmental and private institutions and will encourage increased trade between the two countries.

They consider encouragement of exchanges and joint research in the scientific and technical field as an important mutual aim and will take appropriate concrete steps for this purpose.

They will deepen cultural ties through exchanges of scholars, students and other representatives of the cultures of both countries.

They will make special efforts to increase tourism in both directions, and to amplify person-to-person contact among their citizens.

They will take measures to improve air

and maritime communications between them.

They will seek to establish a broad range of working relationships and will look particularly to their respective Foreign Ministers and Ambassadors and to the Joint Commission on Cooperation, as well as to other officials and organizations, and private individuals and groups as appropriate, to implement the various aspects of the above principles.

## II. Joint Cooperation Commission

The two Governments have agreed that the intensive review of the areas of economic cooperation held by President Nixon and President Sadat on June 12 constituted the first meeting of the Joint Cooperation Commission, announced May 31, 1974. This Commission will be headed by the Secretary of State of the United States and the Minister of Foreign Affairs of Egypt. To this end, they have decided to move ahead rapidly on consultations and coordination to identify and implement programs agreed to be mutually beneficial in the economic, scientific and cultural fields.

The United States has agreed to help strengthen the financial structure of Egypt. To initiate this process, United States Secretary of the Treasury William Simon will visit Egypt in the near future for high level discussions.

## III. Nuclear energy

Since the atomic age began, nuclear energy has been viewed by all nations as a double-edged sword, offering opportunities for peaceful applications, but raising the risk of nuclear destruction. In its international programs of cooperation, the United States Government has made its nuclear technology available to other nations under safeguard conditions. In this context, the two Governments will begin negotiations of an Agreement for Cooperation in the field of nuclear energy under agreed safeguards. Upon conclusion of such an agreement, the United States is

prepared to sell nuclear reactors and fuel to Egypt, which will make it possible for Egypt by the early 1980s to generate substantial additional quantities of electric power to support its rapidly growing development needs. Pending conclusion of this Agreement, the United States Atomic Energy Commission and the Egyptian Ministry of Electricity will this month conclude a provisional agreement for the sale of nuclear fuel to Egypt.

## IV. Working groups

The two Governments have agreed to set up Joint Working Groups to meet in the near future to prepare concrete projects and proposals for review by the Joint Commission at a meeting to be held later this year in Washington, D.C. These Joint Working Groups will be composed of governmental representatives from each country and will include the following:

(1) A Joint Working Group on Suez Canal Reconstruction and Development to consider and review plans for reopening the Suez Canal and reconstruction of the cities along the Canal, and the United States role in this endeavor.

(2) A Joint Working Group to investigate and recommend measures designed to open the way for United States private investment in joint ventures in Egypt and to promote trade between the two countries. Investment opportunities would be guided by Egypt's need for financial, technical, and material support to increase Egypt's economic growth. The United States regards with favor and supports the ventures of American enterprises in Egypt. It is noted that such ventures, currently being negotiated, are in the field of petrochemicals, transportation, food and agricultural machinery, land development, power, tourism, banking, and a host of other economic sectors. The estimated value of projects under serious consideration exceeds two billion dollars. American technology and capital combined with Egypt's absorptive capacity, skilled manpower and productive investment opportunities can contribute

effectively to the strengthening and development of the Egyptian economy. The United States and Egypt will therefore negotiate immediately a new Investment Guarantee Agreement between them.

(3) A Joint Working Group on Agriculture to study and recommend actions designed to increase Egypt's agricultural production through the use of the latest agricultural technology.

(4) A Joint Working Group on Technology, Research and Development in scientific fields, including space, with special emphasis on exchanges of scientists.

(5) A Joint Working Group on Medical Cooperation to assist the Government of Egypt to develop and strengthen its medical research, treatment and training facilities. These efforts will supplement cooperation in certain forms of medical research already conducted through the Naval Medical Research Unit (NAMRU), whose mutually beneficial work will continue.

(6) A Joint Working Group on Cultural Exchanges to encourage and facilitate exhibitions, visits, and other cultural endeavors to encourage a better understanding of both cultures on the part of the peoples of the United States and Egypt.

The two Governments have agreed to encourage the formation of a Joint Economic Council to include representatives from the private economic sector of both countries to cooperate and promote mutually beneficial cooperative economic arrangements.

In support of their economic cooperation, the United States will make the maximum feasible contribution, in accordance with Congressional authorization, to Egypt's economic development, including clearing the Suez Canal, reconstruction projects, and restoring Egyptian trade. In addition, the United States is prepared to give special priority attention to Egypt's needs for agricultural commodities.

Consistent with the spirit of cultural cooperation, the United States Government has agreed to consider how it might assist the Egyptian Government in the reconstruction of Cairo's Opera House. The Egyptian Government for its part intends to place the 'Treasures of Tutankhamen' on exhibit in the United States.

Both Governments, in conclusion, reiterate their intention to do everything possible to broaden the ties of friendship and cooperation consistent with their mutual interests in peace and security and with the principles set forth in this statement.

In thanking President el-Sadat for the hospitality shown to him and the members of his party, President Nixon extended an invitation to President el-Sadat, which President el-Sadat has accepted, to visit the United States during 1974.

Cairo, Egypt
June 14, 1974

[Signed] Richard Nixon

[Signed] Muhammed Anwar el-Sadat

# Memorandum of Understanding between Israel and the United States on Strategic Cooperation, Washington, 30 November 1981

*Preamble*. This Memorandum of Understanding reaffirms the common bonds of friendship between the United States and Israel and builds on the mutual security relationship that exists between the two nations. The Parties recognize the need to enhance Strategic Cooperation to deter all threats from the Soviet Union to the region. Noting the long-standing and fruitful cooperation for mutual security that has developed between the two countries, the Parties have decided to establish a framework for continued consultation and cooperation to enhance their national security by deterring such threats to the whole region.

The Parties have reached the following agreements in order to achieve the above aims.

*Article I.* United States–Israeli Strategic Cooperation, as set forth in this Memorandum, is designed against the threat to peace and security of the region caused by the Soviet Union or Soviet-controlled forces from outside the region introduced into the region. It has the following broad purposes:

(a) To enable the Parties to act cooperatively and in a timely manner to deal with the above mentioned threat.

(b) To provide each other with military assistance for operations of their forces in the area that may be required to cope with this threat.

(c) The Strategic Cooperation between the Parties is not directed at any State or group of States within the region. It is intended solely for defensive purposes against the above mentioned threat.

*Article II.* 1. The fields in which Strategic Cooperation will be carried out to prevent the above mentioned threat from endangering the security of the region include:

(a) Military cooperation between the Parties, as may be agreed by the Parties.

(b) Joint military exercises, including naval and air exercises in the Eastern Mediterranean Sea, as agreed upon by the Parties.

(c) Cooperation for the establishment and maintenance of joint readiness activities, as agreed upon by the Parties.

(d) Other areas within the basic scope and purpose of this agreement, as may be jointly agreed.

2. Details of activities within these fields of cooperation shall be worked out by the Parties in accordance with the provisions of Article III below. The co-

operation will include, as appropriate, planning, preparations, and exercises.

*Article III.* 1. The Secretary of Defense and the Minister of Defense shall establish a Coordinating Council to further the purposes of this Memorandum:

(a) To coordinate and provide guidance to Joint Working Groups;

(b) To monitor the implementation of cooperation in the fields agreed upon by the Parties within the scope of this agreement;

(c) To hold periodic meetings, in Israel and the United States, for the purposes of discussing and resolving outstanding issues and to further the objectives set forth in this Memorandum. Special meetings can be held at the request of either Party. The Secretary of Defense and Minister of Defense will chair these meetings whenever possible.

2. Joint Working Groups will address the following issues:

(a) Military cooperation between the Parties, including joint US–Israeli exercises in the Eastern Mediterranean Sea.

(b) Cooperation for the establishment of joint readiness activities including access to maintenance facilities and other infrastructure, consistent with the basic purposes of this agreement.

(c) Cooperation in research and development, building on past cooperation in this area.

(d) Cooperation in defense trade.

(e) Other fields within the basic scope and purpose of this agreement, such as questions of prepositioning, as agreed by the Coordinating Council.

3. The future agenda for the work of the Joint Working Groups, their composition, and procedures for reporting to the Coordinating Council shall be agreed upon by the Parties.

*Article IV.* This Memorandum shall enter into force upon exchange of notification that required procedures have been completed by each Party. If either Party considers it necessary to terminate this Memorandum of Understanding, it may do so by notifying the other Party six months in advance of the effective date of termination.

*Article V.* Nothing in the Memorandum shall be considered as derogating from previous agreements and understandings between the Parties.

*Article VI.* The Parties share the understanding that nothing in this Memorandum is intended to or shall in any way prejudice the rights and obligations which devolve or may devolve upon either government under the Charter of the United Nations or under International Law. The Parties reaffirm their faith in the purposes and principles of the Charter of the United Nations and their aspiration to live in peace with all countries in the region.

[For the Government of the United States]
Caspar W. Weinberger
Secretary of Defense

[For the Government of Israel]
Ariel Sharon
Minister of Defense

November 30, 1981

# III · The Soviet treaty system

## Soviet treaties in Eastern Europe

From 1939 to 1945 Stalin sought to regain for the Soviet Union the territory that had once constituted the Tsarist Russian Empire in 1914 with two exceptions: Poland and Finland. Although accepting separate Polish and Finnish States, Stalin was not prepared to recognize as final their frontiers as established after the First World War, not their right to follow policies of enmity to the Soviet Union. The twin impulses of expanding Soviet power for its own sake and of creating a 'buffer' of greater security against the West motivated Soviet policies from 1939 to 1945. Stalin regarded both 'Fascist' and 'bourgeois–democratic' Europe as basically hostile to the Soviet Union; if the 'capitalists' were divided, the Soviet Union, still weaker than the capitalist world, should seek advantage and safety from any capitalist conflicts. Its policy towards them would be governed by the opportunism of Soviet self-interest. From 1939 to 1940 Stalin achieved his territorial objectives in alliance with Hitler.

In September 1939 the Soviet Union occupied eastern Poland and incorporated this territory some weeks later in the Soviet Union. As a result of the Winter War with Finland (November 1939–March 1940) the Soviet Union annexed Finnish territory of strategic importance, especially the Karelian isthmus and, in the extreme north of Finland, Petsamo and its district which gave the Soviet Union a common frontier with Norway in the Arctic. In June 1940, Rumania under Soviet pressure and on German 'advice' returned Bessarabia to Russian rule; in August 1940 Lithuania, Latvia and Estonia were incorporated in the Soviet Union. In 1945, the Soviet Union retained all these gains of 1939–40 and added further relatively small but strategically important areas: Ruthenia, or what was called by the Soviet leaders the Subcarpathian Ukraine, was acquired from Czechoslovakia, and thereby the Soviet Union regained a common frontier with Hungary which had been lost after the First World War. The Soviet Union also administered the northern half of German East Prussia, the southern half being administered by Poland.

A complementary aspect of Soviet policy was to ensure that those independent States on her borders still surviving should be friendly to the Soviet Union and closely linked to her politically, economically and culturally. Before 1939 only Czechoslovakia had pursued a policy of friendship and alliance with the Soviet Union. Stalin was determined that the Soviet Union's neighbours shoud become a source of strength and not of weakness for the Soviet Union, and that the revival of a German military threat be delayed as long as possible. Stalin's diplomatic methods were foreshadowed in the *Soviet–Czechoslovak Treaty of Friendship, 12 December 1943*. By friendly neighbours Stalin meant States which would be bound by political treaties to the Soviet alliance, whose military resources would be dominated by the Soviet Union, and which would permit the stationing or entry of Soviet troops for mutual protection. In evaluating these 'political' treaties it must be remembered that additional 'economic' agreements were just as important in the relationship. 'Friendly' also meant that the economies of Russia's allies would more or less follow the communist pattern; during the Stalinist period these economies were shaped mainly in the interests of the Soviet Union. Whilst in Poland and Czechoslovakia the political leadership at first did not have to be entirely communist in appearance and 'united front' Governments were formed, the economic reorganization and the Soviet presence ensured that real political power lay in the hands of the Soviet Union and with the communist leadership of these countries, most of whom had been trained in Moscow.

*The Soviet Union signed alliances with Poland on 21 April 1945* (p. 143), *and with Yugoslavia on 11 April 1945* (p. 142), in addition to the Czech alliance already cited. These followed a common pattern in that the signatories agreed to collaborate in the event of any renewed aggression on the part of Germany specifically, or in the event of any other State attacking the territorial integrity of the signatories; an agreement on the part of the signatories was included stating that they would not join in alliances directed against the other signatories. The agreement that close political, economic, social and cultural ties would be promoted meant in fact that these countries within a few years became dependent on the Soviet Union;

clauses in the treaty promising non-interference in the domestic affairs of the neighbours of the Soviet Union were in practice not observed. Only Finland and Yugoslavia were allowed some genuine measure of domestic independence.

During the first six months of 1945, under the aegis of the Red Army, communist-controlled Governments were set up in Rumania and Bulgaria. In Poland and Hungary 'united front' Governments were permitted with some non-communist participation until the summer of 1947. In 1948 Czechoslovakia came under complete communist control. In Yugoslavia Marshal Tito had established his communist Government without Russian help. Denounced by Stalin in June 1948 for national deviationism, Tito successfully resisted all Soviet pressure.

*The Soviet Union concluded alliance treaties with Rumania on 4 February 1948* (p. 145), *with Hungary on 18 February and Bulgaria on 18 March 1948.* A few months earlier in *September 1947* the *Communist Information Bureau, Cominform,* had been established with headquarters in Belgrade but with nothing really to do. Tito's successful defiance of Stalin's accusations, which Stalin had delivered through the Cominform, soon made the Cominform totally ineffective, though as an organization it remained formally in being until 1956. Tito's assertion of Yugoslav independence led to Soviet-inspired purges in Hungary, Bulgaria, Albania, Poland, Rumania and Czechoslovakia. Soviet policy was laid down by the Party and backed by Soviet Army units, which could be used as a last resort. Whilst Stalin decided not to attack Yugoslavia he was all the more determined to prevent a spread of a revived Balkan 'nationalism' whether communist or of any other kind.

These developments in Eastern and Central Europe were related to the growing conflict betwen the Western wartime allies and the Soviet Union which became known as the cold war. Western policies were viewed by Stalin as attempts under the leadership of the United States to revive in a new form a capitalist coalition of States, which would encircle the Soviet Union. Stalin saw in the same light Western protests over Russian policy in the Soviet zone of Germany and in Central and Eastern Europe. For Stalin, 20 million Russian war casualties and the destruction of much of European Russia justified and necessitated a post-war policy that would ensure Soviet security and material reparations. Experience during the Second World War of the extent of Allied solidarity did not lessen his deep-rooted fear that in the post-war world an isolated Soviet Russia was facing a more powerful Western coalition possessing the atom bomb.

Stalin interpreted the Marshall Plan (p. 203) and American economic aid as attempts to revive capitalism among Russia's neighbours to the detriment of the security of the Soviet Union. But the event which most alarmed Central and Eastern Europe was the creation of the Federal Republic of Germany and German rearmament (p. 184). The Soviet response was to form an alliance of communist States, ostensibly among equals, with joint responsibilities and mutual decision-making organs giving the appearance of equality. *The Council for Mutual Economic Assistance (Comecon), established in January 1949* was set up as the Soviet counterpart to the *Organization for European Economic Cooperation* created by the Western European States in April 1948 (see p. 204). At first Comecon was little more than a paper organization: it held only two meetings prior to the death of Stalin on 5 March 1953. The founding members were Albania (which left in 1961, but rejoined in 1971), Bulgaria, Czechoslovakia, Hungary, Poland, Rumania and the Soviet Union. East Germany was admitted in 1950, Mongolia in 1962, and Cuba in 1972. After 1956 more life was breathed into the organization, which the U.S.S.R. sought to develop into a closed trading system under its control. But by the 1970s some members, notably Rumania, Poland and Hungary, had succeeded in shaking loose to some extent from the restrictions of the system and built up sizable trading relations with capitalist economies.

In June 1953 the first of a series of upheavals among Russia's satellites was crushed in East Germany. In January–February 1954 the Foreign Ministers of the Big Four met again in Berlin, but could not agree on a solution for a divided Germany. The post-Stalin period of flexibility over Germany drew to a close with the signature by the Western allies of the *Paris Agreements, 23 October 1954,* which came into force in May 1955 and which restored sovereignty to the German Federal Republic and provided for her entry into NATO (p. 188). The Soviet response was to convene a conference in Moscow from 29 November–2 December 1954 attended by Albania, Bulgaria, Czechoslovakia, the German Democratic Republic (East Germany), Hungary, Poland, Rumania and the Soviet Union. They jointly declared that if the Paris Agreements were ratified they would adopt measures to safeguard their security. On 6 May 1955, the day after the ratification of the Paris Agreements, the Soviet Union denounced the Anglo-Soviet Alliance Treaty of 1942. On *14 May 1955* the same eight communist States signed the *Treaty of Friendship, Cooperation and Mutual Assistance* known as the *Warsaw Pact* (p. 147).

The Warsaw Pact is the most important multilateral treaty between the communist States under Soviet leadership both militarily and politically. The treaty refers to a political consultative committee which has the power to set up auxiliary bodies. Militarily it formalized arrangements for Soviet control dating probably three years earlier to about August 1952, when a decision was taken to re-equip the satellite armies and place them under Soviet command. In accordance with the agreement reached in May 1955, the following January a United Military Command was established with headquarters in Moscow. A Soviet officer, Marshal Konev, became commander-in-chief, and the Defence Ministers of participating countries were to be deputy commanders-in-chief. Joint military exercises have been held in member countries since the autumn of 1961.

At first the Asian communist countries – China, North Korea and North Vietnam – sent observers to the Warsaw Pact, but they withdrew by 1962. Albania was excluded and withdrew after 1961, siding with China in the Sino-Soviet conflict.

Following the momentous Twentieth Congress of the Communist Party of the Soviet Union in February 1956, when Nikita Khrushchev attacked the mistakes and cruelty of Stalin's dictatorship, Poland and Hungary sought more independence from Soviet control. Outright Soviet military intervention was only just avoided in Poland; but in November 1956 Soviet troops crushed Hungarian resistance after the Hungarian Government of Imre Nagy on 1 November 1956 had seceded from the Warsaw Pact. The Soviet Union moved back into Hungary just as the Western Suez involvement was reaching its culmination (p. 350).

The limitations of independence and of the alleged equality of Communist States were again exposed when on 21 August 1968 the Soviet Union and the other European Warsaw Pact countries (except Rumania), acting as socialist allies, invaded Czechoslovakia, itself a member of the Warsaw Pact. The reformist communist government of Alexander Dubček was deposed, and a more pliant pro-Soviet régime installed. According to *Pravda,* the 'allied socialist' troops together with the Soviet Union, i.e. the Warsaw Pact countries, had 'a solemn commitment – to stand up in defence of the gains of socialism'. Participants of the Warsaw Treaty Organization were involved, for to tolerate a breach in this organization would contradict the vital interests of all the member countries, including the Soviet Union. Although the Czech Government denounced the invasion as illegal and Rumania also condemned it, Czechoslovakia by the end of August 1968 was occupied and forced to submit. The Soviet justification on the basis of limited sovereignty within the socialist community became known as the Brezhnev Doctrine.

Following the invasion the Soviet Union imposed the *Soviet–Czecho-slovak Treaty on the Stationing of Soviet Troops, 16 October 1968* (p. 150). This was unusual among Soviet treaties with its client states in eschewing the common courtesies of socialist fraternity and detailing the conduct to be observed by the occupied State in its relations with Soviet forces in the country. Only in 1970, when the government installed by the Soviet forces had succeeded in stamping out any tendency towards national self-assertion, did a more cordial public formulation of the relationship emerge in the *Soviet–Czechoslovak Friendship Treaty, 6 May 1970* (p. 153).

Bilateral treaties were concluded between the *Soviet Union and Poland, 17 December 1956*, the *Soviet Union and the German Democratic Republic, 12 March 1957*, the *Soviet Union and Rumania, 15 April 1957*, and the *Soviet Union and Hungary, 27 May 1957*, in the aftermath of the Polish troubles and the Hungarian uprising, to normalize and improve relations, limit Soviet supervision and direct interference, and above all to justify the stationing of Soviet troops ostensibly to fulfil the needs of the Warsaw Pact. The treaty with Poland more specifically stated that the 'temporary stay' of Soviet troops in Poland could neither affect Polish sovereignty nor lead to any interference in the domestic affairs of Poland, and that no Soviet troop movements outside specified areas of Poland would be permitted without Polish authorization. But these provisions were shown to be mere window-dressing when, following an upsurge of Polish national feeling which found expression in the late 1970s in the formation of the Solidarity trade union movement, the U.S.S.R. in December 1981 brought pressure to bear, as a result of which a government headed (uniquely in the Soviet bloc) by the commander-in-chief of the armed forces took office. General Jaruzelski's régime restored order, disbanded Solidarity, curbed freedom of the press, imprisoned political opponents, and made due obeisance to its Soviet masters – very much on the model of events in Hungary after 1956 and in Czechoslovakia after 1968. On this occasion the U.S.S.R. had not formally 'occupied' the country (though large Soviet forces were stationed there throughout), but as on the previous occasions the satellite state's room for independent manoeuvre had been severely limited and an example had been served to other potentially errant members of the Warsaw Pact. Although Hungary succeeded in maintaining a certain degree of economic independence and Rumania remained (in its foreign but not its domestic policies) the political maverick of Eastern Europe, the Warsaw Pact entered its fourth decade in 1985 in solid political and military condition.

Of all the European neighbours of the Soviet Union (apart from Norway, a member of NATO), only Finland was permitted to retain a democratic, multi-party political structure, a (limited) free press, and a liberal economy. The *Soviet–Finnish Treaty, 6 April 1948* (p. 146), extended for a further twenty years on 19 September 1955, provided the basis for relations. On 19 July 1970 the treaty was extended for another twenty years. The 1948 treaty provided that if Finland or the U.S.S.R. were attacked by Germany or any State allied to Germany, Finland would repulse the aggressor, acting within her boundaries with the assistance in case of need of the Soviet Union, or jointly with the Soviet Union (Article I). Finland was not obliged by the treaty to come to the assistance of the Soviet Union if the latter were attacked or at war in any other region. During the post-war period Finland remained neutral, leaning towards the Soviet Union in foreign policy, but towards the West economically and culturally. She became a member of the Nordic Union (p. 245), and an associate of EFTA (p. 238) and later of the EEC (p. 223). It was symbolic of Finland's delicately poised position between East and West that the Finnish capital, Helsinki, became the venue for the *European Security Conference,* of which the *Final Act, 1 August 1975* (p. 463), marked the most significant achievement of the period of East–West détente.

# Treaty of Friendship, Mutual Aid and Post-War Cooperation between the Soviet Union and Yugoslavia, Moscow, 11 April 1945

The Presidium of the Supreme Soviet of the Union of Soviet Socialist Republics and the Regency Council of Yugoslavia,

Resolved to bring the war against the German aggressors to its final conclusion; desirous still further to consolidate the friendship existing between the peoples of the Soviet Union and Yugoslavia, which together are fighting against the common enemy – Hitlerite Germany; desirous to ensure close cooperation between the peoples of the two countries and all United Nations during the war and in peacetime, and to make their contribution to the post-war organization of security and peace; convinced that the consolidation of friendship between the Soviet Union and Yugoslavia corresponds to the vital interests of the two peoples, and best

serves the further economic development of the two countries, have . . . agreed on the following:

*Article 1.* Each of the Contracting Parties will continue the struggle in cooperation with one another and with all the United Nations against Germany until final victory. The two Contracting Parties pledge themselves to render each other military and other assistance and support of every kind.

*Article 2.* If one of the Contracting Parties should in the post-war period be drawn into military operations against Germany, which would have resumed her aggressive policy, or against any other State which would have joined Germany either directly or in any other form in a war of this nature, the other Contracting Party shall immediately render military or any other support with all the means available.

*Article 3.* The two Contracting Parties state that they will participate, in the spirit of closest cooperation, in all international activities designed to ensure peace and security of peoples, and will make their contribution for attaining these lofty purposes.

The Contracting Parties state that the application of the present Treaty will be in accordance with the international principles in the acceptance of which they have participated.

*Article 4.* Each of the Contracting Parties undertakes not to conclude any alliance and not to take part in any coalition directed against the other party.

*Article 5.* The two Contracting Parties state that after the termination of the present war they will act in a spirit of friendship and cooperation for the purpose of further developing and consolidating the economic and cultural ties between the peoples of the two countries.

*Article 6.* The present Treaty comes into force immediately it is signed and is subject to ratification in the shortest possible time. The exchange of ratification documents will be effected in Belgrade as early as possible.

The present Treaty will remain in force for a period of twenty years. If one of the Contracting Parties at the end of this twenty years period does not, one year before the expiration of this term, announce its desire to renounce the Treaty, it will remain in force for the following five years, and so on each time until one of the Contracting Parties gives written notice of its desire to terminate the efficacy of the Treaty one year before the termination of the current five-year period.

## Agreement regarding Friendship, Mutual Assistance and Post-War Cooperation between the Soviet Union and the Polish Republic, Moscow, 21 April 1945

The President of the National Council of the Homeland and the Presidium of the Supreme Council of the Union of Socialist Soviet Republics moved by an unshaken determination to bring, in a common effort, the war with the German aggressors to a complete and final victory;

Wishing to consolidate the fundamental change in the history of the Polish–Soviet relations in the direction of friendly cooperation, which has taken place in the course of a common fight against German imperialism;

Trusting that a further consolidation of good neighbourly relations and friendship between Poland and her direct neighbour – the U.S.S.R. – is vital to the interests of the Polish and Soviet peoples;

Confident that friendship and close cooperation between the Polish people and the Soviet people will serve the cause of successful economic development of both countries during the war as well as after the war;

Wishing to support after the war by all possible means the cause of peace and security of peoples;

Have resolved to conclude this agreement and have...appointed as their plenipotentiaries:

The President of the National Council of the Homeland – Edward Osóbka-Morawski, the President of the Council of Ministers and the Minister of Foreign Affairs of the Polish Republic,

The Presidium of the Supreme Council

of the Union of Socialist Soviet Republics – Joseph Vissarionovitch Stalin, Chairman of the Council of People's Commissars of the U.S.S.R.;

Who, after exchange of full powers which were recognized as being in order and drawn up in due form, have agreed as follows:

*Article 1.* The High Contracting Parties jointly with all United Nations will continue the fight against Germany until final victory. In that fight the High Contracting Parties undertake to give one another mutual military and other assistance using all the means at their disposal.

*Article 2.* The High Contracting Parties, in a firm belief that in the interest of security and successful development of the Polish and Soviet peoples it is necessary to preserve and to strengthen lasting and unshaken friendship during the war as well as after the war, will strengthen the friendly cooperation between the two countries in accordance with the principles of mutual respect for their independence and sovereignty and non-interference in the internal affairs of the other Government.

*Article 3.* The High Contracting Parties further undertake that even after the end of the present war they will jointly use all the means at their disposal in order to eliminate every possible menace of a new aggression on the part of Germany or on the part of any other Government whatsoever which would be directly or in any other manner allied with Germany.

For this purpose the High Contracting Parties will, in a spirit of most sincere collaboration, take part in all international activities aiming at ensuring peace and security of peoples and will contribute their full share to the cause of realization of these high ideals.

The High Contracting Parties will execute this Agreement in compliance with the international principles in the establishment of which both Contracting Parties took part.

*Article 4.* If one of the High Contracting Parties during the post-war period should become involved in war operations against Germany in case she should resume aggressive policy or against any other Government whatsoever which would be allied with Germany directly or in any other form in such a war the other High Contracting Party will immediately extend to the other Contracting Party which is involved in military operations military and other support with all the means at its disposal.

*Article 5.* The High Contracting Parties undertake not to sign without mutual consent an armistice or a peace treaty with the Hitlerite Government or any other authority in Germany which menaces or may menace the independence, territorial integrity or security of either of the two High Contracting Parties.

*Article 6.* Each of the High Contracting Parties undertakes not to enter into any alliance or to take part in any coalition directed against the other High Contracting Party.

*Article 7.* The High Contracting Parties will cooperate in a spirit of friendship also after the end of the present war for the purpose of developing and strengthening the economic and cultural relations between the two countries and will give mutual assistance in the economic reconstruction of the two countries.

*Article 8.* This Agreement comes into force from the moment of signing and is liable to ratification within the shortest possible period. Exchange of ratifying documents will take place in Warsaw as soon as possible.

This Agreement will remain in force for twenty years after the moment of signing.

If one of the High Contracting Parties does not make a statement twelve months before the expiration of the twenty years period to the effect that it wishes to give notice, this Agreement will remain in force for a further period of five years and so on until one of the High Contracting Parties makes a statement in writing twelve months before the expiration of a successive five years period to the effect that it intends to give notice of the Agreement.

In witness whereof the mandatories have signed this Agreement and have apposed their seals thereto.

Drawn up in Moscow on April 21, 1945, in duplicate, each copy in Polish and in Russian, both texts being equally binding.

By authority of the President of the National Council of the Homeland
OSÓBKA-MORAWSKI

By authority of the Presidium of the Supreme Council of the U.S.S.R.
J. STALIN

After consideration this Agreement has been recognized equitable in its whole as well as in individual provisions contained therein; it is, therefore, announced that it has been accepted, ratified and approved and will be strictly complied with.

In witness whereof this Act has been issued with the seal of the Polish Republic duly apposed thereto.

WARSAW, September 19, 1945

President of the National Council of the Homeland
BOLESLAW BIERUT

President of the Council of Ministers
EDWARD OSÓBKA-MORAWSKI

Vice-Minister of Foreign Affairs
p.p. Z. MODZELEWSKI

# Treaty of Friendship, Collaboration and Mutual Assistance between the Rumanian People's Republic and the Soviet Union, Moscow, 4 February 1948

[A treaty in similar terms was concluded between Bulgaria and the Soviet Union, 18 March 1948; and between Hungary and the Soviet Union, 18 February 1948.]

The Praesidium of the Rumanian Popular Republic and the Praesidium of the Supreme Soviet of the Union of Soviet Socialist Republics,

Desirous of consolidating friendly relations between Rumania and the Soviet Union;

Desirous of keeping up close collaboration, with a view to consolidating peace and general security, in accordance with the purposes and principles of the United Nations Organization;

Convinced that the keeping up of friendship and good neighbourliness between Rumania and the Soviet Union is in accordance with the vital interests of the peoples of both States, and will bring the best possible contribution to their economic development;

Have decided to conclude this Treaty, and have to that end full powers:

Article 1. The High Contracting Parties undertake to take jointly all measures in their power to remove any threat of repeated aggression on the part of Germany, or of any State allying itself with Germany directly or in any other way.

The High Contracting Parties state that it is their intention to participate with full sincerity in any international action aimed at ensuring the peace and security of nations, and that they will fully contribute to the carrying out of these great tasks.

Article 2. Should one of the High Contracting Parties be involved in armed conflict with Germany, attempting to renew her policy of aggression, or with any other State allying itself with Germany, directly or in any other way, in her aggressive policy, the other High Contracting Party will lose no time in giving the High Contracting Party involved in a conflict military or other aid with all the means at its disposal.

This Treaty will be applied in accordance with the principles of the United Nations Charter.

*Article 3.* Each of the High Contracting Parties undertakes to conclude no alliance and to participate in no coalition, action or measures directed against the other High Contracting Party.

*Article 4.* The High Contracting Parties will consult with regard to all important international issues concerning the interests of the two countries.

*Article 5.* The High Contracting Parties state that they will act in a spirit of friendship and collaboration, with a view to further developing and strengthening economic and cultural relations between the two States, with due regard for the principles of mutual respect for their independence and sovereignty, and of noninterference in the internal affairs of the other State.

*Article 6.* This Treaty will remain in force for twenty years, as from the date of its signing. If, one year before the expiry of the twenty years, none of the High Contracting Parties expresses the wish to cancel the Treaty, it will remain in force another five years, and so on, until one of the High Contracting Parties, one year before the expiry of the current five-year period, announces in writing its intention to put an end to the validity of the Treaty. . . .

## *Treaty of Friendship, Cooperation and Mutual Assistance between the Soviet Union and the Finnish Republic, Moscow, 6 April 1948*

The Presidium of the Supreme Soviet of the Union of Soviet Socialist Republics and the President of the Finnish Republic,

With the object of further promoting friendly relations between the U.S.S.R. and Finland;

Convinced that consolidation of goodneighbourly relations and cooperation between the Union of Soviet Socialist Republics and the Finnish Republic meets the vital interests of both countries;

Considering Finland's aspiration to stand aside from the contradictions of interests of the Great Powers, and

Expressing their unswerving aspiration to cooperate in the interests of preservation of international peace and security in conformity with the aims and principles of the United Nations Organization;

Have decided to conclude for these ends the present Treaty, and . . . have appointed as their plenipotentiaries:

for the Presidium of the Supreme Soviet of the Union of Soviet Socialist Republics – Vyacheslav Mikhailovich Molotov, vice-chairman of the Council of Ministers and Minister of Foreign Affairs of the U.S.S.R.;

for the President of the Finnish Republic – Mauno Pekkala, Prime Minister of the Finnish Republic,

Who upon exchanging their credentials, found in due form and full order, have agreed upon the following:

*Article 1.* In the event of Finland or the Soviet Union, across the territory of Finland, becoming the object of military aggression on the part of Germany or any State allied to the latter, Finland, loyal to her duty as an independent State, will fight to repulse the aggression. In doing so, Finland will direct all the forces at her disposal to the defence of the inviolability of her territory on land, on sea and in the air, acting within her boundaries in accordance with her obligations under the present Treaty, with the assistance, in case of need, of the Soviet Union or jointly with the latter.

In the cases indicated above, the Soviet Union will render Finland the necessary assistance, in regard to the granting of which the parties will agree between themselves.

*Article II.* The High Contracting Parties will consult each other in the event of a threat of military attack envisaged in Article I being ascertained.

*Article III.* The High Contracting Parties affirm their intention to participate most sincerely in all actions aimed at preserving international peace and security in conformity with the aims and principles of the United Nations Organization.

*Article IV.* The High Contracting Parties reaffirm the undertaking, contained in Article III of the Peace Treaty signed in Paris on 10 February 1947, not to conclude any alliance and not to take part in coalitions aimed against the other High Contracting Party.

*Article V.* The High Contracting Parties affirm their determination to act in the spirit of cooperation and friendship with the object of further promoting and consolidating the economic and cultural ties between the Soviet Union and Finland.

*Article VI.* The High Contracting Parties undertake to observe the principles of mutual respect for their State sovereignty and independence as well as non-interference in the domestic affairs of the other State.

*Article VII.* Implementations of the present Treaty will conform to the principles of the United Nations Organization.

*Article VIII.* The present Treaty is subject to ratification, and will be valid for ten years as from the day of its coming into force. The Treaty will come into force as from the day of the exchange of ratification instruments, which will be effected in Helsinki within the shortest possible time.

Unless either of the High Contracting Parties denounces the Treaty one year before the expiration of the above-mentioned ten-year term, it will remain in force for each of the next five-year terms until either of the High Contracting Parties gives notice in writing of its intention to terminate the operation of the Treaty.

# *Treaty of Friendship, Cooperation and Mutual Assistance between Albania, Bulgaria, Hungary, the German Democratic Republic, Poland, Rumania, the Soviet Union and Czechoslovakia (Warsaw Pact), Warsaw, 14 May 1955*

The Contracting Parties,

Reaffirming their desire to create a system of collective security in Europe based on the participation of all European States, irrespective of their social and political structure, whereby the said

States may be enabled to combine their efforts in the interests of ensuring peace in Europe;

Taking into consideration, at the same time, the situation that has come about in Europe as a result of the ratification of the Paris Agreements, which provide for the constitution of a new military group in the form of a 'West European Union', with the participation of a remilitarized West Germany and its inclusion in the North Atlantic bloc, thereby increasing the danger of a new war and creating a threat to the national security of peace-loving States;

Being convinced that in these circumstances the peace-loving States of Europe must take the necessary steps to safeguard their security and to promote the maintenance of peace in Europe;

Being guided by the purposes and principles of the Charter of the United Nations;

In the interests of the further strengthening and development of friendship, cooperation and mutual assistance in accordance with the principles of respect for the independence and sovereignty of States and of non-intervention in their domestic affairs;

Have resolved to conclude the present Treaty of Friendship, Cooperation and Mutual Assistance and have appointed as their plenipotentiaries...who have agreed as follows:

*Article 1.* The Contracting Parties undertake, in accordance with the Charter of the United Nations, to refrain in their international relations from the threat or use of force and to settle their international disputes by peaceful means in such a manner that international peace and security are not endangered.

*Article 2.* The Contracting Parties declare that they are prepared to participate, in a spirit of sincere cooperation, in all international action for ensuring international peace and security and will devote their full efforts to the realization of these aims.

In this connection, the Contracting Parties shall endeavour to secure, in agreement with other States desiring to cooperate in this matter, the adoption of effective measures for the general reduction of armaments and the prohibition of atomic, hydrogen and other weapons of mass destruction.

*Article 3.* The Contracting Parties shall consult together on all important international questions involving their common interests, with a view to strengthening international peace and security.

Whenever any one of the Contracting Parties considers that a threat of armed attack on one or more of the States parties to the Treaty has arisen, they shall consult together immediately with a view to providing for their joint defence and maintaining peace and security.

*Article 4.* In the event of an armed attack in Europe on one or more of the States parties to the Treaty by any State or group of States, each State party to the Treaty shall, in the exercise of the right of individual or collective self-defence, in accordance with Article 51 of the United Nations Charter, afford the State or States so attacked immediate assistance, individually and in agreement with the other States parties to the Treaty, by all the means it considers necessary, including the use of armed force. The States parties to the Treaty shall consult together immediately concerning the joint measures necessary to restore and maintain international peace and security.

Measures taken under this Article shall be reported to the Security Council in accordance with the provisions of the United Nations Charter. These measures shall be discontinued as soon as the Security Council takes the necessary action to restore and maintain international peace and security.

*Article 5.* The Contracting Parties have agreed to establish a Unified Command, to which certain elements of their armed forces shall be allocated by agreement between the parties, and which shall act in accordance with jointly established principles. The parties shall likewise take such other concerted action as may be necessary to reinforce their defensive strength, in order to defend the peaceful labour of their peoples, guarantee the inviolability of their frontiers and territories and afford protection against possible aggression.

*Article 6.* For the purpose of carrying out the consultations provided for in the present Treaty between the States parties thereto, and for the consideration, of matters arising in connection with the application of the present Treaty, a Political Consultative Committee shall be established, in which each State party to the Treaty shall be represented by a member of the Government or by some other specially appointed representative.

The Committee may establish such auxiliary organs as may prove to be necessary.

*Article 7.* The Contracting Parties undertake not to participate in any coalitions or alliances, and not to conclude any agreements, the purposes of which are incompatible with the purposes of the present Treaty.

The Contracting Parties declare that their obligations under international treaties at present in force are not incompatible with the provisions of the present Treaty.

*Article 8.* The Contracting Parties declare that they will act in a spirit of friendship and cooperation to promote the further development and strengthening of the economic and cultural ties among them, in accordance with the principles of respect for each other's independence and sovereignty and of non-intervention in each other's domestic affairs.

*Article 9.* The present Treaty shall be open for accession by other States, irrespective of their social and political structure, which express their readiness by participating in the present Treaty, to help in combining the efforts of the peaceloving States to ensure the peace and security of the peoples. Such accessions shall come into effect with the consent of the States parties to the Treaty after the instruments of accession have been deposited with the Government of the Polish People's Republic.

*Article 10.* The present Treaty shall be subject to ratification, and the instruments of ratification shall be deposited with the Government of the Polish People's Republic.

The Treaty shall come into force on the date of deposit of the last instrument of ratification. The Government of the Polish People's Republic shall inform the other States parties to the Treaty of the deposit of each instrument of ratification.

*Article 11.* The present Treaty shall remain in force for twenty years. For Contracting Parties which do not, one year before the expiration of that term, give notice of termination of the Treaty to the Government of the Polish People's Republic, the Treaty shall remain in force for a further ten years.

In the event of the establishment of a system of collective security in Europe and the conclusion for that purpose of a General European Treaty concerning collective security, a goal which the Contracting Parties shall steadfastly strive to achieve, the present Treaty shall cease to have effect as from the date on which the General European Treaty comes into force.

Done at Warsaw, this fourteenth day of May 1955, in one copy, in the Russian, Polish, Czech and German languages, all the texts being equally authentic. Certified copies of the present Treaty shall be transmitted by the Government of the Polish People's Republic to all the other parties to the Treaty.

# Soviet–Czechoslovak Treaty on Stationing of Soviet Troops, Prague, 16 October 1968

The Government of the Union of Soviet Socialist Republics and the Government of the Czechoslovak Socialist Republic,

Being firmly resolved to make every effort to strengthen friendship and cooperation between the Union of Soviet Socialist Republics and Czechoslovakia, as well as between all the countries of the socialist commonwealth, and to defend the gains of socialism, strengthen peace and security in Europe and throughout the world, in conformity with the Statement of the Bratislava Conference of August 3, 1968,

Taking into consideration the Treaty on Friendship, Mutual Assistance and Post-War Cooperation of December 12, 1943, as extended by the Protocol of November 27, 1963,

In conformity with the arrangement achieved during the Soviet–Czechoslovak negotiations held in Moscow on August 23–6 and October 3–4, 1968,

Have decided to conclude the present Treaty and have agreed upon the following:

*Article 1.* The Government of the Union of Soviet Socialist Republics, acting with the consent of the Governments of the People's Republic of Bulgaria, the People's Republic of Hungary, the German Democratic Republic, the People's Republic of Poland, and the Government of the Czechoslovak Socialist Republic have agreed that part of the Soviet forces situated in the Czechoslovak Socialist Republic shall remain temporarily on the territory of the Czechoslovak Socialist Republic for the purposes of ensuring the security of the countries of the socialist commonwealth against the increasing revanchist aspirations of the West German militarist forces.

The rest of the forces of the Union of Soviet Socialist Republics, as well as the forces of the People's Republic of Bulgaria, the People's Republic of Hungary,

the German Democratic Republic, and the People's Republic of Poland, will be withdrawn from the territory of Czechoslovakia in accordance with the documents of the Moscow negotiations of August 23–6 and October 3–4, 1968. The withdrawal of these forces shall begin after the ratification of the present Treaty by both Parties and shall be carried out by stages within two months.

The number and places of distribution of Soviet forces which remain temporarily on the territory of the Czechoslovak Socialist Republic shall be determined by agreement between the Governments of the Union of Soviet Socialist Republics and the Czechoslovak Socialist Republic.

The Soviet forces temporarily situated on the territory of the Czechoslovak Socialist Republic shall remain subordinated to the Soviet Military Command.

*Article 2.* 1. The temporary presence of Soviet forces on the territory of the Czechoslovak Socialist Republic does not violate its sovereignty. Soviet forces shall not interfere in the internal affairs of the Czechoslovak Socialist Republic.

2. Soviet forces, persons serving [with Soviet forces], and members of their families situated on the territory of the Czechoslovak Socialist Republic will observe legislation in force in the Czechoslovak Socialist Republic.

*Article 3.* 1. The Soviet Side shall bear the expenses for maintenance of Soviet forces on the territory of the Czechoslovak Socialist Republic.

2. The Government of the Czechoslovak Socialist Republic shall grant Soviet forces, persons serving [with Soviet forces], and members of their families, for the period of their temporary sojourn in the Czechoslovak Socialist Republic, with barrack accommodations and housing in garrison settlements, official, warehouse, and other premises, airfields with hospital

structures and equipment, means of the State network of communications and transport, electric power, and other services.

Proving grounds, firing ranges, and training grounds will be used jointly with the Czechoslovak People's Army.

The procedure and conditions for use of the aforementioned facilities, as well as municipal, trade, and other services will be determined by agreement of the Contracting Parties.

*Article 4.* Soviet military units, persons serving with Soviet forces, and members of their families may travel to the Czechoslovak Socialist Republic to the places of distribution of Soviet forces and from the Czechoslovak Socialist Republic in through trains and railway cars belonging to the Soviet Union or transfer from the railway cars of one country to the railway cars of the other country, as well as by motor vehicle and air transport.

Persons serving with Soviet forces and members of their families shall be exempt from passport or visa control when entering, staying in, or leaving the Czechoslovak Socialist Republic.

Localities and the procedure for crossing the Soviet–Czechoslovak frontier, the methods of control, as well as types and forms of corresponding documents, shall be determined by agreement of the Contracting Parties.

*Article 5.* The Czechoslovak Side agrees to admit across the State frontier of the Czechoslovak Socialist Republic without levying duties, and without customs and border inspection:

Soviet forces and persons serving [with Soviet forces] who are traveling with military units, contingents, and commands;

All military freight, including freight destined for trade and other services for Soviet troops;

Persons serving with the Soviet forces traveling to the Czechoslovak Socialist Republic or leaving the Czechoslovak Socialist Republic alone or together with members of their families, with their personal belongings, upon presentation to customs agencies of documents certifying their right to cross the State frontier of the Czechoslovak Socialist Republic.

Property, and military equipment and materiel imported into the Czechoslovak Socialist Republic by the Soviet Side may be taken back to the Union of Soviet Socialist Republics without imposition of duties and charges.

*Article 6.* 1. Trade and other services for the personnel of Soviet forces temporarily situated on the territory of the Czechoslovak Socialist Republic and members of the families of persons serving with Soviet forces will be provided through Soviet trade and service enterprises.

2. The Czechoslovak Side will supply Soviet trade and service enterprises goods within the limits of quantities agreed upon between competent trade organizations of the Union of Soviet Socialist Republics and the Czechoslovak Socialist Republic at State retail prices in effect in the Czechoslovak Socialist Republic and at a trade discount adopted for corresponding trade enterprises of the Czechoslovak Socialist Republic.

Payment for deliveries shall be made in the currency of the Czechoslovak Socialist Republic.

3. Under contracts concluded between appropriate Soviet and Czechoslovak foreign trade organizations and at prices in effect in trade relations between the Union of Soviet Socialist Republics and the Czechoslovak Socialist Republic, the Czechoslovak Side will deliver agreed quantities of foodstuffs and manufactured goods, including fuel (coal, coke, firewood), for the planned supply of Soviet forces.

*Article 7.* The Government of the Czechoslovak Socialist Republic will grant to the Government of the Union of Soviet Socialist Republics the necessary sums in Czechoslovak crowns for expenses connected with the temporary sojourn of Soviet forces on the territory of Czechoslovakia. The amount of these sums will be established by agreement between the competent agencies of the Contracting Parties.

*Article 8.* The procedure of payment for services provided for by Article 3, as well as the sums in Czechoslovak crowns in accordance with Article 7 of the present Treaty, will be established by an additional Agreement between the Contracting Parties within six weeks after the entry of the present Treaty into force. The said sums in Czechoslovak crowns will be recomputed into convertible rubles on the basis of the ratio of internal prices and tariffs of the Czechoslovak Socialist Republic and of foreign trade prices.

*Article 9.* Questions of jurisdiction connected with the temporary sojourn of Soviet forces on the territory of the Czechoslovak Socialist Republic shall be regulated as follows:

1. In cases concerning crimes and offenses committed by persons serving with Soviet forces, or members of their families, on the territory of the Czechoslovak Socialist Republic, Czechoslovak legislation shall be applied and Czechoslovak courts, the procuracy, and other Czechoslovak agencies competent to prosecute for punishable acts shall function.

Cases concerning crimes committed by Soviet servicemen shall be investigated by the military procuracy and shall be considered by agencies of military justice of the Czechoslovak Socialist Republic.

2. The provisions of point one of the present Article shall not apply:

(a) in the event of the commission by persons serving with Soviet forces or by members of their families of crimes or offenses only against the Soviet Union, as well as against persons serving with Soviet forces or members of their families;

(b) in the event of the commission by persons serving with Soviet forces of crimes or offenses while executing official duties in areas of distribution of military units.

In cases specified in subpoints (a) and (b), the competent Soviet courts, pro-

curacy, and other agencies shall act on the basis of Soviet legislation.

3. In the event of the commission of punishable acts against Soviet forces temporarily situated on the territory of the Czechoslovak Socialist Republic, as well as against persons serving [with Soviet forces], the persons guilty of such actions will bear the same responsibility as for punishable acts against the armed forces of the Czechoslovak Socialist Republic and persons serving [with Czechoslovak forces].

4. Competent Soviet and Czechoslovak agencies may mutually request each other for transfer or acceptance of jurisdiction with respect to individual cases provided for in points 1 and 2 of the present Article. Such requests will be considered favorably.

5. Competent Soviet and Czechoslovak agencies will mutually render to each other legal and any kind of other assistance concerning questions of prosecuting punishable acts specified in points 1, 2, and 3 of the present Article.

*Article 10.* 1. The Government of the Union of Soviet Socialist Republics agrees to compensate the Government of the Czechoslovak Socialist Republic for the material damage which may be inflicted upon the Czechoslovak State by actions or omissions of Soviet military units or persons serving with them, as well as for the damage which may be inflicted by Soviet military units or persons serving with them while executing their official duties to Czechoslovak citizens, institutions, or citizens of third States situated on the territory of the Czechoslovak Socialist Republic – in both instances within amounts established (on the basis of submitted claims and with due account for provisions of Czechoslovak legislation) by Plenipotentiary representatives for the affairs of the temporary sojourn of Soviet forces in the Czechoslovak Socialist Republic, appointed in accordance with Article 13 of the present Treaty.

Disputes which might arise from the

duties of Soviet military units are subject to consideration on the same grounds.

2. The Government of the Union of Soviet Socialist Republics also agrees to compensate the Government of the Czechoslovak Socialist Republic for damage which may be inflicted upon Czechoslovak institutions and citizens, as well as citizens of third States, situated on the territory of the Czechoslovak Socialist Republic, as a result of actions or omissions of persons serving with Soviet forces which were not committed while executing official duties, as well as a result of actions or omissions of members of the families of persons serving with Soviet forces – in both instances within amounts established by a competent Czechoslovak court on the basis of claims made to persons who caused the damage.

*Article 11.* 1. The Government of the Czechoslovak Socialist Republic agrees to compensate the Government of the Union of Soviet Socialist Republics for damage which may be inflicted upon the property of Soviet military units temporarily situated on the territory of the Czechoslovak

Socialist Republic or upon persons serving with Soviet forces by actions or omissions of Czechoslovak State institutions – in amounts established by Plenipotentiary representatives for the affairs of the temporary sojourn of Soviet forces in the Czechoslovak Socialist Republic on the basis of the submitted claims and taking into account Czechoslovak legislation.

Disputes which may arise from the duties of Czechoslovak institutions to Soviet military units are subject to consideration on the same grounds.

2. The Government of the Czechoslovak Socialist Republic also agrees to compensate the Government of the Union of Soviet Socialist Republics for damage which may be inflicted upon Soviet military units temporarily situated on the territory of the Czechoslovak Socialist Republic or persons serving with Soviet forces and members of their families by actions or omissions of Czechoslovak citizens – in amounts established by a Czechoslovak court on the basis of claims made to persons who caused the damage.

. . .

Translation by William E. Butler, © American Society of International Law.

# *Treaty of Friendship, Cooperation and Mutual Aid between the Union of Soviet Socialist Republics and the Czechoslovak Socialist Republic, Prague, 6 May 1970*

The Union of Soviet Socialist Republics and the Czechoslovak Socialist Republic,

Affirming their fidelity to the aims and principles of the Soviet–Czechoslovak Treaty of Friendship, Mutual Aid and Post-War Cooperation, concluded on December 12, 1943, and extended on November 27, 1963, a treaty that played a historic role in the development of friendly relations between the peoples of the two States and laid a solid foundation for the further strengthening of fraternal friendship and all-round cooperation between them;

Profoundly convinced that the indestructible friendship between the Union of Soviet Socialist Republics and the Czechoslovak Socialist Republic, which was cemented in the joint struggle against Fascism and has received further deepening in the years of the construction of socialism and communism, as well as the fraternal mutual assistance and all-round cooperation between them, based on the teachings of Marxism-Leninism and the immutable principles of socialist internationalism, correspond to the fundamental interests of the peoples of both countries and of the entire socialist commonwealth;

Affirming that the support, strengthening and defence of the socialist gains achieved at the cost of the heroic efforts and selfless labour of each people are the common internationalist duty of the socialist countries;

Consistently and steadfastly favouring the strengthening of the unity and solidarity of all countries of the socialist commonwealth, based on the community of their social systems and ultimate goals;

Firmly resolved strictly to observe the obligations stemming from the May 14, 1955, Warsaw Treaty of Friendship, Cooperation and Mutual Aid;

Stating the economic cooperation between the two States facilitates their development, as well as the further improvement of the international socialist division of labour and socialist economic integration within the framework of the Council for Mutual Economic Aid;

Expressing the firm intention to promote the cause of strengthening peace and security in Europe and throughout the world, to oppose imperialism, revanchism and militarism;

Guided by the goals and principles proclaimed in the United Nations Charter;

Taking into account the achievements of socialist and communist construction in the two countries, the present situation and the prospects for all-round cooperation, as well as the changes that have taken place in Europe and throughout the world since the conclusion of the Treaty of December 12, 1943;

Have agreed on the following:

*Article 1.* In accordance with the principles of socialist internationalism, the High Contracting Parties will continue to strengthen the eternal, indestructible friendship between the peoples of the Union of Soviet Socialist Republics and the Czechoslovak Socialist Republic, to develop all-round cooperation between the two countries and to give each other fraternal assistance and support, basing their actions on mutual respect for State sovereignty and independence, on equal rights and non-interference in one another's internal affairs.

*Article 2.* The High Contracting Parties will continue, proceeding from the principles of friendly mutual assistance and the international socialist division of labour, to develop and deepen mutually advantageous bilateral and multilateral economic, scientific and technical cooperation with the aim of developing their national economies, achieving the highest possible scientific and technical level and efficiency of social production, and increasing the material well-being of the working people of their countries.

The two sides will promote the further development of economic ties and cooperation and the socialist economic integration of the member countries of the Council for Mutual Economic Aid.

*Article 3.* The High Contracting Parties will continue to develop and expand cooperation between the two countries in the fields of science and culture, education, literature and the arts, the press, radio, motion pictures, television, public health, tourism and physical culture and in other fields.

*Article 4.* The High Contracting Parties will continue to facilitate the expansion of cooperation and direct ties between the bodies of State authority and the public organizations of the working people, with the aim of achieving a deeper mutual familiarization and a closer drawing together between the peoples of the two States.

*Article 5.* The High Contracting Parties, expressing their unswerving determination to proceed along the path of the construction of socialism and communism, will take the necessary steps to defend the socialist gains of the peoples and the security and independence of the two countries, will strive to develop all-round relations among the States of the socialist commonwealth, and will act in a spirit of the consolidation of the unity, friendship and fraternity of these States.

*Article 6.* The High Contracting Parties proceed from the assumption that the Munich Pact of September 29, 1938, was signed under the threat of aggressive war and the use of force against Czechoslovakia, that it was a component part of Hitler Germany's criminal conspiracy against peace and was a flagrant violation of the basic norms of international law, and hence was invalid from the very outset, with all the consequences stemming therefrom.

*Article 7.* The High Contracting Parties, consistently pursuing a policy of the peaceful coexistence of States with different social systems, will exert every effort for the defence of international peace and the security of the peoples against encroachments by the aggressive forces of imperialism and reaction, for the relaxation of international tension, the cessation of the arms race and the achievement of general and complete disarmament, the final liquidation of colonialism in all its forms and manifestations, and the giving of support to countries that have been liberated from colonial domination and are marching along the path of strengthening national independence and sovereignty.

*Article 8.* The High Contracting Parties will jointly strive to improve the situation and to ensure peace in Europe, to strengthen and develop cooperation among the European States, to establish good-neighbour relations among them and to create an effective system of European security on the basis of the collective efforts of all European States.

*Article 9.* The High Contracting Parties declare that one of the main preconditions for ensuring European security is the immutability of the State borders that were formed in Europe after the Second World War. They express their firm resolve, jointly with the other Member States of the May 14, 1955, Warsaw Treaty of Friendship, Cooperation and Mutual Aid and in accordance with this Treaty, to ensure the inviolability of the borders of the Member States of this Treaty and to take all necessary steps to prevent aggression on the part of any forces of militarism and revanchism and to rebuff the aggressor.

*Article 10.* In the event that one of the High Contracting Parties is subjected to an armed attack by any States or group of States, the other Contracting Party, regarding this as an attack against itself, will immediately give the first party all possible assistance, including military aid, and will also give it support with all means at its disposal, by way of implementing the right to individual or collective self-defence in accordance with Article 51 of the United Nations Charter.

The High Contracting Parties will without delay inform the United Nations Security Council of steps taken on the basis of this Article, and they will act in accordance with the provisions of the United Nations Charter.

*Article 11.* The High Contracting Parties will inform each other and consult on all important international questions affecting their interests and will act on the basis of common positions agreed upon in accordance with the interests of both States.

*Article 12.* The High Contracting Parties declare that their obligations under existing international treaties are not at variance with the provisions of this Treaty.

*Article 13.* This Treaty is subject to ratification and will enter into force on the day of the exchange of instruments of ratification, which will be conducted in Moscow in a very short time.

*Article 14.* This Treaty is concluded for a period of twenty years and will be automatically extended every five years thereafter, if neither of the High Contracting Parties gives notice that it is denouncing the Treaty twelve months before the expiration of the current period.

[Signed]   L.   BREZHNEV   and   A. KOSYGIN;   G.   HUSAK   and   L. STROUGAL.

## Soviet treaties in the Third World

Ever since the Baku Congress of Peoples of the East in September 1920, at which Zinoviev, the head of Comintern, proclaimed a 'holy people's war against the robbers and oppressors', communist Russia had posed as a champion of anti-colonial nationalism everywhere (save within its own borders). Until the end of the Second World War Soviet support for anti-colonial movements was largely confined to the realm of propaganda. In one notable instance, that of China in 1927, Comintern opposed a communist rising as 'opportunist'.

With the emergence of the Soviet Union as a major actor on the international stage after 1945, rhetoric began to be translated more effectively into reality, as Stalin and his successors saw Soviet support for anti-imperialist liberation movements in Asia and Africa as a convenient weapon in the cold war. But although usually aligned with anti-colonial movements, the Soviet Union generally pursued a policy based primarily on the national interests of the Soviet State and only secondarily on consistent ideological premises. Thus in its policy towards China and Japan, the Soviet Union sought to restore or maintain Russian sovereignty over disputed border regions and initially promised support to the Chinese Nationalists rather than their communist rivals. Similarly in the Middle East, the Soviet Union in the late 1940s supported Zionism (apparently in the hope of removing the British from Palestine) rather than its opponents, only later switching to support of Arab nationalist régimes. In its backing of Arab anti-Western States in the Middle East, the Soviet Union often closed its eyes to the suppression by these States of their native communist parties.

## THE SOVIET UNION AND CHINA

Concern for the security of the Soviet Union's frontier in Asia has been a constant preoccupation of Soviet leaders. Stalin was seriously worried after 1931 by Japanese ascendancy in Manchuria, and armed conflicts occurred on the frontiers of Mongolia and Manchuria in 1939. But the growing European dangers led the Soviet Union to conciliate Japan, a new policy marked by the signature of the *Soviet–Japanese Neutrality Pact, 13 April 1941*. The Soviet Union ceased to aid Nationalist China in resisting Japanese aggression. As the Germans advanced through Greece and Yugoslavia, Stalin sought security on his Asian frontiers through a policy of friendship with Japan, and signed the extensive *Soviet–Japanese*

*Commercial Agreement, 11 June 1941,* providing for exchange of goods and reciprocal most-favoured-nation treatment. With the German attack on the Soviet Union on 22 June 1941, the Soviet Union first became Britain's ally in the war in Europe and later that of the Union States also. But Stalin did not extend the Grand Alliance to Asia where Britain and the United States were also allied with China in the war against Japan. Relations between China and the Soviet Union steadily deteriorated from June 1941 to the spring of 1945. Nationalist China by October 1943 had forced Soviet influence out of the Chinese province of Sinkiang, where Stalin hoped to build up a strong economic base. The Soviet Union continued to pursue friendly relations with Japan and concluded another *Soviet–Japanese Agreement on 30 March 1944,* whereby Japan returned to Russia the oil and coal concession in northern Sakhalin which she had secured from Russia in 1925, and the Soviet Union renewed the Fisheries Convention and undertook to pay Japan an annual sum of 5 million roubles and to deliver 50,000 metric tons of oil.

At the *Yalta Conference in February 1945* (p. 27) a secret agreement was reached between Britain, the United States and the Soviet Union; the Soviet Union would enter the war against Japan two or three months after the surrender of Germany; the Soviet Union also promised to conclude an alliance with the Nationalist Government of China; in return the Soviet Union was to secure extensive rights in Chinese Manchuria similar to those Tsarist Russia had once enjoyed before the Russo-Japanese war of 1904–5. The agreement about Russian rights in China was made subject to Chiang Kai-shek's concurrence since he had not been consulted, but the President of the United States promised to 'take measures in order to obtain this concurrence on advice from Marshal Stalin'. The agreement was kept secret until February 1946, but Stalin's breach with Japan became public when on 5 April 1945 he unilaterally denounced the Russo-Japanese Neutrality Pact. On 8 August 1945 Russia declared war on Japan shortly after the atomic bomb had been dropped on Hiroshima.

The Soviet Union was only at war one week before the unconditional surrender of Japan on 14 August 1945. On the same day the *Soviet–Chinese Treaty of Alliance and Friendship, 14 August 1945* (p. 51), was signed. The treaty had lost its purpose as a wartime alliance, but fears of a Japanese military revival remained strong in Asia for some time. For the Soviet Union the treaty gave her those rights in China promised at Yalta. The Nationalist Chinese also valued the treaty, for in the summer of 1945 the Nationalist Government of Chiang Kai-shek was faced not only with the problem of regaining control over the Japanese-occupied regions of China, but also with the Communist Chinese rival bid for power in North China; and a third difficulty was the continued unrest and doubtful Chinese control of the province of Sinkiang. The treaty with Russia held out hope of support in all these problems. The Soviet Union undertook to pursue a friendly policy toward the Nationalist Government and to aid the nationalists alone (and not the communists); the treaty contained a Soviet recognition of sovereignty over all the regions of China occupied by Japan. Though extensive rights were granted to the Soviet Union, actual occupation of Chinese territory by Soviet troops was to last for a limited period of time and ostensibly Chinese sovereignty was not thereby diminished.

The Chinese Nationalist Government for their part in an exchange of notes agreed to recognize the independence of Outer Mongolia after the wishes of the Mongolian people had been tested. Formal Chinese recognition of Mongolian independence, and with it a renunciation of earlier suzerain claims, was accorded by the Nationalist Chinese Government on 5 January 1946; *on 27 February 1946 the Soviet Union and Outer Mongolia signed a treaty of friendship and mutual aid.* Mongolia was drawn securely into the Russian (as distinct from the Chinese) orbit by a trade treaty in 1957 and an economic assistance treaty in 1960. The *Mongolia–U.S.S.R. Friendship Treaty, signed at Ulan Bator on 15 January 1966,* further consolidated Mongolia's position as a Soviet buffer State against China.

Meanwhile the Soviet relationship with China had passed through two major transformations. The first involved a Soviet switch in the late 1940s to support for the Chinese communists in their struggle against the Nationalist Government of Chiang Kai-shek. Despite the 1945 Sino-Soviet treaty, relations between the Soviet Union and Nationalist China had soon become acrimonious. There were disputes over the delayed Soviet evacuation of northern China, over Soviet expropriation of Manchurian industry as war booty, and the Nationalists charged that the Soviet Union was aiding the Chinese communists in violation of the 1945 treaty.

The victory of the Chinese Communists in 1949 under Mao Tse-tung's leadership opened a new chapter in Sino-Soviet relations. In December 1949 Mao Tse-tung led a delegation to Moscow to negotiate another alliance treaty with the Soviet Union. A *Treaty of Friendship, Alliance and Mutual Assistance and a number of associated agreements were signed on 14 February 1950* (p. 165). The Sino-Soviet Alliance of 14 August 1945 was declared null and void, but Chinese recognition of the independence of Outer Mongolia was reaffirmed. The alliance was directed to resisting any renewed Japanese aggression and extended to any State collaborating with Japan. This reflected the new realities of the cold war and Soviet–

American hostility. The Soviet Union also abandoned many of her rights in northern China acquired in 1945. (The actual transfer of the Manchurian railway to China occurred in 1952 and of Port Arthur by 1955.) The Soviet Union extended a credit to China and promised economic aid. Whilst the 1950 treaty changed the Sino-Soviet relationship, the Soviet Union continued to retain a privileged position in China and was the acknowledged leader of the communist world movement for the next decade. Until 1956 the Soviet Union and Communist China acted in close collaboration internationally and domestically.

But from the late 1950s onwards a steadily widening rift became apparent between the two communist nations, with the Chinese refusing to acknowledge Soviet pre-eminence in the world communist movement and decrying the post-Stalin Soviet régime as 'revisionist'. In 1958 and 1959 the U.S.S.R. would not provide nuclear assistance to China on terms acceptable to the Chinese leaders. In August 1960 Soviet technicians were withdrawn, an indication of how far Sino-Soviet relations had deteriorated. The Chinese denounced the efforts of the Soviet leader, Khrushchev, to improve relations with the United States in a new era of Soviet–United States 'peaceful co-existence'. The Chinese deeply resented Soviet military and economic aid to India which continued despite the Sino-Indian border conflict of 1962.

In March 1963 the Chinese publicly described the treaties signed by Imperial China with Tsarist Russia – the treaties of Aigun (1858), Peking (1860) and St Petersburg (1881) – as among the 'unequal treaties' imposed by imperialists on China. Mao Tse-tung added that they raised outstanding issues that ought to be settled by peaceful negotiation. The Soviet Union denied the Chinese claim challenging the Russian–Chinese frontiers settled by these treaties, but was ready to negotiate on specific points. These negotiations broke down in 1964.

The Sino-Soviet border can be divided into three sections: the Sinkiang sector running from the disputed frontier regions of the Pamirs where Afghanistan, Russia and Kashmir meet, northward to Mongolia; the Mongolian sector, strictly speaking not a Soviet frontier but the frontier between the Mongolian Republic (allied to the Soviet Union) and China; and thirdly, the Manchurian sector running in a great arc from the Mongolian frontier to North Korea, along the banks of the rivers Argun and Amur and down the Ussuri to Lake Khank.

Chinese efforts to place Sinkiang firmly under Chinese administration led to conflict with India in 1962. In the 1960s the Sino-Russian border on the Ili was the scene of many 'incidents'. The Chinese accused the Russians of 'unbridled subversive activities' in China's borderland among the non-Chinese minorities, about whose loyalty the Chinese are especially sensitive.

The independence of Outer Mongolia recognized in the Sino-Soviet treaties of 1945 and 1950 continued to rankle with the Chinese. Despite these treaties Mao Tse-tung in July 1964 mentioned the question of Outer Mongolia as open to further discussion. On the other hand in 1962 a Sino-Mongolian boundary treaty was signed, and China made numerous territorial concessions to Mongolia.

The third section of the Sino-Russian frontier separates Manchuria from Russia. The Ussuri river and some islands in it became the scene of incidents culminating in violence in March 1969.

The Sino-Soviet frontier dispute appeared to be mainly a conflict of principle in the eyes of the Chinese, who demanded from the Soviet Union an admission that the 'unequal' treaties were not valid and that only freely negotiated treaties between the U.S.S.R. and China could be made valid. The Soviet claim to these frontiers was based on orthodox international law relating to the validity of treaties (the U.S.S.R. being happy, for these purposes, to claim rights of succession to the Tsarist empire), and to the Russian period of possession and effective occupation.

But in the last resort the frontier differences were more a symptom than a cause of the conflict. China's explosion of an atom bomb in 1964 and of a hydrogen bomb in 1967 intensified the Chinese determination to gain recognition as an independent communist power. Meanwhile the period of 'cultural revolution' in China in the late 1960s accentuated the radical elements in Chinese communism.

Sino-Soviet talks in the years after 1969 failed to produce a resolution of the border issue. The rapprochement between China and the United States in the 1970s (see p. 298) brought a new – and to the Russians, ominous – element into Sino-Soviet relations. Nevertheless, after the death of Mao Tse-tung in 1976, and particularly after the accession to effective power in the late 1970s of the pragmatic wing of the Chinese communist party, associated with Deng Xiao-ping, some signs of improvement in the atmosphere became evident. Although there was no sudden healing of the breach, the stridency of Chinese anti-Soviet rhetoric of the 1960s was replaced by a more cautious approach. Symptomatic of the new mood were the *Chinese–Soviet Economic Cooperation Agreement, 28 December 1984* and the *Chinese–Soviet Scientific Cooperation Agreement, 28 December 1984*. These were followed by the *Chinese–Soviet Agreement on Economic and Technical Cooperation, 10 July 1985*.

## THE SOVIET UNION AND ASIA

Elsewhere in Asia the Soviet Union found several opportunities after the Second World War to broaden its influence. In North Korea, occupied by Soviet forces until September 1948, a communist régime was established under the leadership of a Korean-born Soviet army officer, Kim Il-sung. After the Korean War (p. 296) the country remained securely in the communist orbit, without, however, taking sides in the Sino-Soviet quarrel. A *Treaty of Friendship between the Soviet Union and North Korea was signed on 6 July 1961*. This was balanced by a similar *Chinese–North Korean Treaty, 11 July 1961*. North Korea signed trade agreements with both of its communist neighbours.

In Vietnam the Soviet Union gave support to the forces under Ho Chi Minh who declared an independent republic in September 1945. A bitter war between Ho's communists and the French army ended in defeat for the French and their recognition, in the Geneva Agreements of 1954 (p. 274), that their colonial rule in the country was at an end. *The U.S.S.R. signed Economic Aid Agreements with North Vietnam in 1965 and 1966.* Following the communist victory in the Vietnam war (p. 273), a *Treaty of Friendship and Cooperation between Vietnam and the Soviet Union was signed on 3 November 1978* (p. 172). The next month Vietnamese forces attacked Cambodia, occupied the country, and installed a puppet régime. In this conflict, and in associated military encounters between Vietnamese and Chinese forces, the Soviet Union gave strong diplomatic support to the Vietnamese.

India, from independence in 1947 onwards, pursued a policy of non-alignment with either bloc in the East–West conflict. But in the course of the 1960s, as a result of her wars with China and with Pakistan (see p. 261), India moved closer towards the Soviet Union. The *Soviet Union and India signed a Treaty of Peace, Friendship and Cooperation on 9 August 1971* (p. 170). This treaty strengthened India's hand in its confrontation with Pakistan. The terms of the treaty were 'negative' in character. The two signatories undertook not to join any military alliances directed against each other (Article 8), and not to provide assistance to any other State engaged in armed conflict with one of the signatories, but immediately to consult with each other if one of the signatories were attacked or under threat of attack (Article 9). The treaty thus fell short of constituting a full-fledged alliance, since neither signatory was committed to come to the aid of its treaty partner.

During much of the nineteenth and early twentieth centuries the rugged mountain country of Afghanistan had served as a buffer between the Russian empire and the British empire in India. From 1953 onwards Afghanistan received Soviet economic aid, but the country was not drawn into the Soviet political orbit. In 1979, however, the Soviet Union seized the opportunity of internal chaos in neighbouring Iran and allowed itself to be sucked into the murderous internal politics of Afghanistan. *On 5 December 1978 the Soviet Union and Afghanistan signed a Treaty of Friendship, Goodneighbourliness and Cooperation* (p. 174). Article 1 of this treaty contained a declaration of respect for each other's national sovereignty, territorial integrity and non-interference in each other's internal affairs. Nevertheless, in December 1979 the Soviet Union intervened in Afghanistan in massive military force in support of a pro-Moscow faction. A statement was issued, allegedly in the name of the Afghan Government, declaring that military assistance had been requested from the U.S.S.R. 'proceeding from the December 5, 1978 Treaty'. Soviet involvement in the ensuing civil war inflicted large-scale casualties, produced a horde of millions of refugees who fled to Pakistan, and gravely complicated the Soviet Union's relations with Islamic and Third World countries. But in the course of the early 1980s the Soviet forces resolutely ground down American-backed resistance and began the task of casting the institutions of the country in the familiar Soviet mould.

## SOVIET TREATY RELATIONS IN THE MIDDLE EAST

Before 1955 most of the States of the Middle East viewed the Soviet Union with hostility, and several of them entered defensive alliances with the United States or Britain (see pp. 126 and 347). In 1947 and 1948 the Soviet Union gave strong support to the Zionists in Palestine, facilitating the supply of arms to the nascent Jewish State by Czechoslovakia, and racing with the U.S.A. to be the first major power to recognize Israel in May 1948. But from the early 1950s the Soviet Union pursued a policy more favourable to Israel's Arab opponents, hoping thereby to undermine the influence of Western powers in the region. The Suez crisis of 1956 (p. 349) provided the U.S.S.R. with its first major opportunity in the area. Egypt became the focal point of Soviet efforts. In September 1955 an agreement was concluded for Czechoslovak arms supplies to Egypt. When the U.S.A. thereupon cancelled plans for American financial assistance in the building of the Aswan High Dam, the Soviet Union stepped into the breach. Soviet experts were sent to Egypt and the dam, built mainly with Soviet equipment and funds, was constructed in the course of the 1960s.

The U.S.S.R. became a major arms supplier to Egypt, particularly after the 'Six-Day War' of 1967. During the years 1967–71 Soviet influence in Egypt reached its apogee, and in the 'War of Attrition' between Israel and Egypt in 1969–70, some Soviet pilots and planes took an active part in combat. The *Soviet–Egyptian Treaty of Friendship, 27 May 1971*, (p. 168) marked the high point of the relationship. But thereafter relations began to cool, as the Egyptians became restive with what was seen as Soviet domination; over the next few years, under the leadership of President Sadat, the Egyptians undertook a daring switch of alliances from the Soviet Union to the U.S.A. (see p. 353).

Elsewhere in the Arab world the Soviet Union succeeded in winning friends in several countries. A *Soviet–Iraqi Treaty of Friendship was signed on 9 April 1972*. Iraq became one of the Soviet Union's closest followers in the region, and the U.S.S.R. provided Iraq with considerable help in its war with Iran in the early 1980s. Although Syria was at loggerheads with Iraq during much of the 1960s and 1970s, the U.S.S.R. managed to cultivate good relations with both countries. Syria too became heavily dependent on Soviet military equipment. A *Treaty of Friendship between the Soviet Union and Syria was signed on 8 October 1980*. While most of the Arabian peninsula remained strongly in the Western camp (Saudi Arabia did not even have diplomatic relations with the U.S.S.R.), an exception was the Marxist state of South Yemen which achieved independence from Britain upon the British withdrawal from Aden on 29 November 1967. On *25 October 1979 the Soviet Union and South Yemen signed a Treaty of Friendship* (p. 176).

## SOVIET TREATY RELATIONS IN AFRICA

Soviet involvement in independent Africa was at first a relatively minor aspect of Soviet diplomacy, but strong Soviet support (including arms supplies, training, propaganda and diplomatic aid) for anti-colonial liberation movements in the continent eventually reaped considerable rewards. After the independence of Ghana in 1957 (see p. 319), the country established good relations with the U.S.S.R., although these deteriorated after the fall of President Kwame Nkrumah in 1966. In North Africa the U.S.S.R. found its most erratic partner in President Qadhafi of Libya, who seized power in 1969. It also developed cordial relations with Algeria; a string of agreements for the expansion of trade and for Soviet military equipment failed, however, to turn Algeria into a reliable ally of the U.S.S.R.

The conflicts in the Horn of Africa afforded the Soviet Union more fruitful opportunities. A *Soviet–Somali Friendship Treaty was signed on 11 July 1974,* but when war broke out in 1977 between the Somalis and Ethiopia, the Soviet Union backed Ethiopia, whereupon the Somalis terminated the treaty. *On 20 November 1978 the Soviet Union signed a Friendship Treaty with Ethiopia.*

Elsewhere in Africa Russian courtship found many countries willing to be wooed, but few ready to tie the knot on a permanent basis. In the early stages of the Congo imbroglio (see p. 321) the Soviet Union seemed to have found a protégé in the country's first Prime Minister, Patrice Lumumba; but under the military government which soon took control the country (later known as Zaire) slid towards the Western camp.

The U.S.S.R.'s most important diplomatic gains were in southern Africa, where its strong support of the liberation movements in the Portuguese colonies of Mozambique and Angola paid off after independence in the form of close relations which found formal expression in *Treaties of Friendship between the Soviet Union and Angola, 8 October 1976 and between the Soviet Union and Mozambique, 31 March 1977.*

In the struggle for power inside South Africa, the Soviet Union supported the African National Congress, originally a non-communist organization, and in the 1980s began to supply arms to guerillas operating in South-West Africa (Namibia) and across the South African borders. But here (as in the case of the Palestine Liberation Organization to which the U.S.S.R. gave similar diplomatic and other aid) the relationship remained a marriage more of convenience than of conviction, with the recipients maintaining an ideological stance distinct from that of Moscow.

Strange to relate, one of the Soviet Union's most reliable allies in Africa was not an African State at all but Cuba, communist and pro-Soviet since 1961, which in the 1970s sent military aid, including large numbers of troops, to Angola as well as other African States. These efforts in support of Soviet clients were repaid by massive economic aid by the Soviet Union to Cuba. Cuba was, in effect, transformed into a Soviet economic satellite, and indeed became a member of Comecon in 1972. Meanwhile Cuba had developed into the U.S.S.R.'s only long-term ally in the Americas, although after the Cuban missile crisis of October 1962 the Soviet Union moved with some circumspection. Soviet influence in Cuba remained paramount in the 1970s and early 1980s, but the details of Soviet–Cuban relations in military and security matters were not given publicity in the form of an open treaty.

# Treaty of Friendship, Alliance and Mutual Assistance between the People's Republic of China and the Soviet Union, Moscow, 14 February 1950

The Central People's Government of the People's Republic of China and the Presidium of the Supreme Soviet of the Union of Soviet Socialist Republics, fully determined to prevent jointly, by strengthening friendship and cooperation between the People's Republic of China and the Union of Soviet Socialist Republics, the revival of Japanese imperialism and the resumption of aggression on the part of Japan or any other State that may collaborate in any way with Japan in acts of aggression; imbued with the desire to consolidate lasting peace and universal security in the Far East and throughout the world in conformity with the aims and principles of the United Nations; profoundly convinced that the consolidation of good neighbourly relations and friendship between the People's Republic of China and the Union of Soviet Socialist Republics meets the vital interests of the peoples of China and the Soviet Union, have towards this end decided to conclude the present Treaty and have appointed as their plenipotentiary representatives: Chou En-lai, Premier of the Government Administration Council and Minister of Foreign Affairs, acting for the Central People's Government of the People's Republic of China; and Andrei Yanuaryevich Vyshinsky, Minister of Foreign Affairs of the U.S.S.R., acting for the Presidium of the Supreme Soviet of the Union of Soviet Socialist Republics. Both plenipotentiary representatives having communicated their full powers found them in good and due form, have agreed upon the following:

*Article 1.* Both Contracting Parties undertake jointly to adopt all necessary measures at their disposal for the purpose of preventing the resumption of aggression and violation of peace on the part of Japan or any other State that may collaborate with Japan directly or indirectly in acts of aggression. In the event of one of the Contracting Parties being attacked by Japan or any State allied with her and thus being involved in a state of war, the other Contracting Party shall immediately render military and other assistance by all means at its disposal.

The Contracting Parties also declare their readiness to participate in a spirit of sincere cooperation in all international actions aimed at ensuring peace and security throughout the world and to contribute their full share to the earliest implementation of these tasks.

*Article 2.* Both Contracting Parties undertake in a spirit of mutual agreement to bring about the earliest conclusion of a peace treaty with Japan jointly with other Powers which were allies in the Second World War.

*Article 3.* Each Contracting Party undertakes not to conclude any alliance directed against the other Contracting Party and not to take part in any coalition or in any actions or measures directed against the other Contracting Party.

*Article 4.* Both Contracting Parties, in the interests of consolidating peace and universal security, will consult with each other in regard to all important international problems affecting the common interests of China and the Soviet Union.

*Article 5.* Each Contracting Party undertakes, in a spirit of friendship and cooperation and in conformity with the principles of equality, mutual benefit and mutual respect for the national sovereignty and territorial integrity and non-interference in the internal affairs of the other Contracting Party, to develop and consolidate economic and cultural ties between China and the Soviet Union, to render the other all possible economic assistance and to carry out necessary economic cooperation.

*Article 6.* The present Treaty shall come into force immediately after its ratification; the exchange of instruments of ratification shall take place in Peking.

The present Treaty shall be valid for thirty years. If neither of the Contracting Parties gives notice a year before the expiration of this term of its intention to denounce the Treaty, it shall remain in force for another five years and shall be further extended in compliance with this provision.

Done in Moscow on 14 February 1950, in two copies, each in the Chinese and Russian languages, both texts being equally valid.

*On the authorization of the Central People's Government of the People's Republic of China*

CHOU EN-LAI

*On the authorization of the Presidium of the Supreme Soviet of the Union of Soviet Socialist Republics*

A.Y. VYSHINSKY

## Agreement between the People's Republic of China and the Union of Soviet Socialist Republics on the Chinese Changchun Railway, Port Arthur and Dairen

The Central People's Government of the People's Republic of China and the Presidium of the Supreme Soviet of the Union of Soviet Socialist Republics record that since 1945, fundamental changes have occurred in the situation in the Far East, namely: imperialist Japan has suffered defeat; the reactionary Kuomintang Government has been overthrown; China has become a People's Democratic Republic; a new People's Government has been established in China which has unified the whole of China, has carried out a policy of friendship and cooperation with the Soviet Union and has proved its ability to defend the national independence and territorial

integrity of China and the national honour and dignity of the Chinese people.

The Central People's Government of the People's Republic of China and the Presidium of the Supreme Soviet of the Union of Soviet Socialist Republics consider that this new situation permits a new approach to the question of the Chinese Changchun Railway, Port Arthur and Dairen.

In conformity with these new circumstances the Central People's Government of the People's Republic of China and the Presidium of the Supreme Soviet of the Union of Soviet Socialist Republics have decided to conclude the present Agreement on the Chinese Changchun Railway, Port Arthur and Dairen:

*Article 1.* Both Contracting Parties agree that the Soviet Government transfer without compensation to the Government of the People's Republic of China all its rights to joint administration of the Chinese Changchun Railway with all the property belonging to the Railway. The transfer shall be effected immediately after the conclusion of a peace treaty with Japan, but not later than the end of 1952.

Pending the transfer, the existing Sino-Soviet joint administration of the Chinese Changchun Railway shall remain unchanged. After this Agreement becomes effective, posts (such as manager of the Railway, chairman of the Central Board, etc.) will be periodically alternated between representatives of China and the U.S.S.R.

As regards concrete methods of effecting the transfer, they shall be agreed upon and determined by the Governments of both Contracting Parties.

*Article 2.* Both Contracting Parties agree that Soviet troops be withdrawn from the jointly utilized naval base Port Arthur, and that the installations in this area be handed over to the Government of the People's Republic of China immediately on the conclusion of a peace treaty with Japan, but not later than the end of 1952.

The Government of the People's Republic of China will compensate the Soviet Union for expenses which it has incurred in restoring and constructing installations since 1945.

For the period pending the withdrawal of Soviet troops and the transfer of the above-mentioned installations the Governments of China and the Soviet Union will each appoint an equal number of military representatives to form a joint Chinese–Soviet Military Commission which will be alternately presided over by each side and which will be in charge of military affairs in the area of Port Arthur; concrete measures in this sphere will be drawn up by the joint Chinese–Soviet Military Commission within three months after the present Agreement becomes effective and shall be put into force upon approval of these measures by the Governments of both countries.

The civil administration in the aforementioned area shall be under the direct authority of the Government of the People's Republic of China. Pending the withdrawal of Soviet troops, the zone for billeting Soviet troops in the area of Port Arthur will remain unaltered in conformity with existing frontiers.

In the event of either of the Contracting Parties becoming the victim of aggression on the part of Japan or any State that may collaborate with Japan, and as a result thereof becoming involved in hostilities, China and the Soviet Union may, on the proposal of the Government of the People's Republic of China and with the agreement of the Government of the U.S.S.R., jointly use the naval base Port Arthur for the purpose of conducting joint military operations against the aggressor.

*Article 3.* Both Contracting Parties agree that the question of Dairen harbour be further considered on the conclusion of a peace treaty with Japan. As regards the administration of Dairen, it is in the hands of the Government of the People's Republic of China. All the property in Dairen now temporarily administered by or leased to the Soviet Union, shall be taken over by the Government of the People's Republic of China. To carry out the transfer of the aforementioned property, the Governments of China and the Soviet Union shall appoint three representatives each to form a Joint Commission which, within three months after the present Agreement comes into effect, shall draw up concrete measures for the transfer of the property; and these measures shall be fully carried out in the course of 1950 after their approval by the Governments of both countries upon the proposal of the Joint Commission.

[*Article 4.* Ratification.]

## Agreement between the Central People's Government of the People's Republic of China and the Government of the Union of Soviet Socialist Republics on the granting of credit to the People's Republic of China

In connection with the consent of the Government of the Union of Soviet Socialist Republics to grant the request of the Central People's Government of the People's Republic of China for a credit to pay for the equipment and other materials which the Soviet Union has agreed to deliver to China, both Governments have agreed upon the following:

*Article 1.* The Government of the Union of Soviet Socialist Republics grants to the Central People's Government of the People's Republic of China a credit which in terms of American dollars, amounts to U.S. $300,000,000, taking 35 American dollars to one ounce of fine gold.

In view of the extraordinary devastation of China as a result of prolonged hostilities on its territory, the Soviet Government has agreed to grant the credit at the favourable rate of interest of 1 per cent per annum.

. . .

*Article 3.* The Central People's Government of the People's Republic of China shall repay the credit mentioned in Article 1, together with the interest thereon, in deliveries of raw materials, tea, gold and American dollars. Prices for raw materials and tea and their quantities and dates of delivery shall be determined by special agreement, with prices to be determined on the basis of prices on the world markets.

The credit shall be repaid in ten equal annual instalments...

[In the communiqué issued at the time of the signature of the treaty the following statements were made.]

...

In connection with the signing of the Treaty of Friendship, Alliance and Mutual Assistance, and the Agreement on the Chinese Changchun Railway, Port Arthur and Dairen, Chou En-lai, Premier and Minister of Foreign Affairs, and A.Y. Vyshinsky, Minister of Foreign Affairs, exchanged notes to the effect that the respective Treaty and Agreements concluded on August 14, 1945, between China and the Soviet Union are now null and void, and also that both Governments affirm that the independent status of the Mongolian People's Republic is fully guaranteed as a result of the plebiscite of 1945 and the establishment with it of diplomatic relations by the People's Republic of China.

At the same time, A.Y. Vyshinsky, Minister of Foreign Affairs, and Chou En-lai, Premier and Minister of Foreign Affairs, also exchanged notes on the decision of the Soviet Government to transfer without compensation to the Government of the People's Republic of China the property acquired in Manchuria from Japanese owners by Soviet economic organizations, and also on the decision of the Soviet Government to transfer without compensation to the Government of the People's Republic of China all the buildings in the former military compound in Peking...

## Soviet–Egyptian Treaty of Friendship and Cooperation, Cairo, 27 May 1971

The Union of Soviet Socialist Republics and the United Arab Republic,

Being firmly convinced that the further development of friendship and all-round cooperation between the Union of Soviet Socialist Republics and the United Arab Republic is responsive to the interests of the peoples of both States and serves the cause of strengthening universal peace,

Being inspired by the ideals of the struggle against imperialism and colonialism, and for the freedom, independence and social progress of peoples,

Being determined to wage persistently the struggle for the consolidation of international peace and security in accordance with the invariable course of their peace-loving foreign policies,

Reaffirming their loyalty to the aims and principles of the United Nations Charter,

And being motivated by the aspiration to strengthen and consolidate the traditional relations of sincere friendship between the two States and peoples by concluding a Treaty on Friendship and Cooperation and thus creating a basis for their further development,

Have agreed on the following:

*Article 1.* The high contracting parties solemnly declare that unbreakable friendship will always exist between the two countries and their peoples. They will continue to develop and strengthen the existing relations of friendship and all-round cooperation between them in the political, economic, scientific, technological, cultural and other fields on the basis of the principles of respect for sovereignty, territorial integrity, non-interference in one another's internal affairs, equality and mutual benefit.

*Article 2.* The Union of Soviet Socialist Republics, as a socialist State, and the United Arab Republic, which has set itself the aim of the socialist reconstruction of society, will cooperate closely and in all fields in ensuring conditions for preserving and further developing the social and economic gains of their peoples.

*Article 3.* Guided by the aspiration to promote in every way the maintenance of international peace and the security of peoples, the Union of Soviet Socialist Republics and the United Arab Republic will continue with the utmost determination to exert efforts toward achieving and ensuring a lasting and just peace in the Middle East in accordance with the aims and principles of the United Nations Charter.

In conducting a peace-loving foreign policy, the high contracting parties will come out in favor of peace, the relaxation of international tension, the achieving of general and complete disarmament and the prohibition of nuclear and other types of weapons of mass destruction.

*Article 4.* Guided by the ideals of the freedom and equality of all peoples, the high contracting parties condemn imperialism and colonialism in all their forms and manifestations. They will continue to come out against imperialism and for the complete and final liquidation of colonialism in pursuance of the U.N. Declaration on the Granting of Independence to All Colonial Countries and Peoples, and will wage an unswerving struggle against racism and apartheid.

*Article 5.* The high contracting parties also will continue to expand and deepen all-round cooperation and the exchange of experience in the economic, scientific and technological fields – in industry, agricul-

ture, water conservation, irrigation, the development of natural resources, the development of power engineering, the training of national cadres, and other branches of the economy.

The two sides will expand trade and maritime shipping between the two States on the basis of the principles of mutual benefit and most-favored-nation treatment.

*Article 6.* The high contracting parties will promote further cooperation between them in the fields of science, the arts, literature, education, public health, the press, radio, television, cinema, tourism, physical education, and other fields.

The parties will promote wider cooperation and direct contacts between political and social organizations of the working people, enterprises and cultural and scientific institutions for the purpose of achieving a deeper mutual acquaintance with the life, work and achievements of the peoples of the two countries.

*Article 7.* Being deeply interested in ensuring peace and the security of peoples and attaching great importance to the concerted nature of their actions in the international arena in the struggle for peace, the high contracting parties will, for this purpose, regularly consult each other at various levels on all important questions affecting the interests of both States.

In the event of situations arising which, in the opinion of both sides, create a danger to peace or a breach of peace, they will contact each other without delay in order to concert their positions with a view to removing the threat that has arisen or restoring peace.

*Article 8.* In the interests of strengthening the defense capability of the United Arab Republic, the high contracting parties will continue to develop cooperation in the military field on the basis of appropriate agreements between them. Such cooperation will provide, in particular, for assistance in the training of U.A.R. military personnel and in mastering the armaments and equipment supplied to the United Arab Republic for the purpose of strengthening its capability in the cause of eliminating the consequences of aggression as well as increasing its ability to stand up to aggression in general.

*Article 9.* Proceeding from the purposes and principles of this Treaty,

Each of the high contracting parties states that it will not enter into alliances or take part in any groupings of States, or in actions or measures directed against the other high contracting party.

*Article 10.* Each of the high contracting parties declares that its obligations under existing international treaties are not in contradiction with the provisions of this Treaty and it undertakes not to enter into any international agreements incompatible with it.

*Article 11.* The present Treaty shall be valid for 15 years from the day it enters into force.

If neither of the high contracting parties announces, a year before the expiry of this term, its desire to terminate the Treaty, it shall remain in force for the next five years and so henceforward, until one of the high contracting parties, a year before the expiry of the current five-year period, gives a written warning of its intention to terminate its validity.

*Article 12.* The present Treaty is subject to ratification and shall enter into force on the day of the exchange of the instruments of ratification, which will take place in Moscow in the very near future.

The present Treaty is done in two copies, each in Russian and Arabic, both texts being equally authentic.

DONE in the city of Cairo on May 27, 1971, which corresponds to 3 Rabia as-Sani, 1913, Hidjra.

[For the Union of Soviet Socialist Republics]
N. Podgornyi

[For the United Arab Republic]
Anwar Sadat

Translation by William E. Butler, © American Society of International Law.

# Treaty of Peace, Friendship and Cooperation between India and the Soviet Union, New Delhi, 9 August 1971

*Desirous* of expanding and consolidating the existing relations of sincere friendship between them,

*Believing* that further development of friendship and cooperation meets the basic national interests of both States as well as the interests of lasting peace in Asia and the World,

*Determined* to promote the consolidation of universal peace and security and to make steadfast efforts for the relaxation of international tensions and final elimination of the remnants of colonialism,

*Upholding* their firm faith in the principles of peaceful coexistence and cooperation between States with different political and social systems,

*Convinced* that in the world today inter-national problems can only be solved by cooperation and not by conflict,

*Reaffirming* their determination to abide by the purposes and the principles of the United Nations Charter,

The Republic of India on one side and the Union of Soviet Socialist Republics on the other side, have decided to conclude the present Treaty, for which purpose the following plenipotentiaries have been appointed:

[On behalf of the Republic of India]
Sardar Swaran Singh, Minister of External Affairs.

[On behalf of the Union of Soviet Socialist Republics]

Mr. A. Gromyko, Minister of Foreign Affairs,

who having each presented their credentials, which are found to be in proper form and due order, have agreed as follows.

*Article 1.* The High Contracting Parties solemnly declare that enduring peace and friendship shall prevail between the two countries and their peoples. Each Party shall respect the independence, sovereignty and territorial integrity of the other Party and refrain from interfering in the other's internal affairs. The High Contracting Parties shall continue to develop and consolidate relations of sincere friendship, good neighbourliness and comprehensive cooperation existing between them on the basis of the aforesaid principles as well as those of equality and mutual benefit.

*Article 2.* Guided by a desire to contribute in every possible way to ensure an enduring peace and security of their people, the High Contracting Parties declare their determination to continue their efforts to preserve and to strengthen peace in Asia and throughout the world, to halt the arms race and to achieve a general and complete disarmament, including both nuclear and conventional, under effective international control.

*Article 3.* Guided by their loyalty to the lofty ideal of equality of all peoples and nations, irrespective of race or creed, the High Contracting Parties condemn colonialism and racialism in all forms and manifestations and reaffirm their determination to strive for their final and complete elimination.

The High Contracting Parties shall cooperate with other States to achieve these aims and to support just aspirations of the peoples in their struggle against colonialism and racial domination.

*Article 4.* The Republic of India respects the peace-loving policy of the Union of Soviet Socialist Republics aimed at strengthening friendship and cooperation with all nations.

The Union of Soviet Socialist Republics respects India's policy of non-alignment and reaffirms that this policy constitutes an important factor in the maintenance of universal peace and international security and in lessening of tensions in the world.

*Article 5.* Deeply interested in ensuring universal peace and security, attaching great importance to their mutual cooperation in the international field for achieving these aims, the High Contracting Parties will maintain regular contacts with each other on major international problems affecting the interests of both States by means of meetings and exchanges of views between their leading statesmen, visits by official delegations and special envoys of the two Governments and through diplomatic channels.

. . .

[*Article 6.* Expansion of trade relations etc.

*Article 7.* Expansion of scientific and cultural relations etc.]

*Article 8.* In accordance with the traditional friendship established between the two countries, each of the High Contracting Parties solemnly declares that it shall not enter into or participate in any military alliance directed against the other Party.

Each High Contracting Party undertakes to abstain from any aggression against the other Party and to prevent the use of its territory for the commission of any act which might inflict military damage on the other High Contracting Party.

*Article 9.* Each High Contracting Party undertakes to abstain from providing any assistance to any third party that engages in armed conflict with the other Party. In the event of either Party being subjected to an attack or a threat thereof, the High Contracting Parties shall immediately enter into mutual consultations in order to remove such a threat and to take appropriate effective measures to ensure peace and security of their countries.

*Article 10.* Each High Contracting Party solemnly declares that it shall not enter into any obligation secret or public with one or more States which is incompatible with this Treaty. Each High Contracting Party further declares that no obligation exists nor shall any obligation be entered into between itself and any other State or States which might cause military damage to the other Party.

*Article 11.* This Treaty is concluded for a duration of twenty years and will be automatically extended for each successive period of five years unless either High Contracting Party declares its desire to terminate it by giving a notice to the other High Contracting Party twelve months prior to expiration of the Treaty. The Treaty will be subject to ratification and will come into force on the date of exchange of Instruments of Ratification which will take place in Moscow within one month of the signing of this Treaty

. . .

# Treaty of Friendship and Cooperation between the Soviet Union and Vietnam, Moscow, 3 November 1978

The Socialist Republic of Viet Nam and the Union of Soviet Socialist Republics,

Proceeding from the close cooperation in all fields in a fraternal spirit, from the unshakable friendship and solidarity between the two countries on the basis of the principles of Marxism–Leninism and socialist internationalism,

Firmly convinced that the endeavour to consolidate the solidarity and friendship between the Socialist Republic of Viet Nam and the Union of Soviet Socialist Republics is in conformity with the basic interests of the two peoples and in the interests of the consolidation of the fraternal friendship and one-mindedness among the countries in the socialist community,

In keeping with the principles and objectives of the socialist foreign policy and the desire to ensure the most favourable international conditions for the building of socialism and communism,

Confirming that the signatories to the Treaty acknowledge their international obligation to assist each other in the consolidation and preservation of the socialist achievements recorded by the two peoples through their heroic efforts and selfless labour,

Determined to work for the unity of all forces struggling for peace, national independence, democracy and social progress,

Expressing their iron-like determination to contribute to the consolidation of peace in Asia and throughout the world, and to the development of good relations and mutually beneficial cooperation among countries with different social systems,

Hoping to develop further and perfect the all-round cooperation between the two countries,

Attaching importance to the continued development and consolidation of the juridical basis of the bilateral relations,

In keeping with the objectives and principles of the United Nations Charter,

Have resolved to sign this Treaty of Friendship and Cooperation and have agreed as follows:

*Article 1.* In keeping with the principles of socialist internationalism, the two parties signatory to the present Treaty shall continue to consolidate the unshakable friendship and solidarity and assist each other in a fraternal spirit. The two parties shall unceasingly develop political relations and cooperation in all fields and endeavour to assist each other on the basis of respect for each other's national independence and sovereignty, equality and non-interference in each other's internal affairs.

*Article 2.* The two parties signatory to the present Treaty shall join efforts to consolidate and broaden the mutually beneficial cooperation in the economic and scientific–technological fields in order to push forward the building of socialism and communism and to raise constantly the material and cultural standards of the two peoples. The two parties shall continue to coordinate their long-term national economic plans, agree upon long-term measures aimed at developing the most important sectors of the economy, science and technology, and exchange knowledge and experience accumulated in the building of socialism and communism.

*Article 3.* The two parties signatory to the Treaty shall promote cooperation between their State bodies and mass organizations, and develop broad relations in the fields of science and culture, education, literature and art, press, broadcasting and television, health service, environmental protection, tourism, sports and physical training and others. The two parties shall encourage the development of contacts between the working people of the two countries.

*Article 4.* The two parties signatory to the Treaty shall consistently strive further to consolidate their fraternal relations, and to strengthen the solidarity and one-mindedness among the socialist countries on the basis of Marxism–Leninism and socialist internationalism.

The two parties shall do their utmost to consolidate the world socialist system and actively contribute to the development and defence of the socialist gains.

*Article 5.* The two parties signatory to the Treaty shall continue doing their utmost to contribute to defending world peace and the security of all nations. They shall actively oppose all schemes and manoeuvres of imperialism and reactionary forces, support the just struggle for the complete eradication of all forms and colours of colonialism and racism, support the struggle waged by non-aligned countries and the peoples of Asian, African and Latin American coun-

tries against imperialism, colonialism and neo-colonialism, for the consolidation of independence and the defence of sovereignty, for mastery over their natural resources, and for the establishment of a new world economic relationship with no inequity, oppression and exploitation, and support the aspirations of the Southeast Asian peoples for peace, independence and cooperation among countries in this region.

The two parties shall strive to develop the relations between countries with different social systems on the basis of the principles of peaceful coexistence, for the purpose of broadening and consolidating the process of easing tension in international relations and radically eliminating aggressions and wars of aggression from the life of all nations, for the sake of peace, national independence, democracy and socialism.

*Article 6.* The two parties signatory to the Treaty shall exchange views on all important international questions relating to the interests of the two countries. In case either party is attacked or threatened with attack, the two parties signatory to the Treaty shall immediately consult each other with a view to eliminating that threat, and shall take appropriate and effective measures to safeguard peace and the security of the two countries.

*Article 7.* The present Treaty does not concern the two parties' rights and obligations stemming from the bilateral or multilateral agreements to which they are signatories and is not intended to oppose any third country.

*Article 8.* The present Treaty shall be ratified and shall enter into force on the date of the exchange of instruments of ratification, which shall take place in Ha Noi as early as possible.

*Article 9.* The present Treaty shall remain in force for 25 years and thereafter shall be automatically extended for periods of 10 years if neither signatory party declares its desire to terminate the present Treaty by informing the other party 12 months before the Treaty expires.

Done in duplicate in the Vietnamese and Russian languages, both texts being equally authentic, in Moscow, this third day of November 1978.

FOR THE SOCIALIST REPUBLIC OF VIET NAM: [Signed] Le Duan
　　　　　Pham Van Dong

FOR THE UNION OF SOVIET SOCIALIST REPUBLICS:
[Signed] L.I. Brezhnev
　　　　　A.N. Kosygin

# Treaty of Friendship, Goodneighbourliness and Cooperation between the Soviet Union and Afghanistan, Moscow, 5 December 1978

The Union of Soviet Socialist Republics and
The Democratic Republic of Afghanistan,

Reaffirming their commitment to the aims and principles of the Soviet–Afghan Treaties of 1921 and 1931, which laid the basis for friendly and good neighbour relations between the Soviet and Afghan peoples and which meet their basic national interests,

Willing to strengthen in every way friendship and all-round cooperation between the two countries,

Being determined to develop social and economic achievements of the Soviet and Afghan peoples, to safeguard their security and independence, to come out resolutely for the cohesion of all the forces fighting for peace, national independence, democracy and social progress,

Expressing their firm determination to facilitate the strengthening of peace and security in Asia and the whole world, to make their contribution toward developing relations among states and strengthening fruitful and mutually beneficial cooperation in Asia, attaching great importance to the further consolidation of the contractual–legal basis of their relations,

Reaffirming their dedication to the aims and principles of the United Nations Charter,

Decided to conclude the present Treaty of Friendship, Goodneighbourliness and Cooperation and agreed on the following:

*Article 1.* The High Contracting Parties solemnly declare their determination to strengthen and deepen the inviolable friendship between the two countries and to develop all-round cooperation on the basis of equality, respect for national sovereignty, territorial integrity and non-interference in each other's internal affairs.

*Article 2.* The High Contracting Parties shall make efforts to strengthen and broaden mutually beneficial economic, scientific and technical cooperation between them. With these aims in view, they shall develop and deepen cooperation in the fields of industry, transport and communications, agriculture, the use of natural resources, development of the power-generating industry and other branches of economy, to give each other assistance in the training of national personnel and in planning the development of the national economy. The two sides shall expand trade on the basis of the principles of equality, mutual benefit, and most-favoured-nation treatment.

*Article 3.* The High Contracting Parties shall promote the development of cooperation and exchange of experience in the fields of science, culture, art, literature, education, health services, the press, radio, television, cinema, tourism, sport, and other fields.

The two sides shall facilitate the expansion of cooperation between organs of State power and public organizations, enterprises, cultural and scientific institutions with a view to making a deeper acquaintance of the life, work experience and achievements of the peoples of the two countries.

*Article 4.* The High Contracting Parties, acting in the spirit of the traditions of friendship and goodneighbourliness, as well as the U.N. Charter, shall consult each other and take by agreement appropriate measures to ensure the security, independence, and territorial integrity of the two countries.

In the interests of strengthening the defence capacity of the High Contracting Parties, they shall continue to develop cooperation in the military field on the basis of appropriate agreements concluded between them.

*Article 5.* The Union of Soviet Socialist Republics respects the policy of non-alignment which is pursued by the Democratic Republic of Afghanistan and which is an important factor for maintaining international peace and security.

The Democratic Republic of Afghanistan respects the policy of peace pursued by the Union of Soviet Socialist Republics and aimed at strengthening friendship and cooperation with all countries and peoples.

*Article 6.* Each of the High Contracting Parties solemnly declares that it shall not join any military or other alliances or take part in any groupings of States, as well as in actions or measures directed against the other High Contracting Party.

*Article 7.* The High Contracting Parties shall continue to make every effort to defend international peace and the security of the peoples, to deepen the process of relaxation of international tension, to spread it to all areas of the world, including Asia, to translate it into concrete forms of mutually beneficial cooperation among States and to settle international disputed issues by peaceful means.

The two sides shall actively contribute toward general and complete disarmament, including nuclear disarmament, under effective international control.

*Article 8.* The High Contracting Parties shall facilitate the development of cooperation among Asian States and the establishment of relations of peace, good-neighbourliness and mutual confidence among them and the creation of an effective security system in Asia on the basis of joint efforts by all countries of the continent.

*Article 9.* The High Contracting Parties shall continue their consistent struggle against machinations by the forces of aggression, for the final elimination of colonialism and racism in all their forms and manifestations.

The two sides shall cooperate with each other and with other peace-loving States in supporting the just struggle of the peoples for their freedom, independence, sovereignty and social progress.

*Article 10.* The High Contracting Parties shall consult each other on all major international issues affecting the interests of the two countries.

*Article 11.* The High Contracting Parties state that their commitments under the existing international treaties do not contradict the provisions of the present Treaty and undertake not to conclude any international agreements incompatible with it.

*Article 12.* Questions which may arise between the High Contracting Parties concerning the interpretation or application of any provision of the present Treaty, shall be settled bilaterally, in the spirit of friendship, mutual understanding and respect.

*Article 13.* The present Treaty shall remain in force within twenty years of the day it becomes effective.

Unless one of the High Contracting Parties declares six months before the expiration of this term its desire to terminate the Treaty, it shall remain in force for the next five years until one of the High Contracting Parties warns in writing the other Party, six months before the expiration of the current five-year term, about its intention to terminate the Treaty.

*Article 14.* If one of the High Contracting Parties expresses the wish in the course of the twenty-year term of the Treaty to terminate it before its expiration date, it shall notify in writing the other Party, six months before its suggested date of expiration of the Treaty, about its desire to terminate the Treaty before the expiration of the term and may consider the Treaty terminated as of the date thus set.

*Article 15.* The present Treaty shall be ratified and take effect on the day of exchange of the instruments of ratification, which is to take place in Kabul.

Done in duplicate, each in the Russian and Dari languages, both texts being equally authentic.

Done in Moscow on December 5, 1978.

[For the Union of Soviet Socialist Republics]
L. Brezhnev

[For the Democratic Republic of Afghanistan]
N. Mohammad Tarakki

# *Treaty of Friendship and Cooperation between the Soviet Union and South Yemen, Moscow, 25 October 1979*

The Union of Soviet Socialist Republics and the People's Democratic Republic of Yemen,

Considering that the further development and strengthening of the relations of friendship and all-round cooperation which have been formed between them meet the basic national interest of the peoples of both countries and serve the cause of consolidating peace and security in the entire world,

Moved by the aspiration to promote in every possible way the development of peaceful relations between states and fruitful international cooperation,

Formally resolve to develop the socio-economic achievements of the peoples of the U.S.S.R. and the P.D.R.Y., and to support the unity and cooperation of all the forces which struggle for peace and national independence, democracy, and social progress.

Inspired by the ideals of the struggle against imperialism, colonialism, and racism in all their forms and manifestations,

Confirming their loyalty to the purposes and principles of the United Nations Charter, including the principles of respect for sovereignty, territorial integrity, and non-interference in internal affairs,

Desiring to develop and strengthen existing relations of friendship and cooperation between both countries,
have agreed on the following:

*Article 1.* The High Contracting Parties solemnly declare their resolve to strengthen the indestructible friendship between both countries, steadfastly develop political relations and all-round cooperation on the basis of equality, respect for national sovereignty, territorial integrity, and non-interference in each other's internal affairs.

*Article 2.* The High Contracting Parties will cooperate closely and comprehensively to ensure conditions for the preservation and further development of the socio-economic conquests of their peoples and respect for sovereignty by each of them over all their natural resources.

*Article 3.* The High Contracting Parties will undertake efforts to strengthen and expand mutually advantageous economic and scientific technical cooperation between them. To this end the parties will develop and deepen cooperation in the domain of industry, agriculture, fisheries, the use of natural resources, planning the development of the national economy, and any other branches of the economy, as well as in the training of national cadres. The parties will expand trade and navigation on the basis of principles of equality, mutual advantage, and most-favored-nation terms.

*Article 4.* The High Contracting Parties will promote the development of cooperation and the exchange of experience in the domains of science, culture, art, literature, education, public health, the press, radio, television, the cinema, tourism, sport, and other domains.

The parties will promote the development of contacts and cooperation between agencies of state power, trade union, and other social organizations, and also the expansion of direct links between enterprises and cultural and scientific institutions for the purpose of a deeper familiarity with the life, labor, experience, and achievements of the peoples of both countries. The parties will stimulate the development of contacts between the working people of both countries.

*Article 5.* The High Contracting Parties will continue to develop cooperation in the military sphere on the basis of the respective agreements concluded between them in the interests of strengthening their defense capability.

*Article 6.* The Union of Soviet Socialist Republics shall respect the policy of non-alignment conducted by the People's Democratic Republic of Yemen, which is an important factor in the development of international cooperation and peaceful co-existence.

The People's Democratic Republic of Yemen shall respect the peace-loving foreign policy being conducted by the Union of Soviet Socialist Republics, which is directed toward strengthening friendship and cooperation of all countries and peoples.

*Article 7.* The High Contracting Parties will make every effort to defend international peace and the security of peoples, to deepen the reduction of international tension, to extend it to all areas of the world, to embody it in specific forms of mutually advantageous cooperation between states, to settle controversial international questions by peaceful means in order to transform the principle of the non-use of force into an actual law of international life and to eradicate from the practice of international relations any manifestations of the policy of hegemony and expansionism. The parties will actively promote the cause of general and complete disarmament, including nuclear, under effective international control.

*Article 8.* The High Contracting Parties will continue the active struggle against the intrigues of imperialism and for the final elimination of colonialism and racism in all their forms and manifestations.

The parties will cooperate with one another and with other peace-loving states in support of the just struggle of peoples for their freedom, independence, sovereignty and social progress.

*Article 9.* The High Contracting Parties will promote in every possible way the ensuring of a firm and just peace in the Near East and the achievement for this purpose of a comprehensive Near Eastern settlement.

*Article 10.* The High Contracting Parties will promote the development of cooperation among Asian States and the establishment among them of relations of peace, goodneighborliness and mutual trust, and the creation of an effective security system in Asia on the basis of the joint efforts of all States of this continent.

*Article 11.* The High Contracting Parties will consult with one another on important international questions directly affecting the interests of both countries.

In the event situations arise which create a threat to the peace or a breach of international peace, the parties will endeavor to be in contact immediately with one another for the purpose of coordinating their position in the interests of eliminating the threat which arose or the restoration of peace.

*Article 12.* Each of the High Contracting Parties solemnly declares that it will not enter into military or other alliances nor take part in any groupings of States nor any actions or measures directed against the other High Contracting Party.

. . .

*Article 15.* The present Treaty will be valid for 20 years from the date of its entry into force.

. . .

Translation by William E. Butler, © American Society of International Law.

# IV · The German question

The German question was the greatest and most intractable issue to bedevil East–West relations during the quarter century after the end of the Second World War. The collapse of the Grand Alliance and its transformation into bitter enmity was symbolized by the failure of the erstwhile allies to agree on the terms of a peace treaty with their chief common enemy, Germany. Thus, in spite of the total defeat of the Third Reich in May 1945, no peace treaty was ever signed. Instead, in a succession of crises, most notably in 1948, 1958, and 1961, Berlin, the former capital of a united Germany, became a flashpoint highlighting the division of the country. Although Russian and Western forces did not engage in hostilities at any stage, the Berlin crises, and the larger question of the future political shape of Germany, repeatedly heightened East–West tension. Only in the early 1970s did the U.S.S.R. and the Western powers, as well as the two German States and States bordering on Germany, sign a series of agreements, amounting to a pragmatic acceptance of the status quo of a Germany bifurcated into a communist east (the German Democratic Republic) and a non-communist west (the Federal Republic of Germany).

## The division of Germany and the three Berlin crises

The frontiers of the Federal Republic of Germany and the German Democratic Republic have their origins in Allied decisions reached in 1944 before the end of the war, and in the actions of the Allies jointly and individually in 1945. The Moscow Conference in October 1943 had set up the European Advisory Commission, which prepared draft agreements delimiting the three zones of Germany respectively to be occupied by the U.S.S.R., the United States and Great Britain. The commission also proposed three zones of occupation for Greater Berlin, which was treated separately. To have allowed one Power (and geography would have decreed that this must be the U.S.S.R.) the sole right to occupy the capital would, in the view of the other two Powers, have allowed too much weight and prestige in Germany as a whole to the U.S.S.R. In these original agreements, based on the proposals of the European Advisory Commission dated 12 September 1944 and amended and made more specific in a supplementary agreement on 14 November 1944, the occupying forces of each zone were placed under the authority of a Commander-in-Chief of the country occupying the zone. Berlin was placed under the joint control of an Allied governing authority composed of three Commandants appointed by their respective Commanders-in-Chief. This distinction remains an important fact relating to the status of Berlin.

The Yalta Conference in February 1945 (p. 27) confirmed and expanded the agreements reached by the European Advisory Commission. The Russian, British and American zones of Germany, and the joint control and individual zones of the three Powers in Berlin, were agreed upon. Agreement was reached on inviting France to become the fourth occupying Power of Germany with equal rights. The French zone was to be formed out of the British and American zones. The Russian zone extended to the eastern frontiers of Germany of 31 December 1931. The Yalta Agreement, however, envisaged that territory of eastern Germany would be transferred to Poland: 'The three Heads of Government. . . recognize that Poland must receive substantial accessions of territory in the North and West. They feel that the opinion of the new Polish Provisional Government of National Unity should be sought in due course on the extent of these accessions and that the final delimitation of the western frontier of Poland should thereafter await the peace conference.' At Yalta the establishment of an Allied Control Council for Germany was briefly referred to in connection with inviting French membership.

On 1 June 1945 the Four Powers were still not in occupation of the precise zones assigned to them; when hostilities ended American and British troops held portions of the zone assigned to the U.S.S.R., and the zonal division of Berlin by the Four Powers remained to be completed. On 5 June 1945 the four Commanders-in-Chief met in Berlin and signed a *Four-Power Declaration on the assumption of supreme authority in Germany*

(p. 186), which also set out guidelines for the behaviour of the Germans. But the Soviet Marshal Zhukov rejected the setting up of the Allied Control Council until still unsettled boundaries had been determined (French zone) and the forces of each occupying Power had withdrawn within their zonal boundaries. A joint statement was also issued on 5 June 1945 by the Allies concerning the agreements so far reached on zones of occupation and the administration of Germany. It described the function and composition of the Allied Control Council for Germany, composed of the four Commanders-in-Chief, which was to be paramount in matters affecting Germany as a whole; but the Commanders-in-Chief were the supreme authority, each in his own sphere. Berlin would be administered by the Four Powers jointly, the four appointed Commandants constituting an Allied *Kommandatura* responsible to an Allied Control Council for Greater Berlin. A timetable for effecting the military withdrawals was agreed. The American and British forces were back in their zones and their garrisons in their respective Berlin sectors by 4 July 1945, and on 30 August 1945 the Allied Council proclaimed that it had begun to function. Since each Commander-in-Chief was supreme in his own zone, any disagreement at the Allied Control Council could only have the negative effect of preventing action on 'matters affecting Germany as a whole' without limiting the supreme authority of each Commander-in-Chief in his zone.

In the summer of 1945 a number of important issues remained to be settled. The question of U.S., British and French access to their three sectors in Berlin, embedded as they were in the Soviet zone of Germany, was first resolved in a preliminary way at a conference between the Allied Commanders in Berlin on 29 June 1945, which guaranteed the use of one main rail line, one highway and two air corridors to the three Western Powers. At meetings of the Allied Control Council these agreements were finalized and approved. A few months later, on 30 November, the Allied Control Council provided three air corridors (in place of two) between Berlin and the British and American zones, and it was specifically stated that 'flight over these routes (corridors) will be conducted without previous notice being given, by aircraft of the nations governing Germany'. An Allied Berlin Air Safety Centre was established to ensure the safety of all flights in the Berlin area. These rights of access derived from the arrangement for joint occupation and joint control of 'Greater Berlin' which France, Britain and the United States have continued to maintain.

The eastern frontier of Germany (western frontier of Poland) was one of the principal issues of the Potsdam Conference of July 1945 (p. 32). By the time the leaders of the Big Three, the U.S., U.S.S.R., and Great Britain, attended the conference, the Red Army was in occupation of the whole of its German zone of occupation, as defined in inter-Allied agreements before Yalta and confirmed at the Yalta Conference; but the Soviet authorities had already handed a part of their zone over to the Poles in unilateral fulfilment of the general promise made at Yalta that Poland 'must receive substantial accessions of territory'. The *fait accompli* was partially accepted in section VIII of the Potsdam Conference Protocol. The German territories were not annexed and did not formally become a part of Poland since the Protocol stated 'that the final delimitation of the western frontier of Poland should await the peace settlement'; the extent of German territory handed over to Poland was agreed at Potsdam, and this territory was placed 'under the administration of the Polish State'; it was separated from the rest of Germany by a specific statement that it did not form part of the Soviet zone of occupation. The present frontier between the German Democratic Republic and Poland corresponds to the Potsdam provisional delimitation; the relevant Potsdam section VIII did not mention the German town of Stettin which lies *west* of the Oder, but an earlier Western memorandum had specifically included Stettin as falling into Polish-administered territory, and it is now Polish Szczecin.

The western frontier of the present Federal Republic of Germany also corresponds to the western zonal boundaries that Britain and the United States confirmed at Yalta and Potsdam, with some minor adjustments in favour of the Netherlands and Belgium agreed as 'provisional rectifications' in March 1949. More important, the Saar region (a territory larger than the pre-war Saar) was for a time integrated economically with France but given autonomous status by the French from 1947 to 1956. With the adoption of the Schuman Plan in April 1951, which led to the setting up of the High Authority of the European Coal and Steel Community controlling the pooled Franco-German iron and steel production, including that of the Saar, the Saar problem as a cause of Franco-German contention lost some of its significance (p. 209). An agreement between France and Germany, leading to a plebiscite in October 1955 and elections soon after, closed the issue and the Saar region was reunited with the Federal Republic of Germany on 1 January 1957.

The creation of the Federal Republic of Germany as an independent sovereign State came about in a number of stages. The gradual recovery of West German sovereignty was closely bound up both with the 'cold war' situation and the movement towards Western European integration (see

Chapter 5). Disagreements between the four Powers responsible for Germany, especially between the Soviet Union and the Western Allies, were reflected in the inability of the Council of Foreign Ministers during 1946 and 1947 to make any real progress towards a peace settlement for Germany as a whole. The breakdown of inter-Allied control of Germany in 1948 accentuated the different interpretations and applications of Allied agreements in the respective zones of the occupying Powers.

On 30 March 1948 the Russians imposed restrictions on Western access to Berlin by rail. In June they tightened the noose by barring road access from the West. The Western Powers determined to maintain their position in what was now a vulnerable island of Western influence deep within Soviet-controlled territory. Rather than attempt to break the blockade on land (it was feared that such an effort might produce large-scale hostilities), the British and Americans embarked on a massive airlift of food and other essential supplies along the air corridors to Berlin. The Russians gave way and lifted the blockade on 12 May 1949 after 318 days. During the blockade, however, the Soviet authorities set up a separate communist municipal Government in Berlin on 30 November 1948. The unity of the city under joint Allied authority was thus disrupted.

Meanwhile, in June 1948, the U.S.A., Britain and France took the first steps towards the establishment of a unified central Government for the three Western zones of Germany. The Russians undertook parallel measures in the Eastern zone to formalize the pro-communist Government there. The inauguration of the Federal Republic of Germany on 21 September 1949, with Konrad Adenauer as its first Chancellor, was followed on 7 October by the establishment of the German Democratic Republic as its eastern neighbour.

The Soviet desire to legitimize the Older–Neisse line as the eastern frontier of Germany was reflected in the terms of the *Agreement between Poland and the German Democratic Republic of 6 July 1950* (p. 187). This paid tribute to the 'defeat of German fascism by the U.S.S.R.' (note the absence of any reference to Russia's erstwhile allies) and pronounced the Oder–Neisse line 'the inviolable frontier of peace and friendship, which does not divide but unites both nations'.

The death of Stalin in March 1953 aroused hopes in Eastern Europe of relief from the grim tyranny of the Stalinist régimes. But Stalin's successors demonstrated their determination to hold on to the reins of power by sending in Russian forces to crush a rising in East Germany. A conference of the foreign ministers of the U.S.S.R., France, Britain, and the United States took place in Berlin in January 1954 but without reaching any agreement on a solution of the German question. Both Russia and the Western Powers paid lip-service to the objective of a reunified Germany – but each side insisted on a Germany cast in its own image. The reality of a more or less permanently divided Germany now hardened into being: two German States gained formal sovereignty, mutually antagonistic and neither recognizing the other.

*On 23 October 1954, Britain, the United States, France, and the Federal Republic of Germany signed a Protocol on the termination of the occupation régime in western Germany* (p. 188). On 5 May 1955, ten years almost to the day after the defeat of the Third Reich, the Federal Republic became an independent and sovereign State.

The Soviet Union had issued a declaration on 25 March 1954 promising that it would 'establish relations with the German Democratic Republic on the same basis as with other sovereign States'. The declaration specified, however, that the U.S.S.R. would retain in the German Democratic Republic 'those functions which are related to guaranteeing security'. *On 20 September 1955 the U.S.S.R. and the German Democratic Republic signed a treaty* which came into force on 6 October. This recognized the G.D.R. as a sovereign republic – although the United States, Britain, and most other non-communist countries refused to recognize the new State. At the same time the U.S.S.R. established diplomatic relations with West Germany.

A solution of one peripheral aspect of the German question, namely Austria, was found in the same year. The Four-Power occupation administration was ended by the *Austrian State Treaty, 15 May 1955* (p. 189). All foreign troops were to be withdrawn and Austria regained the independence she had lost at the time of the *Anschluss* in 1938. A democratic constitution was to be established and the country neutralized. As after the First World War, Austria was forbidden to rejoin a pan-German State. This treaty, the only occasion after the Second World War on which the U.S.S.R. agreed to withdraw troops in Europe and permit the establishment of democratic institutions in territory thus vacated, seemed to promise further progress towards a resolution of the German problem. Any such expectations were soon dashed.

In November 1958 a renewed crisis loomed over Berlin, when the Soviet Prime Minister, Nikita Khrushchev, precipitately demanded that Western occupation forces withdraw from Berlin. Western forces stayed put, however, and after a period of high tension the crisis waned.

But the anomalous situation in Berlin remained a potentially explosive powder keg, as was shown three years later in the third and last major

Berlin crisis. On 13 August 1961 the East German authorities began construction of a fortified wall sealing off East from West Berlin. The purpose of this action was to prevent the massive drain of population through this chink in the iron curtain (more than three million people had left East Germany for the West prior to the erection of the wall). The flow to the West was abruptly halted. Bloody scenes at the wall, when East German border guards shot and sometimes killed would-be escapers, aroused bitter indignation in the West. But the Western Powers took no effective retaliatory action in response to the building of the Berlin wall. In the long run, the building of the wall ultimately stabilized the status quo in Berlin and confirmed the survival of the German Democratic Republic as a separate State, although the West withheld recognition until the 1970s.

The *Soviet–East German Treaty of 12 June 1964* (p. 190) marked a further effort by the U.S.S.R. to consolidate the existing position in Germany. The treaty evoked a statement by France, Britain and the United States on 26 June 1964 commenting on the 'agreement signed by the Soviet Union and the so-called "German Democratic Republic"'. The three Western powers insisted that the treaty did not affect the validity of existing agreements, particularly those under which the Soviet Union was bound regarding Berlin. The statement rejected Article 6 of the treaty in which West Berlin had been declared to be an 'independent political unit'. And the three Powers reiterated that they did not recognize the G.D.R., asserting that a 'final determination of the frontiers of Germany must await a peace settlement for the whole of Germany'. (The G.D.R.– U.S.S.R. Treaty of 1964 was replaced in October 1975 by a similar treaty containing a stronger mutual military assistance clause.)

After 1964 the German problem congealed until the end of the 1960s. The election in West Germany in 1969 which brought to power a Government headed by the Social Democrat Willy Brandt, marked a turning-point. Brandt's policy of *Ostpolitik* (cautiously introduced during his period of office as Foreign Minister from 1966 to 1969) represented a new departure from the sterile policies of non-recognition of existing realities pursued in Bonn for the previous two decades. In the new international atmosphere of *détente* (see Chapter 10), the readiness of the Brandt Government to explore openings in the East led to accelerating progress towards a solution of the German problem.

## Statement by the Governments of the United States of America, the United Kingdom, the Union of Soviet Socialist Republics, and the Provisional Government of the French Republic on zones of occupation in Germany, 5 June 1945

1. Germany, within her frontiers as they were on 31 December 1937, will, for the purposes of occupation, be divided into four zones, one to be allotted to each Power as follows:

an eastern zone to the Union of Soviet Socialist Republics;
a north-western zone to the United Kingdom;
a south-western zone to the United States of America;
a western zone to France.

The occupying forces in each zone will be under a Commander-in-Chief designated by the responsible Power. Each of the Four Powers may, at its discretion, include among the forces assigned to occupation duties under the command of its Commander-in-Chief, auxiliary contingents from the forces of any other Allied Power which has actively participated in military operations against Germany.

2. The area of 'Greater Berlin' will be occupied by forces of each of the Four Powers. An Inter-Allied Governing Authority (in Russian, *Komendatura*) consisting of four Commandants, appointed by their respective Commanders-in-Chief, will be established to direct jointly its administration.

## Statement by the Governments of the United States of America, the United Kingdom, the Union of Soviet Socialist Republics, and the Provisional Government of the French Republic on control machinery in Germany, 5 June 1945

. . .

In the period when Germany is carrying out the basic requirements of unconditional surrender, supreme authority in Germany will be exercised, on instructions from their Governments, by the British, United States, Soviet and French Commanders-in-Chief, each in his own zone of occupation, and also jointly, in matters affecting Germany as a whole. The four Commanders-in-Chief will together constitute the Control Council. Each Commander-in-Chief will be assisted by a Political Adviser.

2. The Control Council, whose decisions shall be unanimous, will ensure appropriate uniformity of action by the Commanders-in-Chief in their respective zones of occupation and will reach agreed decisions on the chief questions affecting Germany as a whole.

3. Under the Control Council there will be a permanent Coordinating Committee composed of one representative of each of the four Commanders-in-Chief, and a Control Staff organized in the following Divisions (which are subject to adjustment in the light of experience):

Military; Naval; Air; Transport; Political; Economic; Finance; Reparation, Deliveries and Restitution; Internal Affairs and Communications; Legal; Prisoners of War and Displaced Persons; Manpower. There will be four heads of each Division, one designated by each Power. The staffs of the Divisions may include civilian as well as military personnel, and may also in special cases include nationals of other United Nations appointed in a personal capacity.

4. The functions of the Coordinating Committee and of the Control Staff will be to advise the Control Council, to carry out the Council's decisions and to transmit them to the appropriate German organs, and to supervise and control the day-to-day activities of the latter.

5. Liaison with the other United Nations Governments chiefly interested will be established through the appointment by such Governments of military missions (which may include civilian members) to the Control Council. These missions will have access through the appropriate channels to the organs of control.

6. United Nations organizations will, if admitted by the Control Council to operate in Germany, be subordinate to the Allied control machinery and answerable to it.

7. The administration of the 'Greater Berlin' area will be directed by an Inter-Allied Governing Authority, which will operate under the general direction of the Control Council, and will consist of four Commandants, each of whom will serve in rotation as Chief Commandant. They will be assisted by a technical staff which will supervise and control the activities of the local German organs.

8. The arrangements outlined above will operate during the period of occupation following German surrender, when Germany is carrying out the basic requirements of unconditional surrender. Arrangements for the subsequent period will be the subject of a separate agreement.

## Agreement between Poland and the German Democratic Republic, 6 July 1950

The President of the Republic of Poland and the President of the Democratic Republic of Germany,

Desirous of proving their will to consolidate universal peace and wishing to contribute their share to the great work of harmonious cooperation carried on by peace-loving nations,

Considering that this cooperation between the Polish people and the German people has become possible, thanks to the defeat of German fascism by the U.S.S.R. and to the progressive development of democratic forces in Germany, and

Wishing to create — after the tragic experiences of Hitlerism — unshakeable foundations for a peaceful and good-neighbour relationship between the two nations,

Wishing to stabilize and strengthen mutual relations on the basis of the Potsdam Agreement, which established the frontiers along the Odra and Nysa Luzycka rivers,

Executing the decisions contained in the Warsaw Declaration by the Government of the Republic of Poland and the Delegation of the Provisional Government of the Democratic Republic of Germany on June 6, 1950,

Recognizing the established and existing frontier as the inviolable frontier of peace and friendship, which does not divide but unites both nations. . . .

*Article 1.* The High Contracting Parties jointly declare that the established and existing frontier running from the Baltic Sea along the line west of Swinoujscie and along the Odra river to the place where the Nysa Luzycka river flows into the Odra river and then along the Nysa Luzycka river to the Czechoslovak frontier, constitutes the State frontier between Poland and Germany.

[*Articles 2–7* concern Demarcation Commission, airspace and ratification.]

# Protocol between Britain, the United States, France, and the Federal Republic of Germany on the termination of the occupation régime, Paris, 23 October 1954

The United States of America, the United Kingdom of Great Britain and Northern Ireland, the French Republic and the Federal Republic of Germany agree as follows:

*Article 1.* The Convention on Relations between the Three Powers and the Federal Republic of Germany, the Convention on the Rights and Obligations of Foreign Forces and their Members in the Federal Republic of Germany, the Finance Convention, the Convention on the Settlement of Matters arising out of the War and the Occupation, signed at Bonn on 26 May 1952, the Protocol signed at Bonn on 27 June 1952 to correct certain textual errors in the aforementioned Conventions, and the Agreement on the Tax Treatment of the Forces and their Members signed at Bonn on 26 May 1952, as amended by the Protocol signed at Bonn on 26 July 1952, shall be amended in accordance with the five Schedules to the present Protocol and as so amended shall enter into force (together with subsidiary documents agreed by the signatory States relating to any of the aforementioned instruments) simultaneously with it.

*Article 2.* Pending the entry into force of the arrangements for the German Defence Contribution, the following provisions shall apply:
1. The rights heretofore held or exercised by the United States of America, the United Kingdom of Great Britain and Northern Ireland and the French Republic relating to the fields of disarmament and demilitarization shall be retained and exercised by them, and nothing in any of the instruments mentioned in Article 1 of the present Protocol shall authorize the enactment, amendment, repeal or deprivation of effect of legislation or, subject to the provisions of paragraph 2 of this Article, executive action in those fields by any other authority.
2. On the entry into force of the present Protocol, the Military Security Board shall be abolished (without prejudice to the validity of any action or decisions taken by it) and the controls in the fields of disarmament and demilitarization shall thereafter be applied by a Joint Four-Power Commission to which each of the signatory States shall appoint one representative and which shall take its decisions by majority vote of the four members.
3. The Governments of the signatory States will conclude an administrative agreement which shall provide, in conformity with the provisions of this Article, for the establishment of the Joint Four-Power Commission and its staff and for the organization of its work.

*Article 3.* 1. The present Protocol shall be

ratified or approved by the signatory States in accordance with their respective constitutional procedures. The Instruments of Ratification or Approval shall be deposited by the signatory States with the Government of the Federal Republic of Germany.

2. The present Protocol and subsidiary documents relating to it agreed between the signatory States shall enter into force upon the deposit by all the signatory States of the instruments of ratification or approval as provided in paragraph 1 of this Article.

3. The present Protocol shall be deposited in the Archives of the Government of the Federal Republic of Germany, which will furnish each signatory State with certified copies thereof and notify each State of the date of entry into force of the present Protocol.

[Signed] Dulles, Eden, Mendès-France, Adenauer.

# Austrian State Treaty, Vienna, 15 May 1955

...Whereas on 13th March 1938, Hitlerite Germany annexed Austria by force and incorporated its territory in the German Reich;

Whereas in the Moscow Declaration published on 1st November 1943 the Governments of the Union of Soviet Socialist Republics, the United Kingdom and the United States of America declared that they regarded the annexation of Austria by Germany on 13th March 1938 as null and void and affirmed their wish to see Austria re-established as a free and independent State, and the French Committee of National Liberation made a similar declaration on 16th November 1943...

## Part I · Political and territorial clauses

*Article 1. Re-establishment of Austria as a free and independent State.* The Allied and Associated Powers recognize that Austria is re-established as a sovereign, independent and democratic State.

*Article 2. Maintenance of Austria's independence.* The Allied and Associated Powers declare that they will respect the independence and territorial integrity of Austria as established under the present Treaty.

*Article 3. Recognition by Germany of Austrian independence* [to be included in German peace treaty].

*Article 4. Prohibition of Anschluss.* 1. The Allied and Associated Powers declare that political or economic union between Austria and Germany is prohibited. Austria fully recognizes its responsibilities in this matter and shall not enter into political or economic union with Germany in any form whatsoever...[Austria not to promote union by any means whatever].

*Article 5. Frontiers of Austria.* The frontiers of Austria shall be those existing on 1st January 1938.

*Article 6. Human rights* [guarantee of].

*Article 7. Rights of the Slovene and Croat minorities* [guarantee of].

*Article 8. Democratic institutions.* Austria shall have a democratic Government based on elections by secret ballot and shall guarantee to all citizens free, equal and universal suffrage as well as the right to be elected to public office without discrimination as to race, sex, language, religion or political opinion.

*Article 9. Dissolution of Nazi organizations* [measures to be taken].

[*Article 10. Special clauses on legislation.*
1. To liquidate remnants of Nazi régime and re-establish a democratic system.
2. To maintain law of 3 April 1919, concerning the House of Hapsburg-Lorraine.]

[*Article 11.* Austria to recognize all peace treaties between other belligerents of the Second World War.]

## Part II · Military and air clauses

[*Articles 12–16.* Restriction on possession of weapons including prohibition of nuclear weapons; restrictions on former Nazis serving in armed services. Austria to cooperate in preventing German re-armament.]

*Article 17. Duration of limitations.* Each of the military and air clauses of the present Treaty shall remain in force until modified in whole or in part by agreement between the Allied and Associated Powers and Austria or, after Austria becomes a member of the United Nations, by agreement between the Security Council and Austria.

[*Article 18. Repatriation of prisoners of war.*]

[*Article 19. Maintenance of war graves.*]

## Part III

*Article 20. Withdrawal of Allied forces.* ...The forces of the Allied and Associated Powers and members of the Allied Commission for Austria shall be with-drawn from Austria within ninety days from the coming into force of the present Treaty, and in so far as possible not later than 31st December 1955....

## Part IV · Claims arising out of the war.

*Article 21. Reparation.* No reparation shall be exacted from Austria arising out of the existence of a state of war in Europe after 1st September 1939.

*Article 22. German assets in Austria.* The Soviet Union, the United Kingdom, the United States of America and France have the right to dispose of all German assets in Austria in accordance with the Protocol of the Berlin Conference of 2nd August 1945.

1. The Soviet Union shall receive for a period of validity of thirty years concessions to oilfields equivalent to 60 per cent of the extraction of oil in Austria for 1947, as well as property rights to all buildings, constructions, equipment, and other property belonging to these oilfields, in accordance with list No. 1 and map No. 1 annexed to the Treaty...[details of other payments to the Soviet Union].

The United Kingdom, the United States of America and France hereby transfer to Austria all property, rights and interests held or claimed by her on behalf of any of them in Austria as former German assets or war booty.

. . .

# Treaty of Friendship, Mutual Assistance and Cooperation between the Soviet Union and the German Democratic Republic (East Germany), Moscow, 12 June 1964

The Union of Soviet Socialist Republics and the German Democratic Republic, guided by the desire to continue to develop and strengthen the fraternal friendship between the Union of Soviet Socialist Republics and the German

Democratic Republic, which is in line with the basic interests of the peoples of both countries and of the socialist community as a whole,

On the basis of the fraternal all-round cooperation which is the cornerstone of the policy determining the relations between both States and which has assumed a still closer and cordial nature after the conclusion of the Treaty on the Relations Between the Union of Soviet Socialist Republics and the German Democratic Republic of September 20, 1955,

Expressing firm intention to contribute to the cause of consolidating peace in Europe and throughout the world and to follow unswervingly a policy of peaceful coexistence of States with different social systems,

Fully determined to unite their efforts in order to counteract effectively – on the basis of the Warsaw Treaty of Friendship, Cooperation and Mutual Assistance of May 14, 1955 – the threat to international security and peace created by the revanchist and militarist forces which are striving for a revision of the results of World War II, and to defend the territorial integrity and sovereignty of both States from any attack,

Being of unanimous opinion that the German Democratic Republic – the first State of workers and peasants in the history of Germany – which has carried into life the principles of the Potsdam Agreement, follows the path of peace and is an important factor for ensuring security in Europe and aversion of the war danger,

Striving to facilitate the conclusion of a German peace treaty and to conduce to the realization of Germany's unity on peaceful and democratic principles,

Guided by the aims and principles of the United Nations Charter, agreed on the following:

*Article 1.* The High Contracting Parties, on the basis of full equality, mutual respect for the State sovereignty, non-interference in internal affairs and the lofty principles of socialist internationalism, implementing the principles of mutual advantage and mutual fraternal assistance, will continue to develop and consolidate the relations of friendship and close cooperation in all spheres.

*Article 2.* In the interests of peace and peaceful future of the peoples, including the German people, the High Contracting Parties will unswervingly work for the elimination of the vestiges of World War II, for conclusion of a German peace treaty and for the normalization of the situation in West Berlin on this basis.

The Sides proceed from the premise that, pending the conclusion of a German peace treaty, the United States of America, Great Britain and France continue to bear their responsibility for the realization on the territory of the Federal Republic of Germany of the demands and commitments jointly assumed by the Governments of four powers under the Potsdam and other international agreements directed towards eradication of German militarism and nazism and towards prevention of German aggression.

*Article 3.* The High Contracting Parties join their efforts directed towards ensuring peace and security in Europe and throughout the world in accordance with the aims and principles of the United Nations Charter. They will take all measures in their power to conduce to the settlement, on the basis of the principles of peaceful coexistence, of the cardinal international problems such as general and complete disarmament, including partial measures facilitating the discontinuation of the arms race and relaxation of international tensions, abolition of colonialism and settlement of territorial and border disputes between States by peaceful means.

*Article 4.* In the face of the existing danger of an aggressive war on the part of the militarist and revanchist forces the High Contracting Parties solemnly declare that the integrity of the State frontiers of the German Democratic Republic is one of the basic factors of European security. They confirm their firm determination jointly to guarantee the inviolability of these frontiers in accordance with the Warsaw Treaty of Friendship, Cooperation and Mutual Assistance.

The High Contracting Parties will also undertake all necessary measures for preventing aggression on the part of the forces of militarism and revanchism which are striving for a revision of the results of the World War II.

*Article 5.* In case one of the High Contracting Parties becomes an object of an armed attack in Europe by some State or a group of States, the other High Contracting Party will render it immediate assistance in accordance with the provisions of the Warsaw Treaty of Friendship, Cooperation and Mutual Assistance.

The Security Council will be informed of the measures taken, in accordance with the provisions of the United Nations Charter. These measures will be discontinued as soon as the Security Council takes measures necessary for restoring and maintaining international peace and security.

*Article 6.* The High Contracting Parties will regard West Berlin as an independent political unit.

*Article 7.* The High Contracting Parties confirm their opinion that in view of the existence of the two sovereign German States – the German Democratic Republic and the Federal Republic of Germany – the creation of a peace-loving democratic united German State can be achieved only through negotiations on an equal footing and agreement between both sovereign German States.

. . .

[For the Union of Soviet Socialist Republics]
Chairman of the Council
of Ministers of the Union
of Soviet Socialist Republics
N. KHRUSHCHEV

[For the German Democratic Republic]
Chairman of the State
Council of the German
Democratic Republic
W. ULBRICHT

## The settlement of the German question

The first tangible fruit of *Ostpolitik* was *the signature in Moscow on 12 August 1970 of a treaty between the Federal Republic of Germany and the Soviet Union* (p. 194). In Article 3 of this treaty the Soviet Union gained its objective of securing acceptance of the territorial status quo, most notably in regard to the Oder–Neisse line. An accompanying letter from the West German Foreign Minister to his Soviet counterpart stressed that the Federal Republic still remained committed to the ultimate objective of German reunification – but this utterance was recognized by all concerned as designed primarily for internal consumption in West Germany.

The Soviet–West German treaty paved the way for the *Treaty between the Federal Republic and Poland, signed on 7 December 1970* (p. 195). The terms were similar to those of the Soviet–German treaty, including an explicit recognition by West Germany of the Oder–Neisse line as Poland's western border.

These two agreements greatly improved the atmosphere and facilitated progress in negotiations, begun by the four occupying Powers in March 1970, concerning the Berlin problem. The *Four-Power Agreement on Berlin, signed on 3 September 1971* (p. 196), crystallized the essence of the status quo in the city, while humanizing some of the arrangements concerning daily life there. The U.S.S.R., France, the United States, and Britain accepted their responsibilities and reaffirmed their joint rights in Berlin as unchanged. The U.S.S.R. declared that transport between the Western sectors of Berlin and the Federal Republic of Germany would be unimpeded. The Western Powers declared that the ties between West Berlin and the Federal Republic would be developed, but that their sectors did not form a constituent part of the Federal Republic and would not be governed by it. It was agreed that a Soviet Consulate-General would be established in West Berlin.

The next stage in this complex round of negotiations was direct discussion between the two German States with a view to implementing the principles laid down in the quadripartite agreement. *On 17 December 1971 the G.D.R. and the Federal Republic signed an agreement on the transit traffic of civilian persons and goods between the Federal Republic and West Berlin. On 20 December 1971* a set of documents received signature constituting an 'Arrangement' between the Government of the G.D.R. and the Senate of West Berlin on facilitating and improving the traffic of travellers and visitors. A further 'arrangement' reached at this time between the G.D.R. and the West Berlin Senate settled the question of enclaves by the exchange of small pieces of territory.

*On 12 May 1972 the G.D.R. and the Federal Republic initialled a treaty on questions relating to surface traffic.* Subsequently, the Federal Republic ratified (on 17 and 19 May respectively) the treaties concluded with the U.S.S.R. in August 1970 and with Poland in December 1970. Following these ratifications the treaty of 12 May 1972 was signed on 26 May; the ratification of this treaty in September 1972 marked the implicit recognition of the G.D.R. by the Federal Republic as a sovereign State capable of signing treaties.

*The Final Protocol of the Quadripartite Agreement on Berlin, signed on 3 June 1972*, noted with satisfaction the conclusion of these various intra-German agreements, and declared that as a result of those agreements the four Governments would immediately regard the Four-Power Berlin Agreement as having entered into force. A common declaration of the four Powers on 9 November 1972 supported the applications of the two German States for membership of the United Nations. The culmination of this cascade of diplomatic documents was the *Treaty on the basis of relations between the German Democratic Republic and the Federal Republic of Germany, signed at Berlin on 21 December 1972* (p. 198). The two Germanies agreed on 14 March 1974 to exchange diplomatic missions; on 4 September 1974 the United States and the G.D.R. agreed to establish diplomatic relations.

Meanwhile *the Federal Republic had normalized its relations with Czechoslovakia by the signature of a treaty in Prague on 11 December 1973* (p. 199). This treaty contained a declaration by the Federal Republic that the Munich Agreement of 29 September 1938 (by which Czechoslovakia had been compelled to yield territory to Germany) was void. Willy Brandt, the architect of all these agreements, felt obliged to resign his office as Federal German Chancellor on 6 May 1974 as the result of a spy scandal. The achievement, however, endured: what amounted, in effect, to the solution of the German problem – and, by extension, of the most important territorial consequences of the Second World War. This was, in all but name, the long-delayed peace settlement in central Europe, and it was enshrined in the *Final Act of the Helsinki Conference on European Security and Cooperation on 1 August 1975* (p. 463).

## Treaty between the Federal Republic of Germany and the Soviet Union, Moscow, 12 August 1970

The High Contracting Parties

*Anxious* to contribute to strengthening peace and security in Europe and the world,

*Convinced* that peaceful cooperation among States on the basis of the purposes and principles of the Charter of the United Nations complies with the ardent desire of nations and the general interests of international peace,

*Appreciating* the fact that the agreed measures previously implemented by them, in particular the conclusion of the Agreement of 13 September 1955 on the Establishment of Diplomatic Relations, have created favourable conditions for new important steps destined to develop further and to strengthen their mutual relations,

*Desiring* to lend expression, in the form of a treaty, to their determination to

improve and extend cooperation between them, including economic relations as well as scientific, technological and cultural contacts, in the interest of both States,

Have agreed as follows:

*Article 1.* The Federal Republic of Germany and the Union of Soviet Socialist Republics consider it an important objective of their policies to maintain international peace and achieve détente.

They affirm their endeavour to further the normalization of the situation in Europe and the development of peaceful relations among all European States, and in so doing proceed from the actual situation existing in this region.

*Article 2.* The Federal Republic of Germany and the Union of Soviet Socialist Republics shall in their mutual relations as well as in matters of ensuring European and international security be guided by the purposes and principles embodied in the Charter of the United Nations. Accordingly they shall settle their disputes exclusively by peaceful means and undertake to refrain from the threat or use of force, pursuant to Article 2 of the Charter of the United Nations, in any matters affecting security in Europe or international security, as well as in their mutual relations.

*Article 3.* In accordance with the foregoing purposes and principles the Federal Republic of Germany and the Union of Soviet Socialist Republics share the realization that peace can only be maintained in Europe if nobody disturbs the present frontiers.

• They undertake to respect without restriction the territorial integrity of all States in Europe within their present frontiers;

• they declare that they have no territorial claims against anybody nor will assert such claims in the future;

• they regard today and shall in future regard the frontiers of all States in Europe as inviolable such as they are on the date of signature of the present Treaty, including the Oder–Neisse line which forms the western frontier of the People's Republic of Poland and the frontier between the Federal Republic of Germany and the German Democratic Republic.

*Article 4.* The present Treaty between the Federal Republic of Germany and the Union of Soviet Socialist Republics shall not affect any bilateral or multilateral treaties or arrangements previously concluded by them.

*Article 5.* [Ratification.]

## Accompanying letter from the West German Foreign Minister, Walter Scheel, to the Soviet Foreign Minister

In connection with today's signature of the Treaty between the Federal Republic of Germany and the Union of Soviet Socialist Republics the Government of the Federal Republic of Germany has the honour to state that this Treaty does not conflict with the political objective of the Federal Republic of Germany to work for a state of peace in Europe in which the German nation will recover its unity in free self-determination.

# Treaty between the Federal Republic of Germany and Poland concerning basis for normalizing relations, Warsaw, 7 December 1970

### The Federal Republic of Germany and the People's Republic of Poland

*Considering* that more than 25 years have passed since the end of the Second World War of which Poland became the first victim and which inflicted great suffering on the nations of Europe,

*Conscious* that in both countries a new generation has meanwhile grown up to whom a peaceful future should be secured,

*Desiring* to establish durable foundations for peaceful coexistence and the development of normal and good relations between them,

*Anxious* to strengthen peace and security in Europe,

*Aware* that the inviolability of frontiers and respect for the territorial integrity and sovereignty of all States in Europe within their present frontiers are a basic condition for peace,

Have agreed as follows:

*Article I.* 1. The Federal Republic of Germany and the People's Republic of Poland state in mutual agreement that the existing boundary line the course of which is laid down in Chapter IX of the Decisions of the Potsdam Conference of 2 August 1945 as running from the Baltic Sea immediately west of Swinemunde, and thence along the Oder River to the confluence of the western Neisse River and along the western Neisse to the Czechoslovak frontier, shall constitute the western State frontier of the People's Republic of Poland.

2. They reaffirm the inviolability of their existing frontiers now and in the future and undertake to respect each other's territorial integrity without restriction.

3. They declare that they have no territorial claims whatsoever against each other and that they will not assert such claims in the future.

*Article II.* 1. The Federal Republic of Germany and the People's Republic of Poland shall in their mutual relations as well as in matters of ensuring European and international security be guided by the purposes and principles embodied in the Charter of the United Nations.

2. Accordingly they shall, pursuant to Articles 1 and 2 of the Charter of the United Nations, settle all their disputes exclusively by peaceful means and refrain from any threat or use of force in matters affecting European and international security and in their mutual relations.

*Article III.* 1. The Federal Republic of Germany and the People's Republic of Poland shall take further steps towards full normalization and a comprehensive development of their mutual relations of which the present Treaty shall form the solid foundation.

2. They agree that a broadening of their cooperation in the sphere of economic, scientific, technological, cultural and other relations is in their mutual interest.

*Article IV.* The present Treaty shall not affect any bilateral or multilateral international arrangements previously concluded by either Contracting Party or concerning them.

*Article V.* [Ratification.]


## Four-Power Agreement on Berlin, Berlin (American Sector), 3 September 1971

The Governments of the United States of America, the French Republic, the Union of Soviet Socialist Republics, and the United Kingdom of Great Britain and Northern Ireland, represented by their Ambassadors, who held a series of meetings in the building formerly occupied by the Allied Control Council in the American Sector of Berlin,

Acting on the basis of their quadripartite rights and responsibilities, and of the corresponding wartime and post-war agreements and decisions of the Four Powers, which are not affected,

Taking into account the existing situation in the relevant area,

Guided by the desire to contribute to practical improvements of the situation,

Without prejudice to their legal positions,

Have agreed on the following:

## Part I

GENERAL PROVISIONS

1. The four Governments will strive to promote the elimination of tension and the prevention of complications in the relevant area.

2. The four Governments, taking into account their obligations under the Charter of the United Nations, agree that there shall be no use or threat of force in the area and that disputes shall be settled solely by peaceful means.

3. The four Governments will mutually respect their individual and joint rights and responsibilities, which remain unchanged.

4. The four Governments agree that, irrespective of the differences in legal views, the situation which has developed in the area, and as it is defined in this Agreement as well as in the other agreements referred to in this Agreement, shall not be changed unilaterally.

## Part II

PROVISIONS RELATING TO THE WESTERN SECTORS OF BERLIN

(a) The Government of the Union of Soviet Socialist Republics declares that transit traffic by road, rail and waterways through the territory of the German Democratic Republic of civilian persons and goods between the Western Sectors of Berlin and the Federal Republic of Germany will be unimpeded; that such traffic will be facilitated so as to take place in the most simple and expeditious manner; and that it will receive preferential treatment.

Detailed arrangements concerning this civilian traffic, as set forth in Annex I, will be agreed by the competent German authorities.

(b) The Governments of the French Republic, the United Kingdom and the United States of America declare that the ties between the Western Sectors of Berlin and the Federal Republic of Germany will be maintained and developed, taking into account that these Sectors continue not to be a constituent part of the Federal Republic of Germany and not to be governed by it.

Detailed arrangements concerning the relationship between the Western Sectors of Berlin and the Federal Republic of Germany are set forth in Annex II.

(c) The Government of the Union of Soviet Socialist Republics declares that communications between the Western Sectors of Berlin and areas bordering on these Sectors and those areas of the German Democratic Republic which do not border on these Sectors will be improved. Permanent residents of the Western Sectors of Berlin will be able to travel to and visit such areas for compassionate, family, religious, cultural or commercial reasons, or as tourists, under conditions comparable to those applying to other persons entering these areas.

The problems of the small enclaves, including Steinstücken, and of other small areas may be solved by exchange of territory.

Detailed arrangements concerning travel, communications and the exchange of territory, as set forth in Annex III, will be agreed by the competent German authorities.

(d) Representation abroad of the interests of the Western Sectors of Berlin and consular activities of the Union of Soviet Socialist Republics in the Western Sectors of Berlin can be exercised as set forth in Annex IV.

## Part III

FINAL PROVISIONS

This Quadripartite Agreement will enter into force on the date specified in a Final Quadripartite Protocol to be concluded when the measures envisaged in Part II of this Quadripartite Agreement and in its Annexes have been agreed.

Done at the building formerly occupied by the Allied Control Council in the American Sector of Berlin, this 3rd day of September, 1971, in four originals, each in the English, French and Russian languages, all texts being equally authentic.

[Four annexes, two agreed minutes, and one final quadripartite protocol were attached to the agreement: these set out the detailed provisions for giving effect to the general principles outlined in the agreement.]

# Treaty on the basis of relations between the Federal Republic of Germany and the German Democratic Republic, East Berlin, 21 December 1972

The High Contracting Parties,

Conscious of their responsibility for the preservation of peace,

Anxious to render a contribution to détente and security in Europe,

Aware that the inviolability of frontiers and respect for the territorial integrity and sovereignty of all States in Europe within their present frontiers are a basic condition for peace,

Recognizing that therefore the two German States have to refrain from the threat or use of force in their relations,

Proceeding from the historical facts and without prejudice to the different views of the Federal Republic of Germany and the German Democratic Republic on fundamental questions, including the national question,

Desirous to create the conditions for cooperation between the Federal Republic of Germany and the German Democratic Republic for the benefit of the people in the two German States,

Have agreed as follows:

*Article 1.* The Federal Republic of Germany and the German Democratic Republic shall develop normal, good-neighbourly relations with each other on the basis of equal rights.

*Article 2.* The Federal Republic of Germany and the German Democratic Republic will be guided by the aims and principles laid down in the United Nations Charter, especially those of the

sovereign equality of all States, respect for their independence, autonomy and territorial integrity, the right of self-determination, the protection of human rights, and non-discrimination.

*Article 3.* In conformity with the United Nations Charter the Federal Republic of Germany and the German Democratic Republic shall settle any disputes between them exclusively by peaceful means and refrain from the threat or use of force.

They reaffirm the inviolability now and in the future of the frontier existing between them and undertake fully to respect each other's territorial integrity.

*Article 4.* The Federal Republic of Germany and the German Democratic Republic proceed on the assumption that neither of the two States can represent the other in the international sphere or act on its behalf.

*Article 5.* The Federal Republic of Germany and the German Democratic Republic shall promote peaceful relations between the European States and contribute to security and cooperation in Europe.

They shall support efforts to reduce forces and arms in Europe without allowing disadvantages to arise for the security of those concerned.

The Federal Republic of Germany and the German Democratic Republic shall support, with the aim of general and complete disarmament under effective international control, efforts serving international security to achieve armaments limitation and disarmament, especially with regard to nuclear weapons and other weapons of mass destruction.

*Article 6.* The Federal Republic of Germany and the German Democratic Republic proceed on the principle that the sovereign jurisdiction of each of the two States is confined to its own territory. They respect each other's independence and autonomy in their internal and external affairs.

*Article 7.* The Federal Republic of Germany and the German Democratic Republic declare their readiness to regulate practical and humanitarian questions in the process of the normalization of their relations. They shall conclude agreements with a view to developing and promoting on the basis of the present Treaty and for their mutual benefit cooperation in the fields of economics, science and technology, transport, judicial relations, posts and telecommunica-

tions, health, culture, sport, environmental protection, and in other fields. The details have been agreed in the Supplementary Protocol.

*Article 8.* The Federal Republic of Germany and the German Democratic Republic shall exchange Permanent Missions. They shall be established at the respective Government's seat.

Practical questions relating to the establishment of the Missions shall be dealt with separately.

[A number of documents were exchanged at the same time as the treaty. These included the supplementary protocol which dealt with the detailed application of Articles 3 and 7 of the treaty. The other documents included correspondence concerning the applications by the two states for membership of the United Nations, correspondence on the reunification of families, and exchanges concerning the improvement of travel and communications facilities between East and West Germany.]

## *Treaty establishing normal relations between the Federal Republic of Germany and Czechoslovakia, Prague, 11 December 1973*

*Preamble.* The Federal of Republic of Germany and the Czechoslovak Socialist Republic,

*In the historic awareness* that the harmonious coexistence of the nations in Europe is a necessity for peace,

*Determined* to put an end once and for all to the disastrous past in their relations, especially in connection with the Second World War which has inflicted immeasurable suffering on the peoples of Europe,

*Recognizing* that the Munich Agreement of 29 September 1938 was imposed on the Czechoslovak Republic by the National

Socialist régime under the threat of force,

*Considering the fact* that a new generation has grown up in both countries which has a right to a secure and peaceful future,

*Intending* to create lasting foundations for the development of good-neighbourly relations,

*Anxious* to strengthen peace and security in Europe,

*Convinced* that peaceful cooperation on the basis of the purposes and principles of the United Nations Charter complies with the wishes of nations and the interests of peace in the world,

Have agreed as follows:

*Article I.* The Federal Republic of Germany and the Czechoslovak Socialist Republic, under the present Treaty, deem the Munich Agreement of 29 September 1938 void with regard to their mutual relations.

*Article II.* 1. The present Treaty shall not affect the legal effects on natural or legal persons of the law as applied in the period between 30 September 1938 and 9 May 1945.

This provision shall exclude the effects of measures which both Contracting Parties deem to be void owing to their incompatibility with the fundamental principles of justice.

2. The present Treaty shall not affect the nationality of living or deceased persons ensuing from the legal system of either of the two Contracting Parties.

3. The present Treaty, together with its declarations on the Munich Agreement, shall not constitute any legal basis for material claims by the Czechoslovak Socialist Republic and its natural and legal persons.

*Article III.* 1. The Federal Republic of Germany and the Czechoslovak Socialist Republic shall in their mutual relations as well as in matters of ensuring European and international security be guided by the purposes and principles embodied in the United Nations Charter.

2. Accordingly they shall, pursuant to Articles 1 and 2 of the United Nations Charter, settle all their disputes exclusively by peaceful means and shall refrain from any threat or use of force in matters affecting European and international security, and in their mutual relations.

*Article IV.* 1. In conformity with the said purposes and principles, the Federal Republic of Germany and the Czechoslovak Socialist Republic reaffirm the inviolability of their common frontier now and in the future and undertake to respect each other's territorial integrity without restriction.

2. They declare that they have no territorial claims whatsoever against each other and that they will not assert any such claims in the future.

*Article V.* 1. The Federal Republic of Germany and the Czechoslovak Socialist Republic will undertake further steps for the comprehensive development of their mutual relations.

2. They agree that an extension of their neighbourly cooperation in the economic and scientific fields, in their scientific and technological relations, and in the fields of culture, environmental protection, sport, transport and in other sectors of their relations, is in their mutual interest.

. . .

# V · West European integration

Among the major changes in the world since the Second World War the developing integration of Western Europe is one of the most important. The onset of the 'cold war' and the break-up of Allied unity led to the realignment of European Powers and the rehabilitation of West Germany much earlier than anyone anticipated in 1945. The economic success of collaboration and the lessening of destructive nationalist feelings provided positive and fresh idealistic goals for greater West European unity.

## The first phase, 1947–50: the split of Europe into East and West

During the first five years following the defeat of Germany some basic characteristics of European integration began to emerge. First and most important, these years marked the political division of Europe, which made possible a separate evolution of Western Europe.

As one by one the interrelationships of Western Europe's economic, political, social and international problems were perceived by the national governments of Western Europe, by German leaders and by the American administration anxious to aid West European recovery and the Western capacity for self-defence, so varied solutions were found to deal with these problems. The variety of the solutions, in several complex treaties and in the setting up of numerous apparently overlapping institutions, reveals the different attitudes towards European integration adopted by the West European States.

In reconstructing post-war Europe, the political leaders of the wartime alliance were faced with a number of immediate problems for which they had no clear-cut answers during the first two years after the war. First and foremost was the question of the policy to be adopted towards Germany. Would Allied cooperation lead eventually to a restored united Germany? The considerations applying to Germany's future to a lesser extent also applied to Austria. With the onset of the 'cold war' a new relationship was established between the occupying Allied authorities in Western Germany and the German political leaders. Efforts to bring about European economic recovery too were dependent on the policies to be adopted towards the great industrial complexes in West Germany's Ruhr valley. During the years from 1945 to 1950, many uncertainties on these issues gave way to settled policies.

The changing attitudes of these years are exemplified by French thinking, which to begin with was dominated by a traditional fear of German revival and renewed aggression. *The Treaty of Dunkirk concluded between Britain and France, 4 March 1947* (p. 206), bound the two signatories to come to each other's aid if attacked by Germany, and pledged them to common action if Germany should fail to fulfil her economic obligations. The treaty also looked forward to a new Europe with provisions for Anglo-French economic cooperation. It became characteristic of later treaties that they were not purely military but also provided for economic and social cooperation and political consultation. The breakdown of Allied cooperation in Germany, the Berlin blockade, and the onset of the cold war rendered outdated the ordering of defence priorities that lay behind the making of the Treaty of Dunkirk.

In the new realities of politics and power as perceived from 1947 to 1950, a programme for West European, including West German, economic recovery was launched. A process leading eventually to the full restoration of West German sovereignty was started, Western European defence was coordinated and brought into association with the United States and Canada, and the first vital steps taken that were to lead to the close association of the West European States in the European Economic Community.

Lack of Allied progress in settling the German question from 1945 to 1947, the Western response to Soviet policies in Central and Eastern Europe, and civil war in Greece, all led the United States into commitments to provide more military and economic aid to Governments in conflict with communism within their States, and to strengthen their capacity to resist attack from without; this was the purpose of the *Truman Doctrine, 12 March 1947* (p. 103). It was followed by the Harvard speech of the Secretary of State, George C. Marshall, on 5 June 1947 in which he first offered a massive programme of United States economic aid to all

Europe (including Germany but excepting Spain). The resulting programme became known as the *Marshall Plan*. The prime condition on which such aid would be made available, Marshall had stated, was that the joint aid programme should be agreed to by a number of, if not all, European nations. The thinking behind American policy at the time confidentially set out by George Kennan, the head of a planning staff advising Marshall, was that American aid to Europe should be directed not to combating communism as such but to the restoration of the economic health and vigour of European society. If this could be achieved it would remedy the economic distress which was believed to be making European society vulnerable to communism and totalitarian exploitation. The Marshall Plan intentionally provided a powerful stimulus to West European cooperation, since American aid was to be furnished not for individual national economic programmes but for a programme agreed to by West European Governments acting together.

Ernest Bevin, Britain's Foreign Secretary, took the lead in response, and together with Georges Bidault, the French Foreign Minister, invited twenty-two European nations (but not Spain) to a conference to work out a recovery programme. The Western European States accepted the invitation to the conference, and Poland and Czechoslovakia also wished to attend. The Soviet Foreign Minister, Molotov, on behalf of the Soviet Union, agreed to meet Bevin and Bidault in Paris beforehand to work out the agenda and procedure for the conference. These tripartite discussions soon broke down and Molotov condemned the principle of a 'European plan'; he insisted on separate and bilateral negotiations between European States and the United States for American aid. The Soviet Union together with Poland and Czechoslovakia and the States within the Soviet sphere refused to cooperate on the basis of the American proposal after Molotov's departure from Paris.

This marked an irrevocable breach between the post-war economic development of Eastern and Western Europe. Separate development was dictated by political and ideological considerations. It also meant that the United Nations' Economic Commission for Europe, set up in Geneva in 1947 and concerned with Europe as a whole, would be stillborn. Separate organizations were set up to handle the economic policies of Communist Europe and of Western Europe. In Western Europe the organization required to handle American aid and the recovery programme was fashioned at a conference of Western Powers held in Paris during the summer of 1947.

The Paris Conference, 12 July–22 September 1947, was attended by sixteen nations: Austria, Belgium, Britain, Denmark, France, Greece, Iceland, Ireland, Italy, Luxemburg, the Netherlands, Norway, Portugal, Sweden, Switzerland and Turkey. The main result of the conference was the report of the Committee of Economic Cooperation, 22 September 1947, which outlined a four-year European recovery programme and proposed the creation of a permanent organization of the sixteen participating nations. At a second Conference in Paris, 15–16 March 1948, a working party was set up by the representatives of the same sixteen nations together with the military representatives of the Anglo-American and French zones of Germany, to draft the convention for economic cooperation which led in turn to the treaty setting up the *Organization for European Economic Cooperation (O.E.E.C.), 16 April 1948.* In October 1949, the German Federal Republic acceded to O.E.E.C. as a full member. Associated with the work of the O.E.E.C. were the following countries: the United States, Canada, Yugoslavia and Finland.

The O.E.E.C. worked out programmes for the participating States which were submitted for approval to the United States Economic Cooperation Administration, set up by Congress in 1948. Between 1948 and 1952 American aid to Western Europe amounted to $13,812 million, in addition to technical and administrative assistance. Successful as the O.E.E.C. proved to be in channelling American aid to Western Europe, this aid was applied essentially to support the individual economies of the participating States. Little Western European economic integration was achieved.

West European recovery was intimately dependent on West German recovery. At a number of conferences held in London in 1948, Britain, France and the Benelux countries reached agreement on the steps that were to lead to a Federal West German constitution, the fusion of all three Western zones of occupation and the establishment of an international authority for the Ruhr. The lessening of tension with the Soviet Union after the raising of the Berlin blockade (12 May 1949) did not divert the three Western allies from steps towards setting up a West German State. In May 1949 the three Allied Military Governors approved the Federal West German constitutional draft entitled the *Basic Law*; in addition the *Occupation Statute* laid down the new relationship between the Western occupying Powers, the rights they reserved to themselves and the jurisdiction to be granted to a West German Federal Government; finally the French zone of occupation was merged with the Anglo-American 'Bizone'. On 21 September 1949 Western Germany passed from Allied Military Government to a supervised West German democracy, when the

Western allies assumed their new function as the Allied High Commission on the basis of the Occupation Statute, and a Federal German Government headed by Chancellor Konrad Adenauer was inaugurated (p. 183).

Simultaneously with the changing relationship between the three Western Powers and West Germany, the Western European States placed their military, political and economic cooperation on a new footing. Bevin, in a speech on 24 January 1948, launched a plan to expand the Anglo-French partnership established by the Treaty of Dunkirk into a more comprehensive Western union. The communist takeover in Czechoslovakia in February 1948 lent urgency to the discussions. Negotiations in Brussels in March 1948 between Britain, France and the Benelux countries (the customs union of Netherlands, Belgium and Luxemburg, formed on the basis of a convention signed on 5 September 1944) were brought to a conclusion with the signature of the *Brussels Treaty, 17 March 1948* (p. 207). The military alliance between the signatories was no longer solely directed against the possibility of renewed German aggression but provided for defence against any aggressor. The signatories also pledged themselves to collaborate in economic, social and cultural fields. A Consultative Council of the five Foreign Ministers was established, but it had no supranational powers; it was a body which would make recommendations to individual Governments.

The European Movement, founded at the Hague in 1948 to mobilize public opinion, aimed at much closer European political union. The Consultative Council of the Brussels Treaty Powers in January 1949 agreed that a Council of Europe should be established consisting of a Ministerial Committee meeting in private and a Consultative Body meeting in public. At the conclusion of a conference in London, the five Brussels Treaty Powers, the Benelux countries, Britain and France, joined by Denmark, Ireland, Italy, Norway and Sweden, agreed on the *Statute of the Council of Europe, 5 May 1949*, as the constitution of the Council of Europe was entitled. The constitution did not provide for the merging of national sovereignties in the political and economic fields as many of the sponsors of the European movement hoped. The Committee of Ministers (the Council's Executive Organ) could consult, cooperate and discuss, but could only recommend action to Member Governments for decision; the Council itself could not reach binding decisions. An assembly consisting of Parliamentarians had little real power. This assembly was not to be elected by direct European elections but was composed of delegations sent by member national Parliaments. By 1984 the Council had concluded 116 treaties, conventions and agreements on European cooperation. Among these was the *European Convention for the Protection of Human Rights, 4 November 1950*, acceptance of which was made a condition of membership. (When the Greek Government was found to have violated the convention, Greece resigned in 1969.) A *European Social Charter was concluded on 18 October 1961*, and came into effect on 26 February 1965. A *European Convention on Social Security* came into force in 1977. The ten founding members of the Council of Europe were Belgium, Britain, Denmark, France, Irish Republic, Italy, Luxemburg, the Netherlands, Norway and Sweden. By 1984 nearly all non-communist States in Europe had joined the Council of Europe, the number of members having risen to twenty-one. Soon after its foundation, however, the Council of Europe found itself outflanked by other, much more tightly organized functional institutions of European cooperation. In defence the key institution was NATO (see pp. 106 and 211). And in economic (and later political matters) a smaller, more cohesive group of States laid the groundwork for what was to develop into the European Community.

## Treaty of Alliance and Mutual Assistance between Britain and France (Treaty of Dunkirk), 4 March 1947

. . . Determined to collaborate in measures of mutual assistance in the event of any renewal of German aggression, while considering most desirable the conclusion of a Treaty between all the Powers having responsibility for action in relation to Germany with the object of preventing Germany from becoming again a menace to peace;

Having regard to the Treaties of Alliance and Mutual Assistance which they have respectively concluded with the Union of Soviet Socialist Republics;

Intending to strengthen the economic relations between the two countries to their mutual advantage and in the interests of general prosperity;

Have decided to conclude a Treaty with these objects. . .

*Article 1.* Without prejudice to any arrangements that may be made, under any Treaty concluded between all the Powers having responsibility for action in relation to Germany under Article 107 of the Charter of the United Nations, for the purpose of preventing any infringements by Germany of her obligations with regard to disarmament and demilitarization and generally of ensuring that Germany shall not again become a menace to peace, the High Contracting Parties will, in the event of any threat to the security of either of them arising from the adoption by Germany of a policy of aggression or from action by Germany designed to facilitate such a policy, take, after consulting with each other and where appropriate with the other Powers having responsibility for action in relation to Germany, such agreed action (which so long as the said Article 107 remains operative shall be action under that Article) as is best calculated to put an end to this threat.

*Article II.* Should either of the High Contracting Parties become again involved in hostilities with Germany, either in consequence of an armed attack, within the meaning of Article 51 of the Charter of the United Nations, by Germany against that party, or as a result of agreed action taken against Germany under Article I of this Treaty, or as a result of enforcement action taken against Germany by the United Nations Security Council, the other High Contracting Party will at once give the High Contracting Party so involved in hostilities all the military and other support and assistance in his power.

*Article III.* In the event of either High Contracting Party being prejudiced by the failure of Germany to fulfil any obligation of an economic character imposed on her as a result of the Instrument of Surrender or arising out of any subsequent settlement, the High Contracting Parties will consult with each other and where appropriate with the other Powers having responsibility for action in relation to Germany, with a view to taking agreed action to deal with the situation.

*Article IV.* Bearing in mind the interests of the other members of the United Nations, the High Contracting Parties will by constant consultation on matters affecting their economic relations with each other take all possible steps to promote the prosperity and economic security of both countries and thus enable each of them to contribute more effectively to the economic and social objectives of the United Nations.

*Article V.* 1. Nothing in the present Treaty should be interpreted as derogating in any way from the obligations devolving upon the High Contracting Parties from the provisions of the Charter of the United Nations or from any special agreements concluded in virtue of Article 43 of the Charter.

2. Neither of the High Contracting Parties will conclude any alliance or take part in any coalition directed against the other High Contracting Party; nor will they enter into any obligation inconsistent with the provisions of the present Treaty.

*Article VI.* 1. The present Treaty is subject to ratification and the instruments of ratification will be exchanged in London as soon as possible.

2. It will come into force immediately on the exchange of the instruments of ratification and will remain in force for a period of fifty years... [Thereafter in perpetuity unless one year's notice of the desire to end the Treaty is given by one of the signatories.]

# Treaty between Belgium, France, Luxemburg, the Netherlands and Britain (Brussels Treaty), Brussels, 17 March 1948

...Resolved

To reaffirm their faith in fundamental human rights, in the dignity and worth of the human person and in the other ideals proclaimed in the Charter of the United Nations;

To fortify and preserve the principles of democracy, personal freedom and political liberty, the constitutional traditions and the rule of law, which are their common heritage;

To strengthen, with these aims in view, the economic, social and cultural ties by which they are already united;

To cooperate loyally and to coordinate their efforts to create in Western Europe a firm basis for European economic recovery;

To afford assistance to each other, in accordance with the Charter of the United Nations, in maintaining international peace and security and in resisting any policy of aggression;

To take such steps as may be held to be necessary in the event of a renewal by Germany of a policy of aggression;

To associate progressively in the pursuance of these aims other States inspired by the same ideals and animated by the like determination;

Desiring for these purposes to conclude a Treaty for collaboration in economic, social and cultural matters and for collective self-defence...

*Article I.* Convinced of the close community of their interests and of the necessity of uniting in order to promote the economic recovery of Europe, the High Contracting Parties will so organize and coordinate their economic activities as to produce the best possible results, by the elimination of conflict in their economic policies, the coordination of production and the development of commercial exchanges.

The cooperation provided for in the preceding paragraph, which will be effected through the Consultative Council referred to in Article VII as well as through other bodies, shall not involve any duplication of, or prejudice to, the work of other economic organizations in which the High Contracting Parties are or may be represented but shall on the contrary assist the work of those organizations.

*Article II.* The High Contracting Parties will make every effort in common, both by direct consultation and in specialized agencies, to promote the attainment of a higher standard of living by their peoples and to develop on corresponding lines the social and other related services of their countries.

The High Contracting Parties will consult with the object of achieving the earliest possible application of recom-

mendations of immediate practical interest, relating to social matters, adopted with their approval in the specialized agencies.

They will endeavour to conclude as soon as possible conventions with each other in the sphere of social security.

*Article III.* The High Contracting Parties will make every effort in common to lead their peoples towards a better understanding of the principles which form the basis of their common civilization and to promote cultural exchanges by conventions between themselves or by other means.

*Article IV.* If any of the High Contracting Parties should be the object of an armed attack in Europe, the other High Contracting Parties will, in accordance with the provisions of Article 51 of the Charter of the United Nations, afford the Party so attacked all the military and other aid and assistance in their power.

*Article V.* All measures taken as a result of the preceding Article shall be immediately reported to the Security Council. They shall be terminated as soon as the Security Council has taken the measures necessary to maintain or restore international peace and security.

The present Treaty does not prejudice in any way the obligations of the High Contracting Parties under the provisions of the Charter of the United Nations. It shall not be interpreted as affecting in any way the authority and responsibility of the Security Council under the Charter to take at any time such action as it deems necessary in order to maintain or restore international peace and security.

*Article VI.* The High Contracting Parties declare, each so far as he is concerned, that none of the international engagements now in force between him and any other of the High Contracting Parties or any third State is in conflict with the provisions of the present Treaty.

None of the High Contracting Parties will conclude any alliance or participate in any coalition directed against any other of the High Contracting Parties.

*Article VII.* For the purpose of consulting together on all the questions dealt with in the present Treaty, the High Contracting Parties will create a Consultative Council, which shall be so organized as to be able to exercise its functions continuously. The Council shall meet at such times as it shall deem fit.

At the request of any of the High Contracting Parties, the Council shall be immediately convened in order to permit the High Contracting Parties to consult with regard to any situation which may constitute a threat to peace, in whatever area this threat should arise; with regard to the attitude to be adopted and the steps to be taken in case of a renewal by Germany of an aggressive policy; or with regard to any situation constituting a danger to economic stability.

[*Article VIII.* Provisions for settling disputes among signatories by peaceful means.]

*Article IX.* The High Contracting Parties may, by agreement, invite any other State to accede to the present Treaty on conditions to be agreed between them and the States so invited. . . .

[*Article X.* Ratification.]

## The second phase, 1951–5: Western Europe divides

The Brussels Treaty and NATO provided the military alliance shield for Western Europe. The Council of Europe and the O.E.E.C. represented the degree of economic and cultural cooperation on which the Western European States could agree. In March 1951 France and Germany took another decisive step forward. They began negotiations for an integration of economic policies which envisaged a transfer of national decision-making to an international authority. Such a diminution of sovereignty was unacceptable to Britain and some other European States. The group which became known as the Six proceeded without Britain. *The Paris Treaty of 18 April 1951*, signed by France, the Federal (West) German Republic, Italy, Belgium, Luxemburg and the Netherlands, embodied their agreement to set up a *European Coal and Steel Community* (E.C.S.C., p. 214). The negotiations were based on the initiative taken by the French Foreign Minister, Robert Schuman, who at a press conference on 9 May 1950 had outlined a French Government plan 'to place all Franco-German coal and steel production under a common High Authority, in an organization open to the participation of the other countries of Europe'. The adoption of such a plan would be the first step towards European federation, Schuman declared, and would 'change the destiny of regions that have long been devoted to the production of war armaments of which they themselves have been the constant victims'. Schuman's objective was primarily political in that he wished to transform Franco-German relations, to bring to an end their hostility by making war impossible between them, since coal and steel essential for war production would cease to be under national control. The adoption of the plan transformed the problems associated with the future of the Saar, the control of the Ruhr, German rearmament and the status of the Federal Republic of Germany, which now became an equal member of the European Coal and Steel Community. The blueprint for the Schuman plan had been worked out by Jean Monnet and a few close collaborators in the offices of the Commissariat du Plan de Modernisation et d'Equipement. It represented the approach of the 'functionalists' who believed the political union of the European States was too high a hurdle to overcome immediately and who wished to proceed step by step. A beginning would be made by pooling some aspects of sovereignty to international institutions with limited functions but real power. The Paris Treaty emphasized the supranational aspect of the E.C.S.C., and its organization was deliberately designed to serve as a model for future European institutions. After ratification by the six national Parliaments the treaty came into force on 25 July 1952 and Monnet was made the first president of E.C.S.C. Britain held aloof. One link that was maintained between the Europe of the Council of Europe and the Europe of the Six, the E.C.S.C., was that the Assembly of the E.C.S.C. would be composed of the parliamentary representatives of the six who sat in the Assembly of the Council of Europe; but neither Assembly had much practical control over policy-making.

The formation of the E.C.S.C. from 1950 to 1952 was a crucial part of a Western policy supported by France, of restoring West German sovereignty provided a West German Republic remained closely tied by treaty to Western Europe. Additional safeguards were sought from Britain and the United States so that no revived West German State would be able either to dominate Western Europe or to play off East against West in following an independent policy towards the Soviet Union. The West German Government for its part was ready to accept this new West European role. Adenauer believed that only by identifying West Germany loyally with the West could Germany be secured from the threat of Soviet domination. Only if he could gain the trust of Germany's wartime enemies would it be possible to end the Allied occupation of West Germany.

With the communist takeover in Czechoslovakia in February 1948, the Berlin blockade in 1948–9, and the outbreak of the Korean War in June 1950, the administration of the United States became so alarmed at this evidence of aggressiveness of world communism that it took the lead in arguing the necessity of German rearmament as an indispensable condition of West European defence. These strands, the European and the

American, came together in the signature of two treaties between West Germany and her former enemies, signed on successive days in Bonn and Paris. The *Bonn Agreements, 26 May 1952*, consisted of a number of treaties which provided for the ending of the Occupation Statute, the abolition of the High Commission, and the restoration of German sovereignty subject to new contractual agreements between the Allies and West Germany. But the ratification or coming into force of the Bonn Agreements depended on the ratification of another treaty signed on the following day in Paris, 27 May 1952, establishing the European Defence Community which allowed for a German military contribution within the framework of the combined defensive efforts of the Six.

On 24 October 1950 the French Prime Minister, René Pleven, had proposed to the French Assembly the creation of a European army linked to political institutions of a united Europe. Negotiations concerning the rearming of Germany, and the incorporation of German divisions in a European army, proved especially difficult, but in the end accord was reached in Paris on a *Treaty establishing the European Defence Community (E.D.C.), 27 May 1952*, between Belgium, France, West Germany, the Netherlands, Italy and Luxemburg. A number of agreements particularly designed to reassure the French accompanied the treaty. First there was a Three Power agreement of France, Britain and the United States concerning stationing of their troops in Europe; it stated that any threat to the security of the E.D.C. would be regarded as a threat to their own security. Secondly, although Britain was not prepared to fuse its defence entirely with Western Europe's, the British Government signed an agreement with the six E.D.C. countries stating that while Britain was a member of NATO it would render all military and other aid in its power to any signatory of the E.D.C. which became the victim of an armed attack in Europe. Another protocol to the treaty promised reciprocal aid as between members of NATO or E.D.C. if attacked. A year later, in March 1953, a draft treaty was signed establishing a political community between them to which the E.D.C. would be subject. But throughout this period no French Government could be sure of securing the necessary majority in the French Assembly to secure ratification of the E.D.C. treaty, involving as it did the abandonment of an independent French army in Europe under exclusive French command. Although the Benelux countries and West Germany had secured parliamentary ratification of the treaties, the French National Assembly rejected it on 30 August 1954. This meant that the *Bonn Agreements* of 1952 ending the Allied occupation of Western Germany and bringing about the restoration of West German sovereignty could not be ratified. It also meant that the contribution of a revived but controlled German armaments industry and reconstituted West German armed forces could not be made available for the mutual defence of Western Europe through the planned supranational arrangements of the Six in alliance with the other NATO Powers. If a West German contribution was regarded as essential for the defence of Western Europe then an entirely new treaty framework had to be found to replace the many-sided commitments of the Paris Treaty of 1952. The West European States found this framework in the *Brussels Treaty Alliance of 17 March 1948* (p. 207).

On Britain's initiative, the Brussels Treaty, which complemented but in military significance had been superseded by NATO was revived in the autumn of 1954 and expanded. Multilateral negotiations were conducted at the Nine Power *London Conference, 28 September–3 October 1954*, attended by Belgium, Britain, Canada, France, the German Federal Republic, Italy, Luxemburg, the Netherlands and the United States. Pierre Mendès-France, for France, insisted that West German rearmament and the accession of West Germany to NATO would be assented to by France only if Britain and the United States undertook to maintain their troops in Europe, if German rearmament were controlled, and if an agreement could be reached on the Saar. At the London Conference it was agreed that at a subsequent conference in Paris a comprehensive set of agreements were to be drawn up in binding legal form. After further negotiations, the *Paris Agreements, 23 October 1954, were signed.* The Brussels Treaty Organization was renamed and reconstituted as the *West European Union* by four Protocols:

*Protocol I.* The German Federal Republic and Italy were added to the original Brussels Treaty Powers (the Six and Britain). The Consultative Council of the Brussels Treaty became the Council of Western European Union.

*Protocol II.* This laid down the maximum strength of land and air forces to be maintained in time of peace by each signatory of the W.E.U. under the supreme command of NATO. Britain undertook to maintain in Europe a stated minimum of four divisions together with tactical air support which would not be withdrawn without the consent of the majority of the W.E.U.

*Protocol III.* This consisted of resolutions concerning the control of West German armaments; the German Federal Republic was forbidden to manufacture atomic, biological or chemical weapons, and other limitations were also placed on German rearmament.

*Protocol IV.* This set up an agency for the control of West German armament.

The W.E.U. was headed by a Council consisting of the Foreign Ministers of Member States, a Permanent Council consisting of the Ambassadors of Member States and a Secretariat. An Assembly was added consisting of the representatives of the W.E.U. at the Consultative Assembly of the Council of Europe. The Agency for the Control of Armaments was attached to the Secretariat responsible to the Council. The W.E.U. gave the Assembly no real powers and the Council was a conference of allied Foreign Ministers whose decisions depended on individual Government policies and approval. The W.E.U. thus lacked the supranational character of E.C.S.C. and the rejected E.D.C. The military functions of W.E.U. came to be exercised in practice by NATO. Economic questions and negotiations were conducted by other specialized organizations like the E.E.C., and so the W.E.U. did little to bridge the gap developing between the Six on the one hand and Britain and the remaining West European States on the other. Subsequent attempts to use the W.E.U. as a West European political forum were not successful. The most important later decisions of the W.E.U. were those that lifted many of the restrictions on the rearmament of the Federal Republic of Germany after 1959. The importance of the W.E.U. lies in the fact that it established a treaty framework making possible West German rearmament and the restoration of German sovereignty.

The *Paris Agreements, 23 October 1954*, thus restored the objectives of the abortive *Bonn Agreements of 1952*, abrogating the Occupation Statute and abolishing the Allied High Commission. The three wartime allies, Britain, France and the United States, retained their rights regarding Berlin, German reunification and the prospective German peace treaty. In a declaration, Britain, France and the United States recognized the Government of the Federal Republic of Germany as the only legitimate one entitled to speak for the whole of Germany; the Federal Republic for its part agreed never to use force to alter its frontiers or to bring about the reunification of Germany, and promised to solve by peaceful means all international differences. The Federal Republic at the same time was admitted to membership of NATO in the winter of 1954. Finally Germany and France signed an agreement covering the Saar (p. 182). After the ratification of the Paris Agreements by the Member States, including the French Assembly and the Bundestag, they entered into force on 5 May 1955. On that day the Federal Republic of Germany regained its sovereignty with the ending of the occupation by Britain, France and the United States.

# Treaty instituting the European Coal and Steel Community, Paris, 18 April 1951

...

Considering that world peace may be safeguarded only by creative efforts equal to the dangers which menace it;

Convinced that the contribution which an organized and vital Europe can bring to civilization is indispensable to the maintenance of peaceful relations;

Conscious of the fact that Europe can be built only by concrete actions which create a real solidarity and by the establishment of common bases for economic development;

Desirous of assisting through the expansion of their basic production in raising the standard of living and in furthering the works of peace;

Resolved to substitute for historic rivalries a fusion of their essential interests; to establish, by creating an economic community, the foundation of a broad and independent community among peoples long divided by bloody conflicts; and to lay the bases of institutions capable of giving direction to their future common destiny;

Have decided to create a European Coal and Steel Community. . . .

TITLE ONE: The European Coal and Steel Community

*Article 1.* By the present Treaty the HIGH CONTRACTING PARTIES institute among themselves a EUROPEAN COAL AND STEEL COMMUNITY, based on a common market, common objectives, and common institutions.

*Article 2.* The mission of the European Coal and Steel Community is to contribute to economic expansion, the development of employment and the improvement of the standard of living in the participating countries through the institution, in harmony with the general economy of the Member States, of a common market as defined in Article 4.

The Community must progressively establish conditions which will in themselves assure the most rational distribution of production at the highest possible level of productivity, while safeguarding the continuity of employment and avoiding the creation of fundamental and persistent disturbances in the economies of the Member States.

*Article 3.* Within the framework of their respective powers and responsibilities and in the common interest, the institutions of the Community shall:

(a) see that the common market is regularly supplied, taking account of the needs of third countries;

(b) assure to all consumers in comparable positions within the common market equal access to the sources of production;

(c) seek the establishment of the lowest prices which are possible without requiring any corresponding rise either in the prices charged by the same enterprises in other transactions or in the price level as a whole in another period, while at the same time permitting necessary amortization and providing normal possibilities of remuneration for capital invested;

(d) see that conditions are maintained which will encourage enterprises to expand and improve their ability to produce and to promote a policy of rational development of natural resources, avoiding inconsiderate exhaustion of such resources;

(e) promote the improvement of the living and working conditions of the labour force in each of the industries under its jurisdiction so as to make possible the equalization of such conditions in an upward direction;

(f) further the development of international trade and see that equitable limits are observed in prices charged on external markets;

(g) promote the regular expansion and the modernization of production as well as the improvement of its quality, under conditions which preclude any protection against competing industries except where justified by illegitimate action on the part of such industries or in their favour.

*Article 4.* The following are recognized to be incompatible with the common market for coal and steel, and are, therefore, abolished and prohibited within the Community in the manner set forth in the present Treaty:

(a) import and export duties, or charges with an equivalent effect, and quantitative restrictions on the movement of coal and steel;

(b) measures or practices discriminating among producers, among buyers or among consumers, specifically as concerns prices, delivery terms and transportation rates, as well as measures or practices which hamper the buyer in the free choice of his supplier;

(c) subsidies or State assistance, or special charges imposed by the State, in any form whatsoever;

(d) restrictive practices tending towards the division of markets or the exploitation of the consumer.

*Article 5.* The Community shall accomplish its mission, under the conditions provided for in the present Treaty, with limited direct intervention.

To this end, the Community will:

enlighten and facilitate the action of the interested parties by collecting information, organizing consultations and defining general objectives;

place financial means at the disposal of enterprises for their investments and participate in the expenses of readaptation;

assure the establishment, the maintenance and the observance of normal conditions of competition and take direct action with respect to production and the operation of the market only when circumstances make it absolutely necessary;

publish the justifications for its action and take the necessary measures to ensure observance of the rules set forth in the present Treaty.

The institutions of the Community shall carry out these activities with as little administrative machinery as possible and in close cooperation with the interested parties.

*Article 6.* The Community shall have juridical personality . . . .

TITLE TWO: The institutions of the Community

*Article 7.* The institutions of the Community shall be as follows:

a HIGH AUTHORITY, assisted by a *Consultative Committee*;

a COMMON ASSEMBLY, hereafter referred to as 'the Assembly';

a SPECIAL COUNCIL, composed of MINISTERS, hereafter referred to as 'the Council';

a COURT OF JUSTICE, hereafter referred to as 'the Court'.

*Chapter 1: The High Authority*

*Article 8.* The High Authority shall be responsible for assuring the fulfilment of the purposes stated in the present Treaty under the terms thereof.

*Article 9.* The High Authority shall be composed of nine members designated for six years and chosen for their general competence.

A member shall be eligible for reappointment. The number of members of the High Authority may be reduced by unanimous decision of the Council.

Only nationals of the Member States may be members of the High Authority.

The High Authority may not include more than two members of the same nationality.

The members of the High Authority shall exercise their functions in complete independence, in the general interest of the Community. In the fulfilment of their duties, they shall neither solicit nor accept instructions from any Government or from any organization. They will abstain from all conduct incompatible with the supranational character of their functions.

Each Member State agrees to respect this supranational character and to make no effort to influence the members of the

High Authority in the execution of their duties.

The members of the High Authority may not exercise any business or professional activities, paid or unpaid, nor acquire or hold, directly or indirectly, any interest in any business related to coal and steel during their term of office or for a period of three years thereafter.

*Article 10.* The Governments of the Member States shall designate eight members of the High Authority by agreement among themselves. These eight members will elect a ninth member, who shall be deemed elected if he receives at least five votes.

The members thus designated will remain in office for six years following the date of the establishment of the common market.

In case a vacancy should occur during this first period for one of the reasons set forth in Article 12, it will be filled under the provisions of the third paragraph of that Article, by common agreement among the Governments of the Member States. . . .

*Article 11.* The President and the Vice President of the High Authority shall be designated from among the membership of the High Authority for two years, in accordance with the procedure provided for the designation of the members of the High Authority by the Governments of the Member States. They may be re-elected.

Except in the case of a complete redesignation of the membership of the High Authority, the designation of the President and Vice President shall be made after consultation with the High Authority.

*Article 12.* In addition to the provisions for regular redesignation, the terms of office of a member of the High Authority may be terminated by death or resignation. . . .

*Article 13.* The High Authority shall act by vote of a majority of its membership.

Its quorum shall be fixed by its rules of procedure. However, this quorum must be greater than one-half of its membership.

*Article 14.* In the execution of its responsibilities under the present Treaty and in accordance with the provisions thereof, the High Authority shall issue decisions, recommendations and opinions.

Decisions shall be binding in all their details.

Recommendations shall be binding with respect to the objectives which they specify but shall leave to those to whom they are directed the choice of appropriate means for attaining these objectives.

Opinions shall not be binding.

When the High Authority is empowered to issue a decision, it may limit itself to making a recommendation.

*Article 15.* The decisions, recommendations and opinions of the High Authority shall state the reasons therefor, and shall take note of the opinions which the High Authority is required to obtain.

When such decisions and recommendations are individual in character, they shall be binding on the interested party upon their notification to him.

In other cases, they shall take effect automatically upon publication.

The High Authority shall determine the manner in which the provisions of the present Article are to be carried out.

*Article 16.* The High Authority shall take all appropriate measures of an internal nature to assure the functioning of its services. . . .

*Article 17.* The High Authority shall publish annually, at least a month before the meeting of the Assembly, a general report on the activities of the Community and on its administrative expenditures.

*Article 18.* There shall be created a Consultative Committee, attached to the High Authority. It shall consist of not less than thirty and not more than fifty-one members, and shall include producers, workers and consumers and dealers in equal numbers.

The members of the Consultative Committee shall be appointed by the Council.

As concerns producers and workers, the Council shall designate the representative organizations among which it shall allocate the seats to be filled. Each organization shall be asked to draw up a list comprising twice the number of seats allocated to it. Designations shall be made from this list.

The members of the Consultative Committee shall be designated in their individual capacity. They shall not be bound by any mandate or instruction from the organizations which proposed them as candidates.

A President and officers shall be elected for one-year terms by the Consultative Committee from its own membership. The Committee shall fix its own rules of procedure.

The allowances of members of the Consultative Committee shall be determined by the Council on proposal by the High Authority.

*Article 19.* The High Authority may consult the Consultative Committee in any case it deems proper. It shall be required to do so whenever such consultation is prescribed by the present Treaty.

The High Authority shall submit to the Consultative Committee the general objectives and programme established under the terms of Article 46, and shall keep the Committee informed of the broad lines of its action under the terms of Articles 54, 65 and 66.

If the High Authority deems it necessary, it shall give the Consultative Committee a period in which to present its opinion of not less than ten days from the date of the notification to that effect addressed to the President of the Committee.

The Consultative Committee shall be convoked by its President, either at the request of the High Authority or at the request of a majority of its members,

for the purpose of discussing a given question.

The minutes of the meetings shall be transmitted to the High Authority and to the Council at the same time as the opinions of the Committee.

*Chapter II: The Assembly*

*Article 20.* The Assembly, composed of representatives of the peoples of the Member States of the Community, shall exercise the supervisory powers which are granted to it by the present Treaty.

*Article 21.* The Assembly shall be composed of delegates whom the Parliaments of each of the Member States shall be called upon to designate once a year from among their own membership, or who shall be elected by direct universal suffrage, according to the procedure determined by each respective High Contracting Party.

The number of delegates is fixed as follows:

| | |
|---|---|
| Germany | 18 |
| Belgium | 10 |
| France | 18 |
| Italy | 18 |
| Luxemburg | 4 |
| Netherlands | 10 |

The representatives of the people of the Saar are included in the number of delegates attributed to France.

*Article 22.* The Assembly shall hold an annual session. It shall convene regularly on the second Tuesday in May. Its session may not last beyond the end of the then current fiscal year.

The Assembly may be convoked in extraordinary session on the request of the Council in order to state its opinion on such questions as may be put to it by the Council.

It may also meet in extraordinary session on the request of a majority of its members or of the High Authority.

*Article 23.* The Assembly shall designate its President and officers from among its membership.

The members of the High Authority may attend all meetings. The President of the High Authority or such of its members as it may designate shall be heard at their request.

The High Authority shall reply orally or in writing to all questions put to it by the Assembly or its members.

The members of the Council may attend all meetings and shall be heard at their request.

*Article 24.* The Assembly shall discuss in open session the general report submitted to it by the High Authority.

If a motion of censure on the report is presented to the Assembly, a vote may be taken thereon only after a period of not less than three days following its introduction, and such vote shall be by open ballot.

If the motion of censure is adopted by two-thirds of the members present and voting, representing a majority of the total membership, the members of the High Authority must resign in a body. They shall continue to carry out current business until their replacement in accordance with Article 10.

*Article 25.* The Assembly shall fix its own rules of procedure, by vote of a majority of its total membership.

The acts of the Assembly shall be published in a manner to be prescribed in such rules of procedure.

*Chapter III: The Council*

*Article 26.* The Council shall exercise its functions in the events and in the manner provided in the present Treaty in particular with a view to harmonizing the action of the High Authority and that of the Governments, which are responsible for the general economic policy of their countries.

To this end, the Council and the High Authority shall consult together and exchange information.

The Council may request the High Authority to examine all proposals and measures which it may deem necessary or appropriate for the realization of the common objectives.

*Article 27.* The Council shall be composed of representatives of the Member States. Each State shall designate thereto one of the members of its Government.

The Presidency of the Council shall be exercised for a term of three months by each member of the Council in rotation in the alphabetical order of the Member States.

*Article 28.* Meetings of the Council shall be called by its President on the request of a State or of the High Authority.

When the Council is consulted by the High Authority, it may deliberate without necessarily proceeding to a vote. The minutes of its meetings shall be forwarded to the High Authority.

Wherever the present Treaty requires the concurrence of the Council, this concurrence shall be deemed to have been granted if the proposal submitted by the High Authority is approved:

– by an absolute majority of the representatives of the Member States, including the vote of the representative of one of the States which produces at least 20 per cent of the total value of coal and steel produced in the Community;

– or, in case of an equal division of votes, and if the High Authority maintains its proposal after a second reading, by the representatives of two Member States, each of which produces at least 20 per cent of the total value of coal and steel in the Community.

Wherever the present Treaty requires a unanimous decision or unanimous concurrence, such decision or concurrence will be adopted if supported by the votes of all of the members of the Council.

The decisions of the Council, other than those which require a qualified majority or a unanimous vote, will be taken by a vote of the majority of the total membership. This majority shall be deemed to exist if it includes the absolute majority of the representatives of the

Member States including the vote of the representative of one of the States which produces at least 20 per cent of the total value of coal and steel produced in the Community.

In case of a vote, any member of the Council may act as proxy for not more than one other member.

The Council shall communicate with the Member States through the intermediary of its President.

The acts of the Council shall be published under a procedure which it shall establish.

*Article 29.* The Council shall fix the salaries, allowances and pensions of the President of the High Authority, and of the President, the Judges, the Court Advocates and the Clerk of the Court.

*Article 30.* The Council shall establish its own rules of procedure.

*Chapter IV: The Court*

*Article 31.* The function of the Court is to ensure the rule of law in the interpretation and application of the present Treaty and of its implementing regulations.

*Article 32.* The Court shall be composed of seven Judges, appointed for six years by agreement among the Governments of the Member States from among persons of recognized independence and competence.

A partial change in membership of the Court shall occur every three years, affecting alternatively three members and four members. The three members whose terms expire at the end of the first period of three years shall be designated by lot.

Judges shall be eligible for reappointment.

The number of Judges may be increased by unanimous vote of the Council on proposal by the Court.

## The third phase, 1955–60: the Six establish the Common Market (E.E.C.); the Seven establish E.F.T.A.

The success of the European Coal and Steel Community from 1955–7 and the unprecedented growth of economic recovery among the Six stimulated new efforts to take further the integration of the Six. At a meeting of the Foreign Ministers of the Six at Messina on 3 June 1955 a resolution was adopted pledging their determination to work 'toward the establishment of a United Europe, through the development of common institutions, the gradual merger of national economies, the creation of a common market and increasing harmonization of social policies'. Support for this policy was given by the European Movement. Strong support too was provided by the parliamentarians of the Six who were members of the Common Assembly of the E.C.S.C.

### 1. The treaties

After negotiations extending over nearly two years, the *Treaty of Rome was signed, 25 March 1957* (p. 223) by the Six, namely Belgium, France, the Federal Republic of Germany, Italy, Luxemburg and the Netherlands.

The Treaty of Rome established the *European Economic Community* (*E.E.C.*). On the same day, also in Rome, the Six signed the *Euratom Treaty* creating the *European Atomic Energy Community*. Euratom was designed to develop the peaceful uses of nuclear energy; it was regarded by the Six as of great future importance in building up European union. In practice it failed to develop as anticipated. Nuclear work for military purposes became a national enterprise in France (as in Britain, a non-member until 1973), and despite expensive budgets for research centres in the 1950s and 1960s, national policies, even in the non-military nuclear field, predominated over cooperative joint efforts. By the close of the 1960s Euratom was bypassed and its members could no longer agree on expensive budgets. A great drawback for Euratom at the very start was that the European State with the most advanced nuclear technology, Britain, was not a member. The European Economic Community, by way of contrast, although Britain would not join at its inception, successfully did, in the words of the preamble to the treaty, 'establish the foundations of an ever closer union among the European peoples'.

## 2. *The objectives of the treaties*

The Treaty of Rome is based on the objective of achieving freedom of market and competition within the Member States and a common external tariff with the rest of the world. In some respects the treaty was precise. It set out timetables for the reduction of internal tariffs, for the removal of quotas internally and for the creation of a common external tariff. These objectives were all achieved in July 1968 ahead of the timetable of the Treaty of Rome. Other objectives of the Rome Treaty, set out in Articles 2 and 3, were to lead the Six to complete economic integration; these proved slow to be realized. To this group of activities belonged many questions of economic and social policy which continued to be dealt with on a national basis. A common monetary policy proved an especially thorny problem, involving as it did supranational regulation of those financial policies by which individual Governments attempt to regulate their employment, balance of payments and inflation. Two other cardinal tenets of the Treaty of Rome were the establishment of a common agricultural policy (Articles 38 to 47) and free movement of labour and capital (Articles 48 to 84).

## 3. *The decision-making process of the E.E.C.*

The supranational core of the European Economic Community is the *Commission*, supported by its own civil service several thousand strong. It has its headquarters in Brussels. The number of Commissioners was initially nine. At least one Commissioner (and not more than two) had to be a national of each Member State. The Commissioners were to be appointed for four years by the common agreement of all Member States, and the appointment was renewable. The treaty lays down that the Commissioners shall act in the Community's interest and are not to be influenced by the Government of a Member State. The Commission has considerable powers. It can initiate proposals for legislation, and its duty is to implement the treaty as supplemented by policy agreements. It can impose fines on individual firms judged in default of the terms of the treaty.

The *European Community Court of Justice* sitting in Luxemburg gives final rulings when appealed to by Member States, by individual firms or by the Commission, concerning the application of the Treaty of Rome. So fines imposed by the Commission, for instance, can be appealed against before the Court of Justice. Both the Commission and Member States have brought a number of cases against each other before the Court.

The Commission submits proposals to the *Council of Ministers*. It is in the *Council* that final decisions are made. The Council is not supranational but consists of one Minister sent by each National Government that is a Member State.

The Commission was theoretically answerable to the *European Parliament*, which held its first meeting on 19 March 1958 at Strasbourg. The Parliament was in its early years composed, like the Council of Europe, not of members directly elected by popular suffrage, but of delegates sent by the Parliaments of member countries. It consisted initially of 142 members. In reality, during the first two decades of its existence, the Parliament exercised little effective power.

### 4. The establishment of E.F.T.A.

*The European Free Trade Association* (E.F.T.A.) was established by the *Treaty of Stockholm, signed on 4 January 1960 and ratified 3 May 1960* (p. 238), by Austria, Britain, Denmark, Norway, Portugal, Sweden and Switzerland. Finland became an associate member in 1961. Its establishment marked the split of the Western European States into two distinct groups. The E.E.C. had been developing integrated economic policies among its six members and had been moving towards 'European union', with some institutions such as the original High Authority of the European Coal and Steel Community and the Commission of the E.E.C.

possessing supranational characteristics. During the 1950s, which saw the creation of the E.E.C. and the working together of the six continental European Powers, Britain emphasized her separate world position as the centre of the Commonwealth, enjoying a special relationship with the U.S. Britain regarded herself as a Great Power with global responsibilities, and successive governments before 1960 rejected Britain's submitting her economic and defence policies to any supranational European bodies. With strong economic Commonwealth links and trading with the United States, the policy of a common external tariff for agricultural and industrial goods did not appear advantageous to British Governments. Finland and Sweden, as well as Switzerland and Austria, did not wish to or could not compromise their political neutrality by joining a Western group of nations. Attempts at meetings of the O.E.E.C. in 1957 and 1958 to create a European industrial free trade area to exist parallel with the E.E.C. failed. Subsequent rounds of negotiations among the 'Outer Seven' (Austria, Britain, Denmark, Norway, Portugal, Sweden and Switzerland) from December 1958 to December 1959 led to the establishment of E.F.T.A. Its objectives were limited. With headquarters in Geneva, a small Secretariat and a Council of representatives from Member States acting unanimously where decisions involving new obligations were concerned, the machinery lacked supranational decision-making institutions. It established by progressive reduction of tariffs between members on industrial goods a common market in industrial goods. This progress was in fact accelerated so that with few exceptions these tariffs had been entirely removed by 1 January 1967. There was, however, no attempt to apply an agreed common external tariff to non-E.F.T.A. members. (The common external tariff is an essential feature of the E.E.C.) Each E.F.T.A. State regulated tariffs with non-members according to its individual trade policies. E.F.T.A. succeeded in expanding trade between its members during the 1960s; but the applications of Britain, Denmark, Norway and Ireland to join the E.E.C. in 1961 and 1967 underlined the 'temporary' nature of E.F.T.A., which was always seen as a first step to a larger European grouping.

# Treaty between Belgium, the Federal Republic of Germany, France, Italy, Luxemburg and the Netherlands establishing the European Economic Community (Treaty of Rome), 25 March 1957

## Part One · Principles

*Article 1.* By this Treaty, the High Contracting Parties establish among themselves a European Economic Community.

*Article 2.* The Community shall have as its task, by establishing a common market and progressively approximating the economic policies of Member States, to promote throughout the Community a harmonious development of economic activities, a continuous and balanced expansion, an increase in stability, an accelerated raising of the standard of living and closer relations between the States belonging to it.

*Article 3.* For the purposes set out in Article 2, the activities of the Community shall include, as provided in this Treaty and in accordance with the timetable set out therein:

(a) the elimination, as between Member States, of customs duties and of quantitative restrictions on the import and export of goods, and of all other measures having equivalent effect;

(b) the establishment of a common customs tariff and of a common commercial policy towards third countries;

(c) the abolition, as between Member States, of obstacles to freedom of movement for persons, services and capital;

(d) the adoption of a common policy in the sphere of agriculture;

(e) the adoption of a common policy in the sphere of transport;

(f) the institution of a system ensuring that competition in the common market is not distorted;

(g) the application of procedures by which the economic policies of Member States can be coordinated and disequi-

libria in their balances of payments remedied;

(h) the approximation of the laws of Member States to the extent required for the proper functioning of the common market;

(i) the creation of a European Social Fund in order to improve employment opportunities for workers and to contribute to the raising of their standard of living;

(j) the establishment of a European Investment Bank to facilitate the economic expansion of the Community by opening up fresh resources;

(k) the association of the overseas countries and territories in order to increase trade and to promote jointly economic and social development.

*Article 4.* 1. The tasks entrusted to the Community shall be carried out by the following institutions:

an Assembly,
a Council,
a Commission,
a Court of Justice.

Each institution shall act within the limits of the powers conferred upon it by this Treaty.

2. The Council and the Commission shall be assisted by an Economic and Social Committee acting in an advisory capacity.

*Article 5.* Member States shall take all appropriate measures, whether general or particular, to ensure fulfilment of the obligations arising out of this Treaty or resulting from action taken by the institutions of the Community. They shall facilitate the achievement of the Community's tasks.

They shall abstain from any measure which could jeopardize the attainment of the objectives of this Treaty.

*Article 6.* 1. Member States shall, in close cooperation with the institutions of the Community, coordinate their respective economic policies to the extent necessary to attain the objectives of this Treaty.

2. The institutions of the community shall take care not to prejudice the internal and external financial stability of the Member States.

*Article 7.* Within the scope of application of this Treaty, and without prejudice to any special provisions contained therein, any discrimination on grounds of nationality shall be prohibited.

The Council may, on a proposal from the Commission and after consulting the Assembly, adopt, by a qualified majority, rules designed to prohibit such discrimination.

*Article 8.* 1. The common market shall be progressively established during a transitional period of twelve years. [Note: this period in practice was shortened to end on 1 July 1968.]

This transitional period shall be divided into three stages of four years each; the length of each stage may be altered in accordance with the provisions set out below.

2. To each stage there shall be assigned a set of actions to be initiated and carried through concurrently....

## Part Two · Foundations of the Community

TITLE I: Free movement of goods

*Article 9.* 1. The Community shall be based upon a customs union which shall cover all trade in goods and which shall involve the prohibition between Member States of customs duties on imports and exports and of all charges having equivalent effect, and the adoption of a common customs tariff in their relations with third countries.

2. The provisions of Chapter 1, Section 1, and of Chapter 2 of this Title shall apply to products originating in Member States and to products coming from third countries which are in free circulation in Member States.

*Article 10.* 1. Products coming from a third country shall be considered to be in free circulation in a Member State if the import formalities have been complied with and any customs duties or charges having equivalent effect which are payable have been levied in that Member State, and if they have not benefited from a total or partial drawback of such duties or charges....

*Article 11.* Member States shall take all appropriate measures to enable Governments to carry out, within the periods of time laid down, the obligations with regard to customs duties which devolve upon them pursuant to this Treaty.

*Chapter 1: The Customs Union*

SECTION 1 · ELIMINATION OF CUSTOMS DUTIES BETWEEN MEMBER STATES

*Article 12.* Member States shall refrain from introducing between themselves any new customs duties on imports or exports or any charges having equivalent effect, and from increasing those which they already apply in their trade with each other.

*Article 13.* 1. Customs duties on imports in force between Member States shall be progressively abolished by them during the transitional period in accordance with Articles 14 and 15....

[*Article 14.* Sets out timetable of reductions.]

...

SECTION 2 · SETTING UP OF THE COMMON CUSTOMS TARIFF

*Article 18.* The Member States declare their readiness to contribute to the development of international trade and the lowering of barriers to trade by entering into agreements designed, on a basis of reciprocity and mutual advantage, to reduce customs duties below the general level of which they could avail themselves as a result of the establishment of a customs union between them.

[*Articles 19—28*. Provide for the setting up of an external trade barrier between the Common Market and the rest of the world – the common external tariff – and these articles also set out the detailed provisions of the tariffs.]

*Article 29*. In carrying out the tasks entrusted to it under this Section the Commission shall be guided by:

(a) the need to promote trade between Member States and third countries;

(b) developments in conditions of competition within the Community in so far as they lead to an improvement in the competitive capacity of undertakings;

(c) the requirements of the Community as regards the supply of raw materials and semi-finished goods; in this connection the Commission shall take care to avoid distorting conditions of competition between Member States in respect of finished goods;

(d) the need to avoid serious disturbances in the economies of Member States and to ensure rational development of production and an expansion of consumption within the Community.

*Chapter 2: Elimination of quantitative restrictions between Member States*

*Article 30*. Quantitative restrictions on imports and all measures having equivalent effect shall, without prejudice to the following provisions, be prohibited between Member States.

*Article 31*. Member States shall refrain from introducing between themselves any new quantitative restrictions or measures having equivalent effect.

This obligation shall, however, relate only to the degree of liberalization attained in pursuance of the decisions of the Council of the Organization for European Economic Cooperation of 14 January 1955. Member States shall supply the Commission, not later than six months after the entry into force of this Treaty, with lists of the products liberalized by them in pursuance of these decisions. These lists shall be consolidated between Member States.

*Article 32*. In their trade with one another Member States shall refrain from making more restrictive the quotas and measures having equivalent effect existing at the date of the entry into force of this Treaty.

These quotas shall be abolished by the end of the transitional period at the latest. During that period, they shall be progressively abolished in accordance with the following provisions. [These are set out in Articles 33 to 36.]

. . .

*Article 37*. 1. Member States shall progressively adjust any State monopolies of a commercial character so as to ensure that when the transitional period has ended no discrimination regarding the conditions under which goods are procured and marketed exists between nationals of Member States. . . .

TITLE II: Agriculture

*Article 38*. 1. The common market shall extend to agriculture and trade in agricultural products. 'Agricultural products' means the products of the soil, of stock-farming and of fisheries and products of first-stage processing directly related to these products. . . .

*Article 39*. 1. The objectives of the common agricultural policy shall be:

(a) to increase agricultural productivity by promoting technical progress and by ensuring the rational development of agricultural production and the optimum utilization of the factors of production, in particular labour;

(b) thus to ensure a fair standard of living for the agricultural community, in particular by increasing the individual earnings of persons engaged in agriculture;

(c) to stabilize markets;

(d) to assure the availability of supplies;

(e) to ensure that supplies reach consumers at reasonable prices.

2. In working out the common agricultural policy and the special methods for its application, account shall be taken of:

(a) the particular nature of agricultural activity, which results from the social structure of agriculture and from structural and natural disparities between the various agricultural regions;

(b) the need to effect the appropriate adjustments by degrees;

(c) the fact that in the Member States agriculture constitutes a sector closely linked with the economy as a whole.

*Article 40.* 1. Member States shall develop the common agricultural policy by degrees during the transitional period and shall bring it into force by the end of that period at the latest.

2. In order to attain the objectives set out in Article 39 a common organization of agricultural markets shall be established. . . .

. . .

*Article 42.* The provisions of the Chapter relating to rules on competition shall apply to production of and trade in agricultural products only to the extent determined by the Council within the framework of Article 43 (2) and (3) and in accordance with the procedure laid down therein, account being taken of the objectives set out in Article 39.

The Council may, in particular, authorize the granting of aid:

(a) for the protection of enterprises handicapped by structural or natural conditions;

(b) within the framework of economic development programmes.

. . .

[*Article 43.* Details of procedural steps to be taken by the Commission and Council to create the Common Agricultural Policy and to form the common agricultural market.]

*Article 44.* 1. In so far as progressive abolition of customs duties and quantita-

tive restrictions between Member States may result in prices likely to jeopardize the attainment of the objectives set out in Article 39, each Member State shall, during the transitional period, be entitled to apply to particular products, in a non-discriminatory manner and in substitution for quotas and to such an extent as shall not impede the expansion of the volume of trade provided for in Article 45 (2), a system of minimum prices below which imports may be either:

temporarily suspended or reduced; or allowed, but subjected to the condition that they are made at a price higher than the minimum price for the product concerned.

In the latter case the minimum prices shall not include customs duties.

2. Minimum prices shall neither cause a reduction of the trade existing between Member States when this Treaty enters into force nor form an obstacle to progressive expansion of this trade. Minimum prices shall not be applied so as to form an obstacle to the development of a natural preference between Member States.

3. As soon as this Treaty enters into force the Council shall, on a proposal from the Commission, determine objective criteria for the establishment of minimum price systems and for the fixing of such prices.

These criteria shall in particular take account of the average national production costs in the Member State applying the minimum price, of the position of the various undertakings concerned in relation to such average production costs, and of the need to promote both the progressive improvement of agricultural practice and the adjustments and specialization needed within the common market. . . .

*Article 45.* 1. Until national market organizations have been replaced by one of the forms of common organization referred to in Article 40 (2), trade in products in respect of which certain Member States:

have arrangements designed to guarantee national producers a market for their products; and

are in need of imports,

shall be developed by the conclusion of long-term agreements or contracts between importing and exporting Member States.

These agreements or contracts shall be directed towards the progressive abolition of any discrimination in the application of these arrangements to the various producers within the Community.

Such agreements or contracts shall be concluded during the first stage; account shall be taken of the principle of reciprocity.

2. As regards quantities, these agreements or contracts shall be based on the average volume of trade between Member States in the products concerned during the three years before the entry into force of this Treaty and shall provide for an increase in the volume of trade within the limits of existing requirements, account being taken of traditional patterns of trade.

As regards prices, these agreements or contracts shall enable producers to dispose of the agreed quantities at prices which shall be progressively approximated to those paid to national producers on the domestic market of the purchasing country.

This approximation shall proceed as steadily as possible and shall be completed by the end of the transitional period at the latest.

Prices shall be negotiated between the parties concerned within the framework of directives issued by the Commission for the purpose of implementing the two preceding sub-paragraphs....

*Article 46.* Where in a Member State a product is subject to a national market organization or to internal rules having equivalent effect which affect the competitive position of similar production in another Member State, a countervailing charge shall be applied by Member States to imports of this product coming from the Member State where such organization or rules exist, unless that State applies a countervailing charge on export.

The Commission shall fix the amount of these charges at the level required to redress the balance; it may also authorize other measures, the conditions and details of which it shall determine.

*Article 47.* As to the functions to be performed by the Economic and Social Committee in pursuance of this Title, its agricultural section shall hold itself at the disposal of the Commission to prepare, in accordance with the provisions of Articles 197 and 198, the deliberations of the Committee.

TITLE III: Free movement of persons, services and capital

*Chapter 1: Workers*

*Article 48.* 1. Freedom of movement for workers shall be secured within the Community by the end of the transitional period at the latest.

2. Such freedom of movement shall entail the abolition of any discrimination based on nationality between workers of the Member States as regards employment, remuneration and other conditions of work and employment.

3. It shall entail the right, subject to limitations justified on grounds of public policy, public security or public health:

(a) to accept offers of employment actually made;

(b) to move freely within the territory of Member States for this purpose;

(c) to stay in a Member State for the purpose of employment in accordance with the provisions governing the employment of nationals of that State laid down by law, regulation or administrative action;

(d) to remain in the territory of a Member State after having been employed in that State, subject to conditions which shall be embodied in implementing regulations to be drawn up by the Commission.

4. The provisions of this Article shall not apply to employment in the public service.

*Article 49.* As soon as this Treaty enters

into force, the Council shall, acting on a proposal from the Commission and after consulting the Economic and Social Committee, issue directives or make regulations setting out the measures required to bring about, by progressive stages, freedom of movement for workers, as defined in Article 48, in particular:

(a) by ensuring close cooperation between national employment services;

(b) by systematically and progressively abolishing those administrative procedures and practices and those qualifying periods in respect of eligibility for available employment, whether resulting from national legislation or from agreements previously concluded between Member States, the maintenance of which would form an obstacle to liberalization of the movement of workers;

(c) by systematically and progressively abolishing all such qualifying periods and other restrictions provided for either under national legislation or under agreements previously concluded between Member States as impose on workers of other Member States conditions regarding the free choice of employment other than those imposed on workers of the State concerned;

(d) by setting up appropriate machinery to bring offers of employment into touch with applications for employment and to facilitate the achievement of a balance between supply and demand in the employment market in such a way as to avoid serious threats to the standard of living and level of employment in the various regions and industries.

*Article 50.* Member States shall, within the framework of a joint programme, encourage the exchange of young workers.

*Article 51.* The Council shall, acting unanimously on a proposal from the Commission, adopt such measures in the field of social security as are necessary to provide freedom of movement for workers; to this end, it shall make arrangements to secure for migrant workers and their dependants:

(a) aggregation, for the purpose of

acquiring and retaining the right to benefit and of calculating the amount of benefit, of all periods taken into account under the laws of the several countries;

(b) payment of benefits to persons resident in the territories of Member States.

*Chapter 2: Right of establishment*

*Article 52.* Within the framework of the provisions set out below, restrictions on the freedom of establishment of nationals of a Member State in the territory of another Member State shall be abolished by progressive stages in the course of the transitional period. Such progressive abolition shall also apply to restrictions on the setting up of agencies, branches or subsidiaries by nationals of any Member State established in the territory of any Member State.

Freedom of establishment shall include the right to take up and pursue activities as self-employed persons and to set up and manage undertakings, in particular companies of firms within the meaning of the second paragraph of Article 58, under the conditions laid down for its own nationals by the law of the country where such establishment is effected, subject to the provisions of the Chapter relating to capital.

. . .

[*Articles 53—8.* Set out details of implementation.]

*Chapter 3: Services*

*Article 59.* Within the framework of the provisions set out below, restrictions on freedom to provide services within the Community shall be progressively abolished during the transitional period in respect of nationals of Member States who are established in a State of the Community other than that of the person for whom the services are intended.

The Council may, acting unanimously on a proposal from the Commission, extend the provisions of this Chapter to nationals of a third country who provide services and who are established within the Community.

. . .

[*Articles 60–6.* Set out details of implementation.]

*Chapter 4: Capital*

*Article 73.* 1. During the transitional period and to the extent necessary to ensure the proper functioning of the common market, Member States shall progressively abolish between themselves all restrictions on the movement of capital belonging to persons resident in Member States and any discrimination based on the nationality or on the place of residence of the parties or on the place where such capital is invested.

. . .

[*Articles 68–72.* Set out details of implementation.]

*Article 73.* 1. If movements of capital lead to disturbances in the functioning of the capital market in any Member State, the Commission shall, after consulting the Monetary Committee, authorize that State to take protective measures in the field of capital movements, the conditions and details of which the Commission shall determine.

The Council may, acting by a qualified majority, revoke this authorization or amend the conditions or details thereof.

2. A Member State which is in difficulties may, however, on grounds of secrecy or urgency, take the measures mentioned above, where this proves necessary, on its own initiative. The Commission and the other Member States shall be informed of such measures by the date of their entry into force at the latest. In this event the Commission may, after consulting the Monetary Committee, decide that the State concerned shall amend or abolish the measures.

TITLE IV: Transport

[*Articles 74–84.* Set out objectives and means of implementing a common trans-

port policy covering road, rail, waterways and air transport.]

. . .

# Part Three · Policy of the Community

TITLE I: Common rules

*Chapter 1: Rules on competition*

SECTION 1 · RULES APPLYING TO UNDERTAKINGS

*Article 85.* 1. The following shall be prohibited as incompatible with the common market: all agreements between undertakings, decisions by associations of undertakings and concerted practices which may affect trade between Member States and which have as their object or effect the prevention, restriction or distortion of competition within the common market, and in particular those which:

(a) directly or indirectly fix purchase or selling prices or any other trading conditions;

(b) limit or control production, markets, technical development, or investment;

(c) share markets or sources of supply. . . .

*Article 86.* Any abuse by one or more undertakings of a dominant position within the common market or in a substantial part of it shall be prohibited as incompatible with the common market in so far as it may affect trade between Member States. Such abuse may, in particular, consist in:

(a) directly or indirectly imposing unfair purchase or selling prices or other unfair trading conditions;

(b) limiting production, markets or technical development to the prejudice of consumers. . .

*Article 87.* 1. Within three years of the entry into force of this Treaty the Council shall, acting unanimously on a proposal from the Commission and after consulting the Assembly, adopt any appropriate regulations or directives to give effect to the principles set out in Articles 85 and 86. . . .

[*Articles 89–90*. Commission's powers of supervision and control.]

[*Article 91*. Commission's powers of supervision of injurious practices of dumping.]

SECTION 3 · AIDS GRANTED BY STATE

*Article 92*. 1. Save as otherwise provided in this Treaty, any aid granted by a Member State or through State resources in any form whatsoever which distorts or threatens to distort competition by favouring certain undertakings or the production of certain goods shall, in so far as it affects trade between Member States, be incompatible with the common market.
. . .[Exceptions are set out such as disaster aid and aid to promote economic development where standards of living are exceptionally low.]

*Article 93*. 1. The Commission shall, in cooperation with Member States, keep under constant review all systems of aid existing in those States. It shall propose to the latter any appropriate measures required by the progressive development or by the functioning of the common market. . .
3. The Commission shall be informed, in sufficient time to enable it to submit its comments, of any plans to grant or alter aid. If it considers that any such plan is not compatible with the common market having regard to Article 92, it shall without delay initiate the procedure provided for in paragraph 2. The Member State concerned shall not put its proposed measures into effect until this procedure has resulted in a final decision.

*Article 94*. The Council may, acting by a qualified majority on a proposal from the Commission, make any appropriate regulations for the application of Articles 92 and 93 and may in particular determine the conditions in which Article 93 (3) shall apply and the categories of aid exempted from this procedure.

*Chapter 2: Tax provisions*

*Article 95*. No Member State shall impose, directly or indirectly, on the products of other Member States any internal taxation of any kind in excess of that imposed directly or indirectly on similar domestic products.
Furthermore, no Member State shall impose on the products of other Member States any internal taxation of such a nature as to afford indirect protection to other products.
Member States shall, not later than at the beginning of the second stage, repeal or amend any provisions existing when this Treaty enters into force which conflict with the preceding rules.

*Article 96*. Where products are exported to the territory of any Member State, any repayment of internal taxation shall not exceed the internal tax imposed on them, whether directly or indirectly.

. . .

[*Articles 97–9*. Details concerning introduction of value added tax.]

*Chapter 3: Approximation of laws*

*Article 100*. The Council shall, acting unanimously on a proposal from the Commission, issue directives for the approximation of such provisions laid down by law, regulation or administrative action in Member States as directly affect the establishment or functioning of the common market.
The Assembly and the Economic and Social Committee shall be consulted in the case of directives whose implementation would, in one or more Member States, involve the amendment of legislation.

*Article 101*. Where the Commission finds that a difference between the provisions laid down by law, regulation or administrative action in Member States is distorting the conditions of competition in the common market and that the resultant distortion needs to be eliminated, it shall consult the Member States concerned.
If such consultation does not result in an agreement eliminating the distortion in question, the Council shall, on a proposal from the Commission, acting unanimously during the first stage and by

a qualified majority thereafter, issue the necessary directives. The Commission and the Council may take any other appropriate measures provided for in this Treaty.

...

TITLE II: Economic policy

*Chapter 1: Conjunctural policy*

*Article 103.* 1. Member States shall regard their conjunctural policies as a matter of common concern. They shall consult each other and the Commission on the measures to be taken in the light of the prevailing circumstances....

*Chapter 2: Balance of payments*

*Article 104.* Each Member State shall pursue the economic policy needed to ensure the equilibrium of its overall balance of payments and to maintain confidence in its currency, while taking care to ensure a high level of employment and a stable level of prices.

*Article 105.* 1. In order to facilitate attainment of the objectives set out in Article 104, Member States shall coordinate their economic policies. They shall for this purpose provide for cooperation between their appropriate administrative departments and between their central banks.

The Commission shall submit to the Council recommendations on how to achieve such cooperation....

[*Article 106.* Abolition of restrictions on transfers of currency.]

*Article 107.* 1. Each Member State shall treat its policy with regard to rates of exchange as a matter of common concern.

2. If a Member State makes an alteration in its rate of exchange which is inconsistent with the objectives set out in Article 104 and which seriously distorts conditions of competition, the Commission may, after consulting the Monetary Committee, authorize other Member States to take for a strictly limited period the necessary measures, the conditions and details of which it shall determine, in order to counter the consequences of such alteration.

*Article 108.* 1. Where a Member State is in difficulties or is seriously threatened with difficulties as regards its balance of payments either as a result of an overall disequilibrium in its balance of payments, or as a result of the type of currency at its disposal, and where such difficulties are liable in particular to jeopardize the functioning of the common market or the progressive implementation of the common commercial policy, the Commission shall immediately investigate the position of the State in question and the action which, making use of all the means at its disposal, that State has taken or may take in accordance with the provisions of Article 104. The Commission shall state what measures it recommends the State concerned to take.... [The Commission may authorize the State in difficulties to take protective measures.]

*Article 109.* 1. Where a sudden crisis in the balance of payments occurs and a decision within the meaning of Article 108 (2) is not immediately taken, the Member State concerned may, as a precaution, take the necessary protective measures. Such measures must cause the least possible disturbance in the functioning of the common market and must not be wider in scope than is strictly necessary to remedy the sudden difficulties which have arisen....

3. After the Commission has delivered an opinion and the Monetary Committee has been consulted, the Council may, acting by a qualified majority, decide that the State concerned shall amend, suspend or abolish the protective measures referred to above.

*Chapter 3: Commercial policy*

*Article 110.* By establishing a customs union between themselves Member States aim to contribute, in the common interest, to the harmonious development of world trade, the progressive abolition of restrictions on international trade and the lowering of customs barriers.

The common commercial policy shall take into account the favourable effect which the abolition of customs duties between Member States may have on the increase in the competitive strength of undertakings in those States.

. . .

[*Articles 111–12.* Implementation.]

*Article 113.* 1. After the transitional period has ended, the common commercial policy shall be based on uniform principles, particularly in regard to changes in tariff rates, the conclusion of tariff and trade agreements, the achievement of uniformity in measures of liberalization, export policy and measures to protect trade such as those to be taken in case of dumping or subsidies.

2. The Commission shall submit proposals to the Council for implementing the common commercial policy.

3. Where agreements with third countries need to be negotiated, the Commission shall make recommendations to the Council, which shall authorize the Commission to open the necessary negotiations.

The Commission shall conduct these negotiations in consultation with a special committee appointed by the Council to assist the Commission in this task and within the framework of such directives as the Council may issue to it.

4. In exercising the powers conferred upon it by this Article, the Council shall act by a qualified majority.

*Article 114.* The agreements referred to in Article 111 (2) and in Article 113 shall be concluded by the Council on behalf of the Community, acting unanimously during the first two stages and by a qualified majority thereafter.

. . .

TITLE III: Social policy

*Chapter 1: Social provisions*

*Article 117.* Member States agree upon the need to promote improved working conditions and an improved standard of living for workers, so as to make possible their harmonization while the improvement is being maintained.

They believe that such a development will ensue not only from the functioning of the common market, which will favour the harmonization of social systems, but also from the procedures provided for in this Treaty and from the approximation of provisions laid down by law, regulation or administrative action.

*Article 118.* Without prejudice to the other provisions of this Treaty and in conformity with its general objectives, the Commission shall have the task of promoting close cooperation between Member States in the social field. . . .

*Article 119.* Each Member State shall during the first stage ensure and subsequently maintain the application of the principle that men and women should receive equal pay for equal work. . . .

*Chapter 2: The European Social Fund*

*Article 123.* In order to improve employment opportunities for workers in the common market and to contribute thereby to raising the standard of living, a European Social Fund is hereby established in accordance with the provisions set out below; it shall have the task of rendering the employment of workers easier and of increasing their geographical and occupational mobility within the Community.

*Article 124.* The Fund shall be administered by the Commission.

The Commission shall be assisted in this task by a Committee presided over by a member of the Commission and composed of representatives of Governments, trade unions and employers' organizations.

. . .

TITLE IV: The European Investment Bank

*Article 129.* A European Investment Bank is hereby established; it shall have legal personality.

The members of the European Investment Bank shall be the Member States.

The Statute of the European Investment Bank is laid down in a Protocol annexed to this Treaty.

*Article 130.* The task of the European Investment Bank shall be to contribute, by having recourse to the capital market and utilizing its own resources, to the balanced and steady development of the common market in the interest of the Community. For this purpose the Bank shall, operating on a non-profit-making basis, grant loans and give guarantees which facilitate the financing of the following projects in all sectors of the economy:

(a) projects for developing less developed regions;

(b) projects for modernizing or converting undertakings or for developing fresh activities called for by the progressive establishment of the common market, where these projects are of such a size or nature that they cannot be entirely financed by the various means available in the individual Member States;

(c) projects of common interest to several Member States which are of such a size or nature that they cannot be entirely financed by the various means available in the individual Member States.

## Part Four · Association of the overseas countries and territories

*Article 131.* The Member States agree to associate with the Community the non-European countries and territories which have special relations with Belgium, France, Italy and the Netherlands. These countries and territories (hereinafter called 'the countries and territories') are listed in Annex IV to this Treaty.

The purpose of association shall be to promote the economic and social development of the countries and territories and to establish close economic relations between them and the Community as a whole.

In accordance with the principles set out in the Preamble to this Treaty, association shall serve primarily to further the interests and prosperity of the inhabitants of these countries and territories in order to lead them to the economic,

social and cultural development to which they aspire.

. . .

## Part Five · Institutions of the Community

TITLE 1:  Provisions governing the institutions

*Chapter 1: The institutions*

SECTION 1 · THE ASSEMBLY

*Article 137.* The Assembly, which shall consist of representatives of the peoples of the States brought together in the Community, shall exercise the advisory and supervisory powers which are conferred upon it by this Treaty.

*Article 138.* 1. The Assembly shall consist of delegates who shall be designated by the respective Parliaments from among their members in accordance with the procedure laid down by each Member State.

. . .

[*Articles 139–43.* Procedures of Assembly.]

*Article 144.* If a motion of censure on the activities of the Commission is tabled before it, the Assembly shall not vote thereon until at least three days after the motion has been tabled and only by open vote.

If the motion of censure is carried by a two-thirds majority of the votes cast, representing a majority of the members of the Assembly, the members of the Commission shall resign as a body. They shall continue to deal with current business until they are replaced in accordance with Article 158.

*Article 145.* To ensure that the objectives set out in this Treaty are attained, the Council shall, in accordance with the provisions of this Treaty:

ensure coordination of the general economic policies of the Member States; have power to take decisions.

*Article 146.* The Council shall consist of representatives of the Member States. Each Government shall delegate to it one of its members.

The office of president shall be held for a term of six months by each member of the Council in turn...

*Article 147.* The Council shall meet when convened by its President on his own initiative or at the request of one of its members or of the Commission.

*Article 148.* 1. Save as otherwise provided in this Treaty, the Council shall act by a majority of its members.

2. Where the Council is required to act by a qualified majority, the votes of its members shall be weighted as follows:

| | |
|---|---|
| Belgium | 2 |
| Germany | 4 |
| France | 4 |
| Italy | 4 |
| Luxemburg | 1 |
| Netherlands | 2 |

For their adoption, acts of the Council shall require at least:

twelve votes in favour where this Treaty requires them to be adopted on a proposal from the Commission,
twelve votes in favour, cast by at least four members, in other cases.

3. Abstentions by members present in person or represented shall not prevent the adoption by the Council of acts which require unanimity.

*Article 149.* Where, in pursuance of this Treaty, the Council acts on a proposal from the Commission, unanimity shall be required for an act constituting an amendment to that proposal.

As long as the Council has not acted, the Commission may alter its original proposal, in particular where the Assembly has been consulted on that proposal.

. . .

*Article 155.* In order to ensure the proper functioning and development of the common market, the Commission shall:

ensure that the provisions of this Treaty and the measures taken by the institutions pursuant thereto are applied;
formulate recommendations or deliver opinions on matters dealt with in this Treaty, if it expressly so provides or if the Commission considers it necessary;
have its own power of decision and participate in the shaping of measures taken by the Council and by the Assembly in the manner provided for in this Treaty;
exercise the powers conferred on it by the Council for the implementation of the rules laid down by the latter.

. . .

*Article 157* [as revised by Article 10 of the Merger Treaty of 1965]. 1. The Commission shall consist of nine members, who shall be chosen on the grounds of their general competence and whose independence is beyond doubt.

The number of members of the Commission may be altered by the Council, acting unanimously.

Only nationals of Member States may be members of the Commission.

The Commission must include at least one national of each of the Member States, but may not include more than two members having the nationality of the same State.

2. The members of the Commission shall, in the general interest of the Communities, be completely independent in the performance of their duties.

In the performance of these duties, they shall neither seek nor take instructions from any Government or from any body. They shall refrain from any action incompatible with their duties. Each Member State undertakes to respect this principle and not to seek to influence the members of the Commission in the performance of their tasks.

The members of the Commission may not, during their term of office, engage in any other occupation, whether gainful or not. When entering upon their duties they shall give a solemn undertaking that, both during and after their term of office, they will respect the obligations arising therefrom and in particular their duty to behave with integrity and discretion as regards the acceptance, after they have ceased to hold office, of certain appointments or benefits. In the event of any breach of these obligations, the Court of Justice may, on application by the Council or the Commission, rule that the member concerned be, according to the circumstances, either compulsorily retired in accordance with the provisions of Article 13 or deprived of his right to a pension or other benefits in its stead.

*Article 158.* The members of the Commission shall be appointed by common accord of the Governments of the Member States.

Their term of office shall be four years. It shall be renewable.

. . .

*Article 163.* The Commission shall act by a majority of the number of members provided for in Article 157.

A meeting of the Commission shall be valid only if the number of members laid down in its rules of procedure is present.

SECTION 4 · THE COURT OF JUSTICE

*Article 164.* The Court of Justice shall ensure that in the interpretation and application of this Treaty the law is observed.

*Article 165.* The Court of Justice shall consist of seven Judges...

*Article 166.* The Court of Justice shall be assisted by two Advocates-General.

It shall be the duty of the Advocate-General, acting with complete impartiality and independence, to make, in open court, reasoned submissions on cases brought before the Court of Justice, in order to assist the Court in the performance of the task assigned to it in Article 164. . . .

*Article 167.* The Judges and Advocates-General shall be chosen from persons whose independence is beyond doubt and who possess the qualifications required for appointment to the highest judicial offices in their respective countries or who are jurisconsults of recognized competence; they shall be appointed by common accord of the Governments of the Member States for a term of six years. . . .

*Article 169.* If the Commission considers that a Member State has failed to fulfil an obligation under this Treaty, it shall deliver a reasoned opinion on the matter after giving the State concerned the opportunity to submit its observations.

If the State does not comply with the opinion within the period laid down by the Commission, the latter may bring the matter before the Court of Justice.

*Article 170.* A Member State which considers that another Member State has failed to fulfil an obligation under this Treaty may bring the matter before the Court of Justice.

Before a Member State brings an action against another Member State for an alleged infringement of an obligation under this Treaty, it shall bring the matter before the Commission.

The Commission shall deliver an opinion after each of the States concerned has been given the opportunity to submit its own case and its observations on the other party's case both orally and in writing.

If the Commission has not delivered an opinion within three months of the date on which the matter was brought before it, the absence of such opinion shall not prevent the matter being brought before the Court of Justice.

*Article 171.* If the Court of Justice finds that a Member State has failed to fulfil an obligation under this Treaty, the State shall be required to take the necessary measures to comply with the judgement of the Court of Justice.

*Article 172.* Regulations made by the Council pursuant to the provisions of this Treaty may give the Court of Justice unlimited jurisdiction in regard to the penalties provided for in such regulations.

*Article 173.* The Court of Justice shall review the legality of acts of the Council and the Commission other than recommendations or opinions.

...

*Article 175.* Should the Council or the Commission, in infringement of this Treaty, fail to act, the Member States and the other institutions of the Community may bring an action before the Court of Justice to have the infringement established...

*Article 177.* The Court of Justice shall have jurisdiction to give preliminary rulings concerning:

(a) the interpretation of this Treaty;

(b) the validity and interpretation of acts of the institutions of the Community;

(c) the interpretation of the statutes of bodies established by an act of the Council, where those statutes so provide....

*Article 182.* The Court of Justice shall have jurisdiction in any dispute between Member States which relates to the subject matter of this Treaty if the dispute is submitted to it under a special agreement between the parties.

...

*Chapter 2: Provisions common to several institutions*

*Article 189.* In order to carry out their task the Council and the Commission shall, in accordance with the provisions of this Treaty, make regulations, issue directives, take decisions, make recommendations or deliver opinions.

A regulation shall have general application. It shall be binding in its entirety and directly applicable in all Member States.

A directive shall be binding, as to the result to be achieved, upon each Member State to which it is addressed, but shall leave to the national authorities the choice of form and methods.

A decision shall be binding in its entirety upon those to whom it is addressed.

Recommendations and opinions shall have no binding force.

...

*Article 192.* Decisions of the Council or of the Commission which impose a pecuniary obligation on persons other than States shall be enforceable.

Enforcement shall be governed by the rules of civil procedure in force in the State in the territory of which it is carried out.

*Chapter 3: The Economic and Social Committee*

*Article 193.* An Economic and Social Committee is hereby established. It shall have advisory status.

The Committee shall consist of representatives of the various categories of economic and social activity, in particular, representatives of producers, farmers, carriers, workers, dealers, craftsmen, professional occupations and representatives of the general public.

...

*Article 198.* The Committee must be consulted by the Council or by the Commission where this Treaty so provides. The Committee may be consulted by these institutions in all cases in which they consider it appropriate....

TITLE II: Financial provisions

*Article 199.* All items of revenue and expenditure of the Community, including those relating to the European Social Fund, shall be included in estimates to be drawn up for each financial year and shall be shown in the budget.

The revenue and expenditure shown in the budget shall be in balance.

*Article 200.* 1. The budget revenue shall include, irrespective of any other revenue, financial contributions of Member States on the following scale:

| | |
|---|---|
| Belgium | 7.9 |
| Germany | 28.0 |
| France | 28.0 |

| | |
|---|---|
| Italy | 28.0 |
| Luxemburg | 0.2 |
| Netherlands | 7.9 |

2. The financial contributions of Member States to cover the expenditure of the European Social Fund, however, shall be determined on the following scale:

| | |
|---|---|
| Belgium | 8.8 |
| Germany | 32.0 |
| France | 32.0 |
| Italy | 20.0 |
| Luxemburg | 0.2 |
| Netherlands | 7.0 |

3. The scales may be modified by the Council, acting unanimously.

. . .

## Part Six · General and final provisions

[*Articles 210–40*. These include provisions for regulations covering officials and servants of the Community and official languages.]

*Article 228.* 1. Where this Treaty provides for the conclusion of agreements between the Community and one or more States or an international organization, such agreements shall be negotiated by the Commission. Subject to the powers vested in the Commission in this field, such agreements shall be concluded by the Council, after consulting the Assembly where required by this Treaty. . . .

. . .

*Article 236.* The Government of any Member State or the Commission may submit to the Council proposals for the amendment of this Treaty.

If the Council, after consulting the Assembly and, where appropriate, the Commission, delivers an opinion in favour of calling a conference of representatives of the Governments of the Member States, the conference shall be convened by the President of the Council for the purpose of determining by common accord the amendments to be made to this Treaty.

The amendments shall enter into force after being ratified by all the Member States in accordance with their respective constitutional requirements.

*Article 237.* Any European State may apply to become a member of the Community. It shall address its application to the Council, which shall act unanimously after obtaining the opinion of the Commission.

The conditions of admission and the adjustments to this Treaty necessitated thereby shall be the subject of an agreement between the Member States and the applicant State. This agreement shall be submitted for ratification by all the contracting States in accordance with their respective constitutional requirements.

*Article 238.* The Community may conclude with a third State, a union of States or an international organization agreements establishing an association involving reciprocal rights and obligations, common action and special procedures.

These agreements shall be concluded by the Council, acting unanimously after consulting the Assembly.

Where such agreements call for amendments to this Treaty, these amendments shall first be adopted in accordance with the procedure laid down in Article 236.

. . .

[*Articles 247–8*. Ratification by High Contracting Parties in accordance with their respective constitutional requirements. Dutch, French, German and Italian equally authentic languages of original treaty.]

In witness whereof, the undersigned plenipotentiaries have signed this Treaty.

Done at Rome this twenty-fifth day of March in the year one thousand nine hundred and fifty-seven.

P.H. SPAAK
ADENAUER
PINEAU
Antonio SEGNI
BECH
J. LUNS

J. CH. SNOY et d'OPPUERS
HALLSTEIN
M. FAURE

Gaetano MARTINO
Lambert SCHAUS
J. LINTHORST HOMAN

# Convention establishing the European Free Trade Association (E.F.T.A.), Stockholm, 4 January 1960

[Austria, Denmark, Norway, Portugal, Sweden, Switzerland and Britain...]

Having regard to the Convention for European Economic Cooperation of 16th April 1948, which established the Organization for European Economic Co-operation;

Resolved to maintain and develop the cooperation instituted within that organization;

Determined to facilitate the early establishment of a multilateral association for the removal of trade barriers and the promotion of closer economic cooperation between the Members of the Organization for European Economic Cooperation, including the Members of the European Economic Community;

Having regard to the General Agreement on Tariffs and Trade;

Resolved to promote the objectives of that Agreement;

Have agreed as follows:

*Article 1. The Association.* 1. An international organization to be known as the European Free Trade Association, hereinafter referred to as 'the Association', is hereby established.

2. The Members of the Association, hereinafter referred to as 'Member States', shall be the States which ratify this Convention and such other States as may accede to it.

3. The Area of the Association shall be the territories to which this Convention applies.

4. The Institutions of the Association shall be a Council and such other organs as the Council may set up.

*Article 2. Objectives.* The objectives of the Association shall be

(a) to promote in the Area of the Association and in each Member State a sustained expansion of economic activity, full employment, increased productivity and the rational use of resources, financial stability and continuous improvement in living standards,

(b) to secure that trade between Member States takes place in conditions of fair competition,

(c) to avoid significant disparity between Member States in the conditions of supply of raw materials produced within the Area of the Association, and

(d) to contribute to the harmonious development and expansion of world trade and to the progressive removal of barriers to it.

*Article 3. Import duties.* 1. Member States shall reduce and ultimately eliminate, in accordance with this Article, customs duties and any other charges with equivalent effect, except duties notified in accordance with Article 6 and other charges which fall within that Article, imposed on or in connection with the importation of goods which are eligible for Area tariff treatment in accordance with Article 4. Any such duty or other charge is hereinafter referred to as an 'import duty'.

2. (a) On and after each of the following dates, Member States shall not apply an import duty on any product at a level exceeding the percentage of the basic duty specified against that date [reducing from

80 per cent on 1 July 1960 to 10 per cent on 1 January 1969].

(b) On and after 1st January 1970, Member States shall not apply any import duties....

[*Articles 4–29. Cooperation, trading practices etc.*]

*Article 30. Economic and financial policies.* Member States recognize that the economic and financial policies of each of them affect the economies of other Member States and intend to pursue those policies in a manner which serves to promote the objectives of the Association. They shall periodically exchange views on all aspects of those policies. In so doing, they shall take into account the corresponding activities within the Organization for European Economic Cooperation and other international organizations. The Council may make recommendations to Member States on matters relating to those policies to the extent necessary to ensure the attainment of the objectives and the smooth operation of the Association.

*Article 31. General consultations and complaints procedures.* 1. If any Member considers that any benefit conferred upon it by this Convention or any objective of the Association is being or may be frustrated and if no satisfactory settlement is reached between the Member States concerned, any of those Member States may refer the matter to the Council.

2. The Council shall promptly, by majority vote, make arrangements for examining the matter. Such arrangements may include a reference to an examining committee constituted in accordance with Article 33. Before taking action under paragraph 3 of this Article, the Council shall so refer the matter at the request of any Member State concerned. Member States shall furnish all information which they can make available and shall lend their assistance to establish the facts.

3. When considering the matter, the Council shall have regard to whether it has been established that an obligation under the Convention has not been fulfilled, and whether and to what extent any benefit conferred by the Convention or any objective of the Association is being or may be frustrated. In the light of this consideration and of the report of any examining committee which may have been appointed, the Council may, by majority vote, make to any Member State such recommendations as it considers appropriate.

4. If a Member State does not or is unable to comply with a recommendation made in accordance with paragraph 3 of this Article and the Council finds, by majority vote, that an obligation under this Convention has not been fulfilled, the Council may, by majority decision, authorize any Member State to suspend to the Member State which has not complied with the recommendation the application of such obligations under this Convention as the Council considers appropriate.

5. Any Member State may, at any time while the matter is under consideration, request the Council to authorize, as a matter of urgency, interim measures to safeguard its position. If it appears to the Council that the circumstances are sufficiently serious to justify interim action, and without prejudice to any action which it may subsequently take in accordance with the preceding paragraphs of this Article, the Council may, by majority decision, authorize a Member State to suspend its obligations under this Convention to such an extent and for such a period as the Council considers appropriate.

*Article 32. The Council.* 1. It shall be the responsibility of the Council

(a) to exercise such powers and functions as are conferred upon it by this Convention,

(b) to supervise the application of this Convention and keep its operation under review, and

(c) to consider whether further action should be taken by Member States in order to promote the attainment of the objectives of the Association and to facilitate the establishment of closer links with other States, unions of States or international organizations.

2. Each Member State shall be represented in the Council and shall have one vote.

3. The Council may decide to set up such organs, committees and other bodies as it considers necessary to assist it in accomplishing its tasks.

4. In exercising its responsibility under paragraph 1 of this Article, the Council may take decisions which shall be binding on all Member States and may make recommendations to Member States.

5. Decisions and recommendations of the Council shall be made by unanimous vote, except in so far as this Convention provides otherwise. Decisions or recommendations shall be regarded as unanimous unless any Member State casts a negative vote. Decisions and recommendations which are to be made by majority vote require the affirmative vote of four Member States.

6. If the number of the Member States changes, the Council may decide to amend the number of votes required for decisions and recommendations which are to be made by majority vote.

. . .

[Article 33. Composition of Examining Committees to be appointed by the Council.]

[Article 34. Administrative arrangements of the Association.]

[Article 35. Legal capacity, privileges and immunities.]

[Article 36. Relations with international organizations.]

[Article 37. Obligations under other international agreements.]

[Articles 39–40. Ratification and entry into force.]

Article 41. Accession and association. 1. Any State may accede to this Convention, provided that the Council decides to approve its accession, on such terms and conditions as may be set out in that decision. The instrument of accession shall be deposited with the Government of Sweden which shall notify all other Member States. This Convention shall enter into force in relation to an acceding State on the date indicated in that decision.

2. The Council may negotiate an agreement between the Member States and any other State, union of States or international organization, creating an association embodying such reciprocal rights and obligations, common actions and special procedures as may be appropriate. Such an agreement shall be submitted to the Member States for acceptance and shall enter into force provided that it is accepted by all Member States. Instruments of acceptance shall be deposited with the Government of Sweden which shall notify all other Member States.

Article 42. Withdrawal. Any Member State may withdraw from this Convention provided that it gives twelve months' notice in writing to the Government of Sweden which shall notify all other Member States.

. . .

[Article 43. Territorial application.]

[Article 44. Amendments require agreement of all Member States.]

## Western Europe since the 1960s: expansion and closer integration of the European Community

The division of Western Europe into an 'Inner Six' and an 'Outer Seven' seemed almost from the outset to be an improbable and impractical arrangement. E.F.T.A. was much the weaker (as well as being the less well integrated) of the two trading blocs, boasting only one major economic power, Great Britain, as a member. In August 1961 Britain (as well as Ireland and Denmark) applied for membership of the E.E.C.; Norway lodged an application in May 1962. Subsequently Austria, Sweden, and Switzerland applied separately for association with the E.E.C. But the French President, Charles de Gaulle, opposed British entry, apparently fearing 'Anglo-Saxon' domination of Western Europe. In January 1963 he issued his 'veto' of British membership of the E.E.C., whereupon the negotiations were indefinitely adjourned. Britain renewed her application for membership in May 1967, followed by similar applications by Denmark, Ireland, and Norway. But in December 1967 these negotiations too came to a standstill due to French objections.

The resignation of de Gaulle from the French Presidency in 1969 opened the way for a renewal of negotiations in June 1970 and these were completed in June 1971. *On 22 January 1972 the Treaty of Accession to the Community of Denmark, Ireland, Norway, and the United Kingdom was signed. On 22 July 1972 free trade agreements were signed between the Community and Austria, Iceland, Portugal, Sweden and Switzerland.* The British Parliament completed ratification of the Treaty of Accession on 20 September 1972. Denmark and Ireland also completed ratification before the close of 1972. But on 26 September a referendum in Norway rejected Norwegian accession.

The three countries which joined the E.E.C. on 1 January 1973 obtained a number of special concessions. Of these the most important concerned Britain. A transitional period of five years was granted to Britain for adjustment to E.E.C. tariffs and rules and to the agreed common policies including the common agricultural policy; this period was to be calculated from 1 January 1973. The stages of harmonization were also agreed. Britain undertook to meet the budget costs of the Community on a rising scale (subsequently amended) from 8.64 per cent in 1973 to 18.92 per cent in 1977. Special quantitative guarantees for New Zealand exports of dairy products were granted until 1978 (subsequently extended to 1988). Other arrangements were made for Commonwealth countries and for British dependent territories with close trading relations with the United Kingdom.

*Greece* applied to join the Community on 12 June 1975, *signed the Accession Treaty on 28 May 1979 and its membership took effect on 1 January 1981.* Negotiations for the entry to the Community of Spain and Portugal stretched through 1983 and 1984; the two countries finally joined the Community on 1 January 1986. The original six members had therefore by 1986 expanded to twelve. (The only case of withdrawal from the Community was that of Greenland, which had entered the E.E.C. as a dependency of Denmark in 1973; following the grant by Denmark of autonomy to Greenland, the territory's inhabitants voted in a referendum in February 1982 to end their membership of the Community.)

The expansion of the Community accentuated stresses already apparent within the E.E.C. in the 1960s. In the early period differences over both policy and institutional arrangements most often pitted France against her five partners. For France the Common Agricultural Policy represented the chief economic advantage to be placed against the possible economic disadvantages of a common market without trade barriers. The progressive implementation of the C.A.P. presented the Community with several crises. A French boycott from July 1965 to January 1966 was partly precipitated by the agricultural problem, but it also proved the Community's basic strength in that agreement was reached in the end.

Under the Community's C.A.P. prices were established for agricultural products which were designed to give a proper return to the European farmer. But the prices were generally well above world market prices for these commodities which hitherto could be imported at the lower world price, so the Community raised a protective barrier against imports from non-members. A Farm Fund was established to implement the C.A.P. Member States contributed a fixed proportion of the Fund from their national budgets. The common Farm Fund's purpose was threefold: to support buying when the market price was about to fall below that fixed by the Commission, secondly to provide export subsidies to lower the Community's price when selling abroad and finally to finance modernization and retraining schemes. This policy led to an over-production at the prices fixed, as for example by creating enormous stockpiled 'butter mountains' and 'wine lakes'. The costs of the Farm Fund escalated beyond what had been anticipated. 'Reform' proved difficult. France, the chief beneficiary, wished to safeguard its position. In December 1969 the E.E.C. reached a fundamental agreement for the continuation of C.A.P. and changes in its financing. Funds for the Farm Fund would after 1971 no longer be contributed through the national budgets of the members, but the Community would receive them automatically from the duties

levied on agricultural imports together with a fixed percentage of the
Value Added Tax levied within each Member State. The importance of the
C.A.P. can be gauged from the fact that it has accounted for more than 90
per cent of the Community's total expenditure.

Related to the disputes over issues such as the Common Agricultural
Policy were disputes over institutions. De Gaulle, as an advocate of
'l'Europe des patries', tended to oppose the supranational tendencies
inherent in the Treaty of Rome. These disputes came to a head in 1965
when France abruptly broke off discussions in Brussels about the C.A.P.
For the next six months France boycotted nearly all the Community's
decision-making institutions. The boycott ended in January 1966 with an
agreement negotiated in Luxemburg between France and her partners.
The new agreement marked an acknowledgement by France's partners that
they could not, in effect, impose their views on an unwilling France. The
attempts to enhance the power of the Commission at the expense of that of
the Council of Ministers were halted. Within the Council of Ministers the
'qualified majority' principle, theoretically regnant, was replaced by what
was, in all but name, a unanimity requirement on most important issues.
This veto principle remained in effect for more than two decades. But in
December 1985 an E.E.C. summit in Luxemburg agreed on amendments
to the Rome Treaty (involving changes to six of the 240 Articles as well as
one new Article). Among these was an agreement that the use of the veto
on the Council in matters of vital national interest would be diminished.
Under the new arrangement (expected to take effect on 1 January 1987)
major economic and internal market questions would no longer require
unanimity in the Council of Ministers.

The powers of the European Parliament during the first two decades of
the Community were minimal. Member States, fearful of shedding
sovereignty, were reluctant to agree to measures which would transfer
authority from their national parliaments. The European Parliament itself,
all of whose members were nominated rather than directly elected, lacked
the legitimacy necessary to seek to assert its role. Some countries (in the
early years France, later Britain) resisted efforts to enhance the standing of
the European Parliament. By a decision in the Council of Ministers on 20
September 1976, however, direct elections were laid down as the basis of
membership of the European Parliament (except in the case of West
Berlin, where the special international status of the city made direct
elections impossible). The first such elections took place in all member
countries between 7 and 10 June 1979; more than 100 million electors
cast ballots. At the same time the Parliament was enlarged in size from

198 to 410 members (increased further with the addition of new Member States' representatives). Thenceforth the Parliament began cautiously to flex its muscles. In December 1979 the Parliament took the unprecedented step of rejecting a draft budget submitted by the European Commission. The E.E.C. summit meeting at Luxemburg in December 1985 agreed on measures designed to give some further authority to the European Parliament which was given a right of 'second reading' of legislation. But the Parliament remained a consultative rather than a decision-making institution, impotent to impose its will on the Commission or the Council of Ministers.

In other spheres the Community achieved more significant progress both in rationalizing its institutional structure and in working towards closer integration of its members. *A treaty signed* by the original six members in Brussels *on 8 April 1965 created a single Council and a single Commission of the European Communities*, getting rid of the clumsy triplication of such bodies in the E.E.C, the E.C.S.C., and Euratom. This merger treaty came into effect in 1967. In the early years of the Community, meetings of Heads of Government took place only at irregular intervals; from 1974 onwards regular summit meetings were held three times a year. Other important institutions of the Community which gradually accreted to themselves significant influence were the European Court of Justice and the European Investment Bank. In March 1979 a European Monetary System (E.M.S.) came into being with the object of stabilizing European currencies. All the Member States of the Community became participants in the E.M.S., with the exception of Britain (and, upon gaining membership in the Community, Greece).

Association or cooperation agreements were signed with a very large number of countries both in Europe and elsewhere. Of particular significance was the series of agreements signed with groups of developing countries. The *First Yaoundé Convention, signed on 20 July 1963*, in the capital of Cameroon, extended tariff reductions and development aid to eighteen former French colonies in Africa. The *Second Yaoundé Convention, signed on 29 July 1969* widened the arrangement to include several other African states. These agreements were replaced by the *First Lomé Convention, signed on 28 February 1975*, in the capital of Togo. The Lomé Convention, which came into force on 1 April 1976, established a privileged relationship between the E.E.C. and forty-six States in Africa, the Caribbean, and the Pacific, known collectively as the A.C.P. States. Under this agreement 99 per cent of A.C.P. exports entered the Community duty-free. The convention also provided for development aid to the A.C.P. countries. The *Second Lomé Convention, concluded on 31 October 1979*, came into force on 1 March 1980. Like its predecessor this ran for five years. The second convention was agreed with fifty-eight A.C.P. countries and widened the areas of cooperation a little. *On 8 December 1984, the Third Lomé Convention* was concluded with sixty-five A.C.P. states. This too was to run for a period of five years, ending on 28 February 1990. The agreement provided for a small increase in aid to the A.C.P. countries but for no major changes in trade relationships with the E.E.C.

The first three decades of the Community's existence thus saw patchy and incomplete progress towards economic and political integration in Europe and towards the establishment of satisfactory common external policies. By the mid-1980s the Member States began to evince what was known as 'aid weariness', manifested in their negotiations for 'Lomé III'. More importantly, the severe economic recession after 1973 gradually increased protectionist pressures within the E.E.C., leading by the mid-1980s to the threat of trade war with the U.S.A. and Japan.

If the Community failed during these years to achieve the hopes of some of its more ambitious members for full political integration in a united Europe of federated States, it did succeed in evolving towards common foreign policy positions on most major issues. A major symbolic agreement was the *Franco-German Treaty of Cooperation, signed at Paris on 22 January 1963* by President de Gaulle and Chancellor Adenauer. This contained a common declaration 'that the reconciliation of the German people and the French people, bringing an end to the age-old rivalries, constitutes a historic event which profoundly transforms the relations of the two peoples'. Membership of the Community so intertwined the functional relations of Member States as to render wars between them inconceivable and to assuage even serious disputes involving territorial claims. A case in point was the antagonism between Britain and Spain over Gibraltar: upon Spanish entry to the Community the barriers by which Spain had blockaded Gibraltar for many years (in an effort to assert its claim to the British colony) were perforce lifted in order to comply with the Treaty of Rome, guaranteeing free movement of persons and goods between Member States.

Other agreements between West European States testified to the general tendency in the region towards integration.

The *Nordic Council*, founded in 1952 by Denmark, Iceland, Norway, and Sweden (Finland joined in 1955), promoted cooperation between the Scandinavian States. It was, however, merely advisory and consultative, decisions being binding only in the case of unanimity.

Three recent agreements involving Western European States, each agreement different in character, give further evidence of the lessening of historical antagonisms.

The *Agreement between the Holy See and Italy, signed at Rome on 18 February 1984* (p. 247) (ratifications were exchanged on 3 June 1985) modified the Lateran Concordat of 1929, and marked a significant change in the relationship between the Roman Catholic Church and the Italian Republic. The new agreement repealed the provision of the 1929 Concordat which declared Catholicism the 'sole religion of the State'. The agreement, which was held by observers to indicate a weakening of the secular power of the Church in Italy, made Church annulments of marriages subject to State confirmation. Various special privileges of the Church and of priests were diminished. Withdrawal of children from religious education classes in schools was made easier. Rome's formal status as a 'sacred city' was removed (thus eliminating the Vatican's right to protest against strip-tease shows and other such affronts). And the Jewish catacombs of Rome and southern Italy were removed from Vatican control and handed over to the Italian Government.

The *Anglo-Irish Agreement over Northern Ireland, signed in London on 15 November 1985* (p. 252) by Margaret Thatcher and Garret FitzGerald (respectively British and Irish Prime Ministers), represented an attempt by the British and Irish Governments to end what Margaret Thatcher called the 'cycle of violence' which afflicted Ulster after 1969. A previous agreement in 1973, which provided for power-sharing between the Protestant majority and the Catholic minority in Northern Ireland, came to grief as a result of a massive protest strike by Protestant opponents of the scheme. Protestant opponents of the 1985 agreement immediately denounced it as 'treachery', and some Catholics in Ireland condemned it as a 'sell-out'. But the two Governments appeared determined, in the face of considerable opposition, to give effect to the arrangement which, for the first time, provided a voice for the Irish Republic in the affairs of Northern Ireland (a Council of Ireland, with representatives of both the independent south and the British north, had been proposed at the time of Irish independence, and again in December 1973 by the Prime Ministers of Northern Ireland and the Irish Republic, but on neither occasion had it been implemented). Under the 1985 agreement Ireland did not surrender her claim to sovereignty over the whole island (a claim enshrined in the Republic's constitution), but the Irish Government formally recognized that Irish unity could be brought about only with the consent of the majority of the population of Northern Ireland.

*On 20 January 1986*, in a festive ceremony at the town hall of Lille,

President Mitterrand of France and Mrs Thatcher signed an *agreement approving construction of a railway tunnel under the English Channel*. This agreement seemed likely to bring to ultimate fruition what was almost certainly the most long-drawn-out scheme for European integration ever undertaken. Construction of a Channel tunnel had been proposed in the early nineteenth century, and an Anglo-French agreement to promote the scheme had actually been signed in 1872. But the idea languished after the British War Office lodged objections on security grounds. A renewed *Anglo-French Agreement on a Channel Tunnel was signed at Chequers on 17 November 1973*, but was never ratified: after a vote in the House of Commons opposing the project on 21 January 1975, the agreement was 'regarded as having been abandoned'. It was, however, revived in December 1984 by a preliminary agreement between Mrs Thatcher and President Mitterrand. The tunnel, which President Mitterrand called 'the biggest construction project of the century' was expected to be built by 1993.

Some enthusiasts for European unity complained in the mid-1980s of 'Eurosclerosis', a tendency to allow existing institutions to harden rather than develop into new forms of collaboration and integration. But seen in a longer perspective the resilience of the European idea, particularly against the background of economic recession after 1973, was striking. For nearly a quarter century after the initiation of the Schuman plan, Western Europe enjoyed the most rapid and sustained period of growth in its history. For more than forty years after 1945 no war was fought in Europe – the longest such period in modern history. These were imperfect, but nevertheless impressive, achievements and they owed much to the multifarious treaties signed in the post-war period to promote European integration.

# Agreement between Italy and the Holy See to amend the 1929 Lateran Concordat, Rome, 18 February 1984

The Holy See and the Italian Republic,

Taking into account the process of political and social change that has occurred in Italy over the last decades and the developments which have taken place in the Church since the Second Vatican Council;

Bearing in mind, on the part of the Italian Republic, the principles proclaimed in its Constitution and, on the part of the Holy See, the Second Vatican Ecumenical Council's declarations on religious freedom and on the relations between the Church and the polity, as well as the new codification of canon law;

Considering further that, in accordance with Article 7, paragraph (2) of the Constitution of the Italian Republic, the relations between the State and the Catholic Church are governed by the Lateran Pacts, which, however, can be modified by common agreement of the two Parties without requiring any procedure of Constitutional revision;

Have recognized the opportunity of entering into the following mutually agreed amendments to the Lateran Concordat:

*Article 1.* The Italian Republic and the Holy See reaffirm that the State and the Catholic Church are, each in its own order, independent and sovereign and commit themselves to the full respect of this principle in their mutual relations and to reciprocal collaboration for the promotion of man and the common good of the Country.

*Article 2.* 1. The Italian Republic shall recognize the full freedom of the Church to develop its pastoral, educational, and charitable mission, of evangelization and sanctification. In particular, the Church shall be assured the freedom of organization, of public exercise of worship, of exercise of its magisterium and spiritual ministry as well as of exercise of jurisdiction in ecclesiastical matters.

2. It shall be equally assured the reciprocal freedom of communication and correspondence between the Holy See, the Italian Bishops Conference, the Regional Bishops Conferences, the bishops, the clergy and the faithful, as well as the freedom of printing and circulating acts and documents concerning the mission of the Church.

3. Catholics and their associations and organizations shall be granted the full freedom of assembly and of expression of their thoughts by oral, written, or any other means of publication.

4. The Italian Republic acknowledges the particular significance that Rome, the

Episcopal See of the Supreme Pontiff, has to Catholicism.

*Article 3.* 1. The boundaries of the dioceses and of the parishes shall be freely determined by the ecclesiastical authority. The Holy See commits itself not to include any part of the Italian territory into a diocese whose Episcopal See is in the territory of another State.

2. Appointments to ecclesiastical offices shall be freely made by the ecclesiastical authority. The ecclesiastical authority shall communicate to the competent civil authorities the appointments of the Archbishops and diocesan bishops, of the coadjutors, the abbots and prelates with territorial jurisdiction as well as of the parish priests and the appointments to the other ecclesiastical offices relevant for the State legal order.

3. Except for the diocese of Rome and for the suburban ones, ecclesiastics who are not Italian citizens shall not be appointed to the offices hereof.

*Article 4.* 1. The priests, the deacons, and the members of the religious orders who have taken vows shall have the right to obtain, at their own request, an exemption from the military service or to be assigned to the substitutive Civil Service.

2. In the event of general mobilization, the ecclesiastics who have not been assigned to the care of souls shall be called to exercise their religious office among the troops or, subordinately, they shall be assigned to the medical service.

3. Students of theology, those in the last two years of their theological preparation for ordination and novices of religious institutes and societies for apostolic life may take advantage of the same postponements of military service which are granted to the students of Italian Universities.

4. Ecclesiastics shall not be required to provide to magistrates or other authorities any information regarding persons or matters known to them by reason of their ministry.

*Article 5.* 1. Buildings open to worship

shall not be requisitioned, occupied, expropriated or demolished except for grave reasons and pursuant to a previous agreement with the competent ecclesiastical authority.

2. Except in cases of urgent necessity, the police force shall not enter buildings open to worship for the purpose of carrying out its duties without first advising the ecclesiastical authority thereof.

3. The civil authority shall take into account the religious needs of the people, as presented to it by the competent ecclesiastical authority, in connection with the construction of new buildings for Catholic worship and of the pertinent parish structures.

*Article 6.* The Italian Republic shall recognize as public holidays every Sunday and all the other religious feasts determined by agreement between the Parties.

*Article 7.* 1. The Italian Republic, in accordance with the principle enunciated in Article 20 of its Constitution, reaffirms that the ecclesiastical character and the religious or worship purpose of an association or institution shall not be the motive of special legislative limitations or of special tax exemptions with regard to its constitution, legal capacity, or any other form of activity.

2. The legal personality previously granted to ecclesiastic bodies shall be retained and the Italian Republic, upon request of the ecclesiastical authority or with its consent, shall continue to recognize the legal personality of the ecclesiastical bodies whose See is in Italy, who are constituted or approved according to the norms of canon law and have a religious or worship purpose. A similar procedure shall be followed in order to recognize civil effects to any substantial change of the same bodies.

3. With respect to taxation, ecclesiastical bodies having a religious or devotional purpose, as well as activities directed to that same scope shall be treated in the same manner as those having a beneficent or educational purpose.

The activities carried out by ecclesiastical bodies that are not for religious or devotional purposes shall be subject, in accordance with the structure and purpose of such bodies, to the laws of the State concerning such activities and to the tax burden provided for the same.

4. The buildings open to worship, the publications of acts, the posting of notices in the interior or at the outside doors of the worship or ecclesiastical buildings, and the collections made in the aforesaid buildings shall continue to be subject to the regulations presently in force.

5. The administration of the property owned by ecclesiastical bodies shall be subject to the controls provided by canon law. The acquisitions made by these bodies shall also be subject, however, to the controls provided for in the Italian laws on acquisition by legal persons.

6. On the occasion of the signing of the present agreement, the Parties shall appoint a joint Commission to formulate norms, that will be subsequently submitted for their approval, for the regulation of the whole matter of ecclesiastical bodies and properties and for the revision of the financial obligations of the Italian State and of its intervention into the patrimonial management of ecclesiastical bodies.

Upon a temporary basis and until the entry into force of the new regulation, Articles 17, paragraph (3), 18, 27, 29 and 30 of the previous text of the Concordat shall remain applicable.

*Article 8.* 1. Civil effects shall be recognized for marriages contracted according to the norms of canon law, provided that the act of marriage be entered in the registers of the vital statistics, and the notices of marriage have been previously published at the communal offices. Immediately after the ceremony, the parish priest or his delegate shall explain the civil effects of the marriage to the parties, by reading the Articles of the Civil Code concerning the rights and duties of married people and he shall thereafter draw up, in original duplicate, the certificate of marriage, in which the spouses' declarations permitted by civil law may be inserted.

The Holy See acknowledges that the registration shall not take place:

(a) When the spouses do not meet the requirements of age determined by civil law for celebration;

(b) When an impediment from which, according to civil law, no derogation is permitted, exists between the spouses.

However, registration is permitted when, according to civil law, an action for nullity or annulment can no longer be maintained.

The request for registration shall be made, in writing and within five days from the celebration, by the parish priest of the place where the marriage has been celebrated. If the conditions for registration are satisfied, the vital statistics officer shall record it within 24 hours from the receipt of the act and shall give notice thereof to the parish priest.

The marriage shall have civil effects from the moment of the celebration, even if the vital statistics officer has, for any reason, made the registration after the prescribed term.

The registration can also be made subsequently upon request of the two spouses, or of one of them with the knowledge and without the opposition of the other, provided that both have retained single status without interruption from the moment of the celebration to the request for registration and the rights legally acquired by third parties are not prejudiced.

2. The judgments of nullity of marriage pronounced by ecclesiastical tribunals, together with the decree of execution issued by the superior controlling ecclesiastical authority, shall be declared, at the request of the parties or of one of them, effective within the Italian Republic by judgment of the competent Court of Appeal, upon verifying:

(a) That the ecclesiastical judge was the competent judge to adjudicate the action, the marriage having been celebrated in accordance with the present Article;

(b) That in the proceedings before the ecclesiastical tribunals the right to sue and to defend in Court has been assured to the parties in a way not dissimilar from what is required by the fundamental principles of the Italian legal system;

(c) That the other conditions required by the Italian legislation for the declaration of efficacy of foreign judgments are present.

The Court of Appeal may, with the judgment that recognizes a canonical judgment, take temporary economical measures in favour of one of the two spouses whose marriage has been declared null, referring the parties to the competent judge for a final decision on the matter.

3. In entering into the present regulation of matrimonial matters the Holy See herein reaffirms the unchangeable validity of the Catholic teaching on marriage and the concern of the Church for the dignity and values of the family, foundation of the society.

*Article 9.* 1. The Italian Republic, in conformity with the principle of freedom of schools and teaching and according to the terms provided for in its Constitution, shall guarantee to the Catholic Church the right freely to establish schools of every order and grade and educational institutes.

Full freedom shall be assured to private schools officially recognized by the State and it shall also be assured to their pupils school treatment equivalent to that applied to the pupils of schools run by the State or by the other territorial entities, also with regard to the State exam.

2. The Italian Republic, recognizing the value of the religious culture and considering that the principles of the Catholic Church are part of the historical heritage of the Italian people, shall continue to assure, within the framework of the scope of the schools, the teaching of Catholic religion in the public schools of every order and grade except for Universities.

With respect for the freedom of conscience and educational responsibility of the parents, everyone shall be granted the right to choose whether or not to receive religious instruction. When they enroll, the students or their parents shall exercise this right at the request of the school authority and their choice shall not give rise to any form of discrimination.

*Article 10.* 1. The Universities, seminaries, academies, colleges, and other institutions for ecclesiastics and members of religious orders or for the training in the ecclesiastical disciplines, established according to canon law, shall continue to be subordinate to the ecclesiastical authority alone.

2. The academic degrees in theology and in the other ecclesiastical disciplines, determined by the agreement of the contracting Parties and granted by the faculties approved by the Holy See, shall be recognized by the State. The diplomas of Paleography, Diplomacy, Custody of Historical Documents, and Library Sciences obtained at Vatican schools shall likewise be recognized.

3. The appointment of professors to the Catholic University of the Sacred Heart and the subordinate institutes shall be subject to the approval of the candidates' religious profile by the competent ecclesiastical authority.

*Article 11.* 1. The Italian Republic assures that service in the army, in the police or in any other similar service, time spent in hospitals, in sanatoria or in houses of public assistance and confinement to the institutes for prevention and punishment shall not impede the exercise of religious freedom and the fulfilment of the practices of Catholic worship.

2. The spiritual assistance to the same shall be assured by ecclesiastics appointed by the competent Italian authorities upon designation by the ecclesiastical authority and in accordance with the legal status, the personnel and the formalities determined by common agreement of these authorities.

*Article 12.* 1. The Holy See and the Italian Republic, each in its proper order, shall collaborate for the protection of the historical and artistic heritage.

In order to harmonize the application of Italian law with the religious needs, the competent authorities of the two Parties shall agree upon appropriate provisions for the protection, appraisal, and enjoyment of cultural property of religious interest that belongs to ecclesiastical bodies or institutions.

The preservation and consultation of archives of historical interest and of the libraries of the same bodies and institutions shall be favoured and facilitated on the basis of understandings between the competent authorities of the two Parties.

2. The Holy See shall retain the power to dispose of the Christian catacombs that exist underground at Rome and other parts of the Italian territory, bearing the consequent responsibility for their custody, maintenance and preservation, but it shall waive the power to dispose of the other catacombs.

Subject to the laws of the State and to any rights of third parties, the Holy See shall be at liberty to proceed with any necessary excavation and removal of sacred relics.

*Article 13.* 1. The preceding provisions shall be amendments to the Lateran Concordat accepted by the two Parties and shall enter into force on the exchange of the instruments of ratification. Except for what is provided in Article 7, paragraph (6), the provisions of the Concordat not reproduced in the present text are herein repealed.

2. Additional matters for which a need of collaboration between the Catholic Church and the State might arise, shall be governed by further agreements between the two Parties or by understandings between the competent authorities of the State and of the Italian Bishops Conference.

*Article 14.* If, in the future, any difficulties should arise with regard to the interpretation or application of the preceding provisions, the Holy See and the Italian Republic shall entrust the search for an amicable settlement to a joint Commission appointed by them.

Rome, February 18, 1984

[A protocol to the agreement, signed on the same date, contained further clarifica-tions and explanations concerning Articles 1, 4, 7, 8, 9, 10, and 13. Concerning Article 1 the Protocol declared: 'The principle of the Catholic religion as the sole religion of the Italian State, originally referred to by the Lateran Pacts, shall be considered to be no longer in force.']

Translation by Maurizio Ragazzi, © American Society of International Law.

# Anglo-Irish Agreement on Northern Ireland, Hillsborough Castle, 15 November 1985

## Anglo-Irish Summit Meeting Joint Communiqué

The Prime Minister, the Rt Hon Margaret Thatcher FRS MP, and the Taoiseach, Dr Garret FitzGerald TD, met at Hills-borough on 15 November 1985. It was the third meeting of the Anglo-Irish Intergovernmental Council to be held at the level of Heads of Government.

The Prime Minister was accompanied by the Secretary of State for Foreign and Commonwealth Affairs, the Rt Hon Sir Geoffrey Howe QC MP, and the Secretary of State for Northern Ireland, the Rt Hon Tom King MP. The Taoiseach was accompanied by the Tanaiste, Mr Dick Spring TD, and the Minister for Foreign Affairs, Mr Peter Barry TD.

The Prime Minister and the Taoiseach signed a formal and binding agreement between their two Governments, which will enter into force as soon as each Government has notified the other of acceptance. The Agreement has the aims of promoting peace and stability in Northern Ireland: helping to reconcile the two major traditions in Ireland: creating a new climate of friendship and cooperation between the people of the two countries: and improving cooperation in combating terrorism.

The Agreement deals in particular with the status of Northern Ireland and the establishment of an Intergovernmental Conference in which the Irish Govern-ment will put forward views and proposals concerning stated aspects of Northern Ireland affairs: in which the promotion of cross-border cooperation will be discussed: and in which determined efforts will be made to resolve any differences between the two Governments.

The Prime Minister and the Taoiseach committed themselves to implementing and sustaining the measures set out in the Agreement with determination and imagination and undertook to encourage people of both the unionist and nationalist traditions in Ireland to make new efforts to understand and respect each other's concerns with a view to promoting re-conciliation.

The exchange of notifications of accept-ance will not be completed until the Agreement has been approved by the British Parliament and by Dail Eireann. The two Governments intend that action to implement the provisions of the Agree-ment should begin once the exchange of notifications has been completed. The first meeting of the Intergovernmental Con-ference will take place as soon as possible thereafter. The British side will be led by the Secretary of State for Northern Ireland and the Irish side by the Minister design-ated as the Permanent Irish Ministerial representative.

The two Governments envisage that the meetings and agenda of the Conference will not normally be announced. But they wish it to be known that, at its first meeting, the Conference will consider its future programme of work in all the fields – political, security, legal, economic, social and cultural – assigned to it under the Agreement. It will concentrate at its initial meetings on:

• Relations between the security forces and the minority community in Northern Ireland;

• Ways of enhancing security cooperation between the two Governments; and

• Seeking measures which would give substantial expression to the aim of underlining the importance of public confidence in the administration of justice.

In the interests of all the people of Northern Ireland the two sides are committed to work for early progress in these matters. Against this background, the Taoiseach said that it was the intention of his Government to accede as soon as possible to the European Convention on the suppression of terrorism.

In addressing the improvement of relations between the security forces and the minority community, the Conference at its first meeting will consider:

(a) The application of the principle that the armed forces (which include the Ulster Defence Regiment) operate only in support of the civil power, with the particular objective of ensuring as rapidly as possible that, save in the most exceptional circumstances, there is a police presence in all operations which involve direct contact with the community.

(b) Ways of underlining the policy of the Royal Ulster Constabulary and of the armed forces in Northern Ireland that they discharge their duties even-handedly and with equal respect for the unionist and nationalist identities and traditions.

In its discussion of the enhancement of cross-border cooperation on security, the first meeting of the Intergovernmental Conference will give particular attention to the importance of continuing and enhanced cooperation, as envisaged in Article 9(a) of the Agreement, in the policing of border areas.

In addition to concluding the new Agreement, the Prime Minister and the Taoiseach reviewed the wide range of work being done under the auspices of the Anglo-Irish Intergovernmental Council to develop further the unique relationship between the two countries. The fact that in the past year there have been more than twenty meetings between Ministers of the two Governments demonstrates the closeness of cooperation. The Prime Minister and the Taoiseach decided that this work should be actively continued, in the interests of friendship between all the people of both countries.

The Prime Minister and the Taoiseach agreed to meet again at an appropriate time to take stock of the development of relations between the two countries and of the implementation of the Agreement which they have signed.

# Agreement between the Government of the United Kingdom of Great Britain and Northern Ireland and the Government of the Republic of Ireland

The Government of the United Kingdom of Great Britain and Northern Ireland and the Government of the Republic of Ireland:

• Wishing further to develop the unique relationship between their peoples and the close cooperation between their countries as friendly neighbours and as partners in the European Community;

● Recognizing the major interest of both their countries and, above all, of the people of Northern Ireland in diminishing the divisions there and achieving lasting peace and stability;

● Recognizing the need for continuing efforts to reconcile and to acknowledge the rights of the two major traditions that exist in Ireland, represented on the one hand by those who wish for no change in the present status of Northern Ireland and on the other hand by those who aspire to a sovereign united Ireland achieved by peaceful means and through agreement;

● Reaffirming their total rejection of any attempt to promote political objectives by violence or the threat of violence and their determination to work together to ensure that those who adopt or support such methods do not succeed;

● Recognizing that a condition of genuine reconciliation and dialogue between Unionists and Nationalists is mutual recognition and acceptance of each other's rights;

● Recognizing and respecting the identities of the two communities in Northern Ireland, and the right of each to pursue its aspirations by peaceful and constitutional means;

● Reaffirming their commitment to a society in Northern Ireland in which all may live in peace, free from discrimination and intolerance, and with the opportunity for both communities to participate fully in the structures and processes of Government;

● Have accordingly agreed as follows:

## A.  Status of Northern Ireland

*Article 1.* The two Governments

(a) Affirm that any change in the status of Northern Ireland would only come about with the consent of a majority of the people of Northern Ireland;

(b) Recognize that the present wish of a majority of the people of Northern Ireland is for no change in the status of Northern Ireland;

(c) Declare that, if in the future a majority of the people of Northern Ireland clearly wish for and formally consent to the establishment of a united Ireland, they will introduce and support in the respective Parliaments legislation to give effect to that wish.

## B.  The Intergovernmental Conference

*Article 2.* (a) There is hereby established, within the framework of the Anglo-Irish Intergovernmental Council set up after the meeting between the two Heads of Government on 6 November 1981, an Intergovernmental Conference (hereinafter referred to as 'the Conference'), concerned with Northern Ireland and with relations between the two parts of the island of Ireland, to deal, as set out in this Agreement, on a regular basis with

(i) political matters;

(ii) security and related matters;

(iii) legal matters, including the administration of justice;

(iv) the promotion of cross-border cooperation.

(b) The United Kingdom Government accept that the Irish Government will put forward views and proposals on matters relating to Northern Ireland within the field of activity of the Conference insofar as those matters are not the responsibility of a devolved administration in Northern Ireland. In the interest of promoting peace and stability, determined efforts shall be made through the Conference to resolve any differences. The Conference will be mainly concerned with Northern Ireland: but some of the matters under consideration will involve cooperative action in both parts of the island of Ireland, and possibly also in Great Britain. Some of the proposals considered in respect of Northern Ireland may also be found to have application by the Irish Government. There is no derogation from the sovereignty of either the United Kingdom Government or the Irish Government, and each retains responsibility for the decisions and administration of government within its own jurisdiction.

*Article 3.* The Conference shall meet at Ministerial or official level, as required. The business of the Conference will thus receive attention at the highest level. Regular and frequent Ministerial meetings shall be held: and in particular special meetings shall be convened at the request of either side. Officials may meet in subordinate groups. Membership of the Conference and of sub-groups shall be small and flexible. When the Conference meets at Ministerial level the Secretary of State for Northern Ireland and an Irish Minister designated as the Permanent Irish Ministerial Representative shall be joint Chairmen. Within the framework of the Conference other British and Irish Ministers may hold or attend meetings as appropriate: when legal matters are under consideration the Attorneys General may attend. Ministers may be accompanied by their officials and their professional advisers: for example, when questions of security policy or security cooperation are being discussed, they may be accompanied by the Chief Constable of the Royal Ulster Constabulary and the Commissioner of the Garda Siochana: or when questions of economic or social policy cooperation are being discussed, they may be accompanied by officials of the relevant departments. A Secretariat shall be established by the two Governments to service the Conference on a continuing basis in the discharge of its functions as set out in this Agreement.

*Article 4.* (a) In relation to matters coming within its field of activity, the Conference shall be a framework within which the United Kingdom Government and the Irish Government work together

(i) for the accommodation of the rights and identities of the two traditions which exist in Northern Ireland; and

(ii) for peace, stability and prosperity throughout the island of Ireland by promoting reconciliation, respect for human rights, cooperation against terrorism and the development of economic, social and cultural cooperation.

(b) It is the declared policy of the United Kingdom Government that responsibility in respect of certain matters within the powers of the Secretary of State for Northern Ireland should be devolved within Northern Ireland on a basis which would secure widespread acceptance throughout the community. The Irish Government support that policy.

(c) Both Governments recognize that devolution can be achieved only with the cooperation of constitutional representatives within Northern Ireland of both traditions there. The Conference shall be a framework within which the Irish Government may put forward views and proposals on the modalities of bringing about devolution in Northern Ireland, in so far as they relate to the interests of the minority community.

## C. Political matters

*Article 5.* (a) The Conference shall concern itself with measures to recognize and accommodate the rights and identities of the two traditions in Northern Ireland, to protect human rights and to prevent discrimination. Matters to be considered in this area include measures to foster the cultural heritage of both traditions, changes in electoral arrangements, the use of flags and emblems, the avoidance of economic and social discrimination and the advantages and disadvantages of a Bill of Rights in some form in Northern Ireland.

(b) The discussion of these matters shall be mainly concerned with Northern Ireland, but the possible application of any measures pursuant to this article by the Irish Government in their jurisdiction shall not be excluded.

(c) If it should prove impossible to achieve and sustain devolution on a basis which secures widespread acceptance in Northern Ireland, the Conference shall be a framework within which the Irish Government may, where the interests of the minority community are significantly or especially affected, put forward views on proposals for major legislation and on major policy issues, which are within the purview of the Northern Ireland Departments and which remain the responsibility of the Secretary of State for Northern Ireland.

*Article 6.* The Conference shall be a framework within which the Irish Government may put forward views and proposals on the role and composition of bodies appointed by the Secretary of State for Northern Ireland or by Departments subject to his direction and control including:

The Standing Advisory Commission on Human Rights;
The Fair Employment Agency;
The Equal Opportunities Commission;
The Police Authority for Northern Ireland;
The Police Complaints Board.

## D.  Security and related matters

*Article 7.* (a) The Conference shall consider

(i) Security policy;

(ii) Relations between the security forces and the community;

(iii) Prisons policy.

(b) The Conference shall consider the security situation at its regular meetings and thus provide an opportunity to address policy issues, serious incidents and forthcoming events.

(c) The two Governments agree that there is a need for a programme of special measures in Northern Ireland to improve relations between the security forces and the community, with the object in particular of making the security forces more readily accepted by the nationalist community. Such a programme shall be developed, for the Conference's consideration, and may include the establishment of local consultative machinery, training in community relations, crime prevention schemes involving the community, improvements in arrangements for handling complaints, and action to increase the proportion of members of the minority in the Royal Ulster Constabulary. Elements of the programme may be considered by

the Irish Government suitable for application within their jurisdiction.

(d) The Conference may consider policy issues relating to prisons. Individual cases may be raised as appropriate, so that information can be provided or inquiries instituted.

## E.  Legal matters, including the administration of justice

*Article 8.* The Conference shall deal with issues of concern to both countries relating to the enforcement of the criminal law. In particular it shall consider whether there are areas of the criminal law applying in the North and in the South respectively which might with benefit be harmonized. The two Governments agree on the importance of public confidence in the administration of justice. The Conference shall seek, with the help of advice from experts as appropriate, measures which would give substantial expression to this aim, considering inter alia the possibility of mixed courts in both jurisdictions for the trial of certain offences. The Conference shall also be concerned with policy aspects of extradition and extraterritorial jurisdiction as between North and South.

## F.  Cross-Border cooperation on security, economic, social and cultural matters

*Article 9.* (a) With a view to enhancing cross-border cooperation on security matters, the Conference shall set in hand a programme of work to be undertaken by the Chief Constable of the Royal Ulster Constabulary and the Commissioner of the Garda Siochana and, where appropriate, groups of officials in such areas as threat assessments, exchange of information, liaison structures, technical cooperation, training of personnel, and operational resources.

(b) The Conference shall have no operational responsibilities: responsibility for police operations shall remain with the heads of the respective police forces, the Chief Constable of the Royal Ulster Constabulary maintaining his links with the Secretary of State for Northern Ireland and the Commissioner of the Garda Siochana his links with the Minister for Justice.

*Article 10.* (a) The two Governments shall cooperate to promote the economic and social development of those areas of both parts of Ireland which have suffered most severely from the consequences of the instability of recent years, and shall consider the possibility of securing international support for this work.

(b) If it should prove impossible to achieve and sustain devolution on a basis which secures widespread acceptance in Northern Ireland, the Conference shall be a framework for the promotion of cooperation between the two parts of Ireland concerning cross-border aspects of economic, social and cultural matters in relation to which the Secretary of State for Northern Ireland continues to exercise authority.

(c) If responsibility is devolved in respect of certain matters in the economic, social or cultural areas currently within the responsibility of the Secretary of State for Northern Ireland, machinery will need to be established by the responsible authorities in the North and South for practical cooperation in respect of cross-border aspects of these issues.

## G. Arrangements for review

*Article 11.* At the end of three years from signature of this Agreement, or earlier if requested by either Government, the working of the Conference shall be reviewed by the two Governments to see whether any changes in the scope and nature of its activities are desirable.

## H. Interparliamentary relations

*Article 12.* It will be for Parliamentary decision in Westminster and in Dublin whether to establish an Anglo-Irish Parliamentary body of the kind adumbrated in the Anglo-Irish studies Report of November 1981. The two Governments agree that they would give support as appropriate to such a body, if it were to be established.

## I. Final clauses

*Article 13.* This Agreement shall enter into force on the date on which the two Governments exchange notifications of their acceptance of this Agreement.

# VI · South and East Asia and the Pacific

Since 1945 warfare has never ceased in one or more of the regions of Asia. Internal civil wars, conflicts between the new nation States of Asia, Great Power involvement in the 'cold war' – all of these, often interrelated and occurring simultaneously, have made Asia an area of intense conflict and rivalry in world diplomacy.

In categorizing the conflicts of Asia after the defeat of Japan in 1945, three broad geographical regions may be distinguished. First, the Indian sub-continent, formerly ruled by Britain, now comprising the independent states of India, Pakistan, Bangladesh (before 1971 East Pakistan), and Sri Lanka (known as Ceylon until 1972), as well as the States bordering on the sub-continent, such as Afghanistan. Secondly, the south-east Asian region, including the continental States of Malaysia, Thailand, and the States of Indo-China, as well as the island States of Singapore, Indonesia, and the Philippines. And thirdly, the area of east and north-east Asia and the Pacific, including China, Taiwan, Japan, Korea, and the Soviet Union, and, on the periphery, the island States of the Pacific and Australasia.

## The Indian sub-continent

The transfer of power in the Indian sub-continent to the independent States of India and Pakistan at midnight on 14–15 August 1947 was marred by large-scale bloodshed as Hindus and Muslims attacked one another; during the next few months an estimated two million people were massacred. Britain accepted the claims that a separate Muslim State should be created and that the Muslims could not all be incorporated in an Indian Government. Thus Pakistan as a nation owed its existence to recognition of the separate national right of Muslims. The State carved out of the areas of Muslim majorities in India comprised one region in the west separated by more than 1,000 miles from another region in the east. Despite large population movements in both directions at the time of independence, Hindu minorities remained in what became Pakistan, and millions of Muslims became Indian citizens, India rejecting religion as a basis of the State. The rulers of the 562 Indian States, who had ruled under British paramountcy before 1947, were advised by the British to choose to accede to either Pakistan or India. This process was carried through with surprisingly few complications, except for three States: Hyderabad and Junagarh, both occupied by Indian forces, and the State of Jammu and Kashmir, whose unresolved relationship to India and Pakistan became a dominant issue and cause of conflict between India and Pakistan.

The Maharaja of Kashmir was a Hindu ruling over a population which was predominantly Muslim. He made no choice for either State as in the partition months of August and September 1947 communal strife, armed insurrection and massacres by bands crossing Kashmir, occurred. In October 1947 Pathan tribesmen invaded Kashmir from the territory of Pakistan. This brought the Maharaja's rule to the verge of collapse. In return for Indian military help, *the Maharaja on 26 October 1947 signed a Treaty of Accession with India.* The Indian Prime Minister, Jawaharlal Nehru, at the time promised that the ultimate future fate of Jammu and Kashmir would be left for the inhabitants of the State to decide when law and order had been restored. From 1947 to 1948 India and Pakistan fought in Kashmir. On 1 January 1949 a ceasefire was agreed upon, and a ceasefire line established in Kashmir on 27 July 1949. But the unresolved dispute continued to embitter and dominate the relations between India and Pakistan, and to influence the relations of Pakistan and India with the Great Powers contesting influence in Asia from Korea to Afghanistan.

Pakistan joined the Western anti-communist alliances of SEATO and CENTO, and received arms and economic assistance from the United States intended for anti-communist use, to strengthen its defences against China and the Soviet Union. With the deterioration of Chinese–Indian relations and the outbreak of fighting over the disputed Sino-Indian border, Pakistan drew closer to China as an ally against India, and thus ceased to be regarded as a firm ally of the West.

Indian foreign policy was only partly shaped to meet the threat of conflict with the smaller Pakistan. Nehru in the 1950s espoused the cause of non-aligned nations, neutrals in the conflict between the Western Powers and the Soviet Union, and freedom from colonial rule; he also sought a combination of the less developed African and Asian nations so that they might assert themselves in a world dominated by Great Powers. *The Bandung Conference, April 1955*, attended by the representatives of twenty-nine African and Asian States, meant different things to different participants. To some, including the Chinese Prime Minister, Chou En-lai, who attended the conference, it symbolized anti-Western nationalism. For Nehru it symbolized non-aligned Asian nationalism and Asian cooperation internationally with non-aligned African States (six African States attended). It became the prototype of later Afro-Asian solidarity conferences.

India's espousal of positive neutralism was also illustrated in *April 1954* with the signature of a *Chinese–Indian Commercial Treaty* which recognized Chinese suzerainty over Tibet (occupied by China in 1950). To this treaty were attached the 'Five Principles of Coexistence'. Nehru established better relations with both the Soviet Union and China. Khrushchev's and Bulganin's visit to India in 1955 was utilized to demonstrate Soviet support for India's position as against Pakistan. Pakistan had by then joined SEATO and the Baghdad Pact. Thus the 'cold war' and Kashmir dispute became intertwined as each State attempted to utilize this conflict to further its own objectives.

Fighting broke out again in the autumn of 1962, not over the Kashmir dispute but between India and China over the still unsettled frontiers of India and Kashmir with China. This frontier, running through some of the most desolate regions of the world, had not been entirely delimited or demarcated during the period of British rule or since independence. Legally the issue was exceedingly complex, rival maps making rival claims. The most serious dispute concerned the frontiers of north-eastern Kashmir in a region known as Aksai Chin, through which the Chinese were building a road connecting Chinese Tibet and Sinkiang; the second frontier in dispute lay between Kashmir and Nepal; the third, a very small area, was the Sikkim frontier between Nepal and Bhutan; the fourth and largest area lay between Bhutan and Burma in the Assam Himalayas.

The good relations between China and India began deteriorating after 1959 for several reasons: rivalry between Chinese and Indian influence developed in the independent State of Nepal (the two other Himalayan States, Bhutan and Sikkim, were under Indian control); the Dalai Lama, leader of Tibetan Buddhists, found refuge in India after the Tibetan revolt of 1959 which drew world attention to Chinese subjugation of Tibet; finally, conflict developed over the disputed sections of the Indo-Chinese borders. A Chinese military demonstration in strength in Assam routed the defending Indian troops in October and November 1962, and China invaded India before withdrawing. A ceasefire between China and India was arranged in December 1962. The Chinese invasion led to Indian military reorganization and Britain and the United States sent military equipment and aid to India. Meanwhile *Pakistan signed a border agreement with China on 2 March 1963.*

On 9 April 1965 fighting broke out between Indian and Pakistani forces in a disputed area of the border between West Pakistan and the Indian province of Gujarat, known as the Rann of Kutch. Hostilities rumbled on until the end of June. *On 30 June 1965, Pakistani and Indian representatives signed an agreement in New Delhi* in the presence of the British High Commissioner in New Delhi, John Freeman. The agreement called for a ceasefire and the establishment of an arbitration tribunal to decide on the Rann of Kutch territorial dispute. (An arbitral award on 19 February 1968 gave one tenth of the area, an uninhabited mudflat, to Pakistan, but in December 1971 the entire area was reoccupied by Indian forces.)

Renewed tension along the Indian–West Pakistan frontier erupted into full-scale war between India and Pakistan in September 1965. Neither side could win a decisive victory and both accepted a U.N. 'demand' for a ceasefire which came into force on 23 September 1965. With the Soviet Union acting as mediator, the Soviet Prime Minister, Alexei Kosygin invited Nehru's successor Lal Bahadur Shastri and President Ayub Khan of Pakistan to *a conference at Tashkent, 3 January–10 January 1966*, which resulted in an agreement. The *Tashkent Declaration, 10 January 1966*, placed the Kashmir dispute on ice, restored normal Indian–Pakistan relations, and provided that the armies of both sides would withdraw to the positions they had occupied before the fighting began; discussions were to be continued on all differences.

*India signed a Treaty of Peace and Friendship and Cooperation with the Soviet Union on 9 August 1971* (p. 170), which strengthened its position as it faced a new crisis in relations with Pakistan.

Civil War in Pakistan between the eastern and western parts of the State began in March 1971, and was the cause of the third outbreak of war between Pakistan and India. The Muslims, who formed the Bengali population of East Pakistan, had been at the forefront in 1947 in demanding a separate Muslim Pakistan State and secession from India. But the

Bengalis of East Pakistan soon resented the imposition of rule by the Urdu-speaking West Pakistanis, whose population was smaller than that of East Pakistan but whose share of wealth and area of land was greater. On 25 March 1971 the West Pakistani army began ruthless military operations in East Pakistan to suppress an incipient independence movement. Some ten million refugees fled to India during the course of the following nine months, whilst among the Bengali East Pakistan population, bands of guerrilla freedom-fighters were formed. The Pakistan army, who were supported by some Urdu-speaking Bihari Moslems (the Biharis had originally left India in 1947 to escape Hindu domination), attempted to suppress Bengali nationalism savagely. India meantime housed the refugees and gave increasing support to the Bengali Government in exile – the Bangladesh Government. Pakistan launched air attacks on India, and on 6 December 1971 Pakistan and India were at war. In East Pakistan Indian forces were entirely victorious. The new State of Bangladesh, which had declared its independence on 10 April 1971, was recognized by India on 6 December 1971, the day of the war's outbreak. As a result of the Indian victory, Bangladesh emerged as the third independent State on the sub-continent.

Six months later, at the *Simla Conference, 28 June–3 July 1972*, President Bhutto of Pakistan and Mrs Gandhi, Prime Minister of India, reached an *Agreement on Bilateral Relations* (p. 264). Indian and Pakistani armed forces were to be withdrawn each to their side of the pre-war (5 December 1971) frontier. This was a considerable concession to Pakistan as India was holding far more West Pakistan territory than the Indian territory the Pakistanis were occupying. But the agreement concerning Jammu and Kashmir stated that 'the line of control resulting from the ceasefire line of December 17, 1971, shall be respected by both sides without prejudice to the recognized position of either side'. The exchange of prisoners of war was one of several difficult questions which it was agreed should be left to later negotiations.

These negotiations proved lengthy and difficult. Bangladesh demanded that war crimes trials be held of those accused of atrocities before and during the war. Eventually an *Indian–Pakistani Agreement on Repatriation of Prisoners of War was signed in New Delhi on 28 August 1973*. Three-way repatriation of prisoners began on 19 September 1973. Not all prisoners, however, were covered by this agreement.

In February 1974 Pakistan finally recognized the independence of Bangladesh. This paved the way for a three-way *Bangladesh–India–Pakistan Agreement on the Repatriation of Prisoners of War and Civilian Internees,*

*9 April 1974.* Among those repatriated under this agreement were 195 Pakistani prisoners accused of war crimes in Bangladesh. In the agreement the Prime Minister of Pakistan 'appealed to the people of Bangladesh to forgive and forget the mistakes of the past in order to promote reconciliation'. The Prime Minister of Bangladesh declared 'that he wanted the people to forget the past and to make a fresh start, stating that the people of Bangladesh knew how to forgive'. In the light of these declarations, the Bangladesh Government agreed not to proceed with war crimes trials and to repatriate the 195 accused Pakistani prisoners.

Indian troops withdrew from Bangladesh on 12 March 1972 and a week later *India and Bangladesh signed a Treaty of Friendship and Cooperation, 19 March 1972*, which looked forward to cooperation and which contained the undertaking that neither signatory would join alliances directed against the other or give assistance to an aggressor. In the event of an attack, or threatened attack, both signatories would immediately consult together.

Following these climactic events, relations between India and Pakistan were gradually normalized. Both countries became more absorbed with their turbulent internal politics than with any thought of resuscitating their historic rivalry. India continued to pursue a non-aligned policy in international affairs. Pakistan for a while turned away from the West, withdrawing from both SEATO and CENTO (see pp. 115 and 128). But in the early 1980s Pakistan once again turned towards the U.S.A. for diplomatic support and military supplies.

The main reason for this was the Soviet invasion of Afghanistan in December 1979 (see p. 162). The flood of refugees into Pakistan and the ensuing guerrilla war in Afghanistan (in which the anti-Soviet rebels were supplied via Pakistan) brought Pakistan into a much closer alignment with the U.S.A. The Soviet occupation of Afghanistan brought Russian forces, for the first time in history, to the very edge of the Indian subcontinent. Although Russian armed forces were continually harried by the Afghan rebels they showed no sign of readiness to withdraw. Contacts among the powers concerned (including the U.S.A.) took place from time to time in the early 1980s, but no agreement on a settlement of the Afghan problem was reached.

# Agreement between India and Pakistan on bilateral relations, Simla, 3 July 1972

I. The Government of India and the Government of Pakistan are resolved that the two countries put an end to the conflict and confrontation that have hitherto marred the relations and work for the promotion of a friendly and harmonious relationship and the establishment of a durable peace in the sub-continent, so that both countries may henceforth devote their resources and energies to the pressing task of advancing the welfare of their peoples.

In order to achieve this objective, the Government of India and the Government of Pakistan have agreed as follows:

(1) That the principles and the purposes of the Charter of the United Nations shall govern the relations between the two countries.

(2) That the two countries are resolved to settle their differences by peaceful means through bilateral negotiations or by any other peaceful means mutually agreed upon between them. Pending the final settlement of any of the problems between the two countries, neither side shall unilaterally alter the situation and both shall prevent the organization, assistance or encouragement of any acts detrimental to the maintenance of peaceful and harmonious relations.

(3) That the prerequisite for reconciliation, good neighbourliness and durable peace between them is a commitment by both countries to the peaceful coexistence, respect for each other's territorial integrity and sovereignty and non-interference in each other's internal affairs, on the basis of equality and mutual benefit.

(4) That the basic issues and causes of conflict which have bedevilled the relations between the two countries for the last twenty-five years shall be resolved by peaceful means.

(5) That they shall always respect each other's national unity, territorial integrity, political independence and sovereign equality.

(6) That in accordance with the Charter of the United Nations, they will refrain from the threat or the use of force against the territorial integrity or political independence of each other.

II. Both Governments will take all steps within their power to prevent hostile propaganda directed against each other. Both countries will encourage the dissemination of such information as would promote the development of friendly relations between them.

III. In order progressively to restore and normalize relations between the two countries step by step, it is agreed that:

(1) Steps shall be taken to resume communications – postal, telegraphic, sea, land including border posts and air links including over-flights.

(2) Appropriate steps shall be taken to promote travel facilities for the nationals of the other country.

(3) Trade and cooperation in economic and agreed fields will be resumed as far as possible.

(4) Exchange in the fields of science and culture will be promoted. In this connection, delegations from the two countries will meet from time to time to work out the necessary details.

IV. In order to initiate the process of establishment of a durable peace, both Governments agree that:

(1) The Indian and Pakistani forces shall be withdrawn to their side of the international border.

(2) In Jammu and Kashmir the line of control resulting from the ceasefire of December 17, 1971 shall be respected by both sides without prejudice to the recognized position of the other side. Neither side shall seek to alter it unilaterally irrespective of the mutual difference and legal interpretations. Both

sides further undertake to refrain from the threat or the use of force in violation of this line.

(3) Withdrawals shall commence upon the entry into force of this Agreement and shall be completed within a period of thirty days thereafter.

V. This Agreement will be subject to ratification by both countries in accordance with their respective constitutional procedures and will come into force with effect from the date on which the Instruments of Ratification are exchanged.

VI. Both Governments agree that their respective Heads will meet again at a mutually convenient time in the future and that, in the meanwhile, the representatives of the two sides will meet to discuss further the modalities and arrangements for the establishment of a durable peace and the normalization of relations, including the questions of repatriation of the prisoners-of-war and the civilian internees, a final settlement of Jammu and Kashmir and the resumption of diplomatic relations.

[The agreement was signed by the Prime Minister of India, Mrs Indira Gandhi, and by President Z.A. Bhutto of Pakistan.]

## South-east Asia

### BURMA, MALAYSIA, INDONESIA, AND THE PHILIPPINES

Burma gained independence on 4 January 1948, following *a treaty signed in London on 17 October 1947*. Like India and Ceylon, Burma was determined, after independence, not to become involved in the 'cold war'. But unlike India, Pakistan, and Ceylon, she chose not to join the Commonwealth at the time of independence. The early years of Burmese independence were marred by severe internal and external tension: the Burmese army faced a variety of internal enemies as well as external incursions from nationalist Chinese forces. Burma's international position was strengthened by *the agreement reached in 1960 on the Chinese–Burmese boundary*. Burma remained staunchly neutralist and sought to isolate itself from international conflicts. Relations with China and the Soviet Union were maintained at a cautious level, and *in 1971 Burma signed a renewed friendship agreement with China*.

In Malaya during the closing stages of the Japanese occupation, the Malayan Communists planned to gain power, but failed when the British returned in 1945. In June 1948 the Chinese Communists launched a new insurrection which was not mastered by the British troops until 1954. The insurrection delayed the granting of Malayan independence until 31 August 1957. Malay misgivings delayed further the incorporation of Singapore, with its predominantly Chinese population, in the new State of Malaya. *The final agreement, which set up a greater Malaysia consisting of Malaya, Singapore, Sarawak and Sabah, was signed in London in July 1963*, and on 16 September 1963 the Federation of Malaysia came into being. The defence of Malaya, Singapore and Borneo, and later Malaysia, from

1957 to 1971 was the joint responsibility of Britain, Australia and New Zealand. But in March 1968 the British Government declared its intention to withdraw British garrisons from south-east Asia, including Singapore, by 1971. The involvement of large numbers of British troops in a confrontation with Indonesia (1963–6) was replaced by new defence arrangements between Malaysia and Singapore. The island of Singapore had declared its independence from Malaysia in 1965. The *Singapore Independence Agreement of 7 August 1965* (p. 283) marked Malaysian acceptance of the secession of Singapore. *In 1971 the Five Power Defence Arrangements were concluded* between Australia, Britain, Malaysia, New Zealand and Singapore. But the withdrawal of British forces in 1971 from what had formerly been the major British base at Singapore compelled Singapore and its neighbours to reconsider their defence arrangements (see below).

Two days after the Japanese surrender to the Allies, on 7 August 1945, Indonesian nationalist leaders proclaimed an independent Republic with Ahmed Sukarno as President. The Netherlands refused to accept this declaration and attempted to regain control over the whole of their former Netherlands East Indian Empire. In December 1949 they agreed to pass sovereignty to an independent Indonesia. Conflict with the Netherlands continued in the dispute over the sovereignty of Western New Guinea, whose incorporation became Indonesia's dominant foreign concern. An *Indonesian–Netherlands Agreement, 16 August 1962*, allowed Western New Guinea to pass under Indonesian sovereignty after a brief interim period.

In mid-September 1963, Indonesian hostility to the creation of Malaysia and specifically to the incorporation of the two British States of North Borneo, Sarawak and Sabah, led to a state of undeclared war between Malaysia and Indonesia. British troops became heavily involved in this war as allies of the Malaysians. The overthrow of Sukarno in 1966 was accompanied by a change in Indonesian foreign policy and the ending of the conflict with Malaysia. *On 1 June 1966 Indonesia and Malaysia signed a peace treaty* which brought the border war to an end.

The independent Republic of the Philippines was inaugurated on 4 July 1946. The Philippines retained close links with the United States, leasing bases and concluding defence and assistance treaties with the United States in 1947 and 1951, and as a member of the multilateral SEATO alliance in 1954. The Philippine Government faced a communist-inspired military resistance from the Filipino Communist Party's 'People's Anti-Japanese Resistance Army', 'Huk' for short. A state of incipient civil war had existed between the Huk and other guerrilla forces during the Japanese occupation. After participating in post-war Filipino politics, the Huks decided on armed action on a large scale in 1950, utilizing 12,000 guerrillas. During the following three decades the communist rebels were kept at bay by the Philippine army which also confronted a determined revolt by Muslims in the Mindanao region of the country. But neither revolt was wholly eliminated. In the early 1980s opposition to the Government gathered strength, fuelled by disgust with the massive corruption and spoils system administered by the government of President Ferdinand Marcos. In 1986, after an apparently rigged presidential election, opposition boiled over into a non-violent revolution in which Marcos was overthrown and replaced as President by Corazón Aquino. The Aquino Government made peace overtures to the communist and Muslim guerrillas. At the same time the new régime made clear its continued adherence to the treaties with the United States governing the presence of the great U.S. bases in the Philippines.

The foundation of the *Association of South-East Asian Nations (ASEAN) on 8 August 1967* created a loose regional alliance of Indonesia, Malaysia, the Philippines, Singapore and Thailand. Originally designed primarily as an effort to achieve economic coordination of member countries, ASEAN developed into a political association. On *24 February 1976* the member countries signed a *Treaty of Amity and Cooperation in South-East Asia. On 7 March 1980 ASEAN signed a cooperation agreement with the European Economic Community*. The ASEAN group declared their aspiration to create a 'zone of peace' in south-east Asia. Although the grouping achieved considerable success in coordinating their economic and diplomatic policies, their efforts to maintain peace in the region as a whole were bedevilled by the continuing murderous conflict among their neighbours in Indo-China.

INDO-CHINA

Indo-China has been the cockpit of bitter warfare and the focus of great power rivalries in South-east Asia almost continuously since the end of the Second World War.

Indo-China as one colonial unit ceased to exist in March 1945 when the Japanese removed the Vichy French administration there. The Japanese next induced Vietnam, Laos and Cambodia to proclaim independence. Before Nationalist Chinese forces could occupy northern Vietnam and Britain southern Vietnam in September 1945, in accordance with the Potsdam Agreements, independent Governments were functioning in all three States. In Vietnam Ho Chi Minh, the leader of the Vietminh, had returned to Hanoi as the leader of one of several political groups and proclaimed an independent democratic Republic of Vietnam, with the Emperor Bao Dai abdicating and serving as his 'Supreme Adviser'. The Fourth French Republic under de Gaulle's leadership, however, rejected complete independence, offering instead only limited autonomy. This caused a crucial split and confusion in Vietnam, with the Vietminh, the French, and Vietnamese Nationalists all competing for control. Ho Chi Minh broke off negotiations with the French on the basis of autonomy in the autumn of 1946, and prepared to fight for independence. Bao Dai continued to treat with the French, and eventually in 1949 signed an agreement which granted to Vietnam partial independence within the French union. Similar terms were eventually accepted by Cambodia and Laos. In both countries at first small resistance movements developed: in Cambodia the Khmer Issaraks, and in Laos eventually the Pathet Lao. By far the most important of the forces opposed to the French was the Vietminh, communist dominated, fighting for an independent Vietnam, and led by Ho Chi Minh.

The Vietminh fought a long and brilliantly led guerrilla campaign against the French forces, coupled with a revolutionary campaign among the civilian population. United States involvement in the war began in May 1950, when President Truman announced that the United States was extending economic and military aid to the French and associated States in Vietnam. After several years, despite increasing American aid, the French wished to bring the fighting to an end. In 1953 the French Government declared its intention to grant complete independence to the three associated States. A treaty of independence was signed with Laos in October 1953; the French promised to defend Laos against communist attack. Before French troops left and a general political settlement was reached they hoped to gain a military success against the Vietminh. When the Foreign Ministers of the Four Powers met in Berlin in February 1954 it was the French, with strong British support, who insisted that Indo-China should be placed on the agenda of the Geneva Conference, which was to meet two months later, so that a negotiated settlement could be reached.

The first *Geneva Conference, 26 April–21 July 1954*, was attended by representatives from nine States – France, Britain, the United States, the Soviet Union, the People's Republic of China, the Democratic Republic of Vietnam (Vietminh), the States of Vietnam, Laos and Cambodia – some of which did not recognize each other: for instance, the United States did not recognize the People's Republic of China, and the French did not recognize the Vietminh. Ten documents comprise the various accords reached by the close of the conference: three military agreements, six unilateral declarations, and a *Final Declaration of the Geneva Conference* (p. 274); but two participants, the State of Vietnam (South Vietnam) and the United States, in unilateral declarations repudiated important parts of this Final Declaration. Instead of negotiating from a position of strength, the French Government with the fall of Dien Bien Phu on 7 May, became anxious to end its own direct military involvement as soon as possible.

An armistice throughout Indo-China was agreed to at the conference. It took the form of three military documents signed on 20 and 21 July 1954 between the French High Command and the Vietminh High Command, dealing separately with Vietnam, Cambodia and Laos. The following were the main provisions of the Vietnam military agreement: a demilitarized zone and ceasefire line was established close to the 17th parallel; agreements were reached on a mutual exchange of prisoners, cessation of hostilities, on a period of 300 days during which each side would regroup and withdraw its troops to its own side of the ceasefire line; no fresh troops or bases were to be established, and no alliances would be permitted with outside Powers. A French–Vietnamese Armistice Commission (India, Canada and Poland) was also established; most controversially, elections were to be held throughout Vietnam after two years to determine the final status of Vietnam. In unilateral declarations the State of Vietnam (recognized by France) protested against many aspects of the armistice terms agreed to by the French High Command without reference to the Vietnamese Government, especially the date of the proposed elections, and reserved to itself full liberty of action.

The United States in its unilateral declaration took note of the three armistice agreements and the Final Declaration, and promised to refrain from the threat of force to disturb them, but declared its view that free elections should be supervised by the U.N. (and not the proposed International Supervisory Commission); it also supported the declaration of the State of Vietnam that the people of Vietnam were entitled to determine their own future. The United States indicated its dissociation from the Geneva Agreements not only by its declaration, but by the return to Washington in May of John Foster Dulles, the Secretary of State, when the conference agenda reached Indo-China, though a deputy continued as U.S. representative. The United States refused to sign any of the agreements or the Final Declaration.

The Geneva Agreements as they applied to Laos accorded sovereignty over the whole of Laos to the Royal Government, rejecting claims of a communist Pathet Lao Government in exile; but the Pathet Lao were permitted temporary control of two provinces, a base from which the conflict was later renewed.

The Geneva Agreements were a collection of documents but contained no actual treaty binding all the participants; indeed no *political* treaties were signed. Judged by treaty standards the agreements were unusual. The three military agreements imposed military obligations which were carried out; but they also brought about political changes such as the division of Vietnam into two parts with the Democratic Republic (recognized only by the Soviet Union and China) in *de facto* control of the north, and the State of Vietnam able to exercise authority only in the south. They also provided for elections, a political and not a military matter. The State of Vietnam (finally granted full independence by France on 4 June 1954) was not a signatory of the armistice agreement. The controversial Final Declaration was signed by none of the delegates but merely listed the participants in a preamble. It consisted of nine paragraphs taking note of or concurring with agreements and declarations made during the course of the conference; of one paragraph (8) interpreting the military agreements; of a paragraph (9) imposing certain duties on authorities of both zones; and of other paragraphs (12) and (13) imposing certain duties on members of the conference, two of whom unilaterally declared that they would not feel bound by them. The Geneva Agreements did end the fighting between the French and Vietminh; the partition did occur; and Cambodia and Laos gained independence; but the major provisions concerning Vietnam expressed the intents and desires of some participants whilst being opposed by others. The Final Declaration did not bind all the participants in commitments towards one another.

The Geneva Agreements brought fighting to an end in Indo-China between the opposing French-led and Vietminh armies. But in Laos the Pathet Lao continued to maintain their independent position and retain control of the two northern provinces with Vietminh help. After the conclusion of the Geneva Conference, the *SEATO Alliance was signed, 8 September 1954*, which extended its scope to cover Cambodia, Laos and South Vietnam (p. 120). However, both Cambodia and Laos, after Laos became neutral in 1962, declined SEATO protection.

In South Vietnam the French continued to attempt to assert their influence, and the United States to provide aid. The Government was headed by Ngo Dinh Diem, who turned the State of Vietnam into the

Republic of Vietnam in 1955; American influence began to replace the French, who finally withdrew in May 1956 stating that they no longer accepted any special responsibility concerning the application of the Geneva Agreements. The date for holding elections as set out in the Geneva Agreements (July 1956) passed, but neither North nor South Vietnam proceeded to take any military action against the other. The United States Military Assistance Advisory Group, a small mission, advised the South Vietnamese forces. In 1958 a Vietcong (communist) insurrection began with the assassination of provincial officials. In May 1959 the Central Committee of the Vietnamese Communist Party decided to renew fighting and to support the Vietcong. This decision made itself felt seriously in South Vietnam during the winter of 1959–60.

With the active support of North Vietnam the strength of the Vietcong, which set up a 'National Front for the Liberation of South Vietnam', increased rapidly in 1960 and 1961. During the same period northern and most of central Laos was overrun by the communist Pathet Lao, with the help of the Vietminh and with Soviet supplies. In May 1961 a second Geneva Conference was convened to deal with the Laos crisis, and fourteen months later the delegates from fourteen nations reached the *Geneva Agreement on Laos, 23 July 1962* (p. 282). A Laotian Government of national union was formed from the three warring factions, and Laos was neutralized. This proved to be largely a paper settlement. An uneasy political and military balance between the factions continued but Laos was not neutralized. Its territory played an important role in the Vietnam war, as the major supply route from North to South Vietnam, the 'Ho Chi Minh trail', ran through eastern Laos.

Thailand, a member of SEATO, was alarmed at SEATO's inability to act in neighbouring Laos in 1960 and 1961. Thailand also faced its own insurgency problems in the north-east, the region bordering on Laos. To reassure Thailand, a joint *U.S.–Thai statement was issued in Washington on 6 March 1962*, indicating that the U.S. regarded the SEATO treaty commitment as involving individual as well as collective responsibility in the event of communist aggression in Thailand. In May 1962 the U.S. sent combat forces to Thailand, later followed by small British, Australian, New Zealand and Philippine contingents. From 1965 to 1973, the U.S. utilized bases in Thailand for bombing missions in Vietnam, and U.S. troops were stationed in Thailand.

In South Vietnam, as the situation worsened for Diem's Government, the new Kennedy Administration in May 1961 approved of more (partly open, partly secret) support for the South Vietnamese. From the autumn of 1961 until the death of Kennedy two years later, American military personnel in South Vietnam increased to more than 16,000 men. This growing American commitment of U.S. 'advisers' in South Vietnam was made at a time of unstable internal Vietnamese politics which followed the overthrow of the Diem régime (November 1963). When Johnson followed Kennedy in the White House in the same month he was determined to continue earlier American support for the South Vietnamese Government against the Vietcong and the North Vietnamese, who had sent their troops south of the ceasefire line in support of the Vietcong.

In August 1964 the attack by North Vietnamese warships on U.S. warships engaged on an intelligence mission in the Gulf of Tonkin persuaded Congress, at Johnson's request, to permit the President to take such counter-measures against the North as he thought necessary. The Gulf of Tonkin Resolution was used thereafter by the U.S. Administration as a virtual *carte blanche* authority for waging war in Indo-China – though no formal declaration of war was ever issued. In February 1965 Johnson took a crucial further step, escalating U.S. involvement in order to deter the North Vietnamese from continuing to support the Vietcong; he authorized the bombing of North Vietnam. On 1 April 1965 Johnson took his second crucial decision when he authorized the commitment of U.S. combat troops in the South. From then on both the North Vietnamese and the United States committed ever larger resources and troops to the struggle in South Vietnam, until American forces rose to more than half a million men. Contingents from Australia, New Zealand, the Philippines, Thailand, and sizeable forces from South Korea supported the American–South Vietnamese military effort. General Thieu emerged in South Vietnam as President and a leader in the war against the Vietcong and North Vietnam.

From 1969 to March 1973 the Nixon Administration steadily decreased the participation of American forces in the ground fighting, but continued the air war in South and North Vietnam.

In May 1968 peace talks were begun in Paris between the United States and North Vietnam, later joined by Vietcong and South Vietnamese delegates, whilst the war continued. The Nixon Administration persevered with both the Paris talks and the war, extending the latter to Vietcong supply lines in Cambodia. The peace talks were broken off in May 1972 but resumed in July. They were conducted on the American side by Dr Henry Kissinger and on the North Vietnamese side by Le Duc Tho, with Mrs Nguyen Thi Binh representing the Vietcong. These talks were deadlocked by 13 December 1972, in part owing to the opposition of the

South Vietnamese President Thieu. From 18 December 1972 until mid-January 1973 the United States resumed heavy bombing, including attacks on Hanoi. *The Agreement to end the Vietnam war was signed in Paris on 27 January 1973 between the Vietcong, South Vietnam, the United States and North Vietnam* (p. 284). Despite the ceasefire, fighting continued in South Vietnam between the Vietnamese contestants endeavouring to gain and hold the maximum territory. The last United States combat soldier had left Vietnam by the end of March 1973.

The end of March 1973 thus marked the end of direct military involvement by the United States in Vietnam. The administration of the ceasefire became the responsibility of the South Vietnamese and Vietcong as North Vietnamese and American officials left. *On 2 March 1973 the International Conference on Vietnam, held in Paris, issued a Declaration by Canada, the People's Republic of China, the United States, France, the Vietcong, South Vietnam, Hungary, Indonesia, Poland, North Vietnam, Britain and the Soviet Union* (p. 291). It committed all participants to upholding the Paris Peace Agreement on Vietnam signed on 27 January 1973 between the two Vietnamese States, the Vietcong and the United States; it also endorsed the responsibilities of Canada, Hungary, Indonesia and Poland as members of the *International Commission of Control and Supervision*, to supervise the ceasefire terms and the fragile peace.

In Laos an *Agreement to end the war was concluded between the Laotian Government and the Pathet Lao on 21 February 1973*. It provided for an end to a conflict that had lasted two decades. The agreement stipulated that a new Coalition Government was to be formed within thirty days, that all foreign forces were to withdraw within ninety days and that all Laotian forces were to remain in place. A Council of National Union was to be set up, with half of the members nominated by the Pathet Lao, to assist the Government and to supervise general elections at a time to be arranged. All prisoners of war, including Americans, were to be released within ninety days.

These agreements ended American and other outside involvement in the Indo-Chinese conflict. But they did not end the war. Rather they introduced a new stage of even more horrifying, at times genocidal, internecine fighting throughout the region.

Shorn of their American protective shield, the anti-communist Governments in all three countries soon collapsed. The Thieu régime in South Vietnam proved incapable of withstanding communist assault in spite of a continuing massive flow of United States economic aid and military supplies. In April 1975 Saigon fell to the Vietcong. The following

November the union of North and South Vietnam was proclaimed.

In neighbouring Laos the communist Pathet Lao forces occupied the capital in April 1975 and set up a republican régime. In the same month the capital of Cambodia fell to communist guerrillas known as the Khmer Rouge, at first allied with the mercurial former neutralist leader of the country, Prince Sihanouk. Under the leadership of the Prime Minister, Pol Pot, the Khmer Rouge Government effectively destroyed the country as a social unit. At least one million (perhaps as many as three million) people were massacred or died from a state-induced famine.

In December 1978 Vietnamese forces crossed the frontier into Cambodia and ousted the Pol Pot regime. In his place the Vietnamese installed a puppet government headed by Heng Samrin. *On 18 February 1979 Vietnam and Cambodia* (renamed Kampuchea) *signed a Treaty of Peace, Friendship and Cooperation* (p. 293). The U.S.S.R. gave diplomatic, but not military, support to the Vietnamese. China, on the other hand, reacted violently, and in February 1979 attacked North Vietnam, withdrawing a few weeks later after having dealt heavy blows to the Vietnamese. Fighting in and around Cambodia between the patrons and supporters of the Pol Pot and Heng Samrin régimes continued during the early 1980s resulting in massive loss of life, a virtual collapse of what remained of the social order in Cambodia and vast refugee movements.

## *The Geneva Agreements, 21 July 1954*

### Extracts from verbatim record of Eighth Plenary Session

*The Chairman* (Mr Eden): As I think my colleagues are aware, agreement has now been reached on certain documents. It is proposed that this Conference should take note of these agreements. I accordingly propose to begin by reading out a list of the subjects covered by the documents, which I understand every delegation has in front of them.

First, agreement on the cessation of hostilities in Vietnam; second, agreement on the cessation of hostilities in Laos; third, agreement on the cessation of hostilities in Cambodia. I would draw particular attention to the fact that these three agreements now incorporate the texts which were negotiated separately concerning the supervision of the Armistice in the three countries by the International Commission and the joint committees.

I should also like to draw the attention of all delegations to a point of some importance in connection with the Armistice Agreements and the related maps and documents on supervision. It has been agreed among the parties to each of these Agreements that none of them shall be made public for the present, pending further agreement among the parties. The reason for this, I must explain to my colleagues, is that these Armistice terms come into force at different dates. And it is desired that they should not be made public until they have come into force.

The further documents to which I must draw attention, which are in your possession, are: fourth, declaration by the Government of Laos on elections; fifth, declaration by the Government of Cambodia on elections and integration of all citizens into the national community; sixth, declaration by the Government of Laos on the military status of the country; seventh, declaration by the Government of Cambodia on the military status of the country; eighth, declaration by the Government of the French Republic on the withdrawal of troops from the three countries of Indochina.

Finally, gentlemen, there is the Draft Declaration by the Conference, which takes note of all these documents. I think all my colleagues have copies of this Draft Declaration before them. I will ask my colleagues in turn to express themselves upon this Declaration.

The Representative of France.

*M. Mendès-France* (France): Mr Chairman, the French Delegation approves the terms of this Declaration.

*The Chairman:* The Representative of Laos.

*Mr Phoui Sananikone* (Laos): The Delegation of Laos has no observations to make on this text.

*The Chairman:* The Representative of the People's Republic of China.

*Mr Chou En-Lai* (People's Republic of China): We agree.

*The Chairman:* On behalf of Her Majesty's Government in the United Kingdom, I associate myself with the Final Declaration of this Conference.

The Union of Soviet Socialist Republics.

*M. Molotov* (U.S.S.R.): The Soviet Delegation agrees.

*The Chairman:* The Representative of Cambodia.

*Mr Tep Pham* (Cambodia): The Delegate of Cambodia wishes to state that, among the documents just listed, one is missing. This is a Cambodian Declaration which we have already circulated to all delegations. Its purport is as follows:

Paragraphs 7, 11 and 12 of the Final Declaration stipulate respect for the territorial integrity of Vietnam. The Cambodian Delegation asks the Conference to consider that this provision does not imply the abandonment of such legitimate rights and interests as Cambodia might assert with regard to certain regions of South Vietnam, about which Cambodia has made express reservations, in particular at the time of the signature of the Franco-Khmer Treaty of November 8, 1949, on relations between Cambodia and France and at the time the French law which linked Cochinchina to Vietnam was passed. Faithful to the ideal of peace, and to the international principle of non-interference, Cambodia has no intention of interfering in the internal affairs of the State of Vietnam and associates herself fully with the principle of respect for its integrity, provided certain adjustments and regularizations be arrived at with regard to the borders between this State and Cambodia, borders which so far have been fixed by a mere unilateral act of France.

In support of this Declaration, the Cambodian Delegation communicates to all members of this Conference a note on Cambodian lands in South Vietnam.

*The Chairman:* If this Declaration was not inscribed on the agenda on the list of documents I have read out, it is because it has only at this instant reached me. I do not think it is any part of the task of this Conference to deal with any past controversies in respect of the frontiers between Cambodia and Vietnam.

The Representative of the Democratic Republic of Vietnam.

*Mr Pham Van Dong* (Democratic Republic of Vietnam): Mr Chairman. I agree completely with the words pronounced by you. In the name of the Government of the Democratic Republic of Vietnam we make the most express reservations regarding the statement made by the Delegation of Cambodia just now. I do this in the interests of good relations and understanding between our two countries.

*The Chairman:* I think the Conference can take note of the statements of the Delegation of Cambodia just circulated and of the statement of the Representative of the Democratic Republic of Vietnam.

I will continue calling upon countries to speak on the subject of the Declaration. I call upon the United States of America.

*Mr Bedell Smith* (United States): Mr Chairman, Fellow Delegates, as I stated to my colleagues during our meeting on July 18, my Government is not prepared to join in a Declaration by the Conference such as is submitted. However, the United States makes this Unilateral Declaration of its position in these matters:

DECLARATION

The Government of the United States being resolved to devote its efforts to the strengthening of peace in accordance with the principles and purposes of the United Nations

Takes Note

of the Agreements concluded at Geneva on July 20 and 21, 1954, between (a) the Franco-Laotian Command and the Command of the People's Army of Vietnam; (b) the Royal Khmer Army Command and the Command of the People's Army of Vietnam; (c) Franco-Vietnamese Command and the Command of the People's Army of Vietnam, and of paragraphs 1 to 12 of the Declaration presented to the Geneva Conference on July 21, 1954.

The Government of the United States of America

Declares with regard to the aforesaid Agreements and paragraphs that (i) it will refrain from the threat or the use of force to disturb them, in accordance with Article 2 (Section 4) of the Charter of the United Nations dealing with the obligation of Members to refrain in their international relations from the threat or use of force; and (ii) it would view any renewal of the aggression in violation of the aforesaid Agreements with grave concern and as seriously threatening international peace and security.

In connection with the statement in the Declaration concerning free elections in Vietnam, my Government wishes to make clear its position which it has expressed in a Declaration made in Washington on June 29, 1954, as follows:

In the case of nations now divided against their will, we shall continue to seek to achieve unity through free elections, supervised by the United Nations to ensure that they are conducted fairly.

With respect to the statement made by the Representative of the State of Vietnam, the United States reiterates its traditional position that peoples are entitled to determine their own future and that it will not join in an arrangement which would hinder this. Nothing in its declaration just made is intended to or does indicate any departure from this traditional position.

We share the hope that the agreement will permit Cambodia, Laos and Vietnam to play their part in full independence and sovereignty, in the peaceful community of nations, and will enable the peoples of that area to determine their own future.

Thank you, Mr Chairman.

*The Chairman:* The Conference will, I think, wish to take note of the statement of the Representative of the United States of America.

I call on the Representative of the State of Vietnam.

*Mr Tran Van Do* (State of Vietnam): Mr Chairman, as regards the Final Declaration of the Conference, the Vietnamese Delegation requests the Conference to incorporate in this Declaration after Article 10, the following text:

The Conference takes note of the Declaration of the Government of the State of Vietnam undertaking:

to make and support every effort to re-establish a real and lasting peace in Vietnam;

not to use force to resist the procedures for carrying the ceasefire into effect, in spite of the objections and reservations that the State of Vietnam has expressed, especially in its final statement.

*The Chairman:* I shall be glad to hear any views that my colleagues may wish to express. But, as I understand the position, the Final Declaration has already been drafted and this additional paragraph has only just now been received; indeed, it has been amended since I received the text a few minutes ago. In all the circumstances, I suggest that the best course we can take is that the Conference should take note of the Declaration of the State of Vietnam in this respect. If any of my colleagues has a contrary view, perhaps they would be good enough to say so. (None.) If none of my colleagues wishes to make any other observations, may I pass to certain other points which have to be settled before this Conference can conclude its labours?

The first is that, if it is agreeable to our colleagues, it is suggested that the two Chairmen should at the conclusion of this meeting address telegrams to the Governments of India, Poland and Canada to ask them if they will undertake the duties of supervision which the Conference has invited them to discharge. Is that agreeable? (Agreed.) Thank you.

. . .

# Final Declaration of the Geneva Conference on the problem of restoring peace in Indo-China, in which the representatives of Cambodia, the Democratic Republic of Vietnam, France, Laos, the People's Republic of China, the State of Vietnam, the Union of Soviet Socialist Republics, the United Kingdom and the United States of America took part

1. The Conference takes note of the agreements ending hostilities in Cambodia, Laos and Vietnam and organizing international control and the supervision of the execution of the provisions of these agreements.

2. The Conference expresses satisfaction at the ending of hostilities in Cambodia, Laos and Vietnam; the Conference expresses its conviction that the execution of the provisions set out in the present Declaration and in the agreements on the cessation of hostilities will permit Cambodia, Laos and Vietnam henceforth to play their part, in full independence and sovereignty, in the peaceful community of nations.

3. The Conference takes note of the declarations made by the Governments of Cambodia and of Laos of their intention to adopt measures permitting all citizens to take their place in the national community, in particular by participating in the next general elections, which, in conformity with the constitution of each of these countries, shall take place in the course of the year 1955, by secret ballot and in conditions of respect for fundamental freedoms.

4. The Conference takes note of the clauses in the agreement on the cessation of hostilities in Vietnam prohibiting the introduction into Vietnam of foreign troops and military personnel as well as of all kinds of arms and munitions. The Conference also takes note of the declarations made by the Governments of Cambodia and Laos of their resolution not to request foreign aid, whether in war material, in personnel or in instructors except for the purpose of the effective defence of their territory and, in the case of Laos, to the extent defined by the agreements on the cessation of hostilities in Laos.

5. The Conference takes note of the clauses in the agreement on the cessation of hostilities in Vietnam to the effect that no military base under the control of a foreign State may be established in the regrouping zones of the two parties, the latter having the obligation to see that the zones allotted to them shall not constitute part of any military alliance and shall not be utilized for the resumption of hostilities or in the service of an aggressive policy. The Conference also takes note of the declarations of the Governments of Cambodia and Laos to the effect that they will not join in any agreement with other

States if this agreement includes the obligation to participate in a military alliance not in conformity with the principles of the Charter of the United Nations or, in the case of Laos, with the principles of the agreement on the cessation of hostilities in Laos or, so long as their security is not threatened, the obligation to establish bases on Cambodian or Laotian territory for the military forces of foreign Powers.

6. The Conference recognizes that the essential purpose of the agreement relating to Vietnam is to settle military questions with a view to ending hostilities and that the military demarcation line is provisional and should not in any way be interpreted as constituting a political or territorial boundary. The Conference expresses its conviction that the execution of the provisions set out in the present Declaration and in the agreement on the cessation of hostilities creates the necessary basis for the achievement in the near future of a political settlement in Vietnam.

7. The Conference declares that, so far as Vietnam is concerned, the settlement of political problems, effected on the basis of respect for the principles of independence, unity and territorial integrity, shall permit the Vietnamese people to enjoy the fundamental freedoms, guaranteed by democratic institutions established as a result of free general elections by secret ballot. In order to ensure that sufficient progress in the restoration of peace has been made, and that all the necessary conditions obtain for free expression of the national will, general elections shall be held in July 1956, under the supervision of an international commission composed of representatives of the Member States of the International Supervisory Commission, referred to in the agreement on the cessation of hostilities. Consultations will be held on this subject between the competent representative authorities of the two zones from July 20, 1955, onwards.

8. The provisions of the agreements on the cessation of hostilities intended to ensure the protection of individuals and of property must be most strictly applied and must, in particular, allow everyone in Vietnam to decide freely in which zone he wishes to live.

9. The competent representative authorities of the Northern and Southern zones of Vietnam, as well as the authorities of Laos and Cambodia, must not permit any individual or collective reprisals against persons who have collaborated in any way with one of the parties during the war, or against members of such persons' families.

10. The Conference takes note of the declaration of the Government of the French Republic to the effect that it is ready to withdraw its troops from the territory of Cambodia, Laos and Vietnam, at the request of the Governments concerned and within periods which shall be fixed by agreement between the parties except in the cases where, by agreement between the two parties, a certain number of French troops shall remain at specified points and for a specified time.

11. The Conference takes note of the declaration of the French Government to the effect that for the settlement of all the problems connected with the re-establishment and consolidation of peace in Cambodia, Laos and Vietnam, the French Government will proceed from the principle of respect for the independence and sovereignty, unity and territorial integrity of Cambodia, Laos and Vietnam.

12. In their relations with Cambodia, Laos and Vietnam, each member of the Geneva Conference undertakes to respect the sovereignty, the independence, the unity and the territorial integrity of the above-mentioned States, and to refrain from any interference in their internal affairs.

13. The members of the Conference agree to consult one another on any question which may be referred to them by the International Supervisory Commission, in order to study such measures as may prove necessary to ensure that the agreements on the cessation of hostilities in Cambodia, Laos and Vietnam are respected.

DOCUMENT NO. 3: Agreement on the

cessation of hostilities in Cambodia, 20 July 1954

*Chapter I: Principles and conditions governing execution of the ceasefire*

*Article 1*. As from twenty-third July, 1954, at 0800 hours (Peking mean time) complete cessation of all hostilities throughout Cambodia shall be ordered and enforced by the Commanders of the Armed Forces of the two parties for all troops and personnel of the land, naval and air forces under their control.

*Article 2*. In conformity with the principle of a simultaneous ceasefire throughout Indo-China, there shall be a simultaneous cessation of hostilities throughout Cambodia, in all the combat areas and for all the forces of the two parties.

To obviate any mistake or misunderstanding and to ensure that both the ending of hostilities and all other operations arising from cessation of hostilities are in fact simultaneous...

NHIEK TIOULONG,
General

For the Commander-in-Chief of the Units of the Khmer Resistance Forces and for the Commander-in-Chief of the Vietnamese Military Units:

TA-QUANG-BUU,
Vice-Minister of National Defence of the Democratic Republic of Vietnam

DOCUMENT NO. 4: Agreement on the cessation of hostilities in Laos, 20 July 1954

. . .

For the Commander-in-Chief of the forces of the French Union Forces in Indo-China:

DELTEIL,
Brigadier-General

For the Commander-in-Chief of the fighting units of 'Pathet-Laos' and for the Commander-in-Chief of the People's Army of Vietnam:

TA-QUANG-BUU,
Vice-Minister of National Defence of the Democratic Republic of Vietnam

DOCUMENT NO. 5: Agreement on the cessation of hostilities in Vietnam, 20 July 1954

*Chapter I: Provisional military demarcation line and demilitarized zone*

*Article 1*. A provisional military demarcation line shall be fixed, on either side of which the forces of the two parties shall be regrouped after their withdrawal, the forces of the People's Army of Vietnam to the north of the line and the forces of the French Union to the south.

The provisional military demarcation line is fixed as shown on the map attached...

It is also agreed that a demilitarized zone shall be established on either side of the demarcation line, to a width of not more than 5 km from it, to act as a buffer zone and avoid any incidents which might result in the resumption of hostilities.

*Article 2*. The period within which the movement of all forces of either party into the regrouping zone on either side of the provisional military demarcation line shall be completed shall not exceed three hundred (300) days from the date of the present Agreement's entry into force.

. . .

*Chapter III: Ban on the introduction of fresh troops, military personnel, arms and munitions. Military bases*

*Article 16*. With effect from the date of entry into force of the present Agreement, the introduction into Vietnam of any troop reinforcements and additional military personnel is prohibited.

. . .

*Article 18*. With effect from the date of entry into force of the present Agreement, the establishment of new military bases is prohibited throughout Vietnam territory.

*Article 19*. With effect from the date of

entry into force of the present Agreement, no military base under the control of a foreign State may be established in the regrouping zone of either party; the two parties shall ensure that the zones assigned to them do not adhere to any military alliance and are not used for the resumption of hostilities or to further an aggressive policy.

. . .

*Article 25.* The Commanders of the Forces of the two parties shall afford full protection and all possible assistance and cooperation to the Joint Commission and its joint groups and to the International Commission and its inspection teams in the performance of the functions and tasks assigned to them by the present Agreement.

. . .

*Article 27.* The signatories of the present Agreement and their successors in their functions shall be responsible for ensuring the observance and enforcement of the terms and provisions thereof. The Commanders of the Forces of the two parties shall, within their respective commands, take all steps and make all arrangements necessary to ensure full compliance with all the provisions of the present Agreement by all elements and military personnel under their command.

The procedures laid down in the present Agreement shall, whenever necessary, be studied by the Commanders of the two parties and, if necessary, defined more specifically by the Joint Commission.

*Chapter VI: Joint Commission and International Commission for supervision and control in Vietnam*

*Article 28.* Responsibility for the execution of the agreement on the cessation of hostilities shall rest with the parties.

*Article 29.* An International Commission shall ensure the control and supervision of this execution.

*Article 30.* In order to facilitate, under

the condition shown below, the execution of provisions concerning joint actions by the two parties, a Joint Commission shall be set up in Vietnam.

For the Commander-in-Chief of the French Union Forces in Indo-China:
DELTEIL,
Brigadier-General

For the Commander-in-Chief of the People's Army of Vietnam:
TA-QUANG-BUU,
Vice-Minister of National Defence

. . .

DOCUMENT NO. 6: Declaration by the Royal Government of Cambodia, 21 July 1954

*(Reference: Article 3 of the Final Declaration)*

The Royal Government of Cambodia.

In the desire to ensure harmony and agreement among the peoples of the Kingdom,

Declares itself resolved to take the necessary measures to integrate all citizens, without discrimination, into the national community and to guarantee them the enjoyment of the rights and freedoms for which the Constitution of the Kingdom provides:

DOCUMENT NO. 7: Declaration by the Royal Government of Laos, 21 July 1954

*(Reference: Article 3 of the Final Declaration)*

The Royal Government of Laos,

In the desire to ensure harmony and agreement among the peoples of the Kingdom,

Declares itself resolved to take the necessary measures to integrate all citizens, without discrimination, into the national community and to guarantee them the enjoyment of the rights and freedoms for which the Constitution of the Kingdom provides;

Affirms that all Laotian citizens may freely participate as electors or candidates in general elections by secret ballot. . .

DOCUMENT NO. 8: Declaration by the

Royal Government of Cambodia, 21 July 1954

*(Reference: Articles 4 and 5 of the Final Declaration)*

The Royal Government of Cambodia is resolved never to take part in an aggressive policy and never to permit the territory of Cambodia to be utilized in the service of such a policy.

The Royal Government of Cambodia will not join in any agreement with other States, if this agreement carries for Cambodia the obligation to enter into military alliance not in conformity with the principles of the Charter of the United Nations, or, as long as its security is not threatened, the obligation to establish bases on Cambodian territory for the military forces of foreign Powers.

The Royal Government of Cambodia is resolved to settle its international disputes by peaceful means, in such a manner as not to endanger peace, international security and justice.

During the period which will elapse between the date of the cessation of hostilities in Vietnam and that of the final settlement of political problems in this country, the Royal Government of Cambodia will not solicit foreign aid in war material, personnel or instructors except for the purpose of the effective defence of the territory.

DOCUMENT NO. 9: Declaration by the Royal Government of Laos, 21 July 1954

*(Reference: Articles 4 and 5 of the Final Declaration)*

The Royal Government of Laos is resolved never to pursue a policy of aggression and will never permit the territory of Laos to be used in furtherance of such a policy.

The Royal Government of Laos will never join in any agreement with other States if this agreement includes the obligation for the Royal Government of Laos to participate in a military alliance not in conformity with the principles of the Charter of the United Nations or with the principles of the agreement on the cessation of hostilities or, unless its security is threatened, the obligation to establish bases on Laotian territory for military forces of foreign Powers.

The Royal Government of Laos is resolved to settle its international disputes by peaceful means so that international peace and security and justice are not endangered.

During the period between the cessation of hostilities in Vietnam and the final settlement of that country's political problems, the Royal Government of Laos will not request foreign aid, whether in war material, in personnel or in instructors, except for the purpose of its effective territorial defence and to the extent defined by the agreement on the cessation of hostilities.

DOCUMENT NO. 10: Declaration by the Government of the French Republic, 21 July 1954

*(Reference: Article 10 of the Final Declaration)*

The Government of the French Republic declares that it is ready to withdraw its troops from the territory of Cambodia, Laos and Vietnam, at the request of the Governments concerned and within a period which shall be fixed by agreement between the parties, except in the cases where, by agreement between the two parties, a certain number of French troops shall remain at specified points and for a specified time.

DOCUMENT NO. 11: Declaration by the Government of the French Republic, 21 July 1954

*(Reference: Article 11 of the Final Declaration)*

For the settlement of all the problems connected with the re-establishment and consolidation of peace in Cambodia, Laos and Vietnam, the French Government will proceed from the principle of respect for the independence and sovereignty, the unity and territorial integrity of Cambodia, Laos and Vietnam.

# *Declaration on the neutrality of Laos, Geneva, 23 July 1962*

The Governments of the Union of Burma, the Kingdom of Cambodia, Canada, the People's Republic of China, the Democratic Republic of Vietnam, the Republic of France, the Republic of India, the Polish People's Republic, the Republic of Vietnam, the Kingdom of Thailand, the Union of Soviet Socialist Republics, the United Kingdom of Great Britain and Northern Ireland and the United States of America, whose representatives took part in the International Conference on the Settlement of the Laotian Question, 1961–2;

Welcoming the presentation of the statement of neutrality by the Royal Government of Laos of July 9, 1962, and taking note of this statement, which is, with the concurrence of the Royal Government of Laos, incorporated in the present Declaration as an integral part thereof, and the text of which is as follows:

THE ROYAL GOVERNMENT OF LAOS,

Being resolved to follow the path of peace and neutrality in conformity with the interests and aspirations of the Laotian people, as well as the principles of the Joint Communiqué of Zurich dated June 22, 1961, and of the Geneva Agreements of 1954, in order to build a peaceful, neutral, independent, democratic, unified and prosperous Laos,

Solemnly declares that:

1. It will resolutely apply the five principles of peaceful coexistence in foreign relations, and will develop friendly relations and establish diplomatic relations with all countries, the neighbouring countries first and foremost, on the basis of equality and of respect for the independence and sovereignty of Laos;

2. It is the will of the Laotian people to protect and ensure respect for the sovereignty, independence, neutrality, unity, and territorial integrity of Laos;

3. It will not resort to the use or threat of force in any way which might impair the peace of other countries, and will not interfere in the internal affairs of other countries;

4. It will not enter into any military alliance or into any agreement, whether military or otherwise, which is inconsistent with the neutrality of the Kingdom of Laos; it will not allow the establishment of any foreign military base on Laotian territory, nor allow any country to use Laotian territory for military purposes or for the purposes of interference in the internal affairs of other countries, nor recognize the protection of any alliance or military coalition, including SEATO;

5. It will not allow any foreign interference in the internal affairs of the Kingdom of Laos in any form whatsoever;

6. Subject to the provisions of Article 5 of the Protocol, it will require the withdrawal from Laos of all foreign troops and military personnel, and will not allow any foreign troops or military personnel to be introduced into Laos;

7. It will accept direct and unconditional aid from all countries that wish to help the Kingdom of Laos build up an independent and autonomous national economy on the basis of respect for the sovereignty of Laos;

8. It will respect the treaties and agreements signed in conformity with the interests of the Laotian people and of the policy of peace and neutrality of the Kingdom, in particular the Geneva Agreements of 1962, and will abrogate all treaties and agreements which are contrary to those principles. . . .

[The above-mentioned countries. . .]

2. Undertake, in particular, that

(a) they will not commit or participate in any way in any act which might directly or indirectly impair the sovereignty, independence, neutrality, unity or territorial integrity of the Kingdom of Laos;

(b) they will not resort to the use or threat of force or any other measure which might impair the peace of the Kingdom of Laos;

(c) they will refrain from all direct or indirect interference in the internal affairs of the Kingdom of Laos;

(d) they will not attach conditions of a political nature to any assistance which they may offer or which the Kingdom of Laos may seek;

(e) they will not bring the Kingdom of Laos in any way into any military alliance or any other agreement, whether military or otherwise, which is inconsistent with her neutrality, nor invite or encourage her to enter into any such alliance or to conclude any such agreement;

(f) they will respect the wish of the Kingdom of Laos not to recognize the protection of any alliance or military coalition, including SEATO;

(g) they will not introduce into the Kingdom of Laos foreign troops or military personnel in any form whatsoever, nor will they in any way facilitate or connive at the introduction of any foreign troops or military personnel;

(h) they will not establish nor will they in any way facilitate or connive at the establishment in the Kingdom of Laos of any foreign military base, foreign strong point or other foreign military installation of any kind;

(i) they will not use the territory of the Kingdom of Laos for interference in the internal affairs of other countries;

(j) they will not use the territory of any country, including their own for interference in the internal affairs of the Kingdom of Laos.

. . .

4. Undertake, in the event of a violation or threat of violation of the sovereignty, independence, neutrality, unity or territorial integrity of the Kingdom of Laos, to consult jointly with the Royal Government of Laos and among themselves in order to consider measures which might prove to be necessary to ensure the observance of these principles and the other provisions of the present Declaration.

. . .

# Singapore Independence Agreement, Kuala Lumpur, 7 August 1965

An Agreement dated the 7th day of August, 1965, and made between the Government of Malaysia of the one part and the Government of Singapore of the other part.

*Whereas* Malaysia was established on the 16th day of September, 1963, by a federation of the existing States of the Federation of Malaya and the States of Sabah, Sarawak and Singapore into one independent and sovereign nation;

*And whereas* it has been agreed by the parties hereto that fresh arrangements should be made for the order and good government of the territories comprised in Malaysia by the separation of Singapore from Malaysia upon which Singapore shall become an independent and sovereign State and nation separate from and independent of Malaysia and so recognized by the Government of Malaysia;

*Now* therefore it is agreed and declared as follows:

*Article I.* This Agreement may be cited as the Independence of Singapore Agreement, 1965.

*Article II.* Singapore shall cease to be a State of Malaysia on the 9th day of August, 1965, (hereinafter referred to as 'Singapore Day') and shall become an independent and sovereign State separate from and independent of Malaysia and recognized as such by the Government of Malaysia; and the Government of Malaysia will proclaim and enact the constitutional instruments annexed to this Agreement in the manner hereinafter appearing.

*Article III.* The Government of Malaysia will declare by way of proclamation in the form set out in Annex A to this Agreement that Singapore is an independent and sovereign State separate from and independent of Malaysia and recognized as such by the Government of Malaysia.

*Article IV.* The Government of Malaysia will take such steps as may be appropriate and available to them to secure the enactment by the Parliament of Malaysia of an Act in the form set out in Annex B to this Agreement and will ensure that it is made operative as from Singapore Day, providing for the relinquishment of sovereignty and jurisdiction of the Government of Malaysia in respect of Singapore so that the said sovereignty and jurisdiction shall on such relinquishment vest in the Government of Singapore in accordance with this Agreement and the constitutional instruments annexed.

*Article V.* The parties hereto will enter into a treaty on external defence and mutual assistance providing that:

1. The parties hereto will establish a joint defence council for purposes of external defence and mutual assistance;

2. The Government of Malaysia will afford to the Government of Singapore such assistance as may be considered reasonable and adequate for external defence,

and in consideration thereof, the Government of Singapore will contribute from its own armed forces such units thereof as may be considered reasonable and adequate for such defence;

3. The Government of Singapore will afford to the Government of Malaysia the right to continue to maintain the bases and other facilities used by its military forces within Singapore and will permit the Government of Malaysia to make such use of these bases and facilities as the Government of Malaysia may consider necessary for the purpose of external defence;

4. Each party will undertake not to enter into any treaty or agreement with a foreign country which may be detrimental to the independence and defence of the territory of the other party.

*Article VI.* The parties hereto will on and after Singapore Day cooperate in economic affairs for their mutual benefit and interest and for this purpose may set up such joint committees or councils as may from time to time be agreed upon.

. . .

[The agreement was accompanied by two annexes: Annex A, the proclamation by the Prime Minister, Lee Kuan Yew, of Singapore's independence, dated 9 August 1965; and Annex B, the text of the Act to amend the Constitution of Malaysia and the Malaysia Act; this amending act, providing for the independence of Singapore, received the royal assent on 9 August 1965.]

# Agreement to end the Vietnam war, Paris, 27 January 1973

The Parties participating in the Paris Conference on Vietnam,

With a view to ending the war and restoring peace in Vietnam on the basis of respect for the Vietnamese people's fundamental national rights and the South

Vietnamese people's right to self-determination, and to contributing to the consolidation of peace in Asia and the world,

Have agreed on the following provisions and undertake to respect and to implement them:

## Chapter I

### THE VIETNAMESE PEOPLE'S FUNDAMENTAL NATIONAL RIGHTS

*Article 1.* The United States and all other countries respect the independence, sovereignty, unity, and territorial integrity of Vietnam as recognized by the 1954 Geneva Agreements on Vietnam.

## Chapter II

### CESSATION OF HOSTILITIES— WITHDRAWAL OF TROOPS

*Article 2.* A ceasefire shall be observed throughout South Vietnam as of 2400 hours G.M.T., on January 27, 1973.

At the same hour, the United States will stop all its military activities against the territory of the Democratic Republic of Vietnam by ground, air and naval forces, wherever they may be based, and end the mining of the territorial waters, ports, harbors, and waterways of the Democratic Republic of Vietnam. The United States will remove, permanently deactivate or destroy all the mines in the territorial waters, ports, harbors, and waterways of North Vietnam as soon as this Agreement goes into effect.

The complete cessation of hostilities mentioned in this Article shall be durable and without limit of time.

*Article 3.* The parties undertake to maintain the ceasefire and to ensure a lasting and stable peace.

As soon as the ceasefire goes into effect:

(a) The United States forces and those of the other foreign countries allied with the United States and the Republic of Vietnam shall remain in place pending the implementation of the plan of troop withdrawal. The Four-Party Joint Military Commission described in Article 16 shall determine the modalities.

(b) The armed forces of the two South Vietnamese parties shall remain in place. The Two-Party Joint Military Commission described in Article 17 shall determine the areas controlled by each party and the modalities of stationing.

(c) The regular forces of all services and arms and the irregular forces of the parties in South Vietnam shall stop all offensive activities against each other and shall strictly abide by the following stipulations:

• All acts of force on the ground, in the air, and on the sea shall be prohibited;

• All hostile acts, terrorism and reprisals by both sides will be banned.

*Article 4.* The United States will not continue its military involvement or intervene in the internal affairs of South Vietnam.

*Article 5.* Within sixty days of the signing of this Agreement, there will be a total withdrawal from South Vietnam of troops, military advisers, and military personnel, including technical military personnel and military personnel associated with the pacification program, armaments, munitions, and war material of the United States and those of the other foreign countries mentioned in Article 3 (a). Advisers from the above-mentioned countries to all paramilitary organizations and the police force will also be withdrawn within the same period of time.

*Article 6.* The dismantlement of all military bases in South Vietnam of the United States and of the other foreign countries mentioned in Article 3 (a) shall be completed within sixty days of the signing of this Agreement.

*Article 7.* From the enforcement of the ceasefire to the formation of the government provided for in Articles 9 (b) and 14 of this Agreement, the two South Vietnamese parties shall not accept the introduction of troops, military advisers, and military personnel including technical military personnel, armaments, munitions, and war material into South Vietnam.

The two South Vietnamese parties shall be permitted to make periodic replacement of armaments, munitions and war material which have been destroyed, damaged, worn out or used up after the ceasefire, on the basis of piece-for-piece, of the same characteristics and properties, under the supervision of the Joint Military Commission of the two South Vietnamese parties and of the International Commission of Control and Supervision.

*Chapter III*

THE RETURN OF CAPTURED MILITARY
PERSONNEL AND FOREIGN CIVILIANS,
AND CAPTURED AND DETAINED
VIETNAMESE CIVILIAN PERSONNEL

*Article 8.* (a) The return of captured military personnel and foreign civilians of the parties shall be carried out simultaneously with and completed not later than the same day as the troop withdrawal mentioned in Article 5. The parties shall exchange complete lists of the above-mentioned captured military personnel and foreign civilians on the day of the signing of this Agreement.

(b) The parties shall help each other to get information about those military personnel and foreign civilians of the parties missing in action, to determine the location and take care of the graves of the dead so as to facilitate the exhumation and repatriation of the remains, and to take any such other measures as may be required to get information about those still considered missing in action.

(c) The question of the return of Vietnamese civilian personnel captured and detained in South Vietnam will be resolved by the two South Vietnamese parties on the basis of the principles of Article 21 (b) of the Agreement on the Cessation of Hostilities in Vietnam of July 20, 1954. The two South Vietnamese parties will do so in a spirit of national reconciliation and concord, with a view to ending hatred and enmity, in order to ease suffering and to reunite families. The two South Vietnamese parties will do their utmost to resolve this question within ninety days after the ceasefire comes into effect.

*Chapter IV*

THE EXERCISE OF THE SOUTH
VIETNAMESE PEOPLE'S RIGHT TO
SELF-DETERMINATION

*Article 9.* The Government of the United States of America and the Government of the Democratic Republic of Vietnam undertake to respect the following principles for the exercise of the South Vietnamese people's right to self-determination:

(a) The South Vietnamese people's right to self-determination is sacred, inalienable, and shall be respected by all countries.

(b) The South Vietnamese people shall decide themselves the political future of South Vietnam through genuinely free and democratic general elections under international supervision.

(c) Foreign countries shall not impose any political tendency or personality on the South Vietnamese people.

*Article 10.* The two South Vietnamese parties undertake to respect the ceasefire and maintain peace in South Vietnam, settle all matters of contention through negotiations, and avoid all armed conflict.

*Article 11.* Immediately after the ceasefire, the two South Vietnamese parties will:

• Achieve national reconciliation and concord, end hatred and enmity, prohibit all acts of reprisal and discrimination against individuals or organizations that have collaborated with one side or the other;

• Ensure the democratic liberties of the people: personal freedom, freedom of speech, freedom of the press, freedom of meeting, freedom of organization, freedom of political activities, freedom of belief, freedom of movement, freedom of residence, freedom of work, right to property ownership, and right to free enterprise.

*Article 12.* (a) Immediately after the ceasefire, the two South Vietnamese parties shall hold consultations in a spirit of national reconciliation and concord, mutual respect, and mutual non-elimination to set up a National Council of National Reconciliation and Concord of three equal segments. The Council shall operate on the principle of unanimity.

After the National Council of National Reconciliation and Concord has assumed its functions, the two South Vietnamese parties will consult about the formation of councils at lower levels. The two South Vietnamese parties shall sign an agreement on the internal matters of South Vietnam as soon as possible and do their utmost to accomplish this within ninety days after the ceasefire comes into effect, in keeping with the South Vietnamese people's aspirations for peace, independence and democracy.

(b) The National Council of National Reconciliation and Concord shall have the task of promoting the two South Vietnamese parties' implementation of this Agreement, achievement of national reconciliation and concord and ensurance of democratic liberties. The National Council of National Reconciliation and Concord will organize the free and democratic general elections provided for in Article 9 (b) and decide the procedures and modalities of these general elections. The institutions for which the general elections are to be held will be agreed upon through consultations between the two South Vietnamese parties. The National Council of National Reconciliation and Concord will also decide the procedures and modalities of such local elections as the two South Vietnamese parties agree upon.

*Article 13.* The question of Vietnamese armed forces in South Vietnam shall be settled by the two South Vietnamese parties in a spirit of national reconciliation and concord, equality and mutual respect, without foreign interference, in accordance with the post-war situation. Among the questions to be discussed by the two South Vietnamese parties are steps to reduce their military effectives and to demobilize the troops being reduced. The two South Vietnamese parties will accomplish this as soon as possible.

*Article 14.* South Vietnam will pursue a foreign policy of peace and independence. It will be prepared to establish relations with all countries irrespective of their political and social systems on the basis of mutual respect for independence and sovereignty and accept economic and technical aid from any country with no political conditions attached. The acceptance of military aid by South Vietnam in the future shall come under the authority of the government set up after the general elections in South Vietnam provided for in Article 9 (b).

*Chapter V*

THE REUNIFICATION OF VIETNAM AND THE RELATIONSHIP BETWEEN NORTH AND SOUTH VIETNAM

*Article 15.* The reunification of Vietnam shall be carried out step by step through peaceful means on the basis of discussions and agreements between North and South Vietnam, without coercion or annexation by either party, and without foreign interference. The time for reunification will be agreed upon by North and South Vietnam.

Pending reunification:

(a) The military demarcation line between the two zones at the 17th parallel is only provisional and not a political or territorial boundary, as provided for in paragraph 6 of the Final Declaration of the 1954 Geneva Conference.

(b) North and South Vietnam shall respect the Demilitarized Zone on either side of the Provisional Military Demarcation Line.

(c) North and South Vietnam shall promptly start negotiations with a view to reestablishing normal relations in various fields. Among the questions to be negotiated are the modalities of civilian movement across the Provisional Military Demarcation Line.

(d) North and South Vietnam shall not join any military alliance or military bloc and shall not allow foreign powers to maintain military bases, troops, military advisers, and military personnel on their respective territories, as stipulated in the 1954 Geneva Agreements on Vietnam.

*Chapter VI*

THE JOINT MILITARY COMMISSIONS, THE
INTERNATIONAL COMMISSION OF
CONTROL AND SUPERVISION, THE
INTERNATIONAL CONFERENCE

*Article 16.* (a) The Parties participating in the Paris Conference on Vietnam shall immediately designate representatives to form a Four-Party Joint Military Commission with the task of ensuring joint action by the parties in implementing the following provisions of this Agreement:
• The first paragraph of Article 2, regarding the enforcement of the ceasefire throughout South Vietnam;
• Article 3 (a), regarding the ceasefire by U.S. forces and those of the other foreign countries referred to in that Article;
• Article 3 (c), regarding the ceasefire between all parties in South Vietnam;
• Article 5, regarding the withdrawal from South Vietnam of U.S. troops and those of the other foreign countries mentioned in Article 3 (a);
• Article 6, regarding the dismantlement of military bases in South Vietnam of the United States and those of the other foreign countries mentioned in Article 3 (a);
• Article 8 (a), regarding the return of captured military personnel and foreign civilians of the parties;
• Article 8 (b), regarding the mutual assistance of the parties in getting information about those military personnel and foreign civilians of the parties missing in action.
(b) The Four-Party Joint Military Commission shall operate in accordance with the principle of consultations and unanimity. Disagreements shall be referred to the International Commission of Control and Supervision.
(c) The Four-Party Joint Military Commission shall begin operating immediately after the signing of this Agreement and end its activities in sixty days, after the completion of the withdrawal of U.S. troops and those of the other foreign countries mentioned in Article 3 (a) and the completion of the return of captured military personnel and foreign civilians of the parties.
(d) The four parties shall agree immediately on the organization, the working procedure, means of activity, and expenditures of the Four-Party Joint Military Commission.

*Article 17.* (a) The two South Vietnamese parties shall immediately designate representatives to form a Two-Party Joint Military Commission with the task of ensuring joint action by the two South Vietnamese parties in implementing the following provisions of this Agreement:
• The first paragraph of Article 2, regarding the enforcement of the ceasefire throughout South Vietnam, when the Four-Party Joint Military Commission has ended its activities;
• Article 3 (b), regarding the ceasefire between the two South Vietnamese parties;
• Article 3 (c), regarding the ceasefire between all parties in South Vietnam, when the Four-Party Joint Military Commission has ended its activities;
• Article 7, regarding the prohibition of the introduction of troops into South Vietnam and all other provisions of this Article;
• Article 8 (c), regarding the question of the return of Vietnamese civilian personnel captured and detained in South Vietnam;
• Article 13, regarding the reduction of the military effectives of the two South Vietnamese parties and the demobilization of the troops being reduced.
(b) Disagreements shall be referred to the International Commission of Control and Supervision.
(c) After the signing of this Agreement, the Two-Party Joint Military Commission shall agree immediately on the measures and organization aimed at enforcing the ceasefire and preserving peace in South Vietnam.

*Article 18.* (a) After the signing of this

Agreement, an International Commission of Control and Supervision shall be established immediately.

(b) Until the International Conference provided for in Article 19 makes definitive arrangements, the International Commission of Control and Supervision will report to the four parties on matters concerning the control and supervision of the implementation of the following provisions of this Agreement:

• The first paragraph of Article 2, regarding the enforcement of the ceasefire throughout South Vietnam;

• Article 3 (a), regarding the ceasefire by U.S. forces and those of the other foreign countries referred to in that Article;

• Article 3 (c), regarding the ceasefire between all the parties in South Vietnam;

• Article 5, regarding the withdrawal from South Vietnam of U.S. troops and those of the other foreign countries mentioned in Article 3 (a);

• Article 6, regarding the dismantlement of military bases in South Vietnam of the United States and those of the other foreign countries mentioned in Article 3 (a);

• Article 8 (a), regarding the return of captured military personnel and foreign civilians of the parties.

The International Commission of Control and Supervision shall form control teams for carrying out its tasks. The four parties shall agree immediately on the location and operation of these teams. The parties will facilitate their operation.

(c) Until the International Conference makes definitive arrangements, the International Commission of Control and Supervision will report to the two South Vietnamese parties on matters concerning the control and supervision of the implementation of the following provisions of this Agreement:

• The first paragraph of Article 2, regarding the enforcement of the ceasefire throughout South Vietnam, when the Four-Party Joint Military Commission has ended its activities;

• Article 3 (b), regarding the cease-fire between the two South Vietnamese parties;

• Article 3 (c), regarding the ceasefire between all parties in South Vietnam, when the Four-Party Joint Military Commission has ended its activities;

• Article 7, regarding the prohibition of the introduction of troops into South Vietnam and all other provisions of this Article;

• Article 8 (c), regarding the question of the return of Vietnamese civilian personnel captured and detained in South Vietnam;

• Article 9 (b), regarding the free and democratic general elections in South Vietnam;

• Article 13, regarding the reduction of the military effectives of the two South Vietnamese parties and the demobilization of the troops being reduced.

The International Commission of Control and Supervision shall form control teams for carrying out its tasks. The two South Vietnamese parties shall agree immediately on the location and operation of these teams. The two South Vietnamese parties will facilitate their operation.

(d) The International Commission of Control and Supervision shall be composed of representatives of four countries: Canada, Hungary, Indonesia and Poland. The chairmanship of this Commission will rotate among the members for specific periods to be determined by the Commission.

(e) The International Commission of Control and Supervision shall carry out its tasks in accordance with the principle of respect for the sovereignty of South Vietnam.

(f) The International Commission of Control and Supervision shall operate in accordance with the principle of consultations and unanimity.

(g) The International Commission of Control and Supervision shall begin operating when a ceasefire comes into force in Vietnam. As regards the provisions in Article 18 (b) concerning the four parties, the International Commission of Control and Supervision shall end its activities when the Commission's tasks of control and supervision regarding these provisions have been fulfilled. As regards the provisions in Article 18 (c) concerning the two South Vietnamese parties, the International Commission of Control and Supervision shall end its activities on the request of the government formed after the general elections in South Vietnam provided for in Article 9 (b).

(h) The four parties shall agree immediately on the organization, means of activity, and expenditures of the International Commission of Control and Supervision. The relationship between the International Commission and the International Conference will be agreed upon by the International Commission and the International Conference.

*Article 19.* The parties agree on the convening of an International Conference within thirty days of the signing of this Agreement to acknowledge the signed agreements; to guarantee the ending of the war, the maintenance of peace in Vietnam, the respect of the Vietnamese people's fundamental national rights, and the South Vietnamese people's right to self-determination; and to contribute to and guarantee peace in Indochina.

The United States and the Democratic Republic of Vietnam, on behalf of the parties participating in the Paris Conference on Vietnam, will propose to the following parties that they participate in this International Conference: the People's Republic of China, the Republic of France, the Union of Soviet Socialist Republics, the United Kingdom, the four countries of the International Commission of Control and Supervision, and the Secretary General of the United Nations, together with the parties participating in the Paris Conference on Vietnam.

*Chapter VII*

REGARDING CAMBODIA AND LAOS

*Article 20.* (a) The parties participating in the Paris Conference on Vietnam shall strictly respect the 1954 Geneva Agreements on Cambodia and the 1962 Geneva

Agreements on Laos, which recognized the Cambodian and the Lao peoples' fundamental national rights, i.e., the independence, sovereignty, unity, and territorial integrity of these countries. The parties shall respect the neutrality of Cambodia and Laos.

The parties participating in the Paris Conference on Vietnam undertake to refrain from using the territory of Cambodia and the territory of Laos to encroach on the sovereignty and security of one another and of other countries.

(b) Foreign countries shall put an end to all military activities in Cambodia and Laos, totally withdraw from and refrain from reintroducing into these two countries troops, military advisers and military personnel, armaments, munitions and war material.

(c) The internal affairs of Cambodia and Laos shall be settled by the people of each of these countries without foreign interference.

(d) The problems existing between the Indochinese countries shall be settled by the Indochinese parties on the basis of respect for each other's independence, sovereignty, and territorial integrity, and non-interference in each other's internal affairs.

*Chapter VIII*

THE RELATIONSHIP BETWEEN THE UNITED STATES AND THE DEMOCRATIC REPUBLIC OF VIETNAM

*Article 21.* The United States anticipates that this Agreement will usher in an era of reconciliation with the Democratic Republic of Vietnam as with all the peoples of Indochina. In pursuance of its traditional policy, the United States will contribute to healing the wounds of war and to post-war reconstruction of the Democratic Republic of Vietnam and throughout Indochina.

*Article 22.* The ending of the war, the restoration of peace in Vietnam, and the strict implementation of this Agreement will create conditions for establishing a new, equal and mutually beneficial relationship between the United States and the Democratic Republic of Vietnam on the basis of respect for each other's independence and sovereignty, and non-interference in each other's internal affairs. At the same time this will ensure stable peace in Vietnam and contribute to the preservation of lasting peace in Indochina and Southeast Asia.

*Chapter IX*

OTHER PROVISIONS

*Article 23*. This Agreement shall enter into force upon signature by plenipotentiary representatives of the parties participating in the Paris Conference on Vietnam. All the parties concerned shall strictly implement this Agreement and its Protocols.

Done in Paris this twenty-seventh day of January, One Thousand Nine Hundred and Seventy-Three, in English and Vietnamese. The English and Vietnamese texts are official and equally authentic.

[For the Government of the United States of America]:

William P. Rogers, Secretary of State

[For the Government of the Republic of Vietnam]:
Tran Van Lam, Minister for Foreign Affairs

[For the Government of the Democratic Republic of Vietnam]:
Nguyen Duy Trinh, Minister for Foreign Affairs

[For the Provisional Revolutionary Government of the Republic of South Vietnam]:
Nguyen Thi Binh, Minister for Foreign Affairs

[The agreement was accompanied by four protocols: the first dealt with the return of military and civilian prisoners-of-war; the second with the International Commission of Control and Supervision; the third with the ceasefire in South Vietnam and the Joint Military Commissions; and the fourth with the removal of mines in the territorial waters of North Vietnam.]

# Declaration of the International Conference on Vietnam, Paris, 2 March 1973

The Government of the United States of America;
The Government of the French Republic;
The Provisional Revolutionary Government of the Republic of South Vietnam;
The Government of the Hungarian People's Republic;
The Government of the Republic of Indonesia;
The Government of the Polish People's Republic;
The Government of the Democratic Republic of Vietnam;
The Government of the United Kingdom of Great Britain and Northern Ireland;
The Government of the Republic of Vietnam;
The Government of the Union of Soviet Socialist Republics;

The Government of Canada; and
The Government of the People's Republic of China;
In the presence of the Secretary-General of the United Nations;
With a view to acknowledging the signed agreements guaranteeing the ending of the war, the maintenance of peace in Vietnam, the respect of the Vietnamese people's fundamental national rights, and the South Vietnamese people's right to self-determination, and contributing to and guaranteeing peace in Indochina,

Have agreed on the following provisions, and undertake to respect and implement them:

*Article 1*. The parties to this Act solemnly acknowledge, express their approval of and support the Paris Agreement on Ending the War and Restoring Peace in Vietnam signed in Paris on January 27, 1973, and the four Protocols to the Agreement signed on the same date (hereinafter referred to respectively as the Agreement and the Protocols).

*Article 2.* The Agreement responds to the aspirations and fundamental national rights of the Vietnamese people, i.e. the independence, sovereignty, unity, and territorial integrity of Vietnam, to the right of the South Vietnamese people to self-determination, and to the earnest desire for peace shared by all countries in the world. The Agreement constitutes a major contribution to peace, self-determination, national independence, and the improvement of relations among countries. The Agreement and the Protocols should be strictly respected and scrupulously implemented.

*Article 3.* The parties to this Act solemnly acknowledge the commitments by the parties to the Agreement and the Protocols to strictly respect and scrupulously implement the Agreement and the Protocols.

*Article 4.* The parties to this Act solemnly recognize and strictly respect the fundamental national rights of the Vietnamese people, i.e. the independence, sovereignty, unity, and territorial integrity of Vietnam, as well as the right of the South Vietnamese people to self-determination. The parties to this Act shall strictly respect the Agreement and the Protocols by refraining from any action at variance with their provisions.

*Article 5.* For the sake of a durable peace in Vietnam, the parties to this Act call on all countries to strictly respect the fundamental national rights of the Vietnamese people, i.e. the independence, sovereignty, unity, and territorial integrity of Vietnam, and the right of the South Vietnamese people to self-determination, and to strictly respect the Agreement and the Protocols by refraining from any action at variance with their provisions.

*Article 6.* (a) The four parties to the Agreement or the two South Vietnamese parties may, either individually or through joint action, inform the other parties to this Act about the implementation of the Agreement and the Protocols. Since the reports and views submitted by the International Commission of Control and Supervision concerning the control and supervision of the implementation of those provisions of the Agreement and the Protocols which are within the tasks of the commission will be sent to either the four parties signatory to the Agreement or to the two South Vietnamese parties, those parties shall be responsible, either individually or through joint action, for forwarding them promptly to the other parties to this Act.

(b) The four parties to the Agreement or the two South Vietnamese parties shall also, either individually or through joint action, forward this information and these reports and views to the other participant in the International Conference on Vietnam for his information.

*Article 7.* (a) In the event of a violation of the Agreement or the Protocols which threatens the peace, the independence, sovereignty, unity, or territorial integrity of Vietnam, or the right of the South Vietnamese people to self-determination, the parties signatory to the Agreement and the Protocols shall, either individually or jointly, consult with the other parties to this Act with a view to determining necessary remedial measures.

(b) The International Conference on Vietnam shall be reconvened upon a joint request by the Government of the United States of America and the Government of the Democratic Republic of Vietnam on behalf of the parties signatory to the Agreement or upon a request by six or more of the parties to this Act.

*Article 8.* With a view to contributing to and guaranteeing peace in Indo-China, the parties to this Act acknowledge the commitment of the parties to the Agreement to respect the independence, sovereignty, unity, territorial integrity, and neutrality of Cambodia and Laos as stipulated in the Agreement, agree also to respect them and to refrain from any action at variance with them, and call on other countries to do the same.

*Article 9.* This Act shall enter into force upon signature by plenipotentiary representatives of all twelve parties and shall be strictly implemented by all the parties. Signature of this Act does not constitute recognition of any party in any case in which it has not previously been accorded.

Done in twelve copies in Paris this second day of March, 1973, in English, French, Russian, Vietnamese and Chinese. All texts are equally authentic.

# Treaty of Peace, Friendship and Cooperation between Vietnam and Cambodia (Kampuchea), Phnom Penh, 18 February 1979

The Socialist Republic of Vietnam and the People's Republic of Kampuchea,

Proceeding from the traditions of Vietnam–Kampuchea militant solidarity and fraternal friendship which have overcome many trials and become an unbreakable force ensuring the success of each country's national defence and construction,

Deeply conscious that the independence, freedom, peace and security of the two countries are closely interrelated and that the two sides are duty-bound to help each other whole-heartedly and with all their might to defend and consolidate the great revolutionary gains they have recorded through almost thirty years' struggle full of hardships and sacrifices,

Affirming that the militant solidarity and the long-term and all-round cooperation and friendship between Vietnam and Kampuchea meet the vital interests of the two peoples and, at the same time, are a factor ensuring a durable peace and stability in South-East Asia, and are in keeping with the basic interests of the peoples in this region and contribute to the maintenance of world peace,

Confident that the Kampuchean people's complete victory under the glorious banner of the National United Front for the Salvation of Kampuchea, the correct line for independence, sovereignty and international solidarity of each country, and respect for each other's legitimate interests constitute a firm basis for the constant development of friendship and cooperation between the two countries,

Desirous to strengthen the militant solidarity, the long-term cooperation and friendship and mutual assistance in all fields to consolidate independence, build a prosperous country and a happy life for each people, thus contributing to the maintenance of peace and stability in South-East Asia and the world, in keeping with the objectives of the Non-Aligned Countries' Movement and the Charter of the United Nations,

Have decided to sign this Treaty and have agreed upon the following articles:

*Article 1.* The two sides undertake to do all they can to defend and constantly develop the traditional militant solidarity, friendship and fraternal cooperation between Vietnam and Kampuchea, and mutual trust and assistance in all fields on the basis of respect for each other's independence, sovereignty and legitimate interests, non-interference in each other's internal affairs, equality and mutual benefit.

The two sides shall do all they can to

educate the cadres, fighters and people of their respective countries to preserve the traditional Vietnam–Kampuchea militant solidarity and loyal friendship and make them pure and clear forever.

*Article 2.* On the principle that national defence and construction are the cause of each people, the two sides undertake to whole-heartedly support and assist each other in all domains and in all necessary forms in order to strengthen the capacity to defend the independence, sovereignty, unity, territorial integrity and peaceful labour of the people in each country against all schemes and acts of sabotage by the imperialist and international reactionary forces. The two sides will take effective measures to implement this commitment whenever one of them so requires.

*Article 3.* In order to help each other build a prosperous and powerful country and a happy life free from cold and hunger, the two sides shall strengthen mutually beneficial fraternal exchanges and cooperation and assist each other in the fields of economy, culture, education, public health, science and technology, and in training cadres and exchanging specialists and experience in all fields of national construction.

To attain this objective, the two sides will sign necessary agreements and, at the same time, increase contacts and cooperation between the State offices concerned and between mass organizations of both countries.

*Article 4.* The two sides undertake to solve through peaceful negotiation all the differences which may arise in the relations between the two countries. They will negotiate to sign an agreement on the delineation of the national frontier between the two countries on the basis of the present border line with the determination to turn the present border into a border of lasting peace and friendship between the two countries.

*Article 5.* The two sides fully respect each other's independent and sovereign line.

They persistently pursue a foreign policy of independence, peace, friendship, cooperation and non-alignment, on the principle of non-interference in whatever form in other countries' internal affairs, non-acceptance of any interference in their respective countries' internal affairs, and not allowing any country to use their respective countries' territory to interfere in other countries.

The two sides attach great importance to the long-standing tradition of militant solidarity and fraternal friendship between the Kampuchean, Lao and Vietnamese peoples, and pledge to do their best to strengthen this traditional relationship on the basis of respect for each country's independence, sovereignty and territorial integrity. They will strengthen their relations in all fields with the socialist countries. Being countries in South-East Asia, the Socialist Republic of Vietnam and the People's Republic of Kampuchea persistently pursue a policy of friendship and good neighbourliness with Thailand and the other countries in South-East Asia, and actively contribute to peace, stability and prosperity of the South-East Asian region. The two sides will develop the relations of cooperation with the independent nationalist countries, the national liberation movements and democratic movements, and resolutely support the struggle of nations for peace, national independence, democracy and social progress. They will make positive contributions to the solidarity and growth of the Non-Aligned Movement against imperialism and the other international reactionary forces, to regain and defend national independence and to advance towards the establishment of a new world economic order.

*Article 6.* The two sides will frequently exchange views on the questions concerning the relations between their two countries and other international matters of mutual interest. All problems in the relations between their two countries will be solved through negotiation in the spirit of mutual understanding and respect and with fairness and reason.

*Article 7.* This Treaty is not aimed at opposing any third country and is not related to the right and obligation of each party to abide by the bilateral and multilateral agreements it engages in.

*Article 8.* This Treaty shall take effect right from the day of the exchange of the Ratification Letters: the ratification shall be done according to the procedures of each party.

*Article 9.* This Treaty is valid for twenty-five years and will be automatically prolonged every ten years if neither of the two signatory parties informs the other by writ one year before the expiration of the Treaty about its intention to cancel the Treaty.

This Treaty is done in Phnom Penh, capital of the People's Republic of Kampuchea, on the 18th of February 1979, in the Vietnamese and Khmer languages, which are equally valid.

FOR THE PEOPLE'S REVOLUTIONARY COUNCIL OF THE PEOPLE'S REPUBLIC OF KAMPUCHEA
[Signed] Heng Samrin
President of the People's Revolutionary Council

FOR THE GOVERNMENT OF THE SOCIALIST REPUBLIC OF VIETNAM
[Signed] Pham Van Dong
Premier of the Government

## East Asia and the Pacific

### THE CHINESE CIVIL WAR

The war in China, during the period of the wider global conflict of 1941 to 1945, was fought on three fronts: Nationalist Chinese, Communist Chinese and Japanese. All American efforts to bring about a collaboration of communist and nationalist war efforts against Japan failed. Whereas the United States gave first priority to the defeat of Japan, Chiang Kai-shek and Mao Tse-tung looked beyond the war to the struggle for the control of China, involving the defeat and subordination of either the nationalist or communist cause. Internationally, Chiang Kai-shek's Government was bolstered by the recognition and the support of all the Western Powers, by a permanent seat for China on the Security Council of the U.N. and by the *Sino-Soviet Treaty of 14 August 1945* (p. 51). Mao Tse-tung continued to build up communist strength after the defeat of Japan; time was gained by both sides when General Marshall, on a mediating mission in China, helped to arrange a ceasefire in January 1946. Several months of uneasy truce and apparent communist–nationalist cooperation ended in November 1946, and a full scale Chinese Civil War ensued.

The Chinese Civil War from 1946 to 1949 involved huge armies on each side (at the outset of the war 1 million communist troops against 3 million nationalist troops), and ended on the mainland of China with the collapse of the nationalist armies on several fronts in the autumn of 1949. On 1 October 1949 Mao Tse-tung proclaimed the People's Republic of China.

The Nationalist Government of Chiang Kai-shek settled on Taiwan

(Formosa). It claimed to speak for all China and retained sufficient international recognition to continue to hold the Chinese seat on the Security Council until 1971. After June 1950 the United States protected Taiwan from possible communist attack by the interposition of the American Seventh Fleet in the Taiwan Straits, which prevented both nationalists and communists from attacking each other. Increasing American aid for Chiang Kai-shek was followed by treaty commitments with the signature of the *Mutual Defense Treaty between the United States and China, 2 December 1954* (p. 123).

Although the United States did not participate directly in the Chinese Civil War it was drawn perilously close to full-scale conflict with the Chinese communists as a result of its involvement in the Korean War between 1950 and 1953.


## The Korean War

From 1905 to 1945 Korea had been under Japanese rule. During the Second World War, at the Cairo Conference in 1943, Korea was promised independence 'in due course', a promise confirmed at the Potsdam Conference in 1945, which also attained the agreement that Soviet troops should accept the surrender of Japanese forces in North Korea whilst South Korea should be occupied first by American military forces. The demarcation between the two zones became the 38th parallel. This demarcation soon became a *de facto* political frontier as all negotiations for free elections in the whole of Korea failed. In South Korea, the Republic of Korea came into being on 15 August 1948, and in North Korea a communist State, the Korean People's Republic, was established in September 1948.

On 25 June 1950 the North Korean army invaded South Korea in strength. Because of the international date-line it was 24 June in Washington. The day after the invasion, 26 June in Korea, 25 June in the United States, the Security Council met, passed its first resolution stating that the North Korean attack constituted a 'breach of peace', and called for an immediate end to hostilities and a withdrawal of North Korean forces to their own side of the border. In the absence of the Soviet representative (owing to Soviet protest at the seating of the Nationalist Chinese representative), this resolution was adopted by a vote of 9–0 with Yugoslavia abstaining. The United States decision to provide the South Korean forces south of the 38th parallel with all-out air and naval support was taken by Truman on the evening of 26 June, and orders were issued at once. On the afternoon of 27 June the Security Council adopted a second and stronger resolution calling upon members to give all possible help to the Republic of Korea to repel the invasion and to restore peace and security in the area. On this resolution Yugoslavia dissented and Egypt and India abstained. President Truman announced his order to the United States air and sea forces to support the South Korean Government, and also declared that he had ordered the Seventh Fleet to prevent any attack on Formosa. On 29 and 30 June, Truman decided to commit the United States ground forces in Korea. The United States' call for help was supported by fifteen nations including the British Commonwealth and Turkey, which sent contingents of armed forces, and many more nations sent civilian aid. The bulk of the fighting force was South Korean and American, which formed the United Nations army in Korea under the 'unified command' of General MacArthur.

The Korean War passed through five major phases: 25 June–14 September 1950, when North Korean forces occupied all South Korea but for the Pusan perimeter; 15 September–30 September 1950, when U.N. forces defeated the North Korean troops in the south after the success of the Inchon landing; 25 October 1950, when U.N. forces crossed the 38th parallel and advanced towards the Chinese and Russian frontier; 26 October 1950–25 January 1951, when U.N. forces continued to advance but were defeated as a result of Chinese intervention, and pulled back south of the 38th parallel where a stable line of defence was established; February 1951–July 1953, when heavy fighting north and south of the 38th parallel finally left the U.N. troops almost all along the front to the north of the 38th parallel; the ceasefire line was finally established on 27 July 1953. The Korean War was a major war involving North Korean and Chinese armies of more than 1 million, while some 700,000 men served with the United Nations Command; casualties on both sides, civilian and military, were very heavy. Negotiations for a truce began in Kaesong in July 1951 while fighting continued. These negotiations, suspended several times, led two years later to the *Armistice Agreement signed at Panmunjom, 27 July 1953* (p. 302), providing for a ceasefire line, the suspension of hostilities, and the exchange of prisoners of war voluntarily wishing to return.

The Korean Armistice was never translated into a full-fledged peace treaty. Korea remained divided between north and south, and relations between the two halves were almost non-existent. South Korea remained firmly embedded in the Western camp. In North Korea the communist régime of Kim Il-sung was cautiously neutral in the quarrel between the U.S.S.R. and China. *On 22 June 1965 South Korea and Japan signed a Treaty on Basic Relations.* This was accompanied by agreements on fisheries, property claims, cultural assets and other matters. With this treaty the historic effort of Japan to assert its domination over Korea was formally terminated. An *agreement in July 1972 between North and South Korea*, in which the two States undertook to seek reunification of the country by peaceful means, failed, however, to bring about a similar reconciliation in the peninsula. The Panmunjom dividing line remained frozen for more than three decades without a fundamental change in the political character of the régimes on either side.

## THE CHINESE–AMERICAN RAPPROCHEMENT

During its first decade of power the communist régime in China remained diplomatically aligned with the Soviet Union. The United States refused even to recognize it as the Government of China, continuing to maintain diplomatic relations exclusively with the 'Republic of China', reduced to an American-protected rump on Taiwan. Even after the rupture between the U.S.S.R. and China (see p. 159), there was no immediate rapprochement between the United States and the Chinese communists. The period of the 'cultural revolution' in China from 1965 to 1968 was marked by violent xenophobia and hostility to all things Western.

The first signal of a change in the wind came in early 1971 with an agreement between the United States and China for a visit to China by an American table tennis team. In July 1971 President Nixon's national security adviser, Dr Henry Kissinger, paid a secret visit to Peking. His discussions there paved the way for one of the major shifts in international diplomacy of the post-war period – the renewal of friendly relations between the United States and China.

In February 1972 President Nixon visited China (a country with which the U.S.A. at that time had no diplomatic relations). The *joint U.S.–Chinese communiqué, issued at Shanghai on 28 February 1972* (p. 303) contained separate (and opposing) statements of policy put forward by the U.S. and China; but the communiqué also expressed the common view of both parties that 'progress towards normalization of relations' was a desirable goal. In February 1973 Kissinger visited China again. A *joint U.S.–China communiqué, issued on 22 February 1973* at the conclusion of Kissinger's visit reaffirmed 'their joint commitment to bring about a normalization of relations', and announced an agreement to establish quasi-diplomatic 'liaison offices' in each other's capitals.

The culmination of this process was an *agreement between China and the*

*United States, announced in a joint communiqué on 15 December 1978,* to reestablish diplomatic relations. In the communiqué the United States announced its recognition of the Government of the People's Republic of China as the sole legal Government of China. A United States Government statement issued at the same time announced that the U.S.A. would terminate diplomatic relations with the Taiwan régime. The Mutual Defense Treaty between Taiwan and the United States was also to be terminated. And the United States would withdraw all remaining American military personnel from Taiwan within four months.

Following the reestablishment of diplomatic relations between China and the U.S.A. a number of further agreements were signed. These included agreements on consular relations, on cultural relations, on scientific and technological cooperation, on the settlement of claims, on civil air transport, and other subjects. *On 30 October 1980 China and the United States signed an Investment Incentive Agreement* designed to facilitate the entry of Western capital into China.

China's historic swing towards a renewed openness to Western and other outside influences affected her relations with all the major powers. Even the schism with the Soviet Union seemed gradually to become less deep: propaganda warfare between the two communist neighbours became less shrill; and a few cautious steps began to be made towards some accommodation.

SINO-JAPANESE RAPPROCHEMENT

Meanwhile, China's relations with Japan also underwent a radical transformation. Although the two countries had concluded a commercial agreement in 1962, Japan had continued to maintain diplomatic relations only with the Taiwan régime (with which it had signed a treaty of peace on 28 April 1952). The Japanese were taken aback by the Nixon Administration's sudden moves towards détente with China, and moved quickly to mend their own fences with Peking. Relations with Taiwan were broken off and in January 1974 and April 1977 China and Japan signed trade agreements. *On 12 August 1978 China and Japan signed a Treaty of Peace and Friendship in Peking* (p. 306). This treaty in effect marked the formal ending of the triangular conflict of nationalist Chinese, communist Chinese, and Japanese that had raged between 1931 and 1945 (although the text of the treaty, unlike that of all other 'peace treaties' signed between antagonists after the Second World War, made no reference to the war).

In the early 1980s China sought to improve relations with Taiwan, going so far as to offer Taiwan a form of autonomy and a continuing capitalist economic structure if the Taiwan Government would agree to reunification with the mainland. These approaches were rebuffed. But the Chinese had more success in negotiations with Britain concerning the future of Hong Kong.

## HONG KONG

This British crown colony (one of the last examples of an almost-extinct species) consisted of three main areas: Hong Kong island (area 29 square miles), seized by Britain in 1841, and ceded by the imperial Chinese Government in a charter dated 5 April 1843; the mainland peninsula of Kowloon (area 3½ square miles), acquired by Britain in the Convention of Peking in 1860; and the so-called 'New Territories', mostly on the mainland (area 365½ square miles) which were leased to Britain in a convention signed on 9 June 1898. This lease was to run for 99 years and was therefore expected to run out in 1997. After the communist victory in China in 1949, the Chinese Government laid claim to Hong Kong, denouncing the 'unequal treaties' by which China had been compelled to yield it up to the British. But China took no military or other action to seek to enforce its claim. In fact, Hong Kong's booming capitalist economy provided some useful services to China which had no desire to change the situation precipitately. The prospect of the termination of the lease, however, coupled with the British Government's general policy of decolonization, led Britain and China to open negotiations for a settlement of the Hong Kong issue. *On 19 December 1984 an agreement between Britain and China on the future of Hong Kong was signed in Peking* (p. 307) by the British Prime Minister, Margaret Thatcher, and the Chinese Prime Minister, Zhao Ziyang. The agreement provided for the restoration of the whole of the crown colony (not merely the New Territories) to China on 1 July 1997. At the same time the Chinese undertook, 'taking account of the history of Hong Kong and its realities' to establish Hong Kong as a 'Special Administrative Region' with 'a high degree of autonomy' and a capitalist economic structure. The agreement had been endorsed by the Hong Kong Legislative Council on 18 October 1984. The British Parliament approved it in December 1984 and China ratified it on 10 April 1985. A similar agreement, providing for the return of Macao to China in 1999, was reached between Portugal and China in March 1987.

## THE SOUTH PACIFIC

First moves towards economic and political coordination in the South Pacific region took place in 1947 with the establishment of the *South Pacific Commission*, formed by Australia, France, the Netherlands, New Zealand, Britain and the U.S.A. By 1984 the Commission had twenty-seven member States; its activities were coordinated by a secretariat; the Commission promoted cooperation in development projects, cultural relations, and use of resources. The *South Pacific Forum*, formed at a meeting in New Zealand on 5 August 1971, attempted to bring about closer economic and political cooperation. The members did not include any of the great powers. Australia and New Zealand were the most important of the members (fourteen by 1984) which included most of the independent island States of the region. The *South Pacific Bureau for Economic Cooperation, formed by an agreement among members of the Forum on 17 April 1973* was a trade agreement whereby Australia and New Zealand offered their smaller neighbours preferential access for their exports.

*On 6 August 1985 the South Pacific Nuclear Free Zone Treaty was signed at Raratonga on the Cook Islands.* Among the signatories (all of them members of the South Pacific Forum) were Australia and New Zealand. The treaty obliged signatories not to acquire nuclear weapons, not to permit the stationing of nuclear weapons on their territory, and not to permit testing of nuclear weapons on their territory. Although the treaty was held by the signatories to be fully consistent with their other treaty obligations (such as the ANZUS Treaty), the New Zealand Government soon found itself embroiled in a serious dispute over the nuclear issue with the United States. By 1986 this had brought about the effective expulsion of New Zealand from the ANZUS alliance (see p. 112).

## THE NORTH PACIFIC

The shooting down of a Korean Airlines passenger jet airliner over Soviet territory on 31 August 1983 thrust into the limelight the normally shrouded military confrontation of the U.S.S.R. and the U.S.A. in the barren, but strategically important region of the north Pacific. Although various conspiracy theories were advanced for the straying of the aircraft over Soviet territory, and for the Soviet decision to shoot it down, the most convincing interpretation suggested that the incident resulted from a chain of mistakes. The *Memorandum of Understanding concerning air traffic control in the north Pacific, signed by the U.S.A., U.S.S.R. and Japan on 29*

*July 1985* (p. 316) was designed to help prevent any repetition of such an incident. It also gave evidence of the sensitivity with which all three powers regarded communications in the region, an area of major significance in the East–West strategic balance.

## Military armistice in Korea, Panmunjom, 27 July 1953

...in the interest of stopping the Korean conflict, with its great toll of suffering and bloodshed on both sides, and with the objective of establishing an armistice which will insure a complete cessation of hostilities and of all acts of armed force in Korea until a final peaceful settlement is achieved, do individually, collectively, and mutually agree to...

*Article I: Military demarcation line and demilitarized zone.* 1. A military demarcation line shall be fixed and both sides shall withdraw two (2) kilometres from this line so as to establish a demilitarized zone between the opposing forces. A demilitarized zone shall be established as a buffer zone to prevent the occurrence of incidents which might lead to a resumption of hostilities.

2. The military demarcation line is located as indicated on the attached map...

. . .

24. The general mission of the Military Armistice Commission shall be to supervise the implementation of this Armistice Agreement and to settle through negotiations any violations of this Armistice Agreement.

. . .

[36. A Neutral Nations Supervisory Commission established.]

*Article III: Arrangements relating to prisoners of war.* 51. The release and repatriation of all prisoners of war held in the custody of each side at the time this Armistice Agreement becomes effective shall be effected in conformity with the following provisions agreed upon by both sides prior to the signing of this Armistice Agreement.

(a) Within sixty (60) days after this Armistice Agreement becomes effective, each side shall, without offering any hindrance, directly repatriate and hand over in groups all those prisoners of war in its custody who insist on repatriation to the side to which they belonged at the time of capture. Repatriation shall be accomplished in accordance with the related provisions of this Article. In order to expedite the repatriation process of such personnel, each side shall, prior to the signing of the Armistice Agreement, exchange the total numbers, by nationalities, of personnel to be directly repatriated. Each group of prisoners of war delivered to the other side shall be accompanied by rosters, prepared by nationality, to include name, rank (if any) and internment or military serial number.

(b) Each side shall release all those remaining prisoners of war, who are not directly repatriated, from its military control and from its custody and hand them over to the Neutral Nations Repatriation Commission for disposition in accordance with the provisions in the Annex hereto: 'Terms of Reference for Neutral Nations Repatriation Commission'. . . .

*Article IV: Recommendation to the Governments concerned on both sides.* 60. In order to ensure the peaceful settlement of the Korean question, the Military Commanders of both sides hereby recommend to the Governments of the countries concerned on both sides that, within three (3) months after the Armistice Agreement is signed and becomes effective, a political conference of a higher level of both sides be held by representatives appointed res-

pectively to settle through negotiation the questions of the withdrawal of all foreign forces from Korea, the peaceful settlement of the Korean question, etc.

. . .

# Joint U.S.–Chinese Communiqué, Shanghai, 28 February 1972

## Shanghai, People's Republic of China

President Richard Nixon of the United States of America visited the People's Republic of China at the invitation of Premier Chou En-lai of the People's Republic of China from February 21 to February 28, 1972. Accompanying the President were Mrs. Nixon, U.S. Secretary of State William Rogers, Assistant to the President Dr Henry Kissinger, and other American officials.

President Nixon met with Chairman Mao Tse-tung of the Communist Party of China on February 21. The two leaders had a serious and frank exchange of views on Sino-U.S. relations and world affairs.

During the visit, extensive, earnest and frank discussions were held between President Nixon and Premier Chou En-lai on the normalization of relations between the United States of America and the People's Republic of China, as well as on other matters of interest to both sides. In addition, Secretary of State William Rogers and Foreign Minister Chi Peng-fei held talks in the same spirit.

President Nixon and his party visited Peking and viewed cultural, industrial and agricultural sites, and they also toured Hangchow and Shanghai where, continuing discussions with Chinese leaders, they viewed similar places of interest.

The leaders of the People's Republic of China and the United States of America found it beneficial to have this opportun-

ity, after so many years without contact, to present candidly to one another their views on a variety of issues. They reviewed the international situation in which important changes and great upheavals are taking place and expounded their respective positions and attitudes.

The U.S. side stated: Peace in Asia and peace in the world requires efforts both to reduce immediate tensions and to eliminate the basic causes of conflict. The United States will work for a just and secure peace: just, because it fulfills the aspirations of peoples and nations for freedom and progress; secure, because it removes the danger of foreign aggression. The United States supports individual freedom and social progress for all the peoples of the world, free of outside pressure or intervention. The United States believes that the effort to reduce tensions is served by improving communication between countries that have different ideologies so as to lessen the risks of confrontation through accident, miscalculation or misunderstanding. Countries should treat each other with mutual respect and be willing to compete peacefully, letting performance be the ultimate judge. No country should claim infallibility and each country should be prepared to re-examine its own attitudes for the common good. The United States stressed that the peoples of Indo-China should be allowed to determine their destiny without outside intervention; its constant primary objective has been a negotiated solution; the eight-point proposal put forward by the Republic of Vietnam and the United States on January 27, 1972 represents a basis for the attainment of that objective; in the absence of a negotiated settlement the United States envisages the ultimate withdrawal of all U.S. forces from the region consistent with the aim of self-determination for each country of Indo-China. The United States will maintain its close ties with and support for the Republic of Korea; the United States will support efforts of the Republic of Korea to seek a relaxation of tension and increased communication in the Korean peninsula. The United States places the highest value on its friendly relations with Japan; it will continue to develop the existing close bonds. Consistent with the United Nations Security Council Resolution of December 21, 1971, the United States favors the continuation of the ceasefire between India and Pakistan and the withdrawal of all military forces to within their own territories and to their own sides of the ceasefire line in Jammu and Kashmir; the United States supports the right of the peoples of South Asia to shape their own future in peace, free of military threat, and without having the area become the subject of great power rivalry.

The Chinese side stated: Wherever there is oppression, there is resistance. Countries want independence, nations want liberation and the people want revolution – this has become the irresistible trend of history. All nations, big or small, should be equal; big nations should not bully the small and strong nations should not bully the weak. China will never be a superpower and it opposes hegemony and power politics of any kind. The Chinese side stated that it firmly supports the struggles of all the oppressed people and nations for freedom and liberation and that the people of all countries have the right to choose their social systems according to their own wishes and the right to safeguard the independence,

sovereignty and territorial integrity of their own countries and oppose foreign aggression, interference, control and subversion. All foreign troops should be withdrawn to their own countries.

The Chinese side expressed its firm support to the peoples of Vietnam, Laos and Cambodia in their efforts for the attainment of their goal and its firm support to the seven-point proposal of the Provisional Revolutionary Government of the Republic of South Vietnam and the elaboration of February this year on the two key problems in the proposal, and to the Joint Declaration of the Summit Conference of the Indo-Chinese Peoples. It firmly supports the eight-point program for the peaceful unification of Korea put forward by the Government of the Democratic People's Republic of Korea on April 12, 1971, and the stand for the abolition of the 'U.N. Commission for the Unification and Rehabilitation of Korea'. It firmly opposes the revival and outward expansion of Japanese militarism and firmly supports the Japanese people's desire to build an independent, democratic, peaceful and neutral Japan. It firmly maintains that India and Pakistan should, in accordance with the United Nations resolutions on the India–Pakistan question, immediately withdraw all their forces to their respective territories and to their own sides of the ceasefire line in Jammu and Kashmir and firmly supports the Pakistan Government and people in their struggle to preserve their independence and sovereignty and the people of Jammu and Kashmir in their struggle for the right of self-determination.

There are essential differences between China and the United States in their social systems and foreign policies. However, the two sides agreed that countries, regardless of their social systems, should conduct their relations on the principles of respect for the sovereignty and territorial integrity of all States, non-aggression against other States, non-interference in the internal affairs of other States, equality and mutual benefit, and peaceful coexistence. International disputes should be settled on this basis, without resorting to the use or threat of force. The United States and the People's Republic of China are prepared to apply these principles to their mutual relations.

With these principles of international relations in mind the two sides stated that:

• progress toward the normalization of relations between China and the United States is in the interests of all countries;

• both wish to reduce the danger of international military conflict;

• neither should seek hegemony in the Asia–Pacific region and each is opposed to efforts by any other country or group of countries to establish such hegemony; and

• neither is prepared to negotiate on behalf of any third party or to enter into agreements or understandings with the other directed at other States.

Both sides are of the view that it would be against the interests of the peoples of the world for any major country to collude with another against other countries, or for major countries to divide up the world into spheres of interest.

The two sides reviewed the long-standing serious disputes between China and the United States. The Chinese side reaffirmed its position: The Taiwan question is the crucial question obstructing the normalization of relations between China and the United States; the Government of the People's Republic of China is the sole legal Government of China; Taiwan is a province of China which has long been returned to the motherland; the liberation of Taiwan is China's internal affair in which no other country has the right to interfere; and all U.S. forces and military installations must be withdrawn from Taiwan. The Chinese Government firmly opposes any activities which aim at the creation of 'one China, one Taiwan', 'one China, two Governments', 'two Chinas', and 'independent Taiwan' or advocate that 'the status of Taiwan remains to be determined'.

The U.S. side declared: The United States acknowledges that all Chinese on either side of the Taiwan Strait maintain there is but one China and that Taiwan is a part of China. The United States Government does not challenge that position. It reaffirms its interest in a peaceful settlement of the Taiwan question by the Chinese themselves. With this prospect in mind, it affirms the ultimate objective of the withdrawal of all U.S. forces and military installations from Taiwan. In the meantime, it will progressively reduce its forces and military installations on Taiwan as the tension in the area diminishes.

The two sides agreed that it is desirable to broaden the understanding between the two peoples. To this end, they discussed specific areas in such fields as science, technology, culture, sports and journalism, in which people-to-people contacts and exchanges would be mutually beneficial. Each side undertakes to facilitate the further development of such contacts and exchanges.

Both sides view bilateral trade as another area from which mutual benefit can be derived, and agreed that economic relations based on equality and mutual benefit are in the interest of the peoples of the two countries. They agree to facilitate the progressive development of trade between their two countries.

The two sides agreed that they will stay in contact through various channels, including the sending of a senior U.S. representative to Peking from time to time for concrete consultations to further the normalization of relations between the two countries and continue to exchange views on issues of common interest.

The two sides expressed the hope that the gains achieved during this visit would open up new prospects for the relations between the two countries. They believe that the normalization of relations between the two countries is not only in the interest of the Chinese and American peoples but also contributes to the relaxation of tension in Asia and the world.

President Nixon, Mrs. Nixon and the American party expressed their appreciation for the gracious hospitality shown them by the Government and people of the People's Republic of China.

# Treaty of Peace and Friendship between China and Japan, Peking, 12 August 1978

The People's Republic of China and Japan,

Recalling with satisfaction that since the Government of the People's Republic of China and the Government of Japan issued a Joint Statement in Peking on September 29, 1972, the friendly relations between the two Governments and the peoples of the two countries have developed greatly on a new basis,

Confirming that the above-mentioned Joint Statement constitutes the basis of the relations of peace and friendship between the two countries and that the principles enunciated in the Joint Statement should be strictly observed,

Confirming that the principles of the Charter of the United Nations should be fully respected,

Hoping to contribute to peace and stability in Asia and in the world,

For the purpose of solidifying and developing the relations of peace and friendship between the two countries,

Have resolved to conclude a Treaty of Peace and Friendship and for that purpose have appointed as their Plenipotentiaries:

*The People's Republic of China*: Huang Hua, Minister of Foreign Affairs

*Japan:* Sunao Sonoda, Minister for Foreign Affairs

Who, having communicated to each other their full powers, found to be in good and due form, have agreed as follows:

*Article I.* 1. The Contracting Parties shall develop durable relations of peace and friendship between the two countries on the basis of the principles of mutual respect for sovereignty and territorial integrity, mutual non-aggression, non-interference in each other's internal affairs, equality and mutual benefit and peaceful coexistence.

2. In keeping with the foregoing principles and the principles of the United Nations Charter, the Contracting Parties affirm that in their mutual relations, all disputes shall be settled by peaceful means without resorting to the use or threat of force.

*Article II.* The Contracting Parties declare that neither of them should seek hegemony in the Asia–Pacific region or in any other region and that each is opposed to efforts by any other country or group of countries to establish such hegemony.

*Article III.* The Contracting Parties shall, in a good-neighbourly and friendly spirit and in conformity with the principles of equality and mutual benefit and non-interference in each other's internal affairs, endeavour to further develop economic and cultural relations between the two countries and to promote exchanges between the peoples of the two countries.

*Article IV.* The present Treaty shall not affect the position of either Contracting Party regarding its relations with third countries.

*Article V.* 1. The present Treaty shall be ratified and shall enter into force on the date of the exchange of instruments of ratification which shall take place at Tokyo. The present Treaty shall remain in force for ten years and thereafter shall continue to be in force until terminated in accordance with the provisions of Paragraph 2 of this Article.

2. Either Contracting Party may, by giving one year's written notice to the other Contracting Party, terminate the present Treaty at the end of the initial ten-year period or at any time thereafter.

. . .

# Agreement between Great Britain and China on the Future of Hong Kong, Peking, 19 December 1984

**Joint Declaration of the Government of the United Kingdom of Great Britain and Northern Ireland and the Government of the People's Republic of China on the question of Hong Kong**

The Government of the United Kingdom of Great Britain and Northern Ireland and the Government of the People's Republic of China have reviewed with satisfaction the friendly relations existing between the two Governments and peoples in recent years and agreed that a proper negotiated settlement of the question of Hong Kong, which is left over from the past, is conducive to the maintenance of the prosperity and stability of Hong Kong and to the further strengthening and development of the relations between the two countries on a new basis. To this end, they have, after talks between the delegations of the two Governments, agreed to declare as follows:

1. The Government of the People's Republic of China declares that to recover the Hong Kong area (including Hong Kong Island, Kowloon and the New Territories, hereinafter referred to as Hong Kong) is the common aspiration of the entire Chinese people, and that it has decided to resume the exercise of sovereignty over Hong Kong with effect from 1 July 1997.

2. The Government of the United Kingdom declares that it will restore Hong Kong to the People's Republic of China with effect from 1 July 1997.

3. The Government of the People's Republic of China declares that the basic policies of the People's Republic of China regarding Hong Kong are as follows:

(1) Upholding national unity and territorial integrity and taking account of the history of Hong Kong and its realities, the People's Republic of China has decided to establish, in accordance with the provisions of Article 31 of the Constitution of the People's Republic of China, a Hong Kong Special Administrative Region upon resuming the exercise of sovereignty over Hong Kong.

(2) The Hong Kong Special Administrative Region will be directly under the authority of the Central People's Government of the People's Republic of China. The Hong Kong Special Administrative Region will enjoy a high degree of autonomy, except in foreign and defence affairs which are the responsibilities of the Central People's Government.

(3) The Hong Kong Special Administrative Region will be vested with executive, legislative and independent judicial power, including that of final adjudication. The laws currently in force in Hong Kong will remain basically unchanged.

(4) The Government of the Hong Kong Special Administrative Region will be composed of local inhabitants. The chief executive will be appointed by the Central People's Government on the basis of the results of elections or consultations to be held locally. Principal officials will be nominated by the chief executive of the Hong Kong Special Administrative Region for appointment by the Central People's Government. Chinese and foreign nationals previously working in the public and police services in the government departments of Hong Kong may remain in employment. British and other foreign nationals may also be employed to serve as advisers or hold certain public posts in government departments of the Hong Kong Special Administrative Region.

(5) The current social and economic systems in Hong Kong will remain unchanged, and so will the life-style. Rights and freedoms, including those of the person, of speech, of the press, of assembly,

of association, of travel, of movement, of correspondence, of strike, of choice of occupation, of academic research and of religious belief will be ensured by law in the Hong Kong Special Administrative Region. Private property, ownership of enterprises, legitimate right of inheritance and foreign investment will be protected by law.

(6) The Hong Kong Special Administrative Region will retain the status of a free port and a separate customs territory.

(7) The Hong Kong Special Administrative Region will retain the status of an international financial centre, and its markets for foreign exchange, gold, securities and futures will continue. There will be free flow of capital. The Hong Kong dollar will continue to circulate and remain freely convertible.

(8) The Hong Kong Special Administrative Region will have independent finances. The Central People's Government will not levy taxes on the Hong Kong Special Administrative Region.

(9) The Hong Kong Special Administrative Region may establish mutually beneficial economic relations with the United Kingdom and other countries, whose economic interests in Hong Kong will be given due regard.

(10) Using the name of 'Hong Kong, China', the Hong Kong Special Administrative Region may on its own maintain and develop economic and cultural relations and conclude relevant agreements with states, regions and relevant international organizations.

The Government of the Hong Kong Special Administrative Region may on its own issue travel documents for entry into and exit from Hong Kong.

(11) The maintenance of public order in the Hong Kong Special Administrative Region will be the responsibility of the Government of the Hong Kong Special Administrative Region.

(12) The above-stated basic policies of the People's Republic of China regarding Hong Kong and the elaboration of them in Annex I to this Joint Declaration will be stipulated, in a Basic Law of the Hong Kong Special Administrative Region of the People's Republic of China, by the National People's Congress of the People's Republic of China, and they will remain unchanged for 50 years.

4. The Government of the United Kingdom and the Government of the People's Republic of China declare that, during the transitional period between the date of the entry into force of this Joint Declaration and 30 June 1997, the Government of the United Kingdom will be responsible for the administration of Hong Kong with the object of maintaining and preserving its economic prosperity and social stability; and that the Government of the People's Republic of China will give its cooperation in this connection.

5. The Government of the United Kingdom and the Government of the People's Republic of China declare that, in order to ensure a smooth transfer of government in 1997, and with a view to the effective implementation of this Joint Declaration, a Sino-British Joint Liaison Group will be set up when this Joint Declaration enters into force; and that it will be established and will function in accordance with the provisions of Annex II to this Joint Declaration.

6. The Government of the United Kingdom and the Government of the People's Republic of China declare that land leases in Hong Kong and other related matters will be dealt with in accordance with the provisions of Annex III to this Joint Declaration.

7. The Government of the United Kingdom and the Government of the People's Republic of China agree to implement the preceding declarations and the Annexes to this Joint Declaration.

8. This Joint Declaration is subject to ratification and shall enter into force on the date of the exchange of instruments of ratification, which shall take place in Beijing before 30 June 1985. This Joint Declaration and its Annexes shall be equally binding.

## Annex I

ELABORATION BY THE GOVERNMENT OF
THE PEOPLE'S REPUBLIC OF CHINA OF
ITS BASIC POLICIES REGARDING HONG
KONG

The Government of the People's Republic
of China elaborates the basic policies of
the People's Republic of China regarding
Hong Kong as set out in paragraph 3 of
the Joint Declaration of the Government
of the United Kingdom of Great Britain
and Northern Ireland and the Government of the People's Republic of China
on the Question of Hong Kong as follows:

### I

The Constitution of the People's Republic
of China stipulates in Article 31 that 'the
State may establish special administrative
regions when necessary. The systems to
be instituted in special administrative
regions shall be prescribed by laws enacted by the National People's Congress
in the light of the specific conditions.' In
accordance with this Article, the People's
Republic of China shall, upon the resumption of the exercise of sovereignty
over Hong Kong on 1 July 1997, establish the Hong Kong Special Administrative Region of the People's Republic of
China. The National People's Congress of
the People's Republic of China shall enact
and promulgate a Basic Law of the Hong
Kong Special Administrative Region of
the People's Republic of China (hereinafter referred to as the Basic Law) in
accordance with the Constitution of the
People's Republic of China, stipulating
that after the establishment of the Hong
Kong Special Administrative Region the
socialist system and socialist policies
shall not be practised in the Hong Kong
Special Administrative Region and that
Hong Kong's previous capitalist system
and life-style shall remain unchanged for
50 years.

The Hong Kong Special Administrative Region shall be directly under the
authority of the Central People's Government of the People's Republic of China
and shall enjoy a high degree of autonomy. Except for foreign and defence
affairs which are the responsibilities of the
Central People's Government, the Hong
Kong Special Administrative Region shall
be vested with executive, legislative
and independent judicial power, including that of final adjudication. The Central People's Government shall authorize
the Hong Kong Special Administrative
Region to conduct on its own those
external affairs specified in Section XI
of this Annex.

The Government and legislature of
the Hong Kong Special Administrative
Region shall be composed of local inhabitants. The chief executive of the Hong
Kong Special Administrative Region shall
be selected by election or through consultations held locally and be appointed
by the Central People's Government.
Principal officials (equivalent to Secretaries) shall be nominated by the chief
executive of the Hong Kong Special Administrative Region and appointed by
the Central People's Government. The
legislature of the Hong Kong Special
Administrative Region shall be constituted by elections. The executive authorities shall abide by the law and shall be
accountable to the legislature.

In addition to Chinese, English may
also be used in organs of government and
in the courts in the Hong Kong Special
Administrative Region.

Apart from displaying the national flag
and national emblem of the People's Republic of China, the Hong Kong Special
Administrative Region may use a regional
flag and emblem of its own.

### II

After the establishment of the Hong
Kong Special Administrative Region, the
laws previously in force in Hong Kong
(i.e. the common law, rules of equity,
ordinances, subordinate legislation and

customary law) shall be maintained, save for any that contravene the Basic Law and subject to any amendment by the Hong Kong Special Administrative Region legislature.

The legislative power of the Hong Kong Special Administrative Region shall be vested in the legislature of the Hong Kong Special Administrative Region. The legislature may on its own authority enact laws in accordance with the provisions of the Basic Law and legal procedures, and report them to the Standing Committee of the National People's Congress for the record. Laws enacted by the legislature which are in accordance with the Basic Law and legal procedures shall be regarded as valid.

The laws of the Hong Kong Special Administrative Region shall be the Basic Law, and the laws previously in force in Hong Kong and laws enacted by the Hong Kong Special Administrative Region legislature as above.

## III

After the establishment of the Hong Kong Special Administrative Region, the judicial system previously practised in Hong Kong shall be maintained except for those changes consequent upon the vesting in the courts of the Hong Kong Special Administrative Region of the power of final adjudication.

Judicial power in the Hong Kong Special Administrative Region shall be vested in the courts of the Hong Kong Special Administrative Region. The courts shall exercise judicial power independently and free from any interference. Members of the judiciary shall be immune from legal action in respect of their judicial functions. The courts shall decide cases in accordance with the laws of the Hong Kong Special Administrative Region and may refer to precedents in other common law jurisdictions.

Judges of the Hong Kong Special Administrative Region courts shall be appointed by the chief executive of the Hong Kong Special Administrative Region acting in accordance with the recommendation of an independent commission composed of local judges, persons from the legal profession and other eminent persons. Judges shall be chosen by reference to their judicial qualities and may be recruited from other common law jurisdictions. A judge may only be removed for inability to discharge the functions of his office, or for misbehaviour, by the chief executive of the Hong Kong Special Administrative Region acting in accordance with the recommendation of a tribunal appointed by the chief judge of the court of final appeal, consisting of not fewer than three local judges. Additionally, the appointment or removal of principal judges (i.e. those of the highest rank) shall be made by the chief executive with the endorsement of the Hong Kong Special Administrative Region legislature and reported to the Standing Committee of the National People's Congress for the record. The system of appointment and removal of judicial officers other than judges shall be maintained.

The power of final judgment of the Hong Kong Special Administrative Region shall be vested in the court of final appeal in the Hong Kong Special Administrative Region, which may as required invite judges from other common law jurisdictions to sit on the court of final appeal.

A prosecuting authority of the Hong Kong Special Administrative Region shall control criminal prosecutions free from any interference.

On the basis of the system previously operating in Hong Kong, the Hong Kong Special Administrative Region Government shall on its own make provision for local lawyers and lawyers from outside the Hong Kong Special Administrative Region to work and practise in the Hong Kong Special Administrative Region.

The Central People's Government shall assist or authorize the Hong Kong Special Administrative Region Government to make appropriate arrangements for reciprocal juridical assistance with foreign States.

## IV

After the establishment of the Hong Kong Special Administrative Region, public servants previously serving in Hong Kong in all government departments, including the police department, and members of the judiciary may all remain in employment and continue their service with pay, allowances, benefits and conditions of service no less favourable than before. The Hong Kong Special Administrative Region Government shall pay to such persons who retire or complete their contracts, as well as to those who have retired before 1 July 1997, or to their dependants, all pensions, gratuities, allowances and benefits due to them on terms no less favourable than before, and irrespective of their nationality or place of residence.

The Hong Kong Special Administrative Region Government may employ British and other foreign nationals previously serving in the public service in Hong Kong, and may recruit British and other foreign nationals holding permanent identity cards of the Hong Kong Special Administrative Region to serve as public servants at all levels, except as heads of major government departments (corresponding to branches or departments at Secretary level) including the police department, and as deputy heads of some of those departments. The Hong Kong Special Administrative Region Government may also employ British and other foreign nationals as advisers to government departments and, when there is a need, may recruit qualified candidates from outside the Hong Kong Special Administrative Region to professional and technical posts in government departments. The above shall be employed only in their individual capacities and, like other public servants, shall be responsible to the Hong Kong Special Administrative Region Government.

The appointment and promotion of public servants shall be on the basis of qualifications, experience and ability. Hong Kong's previous system of recruitment, employment, assessment, discipline, training and management for the public service (including special bodies for appointment, pay and conditions of service) shall, save for any provisions providing privileged treatment for foreign nationals, be maintained.

## V

The Hong Kong Special Administrative Region shall deal on its own with financial matters, including disposing of its financial resources and drawing up its budgets and its final accounts. The Hong Kong Special Administrative Region shall report its budgets and final accounts to the Central People's Government for the record.

The Central People's Government shall not levy taxes on the Hong Kong Special Administrative Region. The Hong Kong Special Administrative Region shall use its financial revenues exclusively for its own purposes and they shall not be handed over to the Central People's Government. The systems by which taxation and public expenditure must be approved by the legislature, and by which there is accountability to the legislature for all public expenditure, and the system for auditing public accounts shall be maintained.

## VI

The Hong Kong Special Administrative Region shall maintain the capitalist economic and trade systems previously practised in Hong Kong. The Hong Kong Special Administrative Region Government shall decide its economic and trade policies on its own. Rights concerning the ownership of property, including those relating to acquisition, use, disposal, inheritance and compensation for lawful deprivation (corresponding to the real value of the property concerned, freely convertible and paid without undue delay) shall continue to be protected by law.

The Hong Kong Special Administrative Region shall retain the status of a free port and continue a free trade policy, including the free movement of goods and capital. The Hong Kong Special Administrative Region may on its own maintain and develop economic and trade relations with all States and regions.

The Hong Kong Special Administrative Region shall be a separate customs territory. It may participate in relevant international organizations and international trade agreements (including preferential trade arrangements), such as the General Agreement on Tariffs and Trade and arrangements regarding international trade in textiles. Export quotas, tariff preferences and other similar arrangements obtained by the Hong Kong Special Administrative Region shall be enjoyed exclusively by the Hong Kong Special Administrative Region. The Hong Kong Special Administrative Region shall have authority to issue its own certificates of origin for products manufactured locally, in accordance with prevailing rules of origin.

The Hong Kong Special Administrative Region may, as necessary, establish official and semi-official economic and trade missions in foreign countries, reporting the establishment of such missions to the Central People's Government for the record.

## VII

The Hong Kong Special Administrative Region shall retain the status of an international financial centre. The monetary and financial systems previously practised in Hong Kong, including the systems of regulation and supervision of deposit-taking institutions and financial markets, shall be maintained.

The Hong Kong Special Administrative Region Government may decide its monetary and financial policies on its own. It shall safeguard the free operation of financial business and the free flow of capital within, into and out of the Hong Kong Special Administrative Region. No exchange control policy shall be applied in the Hong Kong Special Administrative

Region. Markets for foreign exchange, gold, securities and futures shall continue.

The Hong Kong dollar, as the local legal tender, shall continue to circulate and remain freely convertible. The authority to issue Hong Kong currency shall be vested in the Hong Kong Special Administrative Region Government. The Hong Kong Special Administrative Region Government may authorize designated banks to issue or continue to issue Hong Kong currency under statutory authority, after satisfying itself that any issue of currency will be soundly based and that the arrangements for such issue are consistent with the object of maintaining the stability of the currency. Hong Kong currency bearing references inappropriate to the status of Hong Kong as a Special Administrative Region of the People's Republic of China shall be progressively replaced and withdrawn from circulation.

The Exchange Fund shall be managed and controlled by the Hong Kong Special Administrative Region Government, primarily for regulating the exchange value of the Hong Kong dollar.

## VIII

The Hong Kong Special Administrative Region shall maintain Hong Kong's previous systems of shipping management and shipping regulation, including the system for regulating conditions of seamen. The specific functions and responsibilities of the Hong Kong Special Administrative Region Government in the field of shipping shall be defined by the Hong Kong Special Administrative Region Government on its own. Private shipping businesses and shipping-related businesses and private container terminals in Hong Kong may continue to operate freely.

The Hong Kong Special Administrative Region shall be authorized by the Central People's Government to continue to maintain a shipping register and issue related certificates under its own legislation in the name of 'Hong Kong, China'.

With the exception of foreign warships, access for which requires the permission of the Central People's Government, ships shall enjoy access to the ports of the Hong Kong Special Administrative Region in accordance with the laws of the Hong Kong Special Administrative Region.

## IX

The Hong Kong Special Administrative Region shall maintain the status of Hong Kong as a centre of international and regional aviation. Airlines incorporated and having their principal place of business in Hong Kong and civil aviation related businesses may continue to operate. The Hong Kong Special Administrative Region shall continue the previous system of civil aviation management in Hong Kong, and keep its own aircraft register in accordance with provisions laid down by the Central People's Government concerning nationality marks and registration marks of aircraft. The Hong Kong Special Administrative Region shall be responsible on its own for matters of routine business and technical management of civil aviation, including the management of airports, the provision of air traffic services within the flight information region of the Hong Kong Special Administrative Region, and the discharge of other responsibilities allocated under the regional air navigation procedures of the International Civil Aviation Organization.

. . .

## X

The Hong Kong Special Administrative Region shall maintain the educational system previously practised in Hong Kong. The Hong Kong Special Administrative Region Government shall on its own decide policies in the fields of culture, education, science and technology, including policies regarding the educational system and its administration, the language of instruction, the allocation of funds, the examination system, the system of academic awards and the recognition of educational and technological qualifications. Institutions of all kinds, including those run by religious and community organizations, may retain their autonomy. They may continue to recruit staff and use teaching materials from outside the Hong Kong Special Administrative Region. Students shall enjoy freedom of choice of education and freedom to pursue their education outside the Hong Kong Special Administrative Region.

## XI

Subject to the principle that foreign affairs are the responsibility of the Central People's Government, representatives of the Hong Kong Special Administrative Region Government may participate, as members of delegations of the Government of the People's Republic of China, in negotiations at the diplomatic level directly affecting the Hong Kong Special Administrative Region conducted by the Central People's Government. The Hong Kong Special Administrative Region may on its own, using the name 'Hong Kong, China', maintain and develop relations and conclude and implement agreements with States, regions and relevant international organizations in the appropriate fields, including the economic, trade, financial and monetary, shipping, communications, touristic, cultural and sporting fields. Representatives of the Hong Kong Special Administrative Region Government may participate, as members of delegations of the Government of the People's Republic of China, in international organizations or conferences in appropriate fields limited to States and affecting the Hong Kong Special Administrative Region, or may attend in such other capacity as may be permitted by the Central People's Government and the organization or conference concerned, and may express their views in the name of 'Hong Kong, China'. The Hong Kong Special Administrative Region may, using the name 'Hong Kong, China', participate in international organizations and conferences not limited to States.

The application to the Hong Kong Special Administrative Region of international agreements to which the People's Republic of China is or becomes a party shall be decided by the Central People's Government, in accordance with the circumstances and needs of the Hong Kong Special Administrative Region, and after seeking the views of the Hong Kong Special Administrative Region Government. International agreements to which the People's Republic of China is not a party but which are implemented in Hong Kong may remain implemented in the Hong Kong Special Administrative Region. The Central People's Government shall, as necessary, authorize or assist the Hong Kong Special Administrative Region Government to make appropriate arrangements for the application to the Hong Kong Special Administrative Region of other relevant international agreements. The Central People's Government shall take the necessary steps to ensure that the Hong Kong Special Administrative Region shall continue to retain its status in an appropriate capacity in those international organizations of which the People's Republic of China is a member and in which Hong Kong participates in one capacity or another. The Central People's Government shall, where necessary, facilitate the continued participation of the Hong Kong Special Administrative Region in an appropriate capacity in those international organizations in which Hong Kong is a participant in one capacity or another, but of which the People's Republic of China is not a member.

Foreign consular and other official or semi-official missions may be established in the Hong Kong Special Administrative Region with the approval of the Central People's Government. Consular and other official missions established in Hong Kong by States which have established formal diplomatic relations with the People's Republic of China may be maintained. According to the circumstances of each case, consular and other official missions of States having no formal diplomatic relations with the People's Republic of China may either be maintained or changed to semi-official missions. States not recognized by the People's Republic of China can only establish non-governmental institutions.

The United Kingdom may establish a Consulate-General in the Hong Kong Special Administrative Region.

## XII

The maintenance of public order in the Hong Kong Special Administrative Region shall be the responsibility of the Hong Kong Special Administrative Region Government. Military forces sent by the Central People's Government to be stationed in the Hong Kong Special Administrative Region for the purpose of defence shall not interfere in the internal affairs of the Hong Kong Special Administrative Region. Expenditure for these military forces shall be borne by the Central People's Government.

## XIII

The Hong Kong Special Administrative Region Government shall protect the rights and freedoms of inhabitants and other persons in the Hong Kong Special Administrative Region according to law. The Hong Kong Special Administrative Region Government shall maintain the rights and freedoms as provided for by the laws previously in force in Hong Kong, including freedom of the person, of speech, of the press, of assembly, of association, to form and join trade unions, of correspondence, of travel, of movement, of strike, of demonstration, of choice of occupation, of academic research, of belief, inviolability of the home, the freedom to marry and the right to raise a family freely.

Every person shall have the right to confidential legal advice, access to the courts, representation in the courts by lawyers of his choice, and to obtain judicial remedies. Every person shall have the right to challenge the actions of the executive in the courts.

Religious organizations and believers may maintain their relations with religious organizations and believers elsewhere, and schools, hospitals and welfare institutions run by religious organizations may be continued. The relationship between religious organizations in the Hong Kong Special Administrative Region and those in other parts of the People's Republic of China shall be based on the principles of non-subordination, non-interference and mutual respect.

The provisions of the International Covenant on Civil and Political Rights and the International Covenant on Economic, Social and Cultural Rights as applied to Hong Kong shall remain in force.

## XIV

The following categories of persons shall have the right of abode in the Hong Kong Special Administrative Region, and, in accordance with the law of the Hong Kong Special Administrative Region, be qualified to obtain permanent identity cards issued by the Hong Kong Special Administrative Region Government, which state their right of abode:

• All Chinese nationals who were born or who have ordinarily resided in Hong Kong before or after the establishment of the Hong Kong Special Administrative Region for a continuous period of 7 years or more, and persons of Chinese nationality born outside Hong Kong of such Chinese nationals;

• All other persons who have ordinarily resided in Hong Kong before or after the establishment of the Hong Kong Special Administrative Region for a continuous period of 7 years or more and who have taken Hong Kong as their place of permanent residence before or after the establishment of the Hong Kong Special Administrative Region, and persons under 21 years of age who were born of

such persons in Hong Kong before or after the establishment of the Hong Kong Special Administrative Region;

• Any other persons who had the right of abode only in Hong Kong before the establishment of the Hong Kong Special Administrative Region.

The Central People's Government shall authorize the Hong Kong Special Administrative Region Government to issue, in accordance with the law, passports of the Hong Kong Special Administrative Region of the People's Republic of China to all Chinese nationals who hold permanent identity cards of the Hong Kong Special Administrative Region, and travel documents of the Hong Kong Special Administrative Region of the People's Republic of China to all other persons lawfully residing in the Hong Kong Special Administrative Region. The above passports and documents shall be valid for all States and regions and shall record the holder's right to return to the Hong Kong Special Administrative Region.

For the purpose of travelling to and from the Hong Kong Special Administrative Region, residents of the Hong Kong Special Administrative Region may use travel documents issued by the Hong Kong Special Administrative Region Government, or by other competent authorities of the People's Republic of China, or of other States. Holders of permanent identity cards of the Hong Kong Special Administrative Region may have this fact stated in their travel documents as evidence that the holders have the right of abode in the Hong Kong Special Administrative Region.

Entry into the Hong Kong Special Administrative Region of persons from other parts of China shall continue to be regulated in accordance with the present practice.

The Hong Kong Special Administrative Region Government may apply immigration controls on entry, stay in and departure from the Hong Kong Special

Administrative Region by persons from foreign States and regions.

Unless restrained by law, holders of valid travel documents shall be free to leave the Hong Kong Special Administrative Region without special authorization.

The Central People's Government shall assist or authorize the Hong Kong Special Administrative Region Government to conclude visa abolition agreements with States or regions.

[Annex II concerned the Sino-British Joint Liaison Group referred to in paragraph 5 of the joint declaration. Annex III concerned land leases in Hong Kong. An exchange of memoranda, attached to the agreement, dealt with the question of residents of Hong Kong holding 'British Dependent Territories Citizen' passports. The Chinese Government declared that such persons would be recognized as Chinese nationals; nevertheless, 'taking account of the historical background of Hong Kong and its realities', the Chinese authorities would permit them to continue after 1 July 1997 to use travel documents issued to them by the British Government. For its part the British Government stated that such persons would continue to enjoy the right to use British-issued passports; these documents would not, however, confer the right of abode in the United Kingdom.]

# Memorandum of Understanding concerning air traffic control in the north Pacific, Tokyo, 29 July 1985

Delegations of the United States of America (U.S.A.), Japan and the Union of Soviet Socialist Republics (U.S.S.R.) met in Washington, D.C., U.S.A., from February 26, 1985, through March 3, 1985; in Moscow, U.S.S.R., from May 20, 1985, through May 25, 1985; and in Tokyo, Japan, from July 17, 1985, through July 29, 1985, to discuss the question of enhancing the safety of flights in the northern part of the Pacific Ocean.

The Parties,

Desiring to enhance the safety of flights assigned to North Pacific (NOPAC) routes,

Recognizing the usefulness of facilitating communications for this purpose,

Taking into account the important role of the Convention on International Civil Aviation and applicable provisions in related documents, and recognizing the need for strict compliance with the said Convention,

Recognizing also the provisions of the said Convention and applicable provisions in related documents regarding the provision of flight information services and alerting services in the respective flight information regions (FIRs) of the U.S.A., Japan and the U.S.S.R. as well as the responsibility to provide air traffic services which is borne by the U.S.A. and Japan on the NOPAC route system, and

Recognizing that each State has complete and exclusive sovereignty over the airspace above its territory,

Have agreed on the following:

1. Anchorage, Tokyo and Khabarovsk area control centers (ACCs) are designated as the points of contact among the air traffic control services of the U.S.A., Japan and the U.S.S.R. respectively. Tokyo ACC will serve as the principal point of contact.

2. Contact among the air traffic control services of the U.S.A., Japan and the U.S.S.R., which shall be conducted on a priority basis, has as its purpose the coordination of actions to assist a civil aircraft which is in an emergency situation. To achieve this end:

2.1 Anchorage and Tokyo ACCs will initiate communication with Khabarovsk ACC to provide all available information regarding such an aircraft assigned to a NOPAC route when they are aware of its possible entry into a U.S.S.R. FIR.

2.2 When necessary, Khabarovsk ACC will initiate communication with Tokyo/Anchorage ACC for the purpose of exchanging information concerning an unidentified aircraft which appears in a U.S.S.R. FIR.

2.3 The following information, to the extent available, will be exchanged: information provided by the appropriate area control center that the situation has occurred; data on the type of aircraft; its radio call sign, transponder code, nationality, operator, location, altitude and speed; the time and nature of the event; the pilot's intentions if known; actions taken and assistance requested; information to the responsible search and rescue agencies.

2.4 The communication facilities between Anchorage, Tokyo and Khabarovsk ACCs shall be available on an around-the-clock basis.

3. A new, dedicated direct speech circuit will be established between Tokyo and Khabarovsk ACCs, using the currently existing telephone cable. The existing HF speech circuit between Khabarovsk and Sapporo ACCs, with the connection to Tokyo ACC using the domestic telephone channel, will be used as a back-up to that circuit.

4. The delegations, in addition to the establishment of contact among the air traffic control services of the U.S.A., Japan and the U.S.S.R., reviewed air traffic service enhancements in the northern part of the Pacific Ocean. It was noted that the U.S.A. had implemented its plans for secondary radar on St Paul Island complemented by the existing Japanese radar coverage of the route system. It was agreed to study the possibility of using the radio broadcasting station in Petropavlovsk-Kamchatskii as a non-directional radio beacon.

5. This Memorandum of Understanding shall enter into force upon a trilateral exchange of diplomatic notes which will take place as soon as possible. Procedures necessary to implement the terms of this Memorandum shall be the subject of a trilateral agreement among Anchorage, Tokyo and Khabarovsk ACCs. Negotiations among the ACCs shall commence, and the agreement shall be finalized, as soon as possible after this Memorandum has entered into force.

Done in Tokyo on July 29, 1985, in English, Japanese and Russian, each text being equally authentic.

[The trilateral agreement referred to in the final paragraph of the memorandum was signed in Washington on 19 November 1985.]

# VII · Africa

## Problems of decolonization

The partition of Africa was largely completed during the last quarter of the nineteenth century, and only modified after the First World War with the distribution of Germany's colonies. Within the European empires the degree of European control varied: colonies were completely dependent; so were African territories such as Portuguese Angola and Mozambique or French Algeria, which were simply regarded as overseas provinces of the motherland; hardly distinguishable was the nominal autonomy of the Sultan of Morocco within the French Protectorate. But between the wars of 1914 and 1939, there was a measure of progress to independence. The relationship between Britain and Egypt changed during these years as Egypt progressed from a Protectorate to the qualified independence granted by the treaty of 1922, and to the much greater independence bestowed by the treaty of 1936, which still, however, permitted Britain to garrison and defend the Suez Canal. Southern Rhodesia came close to independence in 1923 when granted responsible government without Dominion status. (But Southern Rhodesia was the only British colony in Africa to be given this status: as will be seen, this produced great problems later.)

The Union of South Africa, created in 1909, was recognized as enjoying complete sovereign rights by the Statute of Westminster in 1931. It was the only part of Africa, once colonized, which during the period 1900–50 had gained independence. Only two African States escaped the partition process of the later nineteenth century and maintained their independence: Liberia and Ethiopia, though the latter was occupied by Italy from 1936 to 1941.

Britain took the lead before 1939 in having granted South African independence and Rhodesian self-government, thus creating the most intractable problem in African politics since power was transferred to white minorities of European descent.

In West Africa after the Second World War, the colony of the Gold Coast was the first to be granted independence as Ghana on 6 March 1957. Next followed Nigeria, with a population of about 55 million, attaining independence on 1 October 1960; Sierra Leone on 27 April 1961; and the small colony of Gambia on 18 February 1965.

In East Africa, Uganda was accorded independence on 9 October 1962; Tanganyika, a U.N. trusteeship territory, attained independence on 9 December 1961. Independence was a more difficult process for Kenya where a powerful community of white settlers had been accustomed to authority over the Africans. Strong nationalist feelings led some of the Kikuyu into the secret Mau Mau society, which in the years 1952–6 resorted to violent guerrilla activities directed against the white settlers. A period of repression was followed by further progress towards independence. Kenya finally became independent on 12 December 1963. The British Protectorate of Somaliland became independent in June 1960 and joined Somalia to form one State in July 1960. The small island of Mauritius was given independence in 1968.

In south central Africa the process of decolonization proved the most problem-ridden in British Africa. The administrations of Northern and Southern Rhodesia and Nyasaland had been loosely coordinated since 1944; a closer union was formed with the creation of the Central African Federation in August 1953. It lasted ten years. African Nationalists sought independence and majority rule. Northern Rhodesia was acknowledged in 1963 to have the right to secede from the Federation, and became independent on 24 October 1964 taking the name of Zambia. Nyasaland gained independence a few weeks earlier, on 6 July 1964, and took the name of Malawi. In Southern Rhodesia complete independence, which would follow from Britain's readiness to relinquish its 'reserved powers' over legislation under the 1923 arrangement, was prevented by the Southern Rhodesian Government's insistence on the continuation of predominant settler rule in the foreseeable future. The Southern Rhodesian Government headed by Ian Smith, unable to secure a British grant of independence, in November 1965 declared independence unilaterally (U.D.I.). Neither Britain nor the international community recognized this act.

In southern Africa, the former Protectorate of Bechuanaland became the independent Republic of Botswana on 30 September 1966, and Lesotho and Swaziland, enclaves in South Africa, gained independence on 4 October 1966 and 6 September 1968 respectively. But all three remained economically subservient to South Africa.

France granted self-government and independence to its former West and Central African colonies together in 1960 as part of a coordinated policy. General de Gaulle's constitution of 1958 replaced the French Union by the concept of the French Community, which permitted the French overseas territories full internal self-government but left defence, foreign policy and general economic planning in French hands, with the President of France acting as Chairman of a Council of Prime Ministers from the countries of the Community. Only Guinea voted against this constitution, and after being granted independence on 2 October 1958 it was penalized by being immediately deprived of French aid and technical assistance. Guinea turned for help – and received it – from communist States during the early years of independence. It signed agreements with China but also received aid from the United States. The remaining African members of the French Community were not satisfied with their status and worked for complete independence. This was granted by France, and independence was proclaimed on 26 June 1960 in Madagascar, which took the name of Malagasy Republic; in Chad on 1 August 1960; the Central African Republic, 13 August 1960; Congo-Brazzaville, 15 August 1960; and Gabon, 17 August 1960. These States became fully independent, but decided to remain in the French Community and concluded Cooperation and Mutual Defence Agreements with France. The following States on attaining independence remained outside the Community: Dahomey, 1 August 1960; Niger, 2 August 1960; Upper Volta, 5 August 1960; Ivory Coast, 6 August 1960; and Mauritania, 27 November 1960. The short-lived Mali Federation on 20 June 1960 attained independence, but in August 1960 Senegal seceded, was granted French recognition on 11 September 1960, and remained inside the Community whilst Mali left it. The powers of the French Community itself were altered in 1961; France in effect conceded the full exercise of sovereignty to the African States. French aid, and in some instances as in Chad, military support, remained an important influence.

In North Africa the attainment of independence was accompanied by fierce fighting in Algeria, where a large number of French settlers resisted the handing over of power to an Arab majority. France granted independence to Morocco on 2 March 1956, faced with the threat of an armed insurrection. Spain followed suit but retained some small territories: Ceuta, Melilla and Ifni; Tangier was integrated into Morocco.

Tunisia was granted independence on 20 March 1956. Algeria, which was not a colony or Protectorate but constitutionally a part of metropolitan France, faced a bitter struggle before independence. In 1954 the Algerian Arab Nationalists, who had formed the F.L.N. ('National Liberation Front'), began an insurrection against France. After increasingly bitter fighting between the F.L.N., the French army, and the French extremist O.A.S. ('Secret Army Organization'), determined to keep Algeria French, the civil war came to an end on *18 March 1962 when at the second Evian Conference a ceasefire was agreed* (p. 324). In July 1962 Algeria became fully independent.

Belgium's most important African colony was the second largest country in Africa, the Congo. With its production of industrial diamonds, cobalt and copper, its mineral wealth is of world importance. The Congo was ill-prepared for independence, which was granted on 30 June 1960; within a month law and order in the various regions broke down, atrocities were committed, the Congolese army mutinied, and the mineral-rich province of Katanga seceded on 11 July proclaiming its independence. Belgian troops returned to the Congo to protect Belgian nationals and Belgian property interests. The Congolese leaders on 12 July 1960 asked the U.N. for urgent military assistance. The Security Council authorized the Secretary-General to provide technical and military assistance as necessary. On 15 July the first U.N. military forces landed. (They were eventually to reach 20,000.) Not until December 1962 was the Congo question ameliorated with the reunification of Katanga in the Congo. The Secretary-General of the U.N., Dag Hammarskjöld, had been responsible for its energetic response; but in September 1961, while engaged in an attempt to prevent the outbreak of renewed fighting, he and seven staff members of the U.N. lost their lives in a plane crash. The U.N. military operations were controversial: the Soviet Union condemned the policy of the Secretary-General and refused to contribute towards the cost, nearly half of which was paid for by the United States. Internationally the U.N. Congo operation was dragged into the 'cold war' confrontation. The Congo took the name of Zaire. Under the rule of General Joseph Mobutu, order was eventually restored and the country subsided into poverty, corruption, and thralldom to Western economic interests.

Although the United Nations did not play such a conspicuous role in the decolonization process elsewhere in Africa, its function as successor organization to the defunct League of Nations gave it ultimate responsibility for territories formerly administered by European governments under League of Nations mandates. In British- and French-administered

Togoland (a pre-1914 German colonial possession, subsequently a League mandate, and from 1946 a U.N. trusteeship territory), 'British' Togoland integrated with Ghana in March 1957, and 'French' Togoland became independent as Togo on 27 April 1960. 'French' Cameroons achieved independence as the Republic of Cameroon on 1 January 1960; after plebiscites, 'British' Cameroons was divided, the north in June 1961 joining Nigeria, and the south joining the Republic of Cameroon. Somaliland, which had been placed under Italian administration by the U.N., became independent on 1 July 1960 as Somalia, which included the British Protectorate of Somaliland. Belgian-administered Ruanda-Urundi became two independent States in July 1962, Rwanda and Burundi.

By the mid-1960s the process of decolonization was complete in most of north, west, east, and central Africa. But some obstinate colonial bastions remained, impervious to the anti-imperial wind, and determined to hold out against African nationalist revolts. Among these were the Portuguese territories of Angola, Mozambique, and Portuguese Guinea as well as the islands of São Tomé and Príncipe in the Gulf of Guinea. Armed revolt, in Angola from 1961, and in Mozambique from 1964, eventually drew in hundreds of thousands of Portuguese troops and developed into an insupportable burden on the Portuguese economy and body politic. The colonial war sparked off the 'revolution of flowers' which restored democracy in Portugal in April 1974. *On 26 August 1974 Portugal signed an agreement at Algiers with the African Party for the Independence of Guinea-Bissau and the Cape Verde Islands.* The agreement provided for Portuguese recognition of the colony's independence to take effect on 10 September. *Similar agreements were signed with the Mozambique Liberation Front (Frelimo) on 7 September 1974, and with the Liberation Movement of São Tomé and Príncipe on 26 November.* Angolan independence was delayed by the bloody internecine civil war for the succession in which rival guerrilla groups (sponsored by outside powers) battled among themselves for control of the about-to-be-born State. On 10 November 1975 Portugal declared Angola independent and withdrew its forces. A Marxist group succeeded in taking over the levers of power in much of the country, maintaining their position with the help of several thousand troops dispatched to Angola by the Government of Cuba.

Spain granted independence to Equatorial Guinea (including the island of Fernando Pó) on 12 October 1968. In 1975 Spain decided to divest itself of the barren west African territory of Rio de Oro. In a *Declaration of Principles agreed at Madrid on 14 November 1975, Spain, Morocco and*

*Mauritania* (p. 328) agreed that the Spanish would withdraw from the colony not later than 28 February 1976 and that the 'views of the Saharan population' would be respected. *On 14 April 1976 Morocco and Mauritania signed a convention at Rabat* which (after alluding to a token consultation with the local population) agreed to a partition of the territory whereby Morocco would receive about two thirds of it and Mauritania the remaining third. Algeria took offence at this arrangement, and sponsored the Polisario guerrilla movement which declared the independence of the 'Sahrawi Arab Democratic Republic' in February 1976. A bitter war followed between the Polisario (backed by Algeria) and Morocco. Neither side won a clear-cut victory, but in November 1984 Polisario succeeded in persuading the Organization of African States to admit the putative country to membership. Of little importance in itself, the repercussions of the continuing war in the Western Sahara threatened to be serious for several of the surrounding States as well as for the cohesion of the Organization of African Unity.

The most intractable problems of decolonization, however, were those concerning the former British colony of Southern Rhodesia and the former German colony of South-West Africa.

After the First World War the League of Nations granted a mandate for South-West Africa to South Africa. At the end of the Second World War South Africa refused to place the territory under United Nations Trusteeship. The United Nations revoked the mandate in 1966, and thereafter made repeated attempts to assert its authority in the territory (which it renamed 'Namibia'), but without success. The United Nations declared the South-West African Peoples' Organization (SWAPO) the legitimate representative of the population of the country, and a guerrilla war intensified between SWAPO and South African forces. In spite of repeated diplomatic efforts, no settlement of the conflict was reached, and the territory remained in South African possession.

In Rhodesia (the 'Southern' was dropped at the time of U.D.I.), the white minority régime of Ian Smith succeeded in holding on to power, in defiance of Britain and of the United Nations, for more than a decade. Economic sanctions, instituted by the United Nations, and supposedly enforced by British naval patrols, were undercut by various secret trading arrangements and by the assistance of South Africa. In the course of the 1970s, however, the Rhodesian position gradually weakened, particularly after the independence of Mozambique and Angola. A guerrilla war broke out in which the Rhodesian army (primarily drawn from a population of only a quarter million whites) slowly lost ground. In 1976 the U.S.

Secretary of State, Dr Kissinger, secured a statement from Mr Smith undertaking to permit majority rule within two years (Smith had earlier boasted that it would not take place in his lifetime). A peace conference at Geneva, however, failed to reach agreement on a new constitution. In March 1978 Smith reached an accord with some black leaders for a partial handover of power; but the main African nationalist movements were not parties to the 'internal settlement', and so the civil war continued. Finally, in September 1979 another conference was convened by the British Government at Lancaster House in London. After lengthy negotiations, the *Zimbabwe Rhodesia Independence Agreement was signed on 21 December 1979* (p. 329). The agreement afforded the strange spectacle of African nationalists acquiescing in the return of the rebel territory to British colonial status, pending elections (to be held under British supervision) to determine the composition of a majority-rule government. Zimbabwe (as the country was henceforth to be known) at last achieved legally recognized independence on 17 April 1980.

With the independence of Zimbabwe nearly the whole of Africa, except for the continent's richest and most powerful State, South Africa, had come under non-white rule.

## Agreements on Algerian Independence between France and the Algerian National Liberation Front, Evian, 18 March 1962

### General declaration

The French people, by the referendum of January 8, 1961, recognized the right of the Algerians to choose by means of a consultation of direct and universal suffrage their political destiny in relation to the French Republic.

The negotiations that took place at Evian from March 7 to March 18, 1962, between the Government of the French Republic and the F.L.N. [Algerian National Liberation Front] reached the following conclusions:

A ceasefire is concluded. Military operations and the armed struggle will come to an end on March 19 throughout the Algerian territory.

The guarantees relative to the applica-
tion of self-determination and the organization of public powers in Algeria during the transition period have been defined in common agreement.

The formation, after self-determination, of an independent and sovereign State appearing to conform to the realities of the Algerian situation, and in these conditions, cooperation between France and Algeria corresponding to the interests of the two countries, the French Government considers, together with the F.L.N., that the solution of the independence of Algeria in cooperation with France is the one which corresponds to this situation.

The Government and the F.L.N. have therefore defined this solution, in common agreement, in the declarations which will be submitted to the approval of the electors at the time of the self-determination vote.

## Chapter 1

### ORGANIZATION OF PUBLIC POWERS DURING THE TRANSITION PERIOD AND SELF-DETERMINATION GUARANTEES

A. The self-determination consultation will permit the electors to make known whether they want Algeria to be independent and in that case whether they want France and Algeria to cooperate in the conditions defined by the present declarations.

B. This consultation will take place throughout the Algerian territory, that is to say, in the fifteen following departments: Algiers, Batna, Bône, Constantine, Médéa, Mostaganem, Oases, Oran, Orléansville, Saïda, Saoura, Sétif, Tiaret, Tizi-Ouzou, Tlemcen.

The results of the different voting offices will be totalled and proclaimed for the whole territory.

C. The freedom and the genuineness of the consultation will be guaranteed in conformity with the regulations fixing the conditions for the self-determination consultation.

D. Until self-determination has been realized, the organization of public powers in Algeria will be established in accordance with the regulations which accompany the present declaration.

A Provisional Executive and a court of public law and order shall be set up.

The French Republic shall be represented in Algeria by a High Commissioner.

These institutions, in particular the Provisional Executive, will be installed as soon as the ceasefire comes into force.

E. The High Commissioner will be the custodian of the powers of the Republic in Algeria, in particular in matters of defence, security and the maintenance of law and order in the last resort.

F. The Provisional Executive will, in particular, be responsible for:
- Assuring the conduct of Algeria's own public affairs. It will direct the administration of Algeria and will have the task of admitting Algerians to positions in the various branches of this administration;
- Maintaining public law and order. For this purpose, it will have police services and a security force under its authority;
- Preparing and implementing self-determination.

G. The court of public law and order will consist of an equal number of European and Muslim judges.

H. The full exercise of individual and public liberties will be re-established within the shortest possible time.

I. The F.L.N. will be considered a legal political body.

J. Persons interned both in France and Algeria will be released within a maximum period of twenty days from the date of the ceasefire.

K. An amnesty will be proclaimed immediately. Detained persons will be released.

L. Persons in refuge abroad will be able to return to Algeria. Commissions sitting in Morocco and Tunisia will facilitate this return.

Persons who have been relocated will be able to return to their regular place of residence.

The Provisional Executive will take the first social, economic and other measures aimed at assuring the return of these people to a normal life.

M. The self-determination vote will take place within a period of not less than three months and not exceeding six months. The date will be fixed on proposal of the Provisional Executive within the two months following its installation.

## Chapter II

### INDEPENDENCE AND COOPERATION

If the solution of independence and cooperation is adopted, the contents of the present declarations will be binding on the Algerian State.

### A – INDEPENDENCE OF ALGERIA

1 – The Algerian State will exercise its full and complete sovereignty both inter-

nally and externally. This sovereignty will be exercised in all spheres, in particular in defence and foreign affairs.

The Algerian State will freely establish its own institutions and will choose the political and social regime which it deems to be most in conformity with its interests. On the international level, it will define and implement in full sovereignty the policy of its choice.

The Algerian State will subscribe unreservedly to the Universal Declaration of Human Rights and will base its institutions on democratic principles and on equality of political rights between all citizens without discrimination of race, origin or religion. It will, in particular, apply guarantees recognized for citizens of French civil status.

## II – Individual Rights and Liberties and Their Guarantees

*1. Common provisions.* No one shall be subject to police or legal measures, to disciplinary sanctions or to any discrimination on account of:
- Opinions expressed at the time of events that occurred in Algeria before the day of the self-determination vote;
- Acts committed at the time of these same events before the day of the ceasefire proclamation.

No Algerian shall be forced to leave Algerian territory or be prevented from leaving it.

*2. Provisions concerning French citizens of ordinary civil status* (a) Within the framework of Algerian legislation on nationality, the legal situation of French citizens of ordinary civil status shall be regulated according to the following principles:

For a period of three years from the day of self-determination, French citizens of ordinary civil status:
- Born in Algeria and giving proof of ten years of permanent and regular residence on Algerian territory on the day of self-determination;
- Or giving proof of ten years of permanent and regular residence on Algerian territory on the day of self-determination and whose father or mother was born in Algeria and fulfils or could have fulfilled the conditions for exercising civil rights;
- Or giving proof of twenty years of permanent and regular residence on Algerian territory on the day of self-determination,

Will enjoy, by right, Algerian civil rights and will be considered therefore as French nationals exercising Algerian civil rights.

French nationals exercising Algerian civil rights cannot simultaneously exercise French civil rights.

At the end of the above-mentioned three-year period, they shall acquire Algerian nationality by an application for registration or confirmation of their registration on the voters' lists. Failing this application, they shall enjoy the benefits of a resident aliens convention.

(b) In order to assure, during a three-year period, to French nationals exercising Algerian civil rights, and at the end of this period, in a permanent way, to Algerians of French civil status, the protection of their person and their property and their normal participation in Algerian life, the following measures are provided for:

They will have a just and genuine part in public affairs. In the assemblies, their representation shall correspond to their actual numbers. In the various branches of the civil service, they will be assured of fair participation.

Their participation in the municipal life of Algiers and Oran will be the subject of special provisions.

Their property rights will be respected. No dispossession measures will be taken against them without their being granted fair compensation previously agreed upon.

They will receive guarantees appropriate to their cultural, linguistic and religious particularities. They will retain their personal status, which will be respected and enforced by Algerian courts comprised of magistrates of the same status. They will use the French language within the assemblies and in their relations with the public authorities.

An association for the safeguard of their rights will contribute to the protection of the rights which are guaranteed to them.

A Court of Guarantees, an institution of internal Algerian law, will be responsible for seeing that these rights are respected.

## B – COOPERATION BETWEEN FRANCE AND ALGERIA

The relations between the two countries will be founded, in mutual respect of their independence, on the reciprocal exchange of benefits and the interests of the two parties.

Algeria shall guarantee the interests of France and the rights acquired by individuals and legal entities under the conditions fixed by the present declarations. In exchange, France will grant Algeria her technical and cultural assistance and will contribute privileged financial aid for its economic and social development.

1. For a period of three years, which may be renewed, France's aid will be fixed in conditions comparable to and at a level equivalent to those of the programs now under way.

Having in mind respect for Algeria's independence with regard to commerce and customs, the two countries will determine the different fields in which commercial exchanges will benefit from preferential treatment.

Algeria will belong to the franc area. It will have its own monetary unit and its own currency assets. Freedom of transfers will exist between France and Algeria under conditions compatible with the economic and social development of Algeria.

2. In the existing Departments of the Oases and of the Saoura, the development of the wealth of the subsoil will be carried out according to the following principles:

(a) French–Algerian cooperation will be ensured by a technical body for Saharan cooperation. This body will be composed of equal numbers from both sides. Its role will be, in particular, to develop the infrastructure necessary for the exploitation of the subsoil, to give advice on draft bills and regulations relative to mining, to examine requests concerning the granting of mining titles. The Algerian State will issue the mining titles and will enact mining legislation in full sovereignty;

(b) French interests will be assured in particular by:

● The exercise, in accordance with the regulations of the Saharan petroleum code, such as it exists at present, of the rights attached to mining titles granted by France;

● Preference being given, in the case of equal offers, in the granting of new mining titles, to French companies, in accordance with the terms and conditions provided for in Algerian mining legislation;

● Payment in French francs for Saharan hydrocarbons up to the amount of the supply needs of France and other countries of the franc area.

3. France and Algeria will develop their cultural relations.

Each of the countries shall be able to set up on the territory of the other a University and Cultural Bureau whose establishments will be open to all.

France will lend her aid in the training of Algerian technicians.

French personnel, in particular teachers and technicians, will be placed at the disposal of the Algerian Government by agreement between the two countries.

## Chapter III

### SETTLEMENT OF MILITARY QUESTIONS

If the solution of the independence of Algeria and of cooperation between Algeria and France is adopted, military questions will be settled according to the following principles:

● The French forces, whose numbers will gradually be reduced as of the ceasefire, will be withdrawn from the frontiers of Algeria when self-determination is realized. Their total force will be reduced to 80,000 men within a period of 12 months from the time of self-determination. The repatriation of these forces will have to be completed by the end of a second twenty-four-month period. Military installations will be correspondingly evacuated;

● Algeria shall lease to France the use

of the Mers-el-Kébir base for a fifteen-year period, which may be renewed by agreement between the two countries;

• Algeria shall also grant France the use of a number of military airfields, the terrains, sites and installations necessary to her.

### Chapter IV

SETTLEMENT OF LITIGATION

France and Algeria will resolve differences that may arise between them by means of peaceful settlement. They will have recourse either to conciliation or to arbitration. Failing agreement by these procedures, each of the two States shall be able to have recourse directly to the International Court of Justice.

### Chapter V

CONSEQUENCES OF SELF-DETERMINATION

Upon the official announcement provided for in Article 27 of the statutes of self-determination, the instruments corresponding to these results will be drawn up.

If the solution of independence and cooperation is adopted:

• The independence of Algeria will immediately be recognized by France;

• The transfer of jurisdiction will be realized forthwith;

• The regulations set forth in the present general declaration and declarations accompanying it will come into force at the same time.

The Provisional Executive will organize, within three weeks, elections for the designation of the Algerian National Assembly, to which it will hand over its powers.

[Accompanying documents dealt with economic and financial cooperation between France and Algeria, with a ceasefire between the French army and the Algerian rebel forces, with civil rights, cultural cooperation, technical cooperation, and military questions.]

# Declaration of principles on Western Sahara by Morocco, Mauritania, and Spain, Madrid, 14 November 1975

On 14 November 1975, the delegations lawfully representing the Governments of Spain, Morocco and Mauritania, meeting in Madrid, stated that they had agreed in order on the following principles:

1. Spain confirms its resolve, repeatedly stated in the United Nations, to decolonize the Territory of Western Sahara by terminating the responsibilities and powers which it possesses over that Territory as administering Power.

2. In conformity with the aforementioned determination and in accordance with the negotiations advocated by the United Nations with the affected parties, Spain will proceed forthwith to institute a temporary administration in the Territory, in which Morocco and Mauritania will participate in collaboration with the Yema'a and to which will be transferred all the responsibilities and powers referred to in the preceding paragraph. It is accordingly agreed that two Deputy Governors nominated by Morocco and Mauritania shall be appointed to assist the Governor-General of the Territory in the performance of his functions. The termination of the Spanish presence in the Territory will be completed by 28 February 1976 at the latest.

3. The views of the Saharan population expressed through the Yema'a, will be respected.

4. The three countries will inform the Secretary-General of the United Nations of the terms set down in this instrument

as a result of the negotiations entered into in accordance with Article 33 of the Charter of the United Nations.

5. The three countries involved declare that they arrived at the foregoing conclusions in the highest spirit of understanding and brotherhood, with due respect for the principles of the Charter of the United Nations, and as the best possible contribution to the maintenance of international peace and security.

6. This instrument shall enter into force on the date of publication in the *Boletín Oficial* (Official Gazette) of the State of the 'Sahara Decolonization Act' authorizing the Spanish Government to assume the commitments conditionally set forth in this instrument.

# *Zimbabwe (Rhodesia) Independence Agreement, Lancaster House, London, 21 December 1979*

## Report

1. Following the Meeting of Commonwealth Heads of Government held in Lusaka from 1st to 7th August, Her Majesty's Government issued invitations to Bishop Muzorewa and the leaders of the Patriotic Front to participate in a Constitutional Conference at Lancaster House. The purpose of the Conference was to discuss and reach agreement on the terms of an Independence Constitution, and that elections should be supervised under British authority to enable Rhodesia to proceed to legal independence and the parties to settle their differences by political means.

2. The Conference opened on 10th September under the chairmanship of Lord Carrington, Secretary of State for Foreign and Commonwealth Affairs. The Conference concluded on 15th December, after 47 plenary sessions.

. . .

3. In the course of its proceedings the Conference reached agreement on the following issues:
- a Summary of the Independence Constitution (attached as Annex C to this report);
- arrangements for the pre-independence period (Annex D);
- a ceasefire agreement signed by the parties (Annex E).

4. In concluding this agreement and signing this report the parties undertake:
(a) to accept the authority of the Governor;
(b) to abide by the Independence Constitution;
(c) to comply with the pre-independence arrangements;
(d) to abide by the ceasefire agreement;
(e) to campaign peacefully and without intimidation;
(f) to renounce the use of force for political ends;
(g) to accept the outcome of the elections and instruct any forces under their authority to do the same.

Signed at Lancaster House, London, this twenty-first day of December, 1979.

Lord Carrington
Sir I. Gilmour, Bt.
Bishop A.T. Muzorewa
Dr S.C. Mundawarara
Mr R.G. Mugabe
Mr J.M. Nkomo

. . .

## Annex C  The Independence constitution

[The constitution established that the independent State, to be known as Zimbabwe, would be a republic. Every citizen of Rhodesia would automatically become a citizen of Zimbabwe upon independence. The constitution incorporated a Declaration of Rights, guaranteeing (among other rights) freedom from deprivation of property, freedom of expression, freedom of assembly and association, and protection from discrimination. Executive power was to be vested in the President who was to be elected by members of Parliament. A bicameral Parliament would be elected, consisting of a 40-member Senate and a 100-member House of Assembly. Ten seats in the Senate and twenty in the House of Assembly were to be reserved for election by a separate roll of white (plus coloured and Asian) voters. The provisions relating to the separate representation of the white minority were to be protected from amendment (save by a unanimous vote of the House of Assembly) for a period of seven years. The protective provisions of the Declaration of Rights were to be similarly entrenched for a period of ten years.]

## Annex D   The pre-Independence arrangements

1. The British Government put forward the following proposals for implementing the Independence Constitution in amplification of those tabled on 22nd October.

2. Rhodesia continues to be part of Her Majesty's dominions. The Government and Parliament of the United Kingdom have responsibility and jurisdiction for and in respect of it. It is for the British Parliament to grant legal independence to Rhodesia.

3. An Independence Constitution has been agreed by the parties, subject to agreement on the arrangements for implementing it. The Constitution gives full effect to the principle of genuine majority rule and will give the Government of independent Zimbabwe the powers it needs to carry out the policies on the basis of which it is elected.

4. The question of majority rule, which gave rise to the war, has therefore been resolved. The question now at issue is who is to form the future independence government. The British Government's position is that this must be decided by the people of Zimbabwe, in free and fair elections in which all parties will be able to take part on equal terms. The British Government will transfer power to whatever leaders are chosen by the people of Rhodesia in elections held under these conditions and supervised under the British Government's authority. The British Government will not be prepared to transfer power to any party which has not won it in elections. The elections will be held on the basis of the Independence Constitution and all parties will be expected to abide by it. All parties taking part in the election will also be expected to commit themselves to abide by the outcome. Such a commitment will be essential if Zimbabwe is to come to independence in peace and with a prospect of stability and prosperity for all its people.

5. The proposals put to the conference by the Salisbury delegation and the Patriotic Front showed that there was a wide divergence of views on how to create the conditions in which fair elections can be held.

6. The Salisbury delegation maintained that they had been elected to govern Rhodesia, that most of their members had nothing to do with the illegal declaration of independence, that they had a mandate to govern Rhodesia, and that they should do so during the interim period. Elections should be supervised by the British Government, but they would continue to administer the country.

7. The Patriotic Front's position was set out in the paper on transitional arrangements which they circulated early in the course of this Conference and later amplified. Their proposals called for complex power-sharing arrangements in the interim and restructuring of the Police and Security Forces in advance of the election.

8. Against this background the British Government has reached certain conclusions. In the first place, the purpose of the

pre-independence arrangements is to allow the parties to put their case to the people under fair conditions. The pre-independence period should not be concerned with the remodelling of the institutions of government. This will be a matter for the independence government elected by the people of Rhodesia. The essential requirement is that all parties should be free to put their policies to the people and should commit themselves to abide by the people's choice. The purpose of the interim period should be peaceful competition for power.

9. Secondly, the British Government proposes that the administration of Rhodesia during the election should be entrusted to the authority of the British Government, while the leaders of *all* parties explain their case to the people.

10. Thirdly, the British Government has concluded that, against the background of a war and the certain difficulties of a ceasefire, an interim period must not be excessively protracted, but must allow all the political parties adequate time to put their case to the people of Rhodesia. The longer the interim period lasts before the people of Rhodesia are given the chance to decide their political future for themselves, the greater will be the period of political uncertainty and the greater the risk of a breakdown of the ceasefire. It is in the interests of the people of Zimbabwe that they should be enabled to choose their future leaders as soon as is reasonably possible.

11. Finally, it is clear to the British Government that whatever arrangements are proposed for the interim will be effective only if there is a genuine commitment by both sides to make them work. It is in the interests of all the parties to this Conference that there should be an end to the fighting and free and fair elections. The British Government is prepared to ensure the conditions under which those objectives can be achieved. But it can do so only if both sides accept its authority and its determination to ensure the impartiality of the election process.

## THE MACHINERY OF GOVERNMENT

12. The British Government believes that it is only through a direct British involvement that conditions for elections, acceptable to both sides, can be created. To set in train the process which will enable free and fair elections to be supervised under its authority, as was agreed at the Commonwealth Heads of Government meeting at Lusaka, the British Government will appoint a Governor for Rhodesia who will be British. The Governor's instructions will require him to do all things necessary to secure compliance with the conditions for free and fair elections.

13. The Governor will be established under an Order in Council which will confer on him executive and legislative authority. He will act according to the instructions given to him, for the fulfilment of his task, by the British Government. The Governor will have powers to make laws by Ordinance for the peace, order and good governance of the country. Legislative authority will not be exercised by any other body. Executive authority will be vested in the Governor and all public officers and authorities in Rhodesia, including the civil service, the Police and the Defence Forces, will be required to comply with the Governor's directions. The Patriotic Front's forces will also be required to comply with the directions of the Governor.

14. There will be a Deputy Governor who will be British. The Governor will also have a Military Adviser, Police Adviser, Legal Adviser and Political Adviser and such other supporting staff as the British Government may decide are necessary to enable him to discharge his functions effectively, all of whom will be British. In the day-to-day administration of the country, the Governor will, however, work through the existing public service. The British Government see no practical alternative to this. It will be for the Governor to ensure that his authority is effectively and impartially exercised.

15. The Order in Council providing for

the establishment of the office of Governor will serve as the interim constitution of Rhodesia. Provision will be made to carry forward existing laws. It will be for the Parliament to be chosen in free elections to decide which laws shall be continued and which shall be changed. It will be the Governor's duty to ensure that powers conferred by existing laws on public officers and authorities are not used in an arbitrary manner, or in such a way as to affect the conditions for free and fair elections. Allegations of improper activity by any public authority or any political party or its representative in the election campaign may be brought to the attention of the Governor or his Deputy who will cause them to be dealt with.

16. All persons detained arbitrarily and on political grounds by any party will be released. The Governor will order a review of any such cases within his jurisdiction. The British Government will require to be satisfied that similar procedures will apply in the case of persons detained outside Rhodesia.

17. Once the Governor has arrived and his authority has been accepted in Rhodesia, Rhodesia will have returned to lawful government as a part of Her Majesty's dominions.

18. The Governor will proceed to Rhodesia as soon as possible after the conclusion of the Constitutional Conference. He will assume responsibility for the government of Rhodesia. All the political leaders will commit themselves to the election campaign. Bishop Muzorewa and his colleagues will not exercise ministerial functions during this period. The Governor will be responsible for the administration of the country on a caretaker basis. Heads of Ministries will report to him.

### THE RETURN OF CITIZENS LIVING OUTSIDE RHODESIA

19. Many thousands of Rhodesian citizens are at present living outside the country. Most of them wish to return and it will be desirable that as many as possible should do so in order to vote in the election. The return of all refugees will be a task requiring careful organization. But a start should be made in enabling the refugees to return to their homes as soon as possible; and the British Government will be ready to assist with the process. The task of effecting the return of all refugees will need to be completed by the independence government in cooperation with the governments of the neighbouring countries.

### LAW AND ORDER

20. In the event of an effective ceasefire, the necessity for martial law will disappear. The task of maintaining law and order in the pre-independence period will be the responsibility of the civil police. The police will act under the Governor's supervision, exercised through the Police Adviser and other British police officers. Special arrangements will be made by the Governor in consultation with the parties to ensure the protection of the political leaders in this period.

### DEFENCE

21. The negotiation of a ceasefire will be the next task of the Conference as soon as there is agreement on the arrangements for holding elections and on the administration of the country in the interim period. Subject to this, the role of the military forces of both sides in the interim period will be to maintain the ceasefire. The commanders on both sides will be responsible to the Governor for this. The British Government proposes to establish machinery on which the military commanders on both sides will be represented to ensure compliance with the terms of the ceasefire. The success of the arrangements proposed for the administration of Rhodesia in the period before independence will require all parties to commit themselves to accept the Governor's authority.

### LEGISLATIVE PROCEDURES

22. The authority of the United Kingdom Parliament will be sought for the appointment of the Governor, the making of

the Independence Constitution and the holding of elections under it. Legislation will be submitted to Parliament as a matter of urgency so that the Governor may, without loss of time after his arrival, take the steps necessary to allow elections to be held.

23. A bill will subsequently be introduced to provide for Rhodesia to become independent, following the holding of elections supervised by the British Government and held under the British Government's authority, and the establishment of a government of Zimbabwe on the basis of the Independence Constitution.

THE ELECTIONS

24. The administrative arrangements described in this paper will be implemented in such a manner as to ensure that the elections will be held under the following conditions:

• the administration of the elections will be fair and impartial as between all the political parties taking part;

• peaceful political activity will be freely conducted by all the parties to the election;

• there will be freedom of movement, assembly and expression during the election campaign;

• all parties will conduct their political activities within the law;

• all the parties will have free and uncensored access to the public media to put their case to the people of Rhodesia, and there will be freedom to advertise and to publish political views in the press;

• appropriate measures will be taken to ensure the security of all parties taking part in the election campaign.

25. There will be an Election Council, chaired by the Election Commissioner or his nominated deputy, who will be British. The Election Commissioner will invite each party taking part in the elections to be represented on the Council. The Council will have a general consultative function. Its individual members will be able to make representations to the Election Commissioner on any matter concerning the elections. The Election

Commissioner and his staff will ensure that allegations of unfair practices are properly investigated and remedied.

26. Commonwealth Governments will be invited to send observers to the elections. Their role will be to observe that the elections are genuinely free and fair and that the British Government is carrying out its responsibility to supervise them. No restrictions will be placed upon their movements, and every effort will be made to facilitate their task.

27. All political parties which register for elections will be free to take part in the elections. Any order banning or restricting a political party will be revoked.

. . .

## Annex E  Ceasefire agreement

The parties to this ceasefire agreement have agreed as follows:

1. With effect from 2400 hours on 21st December, 1979, all movement by personnel of the Patriotic Front armed forces into Rhodesia and all cross-border military activity by the Rhodesian forces will cease. This agreement will take effect on a basis of strict reciprocity. The British Government will request the governments of countries bordering on Rhodesia to make arrangements to ensure that externally-based forces do not enter Rhodesia. Provision will be made to permit the return of civilian personnel to Rhodesia in order to vote or engage in other peaceful political activity. Border-crossing points will be established, under the supervision of the monitoring force, for this purpose.

2. With effect from 2400 hours on 28th December, 1979, all hostilities in Rhodesia will cease. The Commanders will issue instructions to the forces under their command to ensure that all contact between the respective forces is avoided. A Ceasefire Commission will be established in Salisbury. The Chairman of the Commission will be the Governor's Military Adviser. The Commission will consist of equal numbers of the representatives of the Military Commanders of both sides. The Commission will meet as

required throughout the ceasefire. Its functions will include:

(a) ensuring compliance with agreed arrangements for the security and activities of the forces;

(b) the investigation of actual or threatened breaches of the ceasefire; and

(c) such other tasks as may be assigned to it by the Governor in the interests of maintaining the ceasefire.

The Commission will be independent of existing command structures and the Governor may at his discretion communicate direct with the Commanders of the Rhodesian forces and the Patriotic Front forces concerning the exercise of their respective functions. Any member of the Commission may invite it to discuss any question which appears to him to be relevant to its functions.

3. The British Government will be responsible for the establishment of a monitoring force under the command of the Governor's Military Adviser. This force will assess and monitor impartially all stages of the inception and maintenance of the ceasefire by the forces and assist the Ceasefire Commission in its tasks. The Commanders of the Rhodesian forces and of the Patriotic Front forces undertake to cooperate fully with the monitoring force and to provide it with whatever facilities are necessary to assist it to discharge its functions.

4. Elements of the monitoring force will be assigned:

(a) to maintain contact with the command structures of the Rhodesian forces and Patriotic Front forces throughout Rhodesia;

(b) to monitor and observe the maintenance of the ceasefire by the respective forces; and

(c) to monitor agreed border-crossing points and the use made of them in accordance with such arrangements as may be agreed in the context of the ceasefire.

5. Members of the monitoring force will carry weapons for their personal protection only and will be provided with vehicles and aircraft carrying a distinctive

marking. The force will be equipped with an independent radio communications network.

6. The parties recognize that disengagement of the forces will be essential to an effective cease-fire and the deployment of the monitoring force. At 2400 hours on 28th December, 1979, the Rhodesian armed forces, under the directions of the Governor, will therefore disengage to enable the Patriotic Front forces inside Rhodesia to begin the process of assembly. Elements of the monitoring force will be deployed to the command structure and bases of the Rhodesian forces and to assembly places and rendezvous positions designated for the Patriotic Front forces.

7. The Patriotic Front forces at present in Rhodesia will report with their arms and equipment to rendezvous positions (RPs) and will proceed thereafter to assembly places as indicated in the Appendix to this agreement. The process of assembly will take place under the direction of the Commanders of the Patriotic Front forces and under the auspices of the monitoring force.

8. Movement to assembly places will be completed by 2400 hours on 4th January, 1980. The process of assembly will take place with the assistance of the monitoring force. Arrangements will be made for the accommodation, security and other agreed requirements of the Patriotic Front forces.

9. The Rhodesian armed forces will comply with the directions of the Governor. There will be reciprocal disengagement by the Rhodesian forces, in relation to the successful accomplishment of the assembly process by the Patriotic Front forces.

10. With effect from ceasefire day, all forces will comply with the ceasefire and with the directions of the Governor. Any forces which fail to comply with the ceasefire or with the directions of the Governor will be deemed to be acting unlawfully.

11. The primary responsibility for dealing with breaches of the ceasefire will rest with the Commanders of the forces

through the mechanism of the Ceasefire Commission and with the assistance of liaison officers of the monitoring force. The Commanders will ensure, with the assistance of the monitoring force, that breaches of the ceasefire are contained and dealt with. In the event of more general or sustained breaches of the ceasefire the Governor will decide what action to take to deal with them with the forces which have accepted his authority.

12. The parties undertake to issue clear and precise instructions to all units and personnel under their command to comply scrupulously with the arrangements for bringing the ceasefire into effect. They will make announcements, immediately following the conclusion of this agreement, which will be broadcast regularly through all appropriate channels to assist in ensuring that instructions to maintain the ceasefire reach all the forces under their command and are understood by the public in general.

13. The parties to this agreement renounce the use of force for political objectives. They undertake to accept the outcome of the elections, to comply with the directions of the Governor and to resolve peacefully any questions relating to the future composition of the armed forces and the training and resettlement of military and civilian personnel.

[An appendix to the ceasefire agreement contained a schedule of the assembly places and rendezvous positions referred to in paragraph 7 of the agreement.]

## Efforts to achieve African unity

Pan-Africanism has its roots in the early twentieth century, and is in part a reaction to European nationalism which in its relationship with Africa involved the assertion of white superiority. African nationalism thus found a common cause in unequal treatment of the African, and it appeals to a revival of African pride, the realization of an independent African unity and consciousness. Its leaders were mainly American and West Indian until the Second World War. When Ghana achieved independence the Prime Minister (later President), Kwame Nkrumah, championed Pan-Africanism and invited the independent African States to a conference in Accra in December 1958. But soon after, they split into competing groups differing in the sides they supported in the Congo conflict and the Nigerian Civil War of 1967–70; they differed also in their European cultural backgrounds and were divided by personal rivalries. Many groupings proved temporary, such as the union of Ghana, Guinea and Mali from 1959 to 1963, which it was intended should form the nucleus of a wider African political union and was inspired by Nkrumah. A similar fate awaited the grouping of Kenya, Uganda and Tanzania; the three States signed the *Treaty for East African Cooperation, 6 June 1967*, which established an *East African Economic Community*. This came into force on *1 December 1967*, and established links with the E.E.C. But tensions developed between its members, particularly after the seizure of power in Uganda by the egregious tyrant, Idi Amin, in 1971. The treaty was terminated in 1977. A number of other attempts to achieve regional cooperation or integration met similar fates. An important exception, however, was the *Tanzania Union Law of 25 April 1964* which bound together the former territories of Tanganyika and Zanzibar. In October 1964 the State adopted the name Tanzania.

The most ambitious attempt to achieve pan-African political coordination (and ultimately integration) is represented by the *Organization of African Unity (O.A.U.), founded by a charter dated 25 May 1963* (p. 337). The O.A.U. was established by a conference of African Heads of State and Government, which convened in Addis Ababa in May 1963. Thirty independent African States (not including South Africa) attended; and most independent African States have acceded to it.

The O.A.U. is an organization within the definition of Article 51 of the United Nations Charter. Its purposes, which are set out in Article 2 of its own Charter, are to 'promote the unity and solidarity of African States'; to promote and intensify collaboration to 'achieve a better life for the peoples of Africa'; to defend their sovereignty, territorial integrity and independence; to 'eradicate all forms of colonialism from Africa'; and to promote international cooperation with due regard to the Charter of the U.N. and the Universal Declaration of Human Rights. From these purposes derive the institutions and policies of the O.A.U., set out as 'principles' in Article 3. They include 'peaceful settlement of disputes by negotiation, mediation, conciliation or arbitration'; the condemnation of all forms of subversive activities, political assassination or interference by any State in the internal affairs of another State; the 'absolute dedication to the total emancipation of the African territories which are still dependent'; and the affirmation of a policy of 'non-alignment with regard to all blocs'.

The Assembly of Heads of State and Government is the supreme organ of the O.A.U. and meets at least once a year. Each Member State has one vote, procedural questions are decided by simple majority and resolutions are approved by two-thirds majority.

A Council of Ministers, frequently Foreign Ministers, meets for consultative purposes at least twice a year. It is responsible to the Assembly of the Heads of State and Government.

An Administrative Secretary-General of the Organization, who directs the affairs of the Secretariat, is appointed by the Assembly of the Heads of State and Government.

One of the crucial functions of the O.A.U. is to facilitate the settlement of disputes between its members. 'Mediation' can be undertaken only with the consent of the parties concerned (Article XX of the Protocol);

'conciliation' can be initiated by one party to a dispute provided the other is notified, but the President of the Bureau of the Commission of Mediation, Conciliation and Arbitration is required on receipt of the request to establish a Board of Conciliators 'in agreement with the parties'. Arbitration may be resorted to by agreement of the parties, and 'shall be regarded as submission in good faith to the award of the Arbitral Tribunal' (Article XXVIII). Thus the procedures of mediation and arbitration require the consent of all parties to the dispute; conciliation can be initiated by one party but it clearly cannot be brought to a successful conclusion without the cooperation of all the parties. There is no provision for any enforcement action against a Member State (compare with Organization of American States, p. 91). The emphasis is on peaceful conciliation. The 'resolutions' of the O.A.U. are also advisory.

The O.A.U. has played a helpful role in some disputes, notably in the border conflict between Somalia, Kenya and Ethiopia in 1967. A resolution, adopted at the O.A.U. meeting in July 1964, declared that all Member States 'pledge themselves to respect the frontiers existing on their achievement of national independence'. In regard to the Nigerian conflict a resolution of the O.A.U. during the September meeting in 1967 declared that it was for Nigeria to settle it, but the O.A.U. expressed its confidence in the Federal Government and supported its unity and territorial integrity. Thus the O.A.U. has not been sympathetic to 'tribal' secessions.

On the other hand the O.A.U. failed to bring an end to some ferocious conflicts that broke out within or between States in independent Africa, such as the war in the Horn of Africa after 1977. The organization also failed to achieve effective cooperation between its members in coping with the pan-African problems of rapid population increase, desertification, undeveloped infrastructures, famine and huge refugee movements.


## Charter of the Organization of African Unity, Addis Ababa, 25 May 1963

We, the Heads of African and Malagasy States and Governments assembled in the City of Addis Ababa, Ethiopia;

Convinced that it is the inalienable right of all people to control their own destiny;

Conscious of the fact that freedom, equality, justice and dignity are essential objectives for the achievement of the legitimate aspirations of the African peoples;

Conscious of our responsibility to harness the natural and human resources of our continent for the total advancement of our peoples in spheres of human endeavour;

Inspired by a common determination to promote understanding among our peoples and cooperation among our States in response to the aspirations of our peoples for brotherhood and solidarity, in a larger unity transcending ethnic and national differences;

Convinced that, in order to translate this determination into a dynamic force in the cause of human progress, conditions for peace and security must be established and maintained;

Determined to safeguard and consolidate the hard-won independence as well as the sovereignty and territorial integrity of our States, and to resist neo-colonialism in all its forms;

Dedicated to the general progress of Africa;

Persuaded that the Charter of the United Nations and the Universal Declaration of Human Rights, to the principles of which we reaffirm our adherence, provide a solid foundation for peaceful and positive cooperation among States;

Desirous that all African States should henceforth unite so that the welfare and well-being of their peoples can be assured;

Resolved to reinforce the links between our States by establishing and strengthening common institutions;

Have agreed to the present Charter.

ESTABLISHMENT

*Article I.* 1. The High Contracting Parties do by the present Charter establish an Organization to be known as the *'Organization of African Unity'*.

2. The Organization shall include the Continental African States, Madagascar and other Islands surrounding Africa.

PURPOSES

*Article II.* 1. The Organization shall have the following purposes:

(a) To promote the unity and solidarity of the African States;

(b) To coordinate and intensify their collaboration and efforts to achieve a better life for the peoples of Africa;

(c) To defend their sovereignty, their territorial integrity and independence;

(d) To eradicate all forms of colonialism from Africa; and

(e) To promote international cooperation, having due regard to the Charter of the United Nations and the Universal Declaration of Human Rights.

2. To these ends, the Member States shall coordinate and harmonize their general policies, especially in the following fields:

(a) Political and diplomatic cooperation;

(b) Economic cooperation, including transport and communications;

(c) Educational and cultural cooperation;

(d) Health, sanitation, and nutritional cooperation;

(e) Scientific and technical cooperation; and

(f) Cooperation for defence and security.

PRINCIPLES

*Article III.* The Member States, in pursuit of the purposes stated in Article II, solemnly affirm and declare their adherence to the following principles:

1. The sovereign equality of all Member States;

2. Non-interference in the internal affairs of States;

3. Respect for the sovereignty and territorial integrity of each State and for its inalienable right to independent existence;

4. Peaceful settlement of disputes by negotiation, mediation, conciliation or arbitration;

5. Unreserved condemnation, in all its forms, of political assassination as well as of subversive activities on the part of neighbouring States or any other States;

6. Absolute dedication to the total emancipation of the African territories which are still dependent;

7. Affirmation of a policy of non-alignment with regard to all blocs.

## MEMBERSHIP

*Article IV.* Each independent sovereign African State shall be entitled to become a Member of the Organization.

## RIGHTS AND DUTIES OF MEMBER STATES

*Article V.* All Member States shall enjoy equal rights and have equal duties.

*Article VI.* The Member States pledge themselves to observe scrupulously the principles enumerated in Article III of the present Charter.

## INSTITUTIONS

*Article VII.* The Organization shall accomplish its purposes through the following principal institutions:

1. The Assembly of Heads of State and Government;
2. The Council of Ministers;
3. The General Secretariat;
4. The Commission of Mediation, Conciliation and Arbitration.

## THE ASSEMBLY OF HEADS OF STATE AND GOVERNMENT

*Article VIII.* The Assembly of Heads of State and Government shall be the supreme organ of the Organization. It shall, subject to the provisions of this Charter, discuss matters of common concern to Africa with a view to coordinating and harmonizing the general policy of the Organization. It may in addition review the structure, functions and acts of all the organs and any specialized agencies which may be created in accordance with the present Charter.

*Article IX.* The Assembly shall be composed of the Heads of State and Government or their duly accredited representatives and it shall meet at least once a year. At the request of any Member State and on approval by a two-thirds majority of the Member States, the Assembly shall meet in extraordinary session.

*Article X.* 1. Each Member State shall have one vote.

2. All resolutions shall be determined by a two-thirds majority of the Members of the Organization.

3. Questions of procedure shall require a simple majority. Whether or not a question is one of procedure shall be determined by a simple majority of all Member States of the Organization.

4. Two-thirds of the total membership of the Organization shall form a quorum at any meeting of the Assembly.

*Article XI.* The Assembly shall have the power to determine its own rules of procedure.

## THE COUNCIL OF MINISTERS

*Article XII.* 1. The Council of Ministers shall consist of Foreign Ministers or such other Ministers as are designated by the Governments of Member States.

2. The Council of Ministers shall meet at least twice a year. When requested by any Member State and approved by two-thirds of all Member States, it shall meet in extraordinary session.

*Article XIII.* 1. The Council of Ministers shall be responsible to the Assembly of Heads of State and Government. It shall be entrusted with the responsibility of preparing conferences of the Assembly.

2. It shall take cognisance of any matter referred to it by the Assembly. It shall be entrusted with the implementation of the decisions of the Assembly of Heads of State and Government. It shall coordinate inter-African cooperation in accordance with the instructions of the Assembly and in conformity with Article II (2) of the present Charter.

*Article XIV.* 1. Each Member State shall have one vote.

2. All resolutions shall be determined by a simple majority of the members of the Council of Ministers.

3. Two-thirds of the total membership of the Council of Ministers shall form a quorum for any meeting of the Council.

*Article XV.* The Council shall have the power to determine its own rules of procedure.

## GENERAL SECRETARIAT

*Article XVI.* There shall be an Administrative Secretary-General of the Organization, who shall be appointed by the Assembly of Heads of State and Government. The Administrative Secretary-General shall direct the affairs of the Secretariat.

*Article XVII.* There shall be one or more Assistant Secretaries-General of the Organization, who shall be appointed by the Assembly of Heads of State and Government.

*Article XVIII.* The functions and conditions of services of the Secretary-General, of the Assistant Secretaries-General and other employees of the Secretariat shall be governed by the provisions of this Charter and the regulations approved by the Assembly of Heads of State and Government.

1. In the performance of their duties the Administrative Secretary-General and his staff shall not seek or receive instructions from any Government or from any other authority external to the Organization. They shall refrain from any action which might reflect on their position as international officials responsible only to the Organization.

2. Each Member of the Organization undertakes to respect the exclusive character of the responsibilities of the Administrative Secretary-General and the Staff and not seek to influence them in the discharge of their responsibilities.

## COMMISSION OF MEDIATION, CONCILIATION AND ARBITRATION

*Article XIX.* Member States pledge to settle all disputes among themselves by peaceful means and, to this end, decide to establish a Commission of Mediation, Conciliation and Arbitration, the composition of which and conditions of service shall be defined by a separate Protocol to be approved by the Assembly of Heads of State and Government. Said Protocol shall be regarded as forming an integral part of the present Charter.

## SPECIALIZED COMMISSIONS

*Article XX.* The Assembly shall establish such Specialized Commissions as it may deem necessary, including the following:
1. Economic and Social Commission;
2. Educational and Cultural Commission;
3. Health, Sanitation, and Nutrition Commission;
4. Defence Commission;
5. Scientific, Technical and Research Commission.

*Article XXI.* Each Specialized Commission referred to in Article XX shall be composed of the Ministers concerned or other Ministers or plenipotentiaries designated by the Governments of the Member States.

*Article XXII.* The functions of the Specialized Commissions shall be carried out in accordance with the provisions of the present Charter and of the regulations approved by the Council of Ministers.

## THE BUDGET

*Article XXIII.* The budget of the Organization prepared by the Administrative Secretary-General shall be approved by the Council of Ministers. The budget shall be provided by contributions from Member States in accordance with the scale of assessment of the United Nations; provided, however, that no Member State shall be assessed an amount exceeding 20 per cent of the yearly regular budget of the Organization. The Member States agree to pay their respective contributions regularly.

## SIGNATURE AND RATIFICATION OF CHARTER

*Article XXIV.* 1. This Charter shall be open for signature to all independent sovereign African States and shall be ratified by the signatory States in accordance with their respective constitutional processes.

2. The original instrument, done if possible in African languages, in English and French, all texts being equally

authentic, shall be deposited with the Government of Ethiopia which shall transmit certified copies thereof to all independent sovereign African States.

3. Instruments of ratification shall be deposited with the Government of Ethiopia, which shall notify all signatories of each such deposit.

ENTRY INTO FORCE

*Article XXV.* This Charter shall enter into force immediately upon receipt by the Government of Ethiopia of the instruments of ratification from two-thirds of the signatory States.

REGISTRATION OF THE CHARTER

*Article XXVI.* This Charter shall, after due ratification, be registered with the Secretariat of the United Nations through the Government of Ethiopia in conformity with Article 102 of the Charter of the United Nations.

INTERPRETATION OF THE CHARTER

*Article XXVII.* Any question which may arise concerning the interpretation of this Charter shall be decided by a vote of two-thirds of the Assembly of Heads of State and Government of the Organization.

ADHESION AND ACCESSION

*Article XXVIII.* 1. Any independent sovereign African State may at any time notify the Administrative Secretary-General of its intention to adhere or accede to this Charter.

2. The Administrative Secretary-General shall, on receipt of such notification, communicate a copy of it to all the Member States. Admission shall be decided by a simple majority of the Member States. The decision of each Member State shall be transmitted to the Administrative Secretary-General, who shall, upon receipt of the required number of votes, communicate the decision to the State concerned.

MISCELLANEOUS

*Article XXIX.* The working languages of the Organization and all its institutions shall be, if possible, African languages, English and French.

*Article XXX.* The Administrative Secretary-General may accept on behalf of the Organization gifts, bequests and other donations made to the Organization, provided that this is approved by the Council of Ministers.

*Article XXXI.* The Council of Ministers shall decide on the privileges and immunities to be accorded to the personnel of the Secretariat in the respective territories of the Member States.

CESSATION OF MEMBERSHIP

*Article XXXII.* Any State which desires to renounce its membership shall forward a written notification to the Administrative Secretary-General. At the end of one year from the date of such notification, if not withdrawn, the Charter shall cease to apply with respect to the renouncing State, which shall thereby cease to belong to the Organization.

AMENDMENT TO THE CHARTER

*Article XXXIII.* This Charter may be amended or revised if any Member State makes a written request to the Administrative Secretary-General to that effect; provided, however, that the proposed amendment is not submitted to the Assembly for consideration until all the Member States have been duly notified of it and a period of one year has elapsed. Such an amendment shall not be effective unless approved by at least two-thirds of all the Member States.

IN FAITH WHEREOF, We, the Heads of African State and Government, have signed this Charter.

## South Africa

The greatest challenge to African nationalism, the continuation of the white suprematist régime in South Africa, left the O.A.U. in a posture of total impotence. More speeches were made and more ink spilled in O.A.U. sessions condemning the evils of *apartheid* than on any other single topic. Nothing united all its members more than this issue. Yet they were unable to mount any effective military challenge to South Africa, unable to prevent several of their own number from trading with South Africa, and for many years unable to persuade the rest of the world to do more than join in ritual protest against the South African Government's policies.

Although South Africa had been under white minority rule since achieving independence from Britain, it was the victory of the Afrikaner (Dutch-origin whites) Nationalist Party in the elections of 1948 that inaugurated the movement towards 'separate development' or *apartheid*. Under this system, certain parts of the country (amounting in all to less than 14 per cent of the total area) were to be set aside for eventual self-rule by the black African majority of the population. In the meantime the black population was deprived of many civil rights and condemned to political and economic subjugation to the white minority. Serious riots in 1960 and 1976 aroused indignation outside South Africa against the régime, but did not dent its determination to persist in the course it had set itself. In 1976 the South African Government declared the independence of Transkei, a small area within South Africa which remained effectively dependent on the Pretoria Government. The independence of the Transkei remained a fiction and was not recognized by the international community. Attempts to promote the 'independence' of further such 'Bantustans', named Bophuthatswana and Ciskei, achieved similarly nugatory results.

The independence of Mozambique, Angola, and finally of Rhodesia, brought South Africa by the late 1970s face to face with black African nationalist régimes on its borders. South Africa resorted to a variety of tactics to deal with this looming potential threat. These included political subversion of neighbouring States, support for anti-Government guerrilla movements in such States (where Governments were hostile to South Africa), actual intervention by South African forces from time to time in Mozambique, Angola, and elsewhere, and diplomatic agreements with these same States.

In the case of weak States such as Lesotho, Botswana, Swaziland, and

Malawi, South Africa had little to fear since these countries were economically almost totally dependent on South Africa. The *South Africa–Swaziland Security Agreement, signed at Mbabane in February 1982* reflected such overwhelming South African superiority.

South Africa had rather more to fear from Mozambique, Angola, and Zimbabwe since these States might more readily provide bases and other support to guerrillas operating against South Africa. Against these States South Africa applied a combination of military, economic and diplomatic tactics, with the design of discouraging them from harbouring guerrilla bases. On the diplomatic level, the *Agreement on Non-Aggression and Good Neighbourliness between South Africa and Mozambique, signed at Nkomati River on 16 March 1984*, marked an important success for South Africa, since for the first time the Government of a major black African State had agreed to sign an accord with the South African Government. But the pact was short-lived, and soon broke down in a welter of mutual recrimination.

It was only with the outbreak of serious civil unrest within South Africa in 1984 that the white-controlled power apparatus began to be forced on to the defensive. Reluctant Governments in the U.S.A. and the European Community were compelled by public opinion to institute limited economic sanctions against South Africa. Violence within the country and across its borders increased. And perhaps most ominously for the *apartheid* system, cracks of self-doubt began to become discernible within the hitherto impregnable redoubt of Afrikaner nationalist ideology.

## South Africa–Swaziland Security Agreement, Mbabane, 12–17 February 1982

12 February 1982
His Majesty
King Sobhuza II of Swaziland
Mbabane
Swaziland

Your Majesty
I have the honour to refer to various discussions and correspondence between the Foreign Ministers of the Kingdom of Swaziland and the Republic of South Africa which resulted in mutual agreement between our respective Governments to

the effect that both Governments are aware of the fact that international terrorism, in all its manifestations, poses a real threat to international peace and security and that our respective Governments should take steps to protect our respective States and nationals against this threat.

Therefore, I now have the honour to inform you that the Government of the Republic of South Africa proposes the following Agreement between our respective Governments:

*Article 1.* The Contracting Parties undertake to combat terrorism, insurgency and subversion individually and collectively and shall call upon each other wherever possible for such assistance and steps as may be deemed necessary or expedient to eliminate this evil.

*Article 2.* In the conduct of their mutual relations the Contracting Parties shall furthermore respect each other's independence, sovereignty and territorial integrity and shall refrain from the unlawful threat or use of force and from any other act which is inconsistent with the purposes and principles of good neighbourliness.

*Article 3.* The Contracting Parties shall live in peace and further develop and maintain friendly relations with each other and shall therefore not allow any activities within their respective territories directed towards the commission of any act which involves a threat or use of force against each other's territorial integrity.

*Article 4.* The Contracting Parties shall

not allow within their respective territories the installation or maintenance of foreign military bases or the presence of foreign military units except in accordance with their right of self-defence in the event of armed attacks as provided for in the Charter of the United Nations and only after due notification to the other.

Should the Government of the Kingdom of Swaziland agree with the abovementioned provisions, this letter and your affirmative reply thereto shall constitute an Agreement between our two Governments.

Please accept, Your Majesty, the renewed assurance of my highest consideration.

P.W. Botha
Prime Minister of the
Republic of South Africa

[The Government of Swaziland accepted the agreement on 17 February 1982. The parties agreed, on 31 March 1984, to make public the terms of the agreement.]

# Agreement on Non-Aggression and Good Neighbourliness between South Africa and Mozambique, Nkomati River, 16 March 1984

The Government of the Republic of South Africa and the Government of the People's Republic of Mozambique, hereinafter referred to as the High Contracting Parties;

*Recognizing* the principles of strict respect for sovereignty and territorial integrity, sovereign equality, political independence and the inviolability of the borders of all States;

*Reaffirming* the principle of non-interference in the internal affairs of other States;

*Considering* the internationally recognized principle of the right of peoples to

self-determination and independence and the principle of equal rights of all peoples;

*Considering* the obligation of all States to refrain, in their international relations, from the threat or use of force against the territorial integrity or political independence of any State;

*Considering* the obligation of States to settle conflicts by peaceful means, and thus safeguard international peace and security and justice;

*Recognizing* the responsibility of States not to allow their territory to be used for acts of war, aggression or violence against other States;

*Conscious* of the need to promote relations of good neighbourliness based on the principles of equality of rights and mutual advantage;

*Convinced* that relations of good neighbourliness between the High Contracting Parties will contribute to peace, security, stability and progress in Southern Africa, the Continent and the World;

Have solemnly agreed to the following:

*Article 1.* The High Contracting Parties undertake to respect each other's sovereignty and independence and, in fulfilment of this fundamental obligation, to refrain from interfering in the internal affairs of the other.

*Article 2.* 1. The High Contracting Parties shall resolve differences and disputes that may arise between them and that may or are likely to endanger mutual peace and security or peace and security in the region, by means of negotiation, enquiry, mediation, conciliation, arbitration or other peaceful means, and undertake not to resort, individually or collectively, to the threat or use of force against each other's sovereignty, territorial integrity or political independence.

2. For the purposes of this article, the use of force shall include *inter alia*:

(a) attacks by land, air or sea forces;

(b) sabotage;

(c) unwarranted concentration of such forces at or near the international boundaries of the High Contracting Parties;

(d) violation of the international land, air or sea boundaries of either of the High Contracting Parties.

3. The High Contracting Parties shall not in any way assist the armed forces of any State or group of States deployed against the territorial sovereignty or political independence of the other.

*Article 3.* 1. The High Contracting Parties shall not allow their respective territories, territorial waters or air space to be used as a base, thoroughfare, or in any other way by another State, Government, foreign military forces, organizations or individuals which plan or prepare to commit acts of violence, terrorism or aggression against the territorial integrity or political independence of the other or may threaten the security of its inhabitants.

2. The High Contracting Parties, in order to prevent or eliminate the acts or the preparation of acts mentioned in paragraph 1 of this article, undertake in particular to:

(a) forbid and prevent in their respective territories the organization of irregular forces or armed bands, including mercenaries, whose objective is to carry out the acts contemplated in paragraph 1 of this article;

(b) eliminate from their respective territories bases, training centres, places of shelter, accommodation and transit for elements who intend to carry out the acts contemplated in paragraph 1 of this article;

(c) eliminate from their respective territories centres or depots containing armaments of whatever nature, destined to be used by the elements contemplated in paragraph 1 of this article;

(d) eliminate from their respective territories command posts or other places for the command, direction and coordination of the elements contemplated in paragraph 1 of this article;

(e) eliminate from their respective territories communication and telecommunication facilities between the command and the elements contemplated in paragraph 1 of this article;

(f) eliminate and prohibit the installation in their respective territories of radio broadcasting stations, including unofficial or clandestine broadcasts, for the elements that carry out the acts contemplated in paragraph 1 of this article;

(g) exercise strict control, in their respective territories, over elements which intend to carry out or plan the acts contemplated in paragraph 1 of this article;

(h) prevent the transit of elements who intend or plan to commit the acts contemplated in paragraph 1 of this article, from a place in the territory of either to a place in the territory of the other or to place in the territory of any third State which has a common boundary with the High Contracting Party against which such elements intend or plan to commit the said acts;

(i) take appropriate steps in their respective territories to prevent the recruitment of elements of whatever nationality for the purpose of carrying out the acts contemplated in paragraph 1 of this article;

(j) prevent the elements contemplated in paragraph 1 of this article from carrying out from their respective territories by any means acts of abduction or other acts, aimed at taking citizens of any nationality hostage in the territory of the other High Contracting Party; and

(k) prohibit the provision on their respective territories of any logistic facilities for carrying out the acts contemplated in paragraph 1 of this article.

3. The High Contracting Parties will not use the territory of third States to carry out or support the acts contemplated in paragraphs 1 and 2 of this article.

*Article 4.* The High Contracting Parties shall take steps, individually and collectively, to ensure that the international boundary between their respective territories is effectively patrolled and that the border posts are efficiently administered to prevent illegal crossings from the territory of a High Contracting Party to the territory of the other, and in particular, by elements contemplated in Article Three of this Agreement.

*Article 5.* The High Contracting Parties shall prohibit within their territory acts of propaganda that incite a war of aggression against the other High Contracting Party and shall also prohibit acts of propaganda aimed at inciting acts of terrorism and civil war in the territory of the other High Contracting Party.

. . .

*Article 8.* Nothing in this Agreement shall be construed as detracting from the High Contracting Parties' right of self-defence in the event of armed attacks, as provided for in the Charter of the United Nations.

*Article 9.* 1. Each of the High Contracting Parties shall appoint high-ranking representatives to serve on a Joint Security Commission with the aim of supervising and monitoring the application of this Agreement.

. . .

IN WITNESS WHEREOF, the signatories, in the name of their respective Governments, have signed and sealed this Agreement, in quadruplicate in the English and Portuguese languages, both texts being equally authentic.

THUS DONE AND SIGNED AT the common border on the banks of the Nkomati River, on this the sixteenth day of March 1984.

PIETER WILLEM BOTHA
PRIME MINISTER OF THE
REPUBLIC OF SOUTH AFRICA

SAMORA MOISÉS MACHEL
MARSHAL OF THE REPUBLIC
PRESIDENT OF THE PEOPLE'S REPUBLIC
OF MOZAMBIQUE
PRESIDENT OF THE COUNCIL OF
MINISTERS

# VIII · The Middle East and East Mediterranean

## The Great Powers and the Middle East, 1945–73

Between the two world wars Britain and France had enjoyed a position of predominance in the Middle East. Britain controlled the Suez Canal and with France nearly all the important strategic bases. Italy was the only other colonial power of importance, occupying (after 1936) Abyssinia, Eritrea, Italian Somaliland and Libya. Italy was forced to renounce her colonies in the peace treaty of 1947 (see p. 42). British and French predominance lasted little more than a decade longer.

In the international relations of the Middle East after 1945 the United States and the Soviet Union replaced Britain and France as the most important external Powers. With independence came profound internal changes in many of the Middle Eastern States where conservative monarchies were swept away by revolutionary republican Governments. New discoveries of oil and its constantly increasing use by developed industrial nations transformed the pattern of economic relationships. Finally, the creation of the Jewish State of Israel made a decisive impact and coloured all Arab relations with the outside world.

France and Britain did not reconcile themselves immediately after the Second World War to the loss of military power in the Middle East. Nevertheless the defeat of France in 1940 had weakened France's position as a colonial power. North Africa, Lebanon and Syria had remained in Vichy hands in 1940. In Syria and Lebanon, Vichy France's weakness provided an opportunity for the nationalist movements, and both the Vichy French authorities and the Free-French administration, which took over in 1941, promised to make Syria and Lebanon free sovereign States.

British pressure on the French led to independence being granted during the course of the Second World War; it was confirmed in 1946. The era of the French mandates was past, and Britain had played an important role in their ending.

Although Britain had helped to ease France out of its colonial-type control of Syria and the Lebanon, British Governments were not prepared to liquidate Britain's Middle Eastern position of power. There was a readiness to change the relationship, provided interests regarded vital to Britain were safeguarded. Thus the continued control of the oil industries of Iran through the Anglo-Iranian Oil Company, of Iraq through the Iraq Petroleum Company (though European and American oil interests also held important shares in these enterprises) and the maintenance of British predominance over the 'imperial' arteries now believed vital economically as well, namely the Persian Gulf and the Suez Canal, were considered essential. Moreover, Britain until May 1948 shouldered the responsibility of maintaining law and order in Palestine.

As the Second World War drew to a close, Britain favoured the growth of a semblance of Arab unity whereby Arab Governments favourable to Britain would have a predominance. The *Arab Unity Conference held in Alexandria, Egypt, in September and October 1944,* led to the formation of the *Pact establishing the Arab League, 22 March 1945* (p. 353). Its founder members were Egypt, Iraq, Syria, Lebanon, Transjordan, Saudi Arabia and Yemen. Libya joined in 1953; Sudan in 1955; Morocco and Tunisia in 1958; Algeria in 1962; Kuwait in 1964; South Yemen in 1967; Bahrein, Qatar, and Oman in 1971; the United Arab Emirates in 1972; Mauritania in 1973; Somalia in 1974; Djibouti in 1975; and the Palestine Liberation Organization in 1976. (Egypt's membership was suspended in 1979 following the Israel–Egypt Peace Treaty.)

Rivalries and tensions between members of the Arab League weakened and often made impossible the adoption of common policies. The lack of military and political coordination was revealed in the first Arab–Israeli war of 1948–9. The Arab League did not become the ally Britain hoped for; under Egyptian influence it was used to develop common attitudes directed against the continued British and French military presence in the Middle East, and against Zionism and Israel. Britain therefore continued to rely on bilateral agreements with its friends in the Middle East.

*On 29 July 1953 Britain and Libya signed an alliance treaty* (p. 356) which permitted Britain to keep military bases in Libya. *Britain and Transjordan concluded an alliance on 15 March 1948.* They promised to come to each other's aid if engaged in war; in fulfilment of this pledge Transjordan made bases available for British forces, and permitted the stationing of these forces in Transjordan 'until such a time. . . that the state of the world renders such measures unnecessary'. The treaty was to last at least twenty years. But negotiations with Iraq in 1948 which would have permitted British bases failed.

After the war Egyptian nationalist resentment made Britain's continued presence in the Suez Canal zone increasingly difficult. The Egyptian revolution of July 1952, which eventually brought to power Gamal Abdel Nasser, led to a settlement over the Canal zone between Nasser and Britain embodied in an *Agreement regarding the Suez Canal Base, signed on 19 October 1954* (p. 357). Britain agreed to remove its troops within twenty months, but with the proviso that Egypt continue to offer to Britain 'such facilities as may be necessary in order to place the Base (in the Canal zone) on a war footing and to operate it effectively' if any outside State attacked a member of the Arab League or Turkey. The Anglo-Egyptian differences over the future of the Sudan had been resolved *on 12 February 1953 when Britain and Egypt signed an agreement about Sudan.* This left the choice to the Sudanese. Sudan opted for independence and became a sovereign State in 1956.

Anglo-Egyptian relations did not, however, improve. Britain suspected Nasser of seeking to undermine British influence in the Middle East, especially in Libya, Iraq, Jordan and the Suez Canal zone. The flashpoint came when in July 1956 the United States, Britain and the World Bank withdrew their earlier offer to provide financial aid to build the High Dam at Aswan. Nasser's reply was to proclaim a few days later, on 26 July 1956, that Egypt was nationalizing the Suez Canal Company. John Foster Dulles, the United States Secretary of State, intervened diplomatically to prevent tensions leading to war and involved the 'user nations', including Britain and France, in interminable conferences during the summer months which tried in vain to work out a solution or at least delay the use of force until after the U.S. presidential elections in early November. There was also growing tension between Egypt and Israel. With the French playing a leading role, joint military action was secretly planned against Egypt without fully informing the United States. Britain was contemplating military action with France and was later drawn into the originally independent French–Israeli military discussions culminating in secret meetings between the Israelis, the French and the British, in a villa in the Paris suburb of Sèvres on 22, 23 and 24 October. There an understanding was reached which, for decades, has been the subject of controversy. It is clear, however, that Prime Minister Eden wanted no signed agreement as evidence, that might be found later, of a conspiracy. Nevertheless, a senior Foreign Office representative was prevailed upon by the French and Israelis at Sèvres to sign a secret protocol of their negotiations which, in effect, set out an agreed timetable for Israeli, French and British joint military operations. According to this understanding, the Israelis would attack Egypt on 29 October and send one military force in the direction of the Canal, though Israel's main objective was to open the Straits of Tiran to its shipping. Britain and France would deliver an ultimatum to Egypt and Israel on 30 October requiring each to 'withdraw' from the Canal ostensibly to protect the Canal zone from war; Egypt's expected refusal was designed to give British and French forces a pretext for attacking Egypt. The 'Suez War' began just as planned at Sèvres, with an Israeli attack against Egypt on 29 October; this was followed as agreed by an Anglo-French ultimatum on 30 October to both Egypt and Israel to withdraw ten miles from each side of the Canal (in fact, the Israelis at the Mitla Pass in the Sinai desert were some thirty miles from the Canal); the Egyptians rejected the ultimatum. On 31 October, British and French planes, without declaring war, bombed Egyptian airports. The Israelis had achieved all their military objectives in freeing the Straits of Tiran even before, on 5 November, British and French paratroops, followed on 6 November by the seaborne force, landed at the western end of the Canal. They advanced rapidly from Port Said despite Egyptian resistance. Moving south along the Canal they had to halt on 6 November when United States pressure and political divisions in Britain brought about a reversal of British policy, though Soviet nuclear threats were not taken seriously in London and Paris. Britain agreed to a ceasefire and France, whose military action was integrated with Britain's, was obliged to follow. At the United Nations, the United States and the Soviet Union had acted together to stop the Anglo-French military action. By 23 December 1956 British and French troops withdrew and a United Nations force replaced them.

Elsewhere in the Middle East British military power through alliances and bases greatly diminished during the decade after the Second World War. In Iraq the staunchly pro-British royal Government was bitterly opposed to Nasser's republican Egypt. Popular nationalism, however, prevented this Government from concluding an alliance with Britain on the model of Jordan in 1948. Instead an *Exchange of Notes between Britain and Iraq in April 1955* promised to maintain and develop peace and friendship between the two States. Iraq was also with Turkey a founder member of the *Baghdad Pact* (p. 358) The overthrow of the Iraqi monarchy in July

1958 ended Britain's special influence. With Iran Britain enjoyed good relations, except for the period from 1951–3 when the nationalization of the Anglo-Iranian Oil Company brought about a rupture. In *1954*, by the *Anglo-Iranian Agreement*, Britain accepted nationalization and received agreed compensation. The Shah of Iran aligned Iran with the West and also joined the Baghdad Pact. Britain's special position in Jordan was weakened on 13 March 1957 with the agreement between the two countries to terminate the alliance of 1948. But little more than a year later, in July 1958, Britain at Jordan's request sent troops, at the time of the revolution and murder of King Faisal of Iraq, to support the Jordanian Hashemite royal family.

During the late 1950s and 1960s Britain and France relinquished practically all their remaining military positions in the Middle East. In North Africa, Moroccan and Tunisian nationalist opposition to continued French rule had led to independence for Morocco on 2 March 1956, and for Tunisia on 20 March 1956. But France retained control of the naval base at Bizerta, which France did not evacuate until (after a Tunisian appeal to the Security Council) October 1965. The French conflict in North Africa was most serious in Algeria. A ceasefire was agreed on 18 March 1962, and Algeria became a sovereign State on 3 July 1962 (pp. 321 and 324). By the end of 1968 France had evacuated all its land forces from Algeria and had given up the naval base at Mers-el-Kébir.

The pace of British withdrawal did not slacken during the 1960s. Britain relinquished control of Cyprus, which became independent in August 1960, though retaining sovereignty over two military bases (see p. 392). The British alliance with Libya ended in 1969 when Colonel Gaddafi overthrew King Idris, and Britain withdrew from her extensive air and military training bases in March 1970. Britain gave up the Aden base on the Red Sea in November 1967. The Trucial States on the Persian Gulf, which had for long enjoyed British protection, were left to arrange their own international security when Britain withdrew in 1971. By 1971, therefore, the last vestiges of British and French military paramountcy in the Middle East had been liquidated.

The positions vacated by the old imperial powers were, in large measure, filled by the new superpowers. This was particularly the case after the Suez adventure of 1956, when the United States felt compelled to assume primary responsibility for the defence of Western interests in the region.

Before Suez the United States had not been willing to assume security treaty commitments in the Middle East (except with Turkey, a NATO member from 1951). Thus the U.S.A. was not a party to the *Baghdad Pact* which developed in 1955 from a series of regional alliances: the basis was the *Treaty of Alliance between Iraq and Turkey, 24 February 1955; Britain acceded to this alliance on 4 April 1955; Pakistan acceded on 23 September 1955; and Iran in October 1955.* Thus the Baghdad Pact had become a Five-Power alliance of Britain, Iraq, Turkey and Pakistan. Iraq, the one Arab State in this 'Western alliance', by joining exposed itself to the enmity of 'progressive' Arab states such as Egypt. Jordan, whose Hashemite royal dynasty wished to align itself with the fellow Hashemite kingdom of Iraq, would also have joined the Baghdad Pact but for the nationalist opposition in Jordan inspired by Egypt. The United States was ready to aid the alliance with money and arms but did not formally assume the obligations of membership.

After Suez, however, the U.S.A. found itself drawn into military commitments in the region to an increasing degree. The crisis for the Western diplomatic alignment broke in July 1958. Revolution overthrew the royal Iraqi dynasty and the pro-Western, conservative Government of Nuri al-Said on 14 July 1958. Fearing revolution in their country, the Lebanese asked for United States protection, and the United States Sixth Fleet landed marines in the Lebanon; Britain sent troops to Jordan responding to the appeal of King Hussein. In March 1959 Iraq formally left the Baghdad Pact, which was now renamed as the Central Treaty Organization (CENTO), with new headquarters in Ankara. To strengthen the alliance, the United States linked herself to the four remaining Baghdad Pact Powers by executive agreements on 28 July 1958, two weeks after the revolution in Iraq. Pakistan's participation in CENTO was largely determined by her desire to strengthen her position against India rather than the Soviet Union. CENTO during the 1960s proved of importance not only militarily but also economically to Turkey, the recipient of American and British aid. With the thaw in the 'cold war' Soviet relations with two CENTO Powers, Iran and Turkey, became more friendly and relaxed, and the Soviet Union also began to extend economic aid to Turkey though not on the scale of Western aid and trade. (On American treaty commitments in the Middle East, see also pp. 126–35.)

Soviet diplomacy in the Middle East after Suez was focused in particular on its relationship with Egypt. Between 1956 and 1972 the U.S.S.R. became Egypt's main diplomatic patron and supplier of arms and economic assistance. Between 1958 and 1963 Egypt and Syria were joined in the United Arab Republic under the leadership of Nasser. Nasser emerged as the champion of Arab unity and chief opponent of Western interests in the Middle East. Although nominally non-aligned, Egypt found itself gradually drawn closer to the Soviet Union during the 1960s, by reason of its economic and military weakness.

Egyptian troops were sent to Yemen in 1962 in order to support republican opponents of the feudal monarchy there. But Saudi Arabia intervened on behalf of the monarchists, and Egypt found itself bogged down in a bitter civil war. Egypt here found that the cost of acting as the vanguard of 'progressive' forces in the Middle East was almost too much to bear. *On 24 August 1965 Saudi Arabia and the United Arab Republic signed an agreement at Jeddah calling for self-determination in Yemen.* Following this agreement Egyptian forces were reduced gradually, the last Egyptian troops leaving on 15 December 1967, after the Israeli victory over Egypt in the Six-Day War (see pp. 361–2).

Meanwhile the Soviet Union had acquired other friends in the Middle East, most notably Iraq, Algeria, and South Yemen (formerly Aden). The revolution in Libya in 1969 added another, albeit sometimes erratic, Soviet client to the list, Colonel Gaddafi. Thus the switch in Egyptian policy in 1972 (engineered by President Anwar Sadat who emerged as leader after the death of Nasser in September 1970) from a pro-Soviet to a pro-American alignment was a serious, but not fatal, setback for Soviet interests in the Middle East. (On Soviet treaty commitments in the Middle East, see also pp. 162–3.)

## Pact of the Arab League, Cairo, 22 March 1945

His Excellency the President of the Syrian Republic,
His Royal Highness the Emir of Transjordan,
His Majesty the King of Iraq,
His Majesty the King of Saudi-Arabia,
His Excellency the President of the Lebanese Republic,
His Majesty the King of Egypt,
His Majesty the King of Yemen,

With a view to strengthen the close relations and numerous ties which bind the Arab States,

And out of concern for the cementing and reinforcing of these bonds on the basis of respect for the independence and sovereignty of these States,

And in order to direct their efforts toward the goal of the welfare of all the Arab States, their common weal, the guarantee of their future and the realization of their aspirations,

And in response to Arab public opinion in all the Arab countries,

Have agreed to conclude a pact to this effect and have delegated as their plenipotentiaries...

Who after the exchange of the credentials granting them full authority, which were found valid and in proper form, have agreed upon the following:

*Article 1.* The League of Arab States shall be composed of the independent Arab States that have signed this Pact.

Every independent Arab State shall have the right to adhere to the League. Should it desire to adhere, it shall present an application to this effect which shall be filed with the permanent General Secretariat and submitted to the Council at its first meeting following the presentation of the application.

*Article 2.* The purpose of the League is to draw closer the relations between member States and coordinate their political activities with the aim of realizing a close collaboration between them, to safeguard their independence and sovereignty, and to consider in a general way the affairs and interests of the Arab countries.

It also has among its purposes a close cooperation of the member States with due regard to the structure of each of these States and the conditions prevailing therein, in the following matters:

(a) Economic and financial matters, including trade, customs, currency, agriculture and industry.

(b) Communications, including railways, roads, aviation, navigation, and posts and telegraphs.

(c) Cultural matters.

(d) Matters connected with nationality, passports, visas, execution of judgments and extradition.

(e) Social welfare matters.

(f) Health matters.

*Article 3.* The League shall have a Council composed of the representatives of the member States. Each State shall have one vote, regardless of the number of its representatives.

The Council shall be entrusted with the function of realizing the purpose of the League and of supervising the execution of the agreements concluded between the member States on matters referred to in the preceding article or on other matters.

It shall also have the function of determining the means whereby the League will collaborate with the international organizations which may be created in the future to guarantee peace and security and organize economic and social relations.

*Article 4.* A special Committee shall be formed for each of the categories enumerated in Article 2, on which the member States shall be represented. These committees shall be entrusted with establishing the basis and scope of cooperation in the form of draft agreements which shall be submitted to the Council for its consideration preparatory to their being submitted to the States referred to.

Delegates representing the other Arab countries may participate in these Committees as members. The Council shall determine the circumstances in which the participation of these representatives shall be allowed as well as the basis of the representation.

*Article 5.* The recourse to force for the settlement of disputes between two or more member States shall not be allowed. Should there arise among them a dispute that does not involve the independence of a State, its sovereignty or its territorial integrity, and should the two contending parties apply to the Council for the settlement of this dispute, the decision of the Council shall then be effective and obligatory.

In this case, the States among whom the dispute has arisen shall not participate in the deliberations and decisions of the Council.

The Council shall mediate in a dispute which may lead to war between two member States or between a member State and another State in order to conciliate them.

The decisions relating to arbitration and mediation shall be taken by a majority vote.

*Article 6.* In case of aggression or threat of aggression by a State against a member State, the attacked or threatened with attack may request an immediate meeting of the Council.

The Council shall determine the necessary measures to repel this aggression. Its decision shall be taken unanimously. If the aggression is committed by a member State the vote of that State will not be counted in determining unanimity.

If the aggression is committed in such a way as to render the Government of the State attacked unable to communicate with the Council, the representative of that State in the Council may request the Council to convene for the purpose set forth in the preceding paragraph. If the representative is unable to communicate with the Council, it shall be the right of any member State to request a meeting of the Council.

*Article 7.* The decisions of the Council taken by a unanimous vote shall be binding on all the member States of the League; those that are reached by a majority vote shall bind only those that accept them.

In both cases the decisions of the Council shall be executed in each State in accordance with the fundamental structure of that State.

*Article 8.* Every member State of the League shall respect the form of government obtaining in the other States of the League, and shall recognize the form of government obtaining as one of the rights of those States, and shall pledge itself not to take any action tending to change that form.

*Article 9.* The States of the Arab League that are desirous of establishing among themselves closer collaboration and stronger bonds than those provided for in the present Pact, may conclude among themselves whatever agreements they wish for this purpose.

The treaties and agreements already concluded or that may be concluded in the future between a member State and any other State, shall not be binding on the other members.

*Article 10.* The permanent seat of the League of Arab States shall be Cairo. The Council of the League may meet at any other place it designates.

*Article 11.* The Council of the League shall meet in ordinary session twice a year, during the months of March and October. It shall meet in extraordinary session at the request of two member States whenever the need arises.

*Article 12.* The League shall have a permanent General Secretariat, composed of a Secretary-General, Assistant Secretaries and an adequate number of officials.

The Secretary-General shall be appointed by the Council upon the vote of two-thirds of the States of the League. The Assistant Secretaries and the principal officials shall be appointed by the Secretary-General with the approval of the Council.

. . .

*Article 18.* If one of the member States intends to withdraw from the League, the Council shall be informed of its intention one year before the withdrawal takes effect.

The Council of the League may consider any State that is not fulfilling the obligations resulting from this Pact as excluded from the League, by a decision taken by a unanimous vote of all the States except the State referred to.

. . .

## Annex on Palestine

At the end of the last Great War, Palestine, together with the other Arab States, was separated from the Ottoman Empire. She became independent, not belonging to any other State.

The Treaty of Lausanne proclaimed that her fate should be decided by the parties concerned in Palestine.

Even though Palestine was not able to control her own destiny, it was on the basis of the recognition of her independence that the Covenant of the League of Nations determined a system of government for her.

Her existence and her independence among the nations can, therefore, no more be questioned *de jure* than the independence of any of the other Arab States.

Even though the outward signs of this independence have remained veiled as a result of *force majeure*, it is not fitting that this should be an obstacle to the participation of Palestine in the work of the League.

Therefore, the States signatory to the Pact of the Arab League, consider that in view of Palestine's special circumstances, the Council of the League should designate an Arab delegate from Palestine to participate in its work until this country enjoys actual independence.

. . .

# Alliance Treaty between Libya and Britain, 29 July 1953

. . .

*Article 1.* There shall be peace and friendship and a close alliance between the High Contracting Parties in consecration of their cordial understanding and their good relations.

Each of the High Contracting Parties undertakes not to adopt in regard to foreign countries an attitude which is inconsistent with the alliance or which might create difficulties for the other party thereto.

*Article 2.* Should either High Contracting Party become engaged in war or armed conflict, the other High Contracting Party will, subject always to the provisions of Article 4, immediately come to his aid as a measure of collective defence. In the event of an imminent menace of hostilities involving either of the High Contracting Parties they will immediately concert together the necessary measures of defence.

*Article 3.* The High Contracting Parties recognize that it is in their common interest to provide for their mutual defence and to ensure that their countries are in a position to play their part in the maintenance of international peace and security. To this end each will furnish to the other all the facilities and assistance in his power on terms to be agreed upon. In return for facilities provided by His Majesty The King of Libya for British armed forces in Libya on conditions to be agreed upon, Her Britannic Majesty will provide financial assistance to His Majesty The King of Libya, on terms to be agreed upon as aforesaid.

*Article 4.* Nothing in the present Treaty is intended to, or shall in any way prejudice the rights and obligations which devolve, or may devolve, upon either of the High Contracting Parties under the Charter of the United Nations or under any other existing international agreements, conventions or treaties including, in the case of Libya, the Covenant of the League of Arab States.

*Article 5.* This Treaty shall be ratified and shall come into force upon the exchange of instruments of ratification which shall take place as soon as possible.

*Article 6.* This Treaty shall remain in force for a period of twenty years except in so far as it may be revised or replaced by a new Treaty during that period by agreement of both the High Contracting Parties, and it shall in any case be reviewed at the end of ten years. Each of the High Contracting Parties agrees in this connection to have in mind the extent to which international peace and security can be ensured through the United Nations. Before the expiry of a period of nineteen years either High Contracting Party may give to the other through the diplomatic channel notice of termination at the end of the said period of twenty years. If the Treaty has not been so terminated and subject to any revision or replacement thereof, it shall continue in force after the period of twenty years until the expiry of one year after notice of termination has been given by either High Contracting Party to the other through the diplomatic channel.

*Article 7.* Should any difference arise relative to the application or interpretation of the present Treaty and should the High Contracting Parties fail to settle such difference by direct negotiations, it shall be referred to the International Court of Justice unless the parties agree to another mode of settlement.

. . .

## Anglo-Egyptian Agreement on the Suez Canal Base, Cairo, 19 October 1954

*Article 1.* Her Majesty's Forces shall be completely withdrawn from Egyptian territory in accordance with the Schedule set forth in Part A of Annex I within a period of twenty months from the date of signature of the present Agreement.

*Article 2.* The Government of the United Kingdom declare that the Treaty of Alliance signed in London on the 26th of August, 1936, with the Agreed Minute, Exchanged Notes, Convention concerning the immunities and privileges enjoyed by the British Forces in Egypt and all other subsidiary agreements, is terminated.

*Article 3.* Parts of the present Suez Canal Base, which are listed in Appendix A to Annex II, shall be kept in efficient working order and capable of immediate use in accordance with the provisions of Article 4 of the present Agreement. To this end they shall be organized in accordance with the provisions of Annex II.

*Article 4.* In the event of an armed attack by an outside Power on any country which at the date of signature of the present Agreement is a party to the Treaty of Joint Defence between Arab League States, signed in Cairo on the 13th of April, 1950, or on Turkey, Egypt shall afford to the United Kingdom such facilities as may be necessary in order to place the Base on a war footing and to operate it effectively. These facilities shall include the use of Egyptian ports within the limits of what is strictly indispensable for the above-mentioned purposes.

*Article 5.* In the event of the return of British Forces to the Suez Canal Base area in accordance with the provisions of Article 4, these forces shall withdraw immediately upon the cessation of the hostilities referred to in that Article.

*Article 6.* In the event of a threat of an armed attack by an outside Power on any country which at the date of signature of the present Agreement is a party to the Treaty of Joint Defence between Arab League States or on Turkey, there shall be immediate consultation between Egypt and the United Kingdom.

*Article 7.* The Government of the Republic of Egypt shall afford over-flying, landing and servicing facilities for notified flights of aircraft under Royal Air Force control. For the clearance of any flights of such aircraft, the Government of the Republic of Egypt shall accord treatment no less favourable than that accorded to the aircraft of any other foreign country with the exception of States parties to the Treaty of Joint Defence between Arab League States. The landing and servicing facilities mentioned above shall be afforded at Egyptian Airfields in the Suez Canal Base area.

*Article 8.* The two Contracting Governments recognize that the Suez Maritime Canal, which is an integral part of Egypt, is a waterway economically, commercially and strategically of international importance, and express the determination to uphold the Convention guaranteeing the freedom of navigation of the Canal signed at Constantinople on the 29th of October, 1888.

*Article 9.* (a) The United Kingdom is accorded the right to move any British equipment into or out of the Base at its discretion.

(b) There shall be no increase above the level of supplies as agreed upon in Part C of Annex II without the consent of the Government of the Republic of Egypt.

*Article 10.* The present Agreement does not affect and shall not be interpreted as affecting in any way the rights and

obligations of the parties under the Charter of the United Nations.

. . .

*Article 12.* (a) The present Agreement shall remain in force for the period of seven years from the date of its signature.

(b) During the last twelve months of that period the two Contracting Governments shall consult together to decide on such arrangements as may be necessary upon the termination of the Agreement.

(c) Unless both the Contracting Governments agree upon any extension of the Agreement it shall terminate seven years after the date of signature and the Government of the United Kingdom shall take away or dispose of their property then remaining in the Base.

. . .

[The agreement was accompanied by annexes, exchanges of notes, and an agreed minute.]

# Pact of Mutual Cooperation between Iraq and Turkey (Baghdad Pact), 24 February 1955

Whereas the friendly and brotherly relations existing between Iraq and Turkey are in constant progress, and in order to complement the contents of the Treaty of Friendship and Good Neighbourhood concluded between His Majesty the King of Iraq and His Excellency the President of the Turkish Republic signed in Ankara on the 29th of March 1946, which recognized the fact that peace and security between the two countries is an integral part of the peace and security of all the nations of the world and in particular the nations of the Middle East, and that it is the basis for their foreign policies;

Whereas Article 11 of the Treaty of Joint Defence and Economic Cooperation between the Arab League States provides

that no provision of that Treaty shall in any way affect, or is designed to affect, any of the rights and obligations accruing to the Contracting Parties from the United Nations Charter;

And having realized the great responsibilities borne by them in their capacity as members of the United Nations concerned with the maintenance of peace and security in the Middle East region which necessitate taking the required measures in accordance with Article 51 of the United Nations Charter. . . have agreed as follows:

*Article 1.* Consistent with Article 51 of the United Nations Charter the High Contracting Parties will cooperate for their security and defence. Such measures as they agree to take to give effect to this cooperation may form the subject of special agreements with each other.

*Article 2.* In order to ensure the realization and effect application of the cooperation provided for in Article 1 above, the competent authorities of the High Contracting Parties will determine the measures to be taken as soon as the present Pact enters into force. These measures will become operative as soon as they have been approved by the Governments of the High Contracting Parties.

*Article 3.* The High Contracting Parties undertake to refrain from any interference whatsoever in each other's internal affairs. They will settle any dispute between themselves in a peaceful way in accordance with the United Nations Charter.

*Article 4.* The High Contracting Parties declare that the dispositions of the present Pact are not in contradiction with any of the international obligations contracted by either of them with any third State or States. They do not derogate from, and cannot be interpreted as derogating from, the said international obligations. The High Contracting Parties undertake not to enter into any international obligation incompatible with the present Pact.

*Article 5.* This Pact shall be open for accession to any Member State of the Arab League or any other State actively concerned with the security and peace in this region and which is fully recognized by both of the High Contracting Parties. Accession shall come into force from the date on which the instrument of accession of the State concerned is deposited with the Ministry of Foreign Affairs of Iraq.

Any acceding State party to the present Pact may conclude special agreements in accordance with Article 1, with one or more States parties to the present Pact. The competent authority of any acceding State may determine measures in accordance with Article 2. These measures will become operative as soon as they have been approved by the Governments of the parties concerned.

*Article 6.* A Permanent Council at ministerial level will be set up to function within the framework of the purposes of this Pact when at least four Powers become parties to the Pact.

The Council will draw up its own rules of procedure.

*Article 7.* This Pact remains in force for a period of five years, renewable for other five-year periods. Any Contracting Party may withdraw from the Pact by notifying the other parties in writing of its desire to do so, six months before the expiration of any of the above-mentioned periods, in which case the Pact remains valid for the other parties.

[*Article 8.* Ratification.]

# Israel and the Arabs since 1948

Unwilling to continue to take responsibility as the mandatory authority in Palestine in the face of growing Arab and Zionist conflict, and with the Jewish survivors of Hitler's concentration camps seeking entrance without restriction, the British Government announced in 1947 that British troops would be withdrawn and that the destiny of Palestine would be left to the United Nations.

The United Nations devised a partition plan which was rejected by the Arabs. On 14 May 1948, the Jewish State of Israel was proclaimed. On the following day, military forces from Egypt, Jordan, Syria and Iraq began to advance into Palestine. The Arab forces were weak and divided, and in a series of battles during the next nine months, the Israelis enlarged the territory allotted to them by the U.N. Only the British-armed and British-officered Transjordanian troops had any success. They crossed the river Jordan and occupied the Palestinian West Bank and half of Jerusalem. After the armistice of the spring of 1949 they retained the West Bank, and the country renamed itself Jordan. Some 700,000 Arabs fled from their homes in Israeli-held Palestine and settled among their Arab neighbours, where their continued presence in refugee camps became one of several effective bars to peace between the Arabs and the Jews. (A similar number of Jews fled from Arab lands and found refuge in Israel over the next few years.)

Armistice talks between Israel and Egypt opened on the island of Rhodes under United Nations auspices on 13 January 1949. *On 24 February 1949 the Israel–Egypt General Armistice Agreement was signed.* On 1 March 1949 Israel opened armistice talks with Lebanon at the border point of Ras al-Naqura. *The Israel–Lebanon General Armistice Agreement was signed on 23 March 1949.* Negotiations between Israel and Jordan began on 26 December 1948 (there had been earlier contacts at a local level in Jerusalem), but the official armistice talks did not open until 4 March 1949 in Rhodes. *The Israel–Jordan General Armistice Agreement was signed on 3 April 1949.* Syria was the last Arab country to come to terms with Israel: negotiations for an armistice opened on 5 April, and an *Israel–Syria General Armistice Agreement was signed on 20 July 1949.*

The armistice agreements left Israel in control of more territory than had been allocated to her in the U.N. partition plan. The greater part of former British mandatory Palestine, except the West Bank area and east Jerusalem (incorporated into Jordan) and the Gaza strip (occupied by Egypt), became Israeli. At the time of the armistice agreements it had been expected that they would be succeeded by peace talks with a view to the signature of formal peace treaties between Israel and its neighbours. The United Nations made strenuous efforts to bring about such talks, but in vain. The armistice lines were not translated into agreed frontiers. The Arab States, without exception, refused to recognize Israel, let alone make peace with her.

Consequently, from 1949 to 1956 there existed an armed truce between Israel and her neighbours. In an effort to maintain a rough balance of military strength between the two sides, Britain, France, and the U.S.A. issued a *Tripartite Declaration on 25 May 1950* (p. 366) which had the effect for a while of helping to maintain stability in the area. But defeat at the hands of Israel had greatly discredited the existing régimes in Egypt, Syria and Iraq, and ultimately contributed to the downfall of all of them. In the mid-1950s raids and counter raids across the Israeli borders raised tension and ultimately brought about Israel's participation in the Suez war (known to Israelis as the Sinai campaign) of October–November 1956, in the company of Britain and France (see p. 350). Israel occupied the whole of Sinai (except for the canal zone) as well as the Gaza strip. Under strong international pressure, particularly from the U.S.A., Israel eventually withdrew. Sinai was evacuated by 22 January 1957 and the Gaza strip in March. A United Nations Emergency Force was stationed on the Egyptian side of the frontier, and remained there for the next ten years. Israel received private assurances from the United States and from the Secretary-General of the United Nations concerning freedom of navigation for her shipping through the Straits of Tiran (at the entrance to the Gulf of Aqaba) to her Red Sea port of Eilat. But once again no formal treaty was signed between Israel and Egypt.

For the next ten years the Israeli–Egyptian border was relatively quiet. But in the mid-1960s tension began to rise again as a result of terrorist attacks across Israel's eastern borders by the Palestine Liberation Organization, established in 1964. In May 1967 President Nasser demanded that the U.N. force in Sinai withdraw. The U.N. Secretary-General, U Thant, agreed to the demand. Nasser closed the Gulf of Aqaba to Israeli shipping and uttered bellicose anti-Israeli speeches. *On 30 May 1967 Egypt and Jordan signed a Defence Agreement* (p. 367), placing their forces under a unified command. Faced with this series of challenges, Israel responded on 5 June by launching an all-out war. The air forces of the Arab States near Israel were largely destroyed on the ground by Israeli air strikes at the beginning of the war. Within six days Israel defeated the armies of Egypt, Jordan and Syria in a convincing demonstration of her military superiority. (Lebanon remained uninvolved.) Israel now occupied the whole of former mandatory Palestine, as well as all of Sinai and the Golan Heights (captured from Syria).

During the six years that followed the Arab–Israeli War of 1967 all efforts to reach a peaceful settlement of Arab–Israeli differences failed, despite intensive mediating efforts principally by the U.N. The chief stumbling-blocks were on the one hand the continued Israeli occupation of all the Arab territories captured by Israel in 1967, and on the other the refusal of the Arab States, especially Egypt and Syria, to negotiate a peace settlement directly with Israel. The Arab States insisted that Israel should implement *U.N. Resolution 242, passed unanimously by the Security Council on 22 November 1967,* according to the Arab interpretation of that resolution; they demanded that Israel should withdraw from all Arab territories captured in the 1967 war. The Israelis interpreted the U.N. resolution to mean that their right to safe and secure frontiers, and therefore the extent of withdrawal from occupied Arab territories, was a matter for peace negotiations between Israel and the Arab States which should be entered into by both sides directly without preconditions of any kind. Meanwhile Israel was unwilling to withdraw partially or wholly before a conference met to settle all the issues raised in the U.N. resolution. Syria rejected the resolution, and Egypt and Syria refused to negotiate directly with Israel; Jordan was secretly more accommodating but King Hussein dared not break openly with his former allies. The disputed U.N. resolution, moreover, was worded with deliberate ambiguity so that the Soviet Union and the United States could both express their agreement with it, at the same time making it clear that they differed on the actual meaning of the resolution! The U.N. resolution could thus later be cited by all parties to justify their points of view.

The Palestinian political organizations were a major disturbing factor in the complex diplomacy of the Middle East. They were frequently at 'war' not only with Israel but also with their Arab hosts, first in Jordan from where the militants were expelled after a bloody encounter with the Jordanian army in September 1970, then in Lebanon, which suffered from retaliatory Israeli raids directed against the Palestinian organizations.

The Soviet Union and the United States played a crucial role in the Arab–Israeli conflict. The Soviet Union equipped Egypt and Syria militarily, and Israel relied heavily on the United States.

War erupted again on 6 October 1973 with a simultaneous attack by the Syrians on the Golan Heights and the Egyptians across the Suez Canal. The date was chosen to coincide with the Day of Atonement or Yom Kippur, the most holy of the Jewish religious days. The Israelis were taken by surprise and lost territory in Sinai and on the Golan Heights during the early days of the war. In contrast to the 1967 war, Israeli casualties in 1973 were heavy, as during the next seventeen days they sought to stabilize the lines and then move over to the offensive. The Soviet Union sent in massive arms to the Arabs, and the United States came to the help of Israel with vital supplies without gaining the cooperation of Britain, France or the Federal Republic of Germany. Angered by this aloofness, Secretary of State Kissinger questioned the effectiveness of the alliance partnership. Jordan, whilst maintaining peace on its own frontier with

Israel, sent some armoured units to Syria where they joined Syrian and Iraqi forces defending the road to Damascus. Lebanon was again uninvolved.

At the United Nations, after more than two weeks of negotiation and disagreement, the *Security Council on 21 October 1973 agreed on a draft ceasefire resolution (number 338)* proposed by the United States and the Soviet Union. The resolution called upon all parties to the fighting to terminate all military activity immediately, no later than twelve hours after the moment of the adoption of this decision, in the positions they occupied. All parties were called upon to start immediately after the ceasefire the implementation of Security Council Resolution 242 (1967) in all its parts; immediately and concurrently with the ceasefire, negotiations were to start between the parties concerned under appropriate auspices aimed at establishing a just and durable peace in the Middle East.

Israel accepted the ceasefire provided all Arab States fighting did so. Egypt and Jordan accepted it, Iraq rejected the ceasefire and Syria accepted it after some delay. On 22 October, when the ceasefire was to come into force, the Israelis had recaptured the Golan Heights and in addition were in possession of Syrian territory on the road to Damascus. Along the Suez Canal, the Egyptians held a stretch of the east bank of the Suez Canal north of the Bitter Lake, but the Israelis established a bridgehead on the west bank of the Suez Canal south of the Bitter Lake. Subsequent to the coming into force of the ceasefire, fighting was renewed on the west bank and the Israelis rapidly thrust past Suez, thereby completely cutting off the Egyptian Third Army still on the east bank. Fighting came to an end only on 24 October 1973.

At the U.N., after a brief Soviet–U.S. crisis, *the superpowers agreed on 25 October* on *a new resolution of the Security Council (number 339), put forward by eight non-aligned members* – Guinea, India, Indonesia, Kenya, Panama, Peru, Sudan and Yugoslavia. This demanded an immediate and complete ceasefire and a return to the positions occupied on 22 October 1973; it also authorized the dispatch of U.N. observers to be drawn from members of the U.N. but excluding the permanent members of the Security Council. This resolution removed the danger of the Soviet–U.S. confrontation threatened by the possible dispatch of Soviet troops or observers to Egypt, which had led to a global alert of U.S. military forces. With the help of Kissinger acting as mediator, *on 11 November 1973 Israel and Egypt signed a six-point agreement to stabilize the ceasefire under U.N. auspices.*

On 21 December 1973 the first comprehensive Middle East peace conference assembled at Geneva, attended by Israel, Egypt, Jordan, the

U.S.A. and the U.S.S.R., in the presence of the Secretary-General of the United Nations. Syria refused to participate. The deliberations lasted only part of one day; the conference was thereupon adjourned; although it remained theoretically in being, it was never resumed. The conference did, however, result in agreement to set up a military working group to implement the disengagement of Israeli and Egyptian forces on the Suez front. Following energetic mediation by Kissinger, an *Israel–Egypt Disengagement Agreement was signed on 18 January 1974* (p. 368). Lengthy 'shuttle diplomacy' by Kissinger between Jerusalem and Damascus yielded an *Israel–Syria Disengagement Agreement, signed on 5 June 1974* (p. 369). Fourteen months later, after exhaustive diplomatic activity by Kissinger, *Israel and Egypt signed a further agreement on Sinai and the Suez Canal, 4 September 1975* (p. 371).

These three agreements marked decisive breakthroughs on the road to peace in the Middle East. They were more than armistice agreements, though less than peace treaties. Israel was compelled to yield up some territory, but received massive economic and military aid from the U.S.A. as well as commitments regarding her security. Egypt undertook to reopen the Suez Canal (closed by Nasser in 1967) and to allow ships carrying cargoes to and from Israel to pass through it (Egypt had before 1967 refused passage to Israeli or Israel-bound vessels). In the second Israel–Egypt agreement the United States also made an important symbolic commitment of two hundred civilian personnel to man early warning stations in Sinai.

These were signals of potential changes in the fundamental attitudes of Egypt and Israel. But it was not until the sudden, theatrical visit of President Sadat to Jerusalem in November 1977 that direct Israeli–Egyptian talks on the major political issues between them were initiated. After several months of negotiation, with the U.S. Administration acting as mediator, a conference was convened by President Carter at his retreat at Camp David in Maryland. Twelve days of talks between Carter, Sadat, and the Israeli Prime Minister, Menachem Begin, and their advisers, finally produced an outline 'framework' for a settlement. *The Camp David Agreements were signed on 18 September 1978* (p. 374). Further negotiations were required to translate this into a full *Egypt–Israel peace treaty, signed on 26 March 1979* (p. 381).

These agreements resolved the main bilateral issues dividing Israel from Egypt. Egypt became the first Arab country to recognize Israel and maintain diplomatic relations with her. Israel thus secured the recognition of her legitimacy that she craved. In return Israel agreed to withdraw her forces from Sinai. Demilitarization arrangements for the peninsula were laid down, and came into effect as Israel withdrew. By the spring of 1982 the whole of Sinai had been returned to Egyptian sovereignty (although a number of disputed points remained as to the exact border between Israel and Egypt).

The Peace Treaty provided for the establishment, under United Nations auspices, of a force of U.N. troops and observers to help keep the peace in Sinai. In the event, it proved impossible to reach agreement at the U.N. on the formation of such a force. Consequently, *the U.S.A., Israel and Egypt reached an agreement on a multi-national force and observers for Sinai on 3 August 1981* (p.389), to be established outside the framework of the U.N.

The Israeli–Egyptian peace was denounced by much of the Arab world as a capitulation. Egypt was for several years ostracized by other Arab States; her membership of the Arab League was 'suspended', and the headquarters of the League removed from Cairo. Nearly all Arab States broke off diplomatic relations with Egypt. None volunteered to follow Egypt to the bargaining table with Israel.

The most vociferous condemnations of the peace treaty came from the Palestine Liberation Organization and the so-called 'Rejection Front' Arab States, notably Syria and Libya. The P.L.O., which by this time had grown into a virtual state within the state in Lebanon, was regarded by many in Israel (including the bellicose Defence Minister, Ariel Sharon) as a major potential threat. The terrorist acts organized by the P.L.O. against Israeli and Jewish targets, both within Israel and elsewhere, provoked Israeli retaliations, generally in the form of air raids over Lebanon.

In June 1982 the Israeli Government, dominated by Sharon, launched a full-scale attack against Lebanon, and after several weeks of fighting occupied the whole of the south of the country up to the outskirts of Beirut. Sharon's intention was to install what was ominously termed a 'new order' in Lebanon. But the assassination of Bashir Gemayel, a Christian Lebanese leader and Israeli client, who had been elected President of Lebanon under Israeli pressure, opened the way to further clashes and to a massacre of Palestinian refugees in two camps near Beirut. The slaughter was perpetrated by Lebanese Christian allies of Israel and provoked outrage within Israel itself as well as elsewhere. The Lebanese State had now been shattered by eight years of murderous civil war and by the Israeli invasion. Israel opened negotiations with the Lebanese Government, hoping to secure a peace treaty on the model of the treaty with Egypt. The results were frustrating. An *Israel–Lebanon Agreement was signed on 17 May 1983,* but not long afterwards it was repudiated by the Lebanese Government, under pressure from Syria (whose forces occupied a large part of the country). Eventually, in 1985, Israel withdrew the bulk of her forces from Lebanon without having obtained any diplomatic compensation (see p. 400).

The Lebanon War came close to wrecking the fragile structure of Israeli–Egyptian relations. Egypt withdrew her ambassador from Israel, and talks on outstanding issues were broken off. They resumed haltingly only upon the Israeli withdrawal from Lebanon. Progress was slow but, with the help of further American mediation, *an agreement was signed in September 1986 concerning the disputed Israeli–Egyptian frontier at Taba.* The accord did not actually resolve the dispute (about a tiny area of beach land), but was a *compromis* agreement, whereby the two sides agreed to submit the matter to arbitration.

The larger questions at issue between Israel and the Arabs remained, however, unresolved. Private discussions between Israeli and Jordanian representatives failed to result in any significant agreement concerning the West Bank or the future political status of the Palestinian Arabs. Israel refused to negotiate with the Palestine Liberation Organization. Syria refused to negotiate with Israel. Syria, with Russian help, built up a massive arsenal of modern weapons, and tension remained high along Israel's borders with Lebanon and Syria. Although Jordan reestablished diplomatic relations with Egypt and broke with the P.L.O. in February 1986, there seemed little prospect of progress towards a 'comprehensive' Arab–Israeli peace.

# Tripartite Declaration regarding security in the Near East, 25 May 1950

The Governments of the United Kingdom, France, and the United States, having had occasion during the recent Foreign Ministers meeting in London to review certain questions affecting the peace and stability of the Arab States and of Israel, and particularly that of the supply of arms and war material to these States, have resolved to make the following statements:

1. The three Governments recognize that the Arab States and Israel all need to maintain a certain level of armed forces for the purposes of assuring their internal security and their legitimate self-defence and to permit them to play their part in the defence of the area as a whole. All applications for arms or war material for these countries will be considered in the light of these principles. In this connection the three Governments wish to recall and reaffirm the terms of the statements made by their representatives on the Security Council on August 4, 1949, in which they declared their opposition to the development of an arms race between the Arab States and Israel.

2. The three Governments declare that assurances have been received from all the States in question, to which they permit arms to be supplied from their countries, that the purchasing State does not intend to undertake any act of aggression against any other State. Similar assurances will be requested from any other State in the area to which they permit arms to be supplied in the future.

3. The three Governments take this opportunity of declaring their deep interest in and their desire to promote the establishment and maintenance of peace and stability in the area and their unalterable opposition to the use of force or threat of force between any of the States in that area. The three Governments, should they find that any of these States was preparing to violate frontiers or armistice lines, would, consistently with their obligations as members of the United Nations, immediately take action, both within and outside the United Nations, to prevent such violation.

# Defence Agreement between the United Arab Republic (Egypt) and Jordan, Cairo, 30 May 1967

The Governments of the United Arab Republic and the Hashemite Kingdom of Jordan, in response to the wishes of the Arab people in each of the two brotherly countries, inspired by their absolute faith in the common destiny and unity of the Arab nation, and with a view to unifying their efforts to insure and protect their security and national ideals, have agreed to conclude a joint defence agreement to realize those aims in the following manner:

*Article 1.* The two contracting States shall consider any armed aggression against either as aggression against both countries. Therefore, acting on the basis of the legitimate right of individual and collective self-defence, each is obligated to go to the aid of the State which is the victim of aggression and forthwith take every measure and use all means at its disposal, including the use of armed forces, to repulse the aggression.

*Article 2.* The contracting States shall consult, at the request of either State, on important international conditions affecting the security or independence of either. In the event of impending war or the sudden occurrence of a menacing situation, the two contracting States shall immediately take the preventive and defensive measures warranted by the situation.

*Article 3.* In the event of a sudden attack on either of the two contracting States, the two States shall, in addition to the military measures required to deal with the attack, decide immediately upon other measures to be put into force under the plans concluded under this agreement.

*Article 4.* In pursuit of the aims of this agreement, the two contracting States have decided to establish the following main bodies:

1. A Defence Council
2. A Joint Command which shall consist of:
   A. A Council of the Chiefs of Staff
   B. A Joint General Staff

*Article 5.* The Defence Council shall consist of the ministers of foreign affairs and defence or war in the two countries. The Council of the Chiefs of Staff shall be responsible to the Defence Council.

The functions of the Defence Council shall include:

A. To prescribe the general principles and bases of the policy of cooperation between the two countries at all levels to repulse aggression against them.

B. To make the necessary recommendations for the direction and coordination of the activities of the two States designed to serve and promote the joint military effort.

C. To ratify the decisions of the Council of the Chiefs of Staff in all matters related to the planning of operations and the preparation of the armed forces of the two States.

D. To establish permanent or provisional special committees when necessary.

E. The Council shall meet periodically once every six months, in Cairo and Amman alternately, or when the need arises at the request of either party.

*Article 6.* The Council of the Chiefs of Staff consists of the chief of staff of the armed forces in each of the two countries.

The Council of the Chiefs of Staff shall:

A. Implement the principles and bases established by the Defence Council by issuing the necessary directives and instructions.

B. Approve the plans and studies prepared by the Joint General Staff, and submit what should be submitted to the Defence Council for ratification.

C. Issue decisions concerning the formation and organization of the Joint General Staff and its tasks.

The Council shall meet periodically once every three months or when necessary at the request of either of the chiefs of staff.

*Article 7.* In the event of the beginning of military operations, the chief of staff of the United Arab Republic armed forces shall assume command of the operations in both States.

*Article 8.* Each of the two States shall bear the cost of the military installations necessary for operations in its territory.

*Article 9.* This agreement shall be valid for five years, renewable automatically for subsequent periods of five years. Each of the two contracting States shall be entitled to withdraw from it after informing the other State in writing of its desire to do so one year before the expiration of the above-mentioned periods.

*Article 10.* The provisions of this agreement shall in no way infringe upon the rights and commitments of each State which are based or may be based on special agreements, the Arab League Charter, or the Charter of the United Nations.

*Article 11.* This agreement shall be ratified in accordance with the constitutional procedures in each of the two contracting States. The instruments of ratification shall be exchanged at the United Arab Republic Foreign Ministry. The agreement shall become valid from the date of the exchange of instruments of ratification.

In confirmation of the above, this agreement has been signed and sealed by the seals of the two States.

Done in Cairo on 20 Safar 1387 Hegira, corresponding to 30 May 1967, in two original copies.

Gamal Abdel Nasser
President of the United Arab Republic

Hussein ibn Talal
King of the Hashemite Kingdom of Jordan

'Unofficial translation', © American Society of International Law.

# Egyptian–Israeli Agreement on Disengagement of Forces, Kilometre marker 101, Cairo–Suez Road, 18 January 1974

A. Egypt and Israel will scrupulously observe the ceasefire on land, sea and air called for by the United Nations Security Council and will refrain from the time of the signing of this document from all military or para-military actions against each other.

B. The military forces of Egypt and Israel will be separated in accordance with the following principles:

1. All Egyptian forces on the east side of the canal will be deployed west of the line designated as line A on the attached map. All Israeli forces, including those west of the Suez Canal and the Bitter Lakes, will be deployed east of the line designated as line B on the attached map.

2. The area between the Egyptian and Israeli lines will be a zone of disengagement in which the United Nations Emergency Force (UNEF) will be stationed. The UNEF will continue to consist of units from countries that are not permanent members of the Security Council.

3. The area between the Egyptian line and the Suez Canal will be limited in armament and forces.

4. The area between the Israeli line (B on the attached map) and the line designated as line C on the attached map, which runs along the western base of the mountains where the Gidi and Mitla Passes are located, will be limited in armament and forces.

5. The limitations referred to in paragraphs 3 and 4 will be inspected by UNEF. Existing procedures of the UNEF, including the attaching of Egyptian and Israeli liaison officers to UNEF, will be continued.

6. Air forces of the two sides will be permitted to operate up to their respective lines without interference from the other side.

C. The detailed implementation of the disengagement of forces will be worked out by military representatives of Egypt and Israel, who will agree on the stages of this process. These representatives will meet no later than 48 hours after the signature of this Agreement at kilometre 101 under the aegis of the United Nations for this purpose. They will complete this task within five days. Disengagement will begin within 48 hours after the completion of the work of the military representatives and in no event later than seven days after the signature of this Agreement. The process of disengagement will be completed not later than 40 days after it begins.

D. This Agreement is not regarded by Egypt and Israel as a final peace agreement. It constitutes a first step toward a final, just and durable peace according to the provisions of Security Council resolution 338 and within the framework of the Geneva Conference.

*For Egypt:*
Mohammad Abdel Ghani El-Gamasy, Major-General, Chief of Staff of the Egyptian Armed Forces

*For Israel:*
David Elazar, Lieutenant-General, Chief of Staff of the Israel Defence Forces

*Witness:*
Ensio P.H. Siilasvuo, Lieutenant-General, Commander of the United Nations Emergency Force

[A map was attached.]

# Syria–Israel Disengagement Agreement, Geneva, 5 June 1974

A. Israel and Syria will scrupulously observe the ceasefire on land, sea and air and will refrain from all military actions against each other, from the time of the signing of this document, in implementation of United Nations Security Council resolution 338 dated 22 October 1973.

B. The military forces of Israel and

Syria will be separated in accordance with the following principles:

. . .

D. This Agreement and the attached Map will be signed by the military representatives of Israel and Syria in Geneva not later than 31 May 1974, in the Egyptian–Israeli Military Working Group of the Geneva Peace Conference under the aegis of the United Nations, after that group has been joined by a Syrian military representative, and with the participation of representatives of the United States and the Soviet Union. The precise delineation of a detailed Map and a plan for the implementation of the disengagement of forces will be worked out by military representatives of Israel and Syria in the Egyptian–Israeli Military Working Group who will agree on the stages of this process. The Military Working Group described above will start their work for this purpose in Geneva under the aegis of the United Nations within 24 hours after the signing of this Agreement. They will complete this task within five days. Disengagement will begin within 24 hours after the completion of the task of the Military Working Group. The process of disengagement will be completed not later than 20 days after it begins.

E. The provisions of paragraphs A, B and C shall be inspected by personnel of the United Nations comprising the United Nations Disengagement Observer Force under this Agreement.

F. Within 24 hours after the signing of this Agreement in Geneva all wounded prisoners of war which each side holds of the other as certified by the ICRC will be repatriated. The morning after the completion of the task of the Military Working Group, all remaining prisoners of war will be repatriated.

G. The bodies of all dead soldiers held by either side will be returned for burial in their respective countries within 10 days after the signing of this Agreement.

H. This Agreement is not a Peace Agreement. It is a step towards a just and durable peace on the basis of Security Council resolution 338 dated 22 October 1973.

# Protocol to Agreement on Disengagement between Israeli and Syrian Forces concerning the United Nations Disengagement Observer Force

Israel and Syria agree that:

The function of the United Nations Disengagement Observer Force (UNDOF) under the agreement will be to use its best efforts to maintain the ceasefire and to see that it is scrupulously observed. It will supervise the agreement and protocol thereto with regard to the areas of separation and limitation. In carrying out its mission, it will comply with generally applicable Syrian laws and regulations and will not hamper the functioning of local civil administration. It will enjoy freedom of movement and communication and other facilities that are necessary for its mission. It will be mobile and provided with personal weapons of a defensive character and shall use such weapons only in self-defence. The number of the UNDOF shall be about 1,250, who will be selected by the Secretary-General of the United Nations in consultation with the parties from members of the United Nations who are not permanent members of the Security Council.

The UNDOF will be under the command of the United Nations, vested in the Secretary-General, under the authority of the Security Council.

The UNDOF shall carry out inspections under the agreement, and report thereon to the parties, on a regular basis, not less often than once every 15 days, and, in addition, when requested by either party. It shall mark on the ground the respective lines shown on the map attached to the agreement.

Israel and Syria will support a resolution of the United Nations Security Council which will provide for the

UNDOF contemplated by the agreement. The initial authorization will be for six months subject to renewal by further resolution of the Security Council.

# Egyptian–Israeli Agreement on Sinai and the Suez Canal, Geneva, 4 September 1975

The Government of the Arab Republic of Egypt and the Government of Israel have agreed that:

*Article I.* The conflict between them and in the Middle East shall not be resolved by military force but by peaceful means.

The Agreement concluded by the parties 18 January 1974, within the framework of the Geneva Peace Conference, constituted a first step towards a just and durable peace according to the provisions of Security Council resolution 338 of 22 October 1973.

They are determined to reach a final and just peace settlement by means of negotiations called for by Security Council resolution 338, this Agreement being a significant step towards that end.

*Article II.* The parties hereby undertake not to resort to the threat or use of force or military blockage against each other.

*Article III.* The parties shall continue scrupulously to observe the ceasefire on land, sea and air and to refrain from all military or para-military actions against each other. The parties also confirm that the obligations contained in the annex and, when concluded, the Protocol shall be an integral part of this Agreement.

*Article IV.* A [Depolyment of forces and limitations on armament.]

. . .

B. The details concerning the new lines, the redeployment of the forces and its timing, the limitation on armaments and forces, aerial reconnaissance, the operation of the early warning and surveillance installations and the use of the roads, the United Nations functions and other arrangements will all be in accordance with the provisions of the annex and map which are an integral part of this Agreement and of the Protocol which is to result from negotiations pursuant to the annex and which, when concluded, shall become an integral part of this Agreement.

*Article V.* The United Nations Emergency Force is essential and shall continue its functions and its mandate shall be extended annually.

*Article VI.* The parties hereby establish a joint commission for the duration of this Agreement. It will function under the aegis of the chief coordinator of the United Nations peace-keeping missions in the Middle East in order to consider any problem arising from this Agreement and to assist the United Nations Emergency Force in the execution of its mandate. The joint commission shall function in accordance with procedures established in the Protocol.

*Article VII.* Non-military cargoes destined for or coming from Israel shall be permitted through the Suez Canal.

*Article VIII.* This Agreement is regarded by the parties as a significant step toward a just and lasting peace. It is not a final peace agreement.

The parties shall continue their efforts to negotiate a final peace agreement within the framework of the Geneva Peace Conference in accordance with Security Council resolution 338.

*Article IX.* This Agreement shall enter into force upon signature of the Protocol and remain in force until superseded by a new agreement.

. . .

## Annex to the Egypt–Israel Agreement

Within five days after the signature of the Egypt–Israel Agreement, representatives of the two parties shall meet in the Military Working Group of the Middle East peace conference at Geneva to begin preparation of a detailed Protocol for the implementation of the Agreement. The working group will complete the Protocol within two weeks. In order to facilitate preparation of the Protocol and implementation of the Agreement, and to assist in maintaining the scrupulous observance of the ceasefire and other elements of the Agreement, the two parties have agreed on the following principles, which are an integral part of the Agreement, as guidelines for the working group.

[The guidelines referred to definitions of deployment lines, limited forces areas, and buffer zones etc.]

. . .

### 6. PROCESS OF IMPLEMENTATION

The detailed implementation and timing of the redeployment of forces, turnover of oil fields, and other arrangements called for by the Agreement, annex and Protocol shall be determined by the working group, which will agree on the stages of this process, including the phased movement of Egyptian troops to line E and Israeli troops to line J. The first phase will be the transfer of the oil fields and installations to Egypt. This process will begin within two weeks from the signature of the Protocol with the introduction of the necessary technicians, and it will be completed no later than eight weeks after it begins. The details of the phasing will be worked out in the Military Working Group.

Implementation of the redeployment shall be completed within five months after signature of the Protocol.

[The following document was also attached to the Agreement.]

## Proposal

In connexion with the early warning system referred to in Article IV of the Agreement between Egypt and Israel concluded on this date and as an integral part of that Agreement (hereafter referred to as the basic Agreement), the United States proposes the following:

1. The early warning system to be established in accordance with Article IV in the area shown on the map attached to the basic Agreement will be entrusted to the United States. It shall have the following elements:

A. There shall be two surveillance stations to provide strategic early warning, one operated by Egyptian and one operated by Israeli personnel. Their locations are shown on the map attached to the basic Agreement. Each station shall be manned by not more than 250 technical and administrative personnel. They shall perform the functions of visual and electronic surveillance only within their stations.

B. In support of these stations, to provide tactical early warning and to verify access to them, three watch stations shall be established by the United States in the Mitla and Giddi Passes as will be shown on the map attached to the basic Agreement. These stations shall be operated by United States civilian personnel. In support of these stations, there shall be established three unmanned electronic sensor fields at both ends of each Pass and in the general vicinity of each station and the roads leading to and from those stations.

2. The United States civilian personnel shall perform the following duties in connexion with the operation and maintenance of these stations.

A. At the two surveillance stations described in paragraph 1.A. above,

United States civilian personnel will verify the nature of the operations of the stations and all movement into and out of each station and will immediately report any detected divergency from its authorized role of visual and electronic surveillance to the parties to the basic Agreement and to the United Nations Emergency Force.

B. At each watch station described in paragraph 1.B. above, the United States civilian personnel will immediately report to the parties to the basic Agreement and to the United Nations Emergency Force any movement of armed forces, other than the United Nations Emergency Force, into either Pass and any observed preparations for such movement.

C. The total number of United States civilian personnel assigned to functions under this proposal shall not exceed 200. Only civilian personnel shall be assigned to functions under this proposal.

3. No arms shall be maintained at the stations and other facilities covered by this proposal, except for small arms required for their protection.

4. The United States personnel serving the early warning system shall be allowed to move freely within the area of the system.

5. The United States and its personnel shall be entitled to have such support facilities as are reasonably necessary to perform their functions.

6. The United States personnel shall be immune from local criminal, civil, tax and customs jurisdiction and may be accorded any other specific privileges and immunities provided for in the United Nations Emergency Force Agreement of 13 February 1957.

7. The United States affirms that it will continue to perform the functions described above for the duration of the basic Agreement.

8. Notwithstanding any other provision of this proposal, the United States may withdraw its personnel only if it concludes that their safety is jeopardized or that continuation of their role is no longer necessary. In the latter case the parties to the basic Agreement will be informed in advance in order to give them the opportunity to make alternative arrangements. If both parties to the basic Agreement request the United States to conclude its role under this proposal, the United States will consider such requests conclusive.

9. Technical problems including the location of the watch stations will be worked out through consultation with the United States.

Henry A. Kissinger
Secretary of State

[The Protocol, which laid down the precise arrangements for redeployment of forces, for the functions of the U.N. Emergency Force, for the transfer of the Ras Sudar and Abu Rudeis oilfields from Israeli to Egyptian control, for the limitation of armaments, for the establishment of early warning and surveillance stations, for the conduct of the Joint Commission, and for flights and aerial reconnaissance, was agreed on 22 September 1975. Egypt signed on that date; Israel's final signature followed on 10 October upon approval by the United States Congress of the proposals for the U.S. role in the early warning system. On 3 October the Foreign Relations Committee of the U.S. Senate released the text of an agreement, signed by Henry Kissinger (U.S. Secretary of State) and Yigal Allon (Israeli Foreign Minister): this agreement bound the United States to 'view sympathetically' Israeli requests for long-term military supplies; the U.S. also undertook, in the event that Israel found that oil for domestic consumption was 'unavailable for purchase', to make oil available to Israel. The United States, in a separate document, also signed by Allon and Kissinger, undertook that it would 'not recognize or negotiate with the Palestine Liberation Organization so long as the Palestine Liberation Organization does not recognize Israel's right to exist and does not accept Security Council Resolutions 242 and 338'.]

# Camp David Agreements, 17 September 1978

## A Framework For Peace in the Middle East agreed at Camp David

Muhammad Anwar al-Sadat, President of the Arab Republic of Egypt, and Menachem Begin, Prime Minister of Israel, met with Jimmy Carter, President of the United States of America, at Camp David from September 5 to September 17, 1978, and have agreed on the following framework for peace in the Middle East. They invite other parties to the Arab–Israeli conflict to adhere to it.

### PREAMBLE

The search for peace in the Middle East must be guided by the following:

• The agreed basis for a peaceful settlement of the conflict between Israel and its neighbors is United Nations Security Council Resolution 242, in all its parts.

• After four wars during thirty years, despite intensive human efforts, the Middle East, which is the cradle of civilization and the birthplace of three great religions, does not yet enjoy the blessings of peace. The people of the Middle East yearn for peace so that the vast human and natural resources of the region can be turned to the pursuits of peace and so that this area can become a model for coexistence and cooperation among nations.

• The historic initiative of President Sadat in visiting Jerusalem and the reception accorded to him by the Parliament, Government and people of Israel, and the reciprocal visit of Prime Minister Begin to Ismailia, the peace proposals made by both leaders, as well as the warm reception of these missions by the peoples of both countries, have created an unprecedented opportunity for peace which must not be lost if this generation and future generations are to be spared the tragedies of war.

• The provisions of the Charter of the United Nations and the other accepted norms of international law and legitimacy now provide accepted standards for the conduct of relations among all States.

• To achieve a relationship of peace, in the spirit of Article 2 of the United Nations Charter, future negotiations between Israel and any neighbor prepared to negotiate peace and security with it, are necessary for the purpose of carrying out all the provisions and principles of Resolutions 242 and 338.

• Peace requires respect for the sovereignty, territorial integrity and political independence of every State in the area and their right to live in peace within secure and recognized boundaries free from threats or acts of force. Progress toward that goal can accelerate movement toward a new era of reconciliation in the Middle East marked by cooperation in promoting economic development, in maintaining stability, and in assuring security.

• Security is enhanced by a relationship of peace and by cooperation between nations which enjoy normal relations. In addition, under the terms of peace treaties, the parties can, on the basis of reciprocity, agree to special security arrangements such as demilitarized zones, limited armaments areas, early warning stations, the presence of international forces, liaison, agreed measures for monitoring, and other arrangements that they agree are useful.

### FRAMEWORK

Taking these factors into account, the parties are determined to reach a just, comprehensive, and durable settlement of the Middle East conflict through the conclusion of peace treaties based on Security Council Resolutions 242 and 338 in all their parts. Their purpose is to achieve peace and good neighborly relations. They recognize that, for peace to endure, it must involve all those who have been most deeply affected by the conflict. They therefore agree that this framework as appropriate is intended by them to constitute a basis for peace not only between Egypt and Israel, but also between Israel and each of its other neighbors which is prepared to negotiate peace with Israel on this basis. With that objective in mind, they have agreed to proceed as follows:

## A. WEST BANK AND GAZA

1. Egypt, Israel, Jordan and the representatives of the Palestinian people should participate in negotiations on the resolution of the Palestinian problem in all its aspects. To achieve that objective, negotiations relating to the West Bank and Gaza should proceed in three stages:

(a) Egypt and Israel agree that, in order to ensure a peaceful and orderly transfer of authority, and taking into account the security concerns of all the parties, there should be transitional arrangements for the West Bank and Gaza for a period not exceeding five years. In order to provide full autonomy to the inhabitants, under these arrangements the Israeli military government and its civilian administration will be withdrawn as soon as a self-governing authority has been freely elected by the inhabitants of these areas to replace the existing military government. To negotiate the details of a transitional arrangement, the Government of Jordan will be invited to join the negotiations on the basis of this framework. These new arrangements should give due consideration both to the principle of self-government by the inhabitants of these territories and to the legitimate security concerns of the parties involved.

(b) Egypt, Israel, and Jordan will agree on the modalities for establishing the elected self-governing authority in the West Bank and Gaza. The delegations of Egypt and Jordan may include Palestinians from the West Bank and Gaza or other Palestinians as mutually agreed. The parties will negotiate an agreement which will define the powers and responsibilities of the self-governing authority to be exercised in the West Bank and Gaza. A withdrawal of Israeli armed forces will take place and there will be a redeployment of the remaining Israeli forces into specified security locations. The agreement will also include arrangements for assuring internal and external security and public order. A strong local police force will be established, which may include Jordanian citizens. In addition, Israeli and Jordanian forces will participate in joint patrols and in the manning of control posts to assure the security of the borders.

(c) When the self-governing authority (administrative council) in the West Bank and Gaza is established and inaugurated, the transitional period of five years will begin. As soon as possible, but not later than the third year after the beginning of the transitional period, negotiations will take place to determine the final status of the West Bank and Gaza and its relationship with its neighbors, and to conclude a peace treaty between Israel and Jordan by the end of the transitional period. These negotiations will be conducted among Egypt, Israel, Jordan, and the elected representatives of the inhabitants of the West Bank and Gaza. Two separate but related committees will be convened, one committee, consisting of representatives of the four parties which will negotiate and agree on the final status of the West Bank and Gaza, and its relationship with its neighbors, and the second committee, consisting of representatives of Israel and representatives of Jordan to be joined by the elected representatives of the inhabitants of the West Bank and Gaza, to negotiate the peace treaty between Israel and Jordan, taking into account the agreement reached on the final status of the West Bank and Gaza. The negotiations shall be based on all the provisions and principles of U.N. Security Council Resolution 242. The negotiations will resolve, among other matters, the location of the boundaries and the nature of the security arrangements. The solution from the negotiations must also recognize the legitimate rights of the Palestinian people and their just requirements. In this way, the Palestinians will participate in the determination of their own future through:

(i) The negotiations among Egypt,

Israel, Jordan and the representatives of the inhabitants of the West Bank and Gaza to agree on the final status of the West Bank and Gaza and other outstanding issues by the end of the transitional period.

(ii) Submitting their agreement to a vote by the elected representatives of the inhabitants of the West Bank and Gaza.

(iii) Providing for the elected representatives of the inhabitants of the West Bank and Gaza to decide how they shall govern themselves consistent with the provisions of their agreement.

(iv) Participating as stated above in the work of the committee negotiating the peace treaty between Israel and Jordan.

2. All necessary measures will be taken and provisions made to assure the security of Israel and its neighbors during the transitional period and beyond. To assist in providing such security, a strong local police force will be constituted by the self-governing authority. It will be composed of inhabitants of the West Bank and Gaza. The police will maintain continuing liaison on internal security matters with the designated Israeli, Jordanian and Egyptian officers.

3. During the transitional period, representatives of Egypt, Israel, Jordan, and the self-governing authority will constitute a continuing committee to decide by agreement on the modalities of admission of persons displaced from the West Bank and Gaza in 1967, together with necessary measures to prevent disruption and disorder. Other matters of common concern may also be dealt with by this committee.

4. Egypt and Israel will work with each other and with other interested parties to establish agreed procedures for a prompt, just and permanent implementation of the resolution of the refugee problem.

## B. EGYPT–ISRAEL

1. Egypt and Israel undertake not to resort to the threat or the use of force to settle disputes. Any disputes shall be settled by peaceful means in accordance with the provisions of Article 33 of the Charter of the United Nations.

2. In order to achieve peace between them, the parties agree to negotiate in good faith with a goal of concluding within three months from the signing of this Framework a peace treaty between them, while inviting the other parties to the conflict to proceed simultaneously to negotiate and conclude similar peace treaties with a view to achieving a comprehensive peace in the area. The Framework for the Conclusion of a Peace Treaty between Egypt and Israel will govern the peace negotiations between them. The parties will agree on the modalities and the timetable for the implementation of their obligations under the treaty.

## C. ASSOCIATED PRINCIPLES

1. Egypt and Israel state that the principles and provisions described below should apply to peace treaties between Israel and each of its neighbors – Egypt, Jordan, Syria and Lebanon.

2. Signatories shall establish among themselves relationships normal to States at peace with one another. To this end, they should undertake to abide by all the provisions of the Charter of the United Nations. Steps to be taken in this respect include:

(a) Full recognition;

(b) Abolishing economic boycotts;

(c) Guaranteeing that under their jurisdiction the citizens of the other parties shall enjoy the protection of the due process of law.

3. Signatories should explore possibilities for economic development in the context of final peace treaties, with the objective of contributing to the atmosphere of peace, cooperation and friendship which is their common goal.

4. Claims Commissions may be established for the mutual settlement of all financial claims.

5. The United States shall be invited to participate in the talks on matters related to the modalities of the implementation of the agreements and working out the

timetable for the carrying out of the obligations of the parties.

6. The United Nations Security Council shall be requested to endorse the peace treaties and ensure that their provisions shall not be violated. The permanent members of the Security Council shall be requested to underwrite the peace treaties and ensure respect for their provisions. They shall also be requested to conform their policies and actions with the undertakings contained in this Framework.

For the Government of the Arab Republic of Egypt:
A. SADAT

For the Government of Israel:
M. BEGIN

Witnessed by:
JIMMY CARTER
President of the United States of America

[An annex followed containing the texts of U.N. Security Council Resolutions 242 and 338.]

# Framework for the conclusion of a Peace Treaty between Egypt and Israel

In order to achieve peace between them, Israel and Egypt agree to negotiate in good faith with a goal of concluding within three months of the signing of this framework a peace treaty between them.

It is agreed that:

The site of the negotiations will be under a United Nations flag at a location or locations to be mutually agreed.

All of the principles of U.N. Resolution 242 will apply in this resolution of the dispute between Israel and Egypt.

Unless otherwise mutually agreed, terms of the peace treaty will be implemented between two and three years after the peace treaty is signed.

The following matters are agreed between the parties:

(a) the full exercise of Egyptian sovereignty up to the internationally recogn-

ized border between Egypt and mandated Palestine;

(b) the withdrawal of Israeli armed forces from the Sinai;

(c) the use of airfields left by the Israelis near El Arish, Rafah, Ras en Naqb, and Sharm el Sheikh for civilian purposes only, including possible commercial use by all nations;

(d) the right of free passage by ships of Israel through the Gulf of Suez and the Suez Canal on the basis of the Constantinople Convention of 1888 applying to all nations; the Strait of Tiran and the Gulf of Aqaba are international waterways to be open to all nations for unimpeded and nonsuspendable freedom of navigation and overflight;

(e) the construction of a highway between the Sinai and Jordan near Elat with guaranteed free and peaceful passage by Egypt and Jordan; and

(f) the stationing of military forces listed below.

## STATIONING OF FORCES

A. No more than one division (mechanized or infantry) of Egyptian armed forces will be stationed within an area lying approximately 50 kilometers (km) east of the Gulf of Suez and the Suez Canal.

B. Only United Nations forces and civil police equipped with light weapons to perform normal police functions will be stationed within an area lying west of the international border and the Gulf of Aqaba, varying in width from 20 km to 40 km.

C. In the area within 3 km east of the international border there will be Israeli limited military forces not to exceed four infantry battalions and United Nations observers.

D. Border patrol units, not to exceed three battalions, will supplement the civil police in maintaining order in the area not included above.

The exact demarcation of the above areas will be as decided during the peace negotiations.

Early warning stations may exist to insure compliance with the terms of the agreement.

United Nations forces will be stationed: (a) in part of the area in the Sinai lying within about 20 km of the Mediterranean Sea and adjacent to the international border, and (b) in the Sharm el Sheikh area to ensure freedom of passage through the Strait of Tiran; and these forces will not be removed unless such removal is approved by the Security Council of the United Nations with a unanimous vote of the five permanent members.

After a peace treaty is signed, and after the interim withdrawal is complete, normal relations will be established between Egypt and Israel, including: full recognition, including diplomatic, economic and cultural relations; termination of economic boycotts and barriers to the free movement of goods and people; and mutual protection of citizens by the due process of law.

INTERIM WITHDRAWAL

Between three months and nine months after the signing of the peace treaty, all Israeli forces will withdraw east of a line extending from a point east of El Arish to Ras Muhammad, the exact location of this line to be determined by mutual agreement.

For the Government of the Arab Republic of Egypt:
A. SADAT

For the Government of Israel:
M. BEGIN

Witnessed by:
JIMMY CARTER
President of the United States of America

## Accompanying letters
[Sinai Settlements]

[The following letters were exchanged in connection with the agreement:]

MENACHEM BEGIN TO JIMMY CARTER

September 17, 1978
Dear Mr President:
I have the honor to inform you that during two weeks after my return home I will submit a motion before Israel's Parliament (the Knesset) to decide on the following question:

> If during the negotiations to conclude a peace treaty between Israel and Egypt all outstanding issues are agreed upon, 'are you in favor of the removal of the Israeli settlers from the northern and southern Sinai areas or are you in favor of keeping the aforementioned settlers in those areas?'

The vote, Mr President, on this issue will be completely free from the usual Parliamentary Party discipline to the effect that although the coalition is being now supported by 70 members out of 120, every member of the Knesset, as I believe, both on the Government and the Opposition benches will be enabled to vote in accordance with his own conscience.

Sincerely yours,

JIMMY CARTER TO ANWAR SADAT

September 22, 1978
Dear Mr President:
I transmit herewith a copy of a letter to me from Prime Minister Begin setting forth how he proposes to present the issue of the Sinai settlements to the Knesset for the latter's decision.

In this connection, I understand from your letter that Knesset approval to withdraw all Israeli settlers from Sinai according to a timetable within the period specified for the implementation of the peace treaty is a prerequisite to any negotiations on a peace treaty between Egypt and Israel.

Sincerely,

ANWAR SADAT TO JIMMY CARTER

September 17, 1978

Dear Mr President:

In connection with the 'Framework for a Settlement in Sinai' to be signed tonight, I would like to reaffirm the position of the Arab Republic of Egypt with respect to the settlements:

1. All Israeli settlers must be withdrawn from Sinai according to a timetable within the period specified for the implementation of the peace treaty.

2. Agreement by the Israeli Government and its constitutional institutions to this basic principle is therefore a prerequisite to starting peace negotiations for concluding a peace treaty.

3. If Israel fails to meet this commitment, the 'Framework' shall be void and invalid.

Sincerely,

JIMMY CARTER TO MENACHEM BEGIN

September 22, 1978

Dear Mr Prime Minister:

I have received your letter of September 17, 1978, describing how you intend to place the question of the future of Israeli settlements in Sinai before the Knesset for its decision.

Enclosed is a copy of President Sadat's letter to me on this subject.

Sincerely,

## [Jerusalem]

ANWAR SADAT TO JIMMY CARTER

September 17, 1978

Dear Mr President,

I am writing you to reaffirm the position of the Arab Republic of Egypt with respect to Jerusalem:

1. Arab Jerusalem is an integral part of the West Bank. Legal and historical Arab rights in the City must be respected and restored.

2. Arab Jerusalem should be under Arab sovereignty.

3. The Palestinian inhabitants of Arab Jerusalem are entitled to exercise their legitimate national rights, being part of the Palestinian People in the West Bank.

4. Relevant Security Council Resolutions, particularly Resolutions 242 and 267, must be applied with regard to Jerusalem. All the measures taken by Israel to alter the status of the City are null and void and should be rescinded.

5. All peoples must have free access to the City and enjoy the free exercise of worship and the right to visit and transit to the holy places without distinction or discrimination.

6. The holy places of each faith may be placed under the administration and control of their representatives.

7. Essential functions in the City should be undivided and a joint municipal council composed of an equal number of Arab and Israeli members can supervise the carrying out of these functions. In this way, the City shall be undivided.

Sincerely,

MENACHEM BEGIN TO JIMMY CARTER

September 17, 1978

Dear Mr President,

I have the honor to inform you, Mr President, that on 28 June 1967 – Israel's Parliament (The Knesset) promulgated and adopted a law to the effect: 'the Government is empowered by a decree to apply the law, the jurisdiction and administration of the State to any part of Eretz Israel (land of Israel – Palestine), as stated in that decree'.

On the basis of this law, the Government of Israel decreed in July 1967 that Jerusalem is one city indivisible, the Capital of the State of Israel.

Sincerely,

JIMMY CARTER TO ANWAR SADAT

September 22, 1978

Dear Mr President:

I have received your letter of September 17, 1978, setting forth the Egyptian position on Jerusalem. I am transmitting a copy of that letter to Prime Minister Begin for his information.

The position of the United States on Jerusalem remains as stated by Ambassador Goldberg in the United Nations General Assembly on July 14, 1967, and subsequently by Ambassador Yost in the United Nations Security Council on July 1, 1969.

Sincerely,

## [Implementation of Comprehensive Settlement]

ANWAR SADAT TO JIMMY CARTER

September 17, 1978

Dear Mr President:

In connection with the 'Framework for Peace in the Middle East', I am writing you this letter to inform you of the position of the Arab Republic of Egypt, with respect to the implementation of the comprehensive settlement.

To ensure the implementation of the provisions related to the West Bank and Gaza and in order to safeguard the legitimate rights of the Palestinian people, Egypt will be prepared to assume the Arab role emanating from these provisions, following consultations with Jordan and the representatives of the Palestinian people.

Sincerely,

## [Definition of terms]

JIMMY CARTER TO MENACHEM BEGIN

September 22, 1978

Dear Mr Prime Minister:

I hereby acknowledge that you have informed me as follows:

A) In each paragraph of the Agreed Framework Document the expressions 'Palestinians' or 'Palestinian People' are being and will be construed and understood by you as 'Palestinian Arabs'.

B) In each paragraph in which the expression 'West Bank' appears, it is being, and will be, understood by the Government of Israel as Judea and Samaria.

Sincerely,

## [Airbases]

HAROLD BROWN (U.S. SECRETARY OF DEFENSE) TO EZER WEIZMAN (ISRAELI MINISTER OF DEFENCE)

September 28, 1978

Dear Mr Minister:

The U.S. understands that, in connection with carrying out the agreements reached at Camp David, Israel intends to build two military airbases at appropriate sites in the Negev to replace the airbases at Eitam and Etzion which will be evacuated by Israel in accordance with the peace treaty to be concluded between Egypt and Israel. We also understand the special urgency and priority which Israel attaches to preparing the new bases in light of its conviction that it cannot safely leave the Sinai airbases until the new ones are operational.

I suggest that our two Governments consult on the scope and costs of the two new airbases as well as on related forms of assistance which the United States might appropriately provide in light of the special problems which may be presented by carrying out such a project on an urgent basis. The President is prepared to seek the necessary Congressional approvals for such assistance as may be agreed upon by the U.S. side as a result of such consultations.

# Treaty of Peace Between Egypt and Israel, Washington, 26 March 1979

The Government of the Arab Republic of Egypt and the Government of the State of Israel;

PREAMBLE

Convinced of the urgent necessity of the establishment of a just, comprehensive and lasting peace in the Middle East in accordance with Security Council Resolutions 242 and 338;

Reaffirming their adherence to the 'Framework for Peace in the Middle East Agreed at Camp David', dated September 17, 1978;

Noting that the aforementioned Framework as appropriate is intended to constitute a basis for peace not only between Egypt and Israel but also between Israel and each of its other Arab neighbors which is prepared to negotiate peace with it on this basis;

Desiring to bring to an end the state of war between them and to establish a peace in which every state in the area can live in security;

Convinced that the conclusion of a Treaty of Peace between Egypt and Israel is an important step in the search for comprehensive peace in the area and for the attainment of the settlement of the Arab–Israeli conflict in all its aspects;

Inviting the other Arab parties to this dispute to join the peace process with Israel guided by and based on the principles of the aforementioned Framework;

Desiring as well to develop friendly relations and cooperation between themselves in accordance with the United Nations Charter and the principles of international law governing international relations in times of peace;

Agree to the following provisions in the free exercise of their sovereignty, in order to implement the 'Framework for the Conclusion of a Peace Treaty Between Egypt and Israel':

*Article I.* 1. The state of war between the Parties will be terminated and peace will be established between them upon the exchange of instruments of ratification of this Treaty.

2. Israel will withdraw all its armed forces and civilians from the Sinai behind the international boundary between Egypt and mandated Palestine, as provided in the annexed protocol (Annex I), and Egypt will resume the exercise of its full sovereignty over the Sinai.

3. Upon completion of the interim withdrawal provided for in Annex I, the Parties will establish normal and friendly relations, in accordance with Article III (3).

*Article II.* The permanent boundary between Egypt and Israel is the recognized international boundary between Egypt and the former mandated territory of Palestine, as shown on the map at Annex II, without prejudice to the issue of the status of the Gaza Strip. The Parties recognize this boundary as inviolable. Each will respect the territorial integrity of the other, including their territorial waters and airspace.

*Article III.* 1. The Parties will apply between them the provisions of the Charter of the United Nations and the principles of international law governing relations among States in times of peace. In particular:

(a) They recognize and will respect each other's sovereignty, territorial integrity and political independence;

(b) They recognize and will respect each other's right to live in peace within their secure and recognized boundaries;

(c) They will refrain from the threat or use of force, directly or indirectly, against each other and will settle all disputes between them by peaceful means.

2. Each Party undertakes to ensure that acts or threats of belligerency, hostility,

or violence do not originate from and are not committed from within its territory, or by any forces subject to its control or by any other forces stationed in its territory, against the population, citizens or property of the other Party. Each Party also undertakes to refrain from organizing, instigating, inciting, assisting or participating in acts or threats of belligerency, hostility, subversion or violence against the other Party, anywhere, and undertakes to ensure that perpetrators of such acts are brought to justice.

3. The Parties agree that the normal relationship established between them will include full recognition, diplomatic, economic and cultural relations, termination of economic boycotts and discriminatory barriers to the free movement of people and goods, and will guarantee the mutual enjoyment by citizens of the due process of law. The process by which they undertake to achieve such a relationship parallel to the implementation of other provisions of this Treaty is set out in the annexed protocol (Annex III).

*Article IV*. 1. In order to provide maximum security for both Parties on the basis of reciprocity, agreed security arrangements will be established including limited force zones in Egyptian and Israeli territory, and United Nations forces and observers, described in detail as to nature and timing in Annex I, and other security arrangements the Parties may agree upon.

2. The Parties agree to the stationing of United Nations personnel in areas described in Annex I. The Parties agree not to request withdrawal of the United Nations personnel and that these personnel will not be removed unless such removal is approved by the Security Council of the United Nations, with the affirmative vote of the five Permanent Members, unless the Parties otherwise agree.

3. A Joint Commission will be established to facilitate the implementation of the Treaty, as provided for in Annex I.

4. The security arrangements provided

for in paragraphs 1 and 2 of this Article may at the request of either party be reviewed and amended by mutual agreement of the Parties.

*Article V*. 1. Ships of Israel, and cargoes destined for or coming from Israel, shall enjoy the right of free passage through the Suez Canal and its approaches through the Gulf of Suez and the Mediterranean Sea on the basis of the Constantinople Convention of 1888, applying to all nations. Israeli nationals, vessels and cargoes, as well as persons, vessels and cargoes destined for or coming from Israel, shall be accorded non-discriminatory treatment in all matters connected with usage of the canal.

2. The Parties consider the Strait of Tiran and the Gulf of Aqaba to be international waterways open to all nations for unimpeded and non-suspendable freedom of navigation and overflight. The Parties will respect each other's right to navigation and overflight for access to either country through the Strait of Tiran and the Gulf of Aqaba.

*Article VI*. 1. This Treaty does not affect and shall not be interpreted as affecting in any way the rights and obligations of the Parties under the Charter of the United Nations.

2. The Parties undertake to fulfill in good faith their obligations under this Treaty, without regard to action or inaction of any other party and independently of any instrument external to this Treaty.

3. They further undertake to take all the necessary measures for the application in their relations of the provisions of the multilateral conventions to which they are parties, including the submission of appropriate notification to the Secretary-General of the United Nations and other depositaries of such conventions.

4. The Parties undertake not to enter into any obligation in conflict with this Treaty.

5. Subject to Article 103 of the United Nations Charter, in the event of a conflict

between the obligations of the Parties under the present Treaty and any of their other obligations, the obligations under this Treaty will be binding and implemented.

*Article VII.* 1. Disputes arising out of the application or interpretation of this Treaty shall be resolved by negotiations.

2. Any such disputes which cannot be settled by negotiations shall be resolved by conciliation or submitted to arbitration.

*Article VIII.* The Parties agree to establish a claims commission for the mutual settlement of all financial claims.

*Article IX.* 1. This Treaty shall enter into force upon exchange of instruments of ratification.

2. This Treaty supersedes the Agreement between Egypt and Israel of September, 1975.

3. All protocols, annexes, and maps attached to this Treaty shall be regarded as an integral part hereof.

4. The Treaty shall be communicated to the Secretary-General of the United Nations for registration in accordance with the provisions of Article 102 of the Charter of the United Nations.

Done at Washington, D.C. this 26th day of March, 1979, in triplicate in the English, Arabic, and Hebrew languages, each text being equally authentic. In case of any divergence of interpretation, the English text shall prevail.

For the Government of the Arab Republic of Egypt: A. Sadat

For the Government of Israel: M. Begin

Witnessed by: Jimmy Carter, President of the United States of America

[The Treaty was accompanied by a number of protocols, agreed minutes, and other documents. Annex I was a protocol providing for Israeli withdrawal from Sinai not later than three years from the date of exchange of instruments of ratification of the Treaty. This protocol detailed the numbers and types of forces and

weapons to be depolyed in Sinai during and after the Israeli withdrawal. It also provided for the deployment of United Nations forces in interim buffer zones. Annex III was a protocol providing for the establishment of diplomatic and consular relations between Israel and Egypt upon completion of the first stage of Israeli withdrawal. This protocol also specified that economic and cultural relations would be established between the two countries, that the border would be opened to civilian movements, and that transportation, postal, and telecommunications traffic would be resumed. The following were among the other documents exchanged:]

## Egyptian–Israeli letter on future negotiations

[to the President of the U.S.A.]

March 26, 1979

Dear Mr President:
This letter confirms that Egypt and Israel have agreed as follows:

The Governments of Egypt and Israel recall that they concluded at Camp David and signed at the White House on September 17, 1978, the annexed documents entitled 'A Framework for Peace in the Middle East Agreed at Camp David' and 'Framework for the conclusion of a Peace Treaty between Egypt and Israel'.

For the purpose of achieving a comprehensive peace settlement in accordance with the above-mentioned Frameworks, Egypt and Israel will proceed with the implementation of those provisions relating to the West Bank and the Gaza Strip. They have agreed to start negotiations within a month after the exchange of the instruments of ratification of the Peace Treaty. In accordance with the 'Framework for Peace in the Middle East', the Hashemite Kingdom of Jordan is invited to join the negotiations. The Delegations of Egypt and Jordan may include Palestinians from the West Bank and Gaza Strip or other Palestinians as mutually agreed. The purpose of the negotiation shall be to agree, prior to the elections, on the modalities for establishing the elected self-governing authority (administrative issues. In the event Jordan decides not to council), define its powers and responsibilities, and agree upon other related take part in the negotiations, the negotiations will be held by Egypt and Israel.

The two Governments agree to negotiate continuously and in good faith to conclude these negotiations at the earliest possible date. They also agree that the objective of the negotiations is the establishment of the self-governing authority in the West Bank and Gaza in order to provide full autonomy to the inhabitants.

Egypt and Israel set for themselves the goal of completing the negotiations within one year so that elections will be held as expeditiously as possible after agreement has been reached between the parties. The self-governing authority referred to in the 'Framework for Peace in the Middle East' will be established and inaugurated within one month after it has been elected, at which time the transitional period of five years will begin. The Israeli military government and its civilian administration will be withdrawn, to be replaced by the self-governing authority, as specified in the 'Framework for Peace in the Middle East'. A withdrawal of Israeli armed forces will then take place and there will be a redeployment of the remaining Israeli forces into specified security locations.

This letter also confirms our understanding that the United States Government will participate fully in all stages of negotiations.

Sincerely yours,

For the Government of Israel: Menachem Begin

For the Government of the Arab Republic of Egypt: Mohamed Anwar El-Sadat

### President Carter to President Sadat

March 26, 1979

Dear Mr President:

I wish to confirm to you that subject to United States Constitutional processes:

In the event of an actual or threatened violation of the Treaty of Peace between Egypt and Israel, the United States will, on request of one or both of the Parties, consult with the Parties with respect thereto and will take such other action as it may deem appropriate and helpful to achieve compliance with the Treaty.

The United States will conduct aerial monitoring as requested by the Parties pursuant to Annex I of the Treaty.

The United States believes the Treaty provision for permanent stationing of United Nations personnel in the designated limited force zone can and should be implemented by the United Nations Security Council. The United States will exert its utmost efforts to obtain the requisite action by the Security Council. If the Security Council fails to establish and maintain the arrangements called for in the Treaty, the President will be prepared to take those steps necessary to ensure the establishment and maintenance of an acceptable alternative multinational force.

Sincerely,

### Memorandum of Agreement between the Government of the United States and Israel

March 26, 1979

The oil supply arrangement of September 1, 1975, between the Governments of the United States and Israel, annexed hereto, remains in effect. A memorandum of agreement shall be agreed upon and concluded to provide an oil supply arrangement for a total of 15 years, including the 5 years provided in the September 1, 1975, arrangement.

The memorandum of agreement, including the commencement of this arrangement and pricing provisions, will be mutually agreed upon by the parties within sixty days following the entry into force of the Treaty of Peace between Egypt and Israel.

It is the intention of the parties that prices paid by Israel for oil provided by the United States hereunder shall be comparable to world market prices current at the time of transfer, and that in any event the United States will be reimbursed by Israel for the costs incurred by the United States in providing oil to Israel hereunder.

Experts provided for in the September 1, 1975, arrangement will meet on request to discuss matters arising under this relationship.

The United States administration undertakes to seek promptly additional statutory authorization that may be necessary for full implementation of this arrangement.

For the Government of Israel: M. Dayan

For the Government of the United States: Cyrus R. Vance

ANNEX

Israel will make its own independent arrangements for oil supply to meet its requirements through normal procedures. In the event Israel is unable to secure its needs in this way, the United States Government, upon notification of this fact by the Government of Israel, will act as follows for five years, at the end of which period either side can terminate this arrangement on one year's notice.

(a) If the oil Israel needs to meet all its normal requirements for domestic consumption is unavailable for purchase in circumstances where no quantitative restrictions exist on the ability of the United States to procure oil to meet its normal requirements, the United States Government will promptly make oil available for purchase by Israel to meet all of the aforementioned normal requirements of Israel. If Israel is unable to secure the necessary means to transport such oil to Israel, the United States Government will make every effort to help Israel secure the necessary means of transport.

(b) If the oil Israel needs to meet all of its normal requirements for domestic consumption is unavailable for purchase in circumstances where quantitative restrictions through embargo or otherwise also prevent the United States from procuring oil to meet its normal requirements, the United States Government will promptly make oil available for purchase by Israel in accordance with the International Energy Agency conservation and allocation formula, as applied by the United States Government, in order to meet Israel's essential requirements. If Israel is unable to secure the necessary means to transport such oil to Israel, the United States Government will make every effort to help Israel secure the necessary means of transport.

Israeli and United States experts will meet annually or more frequently at the request of either party, to review Israel's continuing oil requirement.

## Mostafa Khalil (Egyptian Prime Minister and Minister of Foreign Affairs) to Cyrus R. Vance (U.S. Secretary of State)

March 25, 1979

Dear Secretary Vance:

It was with great surprise that we learned today of the proposed Memorandum of Agreement between the United States and Israel in connection with the Treaty of Peace between Egypt and Israel. We were never consulted on the substance of the proposed Memorandum which directly affects our position with respect to the implementation of the Treaty.

The content of the draft Memorandum is a source of grave concern to the Government of Egypt. At this critical juncture in the peace-making process, when Egypt has clearly, and with firm determination, opted for peace, the draft Memorandum presumes that Egypt's compliance with its obligations is in doubt. Such an assumption is completely unfounded. It, moreover, contravenes the provisions of Article VI, para. 2, which stipulates that the *Parties* undertake to fulfill *in good faith* their obligations under the Treaty.

I trust that you would agree that this new definition of the United States role constitutes a departure from our understanding of that role as a full partner and not as an arbiter. It also constitutes a distortion of that role in the eyes of others.

The United States assumed for herself the role of the arbiter in determining that there has been a violation or threat of violation of the Treaty. I wish to state that the Treaty provides for settlement of disputes procedured in Article VII. This equal right to have recourse to the procedure specified in the Treaty ensures that the balance of corresponding obligations will be maintained. The proposed Memorandum therefore constitutes a prejudgment of the outcome of future disputes, a matter which, in point of fact, amounts to negating the existence of an article on dispute settlement.

In addition, you have given Israel a commitment to take such remedial measures and to provide appropriate support for proper actions taken by Israel in response to violations of the Treaty. We consider such a commitment exceedingly dangerous as it binds the United States to acquiesce to action taken by Israel, however arbitrary, under the pretext that certain violations have taken place.

We oppose any attempt to tamper with the positions of the parties to the Treaty by putting emphasis on the security of Israel with apparent disregard to the manifold elements contained in the Treaty.

We equally oppose the attempt to put emphasis on certain rights as navigation and overflight with total negation of the rights of the other party.

The draft Memorandum also refers to the action the United States would take in the event of an armed attack on Israel. We consider this concept both inappropriate and untimely as it comes with the signing of the Peace Treaty.

Furthermore, the letter addressed to the Prime Minister of Israel on March 26, 1979, by the President of the United States stipulates that: 'In the event of an actual or threatened violation of the Treaty of Peace between Israel and Egypt, the United States will, on request of one or both of the Parties, consult with the Parties with respect thereto and will take such other action as it may deem appropriate and helpful to achieve compliance with the Treaty.'

The Government of Egypt therefore reiterates that the concept and orientation of the proposed Memorandum is detrimental to the peace process.

Needless to say that Egypt does not consider itself bound by that Memorandum or whatever commitments to which it was not a party or on which it was not consulted.

Mostafa Khalil
Prime Minister
Minister for Foreign Affairs

# Memorandum of Agreement between the Governments of the United States of America and the State of Israel

Recognizing the significance of the conclusion of the Treaty of Peace between Israel and Egypt and considering the importance of full implementation of the Treaty of Peace to Israel's security interests and the contribution of the conclusion of the Treaty of Peace to the security and development of Israel as well as its significance to peace and stability in the region and to the maintenance of international peace and security; and

Recognizing that the withdrawal from Sinai imposes additional heavy security, military and economic burdens on Israel;

The Governments of the United States of America and of the State of Israel, subject to their constitutional processes and applicable law, confirm as follows:

1. In the light of the role of the United

States in achieving the Treaty of Peace and the parties' desire that the United States continue its supportive efforts, the United States will take appropriate measures to promote full observance of the Treaty of Peace.

2. Should it be demonstrated to the satisfaction of the United States that there has been a violation or threat of violation of the Treaty of Peace, the United States will consult with the parties with regard to measures to halt or prevent the violation, ensure observance of the Treaty of Peace, enhance friendly and peaceful relations between the parties and promote peace in the region, and will take such remedial measures as it deems appropriate, which may include diplomatic, economic and military measures as described below.

3. The United States will provide support it deems appropriate for proper actions taken by Israel in response to such demonstrated violations of the Treaty of Peace. In particular, if a violation of the Treaty of Peace is deemed to threaten the security of Israel, including, inter alia, a blockade of Israel's use of international waterways, a violation of the provisions of the Treaty of Peace concerning limitation of forces or an armed attack against Israel, the United States will be prepared to consider, on an urgent basis, such measures as the strengthening of the United States presence in the area, the providing of emergency supplies to Israel, and the exercise of maritime rights in order to put an end to the violation.

4. The United States will support the parties' rights to navigation and overflight for access to either country through and over the Strait of Tiran and the Gulf of Aqaba pursuant to the Treaty of Peace.

5. The United States will oppose and, if necessary, vote against any action or resolution in the United Nations which in its judgment adversely affects the Treaty of Peace.

6. Subject to Congressional authorization and appropriation, the United States will endeavor to take into account and will endeavor to be responsive to military and economic assistance requirements of Israel.

7. The United States will continue to impose restrictions on weapons supplied by it to any country which prohibit their unauthorized transfer to any third party. The United States will not supply or authorize transfer of such weapons for use in an armed attack against Israel, and will take steps to prevent such unauthorized transfer.

8. Existing agreements and assurances between the United States and Israel are not terminated or altered by the conclusion of the Treaty of Peace, except for those contained in Articles 5, 6, 7, 8, 11, 12, 15, and 16 of the Memorandum of Agreement between the Government of the United States and the Government of Israel (United States–Israeli Assurances) of September 1, 1975.

9. This Memorandum of Agreement sets forth the full understandings of the United States and Israel with regard to the subject matters covered between them hereby, and shall be carried out in accordance with its terms.

For the Government of the United States of America: Cyrus R. Vance

For the Government of Israel: M. Dayan

March 26, 1979

## Mostafa Khalil to Cyrus R. Vance

March 26, 1979

Dear Secretary Vance:

Pursuant to my letter of yesterday concerning the proposed Memorandum of Agreement between U.S. and Israel I wish to inform you of the following:

While Egypt does not contest the right of the United States Government, or any other government for that matter, to take the decisions it deems compatible with its foreign policy, the Government of Egypt maintains the right not to accept any decision or action which it considers directed against Egypt. I would like to state that the contents of the proposed Memorandum will have a direct bearing on the Peace Treaty.

You are certainly aware of the keen desire of Egypt to strengthen the friendly relations between our two countries as well as to establish peace and stability in the whole region. This will be furthered by achieving a peace treaty between Egypt and Israel as an important step towards a comprehensive settlement of the conflict in the Middle East. Bearing this in mind, I want you to know that we were deeply disappointed to find the United States accepting to enter into an agreement we consider directed against Egypt. The Memorandum does not serve any useful purpose. On the contrary, its contents and purport would adversely affect the whole process of peace and stability in the area.

Egypt rejects the Memorandum for the following reasons:

1. It is contrary to the spirit existing between our two countries and does not contribute to the strengthening of relations between them. I wish to put on record that Egypt was never consulted on the substance of the proposed Memorandum.

2. The contents of the proposed Memorandum are based upon alleged accusations against Egypt and providing for certain measures to be taken against her in that hypothetical case of violations, the determination of which is largely left to Israel.

3. We have been engaged in the final process of negotiating the Treaty for over a month now, however, we have not been notified of the intention of the United States to agree on such a Memorandum. Moreover, we learned of it by way of information and not consultation. Ambassador Eilts gave it to me at 2:00 p.m., March 25, only 24 hours before the scheduled ceremonies for signature of the Treaty.

4. The United States is supposed to be a partner in a tri-partite effort to achieve peace and not to support the allegations of one side against the other.

5. The proposed Memorandum assumes that Egypt is the side liable to violate its obligations.

6. The proposed Memorandum could be construed as an eventual alliance between the United States and Israel against Egypt.

7. It gives the United States certain rights that were never mentioned or negotiated with us.

8. It gives the United States the power to impose measures, or to put it bluntly, punitive measures, a matter which raises doubts about the future relations and could affect the situation in the whole region.

9. The proposed Memorandum even uses dangerously vague terms as 'threats of violations' against which certain measures would be taken. We consider this to be a matter of grave consequences.

10. It implies that the economic and arms supply are subject to the sole judgment of the United States Government in connection with the alleged threats of violations being attributed to one side.

11. It makes certain aspects of Egyptian–American relations to be subject to elements extraneous to those relations and its commitments made to a third party.

12. It implies the United States acquiescence to Israel's embarking on measures, including military measures, against Egypt on the assumption that there are violations or threats of violation of the Treaty.

13. It gives the United States the right to impose a military presence in the region for reasons agreed between Israel and the United States. A matter which we cannot accept.

14. The proposed Memorandum will cast grave doubts about the real intention of the United States, especially in connection with the peace process. It could be accused of collaboration with Israel to create such circumstances that would lead to American military presence in the area,

a matter which would certainly have serious implications especially on the stability in the whole region.

15. It will have adverse effects in Egypt towards the United States and would certainly drive other Arab countries to take a harder position against the peace process, and would give added reasons for them not to participate in that process.

16. It would also pave the way for other alliances to be formed in the area to counter the one whose seeds could be found in the proposed Memorandum.

For all these reasons, I hereby inform you that the Government of Egypt will not recognize the legality of the Memorandum and considers it null and void and as having no effect whatsoever so far as Egypt is concerned.

Mostafa Khalil

## Agreement on Sinai Multinational Force and Observers, Washington, 3 August 1981

ALEXANDER HAIG (U.S. SECRETARY OF STATE) TO EGYPTIAN AND ISRAELI FOREIGN MINISTERS

Dear Mr Minister:

I wish to confirm the understandings concerning the United States' role reached in your negotiations on the establishment and maintenance of the Multinational Force and Observers:

1. The post of the Director-General will be held by U.S. nationals suggested by the United States.

2. Egypt and Israel will accept proposals made by the United States concerning the appointment of the Director-General, the appointment of the Commander, and the financial issues related to paragraphs 24–26 of the Annex to the Protocol, if no agreement is reached on any of these issues between the Parties. The United States will participate in deliberations concerning financial matters. In the event of differences of view between the Parties over the composition of the MFO, the two sides will invite the United States to join them in resolving any issues.

3. Subject to Congressional authorization and appropriations:

A. The United States will contribute an infantry battalion and a logistics support unit from its armed forces and will provide a group of civilian observers to the MFO.

B. The United States will contribute one-third of the annual operating expenses of the MFO. The United States will be reimbursed by the MFO for the costs incurred in the change of station of U.S. Armed Forces provided to the MFO and for the costs incurred in providing civilian observers to the MFO. For the initial period (July 17, 1981–September 30, 1982) during which there will be exceptional costs connected with the establishment of the MFO, the United States agrees to provide three-fifths of the costs, subject to the same understanding concerning reimbursement.

C. The United States will use its best efforts to find acceptable replacements for contingents that withdraw from the MFO.

D. The United States remains prepared to take those steps necessary to ensure the maintenance of an acceptable MFO.

I wish to inform you that I sent today to the Minister of Foreign Affairs of Israel [of Egypt] an identical letter, and I propose that my letters and the replies thereto constitute an agreement among the three States.

Sincerely,
Alexander M. Haig, Jr.

## Protocol

In view of the fact that the Egyptian–Israeli Treaty of Peace dated March 26, 1979 (hereinafter, 'the Treaty'), provides for the fulfillment of certain functions by the United Nations Forces and Observers and that the President of the Security Council indicated on 18 May 1981, that the Security Council was unable to reach the necessary agreement on the proposal to establish the U.N. Forces and Observers, Egypt and Israel, acting in full respect for the purposes and principles of the United Nations Charter, have reached the following agreement:

1. A Multinational Force and Observers (hereinafter, 'MFO') is hereby established as an alternative to the United Nations Forces and Observers. The two parties may consider the possibility of replacing the arrangements hereby established with alternative arrangements by mutual agreement.

2. The provisions of the Treaty which relate to the establishment and functions and responsibilities of the U.N. Forces and Observers shall apply mutatis mutandis to the establishment and functions and responsibilities of the MFO or as provided in this Protocol.

3. The provisions of Article IV of the Treaty and the Agreed Minute thereto shall apply to the MFO. In accordance with paragraph 2 of this Protocol, the words 'through the procedures indicated in paragraph 4 of Article IV and the Agreed Minute thereto' shall be substituted for 'by the Security Council of the United Nations with the affirmative vote of the five permanent members' in paragraph 2 of Article IV of the Treaty.

4. The Parties shall agree on the nations from which the MFO will be drawn.

. . .

## Greece, Turkey, and Cyprus

At the end of the Second World War deeply ingrained historic national rivalries in the Balkans were partly subsumed in (although not eliminated by) the ideological conflict between left and right, reflecting the larger global confrontation between communism and capitalism. In Greece, Yugoslavia, and Albania the war of resistance against the Axis powers had also been a civil war in which partisans of left and right struggled for the succession. In Yugoslavia the communist partisan movement headed by Josip Broz, who took the name Tito, emerged victorious, and set up a communist-ruled federal republic. This was the one European communist régime to emerge from the war which did not owe its existence to the patronage of a Soviet occupying army. In Greece the communist-dominated partisan movement, known as ELAS, made a bid for power at the end of the war. But Stalin had concluded the so-called 'percentages agreement' with Churchill in October 1944, whereby spheres of interest in post-war Europe were carved out. Greece was acknowledged to lie outside the Russian sphere. Consequently, Stalin did not give any significant aid to the Greek communists in their revolt. After bitter fighting, a pro-Western régime was established in Greece.

The indigenous origins of communist power in Yugoslavia more than anything else explain Tito's success, after 1948, in defying Moscow and hewing to an independent, albeit communist, road. In diplomacy this led him to seek some guarantees of security, short of alignment with the West. Hence the so-called *Second Balkan Pact, 9 August 1954* (p. 393), echoing an earlier agreement of Yugoslavia with its neighbours in 1933. The 1954 agreement, coming after Stalin's death, was seen as a harbinger of greater diplomatic freedom in communist eastern Europe, and indeed was followed soon afterwards by a rapprochement between the U.S.S.R. and Yugoslavia. The agreement represents something of a curiosity in post-war diplomacy, since this was the only alliance treaty signed between a communist and non-communist power.

Although the treaty was primarily an instrument of Yugoslav diplomacy, it also bound together two historic rivals in the east Mediterranean, Greece and Turkey. Turkey, which had been neutral during most of World War Two (she declared war on Germany in February 1945 in order to qualify for membership of the United Nations), shared with Greece (after 1952) membership of NATO and a non-communist political system. Both countries feared a potential Soviet thrust towards the Straits, especially after the U.S.S.R. in 1945 denounced its Treaty of Friendship and Neutrality with Turkey, signed in 1925.

Yet the three signatories to the Balkan Pact in reality were held together by little more than their common fear of the Soviet Union; the treaty, designed to run for twenty years, soon fell into abeyance as Greece and Turkey quarrelled over Cyprus.

Cyprus had been acquired by Disraeli at the Congress of Berlin in 1878, and was formally ceded to Britain by the Ottoman Empire in a convention concluded at Constantinople on 4 June 1878. The island became a British Crown Colony in 1925. The population was about one quarter Turkish Muslim and about three quarters Greek Orthodox. During the 1950s a strong movement among the Greek Cypriots called for *enosis* or union with Greece. But this was bitterly resisted by Turkish Cypriots and by Turkey. In most other areas of intermingled Greek–Turkish population in the region, mutual antagonisms had been resolved in the early 1920s by a Gordian cut: the so-called 'exchange of populations' between Greece and Turkey – in fact, a ruthless expulsion of Muslims from Greece and Christians from Turkey. But Cyprus, as a British possession, had been excluded from this process: the long-term consequences were disastrous for all concerned.

In 1959, after long negotiations, Britain secured an agreement with the Greeks and Turks, whereby Cyprus was to become an independent State;

constitutional guarantees were to be entrenched to protect the Turkish minority; and *enosis* was barred. Britain was to retain sovereign bases on the island after independence. *On 16 August 1960 three treaties were signed: a Treaty of Establishment between Britain, Greece, Turkey and Cyprus*, concerning British bases; a *Treaty of Guarantee* (p. 394) whereby the independence, territorial integrity and security of Cyprus were guaranteed by Britain, Greece and Turkey; and a *Treaty of Alliance between Greece, Turkey and Cyprus*, under which Greece and Turkey were both accorded the right to maintain small armed units in Cyprus.

Cyprus became independent on the same day that these treaties were signed, but political conflict and communal violence soon broke out between Greek and Turkish Cypriots. *On 31 March 1964 an exchange of letters between the U.N. Secretary-General and the Cypriot Foreign Minister* constituted an agreement for the stationing of a U.N. peace-keeping force on Cyprus. On 4 April 1964 President Makarios of Cyprus unilaterally ended the tripartite alliance treaty. In June that year Turkey came close to invading Cyprus, claiming to act under the Treaty of Guarantee; only strong U.S. pressure on Turkey averted hostilities.

The dispute rumbled on for the next ten years. It burst into flame again on 15 July 1974, when a group of Greek nationalist adventurers carried out a coup d'état on the island with the intention of bringing about *enosis*. Britain, which still held large forces on its bases on the island, carried out its obligations under Article IV of the Treaty of Guarantee to 'consult', but otherwise did nothing to implement its guarantee. The British Prime Minister, James Callaghan, took the opportunity, however, to lecture all other parties concerned (prompting one observer to label Britain 'the lion that squeaked'). Five days after the coup, Turkey invaded Cyprus and quickly moved to occupy the northern part of the island. The Turkish invasion brought Greece and Turkey close to full-scale war. Efforts to induce the Turks to withdraw were unsuccessful, and a 'Turkish Federated State' was set up in north Cyprus under the protection of the Turkish occupation force. An 'exchange of populations' (often accompanied by bloodshed) now took place on Cyprus, with Greeks fleeing to the unoccupied south, and Turks to the north. Efforts by the U.N. to resolve the dispute after 1974 were unavailing, although the U.N. peace-keeping force maintained its uneasy vigil.

The Cyprus dispute poisoned Graeco-Turkish relations for more than two decades, and the implications of the quarrel for the cohesion of the south-east flank of NATO worried Western strategists (see p. 105). A further cause of friction between the two neighbours was a dispute over rights in the Aegean Sea, where their borders connected. *On 11 November 1976 Greece and Turkey signed an agreement on procedures for negotiation of the Aegean continental shelf issue* (p. 396) which (at least temporarily) reduced tension. But during the following decade relations between Greece and Turkey were frequently strained, and no long-term solution to the Cyprus issue was found.

## Treaty of Alliance, Political Cooperation and Mutual Assistance between Greece, Turkey and Yugoslavia (Balkan Pact), Bled, 9 August 1954

. . .

*Article I.* The Contracting Parties undertake to settle any international dispute in which they may become involved by peaceful means in conformity with the provisions of the Charter of the United Nations . . .

*Article II.* The Contracting Parties agree that any armed aggression against one or more of them on any part of their territory shall be deemed to constitute aggression against all of them, and the Contracting Parties, exercising the right of individual or collective self-defence recognized by Article 51 of the Charter of the United Nations, shall accordingly, individually and collectively assist the attacked party or parties by immediately taking, by common agreement, all measures, including the use of armed force, which they consider necessary for effective defence.

Without prejudice to Article VII of this Treaty, the Contracting Parties bind themselves not to conclude peace or to make any other arrangement with the aggressor without prior common agreement among themselves.

. . .

[*Article III.* Mutual assistance to strengthen capacity for defence.]

[*Article IV.* Permanent Ministerial Council to meet twice a year and cooperation of General Staffs.]

*Article V.* If the situation referred to in Article II of this Treaty should arise, the Contracting Parties shall forthwith consult with one another and the Permanent Council shall meet without delay to determine what measures, in addition to those already adopted in pursuance of Article II above, should be taken jointly to deal with the situation.

*Article VI.* In the event of a serious deterioration of the international situation, particularly in regions in which such a deterioration might directly or indirectly have an adverse effect on security in their region, the Contracting Parties shall consult with one another with a view to studying the situation and determining their position.

The Contracting Parties, aware that armed aggression against a country other than their own may, if extended, directly or indirectly threaten the security and integrity of one or more of their number, hereby agree as follows:

In the event of armed aggression against a country towards which one or more of the Contracting Parties owes or owe, at the time of the signature of this Treaty, an obligation to render mutual assistance, the Contracting Parties shall consult with one another concerning what measures should be taken, in conformity with the purposes of the United Nations, to deal with the situation thereby created in their region.

It is understood that the consultations contemplated in this Article may include an emergency meeting of the Council.

[*Article VII*. Inform U.N. of conflict or defensive measures.]

*Article VIII*. The Contracting Parties reaffirm their determination not to participate in any coalition directed against any one of them and not to enter into any commitment incompatible with the provisions of this Treaty.

[*Article IX*. U.N. obligations not impaired.]

. . .

*Article XIII*. This Treaty shall remain in effect for a period of twenty years.

If not denounced by one of the Contracting Parties one year before its expiry the Treaty shall be automatically renewed for the ensuing year and so on thereafter until it is denounced by one of the Contracting Parties.

[*Article XIV*. Ratification.]

# Treaty of Guarantee of Cyprus, Nicosia, 16 August 1960

The Republic of Cyprus of the one part, and Greece, Turkey and the United Kingdom of Great Britain and Northern Ireland of the other part,

I. Considering that the recognition and maintenance of the independence, territorial integrity and security of the Republic of Cyprus, as established and regulated by the Basic Articles of its Constitution, are in their common interest,

II. Desiring to cooperate to ensure respect for the state of affairs created by that Constitution,

Have agreed as follows:

*Article I*. The Republic of Cyprus undertakes to ensure the maintenance of its independence, territorial integrity and security, as well as respect for its Constitution.

It undertakes not to participate, in whole or in part, in any political or economic union with any State whatsoever. It accordingly declares prohibited any activity likely to promote, directly or indirectly, either union with any other State or partition of the Island.

*Article II*. Greece, Turkey and the United Kingdom, taking note of the undertakings of the Republic of Cyprus set out in Article I of the present Treaty, recognize and guarantee the independence, territorial integrity and security of the Republic of Cyprus, and also the state of affairs established by the Basic Articles of its Constitution.

Greece, Turkey and the United Kingdom likewise undertake to prohibit, so far as concerns them, any activity aimed at promoting, directly or indirectly, either union of Cyprus with any other State or partition of the Island.

*Article III*. The Republic of Cyprus, Greece and Turkey undertake to respect the integrity of the areas retained under United Kingdom sovereignty at the time of the establishment of the Republic of Cyprus, and guarantee the use and enjoyment by the United Kingdom of the rights to be secured to it by the Republic of Cyprus in accordance with the Treaty concerning the Establishment of the Republic of Cyprus signed at Nicosia on today's date.

*Article IV*. In the event of a breach of the provisions of the present Treaty, Greece, Turkey and the United Kingdom undertake to consult together with respect to the representations or measures necessary to ensure observance of those provisions.

In so far as common or concerted action may not prove possible, each of the three guaranteeing Powers reserves the right to take action with the sole aim of re-establishing the state of affairs created by the present Treaty.

*Article V*. The present Treaty shall enter into force on the date of signature. The original texts of the present Treaty shall be deposited at Nicosia.

The High Contracting Parties shall proceed as soon as possible to the registration of the present Treaty with the Secretariat of the United Nations, in accordance with Article 102 of the Charter of the United Nations.

In witness whereof the undersigned have signed the present Treaty.

Done at Nicosia this sixteenth day of August, 1960, in English and French, both texts being equally authoritative.

For the Republic of Cyprus:
† Ο ΚΥΠΡΟΥ ΜΑΚΑΡΙΟΣ
[Archbishop Makarios]
F. KÜÇÜK

For Greece:
G. CHRISTOPOULOS

For Turkey:
Vecdi TÜREL

For the United Kingdom of Great Britain and Northern Ireland:
Hugh FOOT

# *Treaty of Alliance between Greece, Turkey and Cyprus, Nicosia, 16 August 1960*

The Kingdom of Greece, the Republic of Turkey and the Republic of Cyprus,

I. In their common desire to uphold peace and to preserve the security of each of them,

II. Considering that their efforts for the preservation of peace and security are in conformity with the purposes and principles of the United Nations Charter,

Have agreed as follows:

*Article I*. The High Contracting Parties undertake to cooperate for their common defence and to consult together on the problems raised by that defence.

*Article II*. The High Contracting Parties undertake to resist any attack or aggression, direct or indirect, directed against the independence or the territorial integrity of the Republic of Cyprus.

*Article III*. For the purpose of this alliance, and in order to achieve the object mentioned above, a Tripartite Headquarters shall be established on the territory of the Republic of Cyprus.

*Article IV*. Greece and Turkey shall participate in the Tripartite Headquarters so established with the military contingents laid down in Additional Protocol No. 1 annexed to the present Treaty.

The said contingents shall provide for the training of the army of the Republic of Cyprus.

*Article V*. The Command of the Tripartite Headquarters shall be assumed in rotation, for a period of one year each, by a Greek, Turkish and Cypriot General Officer, who shall be appointed respectively by the Governments of Greece and Turkey and by the President and the Vice-President of the Republic of Cyprus.

. . .

Done at Nicosia on 16 August 1960 in

three copies in the French language, of which one shall be deposited with each of the High Contracting Parties.

For the Kingdom of Greece:
[*Signed*] G. CHRISTOPOULOS

For the Republic of Turkey:
[*Signed*] V. TÜREL

For the Republic of Cyprus:
[*Signed*] MAKARIOS, Archbishop of

Cyprus
F. KÜÇÜK

[Additional Protocol No. I detailed the arrangements for the Tripartite Headquarters. Additional Protocol No. II stated that a committee of Foreign Ministers of the three countries was to be established. This committee would constitute the supreme political body of the alliance.]

# Graeco-Turkish Agreement on procedures for negotiation of Aegean Continental Shelf Issue, Berne, 11 November 1976

1. Both parties agree that negotiations be sincere, detailed and conducted in good faith with a view to reaching an agreement based on mutual consent regarding the delimitation of the Continental Shelf.

2. Both parties agree that these negotiations should, due to their nature, be strictly confidential.

3. Both parties reserve their respective positions regarding the delimitation of the Continental Shelf.

4. Both parties undertake the obligation not to use the details of this agreement and the proposals that each will make during the negotiations in any circumstance outside the context of the negotiations.

5. Both parties agree that no statements or leaks to the press should be made referring to the context of the negotiations unless they commonly agree to do so.

6. Both parties undertake to abstain

from any initiative or act relating to the Continental Shelf of the Aegean Sea which might prejudice the negotiations.

7. Both parties undertake, as far as their bilateral relations are concerned, to abstain from any initiative or act which would tend to discredit the other party.

8. Both parties have agreed to study state practice and international rules on this subject with a view to educing certain principles and practical criteria which could be of use in the delimitation of the Continental Shelf between the two countries.

9. A mixed commission will be set up to this end and will be composed of national representatives.

10. Both parties agree to adopt a gradual approach in the course of the negotiations ahead after consulting each other.

## The Middle East and the Great Powers since 1973

During the decade after 1973 the dominant fact transforming relations between the Middle East and the rest of the world (as well as social relations within the region) was the huge increase in the price of oil, and the sudden vast inflow of wealth to oil-producing countries.

Oil had been discovered in Iran in 1908 and in Iraq in the 1920s. In the late 1930s large discoveries were made in Saudi Arabia; these latter developed into the largest known reserves of oil in the world. The Middle East's share of world oil production rose from 6 per cent in 1938 to more than a third by 1973. Since most oil produced by the two largest producers in the world, the U.S.S.R. and the U.S.A., was consumed at home, Middle East oil (produced mainly for export) dominated the world oil trade by the early 1970s.

In the early years of Middle Eastern oil production the entire process of exploration, extraction, transportation, refining and marketing of petroleum had been controlled by the great European and American oil companies who were granted 'concessions' by the rulers of oil-rich States. The oil companies therefore controlled the market price of oil.

To redress the balance of power which had favoured the oil companies backed by their Governments, five oil-producing States, Iran, Iraq, Kuwait, Saudi Arabia and Venezuela, *in 1960 formed the Organization of Petroleum Exporting Countries (OPEC)*. During the course of the 1960s Qatar, Indonesia, Libya, Abu Dhabi and Algeria joined. In *December 1967*, after the third Arab–Israeli war, Kuwait, Libya, Saudi Arabia, Abu Dhabi, Bahrain, Dubai, Qatar and Algeria also formed the *Organization of Arab Petroleum Exporting Countries (OAPEC)*.

OPEC was designed to act as a producers' cartel, but in its first decade it had little success in controlling the world oil market. At the beginning of the 1970s, however, economic and political conditions changed. The booming world economy demanded each year a new increment of oil exports for the energy-hungry industrial economies of Europe and Japan. The U.S.A., whose own oil resources were being rapidly exhausted, became a net importer of oil. Against this background in 1970 the revolutionary government of Libya succeeded in reaching an agreement with independent oil companies operating in the country which greatly raised the price of Libyan oil. (The high quality of Libyan oil and its proximity to European markets at a time when the Suez Canal was closed helped render this deal profitable to all concerned.) The Libyan example was soon followed by other Middle Eastern countries. *In February 1971 twenty-three oil companies* (including the so-called 'Seven Sisters', the largest of these companies) *signed an agreement at Teheran with six oil-producing countries of the Persian Gulf*. This provided for the price of oil to rise eventually to $1.50 per barrel.

Further modest increases followed, but a sudden breakthrough took place in the autumn of 1973 as a result of the Arab–Israeli war. Middle

East oil producers declared an embargo on oil exports to the U.S.A. and to European countries regarded as favourable to Israel. Panic ensued, and the price of oil rose by leaps and bounds. Saudi Arabia, the largest producer in the region, tried to moderate the rate of increase (its large reserves made it fearful lest too high a price might stimulate a switch in industrial economies to alternative energy sources such as coal), but the OPEC 'hawks', notably Iran and Algeria, pushed the price as high as possible. In 1979, when revolution broke out in Iran, toppling the Shah, production of Iranian oil was disrupted (Iran had been the second-largest producer in the region), and a renewed panic pushed oil prices up again until they reached more than $34 per barrel.

The rise in the oil price was accompanied by attempts by producing countries to gain control of the actual process of production. Oil companies were nationalized and the great international corporations were reduced to acting as transporters, refiners, and marketers of oil. Gradually, the producing countries tried to take over these functions also.

This change in economic relationships had far-reaching political and diplomatic consequences. Saudi Arabia, hitherto a petty desert kingdom of little consequence, became a major force in regional and world affairs. Iran, driven by the Shah's delusions of grandeur, sought to transform itself into a great industrial and military power. Oil importing countries, both the industrial powers of Europe and Japan and desperately poor Third World nations, prostrated themselves before their new masters. At the height of the panic, in the immediate wake of the Arab–Israeli war, *on 6 November 1973 the European Community leaders issued a declaration on the Middle East* in which, for the first time, they recognized 'the legitimate rights of the Palestinians'. During 1974 and 1975 European leaders rushed to ingratiate themselves with the Shah in order to secure guaranteed supplies of oil and orders for arms and industrial goods.

The oil bonanza lasted for only one decade. After 1983 the terms of trade began to turn against OPEC, as new sources of oil were brought into operation, as the world-wide recession of the 1970s reduced anticipated demand for oil, as coal, gas and other fuels were brought into operation, and as 'gas-guzzling' motor cars and machines were replaced by more fuel-efficient vehicles and power sources. OPEC fell apart, riven by the contradictory interests of several of its members. By 1986 the oil price had fallen back to less than $15.

It was against this backcloth that the most notable political event of the decade in the Middle East, the Iranian revolution, erupted. The seizure of power by the brutal and obscurantist forces headed by the

Ayatollah Ruhollah Khomeini, signalled a drastic change in direction in Iranian society and diplomacy, with far-reaching repercussions for the region and the world. In November 1979 Iranian 'students' invaded the American embassy in Teheran and took fifty-three Americans (mainly diplomats) hostage. The Iranian Government took no action against the perpetrators and eventually moved to support them. After fruitless diplomatic efforts to free the hostages, President Carter ordered a military rescue mission to go ahead in April 1980. This was a lamentably inefficient fiasco, whose main consequence was the resignation of the U.S. Secretary of State, Cyrus Vance. Thereafter the Americans made further unsuccessful diplomatic efforts to free the hostages in a crisis which consumed and eventually destroyed the political career of President Carter. The hostages were freed in January 1981, just as Carter handed over power to his successor, Ronald Reagan. The *agreement for their release, 18–20 January 1981* (p. 403) took the form of a declaration by the Algerian Government (since the Iranians apparently could not bring themselves to sign a document with representatives of the 'Great Satan', the United States). The agreement laid down procedures for the return of the hostages in exchange for the release of Iranian assets impounded by the United States. It was an inglorious end to one of the most blatant violations of diplomatic conventions since the Second World War.

Meanwhile, in 1980, war broke out between Iran and Iraq. These two countries had long been at odds concerning their border along the Shatt al-Arab, the waterway at the head of the Persian Gulf (known to Arabs as the Arabian Gulf: to avoid giving offence to either party, some in the West began to refer to it as 'the Gulf' *tout court*). *On 13 June 1975 Iran and Iraq signed a treaty* (p. 401) whereby Iraq agreed to recognize the *thalweg* (a technical term in international law, denoting the mid-stream) as the border, in accordance with the demands of Iran. In return, Iran consented to stop supporting Kurdish rebels operating against the Government of Iraq. The Iranian revolution, and the apparent anarchy in Iran in 1980, seemed to afford Iraq its opportunity to strike. President Saddam Hussein denounced the 1975 treaty and invaded Iran, expecting a quick victory. Instead, the Iranians held their own and then pushed the war on to Iraqi territory. Seven years later there was no end in sight after hundreds of thousands of casualties on both sides. Most Arab States supported Iraq, fearful lest an Iranian victory might help spread revolutionary Islamic fervour to their territories. Syria, however, which nurtured a long-standing grudge against Iraq, backed Iran.

Syria's involvement in Lebanon gave it further reason to seek to turn the flank of Iraq. The origins of Syria's embroilment in Lebanon lay in the collapse of the consensual basis of the Lebanese polity. This was the so-called 'National Compact' of 1943, whereby Christians and Muslims in Lebanon had agreed on a scheme of allocation of posts in the Lebanese Government. By the 1960s the population balance had shifted to the advantage of the Muslims, and the activity of the large numbers of Palestinian refugees in Lebanon, particularly after the expulsion of the P.L.O. from Jordan in September 1970, upset the delicately balanced mechanism of Lebanese politics. Civil war between Christians and Muslims (supported by Druzes and Palestinians) broke out in Lebanon in 1975. In 1976 the Syrian army intervened, ostensibly to protect the Christians who seemed to be in danger of losing the civil war. But the Syrian 'peace-keepers' found themselves unable to halt the conflict, and were eventually themselves drawn to the side of the Muslims. The intervention of Israel in an alliance with some of the main Christian factions in June 1982 temporarily restored the Christian advantage. But (see above p. 365) Israel soon tired of its expensive and unrewarding commitments in Lebanon, and by 1985 had withdrawn the bulk of its forces. *On 28 December 1985 a Syrian-sponsored peace agreement for Lebanon was signed in Damascus* by three prominent Lebanese leaders (a Christian, a Druze, and a Shiite Muslim). But the agreement was denounced by other Christian leaders and soon joined the discarded pile of similar agreements abandoned since 1976. By the autumn of 1986 more than a hundred thousand people were estimated to have died as a result of the war since 1975, and the savage conflict showed no sign of ending.

The positions of both the United States and the U.S.S.R. in the Middle East were adversely affected by the Iranian revolution and the civil war in Lebanon. The new Iranian Government denounced its predecessor's treaties and agreements with the United States. On 5 November 1979 (one day after the seizure of the American hostages in Teheran), Iran denounced two articles of the Iran–Soviet Friendship Treaty of 1921 which gave the U.S.S.R. the right to intervene militarily in Iran in case of aggression. Later the revolution turned savagely against the quasi-communist Tudeh Party in Iran. Thus the two superpowers found themselves strange bedfellows in supporting Iraq during the Iran–Iraq war. The United States' position was also much weakened, and its prestige reduced, by its introduction of U.S. military units into Lebanon in 1982, followed by their precipitate withdrawal in February 1984 in the wake of terrorist attacks on the U.S. Embassy and a U.S. marine base in Beirut.

Nevertheless, in spite of these setbacks for the U.S., and in spite of the Russian advance into Afghanistan in 1979, the United States in the mid-1980s remained in a stronger position in the region than its superpower rival. Turkey, Israel, and Egypt, the three most powerful military powers in the area remained securely in the Western camp. America's loss in Iran had not turned out to be Russia's gain. And the United States continued to act as the main mediator in negotiations between Israel and Arab States.

## Treaty on International Borders and Good Neighbourly Relations between Iran and Iraq, Baghdad, 13 June 1975

The President of the Republic of Iraq and His Imperial Majesty the Shahinshah of Iran, in view of the sincere willingness of the two parties expressed in the Algiers Agreement of March 6, 1975, to reach an ultimate and permanent settlement of all outstanding questions between the two countries;

And in view of the fact that the two parties have conducted a final redemarcation of their land borders on the basis of the Constantinople protocol of 1913 and the minutes of the Border Demarcation Commission's Sessions of 1914 and have demarcated their river borders in accordance with Thalweg line; and in view of their willingness to restore security and mutual confidence along their joint borders;

. . .

Have resolved to conclude this treaty and authorize their commissioned representatives,

President of the Republic of Iraq. . . .
His Excellency Saadoun Hammadi, the Foreign Minister of Iraq;
His Imperial Majesty the Shahinshah of Iran. . . His Excellency Abbas Ali Khalatbari, the Foreign Minister of Iran.

Who, after exchanging instruments of their full authorization, which they have found authentic and consistent with governing principles, have agreed to the following provisions:

*Article 1.* The two supreme contracting parties confirmed that the international land borders between Iraq and Iran are those which have been re-demarcated in accordance with the principles and pursuant to the provisions of protocol for the re-demarcation of land borders and supplements thereto, appended with this treaty.

*Article 2.* The two supreme contracting parties confirmed that the international borders in Shatt al-Arab are those demarcated in accordance with the principles and pursuant to the provisions of protocol for the demarcation of river borders and supplements thereto, appended with this treaty.

*Article 3.* The two supreme contracting parties undertake to practice along the borders in general a firm and effective control for the purpose of stopping all penetrations of subversive nature, wherever they may emanate, on the principles and pursuant to the provisions of protocol on border security appended with this treaty.

*Article 4.* The two supreme contracting parties confirm that provisions of the three protocols and their appendices mentioned in Articles 1, 2 and 3 hereof, supplementary thereto, which constitute an inseparable part thereof, are final and permanent provisions, irrevocable for whatever reason and shall represent undivisible elements for a comprehensive settlement, and consequently any encroachment upon any element of such comprehensive settlement is contradictory in principle to the essence of Algiers Agreement.

*Article 5.* Within the context of non-encroachment on borders and the strict respect for the safety of national territories of both states, the two supreme contracting parties confirmed that the line of their territorial and water borders is unencroachable, permanent and final.

. . .

[*Article 6.* Procedure for resolution of disputes.

*Article 7.* Registration of treaty.

*Article 8.* Ratification.

Three Protocols were attached to the treaty:]

## Protocol on border security

Abdul Aziz Bouteflika RCC member and Foreign Minister of Algeria.

Following is the text of protocol on Border Security between Iraq and Iran.

Pursuant to the resolutions of Algiers Agreement dated March 6, 1975, and proceeding from the keenness to consolidate security and mutual confidence along joint borders;

Proceeding from their determination to exercise firm and effective control along the borders to cease all infiltrations of subversive nature and establish a close cooperation between them, with a view to preventing any infiltration or illegal passage through their common borders, with the purpose of subversion, rebellion or mutiny;

With reference to Teheran protocol dated March 15, 1975, minutes of the Foreign Ministers meeting concluded in Baghdad on April 20, 1975 and minutes of the Foreign Ministers meeting concluded in Algiers on May 20, 1975;

The two contracting parties have agreed to the following provisions.

*Article 1.* The two contracting parties shall exchange information related to the movement of subversive elements which may penetrate into any of the two countries with a view to commit acts of subversion, rebellion or mutiny in that country.

The two contracting parties shall take appropriate measures in respect of the movements of elements referred to in article one hereof.

Each shall notify the other immediately of the identity of such persons; it is agreed that they shall utilize all measures to prevent them from commiting acts of subversion.

The same measures shall be adopted against the persons who gather in the territory of any contracting party with a view to committing acts of sabotage or subversion in the territory of the other party.

*Article 2.* Versatile cooperation established between competent authorities of both contracting parties shall be applicable in respect of border closure with the purpose of preventing the penetration of subversive elements, at the level of border authorities of both countries, through to the highest levels of Ministers of Defence, Foreign Affairs and Interior in each of the contracting parties.

. . .

*Article 5.* 1. Arrested saboteurs shall be handed over to the authorities concerned of the party in the territory of which they are arrested, and shall be subject to the legislations in effect therein.

2. The two contracting parties shall notify each other of the measures adopted in respect of the persons referred to in para. 1 hereof.

3. In the case of border crossing by

wanted saboteurs the authorities of the other party shall be notified, which shall take all necessary measures to help arrest the persons mentioned above.

[The second protocol concerned the demarcation of the land border between Iran and Iraq. The third protocol concerned the demarcation of the water border between Iran and Iraq. This laid down that the border at the Shatt al-Arab would follow the *thalweg,* or deep-water line running down the middle of the main channel.]

# Agreement between the United States and Iran for settlement of hostage crisis, 18–20 January 1981

## Declaration of the Government of the Democratic and Popular Republic of Algeria

The Government of the Democratic and Popular Republic of Algeria, having been requested by the Governments of the Islamic Republic of Iran and the United States of America to serve as an intermediary in seeking a mutually acceptable resolution of the crisis in their relations arising out of the detention of the 52 United States nationals in Iran, has consulted extensively with the two Governments as to the commitments which each is willing to make in order to resolve the crisis within the framework of the four points stated in the resolution of November 2, 1980, of the Islamic Consultative Assembly of Iran. On the basis of formal adherences received from Iran and the United States, the Government of Algeria now declares that the following interdependent commitments have been made by the two Governments:

## General principles

The undertakings reflected in this Declaration are based on the following general principles:

A. Within the framework of and pursuant to the provisions of the two Declarations of the Government of the Democratic and Popular Republic of Algeria, the United States will restore the financial position of Iran, in so far as possible, to that which existed prior to November 14, 1979. In this context, the United States commits itself to ensure the mobility and free transfer of all Iranian assets within its jurisdiction, as set forth in Paragraphs 4–9.

B. It is the purpose of both parties, within the framework of and pursuant to the provisions of the two Declarations of the Government of the Democratic and Popular Republic of Algeria, to terminate all litigation as between the Government of each party and the nationals of the other, and to bring about the settlement and termination of all such claims through binding arbitration. Through the procedures provided in the Declaration, relating to the Claims Settlement Agreement, the United States agrees to terminate all legal proceedings in United States courts involving claims of United States persons and institutions against Iran and its state enterprises, to nullify all attachments and judgments obtained therein, to prohibit all further litigation based on such claims, and to bring about the termination of such claims through binding arbitration.

POINT I: NON-INTERVENTION IN IRANIAN AFFAIRS

1. The United States pledges that it is and from now on will be the policy of the United States not to intervene, directly or

indirectly, politically or militarily, in Iran's internal affairs.

POINTS II AND III: RETURN OF IRANIAN ASSETS AND SETTLEMENT OF U.S. CLAIMS

2. Iran and the United States (hereinafter 'the parties') will immediately select a mutually agreeable central bank (hereinafter 'the Central Bank') to act, under the instructions of the Government of Algeria and the Central Bank of Algeria (hereinafter 'The Algerian Central Bank') as depositary of the escrow and security funds hereinafter prescribed and will promptly enter into depositary arrangements with the Central Bank in accordance with the terms of this Declaration. All funds placed in escrow with the Central Bank pursuant to this Declaration shall be held in an account in the name of the Algerian Central Bank. Certain procedures for implementing the obligations set forth in this Declaration and in the Declaration of the Democratic and Popular Republic of Algeria concerning the settlement of claims by the Government of the United States and the Government of the Islamic Republic of Iran (hereinafter 'the Claims Settlement Agreement') are separately set forth in certain Undertakings of the Government of the United States of America and the Government of the Islamic Republic of Iran with respect to the Declaration of the Democratic and Popular Republic of Algeria.

3. The depositary arrangements shall provide that, in the event that the Government of Algeria certifies to the Algerian Central Bank that the 52 U.S. nationals have safely departed from Iran, the Algerian Central Bank will thereupon instruct the Central Bank to transfer immediately all monies or other assets in escrow with the Central Bank pursuant to this Declaration, provided that at any time prior to the making of such certification by the Government of Algeria, each of the two parties, Iran and the United States, shall have the right on seventy-two hours notice to terminate its commitments under this Declaration.

If such notice is given by the United States and the foregoing certification is made by the Government of Algeria within the seventy-two hour period of notice, the Algerian Central Bank will thereupon instruct the Central Bank to transfer such monies and assets. If the seventy-two hour period of notice by the United States expires without such a certification having been made, or if the notice of termination is delivered by Iran, the Algerian Central Bank will thereupon instruct the Central Bank to return all such monies and assets to the United States, and thereafter the commitments reflected in this Declaration shall be of no further force and effect.

*Assets in the Federal Reserve Bank*

4. Commencing upon completion of the requisite escrow arrangements with the Central Bank, the United States will bring about the transfer to the Central Bank of all gold bullion which is owned by Iran and which is in the custody of the Federal Reserve Bank of New York, together with all other Iranian assets (or the cash equivalent thereof) in the custody of the Federal Reserve Bank of New York, to be held by the Central Bank in escrow until such time as their transfer or return is required by Paragraph 3 above.

*Assets in Foreign Branches of U.S. Banks*

5. Commencing upon the completion of the requisite escrow arrangements with the Central Bank, the United States will bring about the transfer to the Central Bank, to the account of the Algerian Central Bank, of all Iranian deposits and securities which on or after November 14, 1979, stood upon the books of overseas banking offices of U.S. banks, together with interest thereon through December 31, 1980, to be held by the Central Bank, to the account of the Algerian Central Bank, in escrow until such time as their transfer or return is required in accordance with Paragraph 3 of this Declaration.

*Assets in U.S. Branches of U.S. Banks*

6. Commencing with the adherence by Iran and the United States to this Declaration and the claims settlement agreement attached hereto, and following the conclusion of arrangements with the Central Bank for the establishment of the interest-bearing security account specified in that agreement and Paragraph 7 below, which arrangements will be concluded within 30 days from the date of this Declaration, the United States will act to bring about the transfer to the Central Bank, within six months from such date, of all Iranian deposits and securities in U.S. banking institutions in the United States, together with interest thereon, to be held by the Central Bank in escrow until such time as their transfer or return is required by Paragraph 3.

7. As funds are received by the Central Bank pursuant to Paragraph 6 above, the Algerian Central Bank shall direct the Central Bank to (1) transfer one-half of each such receipt to Iran and (2) place the other half in a special interest-bearing security account in the Central Bank, until the balance in the security account has reached the level of $1 billion. After the $1 billion balance has been achieved, the Algerian Central Bank shall direct all funds received pursuant to Paragraph 6 to be transferred to Iran. All funds in the security account are to be used for the sole purpose of securing the payment of, and paying, claims against Iran in accordance with the claims settlement agreement. Whenever the Central Bank shall thereafter notify Iran that the balance in the security account has fallen below $500 million, Iran shall promptly make new deposits sufficient to maintain a minimum balance of $500 million in the account. The account shall be so maintained until the President of the Arbitral Tribunal established pursuant to the claims settlement agreement has certified to the Central Bank of Algeria that all arbitral awards against Iran have been satisfied in accordance with the claims

settlement agreement, at which point any amount remaining in the security account shall be transferred to Iran.

*Other Assets in the U.S. and Abroad*

8. Commencing with the adherence of Iran and the United States to this Declaration and the attached claims settlement agreement and the conclusion of arrangements for the establishment of the security account, which arrangements will be concluded within 30 days from the date of this Declaration, the United States will act to bring about the transfer to the Central Bank of all Iranian financial assets (meaning funds or securities) which are located in the United States and abroad, apart from those assets referred to in Paragraphs 5 and 6 above, to be held by the Central Bank in escrow until their transfer or return is required by Paragraph 3 above.

9. Commencing with the adherence by Iran and the United States to this Declaration and the attached claims settlement agreement and the making by the Government of Algeria of the certification described in Paragraph 3 above, the United States will arrange, subject to the provisions of U.S. law applicable prior to November 14, 1979, for the transfer to Iran of all Iranian properties which are located in the United States and abroad and which are not within the scope of the preceding paragraphs.

*Nullification of Sanctions and Claims*

10. Upon the making by the Government of Algeria of the certification described in Paragraph 3 above, the United States will revoke all trade sanctions which were directed against Iran in the period November 4, 1979, to date.

11. Upon the making by the Government of Algeria of the certification described in Paragraph 3 above, the United States will promptly withdraw all claims now pending against Iran before the International Court of Justice and will thereafter bar and preclude the prosecu-

tion against Iran of any pending or future claim of the United States or a United States national arising out of events occurring before the date of this Declaration related to (A) the seizure of the 52 United States nationals on November 4, 1979, (B) their subsequent detention, (C) injury to United States property or property of the United States nationals within the United States Embassy compound in Teheran after November 3, 1979, and (D) injury to the United States nationals or their property as a result of popular movements in the course of the Islamic Revolution in Iran which were not an act of the Government of Iran. The United States will also bar and preclude the prosecution against Iran in the courts of the United States of any pending or future claim asserted by persons other than the United States nationals arising out of the events specified in the preceding sentence.

## POINT IV: RETURN OF THE ASSETS OF THE FAMILY OF THE FORMER SHAH

12. Upon the making by the Government of Algeria of the certification described in Paragraph 3 above, the United States will freeze, and prohibit any transfer of, property and assets in the United States within the control of the estate of the former Shah or of any close relative of the former Shah served as a defendant in U.S. litigation brought by Iran to recover such property and assets as belonging to Iran. As to any such defendant, including the estate of the former Shah, the freeze order will remain in effect until such litigation is finally terminated. Violation of the freeze order shall be subject to the civil and criminal penalties prescribed by U.S. law.

13. Upon the making by the Government of Algeria of the certification described in Paragraph 3 above, the United States will order all persons within U.S. jurisdiction to report to the U.S. Treasury within 30 days, for transmission to Iran, all information known to them, as of November 3, 1979, and as of the date of

the order, with respect to the property and assets referred to in Paragraph 12. Violation of the requirement will be subject to the civil and criminal penalties prescribed by U.S. law.

14. Upon the making by the Government of Algeria of the certification described in Paragraph 3 above, the United States will make known, to all appropriate U.S. courts, that in any litigation of the kind described in Paragraph 12 above the claims of Iran should not be considered legally barred either by sovereign immunity principles or by the act of state doctrine and that Iranian decrees and judgments relating to such assets should be enforced by such courts in accordance with United States law.

15. As to any judgment of a U.S. court which calls for the transfer of any property or assets to Iran, the United States hereby guarantees the enforcement of the final judgment to the extent that the property or assets exist within the United States.

16. If any dispute arises between the parties as to whether the United States has fulfilled any obligation imposed upon it by Paragraphs 12–15, inclusive, Iran may submit the dispute to binding arbitration by the tribunal established by, and in accordance with the provisions of, the claims settlement agreement. If the tribunal determines that Iran has suffered a loss as a result of a failure by the United States to fulfill such obligation, it shall make an appropriate award in favor of Iran which may be enforced by Iran in the courts of any nation in accordance with its laws.

### Settlement of Disputes

17. If any other dispute arises between the parties as to the interpretation or performance of any provision of this Declaration, either party may submit the dispute to binding arbitration by the tribunal established by, and in accordance with the provisions of, the claims settlement agreement. Any decision of the tribunal with respect to such dispute, including any award of damages to compensate for a loss resulting from a breach of this

Declaration or the claims settlement agreement, may be enforced by the prevailing party in the courts of any nation in accordance with its laws.

## Undertakings of the Government of the United States of America and the Government of the Islamic Republic of Iran with respect to the Declaration of the Government of the Democratic and Popular Republic of Algeria

1. At such time as the Algerian Central Bank notifies the Governments of Algeria, Iran, and the United States that it has been notified by the Central Bank that the Central Bank has received for deposit in dollar, gold bullion, and securities accounts in the name of the Algerian Central Bank, as escrow agent, cash and other funds, 1,632,917.779 ounces of gold (valued by the parties for this purpose at $0.9397 billion), and securities (at face value) in the aggregate amount of $7.955 billion, Iran shall immediately bring about the safe departure of the 52 U.S. nationals detained in Iran. Upon the making by the Government of Algeria of the certification described in Paragraph 3 of the Declaration, the Algerian Central Bank will issue the instructions required by the following paragraph.

2. Iran having affirmed its intention to pay all its debts and those of its controlled institutions, the Algerian Central Bank acting pursuant to Paragraph 1 above will issue the following instructions to the Central Bank:

(A) To transfer $3.667 billion to the Federal Reserve Bank of New York to pay the unpaid principal of and interest through December 31, 1980, on (1) all loans and credits made by a syndicate of banking institutions, of which a U.S. banking institution is a member, to the Government of Iran, its agencies, instrumentalities or controlled entities, and (2) all loans and credits made by such a syndicate which are guaranteed by the Government of Iran or any of its agencies, instrumentalities or controlled entities.

(B) To retain $1.418 billion in the escrow account for the purpose of paying the unpaid principal of the interest owing, if any, on the loans and credits referred to in Paragraph (A) after application of the $3.667 billion and on all other indebtedness held by United States banking institutions of, or guaranteed by, the Government of Iran, its agencies, instrumentalities or controlled entities not previously paid and for the purpose of paying disputed amounts of deposits, assets, and interests, if any, owing on Iranian deposits in U.S. banking institutions. Bank Markazi and the appropriate United States banking institutions shall promptly meet in an effort to agree upon the amounts owing.

In the event of such agreement, the Bank Markazi and the appropriate banking institution shall certify the amount owing to the Central Bank of Algeria which shall instruct the Bank of England to credit such amount to the account, as appropriate, of the Bank Markazi or of the Federal Reserve Bank of New York in order to permit payment to the appropriate banking institution. In the event that within 30 days any U.S. banking institution and the Bank Markazi are unable to agree upon the amounts owed, either party may refer such dispute to binding arbitration by such international arbitration panel as the parties may agree, or failing such agreement within 30 additional days after such reference, by the Iran–United States Claims Tribunal. The presiding officer of such panel or tribunal shall certify to the Central Bank of Algeria the amount, if any, determined by it to be owed, whereupon the Central Bank of Algeria shall instruct the Bank of England to credit such amount to the account of the Bank Markazi or of the Federal Reserve Bank of New York in order to permit payment to the appropriate banking institution. After all disputes are resolved either by agreement or by arbitration award and appropriate payment has been made, the balance of the funds referred to in this Paragraph (B) shall be paid to Bank Markazi.

(C) To transfer immediately to, or upon the order of, the Bank Markazi all assets in the escrow account in excess of the amounts referred to in Paragraphs (A) and (B).

## Declaration of the Government of the Democratic and Popular Republic of Algeria concerning the settlement of claims by the Government of the United States of America and the Government of the Islamic Republic of Iran

The Government of the Democratic and Popular Republic of Algeria, on the basis of formal notice of adherence received from the Government of the Islamic Republic of Iran and the Government of the United States of America, now declares that Iran and the United States have agreed as follows:

*Article I.* Iran and the United States will promote the settlement of the claims described in Article II by the parties directly concerned. Any such claims not settled within six months from the date of entry into force of this agreement shall be submitted to binding third-party arbitration in accordance with the terms of this agreement. The aforementioned six months' period may be extended once by three months at the request of either party.

*Article II.* 1. An International Arbitral Tribunal (the Iran–United States Claims Tribunal) is hereby established for the purpose of deciding claims of nationals of the United States against Iran and claims of nationals of Iran against the United States, and any counterclaim which arises out of the same contract, transaction or occurrence that constitutes the subject matter of that national's claim, if such claims and counterclaims are outstanding on the date of this agreement, whether or not filed with any court, and arise out of debts, contracts (including transactions which are the subject of letters of credit or bank guarantees), expropriations or other measures affecting property rights, excluding claims described in Paragraph 11 of the Declaration of the Government of Algeria of January 19, 1981, and claims arising out of the actions of the United States in response to the conduct described in such paragraph, and excluding claims arising under a binding contract between the parties specifically providing that any disputes thereunder shall be within the sole jurisdiction of the competent Iranian courts in response to the Majlis position.

2. The Tribunal shall also have jurisdiction over official claims of the United States and Iran against each other arising out of contractual arrangements between them for the purchase and sale of goods and services.

3. The Tribunal shall have jurisdiction, as specified in Paragraphs 16–17 of the Declaration of the Government of Algeria of January 19, 1981, over any dispute as to the interpretation or performance of any provision of that Declaration.

. . .

[*Articles III, IV, V, VI.* Composition, powers, and procedure of the Tribunal.

*Article VII.* Definitions of terms.]

*Article VIII.* This agreement shall enter into force when the Government of Algeria has received from both Iran and the United States a notification of adherence to the agreement.

Initialled on January 19, 1981

[An accompanying document contained an escrow agreement implementing the provisions in the Algerian Government Declaration whereby the establishment of an escrow arrangement for Iranian property was tied to the release of the American nationals held hostage by the Government of Iran. Under the agreement the Iranian property would be held by the Bank of England, acting as depository, for credit to the Central Bank of Algeria, acting as escrow agent under the agreement. Article 4 of the escrow agreement specified: 'As soon as the Algerian Government certifies in writing to the Banque Central d'Algérie that all 52 United States nationals...now being held in Iran have safely departed from Iran, the Banque Centrale d'Algérie will immediately give the instructions to the Bank of England specifically contemplated by the provisions of the Declaration and Undertakings of the Government of the United States of America and the Government of the Islamic Republic of Iran with respect to the Declaration of the Government of the Democratic and Popular Republic of Algeria.']

# IX · Latin America and the South Atlantic

During the post-war period the structure of treaty relationships established in the late 1940s by the Rio and Bogotá Pacts (see Chapter II) remained largely intact. The United States demonstrated its determination to preserve its paramount influence in the Americas by sponsoring the invasions of Guatemala (1954), Cuba (1961), the Dominican Republic (1965), and Grenada (1983), by its 'covert' subversion of the left-wing Allende Government in Chile (1973), and by its support for the right-wing 'contra' rebels in Nicaragua in the mid-1980s. The U.S. also gave solid support to right-wing dictatorships in many Central and South American countries, most notoriously those of Argentina and Chile in the 1970s; long-established repressive régimes with impeccable anti-communist records, such as those of Stroessner in Paraguay, the Somoza dynasty in Nicaragua, or the Duvaliers in Haiti, enjoyed American backing, as did Governments, such as that of El Salvador, faced by far-left guerrilla uprisings.

The two major exceptions to this pattern of American behaviour were the Kennedy and Carter Administrations. But the *Alliance for Progress of 1961* (p. 98) failed to fulfil its initial promise. The Carter Administration's important achievement of the Panama Canal Treaties (see below) seemed to betoken a new type of relationship between the U.S. and its hemispheric neighbours. But after 1981 the Reagan Administration reverted to the more traditional stance of viewing the region primarily in terms of superpower rivalry and resisting what it regarded as Soviet attempts to employ revolutionary surrogates to encroach on the United States' 'back yard'.

## Central America

The flawed alliance between the U.S. and its continental partners was exemplified in the uneasy relations with its closest and most important Central American neighbour, Mexico. This was an alliance imposed more by geography than by mutual conviction, and by the mid-1980s the combined pressures of Mexico's vast debt (particularly to U.S. banks), massive illegal immigration to the U.S. across the Rio Grande, and the flow of drugs on a large scale over the frontier semed to threaten the equilibrium of Mexican–U.S. relations.

In the smaller Central American States the U.S., fearing the contagious spread of revolutionary doctrines from Cuba, gave virtual carte blanche to right-wing régimes which could furnish evidence of their anti-communist zeal by means of vigorous repression of revolutionary (or even liberal-democratic) opposition movements. The 'human rights' policy of the Carter Administration between 1977 and 1981 marked a significant shift in approach. During that period Washington tended to limit itself to exhortation rather than intervention in the hope of securing better behaviour from errant protégés. The murderous 'death squads' in Guatemala and El Salvador paid little heed to such moral pressure. The result was frequently severe embarrassment for the United States. The most notable case was that of Nicaragua where the Carter Administration found itself, against its own inclination, continuing to bestow the patronage furnished by its predecessors since the 1930s to the Somoza dynasty. In 1979 in Nicaragua, the U.S. Government found itself caught on the wrong foot (as it was in Iran) when a régime it disliked but supported was overthrown by revolutionaries even more unpalatable to Washington.

The left-wing 'Sandinista' Government which seized power from Somoza in 1979 found itself confronted from 1981 by CIA-sponsored guerrillas operating in hit-and-run raids across the frontier from Honduras. United States support for the 'contras' was publicly acknowledged by the Administration which organized the mining of Nicaraguan ports in 1984 (the International Court of Justice supported a Nicaraguan complaint, but the U.S. refused to acknowledge the court's jurisdiction in the matter). In 1985 the U.S. terminated its treaty of friendship with Nicaragua (signed on 21 January 1956). Elaborate efforts by the 'Contadora group' of countries (Colombia, Mexico, Panama, and Venezuela) to negotiate a draft treaty for the entire Central American region collapsed in June 1986. Although El Salvador, Honduras, Costa

Rica, and Guatemala at one stage all expressed their readiness to sign the accord, Nicaragua insisted it would not sign until the U.S. stopped aiding the 'contras'. In their hostility to the 'Contadora peace process' the Sandinistas found strange bedfellows in some officials in Washington who feared that the clause in the draft treaty ruling out external support for rebel forces might compel the U.S. to withdraw its backing from the 'contras'. With the failure of the 'Contadora' initiative, a political solution to the Nicaraguan conflict seemed far beyond the horizon.

The U.S. was not, however, drawn into all the inter-State conflicts in the region: some remained home-grown. The two most striking examples were the 'Football War' of 1969 between El Salvador and Honduras, and the territorial dispute between Guatemala and British Honduras.

The "Football War' erupted in the aftermath of a disputed decision in a soccer match between El Salvador and Honduras in the World Cup tournament. Reflecting deeper nationalist resentments, the war resulted in thousands of deaths. On 4 December 1969 the two countries agreed to negotiate their differences, and *on 4 June 1970 an agreement on a security zone for the purposes of pacification was signed by El Salvador and Honduras at San José, Costa Rica*. Nicaragua, Costa Rica, and Guatemala were also parties to this agreement. But the antagonism aroused by the war was not dispelled.

British Honduras, a colony since 1862, had been claimed in its entirety by Guatemala since 1821. In 1965 the United States agreed to mediate in the dispute between Britain and Guatemala, and in 1968 a proposal, in the form of a draft treaty, was submitted by the mediator. No agreement resulted, but in 1973 Britain granted the territory independence, whereupon it took the name Belize.

In spite of the internal and inter-State conflicts in the region, the 1960s and 1970s were marked by attempts to achieve closer economic integration. *On 13 December 1960 El Salvador, Guatemala, Honduras, and Nicaragua signed a treaty establishing a Central American Common Market*. Costa Rica acceded to the treaty in 1962. *On 12 December 1962 the member States signed the Charter of the Organization of Central American States*. This constituted 'an economic–political community' aiming at close political, economic, and defence coordination. Some progress was made in reducing tariff barriers between member States, but otherwise little real integration took place. After the 'Football War', Honduras effectively withdrew from the organization. Although the establishment of the common market was followed by a number of other *agreements among the Central American States on subjects such as industrial development (31 July 1962), basic cereal grains (28 October 1965), telecommunications (26 April 1966), and social security (14*

*October 1967)*, the organization failed to overcome the profound social and national rivalries which characterized the region.

The most notable diplomatic achievement in Central America in recent years was the reformulation of the relationship between the United States and Panama with reference to the Panama Canal Zone. Negotiations on the subject occupied more than fifteen years. In June 1962 the President of Panama visited Washington for talks with President Kennedy; further discussions led to a *Panama–United States Agreement on Certain Procedural Matters in the Canal Zone, 10 January 1963.* But beyond permitting the use of Panamanian postage stamps within the Canal Zone (administered by the United States under the terms of the Hay–Bunau– Varilla Treaty of 17 November 1903), the U.S. made few concessions to insistent Panamanian demands for retrocession of the Zone to Panama. The dispute became so embittered that the two countries broke off diplomatic relations later in 1963. A *Joint Declaration of the United States and Panama, issued on 3 April 1964*, announced that relations would be resumed, and that discussions would begin 'without limitations or preconditions of any kind...with the objective of reaching a just and fair agreement'.

Negotiations over the following decade were punctuated by heated disputes and anti-American demonstrations in Panama City. *On 7 February 1974*, however, *Panama and the United States announced an Agreement on Principles to Guide Negotiators of a New Treaty on the Panama Canal.* The agreement, which took the form of a joint declaration by the Panamanian Foreign Minister and Dr Kissinger, committed the U.S. to abrogation of the 1903 treaty and its replacement by 'an entirely new interoceanic canal treaty'; the U.S. further agreed that 'the Panamanian territory in which the canal is situated shall be returned to the jurisdiction of the Republic of Panama' at a future date which was yet to be decided; for its part, the Panamanian Government undertook to 'grant to the United States of America the rights necessary to regulate the transit of ships through the canal, to operate, maintain, protect and defend the canal, and to undertake any specific activity related to those ends, as may be agreed upon in the treaty'.

After three more years of negotiation *the Panama Canal Treaty was signed on 7 September 1977* (p. 414). At the same time an associated neutrality treaty (p. 417) and other related agreements were also signed. The main treaty, which was based on the principles agreed in 1974, provided for a gradual process whereby the canal would be fully transferred to Panama by 31 December 1999. By that date all U.S. forces were to be withdrawn from the Canal Zone.

The treaty aroused considerable opposition in the U.S., where it was criticized as compromising American interests. The Carter Administration encountered difficulties in securing the necessary two-thirds majority in the Senate for ratification. Accordingly, the Administration was compelled to acquiesce in the passage of a conditional ratification. On 16 March 1978 the Senate ratified the main treaty on the basis of six 'reservations' and a further six 'understandings', which did not, however, alter the essential substance of the agreements. The Senate conditions were incorporated in the United States Instrument of Ratification, signed by President Carter on 15 June 1978; a Panamanian Instrument, issued the following day, contained a declaration by Panama of its interpretation of the treaty and the Senate's conditions. Similar instruments of ratification were exchanged at the same time for the related neutrality treaty.

## Panama Canal Treaties, Washington, 7 September 1977

### Panama Canal Treaty

The United States of America and the Republic of Panama,

*Acting* in the spirit of the Joint Declaration of April 3, 1964, by the Representatives of the Governments of the United States of America and the Republic of Panama, and of the Joint Statement of Principles of February 7, 1974, initialed by the Secretary of State of the United States of America and the Foreign Minister of the Republic of Panama, and

*Acknowledging* the Republic of Panama's sovereignty over its territory,

*Have decided* to terminate the prior Treaties pertaining to the Panama Canal and to conclude a new Treaty to serve as the basis for a new relationship between them and, accordingly, have agreed upon the following:

*Article I: Abrogation of prior treaties and establishment of a new relationship.* 1. Upon its entry into force, this Treaty terminates and supersedes:

(a) The Isthmian Canal Convention between the United States of America and the Republic of Panama, signed at Washington, November 18, 1903;

(b) The Treaty of Friendship and Cooperation signed at Washington, March 2, 1936, and the Treaty of Mutual Understanding and Cooperation and the related Memorandum of Understandings Reached, signed at Panama, January 25, 1955, between the United States of America and the Republic of Panama;

(c) All other treaties, conventions, agreements and exchanges of notes between the United States of America and the Republic of Panama concerning the Panama Canal which were in force prior to the entry into force of this Treaty; and

(d) Provisions concerning the Panama Canal which appear in other treaties, conventions, agreements and exchanges of notes between the United States of America and the Republic of Panama which were in force prior to the entry into force of this Treaty.

2. In accordance with the terms of this Treaty and related agreements, the Republic of Panama, as territorial sovereign, grants to the United States of America,

for the duration of this Treaty, the rights necessary to regulate the transit of ships through the Panama Canal, and to manage, operate, maintain, improve, protect and defend the Canal. The Republic of Panama guarantees to the United States of America the peaceful use of the land and water areas which it has been granted the rights to use for such purposes pursuant to this Treaty and related agreements.

3. The Republic of Panama shall participate increasingly in the management and protection and defense of the Canal, as provided in this Treaty.

4. In view of the special relationship established by this Treaty, the United States of America and the Republic of Panama shall cooperate to assure the uninterrupted and efficient operation of the Panama Canal.

*Article II: Ratification, entry into force, and termination.* 1. This Treaty shall be subject to ratification in accordance with the constitutional procedures of the two Parties. The instruments of ratification of this Treaty shall be exchanged at Panama at the same time as the instruments of ratification of the Treaty Concerning the Permanent Neutrality and Operation of the Panama Canal, signed this date, are exchanged. This Treaty shall enter into force, simultaneously with the Treaty Concerning the Permanent Neutrality and Operation of the Panama Canal, six calendar months from the date of the exchange of the instruments of ratification.

2. This Treaty shall terminate at noon, Panama time, December 31, 1999.

*Article III: Canal operation and management.* 1. The Republic of Panama, as territorial sovereign, grants to the United States of America the rights to manage, operate, and maintain the Panama Canal, its complementary works, installations and equipment and to provide for the orderly transit of vessels through the Panama Canal. The United States of America accepts the grant of such rights

and undertakes to exercise them in accordance with this Treaty and related agreements.

2. In carrying out the foregoing responsibilities, the United States of America may:

(a) Use for the aforementioned purposes, without cost except as provided in this Treaty, the various installations and areas (including the Panama Canal) and waters, described in the Agreement in Implementation of this Article, signed this date, as well as such other areas and installations as are made available to the United States of America under this Treaty and related agreements, and take the measures necessary to ensure sanitation of such areas;

(b) Make such improvements and alterations to the aforesaid installations and areas as it deems appropriate, consistent with the terms of this Treaty;

(c) Make and enforce all rules pertaining to the passage of vessels through the Canal and other rules with respect to navigation and maritime matters, in accordance with this Treaty and related agreements. The Republic of Panama will lend its cooperation, when necessary, in the enforcement of such rules;

(d) Establish, modify, collect and retain tolls for the use of the Panama Canal, and other charges, and establish and modify methods of their assessment;

(e) Regulate relations with employees of the United States Government;

(f) Provide supporting services to facilitate the performance of its responsibilities under this Article;

(g) Issue and enforce regulations for the effective exercise of the rights and responsibilities of the United States of America under this Treaty and related agreements. The Republic of Panama will lend its cooperation, when necessary, in the enforcement of such rules; and

(h) Exercise any other right granted under this Treaty, or otherwise agreed upon between the two Parties.

3. Pursuant to the foregoing grant of rights, the United States of America shall,

in accordance with the terms of this Treaty and the provisions of United States law, carry out its responsibilities by means of a United States Government agency called the Panama Canal Commission, which shall be constituted by and in conformity with the laws of the United States of America.

. . .

*Article IV: Protection and defense.* 1. The United States of America and the Republic of Panama commit themselves to protect and defend the Panama Canal. Each Party shall act, in accordance with its constitutional processes, to meet the danger resulting from an armed attack or other actions which threaten the security of the Panama Canal or of ships transiting it.

2. For the duration of this Treaty, the United States of America shall have primary responsibility to protect and defend the Canal. The rights of the United States of America to station, train, and move military forces within the Republic of Panama are described in the Agreement in Implementation of this Article, signed this date. The use of areas and installations and the legal status of the armed forces of the United States of America in the Republic of Panama shall be governed by the aforesaid Agreement.

3. In order to facilitate the participation and cooperation of the armed forces of both Parties in the protection and defense of the Canal, the United States of America and the Republic of Panama shall establish a Combined Board comprised of an equal number of senior military representatives of each Party. These representatives shall be charged by their respective governments with consulting and cooperating on all matters pertaining to the protection and defense of the Canal, and with planning for actions to be taken in concert for that purpose. Such combined protection and defense arrangements shall not inhibit the identity or lines of authority of the armed forces of the United States of America or the Republic of Panama. The Combined Board shall pro-

vide for coordination and cooperation concerning such matters as:

(a) The preparation of contingency plans for the protection and defense of the Canal based upon the cooperative efforts of the armed forces of both Parties;

(b) The planning and conduct of combined military exercises; and

(c) The conduct of United States and Panamanian military operations with respect to the protection and defense of the Canal.

4. The Combined Board shall, at five-year intervals throughout the duration of this Treaty, review the resources being made available by the two Parties for the protection and defense of the Canal. Also, the Combined Board shall make appropriate recommendations to the two Governments respecting projected requirements, the efficient utilization of available resources of the two Parties, and other matters of mutual interest with respect to the protection and defense of the Canal.

5. To the extent possible consistent with its primary responsibility for the protection and defense of the Panama Canal, the United States of America will endeavor to maintain its armed forces in the Republic of Panama in normal times at a level not in excess of that of the armed forces of the United States of America in the territory of the former Canal Zone immediately prior to the entry into force of this Treaty.

*Article V: Principle of non-intervention.* Employees of the Panama Canal Commission, their dependents and designated contractors of the Panama Canal Commission, who are nationals of the United States of America, shall respect the laws of the Republic of Panama and shall abstain from any activity incompatible with the spirit of this Treaty. Accordingly, they shall abstain from any political activity in the Republic of Panama as well as from any intervention in the internal affairs of the Republic of Panama. The United States of America shall take all measures within its authority to ensure that the provisions of this Article are fulfilled.

. . .

[The treaty was accompanied by an annex concerning the transfer of activities of the Panama Canal Company and by an agreed minute which specified the agreements abrogated under Article I of the treaty.]

## Treaty concerning the permanent neutrality and operation of the Panama Canal

The United States of America and the Republic of Panama have agreed upon the following:

*Article I.* The Republic of Panama declares that the Canal, as an international transit waterway, shall be permanently neutral in accordance with the regime established in this Treaty. The same regime of neutrality shall apply to any other international waterway that may be built either partially or wholly in the territory of the Republic of Panama.

*Article II.* The Republic of Panama declares the neutrality of the Canal in order that both in time of peace and in time of war it shall remain secure and open to peaceful transit by the vessels of all nations on terms of entire equality, so that there will be no discrimination against any nation, or its citizens or subjects, concerning the conditions or charges of transit, or for any other reason, and so that the Canal, and therefore the Isthmus of Panama, shall not be the target of reprisals in any armed conflict between other nations of the world.

. . .

[The neutrality treaty was accompanied by an annex and a protocol. Several other documents, implementing the accord, accompanied the two treaties. These included maps of land and water areas, exchanges of notes concerning environmental questions, economic and military cooperation, and scientific activities, as well as technical agreements implementing the treaties.]

## The Caribbean

Following the Cuba crisis of 1962 (see p. 87), the obsessional concern of the United States with the danger to its security from the existence of a communist régime in Cuba gradually relaxed. As the failure of the Cuban revolution to export its ideology to its neighbours became manifest, and as the Cuban economy became deeply mired in dependence on massive subventions from the Soviet Union, the Cuban 'model' became increasingly unattractive to other Latin American countries. Although the U.S. remained highly sensitive to Russian moves in relation to Cuba (particularly to any signs of Russian military or naval build-up there), there were no further attempts by the U.S. after the Bay of Pigs fiasco to promote an anti-Castro rising on the island. Diplomatic relations between the two countries, severed in January 1961, were not renewed, but agreements were nevertheless reached in some of the most vexed issues in Cuban–American diplomacy.

*On 6 November 1965,* by an exchange of notes in Havana between the Cuban Foreign Ministry and the Swiss Embassy (representing U.S. interests), *Cuba and the United States concluded an agreement on refugees,* whereby Cuba permitted the departure for the U.S. of Cuban citizens: by

1973 more than a quarter of a million had left on planes to Miami. *On 15 February 1973*, by an exchange of notes carried out simultaneously in Washington and Havana, *Cuba and the United States concluded a Memorandum of Understanding on the Hijacking of Aircraft and Vessels* (p. 420). The agreement was designed to put a stop to the plague of hijackings in the area, and was effective in reducing significantly acts of air piracy. *On 27 April 1977 Cuba and the United States concluded a fisheries agreement*; and *on 16 December 1977 an agreement was reached concerning the maritime boundary between the United States and Cuba*.

Elsewhere in the Caribbean the United States generally succeeded in preventing the emergence of left-wing Governments. The liberal-democratic Government of Juan Bosch in the Dominican Republic was overthrown in 1963; an attempt in 1965 to reinstate it was thwarted by the intervention of twenty thousand U.S. troops. In Jamaica a reformist, mildly socialist Government, headed by Michael Manley, succeeded in maintaining power between 1972 and 1980 without direct U.S. interference; Manley's successor, Edward Seaga, reverted to a strongly pro-free enterprise, and pro-American policy. The closest to a pro-Castro Government in the region was the strange amalgam known as the 'New Jewel' movement, headed by Maurice Bishop, which held power in Grenada from 1979 to 1983. Following the U.S. intervention in Grenada in 1983, however, a pro-American Government was restored there.

The most notorious and embarrassing ally of the United States in the Caribbean was the violently repressive régime of 'Papa Doc' François Duvalier in Haiti after 1957. Although Democratic Administrations in Washington repeatedly condemned the Duvalier dictatorship for its human rights abuses, and sought to hinge the continuation of U.S. economic aid on the implementation of reforms, the country stagnated under Duvalier (and under his son 'Baby Doc' Jean-Claude Duvalier, who succeeded him in 1971), remaining the poorest State in the Americas. The horrors of daily life in Haiti prompted a large-scale illegal movement of refugees to the United States in the late 1970s; it was in an effort to staunch this unwelcome flow that *the United States and Haiti concluded an agreement on 23 September 1981 to stop clandestine migration of residents of Haiti to the United States*. On 7 February 1986, after the U.S. finally withdrew support from the régime, Jean-Claude Duvalier fled into exile, leaving behind an anarchic shambles of a State, in a condition of virtual disintegration after three decades of Duvalier misrule.

In the Caribbean, as elsewhere in Latin America, ambitious schemes were launched for economic integration; but as in other cases these were only partially successful. The initial impetus towards integration developed among the British colonial possessions in the Caribbean after the Second World War. The British Government had proposed a federation of the British West Indian colonies in 1945 as a step towards eventual independence. After lengthy discussions the West Indies Federation came into existence on 3 January 1958. The members were Barbados, Jamaica, Trinidad and Tobago, the Leeward Islands (Antigua, St Kitts-Nevis, and Montserrat, but not the British Virgin Islands), and the Windward Islands (Grenada, Dominica, St Lucia, St Vincent and the Grenadines). The Federation enjoyed a considerable degree of internal self-government, but not full sovereignty. A referendum in Jamaica in September 1961 resulted in a vote in favour of withdrawal from the Federation. This effectively doomed the arrangement which was dissolved on 31 May 1962. Jamaica attained full independence on 6 August 1962. Other British colonies in the area followed it to independence in the 1960s and 1970s.

On *30 April 1968* Antigua, Barbados, Guyana (formerly British Guiana), and Trinidad and Tobago agreed to form the *Caribbean Free Trade Association (CARIFTA)*. They were later joined by other Caribbean States, including (in 1968) Jamaica. Barbados, Guyana, Jamaica, and Trinidad and Tobago signed a new agreement, the *Treaty of Chaguaramas on 4 July 1973; this established the Caribbean Community and Common Market (CARICOM)*. Other States joined subsequently. The association was, however, limited to former British-ruled territories. Haiti, much more economically backward than most CARICOM members, was not admitted (although it was granted observer status). CARICOM sought to establish a common external tariff and coordinated development policies. Mutual rivalries prevented the organization from achieving genuine economic integration; for seven years the Heads of Government of member States did not even meet; but after a conference in November 1982 there were some signs of a revivification of the enterprise.

## Cuba—United States Memorandum of Understanding on the hijacking of aircraft and vessels, Washington and Havana, 15 February 1973

Department of State
Washington
February 15, 1973

The Honorable
Jaroslav Zantovsky,
Chargé d'Affaires ad interim
of the Czechoslovak Socialist Republic.

Sir:

I refer to the Memorandum of Understanding on the hijacking of aircraft and vessels and other offenses which has resulted from conversations which have taken place between the Embassy of Switzerland, representative of the interests of the United States of America in Cuba, and representatives of the Government of the Republic of Cuba, the text of which is as follows:

. . .

The Government of the United States of America and the Government of the Republic of Cuba, on the bases of equality and strict reciprocity, agree:

*First*: Any person who hereafter seizes, removes, appropriates or diverts from its normal route or activities an aircraft or vessel registered under the laws of one of the parties and brings it to the territory of the other party shall be considered to have committed an offense and therefore shall either be returned to the party of registry of the aircraft or vessel to be tried by the courts of that party in conformity with its laws or be brought before the courts of the party whose territory he reached for trial in conformity with its laws for the offense punishable by the most severe penalty according to the circumstances and the seriousness of the acts to which this Article refers. In addition, the party whose territory is reached by the aircraft or vessel shall take all necessary steps to facilitate without delay the continuation of the journey of the passengers and crew innocent of the hijacking of the aircraft or vessel in question, with their belongings, as well as the journey of the aircraft or vessel itself with all goods carried with it, including any funds obtained by extortion or other illegal means, or the return of the foregoing to the territory of the first party; likewise, it shall take all steps to protect the physical integrity of the aircraft or vessel and all goods, carried with it, including any funds obtained by extortion or other illegal means, and the physical integrity of the passengers and crew innocent of the hijacking, and their belongings, while they are in its territory as a consequence of or in connection with the acts to which this Article refers.

In the event that the offenses referred to above are not punishable under the laws existing in the country to which the persons committing them arrived, the party in question shall be obligated, except in the case of minor offenses, to return the persons who have committed such acts, in accordance with the applicable legal procedures, to the territory of the other party to be tried by its courts in conformity with its laws.

*Second*: Each party shall try with a view to severe punishment in accordance with its laws any person who, within its territory, hereafter conspires to promote, or promotes, or prepares, or directs, or forms part of an expedition which from its territory or any other place carries out acts of violence or depredation against aircraft or vessels of any kind or registration coming from or going to the territory of the other party or who, within its territory, hereafter conspires to promote, or promotes, or prepares, or directs, or forms part of an expedition which from its territory or any other place carries out such acts or other similar unlawful acts in the territory of the other party.

*Third*: Each party shall apply strictly its own laws to any national of the other party who, coming from the territory of the other party, enters its territory, violating its laws as well as national and international requirements pertaining to immigration, health, customs and the like.

*Fourth*: The party in whose territory the perpetrators of the acts described in Article First arrive may take into consideration any extenuating or mitigating circumstances in those cases in which the persons responsible for the acts were being sought for strictly political reasons and were in real and imminent danger of death without a viable alternative for leaving the country, provided there was no financial extortion or physical injury to the members of the crew, passengers, or other persons in connection with the hijacking.

### Final Provisions

This Agreement may be amended or expanded by decision of the parties.

This Agreement shall be in force for five years and may be renewed for an equal term by express decision of the parties.

Either party may inform the other of its decision to terminate this Agreement at any time while it is in force by written denunciation submitted six months in advance.

This Agreement shall enter into force on the date agreed by the parties.

Done in English and Spanish texts which are equally authentic.

In compliance with the express instructions of my Government, I wish to convey its acceptance of the Memorandum of Understanding transcribed above, as well as its agreement that the simultaneous exchange of notes taking place in Washington between the Department of State and the Embassy of the Czechoslovak Socialist Republic, representative of the interests of the Republic of Cuba in the United States of America, and in Havana between the Embassy of Switzerland, representative of the interests of the United States of America in Cuba, and the Ministry of Foreign Relations, shall constitute the agreement on the hijacking of aircraft and vessels and other offenses between the Government of the United States of America and the Government of the Republic of Cuba, which shall take effect on the date of this note.

Accept, Sir, the renewed assurances of my high consideration.

William P. Rogers

[On the same date the Czechoslovak Ambassador in Washington, representing Cuban interests in the United States, replied to Secretary Rogers, confirming the Cuban Government's acceptance of the memorandum of understanding. A similar exchange took place on the same date in Havana between the Cuban Government and the Swiss Embassy, representing American interests in Cuba.]

# Agreement between Haiti and the United States to stop clandestine migration of residents of Haiti to the United States, Port-au-Prince, 23 September 1981

ERNEST H. PREEG (U.S. AMBASSADOR TO HAITI) TO EDOUARD FRANÇISQUE (HAITIAN MINISTER OF FOREIGN AFFAIRS), 23 SEPTEMBER 1981

Excellency:

I have the honor to refer to the mutual

concern of the Governments of the United States and of the Republic of Haiti to stop the clandestine migration of numerous residents of Haiti to the United States and to the mutual desire of our two countries to cooperate to stop such illegal migration.

The United States Government confirms the understandings discussed by representatives of our two Governments for the establishment of a cooperative program of interdiction and selective return to Haiti of certain Haitian migrants and vessels involved in illegal transport of persons coming from Haiti.

Having regard to the need for international cooperation regarding law enforcement measures taken with respect to vessels on the high seas and the international obligations mandated in the protocol relating to the status of refugees done at New York 31 January 1967, the United States Government confirms with the Government of the Republic of Haiti its understanding of the following points of agreement:

Upon boarding a Haitian flag vessel, in accordance with this agreement, the authorities of the United States Government may address inquiries, examine documents and take such measures as are necessary to establish the registry, condition and destination of the vessel and the status of those on board the vessel. When these measures suggest that an offense against United States immigration laws or appropriate Haitian laws has been or is being committed, the Government of the Republic of Haiti consents to the detention on the high seas by the United States Coast Guard of the vessels and persons found on board.

The Government of Haiti agrees to permit upon prior notification the return of detained vessels and persons to a Haitian port, or if circumstances permit, the United States Government will release such vessels and migrants on the high seas to representatives of the Government of the Republic of Haiti.

The Government of the Republic of Haiti also agrees in the case of a U.S. flag vessel, outbound from Haiti, and engaged in such illegal trafficking, to permit, upon prior notification, the return to a Haitian port of that vessel and those aboard.

In any case where a Haitian flag vessel is detained, the authorities of the United States Government shall promptly inform the authorities of the Government of the Republic of Haiti of the action taken and shall keep them fully informed of any subsequent developments.

The Government of the Republic of Haiti agrees, to the extent permitted by Haitian law, to prosecute illegal traffickers of Haitian migrants who do not have requisite permission to enter the country of the vessel's destination and to confiscate Haitian vessels or stateless vessels involved in such trafficking. The United States Government likewise agrees, to the extent permitted by United States law, to prosecute traffickers of United States nationality and to confiscate United States vessels engaged in such trafficking.

The Government of the United States agrees to the presence of a representative of the Navy of the Republic of Haiti as liaison aboard any United States vessel engaged in the implementation of this cooperative program.

The United States Government appreciates the assurances which it has received from the Government of the Republic of Haiti that Haitians returned to their country and who are not traffickers will not be subject to prosecution for illegal departure.

It is understood that under these arrangements the United States Government does not intend to return to Haiti any Haitian migrants whom the United States authorities determine to qualify for refugee status.

In furtherance of this cooperative undertaking the United States Government formally requests the Government of the Republic of Haiti's consent to the boarding by the authorities of the United States Government of private Haitian flag vessels in which such authorities have reason to believe that the vessels may be involved in the irregular carriage of passengers outbound from Haiti.

I have the honor to propose that, if the foregoing is acceptable to the Government of the Republic of Haiti, this note and your Excellency's confirmatory reply constitute an agreement between the United States Government and the Government of the Republic of Haiti which shall enter into force on the date of your reply and shall continue in force until six months from the date either Government gives notice to the other of its intention to terminate the agreement.

Accept, Excellency, the renewed assurances of my highest consideration.

[The Haitian Foreign Minister sent a confirmatory reply on the same date.]

## South America

The movement for integration in South America, like the similar efforts in Central America and the Caribbean, achieved results which, while impressive on paper, failed to fulfil the hopes of its initiators. The idea of Latin American unity dates back at least to the period of the independence wars and the Pan-American vision of the Liberator, Simón Bolívar. After the Second World War the United Nations Economic Commission for Latin America sponsored moves towards economic coordination. A *Latin American Free Trade Association* (LAFTA) came into existence with the signature of the *Montevideo Treaty on 18 February 1961*. LAFTA made disappointingly slow progress, however, and on *12 August 1980 a new Montevideo Treaty was signed, establishing the Latin American Integration Association* (ALADI). These treaties sought to achieve tariff reductions among members, but since only a small fraction of their trade was with other members the significance of the arrangement was slight. The original signatories of the second Montevideo Treaty were Argentina, Bolivia, Brazil, Chile, Colombia, Ecuador, Mexico, Paraguay, Peru, Uruguay, and Venezuela.

Most of these States as well as some smaller Central American and Caribbean States (including Cuba) signed the *Panama Convention, 17 October 1975*, establishing the *Latin American Economic System* (SELA) which sought to create 'a permanent system of intra-regional economic and social co-operation'. The convention also declared that it was 'imperative to promote greater unity among Latin American countries'. SELA inaugurated an elaborate bureaucratic apparatus in order to achieve these ambitious ends. Once again, however, the results were unimpressive.

Although these large schemes for integration at the sub-continental level came to little, more limited proposals for cooperation at the sub-regional level made some headway.

*The Andean Group* was established by the *Cartagena Agreement, 26 May 1969*, signed by Bolivia, Chile, Colombia, Ecuador, Peru, and (later)

Venezuela. A number of further agreements were signed by five members of the group (the exception was Chile). These included a *Treaty for the creation of the Andean Reserve Fund, 12 November 1976*; a *Treaty creating the Court of Justice of the Cartagena Agreement, signed at Cartagena on 28 May 1979*, almost exactly ten years after the original agreement; a *Treaty establishing the Andean Parliament, signed at La Paz on 25 October 1979*; and an *Agreement establishing the Andean Council, 12 November 1979*. Chile's failure to sign these subsequent treaties indicates the limitations of the arrangement. (Chile withdrew altogether in 1977.) Nationalist antagonisms between members, particularly between Argentina and Chile (see below) remained rife, and pulled them in different directions, preventing progress towards true integration.

The *River Plate Basin Development Group was established by a treaty signed at Brasília, 23 April 1969*. The stated objects included 'harmonious development and physical integration'. The members were Argentina, Bolivia, Brazil, Paraguay and Uruguay.

The *Treaty for Amazonian Cooperation, 3 July 1978*, was signed at Brasília by Bolivia, Brazil, Colombia, Ecuador, Guyana, Peru, Surinam and Venezuela. On *24 October 1980* the pact members adopted the *Belém Declaration*, affirming their intention to cooperate in the development of the Amazon region.

More promising than some of these rhetorical declarations were narrower practical projects transcending national boundaries. Of these, perhaps the most important, certainly the most impressive in its physical results, was the series of agreements between Argentina, Brazil and Paraguay for the construction of the Itaipú Dam on the Paraná River, where the borders of the three countries meet. This was said to be the largest construction project in the world, certainly in the sub-continent, and when complete would supply large quantities of hydro-electric energy to Brazil and Paraguay.

In spite of their professions of enthusiasm for Latin American unity, many of the States of the sub-continent continued to harbour territorial claims against their neighbours. Efforts, especially by the Organization of American States, to moderate disputes among States met with occasional success, but rarely brought permanent agreements.

Two of the longest-standing territorial disputes in South America were those between Britain and Venezuela concerning British Guiana (later Guyana), and between Argentina and Chile concerning the Beagle Channel.

The British Guiana–Venezuela border dispute dates back to the middle of the nineteenth century. Venezuela claimed sovereignty over the Essequibo region in the west of British Guiana (comprising more than half of the entire territory). The United States, in the later part of the nineteenth century, strongly supported Venezuela, asserting the Monroe Doctrine, and demanding that Britain agree to arbitration. An arbitration award in 1899 was largely favourable to Britain and seemed to end the dispute. It was revived in 1962 by Venezuela which renewed its claim as the British colony approached independence. *On 17 February 1966 Britain and Venezuela signed an agreement on procedure for resolving the boundary dispute* (p. 426). Shortly thereafter, on 26 May 1966, British Guiana became independent, taking the name Guyana. By 1970 the Mixed Commission, established under the accord, had failed to reach agreement. Guyana and Venezuela did, however, approve a twelve-year moratorium during which Venezuela would not pursue its claim. At the end of the period a number of border incidents took place. Guyana sought a ruling from the International Court of Justice, but Venezuela demanded recourse to mediation by the U.N. Secretary-General. The two countries agreed to such mediation in March 1983. By the summer of 1987, however, no substantive resolution of the dispute had been attained – well over a century after its initiation.

Hardly less antique was the Beagle Channel dispute between Argentina and Chile which dated back to 1881. The Beagle Channel (discovered by Charles Darwin's *Beagle* in 1830) connects the Atlantic to the Pacific at the south of Tierra del Fuego. On 28 May 1902 Argentina and Chile acceded to a General Treaty of Arbitration under which they signed a *compromis* (see p. 15) in London on 22 July 1971. The British Government was appointed arbitrator and in turn appointed an arbitration court composed of five members (an American, a Briton, a Frenchman, a Nigerian, and a Swede). The arbitrator's decision, rendered on 18 April 1977, was broadly favourable to Chilean territorial claims.

But the arbitration award did not end the matter. On 25 January 1978 the Argentine Foreign Minister informed the Chilean Ambassador that Argentina had 'decided to declare the award insuperably null and void, in accordance with international law'. The dispute severely strained relations between Chile and Argentina. After further exchanges the two countries agreed to accept the mediation of the Holy See; an agreement accepting Papal mediation was signed in Montevideo on 8 January 1979 (p. 428). On 12 December 1980 the Papal proposal for a settlement of the dispute was issued (after the two countries had seemed to come close to war over the question). The Papal proposal confirmed Chilean sovereignty over three disputed islands; Argentina, however, was recognized as having maritime jurisdiction over waters on the Atlantic side of the channel. After further diplomatic activity, the Papal award provided a basis for agreement. On 23 January 1984 Argentina and Chile signed a preliminary Treaty of Peace and Friendship. *On 29 November 1984 a final Peace and Friendship Treaty was signed at the Vatican* under the auspices of Pope John Paul II (p. 429).

# British–Venezuelan Agreement concerning the frontier between British Guiana and Venezuela, Geneva, 17 February 1966

The Government of the United Kingdom of Great Britain and Northern Ireland, in consultation with the Government of British Guiana, and the Government of Venezuela;

Taking into account the forthcoming independence of British Guiana;

Recognizing that closer cooperation between British Guiana and Venezuela could bring benefit to both countries;

Convinced that any outstanding controversy between the United Kingdom and British Guiana on the one hand and Venezuela on the other would prejudice the furtherance of such cooperation and should therefore be amicably resolved in a manner acceptable to both parties;

In conformity with the agenda that was agreed for the governmental conversations concerning the controversy between Venezuela and the United Kingdom over the frontier with British Guiana, in accordance with the joint communiqué of 7 November, 1963, have reached the following agreement to resolve the present controversy:

*Article I.* A Mixed Commission shall be established with the task of seeking satisfactory solutions for the practical settlement of the controversy between Venezuela and the United Kingdom which has arisen as the result of the Venezuelan contention that the Arbitral Award of 1899 about the frontier between British Guiana and Venezuela is null and void.

*Article II.* 1. Within two months of the entry into force of this Agreement, two representatives shall be appointed to the Mixed Commission by the Government of British Guiana and two by the Government of Venezuela.

2. The Government appointing a representative may at any time replace him, and shall do so immediately should one or both of its representatives be unable to act through illness or death or any other cause.

3. The Mixed Commission may by agreement between the representatives appoint experts to assist the Mixed Commission, either generally or in relation to any individual matter under consideration by the Mixed Commission.

*Article III.* The Mixed Commission shall present interim reports at intervals of six months from the date of its first meeting.

*Article IV.* 1. If, within a period of four years from the date of this Agreement, the Mixed Commission should not have arrived at a full agreement for the solution of the controversy it shall, in its final report, refer to the Government of

Guyana and the Government of Venezuela any outstanding questions. Those Governments shall without delay choose one of the means of peaceful settlement provided in Article 33 of the Charter of the United Nations.

2. If, within three months of receiving the final report, the Government of Guyana and the Government of Venezuela should not have reached agreement regarding the choice of one of the means of settlement provided in Article 33 of the Charter of the United Nations, they shall refer the decision as to the means of settlement to an appropriate international organ upon which they both agree or, failing agreement on this point, to the Secretary-General of the United Nations. If the means so chosen do not lead to a solution of the controversy, the said organ or, as the case may be, the Secretary-General of the United Nations shall choose another of the means stipulated in Article 33 of the Charter of the United Nations, and so on until the controversy has been resolved or until all the means of peaceful settlement there contemplated have been exhausted.

*Article V.* 1. In order to facilitate the greatest possible measure of cooperation and mutual understanding, nothing contained in this Agreement shall be interpreted as a renunciation or diminution by the United Kingdom, British Guiana or Venezuela of any basis of claim to territorial sovereignty in the territories of Venezuela or British Guiana, or of any previously asserted rights of or claims to such territorial sovereignty, or as prejudicing their position as regards their recognition or non-recognition of a right of, claim or basis of claim by any of them to such territorial sovereignty.

2. No acts or activities taking place while this Agreement is in force shall constitute a basis for asserting, supporting or denying a claim to territorial sovereignty in the territories of Venezuela or British Guiana or create any rights of sovereignty in those territories, except in so far as such acts or activities result from

any agreement reached by the Mixed Commission and accepted in writing by the Government of Guyana and the Government of Venezuela. No new claim, or enlargement of an existing claim, to territorial sovereignty in those territories shall be asserted while this Agreement is in force, nor shall any claim whatsoever be asserted otherwise than in the Mixed Commission while that Commission is in being.

*Article VI.* The Mixed Commission shall hold its first meeting at a date and place to be agreed between the Governments of British Guiana and Venezuela. This meeting shall take place as soon as possible after its members have been appointed. Thereafter the Mixed Commission shall meet as and when agreed between the representatives.

*Article VII.* This Agreement shall enter into force on the date of its signature.

*Article VIII.* Upon the attainment of independence by British Guiana, the Government of Guyana shall thereafter be a party to this Agreement, in addition to the Government of the United Kingdom of Great Britain and Northern Ireland and the Government of Venezuela.

In witness whereof the undersigned, being duly authorized thereto by their respective Governments, have signed this Agreement.

Done in duplicate at Geneva this 17th day of February, 1966, in the English and Spanish languages, both texts being equally authoritative.

For the Government of the United Kingdom of Great Britain and Northern Ireland:
MICHAEL STEWART
Secretary of State for Foreign Affairs

L.F.S. BURNHAM
Prime Minister of British Guiana

For the Government of Venezuela:
IGNACIO IRIBARREN BORGES
Minister for Foreign Affairs

# Beagle Channel Dispute: Agreement between Argentina and Chile Accepting Papal Mediation, Montevideo, 8 January 1979

## Document I

1. At the invitation of His Eminence Antonio Cardinal Samore, Special Representative of His Holiness Pope John Paul II for a peace mission agreed to by the Governments of the Argentine Republic and of the Republic of Chile, a meeting was held at Montevideo between the Ministers for Foreign Affairs of the two Republics, His Excellency Mr Carlos W. Pastor, and His Excellency Mr Hernán Cubillos Sallato, who, having analysed the dispute and taking into account:

2. That His Holiness Pope John Paul II, in his message to the Presidents of the two countries on 11 December 1978, expressed his conviction that a calm and responsible examination of the problem will make it possible to fulfil 'the requirements of justice, equity and prudence as a sure and stable basis for the fraternal coexistence' of the two peoples;

3. That in his address to the College of Cardinals, on 22 December 1978, the Holy Father recalled the concerns and the hopes he had already expressed with regard to the search for a means of safeguarding peace, which is keenly desired by the peoples of both countries;

4. That His Holiness Pope John Paul II expressed the desire to send to the capitals of the two States a Special Representative to obtain more direct and concrete information on the positions of the two sides and to contribute to the achievement of a peaceful settlement of the dispute;

5. That that noble initiative was accepted by both Governments;

6. That since 26 December 1978 His Eminence Antonio Cardinal Samore, who was appointed to carry out this peace mission, has held talks with the highest authorities of the two countries and with their closest associates;

7. That on 1 January, which by pontifical order was celebrated as 'World Peace Day', His Holiness Pope John Paul II referred to this delicate situation and expressed the hope that the authorities of the two countries, adopting a forward-looking, balanced and courageous approach, would take the path of peace and would be able to achieve, as soon as possible, the goal of a just and honourable settlement;

8. Declare that the two Governments, through this agreement, reiterate their appreciation to the Supreme Pontiff, John Paul II, for his dispatch of a Special Representative. They decide to avail themselves of the Holy See's offer to intervene and, with a view to deriving the greatest benefit from this gesture by the Holy See in making itself available, agree to request it to act as mediator for the purpose of guiding them in the negotiations and assisting them in the search for a settlement of the dispute, to which end the two Governments agreed to seek such method of peaceful settlement as they considered most appropriate. For that purpose, they will carefully take into account the positions maintained and expressed by the parties in the negotiations already held in connexion with the Act of Puerto Montt and the proceedings in pursuance of that Act.

9. The two Governments will inform the Holy See both of the terms of the dispute and of such background information and opinions as they deem relevant, especially those which were considered in the course of the various negotiations, the records, instruments and proposals of which will be placed at its disposal.

10. The two Governments declare that they will raise no objection to the expression by the Holy See, during these proceedings, of such ideas as its thorough

studies on all disputed aspects of the problem of the southern zone may suggest to it, with a view to contributing to a peaceful settlement acceptable to both parties. They declare their readiness to consider such ideas as the Holy See may express.

11. Accordingly, by this agreement which is concluded in the spirit of the norms laid down in international instruments for the preservation of peace, the two Governments associate themselves with the concern of His Holiness Pope John Paul II and consequently reaffirm their will to settle the outstanding issue through mediation.

Done at Montevideo, on 8 January 1979, and signed in six identical copies.

For the Government of the Argentine Republic:

Carlos W. PASTOR
Minister for Foreign Affairs and Worship

For the Government of the Republic of Chile:

Hernán CUBILLOS SALLATO
Minister for Foreign Affairs

## Document II

Antonio Cardinal Samore, Special Envoy of His Holiness Pope John Paul II, in accepting the request for mediation from the Governments of the Argentine Republic and of the Republic of Chile, asks that that request shall be accompanied by an undertaking that the two States will not resort to the use of force in their mutual relations, will bring about a gradual return to the military situation existing at the beginning of 1977 and will refrain from adopting measures that might impair harmony in any sector.

The Ministers for Foreign Affairs of the two Republics, His Excellency Mr Carlos Washington Pastor and His Excellency Mr Hernán Cubillos Sallato, signify their agreement on behalf of their respective Governments and join the Cardinal in signing six identical copies.

Done at Montevideo, on 8 January 1979.

[*Signed*] PASTOR, CUBILLOS, SAMORE

# Treaty of Peace and Friendship between Argentina and Chile, Vatican City, 29 November 1984

IN THE NAME OF ALMIGHTY GOD

The Government of the Argentine Republic and the Government of the Republic of Chile,

Mindful that on January 8th, 1979, they requested the intercession of the Holy See as Mediator in the dispute in the Southern Region, with the purpose of guiding them in their negotiations and assisting them in their search for a solution; and that, furthermore, they solicited the valuable assistance of the Holy See for the purpose of drawing a boundary line, that would determine their respective jurisdictions to the East and West, parting from the termination of the

already existing delimitation;

Convinced that it is the ineluctable duty of both Governments to express the aspirations to peace of their peoples;

Bearing in mind the Boundary Treaty of 1881, which establishes the unmovable basis of relations between the Argentine Republic and the Republic of Chile, as well as its complementary instruments and statements;

Reasserting the commitment always to solve their controversies by peaceful means and never to resort to the threat or use of force in their mutual relations;

Inspired by the purpose of intensifying economic cooperation and the physical integration of their respective countries;

Taking into account, most particularly, the 'Proposal of the Mediator, suggestions and advice', of December 12th, 1980;

Expressing, on behalf of their peoples, their thanks to His Holiness, Pope John Paul II, for his enlightened efforts to achieve a solution to the dispute and strengthen friendship and understanding between both nations;

Have resolved to conclude the following Treaty, which constitutes a compromise:

PEACE AND FRIENDSHIP

*Article 1.* The High Contracting Parties, responding to the basic interests of their peoples, solemnly reassert their commitment to preserve, reinforce, and develop their bonds of unalterable peace and perpetual friendship.

The Parties shall hold periodic consultative meetings in which they shall examine, most particularly, any event or situation which could lead to a disruption of harmony between them, they shall endeavour to avoid that a discrepancy in their points of view give rise to a controversy and shall suggest or adopt specific measures with a view to maintaining and strengthening good relations between the two countries.

*Article 2.* The Parties confirm their obligation to abstain from resorting directly or indirectly to any form of threat, or the use of force, or the adoption of any other measure which might alter harmony in any sector of their mutual relations.

Furthermore, they confirm their commitment always to employ peaceful means to solve all controversies, whatsoever their nature, which for any reason, have arisen or may arise between them, in conformity with the following provisions.

*Article 3.* If a controversy should arise, the Parties shall adopt appropriate measures in order to maintain the best general conditions of coexistence in all aspects of their relations, so as to prevent the controversy from becoming aggravated or prolonged.

. . .

[*Articles 4–6.* Conciliation procedures.

*Articles 7–11.* Delimitation of maritime boundary.

*Articles 12–13.* Economic cooperation and navigation arrangements in the Beagle Channel.]

FINAL PROVISIONS

*Article 14.* The Parties solemnly declare that the present Treaty constitutes the complete and definitive solution to the questions referred therein.

The boundary lines established by this Treaty constitute definitive and unmovable boundaries between the sovereignties of the Argentine Republic and the Republic of Chile. The Parties agree not to present claims or interpretations which are incompatible with the provisions of this Treaty.

*Article 15.* In the Antarctic, Articles 1 to 6 of the present Treaty shall apply. The remaining provisions in no way affect, or may be interpreted in a sense that may affect, directly or indirectly, the sovereignty, rights or legal positions of the Parties or delimitations in the Antarctic or in their adjacent maritime areas, including the soil and subsoil thereof.

*Article 16.* Taking up the generous offer of the Holy Father, the High Contracting Parties place the present Treaty under the spiritual protection of the Holy See.

. . .

[The treaty was accompanied by two annexes and by maps.]

Translation by Evelina Teubal de Alhadeff, © American Society of International Law.

## The South Atlantic

Before the 1980s the South Atlantic was not regarded as an area of significant strategic conflict. With the exception of the Beagle Channel dispute between Argentina and Chile, political claims in the area were not pressed with any great urgency. In Antarctica a number of States (including Argentina, Australia, Chile, France, New Zealand, Norway, the United Kingdom, and the U.S.S.R.) advanced territorial claims at various periods. But by the *Antarctic Treaty of 1 December 1959* twelve states with interests in the region agreed in effect (although not *strictu sensu*: see Article IV) to suspend all territorial claims and cooperate in the peaceful exploration and scientific investigation of the southern continent.

The Antarctic Treaty applied only to the area south of the sixtieth latitude: it did not therefore apply to the British-held or British-claimed islands north of that line. These included the South Orkney, South Shetland, and South Sandwich Islands, South Georgia, and the Falklands (the only ones with a permanent population).

The Falklands had been ruled by Britain since 1832; they had a population of about two thousand 'kelpers', nearly all of British origin. Argentina had a long-standing claim to the Falklands (which it called the Malvinas), but nevertheless was prepared to make practical arrangements for communications and supplies to the islands from Argentina. An *Agreement between Argentina and Britain concerning the Falkland Islands was concluded in Buenos Aires in July–August 1971* (p. 433). This did not deal with the question of sovereignty but merely with practical questions of access and technical cooperation. Nevertheless it betokened a readiness by both sides to seek a civilized solution to the dispute.

On 2 April 1982 Argentina invaded and occupied the islands and declared their unification with Argentina. A British task force sailed for the South Atlantic a few days later. Mediation efforts by the United Nations, the United States, and Chile all failed. The O.A.S. gave verbal support to Argentina's claim, but called for a negotiated settlement. Hostilities broke out at the end of April, and a full-scale war in and around the Falklands (but not on the Argentine mainland) developed. By 5 June the Argentine forces on the Falklands had surrendered.

The loss of the Falklands had the salutary consequence in Argentina of bringing about the collapse of the discredited military régime and its eventual replacement by an elected civilian Government. Even after the loss of the war, however, Argentina refused to acknowledge British sovereignty over the Falklands. Efforts to improve relations between

Britain and Argentina achieved little or nothing. Diplomatic relations remained suspended. Britain maintained an expensive garrison (outnumbering civilian residents by two to one) and built a new airport on the island. In the autumn of 1986 tension remained high as a result of incidents involving Argentine fishing boats within the 'exclusion zone' around the Falklands declared by Britain; a negotiated agreement seemed very far away.

# The Antarctic Treaty, Washington, 1 December 1959

The Governments of Argentina, Australia, Belgium, Chile, the French Republic, Japan, New Zealand, Norway, the Union of South Africa, the Union of Soviet Socialist Republics, the United Kingdom of Great Britain and Northern Ireland, and the United States of America,

Recognizing that it is in the interest of all mankind that Antarctica shall continue forever to be used exclusively for peaceful purposes and shall not become the scene or object of international discord;

Acknowledging the substantial contributions to scientific knowledge resulting from international cooperation in scientific investigation in Antarctica;

Convinced that the establishment of a firm foundation for the continuation and development of such cooperation on the basis of freedom of scientific investigation in Antarctica as applied during the International Geophysical Year accords with the interests of science and the progress of all mankind;

Convinced also that a treaty ensuring the use of Antarctica for peaceful purposes only and the continuance of international harmony in Antarctica will further the purposes and principles embodied in the Charter of the United Nations;

Have agreed as follows:

*Article I.* 1. Antarctica shall be used for peaceful purposes only. There shall be prohibited, *inter alia*, any measures of a military nature, such as the establishment of military bases and fortifications, the carrying out of military maneuvers, as well as the testing of any type of weapons.

2. The present Treaty shall not prevent the use of military personnel or equipment for scientific research or for any other peaceful purpose.

*Article II.* Freedom of scientific investigation in Antarctica and cooperation toward that end, as applied during the International Geophysical Year, shall continue, subject to the provisions of the present Treaty.

*Article III.* 1. In order to promote international cooperation in scientific investigation in Antarctica, as provided for in Article II of the present Treaty, the Contracting Parties agree that, to the greatest extent feasible and practicable:

(a) information regarding plans for scientific programs in Antarctica shall be exchanged to permit maximum economy and efficiency of operations;

(b) scientific personnel shall be exchanged in Antarctica between expeditions and stations;

(c) scientific observations and results from Antarctica shall be exchanged and made freely available.

2. In implementing this Article, every encouragement shall be given to the establishment of cooperative working relations with those Specialized Agencies of the United Nations and other inter-

LATIN AMERICA AND THE SOUTH ATLANTIC   433

national organizations having a scientific or technical interest in Antarctica.

*Article IV.* 1. Nothing contained in the present Treaty shall be interpreted as:

(a) a renunciation by any Contracting Party of previously asserted rights of or claims to territorial sovereignty in Antarctica;

(b) a renunciation or diminution by any Contracting Party of any basis of claim to territorial sovereignty in Antarctica which it may have whether as a result of its activities or those of its nationals in Antarctica, or otherwise;

(c) prejudicing the position of any Contracting Party as regards its recognition or non-recognition of any other State's right of or claim or basis of claim to territorial sovereignty in Antarctica.

2. No acts or activities taking place while the present Treaty is in force shall constitute a basis for asserting, supporting or denying a claim to territorial sovereignty in Antarctica or create any rights of sovereignty in Antarctica. No new claim, or enlargement of an existing claim, to territorial sovereignty in Antarctica shall be asserted while the present Treaty is in force.

*Article V.* 1. Any nuclear explosions in Antarctica and the disposal there of radioactive waste material shall be prohibited.

2. In the event of the conclusion of international agreements concerning the use of nuclear energy, including nuclear explosions and the disposal of radioactive waste material, to which all of the Contracting Parties whose representatives are entitled to participate in the meetings provided for under Article IX are parties, the rules established under such agreements shall apply in Antarctica.

*Article VI.* The provisions of the present Treaty shall apply to the area south of 60° South Latitude, including all ice shelves, but nothing in the present Treaty shall prejudice or in any way affect the rights, or the exercise of the rights, of any State under international law with regard to the high seas within that area.

. . .

# Agreement between Argentina and Britain concerning the Falkland Islands, Buenos Aires, July–August 1971

## Joint Statement

Special conversations were continued in Buenos Aires from the 21st until the 30th of June 1971 about communications and movement between the Argentine mainland and the Falkland Islands by delegations of the Government of the United Kingdom of Great Britain and Northern Ireland and of the Argentine Republic, the former including participants from the Islands. The conversations were within the general framework of the negotiations recommended by Resolution No. 2065 (XX) of the General Assembly of the United Nations and in accordance with letters addressed to the Secretary-General of the Organization by the Permanent Representatives of both countries on the 21st of November 1969 and the 11th of December 1970.

The delegates concluded that, subject to the approval of their Governments, the following measures should be adopted on the understanding that they may contribute to the process of a definitive solution to the dispute between the two Governments over the Islands which is referred to in Resolution No. 2065 (XX) mentioned above.

1. In order to deal with questions which might arise over the setting up and promotion of communications between the Argentine mainland and the Falkland Islands in both directions, including questions relating to the movement of persons, those which might arise for residents of the Islands while they were on the mainland and those concerning residents of the mainland while they were in the Islands, a special consultative committee should be set up, consisting of representatives of the Argentine Ministry of Foreign Affairs and the British Embassy, with its headquarters in Buenos Aires. The Committee should have its representatives in Port Stanley who would keep it informed.

2. The Argentine Government should issue a document, in the form annexed, to residents of the Falkland Islands irrespective of their nationality who wished to travel to the Argentine mainland, which would allow them free movement within it. A document in the same form issued by the Argentine Government should be the only document needed by residents of the Argentine mainland for journeys to the Falkland Islands.

3. Residents in the Falkland Islands should be exempted by the Argentine Government from all duties, taxes, and any other obligations arising as a result of activities in the Falkland Islands. In addition, residents of the Falkland Islands who go to the Argentine mainland in order to provide services connected with communications should be exempt from taxes on their salaries and other emoluments which they receive from their British employers. The British Government should make no claim on residents of the Argentine mainland who provide services in the Falkland Islands for activities related to communications for taxes on their salaries and other emoluments which they receive from their Argentine employers.

4. The Argentine Government should take the necessary practical measures so that the normal luggage of residents of the Falkland Islands who travel between the Falkland Islands and the Argentine mainland in either direction should be free from the payment of all duties and taxes. Residents of the Falkland Islands should be exempted from the payment of all Argentine duties and taxes in respect of their luggage, household effects and motor cars passing directly through the Argentine mainland towards the Falkland Islands or going abroad through the Argentine mainland. The British Government should take the necessary measures so that the normal luggage of residents of the Argentine mainland who travel between the Argentine mainland and the Falkland Islands in either direction will be exempted from the payment of all duties and taxes.

5. The Argentine Government should take the necessary measures so that each resident of the Islands who establishes a permanent residence on the Argentine mainland may bring in once only free of all duties and taxes all personal effects, household effects and a motor car. Equally, the British Government should take the necessary measures so that each resident on the Argentine mainland who establishes a permanent residence in the Falkland Islands, may bring in once only free of all duties and taxes all personal effects, household effects and a motor car.

6. The British and Argentine Governments should facilitate in the Falkland Islands and on the Argentine mainland respectively, the transit, residence and work of persons directly concerned with practical measures adopted in order to implement and promote communications and movement.

7. The British Government should take the necessary measures to arrange for a regular shipping service for passengers, cargo and mail between the Falkland Islands and the Argentine mainland.

8. The Argentine Government should take the necessary measures to arrange for a regular service of weekly frequency by air for passengers, cargo and mail between the Argentine mainland and the Falkland Islands.

9. Pending the completion of the

airfield at Port Stanley, the Argentine Government should provide a temporary service by amphibian aircraft between the Argentine mainland and the Falkland Islands for passengers, cargo and mail. This service should be reviewed from time to time in the light of progress in the construction of the airfield mentioned above.

10. Both Governments should co-operate over the simplification of administrative practices, regulations and documentation for sea and air transport bearing in mind the need to promote and speed up communications.

11. In order to facilitate the movement of persons born in the Falkland Islands, the Argentine Government should take the necessary measures to exempt them for all obligations related to enlistment and military service. The British Government should declare that in the Falkland Islands no obligations for enlistment for military service exist.

12. Both Governments should study and exchange views on measures to facilitate trade and to permit a greater ease of commercial transactions.

13. The British and Argentine Governments should take the necessary measures so that postal, telegraphic and telephone communications in both directions between the Argentine mainland and the Falkland Islands are as effective and expeditious as possible.

14. The tariff for postal, telegraphic and telephone communications in both directions between the Argentine mainland and the Falkland Islands should be at a rate equivalent to the internal rate at the place of origin of the communications.

15. Postage stamps on mail travelling between the Argentine mainland and the Falkland Islands in either direction should be cancelled with a mark referring to this joint statement. Mail bags should be similarly marked.

16. The Argentine Government should be prepared to cooperate in the health, educational, agricultural and technical fields if so requested. The Argentine Government should arrange for places to be available in schools on the Argentine mainland for the children of residents of the Falkland Islands and should offer scholarships which should be published from time to time, the number of which should be decided upon in the light of local requirements. Both Governments should continue to exchange views on the matters referred to in this paragraph.

17. Conversations should be continued through the customary diplomatic channels and the next meeting should be held in Port Stanley in 1972.

18. If either Government should decide to terminate the measures referred to above, it should give six months' notice of its decision to the other Government.

INITIALLED in Buenos Aires on the 1st day of July 1971 by the Heads of the respective delegations.

[An annex to the declaration gave the form of the identity document mentioned in paragraph 2.]

## The British Chargé d'Affaires ad interim at Buenos Aires to the Argentine Minister for Foreign Affairs and Worship

British Embassy
Buenos Aires
5 August, 1971

Your Excellency,

I have the honour to refer to the Resolution of the General Assembly of the United Nations number 2065 (XX) of the 16th of December 1965 and the letters dated the 21st of November 1969 and the 11th of December 1970 from the Permanent Representatives to the United Nations of the United Kingdom of Great Britain and Northern Ireland and the Argentine Republic addressed to the Secretary-General of the Organization on the question of the Falkland Islands, and also to the Joint Statement on communications and movement between the Argentine mainland and the Falkland Islands initialled in Buenos Aires by the representatives of the two Governments on the 1st of July 1971, and to inform

Your Excellency that the Government of the United Kingdom are prepared to conclude an agreement with the Government of the Argentine Republic in the following terms:

1. (a) Since divergence remains between the two Governments regarding the circumstances that should exist for a definitive solution to the dispute concerning sovereignty over the Falkland Islands, nothing contained in the Joint Statement referred to above and approved by our two Governments on today's date shall be interpreted as:

(i) a renunciation by either Government of any right of territorial sovereignty over the Falkland Islands; or

(ii) a recognition of or support for the other Government's position with regard to territorial sovereignty over the Falkland Islands.

(b) No acts or activities taking place as a consequence of the Joint Statement referred to above having been put into operation and while it is in operation shall constitute a basis for asserting, supporting, or denying the position of either Government with regard to territorial sovereignty over the Falkland Islands.

2. Either Government may denounce this agreement subject to six months' prior notice in writing.

If the foregoing is acceptable to the Government of the Argentine Republic, I have the honour to propose that this Note together with Your Excellency's reply in that sense shall constitute an agreement between the two Governments which shall enter into force on the date of your reply.

I avail myself of this opportunity to renew to Your Excellency the assurances of my highest consideration.

T. Peters
Her Majesty's Chargé d'Affaires

His Excellency Dr Luis María de
Pablo Pardo
Minister for Foreign Affairs and Worship
Buenos Aires

[The Argentine Minister of Foreign Affairs and Worship replied on the same date, recapitulating the above letter and confirming that the notes together constituted an agreement.]

# X · Détente and arms control

During the height of the cold war period in the 1950s and 1960s, the Western Powers on the one hand and the Communist Powers on the other tended to view every international conflict among smaller States in terms of a global struggle between the 'Free World' and the 'Communist World'. The neutral stance of States calling themselves 'non-aligned' was regarded with suspicion by both sides. But a more traditional division in international relations, often loosely referred to as the 'balance of power', was never quite lost sight of. It made itself felt in the mutual recognition by the 'Great Powers', especially the 'superpowers', the United States and the Soviet Union, that they shared some common interests in their relations with each other and with other States. The most fundamental of these interests is to keep control of issues of war and peace in the hands of Washington and Moscow. Such 'superpower' control remains imperfect. Neither the United States nor the U.S.S.R. wishes to be dragged into conflicts not of their choosing and forced into extreme positions created by the independent policies of other States. Above all, the United States and the Soviet Union are not prepared to risk a nuclear war of destruction between them as a result of decisions taken outside the White House and the Kremlin.

From 1945 until September 1949 the United States enjoyed a nuclear monopoly. The secret Anglo-American wartime executive agreements in Quebec, 19 August 1943, and Hyde Park, U.S.A., September 1944, did not survive Roosevelt, and cooperation and the sharing of atomic information with Britain ceased with the enacting of the United States' Atomic Energy Act (the McMahon Act) in August 1946. But the United States could not prevent the spread of atomic weaponry. Efforts in the

United Nations to secure international control and inspection over the manufacture of atomic energy failed as the U.S.S.R. was determined to make its own bomb and to catch up on the U.S. lead. The U.S.S.R. became the second Atomic Power in the autumn of 1949. Britain was equally determined to attain the status of Atomic Power (the ticket to 'Great Power' status) and reached its goal in October 1952. By November 1952, the U.S. had tested the first hydrogen bomb. France, excluded by the United States and Britain from a share in nuclear weapon technology, succeeded in making its own atomic bomb by 1960.

Meantime, British collaboration with the United States was resumed in 1957, the year after Britain had independently made its own hydrogen bomb. In March 1957 at Bermuda, President Eisenhower agreed in principle to provide guided missiles for Britain's nuclear warheads. An amendment to the Atomic Energy Act gave the President discretion to exchange atomic information with any ally making substantial and material contributions to U.S. defence. Britain accepted U.S. missile bases, though their use in an emergency was to be a joint decision. In return for the close alliance relationship, the U.S. in February 1958 agreed to exchange atomic information, which in practice meant help and cooperation in developing a missile for delivery of the nuclear warhead. The intended missile 'Skybolt' was cancelled, but Macmillan and Kennedy concluded the *Nassau Agreement, December 1962*, whereby American Polaris missiles would be placed in Royal Navy submarines. The missile submarines were to be within the NATO framework, but the British Government retained the ultimate control of these ships. Thus the Polaris submarines, though dependent on a U.S. rocket, gave Britain an independent nuclear deterrent, albeit a small one. De Gaulle rejected dependence on the U.S. for missiles and developed a small independent nuclear capacity for France, the so-called 'force de frappe'. Shortly after the Nassau Agreement he vetoed Britain's application to join the European Economic Community on the ground that Britain preferred a junior partnership with the U.S. to Western European alignment (see p. 241).

During the early 1960s Britain enjoyed a special position. Although not a superpower, Britain engaged in superpower diplomacy. When the Soviet Union and the United States conducted arms control negotiations, Britain acted as a third negotiating partner. The nuclear Power not invited was de Gaulle's France. China was also left out when the Communist Chinese succeeded in their first atomic test in October 1964. Both France and China refused to accept the terms of arms control worked out in the treaties sponsored by the United States, the Soviet Union and Britain. The

Soviet Union had apparently promised help in nuclear manufacture to China in 1957, but after 1960 this assistance came to a virtual halt. Thus both the United States and the Soviet Union, whilst establishing bases among allies, did not share atomic secrets with these allies (except to a limited extent with Britain). In practice therefore, both superpowers followed a non-proliferation policy. They engaged in a nuclear armaments race with each other while doing their best to prevent other States from acquiring nuclear weapon technology.

## From 'peaceful coexistence' to 'détente', 1963–70

The term 'peaceful coexistence' had a long pedigree, but it became part of the current vocabulary of propaganda and diplomacy in the decade after Stalin's death in 1953. It was used, particularly by Soviet spokesmen, to denote the Soviet Union's readiness to live with the capitalist powers in a condition, if not of harmony, then of peaceful rivalry. The doctrine carried with it the corollary that the two sides should eschew territorial aggrandizement and accept the status quo, particularly in Europe. It also seemed to suggest a readiness to curb the arms race. Although such rhetoric struck a responsive chord in the West, some sceptics pointed to Soviet actions in Berlin in 1958 or Cuba in 1962 as indicating that the U.S.S.R. in reality continued to seek to expand its sphere of influence rather than accept the status quo. Moreover, acceptance of the territorial status quo in Europe, particularly in Germany, was regarded in the 1950s and early 1960s by many Western statesmen as unacceptable. As for the arms race, some Western strategic analysts argued that, while the West undoubtedly had the edge in the development of missiles and advanced technological weaponry, the continuation of such a Western pre-ponderance was essential in order to counteract the overwhelming Soviet superiority in conventional forces in Europe.

The first post-war 'summit' conference took place at Geneva between 18 and 23 July 1955 (this was the first top-level conference of which the term 'summit' was used). The U.S.S.R. was represented by Khrushchev and Bulganin, the U.S.A. by Eisenhower, the U.K. by Eden, and France by Edgar Faure. Although there was much inspired talk of a 'spirit of Geneva', the conference in fact achieved next to nothing. The late 1950s were years of high East–West tension, with the succession of crises in Hungary, Suez, and Berlin, played out against the backdrop of repeated large-scale nuclear bomb tests in the atmosphere. The success of the Soviet Union in October 1957 in launching the first artificial satellite into space (followed in April 1961 by the Soviet launching of the first man into space) placed a question mark against Western assumptions of continued technological superiority. A second summit was eventually scheduled for May 1960, but it was rudely broken off by Khrushchev, ostensibly in protest against the U.S.A.'s dispatch of U-2 spy planes over Soviet territory (one was shot down shortly before the conference convened). A superpower summit meeting of Khrushchev and Kennedy took place in Vienna in June 1961 (henceforth the superpowers exhibited no interest in the notion of three- or four-power summits). This gave the two leaders an opportunity to size each other up, but the occasion was otherwise unproductive. The mutual testing of wills during the Cuban missile crisis of October 1962 (see p. 87) marked the climax of the cold war. The glimpse over the edge of the nuclear precipice seemed to sober both superpowers; thereafter tension slowly relaxed and a fitful process of negotiation evolved which gradually produced agreements.

The fears aroused in part by the Cuban missile crisis of an accidental outbreak of nuclear war arising through misunderstanding or faulty communications helped produce the first significant agreement between the superpowers: this was the *agreement on the establishment of a direct communications link between the United States and the Soviet Union*, 20 June 1963 (p. 441). The so-called 'hot line', designed to be used in urgent situations, would enable the Soviet and American leaders to communicate directly.

Shortly afterwards the United States, the Soviet Union and Britain signed the *treaty banning nuclear weapon tests in the atmosphere, in outer space, and under water, 5 August 1963* (p. 442). During the following two years this 'limited nuclear test ban' ('limited' since it did not ban underground tests) was signed by a further ninety States. By 1986 there were 114 signatories. But these did not include France and China which insisted on their right to carry out tests in the atmosphere.

The interest of both superpowers in limiting membership of the 'nuclear club' was reflected in the *Treaty on the non-proliferation of nuclear weapons*, which was concluded, after several years of negotiation, on *1 July 1968* (p. 443). The treaty bound nuclear powers not to transfer nuclear weapons to non-nuclear States and to refrain from assisting non-nuclear States from making such weapons; non-nuclear States undertook not to receive or manufacture nuclear weapons. The treaty provided for an international system of safeguards, to be administered by the International Atomic Energy Agency; these gave the Agency the right to conduct inspections. The original signatories were Britain, the United States, and the Soviet Union. By 1986 a total of 133 States had signed the treaty. The effectiveness of the treaty in its central purpose was, however, flawed. Many of the signatories (for example, the Holy See, San Marino, Tonga, Bhutan, and Tuvalu) were States which had not even the remotest prospect of acquiring nuclear weapons. But others, which were already nuclear powers (such as China) or reported to be on the road to a nuclear capability (such as Brazil, and Pakistan) did not sign. India, which exploded a nuclear device in 1974, declared that it would not arm itself with nuclear weapons, but refused to sign the treaty. Israel (another non-signatory) declared that it would not be the first State to introduce nuclear weapons into the Middle East region, but during the 1970s and 1980s there were frequent (perhaps 'inspired') reports that Israel had a stockpile of nuclear weapons. Moreover, the treaty did not prevent the deployment of nuclear warheads on the territory of non-nuclear States, provided they remained under the control of a nuclear power. Thus nuclear warheads remained available to both NATO and the Warsaw Pact on Russian and American bases stationed in the territory of non-nuclear allies.

## Memorandum of Understanding between the United States and the Soviet Union on the establishment of a direct communications ('hot line') link, Geneva, 20 June 1963

For use in time of emergency, the Government of the United States of America and the Government of the Union of Soviet Socialist Republics have agreed to establish as soon as technically feasible a direct communications link between the two Governments.

Each Government shall be responsible for the arrangements for the link on its own territory. Each Government shall take the necessary steps to ensure continuous functioning of the link and prompt delivery to its head of Government of any communications received by means of the link from the head of Government of the other party.

Arrangements for establishing and operating the link are set forth in the Annex which is attached hereto and forms an integral part hereof.

Done in duplicate in the English and Russian languages at Geneva, Switzerland, this 20th day of June, 1963.

For the Government of the Union of Soviet Socialist Republics:
Semyon Tsarapkin

For the Government of the United States of America:
Charles C. Stelle

[The annex contained technical, organizational, and financial details.]

# Treaty banning nuclear weapon tests in the atmosphere, in outer space, and under water, Moscow, 5 August 1963

The Governments of the United States of America, the United Kingdom of Great Britain and Northern Ireland, and the Union of Soviet Socialist Republics, hereinafter referred to as the 'original parties',

Proclaiming as their principal aim the speediest possible achievement of an agreement on general and complete disarmament under strict international control in accordance with the objectives of the United Nations which would put an end to the armaments race and eliminate the incentive to the production and testing of all kinds of weapons, including nuclear weapons,

Seeking to achieve the discontinuance of all test explosions of nuclear weapons for all time, determined to continue negotiations to this end, and desiring to put an end to the contamination of man's environment by radioactive substances,

Have agreed as follows:

*Article 1.* 1. Each of the parties to this Treaty undertakes to prohibit, to prevent, and not to carry out any nuclear weapon test explosion, or any other nuclear explosion, at any place under its jurisdiction or control:

(a) in the atmosphere; beyond its limits, including outer space; or under water, including territorial waters or high seas; or

(b) in any other environment if such explosion causes radioactive debris to be present outside the territorial limits of the State under whose jurisdiction or control such explosion is conducted. It is understood in this connection that the provisions of this sub-paragraph are without prejudice to the conclusion of a treaty resulting in the permanent banning of all nuclear test explosions, including all such explosions underground, the conclusion of which, as the parties have stated in the Preamble to this Treaty, they seek to achieve.

2. Each of the parties to this Treaty undertakes furthermore to refrain from causing, encouraging, or in any way participating in, the carrying out of any nuclear weapon test explosion, or any other nuclear explosion, anywhere which would take place in any of the environments described, or have the effect referred to, in paragraph 1 of this Article.

[*Article II.* Amendments require a majority of all signatories including the assent of all the original signatories.]

*Article III.* This Treaty shall be open to all States for signature...

*Article IV.* This Treaty shall be of unlimited duration.

Each party shall in exercising its national sovereignty have the right to withdraw from the Treaty if it decides that extraordinary events, related to the subject matter of this Treaty, have jeopardized the supreme interest of its country. It shall give notice of such withdrawal to all other parties to the Treaty three months in advance.

...

[Signed] Rusk, Home, Gromyko.

# Treaty on the non-proliferation of nuclear weapons, 1 July 1968

The States concluding this Treaty, hereinafter referred to as the 'parties to the Treaty',

Considering the devastation that would be visited upon all mankind by a nuclear war and the consequent need to make every effort to avert the danger of such a war and to take measures to safeguard the security of peoples;

Believing that the proliferation of nuclear weapons would seriously enhance the danger of nuclear war;

In conformity with resolutions of the United Nations General Assembly calling for the conclusion of an agreement on the prevention of wider dissemination of nuclear weapons;

Undertaking to cooperate in facilitating the application of International Atomic Energy Agency safeguards on peaceful nuclear activities;

Expressing their support for research, development and other efforts to further the application, within the framework of the International Atomic Energy Agency safeguards system, of the principle of safeguarding effectively the flow of source and special fissionable materials by use of instruments and other techniques at certain strategic points;

Affirming the principle that the benefits of peaceful applications of nuclear technology, including any technological by-products which may be derived by nuclear-weapon States from the development of nuclear explosive devices, should be available for peaceful purposes to all parties to the Treaty, whether nuclear-weapon or non-nuclear-weapon States;

Convinced that, in furtherance of this principle, all parties to the Treaty are entitled to participate in the fullest possible exchange of scientific information for, and to contribute alone or in cooperation with other States to, the further development of the applications of atomic energy for peaceful purposes;

Declaring their intention to achieve at the earliest possible date the cessation of the nuclear arms race and to undertake effective measures in the direction of nuclear disarmament;

Urging the cooperation of all States in the attainment of this objective;

Recalling the determination expressed by the parties to the 1963 treaty, banning nuclear weapon tests in the atmosphere in outer space and under water, in its Preamble to seek to achieve the discontinuance of all test explosions of nuclear weapons for all time and to continue negotiations to this end;

Desiring to further the easing of international tension and the strengthening of trust between States in order to facilitate the cessation of the manufacture of nuclear weapons, the liquidation of all their existing stockpiles, and the elimination from national arsenals of nuclear weapons and the means of their delivery pursuant to a treaty on general and complete disarmament under strict and effective international control;

Recalling that, in accordance with the Charter of the United Nations, States must refrain in their international relations from the threat or use of force against the territorial integrity or political independence of any State, or in any other manner inconsistent with the purposes of the United Nations, and that the establishment and maintenance of international peace and security are to be promoted with the least diversion for armaments of the world's human and economic resources;

Have agreed as follows:

*Article I.* Each nuclear-weapon State party to the Treaty undertakes not to transfer to any recipient whatsoever nuclear weapons or other nuclear explosive devices or control over such weapons or explosive devices directly, or indirectly; and not in any way to assist, encourage, or induce any non-nuclear-weapon State to manufacture or otherwise acquire nuclear weapons or other nuclear explosive devices, or control over such weapons or explosive devices.

*Article II.* Each non-nuclear-weapon State party to the Treaty undertakes not to receive the transfer from any transferor whatsoever of nuclear weapons or other nuclear explosive devices or of control over such weapons or explosive devices directly, or indirectly; not to manufacture or otherwise acquire nuclear weapons or other nuclear explosive devices; and not to seek or receive any assistance in the manufacture of nuclear weapons or other nuclear explosive devices.

*Article III.* 1. Each non-nuclear-weapon State party to the Treaty undertakes to accept safeguards, as set forth in an agreement to be negotiated and concluded with the International Atomic Energy Agency in accordance with the Statute of the International Atomic Energy Agency and the Agency's safeguards system, for the exclusive purpose of verification of the fulfilment of its obligations assumed under this Treaty with a view to preventing diversion of nuclear energy from peaceful uses to nuclear weapons or other nuclear explosive devices. Procedures for the safeguards required by this Article shall be followed with respect to source or special fissionable material whether it is being produced, processed or used in any principal nuclear facility or is outside any such facility. The safeguards required by this Article shall be applied on all source or special fissionable material in all peaceful nuclear activities within the territory of such State, under its jurisdiction, or carried out under its control anywhere.

2. Each State party to the Treaty undertakes not to provide: (a) source of special fissionable material, or (b) equipment or material especially designed or prepared for the processing, use or production of special fissionable material, to any non-nuclear-weapon State for peaceful purposes, unless the source of special

fissionable material shall be subject to the safeguards required by this Article.

3. The safeguards required by this Article shall be implemented in a manner designed to comply with Article IV of this Treaty, and to avoid hampering the economic or technological development of the parties or international cooperation in the field of peaceful nuclear activities, including the international exchange of nuclear material and equipment for the processing, use or production of nuclear material for peaceful purposes in accordance with the provisions of this Article and the principle of safeguarding set forth in the Preamble of the Treaty.

4. Non-nuclear-weapon States party to the Treaty shall conclude agreements with the International Atomic Energy Agency to meet the requirements of this Article either individually or together with other States in accordance with the Statute of the International Atomic Energy Agency. Negotiation of such agreements shall commence within 180 days from the original entry into force of this Treaty. For States depositing their instruments of ratification or accession after the 180-day period, negotiation of such agreements shall commence not later than the date of such deposit. Such agreements shall enter into force not later than eighteen months after the date of initiation of negotiations.

*Article IV.* 1. Nothing in this Treaty shall be interpreted as affecting the inalienable right of all the parties to the Treaty to develop research, production and use of nuclear energy for peaceful purposes without discrimination and in conformity with Articles I and II of this Treaty.

2. All the parties to the Treaty undertake to facilitate, and have the right to participate in, the fullest possible exchange of equipment, materials and scientific and technological information for the peaceful uses of nuclear energy. Parties to the Treaty in a position to do so shall also cooperate in contributing alone or together with other States or international organizations to the further development of the applications of nuclear

energy for peaceful purposes, especially in the territories of non-nuclear-weapon States party to the Treaty, with due consideration for the needs of the developing areas of the world.

*Article V.* Each party to the Treaty undertakes to take appropriate measures to ensure that, in accordance with this Treaty, under appropriate international observation and through appropriate international procedures, potential benefits from any peaceful applications of nuclear explosions will be made available to non-nuclear-weapon States party to the Treaty on a non-discriminatory basis and that the charge of such parties for the explosive devices used will be as low as possible and exclude any charge for research and development. Non-nuclear-weapon States party to the Treaty shall be able to obtain such benefits, pursuant to a special international agreement or agreements, through an appropriate international body with adequate representation of non-nuclear-weapon States. Negotiations on this subject shall commence as soon as possible after the Treaty enters into force. Non-nuclear-weapon States party to the Treaty so desiring may also obtain such benefits pursuant to bilateral agreements.

*Article VI.* Each of the parties to the Treaty undertakes to pursue negotiations in good faith on effective measures relating to cessation of the nuclear arms race at an early date and to nuclear disarmament, and on a treaty on general and complete disarmament under strict and effective international control.

*Article VII.* Nothing in this Treaty affects the right of any group of States to conclude regional treaties in order to assure the total absence of nuclear weapons in their respective territories.

*Article VIII.* 1. Any party to the Treaty may propose amendments to this Treaty. The text of any proposed amendment shall be submitted to the Depositary Governments which shall circulate it to all parties to the Treaty. Thereupon, if requested to do so by one-third or more of the parties to the Treaty, the Depositary Governments shall convene a conference, to which they shall invite all the parties to the Treaty, to consider such an amendment.

2. Any amendment to this Treaty must be approved by a majority of the votes of all the parties to the Treaty, including the votes of all nuclear-weapon States party to the Treaty and all other parties which, on the date the amendment is circulated, are members of the Board of Governors of the International Atomic Energy Agency. The amendment shall enter into force for each party that deposits its instrument of ratification of the amendment upon the deposit of such instruments of ratification by a majority of all the parties, including the instruments of ratification of all nuclear-weapon States party to the Treaty and all other parties which, on the date the amendment is circulated, are members of the Board of Governors of the International Atomic Energy Agency. Thereafter, it shall enter into force for any other party upon the deposit of its instrument of ratification of the amendment.

3. Five years after the entry into force of this Treaty, a conference of parties to the Treaty shall be held in Geneva, Switzerland, in order to review the operation of this Treaty with a view to assuring that the purposes of the Preamble and the provisions of the Treaty are being realized. At intervals of five years thereafter, a majority of the parties to the Treaty may obtain, by submitting a proposal to this effect to the Depositary Governments, the convening of further conferences with the same objective of reviewing the operation of the Treaty.

*Article IX.* 1. This Treaty shall be open to all States for signature. Any State which does not sign the Treaty before its entry into force in accordance with paragraph 3 of this Article may accede to it at any time.

2. This Treaty shall be subject to ratification by signatory States. Instruments of ratification and instruments of accession shall be deposited with the

Governments of the United States of America, the United Kingdom of Great Britain and Northern Ireland and the Union of Soviet Socialist Republics, which are hereby designated the Depositary Governments.

3. This Treaty shall enter into force after its ratification by the States, the Governments of which are designated Depositaries of the Treaty, and forty other States signatory to this Treaty and the deposit of their instruments of ratification. For the purposes of this Treaty, a nuclear-weapon State is one which has manufactured and exploded a nuclear weapon or other nuclear explosive device prior to January 1, 1967.

4. For States whose instruments of ratification or accession are deposited subsequent to the entry into force of this Treaty, it shall enter into force on the date of the deposit of their instruments of ratification or accession.

5. The Depositary Governments shall promptly inform all signatory and acceding States of the date of each signature, the date of deposit of each instrument of ratification or of accession, the date of the entry into force of this Treaty, and the date of receipt of any requests for convening a conference or other notices.

6. This Treaty shall be registered by the Depositary Governments pursuant to Article 102 of the Charter of the United Nations.

*Article X.* 1. Each party shall in exercising its national sovereignty have the right to withdraw from the Treaty if it decides that extraordinary events, related to the subject matter of this Treaty, have jeopardized the supreme interests of its country. It shall give notice of such withdrawal to all other parties to the Treaty and to the United Nations Security Council three months in advance. Such notice shall include a statement of the extraordinary events it regards as having jeopardized its supreme interests.

2. Twenty-five years after the entry into force of the Treaty, a conference shall be convened to decide whether the Treaty shall continue in force indefinitely, or shall be extended for an additional fixed period or periods. This decision shall be taken by a majority of the parties to the Treaty.

[*Article XI.* Authentic texts.]

## The road to SALT I, 1971–2

During the 1970s the process of détente accelerated rapidly. In Europe it was given added momentum by the new *Ostpolitik* of the West German Government from the late 1960s (see Chapter IV).

*On 21 January 1971 the United States and the Soviet Union announced an agreement on cooperation in the exploration and use of outer space.* This agreement in an area of great sensitivity to both sides, on grounds of security and prestige, was a green light for progress in other spheres. In September 1971 Britain, France, the Soviet Union, and the United States signed the four-power Berlin Agreement (p. 196). Meanwhile, *on 11 February 1971, Britain, the Soviet Union and the United States signed a treaty on the prohibition of the emplacement of nuclear weapons and other weapons of mass destruction on the sea bed and the ocean floor and in the sub-soil thereof.* By 1986 a total of eighty-three States had acceded to this treaty. Once again, as in the case of previous nuclear treaties, France and China were not among the signatories. The treaty in fact had little practical importance since there appears to be no longer any sound military reason for anchoring nuclear weapons to the sea bed, although at the time this seemed possible. The treaty did not outlaw one of the most important strategic developments of the past two decades – the deployment, by both the United States and the Soviet Union, of submarines capable of launching missiles carrying nuclear weapons.

Other Soviet–American agreements in 1971–2 pointed to the emergence of a changed relationship. *On 30 September 1971 an agreement on measures to reduce the risk of the outbreak of nuclear war was signed* in Washington by the Soviet and American Foreign Ministers (p. 448). This was accompanied by an agreement to improve the efficiency of the direct communications link ('hot line') between Moscow and Washington established in the 1963.

A visit to Moscow by President Nixon in May 1972 was the occasion for a large number of Soviet–American agreements. Signed in what was apparently an ascending order of importance, these began with an *American–Soviet agreement on environmental protection, 23 May 1972*, and an *American–Soviet agreement on medical science and public health on the same date*. *On 24 May 1972 the U.S.A. and the U.S.S.R. signed an agreement on science and technology*. Also *on 24 May 1972 an American–Soviet agreement on cooperation in space was signed* (p. 450). Article 3 of this agreement provided for the docking in space of an American Apollo spacecraft with a Soviet Soyuz craft, and for mutual visits to each other's vehicle by American and Soviet astronauts. Such a rendezvous in space (of symbolic rather than scientific importance) actually took place on 17 July 1975.

The two landmark treaties signed during Nixon's Moscow visit were the *treaty on the limitation of antiballistic missile systems, 26 May 1972*, known as the A.B.M. treaty (p. 452), and the *Interim Agreement on limitation of strategic offensive arms, 26 May 1972, known as SALT I* (p. 454). Both these treaties owed a great deal to the fertile diplomatic brain of Dr Henry Kissinger.

The A.B.M. treaty, which was the product of four years of Soviet–American negotiations, was based on the concept that defences against intercontinental ballistic missiles must be limited if there was to be any hope of reducing offensive nuclear weapons. The maintenance of the balance of terror between the U.S.A. and the U.S.S.R. depended on 'mutually assured destruction'. If either side developed and deployed defensive systems which might render it capable of surviving nuclear attack, the balance would be upset and war might result. Accordingly, Article III of the A.B.M. treaty limited each side to two anti-missile defence systems, one to protect its capital, and the other to protect a deployment area for intercontinental ballistic missiles. A limit was laid down of one hundred A.B.M. launchers and interceptors in each such area. And Article V stipulated (in terms which were later to be the subject of much debate) that neither side was to 'develop, test, or deploy A.B.M. systems or components which are sea-based, air-based, space-based, or mobile land-based'. The treaty was to be of unlimited duration but could be terminated by either side on six months' notice if that side decided that 'extraordinary events related to the subject matter of this Treaty have jeopardized its supreme interests' (Article XV).

The first SALT agreement (the popular title was an acronym derived from the Strategic Arms Limitation Talks which had begun in November 1969) placed a ceiling on the numbers of intercontinental ballistic missiles (I.C.B.M.s) and submarine-launched ballistic missiles (S.L.B.M.s) to be deployed by the U.S.A. and the U.S.S.R. For the U.S.A. the limit was 1,710; for the U.S.S.R. 2,347. The apparent disparity was explicable on the basis of the United States' lead in multiple warheads capable of being launched on one missile (known as MIRVs – multiple independently targetable reentry vehicles). SALT I broadly speaking froze the missile strengths of the two sides at their existing levels; it was not a disarmament accord. Whereas the A.B.M. treaty was to remain in effect in perpetuity, SALT I was an 'interim' agreement which would remain in effect for only five years. During that period negotiations for a permanent accord would continue.

Nixon's visit to Moscow concluded with a *Soviet–American agreement on basic principles of relations, 29 May 1972* (p. 456). The agreement was declaratory and rhetorical rather than substantial, but taken in conjunction with the other agreements arrived at in Moscow it can be said to mark one of the high points of the period of East–West détente.

## Soviet–American Agreements to reduce risk of nuclear war, Washington, 30 September 1971

**Agreement on measures to reduce the risk of outbreak of nuclear war between the United States of America and the Union of Soviet Socialist Republics**

The United States of America and the Union of Soviet Socialist Republics, here-inafter referred to as the Parties:

Taking into account the devastating consequences that nuclear war would have for all mankind, and recognizing the need to exert every effort to avert the risk of outbreak of such a war, including measures to guard against accidental or unauthorized use of nuclear weapons,

Believing that agreement on measures for reducing the risk of outbreak of nuclear war serves the interests of strengthening international peace and security, and is in no way contrary to the interests of any other country,

Bearing in mind that continued efforts are also needed in the future to seek ways of reducing the risk of outbreak of nuclear war,

Have agreed as follows:

*Article 1.* Each Party undertakes to maintain and to improve, as it deems necessary, its existing organizational and technical arrangements to guard against the accidental or unauthorized use of nuclear weapons under its control.

*Article 2.* The Parties undertake to notify each other immediately in the event of an accidental, unauthorized or any other unexplained incident involving a possible detonation of a nuclear weapon which could create a risk of outbreak of nuclear war. In the event of such an incident, the Party whose nuclear weapon is involved will immediately make every effort to take necessary measures to render harmless or destroy such weapon without its causing damage.

*Article 3.* The Parties undertake to notify each other immediately in the event of detection by missile warning systems of unidentified objects, or in the event of signs of interference with these systems or with related communications facilities, if such occurrences could create a risk of outbreak of nuclear war between the two countries.

*Article 4.* Each Party undertakes to notify the other Party in advance of any planned missile launches if such launches will extend beyond its national territory in the direction of the other Party.

*Article 5.* Each Party, in other situations involving unexplained nuclear incidents, undertakes to act in such a manner as to reduce the possibility of its actions being misinterpreted by the other Party. In any such situation, each Party may inform the other Party or request information when, in its view, this is warranted by the interests of averting the risk of outbreak of nuclear war.

*Article 6.* For transmission of urgent information, notifications and requests for information in situations requiring prompt clarification, the Parties shall make primary use of the Direct Communications Link between the Governments of the United States of America and the Union of Soviet Socialist Republics.

For transmission of other information, notifications and requests for information, the Parties, at their own discretion, may use any communications facilities, including diplomatic channels, depending on the degree of urgency.

*Article 7.* The Parties undertake to hold consultations, as mutually agreed, to consider questions relating to implementation of the provisions of this Agreement, as well as to discuss possible amendments thereto aimed at further implementation of the purposes of this Agreement.

*Article 8.* This Agreement shall be of unlimited duration.

*Article 9.* This Agreement shall enter into force upon signature.

Done at Washington on September 30, 1971, in two copies, each in the English and Russian languages, both texts being equally authentic.

For the United States of America:
WILLIAM P. ROGERS

For the Union of Soviet Socialist Republics:
A. GROMYKO

## Agreement between the United States of America and the Union of Soviet Socialist Republics on measures to improve the U.S.A.–U.S.S.R. Direct Communications Link

The United States of America and the

Union of Soviet Socialist Republics, hereinafter referred to as the Parties,

Noting the positive experience gained in the process of operating the existing Direct Communications Link between the United States of America and the Union of Soviet Socialist Republics, which was established for use in time of emergency pursuant to the Memorandum of Understanding Regarding the Establishment of a Direct Communications Link, signed on June 20, 1963,

Having examined, in a spirit of mutual understanding, matters relating to the improvement and modernization of the Direct Communications Link,

Have agreed as follows:

*Article 1.* For the purpose of increasing the reliability of the Direct Communications Link, there shall be established and put into operation the following:

(a) two additional circuits between the United States of America and the Union of Soviet Socialist Republics each using a satellite communications system, with each Party selecting a satellite communications system of its own choice,

(b) a system of terminals (more than one) in the territory of each Party for the Direct Communications Link, with the locations and number of terminals in the United States of America to be determined by the United States side, and the locations and number of terminals in the Union of Soviet Socialist Republics to be determined by the Soviet side.

2. Matters relating to the implementation of the aforementioned improvements of the Direct Communications Link are set forth in the Annex which is attached hereto and forms an integral part hereof.

*Article 2.* Each Party confirms its intention to take all possible measures to assure the continuous and reliable operation of the communications circuits and the system of terminals of the Direct Communications Link for which it is responsible in accordance with this Agreement and the Annex hereto, as well as to communicate to the head of its Government any messages received via the Direct Communications Link from the head of Government of the other Party.

*Article 3.* The Memorandum of Understanding Between the United States of America and the Union of Soviet Socialist Republics Regarding the Establishment of a Direct Communications Link, signed on June 20, 1963, with the Annex thereto, shall remain in force, except to the extent that its provisions are modified by this Agreement and Annex hereto.

*Article 4.* The undertakings of the Parties hereunder shall be carried out in accordance with their respective Constitutional processes.

*Article 5.* This Agreement, including the Annex hereto, shall enter into force upon signature.

. . .

[The attached Annex set out details of the proposed enhancement of the direct communications link.]

# American–Soviet Agreement on Cooperation in Space, Moscow, 24 May 1972

The United States of America and the Union of Soviet Socialist Republics;

Considering the role which the U.S.A. and the U.S.S.R. play in the exploration and use of outer space for peaceful purposes;

Striving for a further expansion of cooperation between the U.S.A. and the

U.S.S.R. in the exploration and use of outer space for peaceful purposes;

Noting the positive cooperation which the parties have already experienced in this area;

Desiring to make the results of scientific research gained from the exploration and use of outer space for peaceful purposes available for the benefit of the peoples of the two countries and of all peoples of the world;

Taking into consideration the provisions of the Treaty on Principles Governing the Activities of States in the Exploration and Use of Outer Space, including the Moon and Other Celestial Bodies, as well as the Agreement on the Rescue of Astronauts, the Return of Astronauts, and the Return of Objects Launched into Outer Space;

In accordance with the Agreement between the United States of America and the Union of Soviet Socialist Republics on Exchanges and Cooperation in Scientific, Technical, Educational, Cultural, and Other Fields, signed April 11, 1972, and in order to develop further the principles of mutually beneficial cooperation between the two countries;

Have agreed as follows:

*Article 1.* The Parties will develop cooperation in the fields of space meteorology; study of the natural environment; exploration of near earth space, the moon and the planets; and space biology and medicine; and, in particular, will cooperate to take all appropriate measures to encourage and achieve the fulfillment of the Summary of Results of Discussion on Space Cooperation Between the U.S. National Aeronautics and Space Administration and the Academy of Sciences of the U.S.S.R. dated January 21, 1971.

*Article 2.* The Parties will carry out such cooperation by means of mutual exchanges of scientific information and delegations, through meetings of scientists and specialists of both countries, and also in such other ways as may be mutually agreed. Joint working groups may be created for the development and implementation of appropriate programs of cooperation.

*Article 3.* The Parties have agreed to carry out projects for developing compatible rendezvous and docking systems of United States and Soviet manned spacecraft and stations in order to enhance the safety of manned flight in space and to provide the opportunity for conducting joint scientific experiments in the future. It is planned that the first experimental flight to test these systems be conducted during 1975, envisaging the docking of a United States Apollo-type spacecraft and a Soviet Soyuz-type spacecraft with visits of astronauts in each other's spacecraft. The implementation of these projects will be carried out on the basis of principles and procedures which will be developed in accordance with the Summary of Results of the Meeting Between Representatives of the U.S. National Aeronautics and Space Administration and the U.S.S.R. Academy of Sciences on the Question of Developing Compatible Systems for Rendezvous and Docking of Manned Spacecraft and Space Stations of the U.S.A. and the U.S.S.R. dated April 6, 1972.

*Article 4.* The Parties will encourage international efforts to resolve problems of international law in the exploration and use of outer space for peaceful purposes with the aim of strengthening the legal order in space and further developing international space law and will cooperate in this field.

*Article 5.* The Parties may by mutual agreement determine other areas of cooperation in the exploration and use of outer space for peaceful purposes.

*Article 6.* This Agreement shall enter into force upon signature and shall remain in force for five years. It may be modified or extended by mutual agreement of the Parties.

# American–Soviet Treaty on the Limitation of Anti-Ballistic Missile Systems, Moscow, 26 May 1972

The United States of America and the Union of Soviet Socialist Republics, hereinafter referred to as the Parties,

Proceeding from the premise that nuclear war would have devastating consequences for all mankind,

Considering that effective measures to limit anti-ballistic missile systems would be a substantial factor in curbing the race in strategic offensive arms and would lead to a decrease in the risk of outbreak of war involving nuclear weapons,

Proceeding from the premise that the limitation of anti-ballistic missile systems, as well as certain agreed measures with respect to the limitation of strategic offensive arms, would contribute to the creation of more favorable conditions for further negotiations on limiting strategic arms,

Mindful of their obligations under Article VI of the Treaty on the Non-Proliferation of Nuclear Weapons,

Declaring their intention to achieve at the earliest possible date the cessation of the nuclear arms race and to take effective measures toward reductions in strategic arms, nuclear disarmament, and general and complete disarmament,

Desiring to contribute to the relaxation of international tension and the strengthening of trust between States,

Have agreed as follows:

*Article 1.* 1. Each Party undertakes to limit anti-ballistic missile (A.B.M.) systems and to adopt other measures in accordance with the provisions of this Treaty.

2. Each Party undertakes not to deploy A.B.M. systems for a defense of the territory of its country and not to provide a base for such a defense, and not to deploy A.B.M. systems for defense of an individual region except as provided for in Article III of this Treaty.

*Article II.* 1. For the purposes of this Treaty an A.B.M. system is a system to counter strategic ballistic missiles or their elements in flight trajectory, currently consisting of:

(a) A.B.M. interceptor missiles, which are interceptor missiles constructed and deployed for an A.B.M. role, or of a type tested in an A.B.M. mode;

(b) A.B.M. launchers, which are launchers constructed and deployed for launching A.B.M. interceptor missiles; and

(c) A.B.M. radars, which are radars constructed and deployed for an A.B.M. role, or of a type tested in an A.B.M. mode.

2. The A.B.M. system components listed in paragraph 1 of this Article include those which are:

(a) operational;

(b) under construction;

(c) undergoing testing;

(d) undergoing overhaul, repair or conversion; or

(e) mothballed.

*Article III.* Each Party undertakes not to deploy A.B.M. systems or their components except that:

(a) within one A.B.M. system deployment area having a radius of one hundred and fifty kilometers and centered on the Party's national capital, a Party may deploy: (1) no more than one hundred A.B.M. launchers and no more than one hundred A.B.M. interceptor missiles at launch sites, and (2) A.B.M. radars within no more than six A.B.M. radar complexes, the area of each complex being circular and having a diameter of no more than three kilometers; and

(b) within one A.B.M. system deployment area having a radius of one hundred and fifty kilometers and containing I.C.B.M. silo launchers, a Party may deploy: (1) no more than one hundred A.B.M. launchers and no more than one hundred A.B.M. interceptor missiles at launch sites, (2) two large phased-array A.B.M. radars comparable in potential to corresponding A.B.M. radars operational or under construction on the date of signature of the Treaty in an A.B.M. system deployment area containing I.C.B.M. silo launchers, and (3) no more than eighteen A.B.M. radars each having a potential less than the potential of the smaller of the above-mentioned two large phased-array A.B.M. radars.

*Article IV.* The limitations provided for in Article III shall not apply to A.B.M. systems or their components used for development or testing, and located within current or additionally agreed test ranges. Each Party may have no more than a total of fifteen A.B.M. launchers at test ranges.

*Article V.* 1. Each Party undertakes not to develop, test, or deploy A.B.M. systems or components which are sea-based, air-based, space-based, or mobile land-based.

2. Each Party undertakes not to develop, test, or deploy A.B.M. launchers for launching more than one A.B.M. interceptor missile at a time from each launcher, nor to modify deployed launchers to provide them with such a capability, nor to develop, test, or deploy automatic or semi-automatic or other similar systems for rapid reload of A.B.M. launchers.

*Article VI.* To enhance assurance of the effectiveness of the limitations on A.B.M. systems and their components provided by this Treaty, each Party undertakes:

(a) not to give missiles, launchers, or radars, other than A.B.M. interceptor missiles, A.B.M. launchers, or A.B.M. radars, capabilities to counter strategic ballistic missiles or their elements in flight trajectory, and not to test them in an A.B.M. mode; and

(b) not to deploy in the future radars for early warning of strategic ballistic missile attack except at locations along the periphery of its national territory and oriented outward.

*Article VII.* Subject to the provisions of this Treaty, modernization and replacement of A.B.M. systems or their components may be carried out.

*Article VIII.* A.B.M. systems or their components in excess of the numbers or outside the areas specified in this Treaty, as well as A.B.M. systems or their components prohibited by this Treaty, shall be destroyed or dismantled under agreed procedures within the shortest possible agreed period of time.

*Article IX.* To assure the viability and effectiveness of this Treaty, each Party undertakes not to transfer to other States, and not to deploy outside its national territory, A.B.M. systems or their components limited by this Treaty.

*Article X.* Each Party undertakes not to assume any international obligations which would conflict with this Treaty.

*Article XI.* The Parties undertake to continue active negotiations for limitations on strategic offensive arms.

*Article XII.* 1. For the purpose of providing assurance of compliance with the provisions of this Treaty, each Party shall use national technical means of verification at its disposal in a manner consistent with generally recognized principles of international law.

2. Each Party undertakes not to interfere with the national technical means of verification of the other Party operating in accordance with paragraph 1 of this Article.

3. Each Party undertakes not to use deliberate concealment measures which impede verification by national technical means of compliance with the provisions of this Treaty. This obligation shall not require changes in current construction, assembly, conversion, or overhaul practices.

*Article XIII.* 1. To promote the objectives and implementation of the provisions of this Treaty, the Parties shall establish promptly a Standing Consultative Commission, within the framework of which they will:

(a) consider questions concerning compliance with the obligations assumed and related situations which may be considered ambiguous;

(b) provide on a voluntary basis such information as either Party considers necessary to assure confidence in compliance with the obligations assumed;

(c) consider questions involving unintended interference with national technical means of verification;

(d) consider possible changes in the strategic situation which have a bearing on the provisions of this Treaty;

(e) agree upon procedures and dates for destruction or dismantling of A.B.M. systems or their components in cases provided for by the provisions of this Treaty;

(f) consider, as appropriate, possible proposals for further increasing the viability of this Treaty, including proposals for amendments in accordance with the provisions of this Treaty;

(g) consider, as appropriate, proposals for further measures aimed at limiting strategic arms.

2. The Parties through consultation shall establish, and may amend as appropriate, Regulations for the Standing Consultative Commission governing procedures, composition and other relevant matters.

*Article XIV.* 1. Each Party may propose amendments to this Treaty. Agreed amendments shall enter into force in accordance with the procedures governing the entry into force of this Treaty.

2. Five years after entry into force of this Treaty, and at five year intervals thereafter, the Parties shall together conduct a review of this Treaty.

*Article XV.* 1. This Treaty shall be of unlimited duration.

2. Each Party shall, in exercising its national sovereignty, have the right to withdraw from this Treaty if it decides that extraordinary events related to the subject matter of this Treaty have jeopardized its supreme interests. It shall give notice of its decision to the other Party six months prior to withdrawal from the Treaty. Such notice shall include a statement of the extraordinary events the notifying Party regards as having jeopardized its supreme interests.

[*Article XVI.* Ratification.]

. . .

[The agreement was accompanied by several 'agreed interpretations'. The United States made five 'unilateral statements' in connection with the treaty. The U.S.S.R. made one 'unilateral statement' which was rejected by the U.S., repeated by the U.S.S.R., and again rejected by the U.S. These differences, however, did not impair the general validity of the treaty.]

# Interim Agreement ('SALT I') between the United States and the Soviet Union on limitation of strategic offensive arms, Moscow, 26 May 1972

The United States of America and the Union of Soviet Socialist Republics, hereinafter referred to as the Parties,

Convinced that the Treaty on the Limitation of Anti-Ballistic Missile Systems and this Interim Agreement on Certain Measures with Respect to the Limitation of Strategic Offensive Arms will contribute to the creation of more favorable conditions for active negotiations on limiting strategic arms as well as to the relaxation of international tension and the strengthening of trust between States,

Taking into account the relationship between strategic offensive and defensive arms,

Mindful of their obligations under Article VI of the Treaty on the Non-Proliferation of Nuclear Weapons,

Have agreed as follows:

*Article 1.* The Parties undertake not to start construction of additional fixed land-based intercontinental ballistic missile (I.C.B.M.) launchers after July 1, 1972.

*Article II.* The Parties undertake not to convert land-based launchers for light I.C.B.M.s, or for I.C.B.M.s of older types deployed prior to 1964, into land-based launchers for heavy I.C.B.M.s of types deployed after that time.

*Article III.* The Parties undertake to limit submarine-launched ballistic missile (S.L.B.M.) launchers and modern ballistic missile submarines to the numbers operational and under construction on the date of signature of this Interim Agreement, and in addition to launchers and submarines constructed under procedures established by the Parties as replacements for an equal number of I.C.B.M. launchers of older types deployed prior to 1964 or for launchers on older submarines.

*Article IV.* Subject to the provisions of this Interim Agreement, modernization and replacement of strategic offensive ballistic missiles and launchers covered by this Interim Agreement may be undertaken.

*Article V.* 1. For the purpose of providing assurance of compliance with the provisions of this Interim Agreement, each Party shall use national technical means of verification at its disposal in a manner consistent with generally recognized principles of international law.

2. Each Party undertakes not to interfere with the national technical means of verification of the other Party operating in

accordance with paragraph 1 of this Article.

3. Each Party undertakes not to use deliberate concealment measures which impede verification by national technical means of compliance with the provisions of this Interim Agreement. This obligation shall not require changes in current construction, assembly, conversion, or overhaul practices.

*Article VI.* To promote the objectives and implementation of the provisions of this Interim Agreement, the Parties shall use the Standing Consultative Commission established under Article XIII of the Treaty on the Limitation of Anti-Ballistic Missile Systems in accordance with the provisions of that Article.

*Article VII.* The Parties undertake to continue active negotiations for limitations on strategic offensive arms. The obligations provided for in this Interim Agreement shall not prejudice the scope or terms of the limitations on strategic offensive arms which may be worked out in the course of further negotiations.

*Article VIII.* 1. This Interim Agreement shall enter into force upon exchange of written notices of acceptance by each Party, which exchange shall take place simultaneously with the exchange of instruments of ratification of the Treaty on the Limitation of Anti-Ballistic Missile Systems.

2. This Interim Agreement shall remain in force for a period of five years unless replaced earlier by an agreement on more complete measures limiting strategic offensive arms. It is the objective of the Parties to conduct active follow-on negotiations with the aim of concluding such an agreement as soon as possible.

3. Each Party shall, in exercising its national sovereignty, have the right to withdraw from this Interim Agreement if it decides that extraordinary events related to the subject matter of this Interim Agreement have jeopardized its supreme interests. It shall give notice of its decision to the other Party six months

prior to withdrawal from this Interim Agreement. Such notice shall include a statement of the extraordinary events the notifying Party regards as having jeopardized its supreme interests.

Done at Moscow on May 26, 1972, in two copies, each in the English and Russian languages, both texts being equally authentic.

## Protocol

The United States of America and the Union of Soviet Socialist Republics, hereinafter referred to as the Parties,

Having agreed on certain limitations relating to submarine-launched ballistic missile launchers and modern ballistic missile submarines, and to replacement procedures, in the Interim Agreement,

Have agreed as follows:

The Parties understand that, under Article III of the Interim Agreement, for the period during which that Agreement remains in force:

The U.S. may have no more than 710 ballistic missile launchers on submarines

(S.L.B.M.s) and no more than 44 modern ballistic missile submarines. The Soviet Union may have no more than 950 ballistic missile launchers on submarines and no more than 62 modern ballistic missile submarines.

Additional ballistic missile launchers on submarines up to the above-mentioned levels, in the U.S. – over 656 ballistic missile launchers on nuclear-powered submarines, and in the U.S.S.R. – over 740 ballistic missile launchers on nuclear-powered submarines, operational and under construction, may become operational as replacements for equal numbers of ballistic missile launchers of older types deployed prior to 1964 or of ballistic missile launchers on older submarines.

The deployment of modern S.L.B.M.s on any submarine, regardless of type, will be counted against the total level of S.L.B.M.s permitted for the U.S. and the U.S.S.R.

This Protocol shall be considered an integral part of the Interim Agreement.

Done at Moscow this 26th day of May, 1972.

# Soviet–American Agreement on basic principles of relations, Moscow, 29 May 1972

The United States of America and the Union of Soviet Socialist Republics,

Guided by their obligations under the Charter of the United Nations and by a desire to strengthen peaceful relations with each other and to place these relations on the firmest possible basis,

Aware of the need to make every effort to remove the threat of war and to create conditions which promote the reduction of tensions in the world and the strengthening of universal security and international cooperation,

Believing that the improvement of U.S.–Soviet relations and their mutually advantageous development in such areas

as economics, science and culture, will meet these objectives and contribute to better mutual understanding and businesslike cooperation, without in any way prejudicing the interests of third countries,

Conscious that these objectives reflect the interests of the peoples of both countries,

Have agreed as follows:

*First.* They will proceed from the common determination that in the nuclear age there is no alternative to conducting their mutual relations on the basis of peaceful coexistence. Differences in ideology and in the social systems of the

U.S.A. and the U.S.S.R. are not obstacles to the bilateral development of normal relations based on the principles of sovereignty, equality, non-interference in internal affairs and mutual advantage.

*Second.* The U.S.A. and the U.S.S.R. attach major importance to preventing the development of situations capable of causing a dangerous exacerbation of their relations. Therefore, they will do their utmost to avoid military confrontations and to prevent the outbreak of nuclear war. They will always exercise restraint in their mutual relations, and will be prepared to negotiate and settle differences by peaceful means. Discussions and negotiations on outstanding issues will be conducted in a spirit of reciprocity, mutual accommodation and mutual benefit.

Both sides recognize that efforts to obtain unilateral advantage at the expense of the other, directly or indirectly, are inconsistent with these objectives. The prerequisites for maintaining and strengthening peaceful relations between the U.S.A. and the U.S.S.R. are the recognition of the security interests of the Parties based on the principle of equality and the renunciation of the use or threat of force.

*Third.* The U.S.A. and the U.S.S.R. have a special responsibility, as do other countries which are permanent members of the United Nations Security Council, to do everything in their power so that conflicts or situations will not arise which would serve to increase international tensions. Accordingly, they will seek to promote conditions in which all countries will live in peace and security and will not be subject to outside interference in their internal affairs.

*Fourth.* The U.S.A. and the U.S.S.R. intend to widen the juridical basis of their mutual relations and to exert the necessary efforts so that bilateral agreements which they have concluded and multilateral treaties and agreements to which they are jointly parties are faithfully implemented.

*Fifth.* The U.S.A. and the U.S.S.R. reaffirm their readiness to continue the practice of exchanging views on problems of mutual interest and, when necessary, to conduct such exchanges at the highest level, including meetings between leaders of the two countries.

The two Governments welcome and will facilitate an increase in productive contacts between representatives of the legislative bodies of the two countries.

*Sixth.* The Parties will continue their efforts to limit armaments on a bilateral as well as on a multilateral basis. They will continue to make special efforts to limit strategic armaments. Whenever possible, they will conclude concrete agreements aimed at achieving these purposes.

The U.S.A. and the U.S.S.R. regard as the ultimate objective of their efforts the achievement of general and complete disarmament and the establishment of an effective system of international security in accordance with the purposes and principles of the United Nations.

*Seventh.* The U.S.A. and the U.S.S.R. regard commercial and economic ties as an important and necessary element in the strengthening of their bilateral relations and thus will actively promote the growth of such ties. They will facilitate cooperation between the relevant organizations and enterprises of the two countries and the conclusion of appropriate agreements and contracts, including long-term ones.

The two countries will contribute to the improvement of maritime and air communications between them.

*Eighth.* The two sides consider it timely and useful to develop mutual contacts and cooperation in the fields of science and technology. Where suitable, the U.S.A. and the U.S.S.R. will conclude appropriate agreements dealing with concrete cooperation in these fields.

*Ninth.* The two sides reaffirm their intention to deepen cultural ties with one another and to encourage fuller familiarization with each other's cultural values. They will promote improved conditions for cultural exchanges and tourism.

*Tenth.* The U.S.A. and the U.S.S.R. will seek to ensure that their ties and cooperation in all the above-mentioned fields and in any others in their mutual interest are built on a firm and long-term basis. To give a permanent character to these efforts, they will establish in all fields where this is feasible joint commissions or other joint bodies.

*Eleventh.* The U.S.A. and the U.S.S.R. make no claim for themselves and would not recognize the claims of anyone else to any special rights or advantages in world affairs. They recognize the sovereign equality of all States.

The development of U.S.–Soviet relations is not directed against third countries and their interests.

*Twelfth.* The basic principles set forth in this document do not affect any obligations with respect to other countries earlier assumed by the U.S.A. and the U.S.S.R.

## From SALT I to SALT II, 1972–9

Following the Moscow agreements of May 1972 (which received the ratification of the U.S. Senate) there followed a period of intensive East–West negotiations on political and trade relations as well as mutual security. *On 18 October 1972 the U.S.A. and the U.S.S.R. signed a trade agreement* which was intended to treble the volume of trade between the two countries by 1975. Also, *on 18 October 1972 the U.S.A. and the U.S.S.R. signed an agreement regarding the settlement of lend-lease, reciprocal aid and claims.* Under this agreement the U.S.S.R. undertook to pay the U.S.A. $722 million as a settlement of all claims arising from transfers made to the U.S.S.R. during the Second World War under 'lend-lease' and related arrangements. *On 21 December 1972 the U.S.A. and U.S.S.R. reached an agreement to establish a standing consultative commission to promote the implementation of arms control agreements.* The commission was to monitor, in particular, the agreements of 30 September 1971 (on measures to reduce the risk of nuclear war) and of 26 May 1972 (the A.B.M. and SALT 1 agreements).

In June 1973, Leonid Brezhnev, General Secretary of the Communist Party of the Soviet Union, accompanied by the Soviet Foreign Minister, Andrei Gromyko, paid a return visit to President Nixon in Washington. Eleven agreements or protocols were concluded during this visit including *an agreement on the prevention of nuclear war, 22 June 1973, an agreement on basic principles of negotiations on the further limitation of strategic offensive arms, 21 June 1973* (which laid the groundwork for further SALT II discussions, but otherwise added little of substance to SALT I), and accords on such matters as civil aviation, taxation, trade, agriculture, cultural exchanges and oceanographic research.

One year later Nixon paid a further visit to Moscow, in the course of which a new batch of documents received signature. Among these were politically uncontentious agreements on such subjects as cooperation in artificial heart research. Two important security agreements were, however, signed, which refined earlier Soviet–American treaties. A *Protocol to the 1972 A.B.M. Treaty*, signed by Nixon and Brezhnev on 3 July 1974, modified the terms of the A.B.M. treaty by limiting each side to a single area for the deployment of A.B.M. systems, rather than the two envisaged in Article III of the original agreement (see p. 447).

At the same time *the United States and the Soviet Union signed a treaty on the limitation of underground nuclear weapon tests, 3 July 1974* (p. 462). The treaty did not bar such tests altogether but limited them to devices having a yield of less than 150 kilotons. The United States Senate, however, did not ratify this treaty. Two years later *the Soviet Union and the United States signed a treaty on underground nuclear explosions for peaceful purposes, 28 May 1976*. This banned such explosions above a 150-kiloton yield. The two treaties together were forwarded to the U.S. Senate for ratification on 29 July 1976. Neither treaty received Senate approval; both therefore fell into abeyance.

While bilateral negotiations between the U.S.A. and the U.S.S.R. on arms control and other issues thus proceeded at a rapid pace in the early 1970s, another set of talks on European security issues took shape after 1972. This parallel track of discussions originated in the success of the negotiations for a settlement of the German question (see Chapter IV). The Helsinki Conference on Security and Cooperation in Europe met from 3 July 1973 to 1 August 1975 (from 18 September 1973 to 21 July 1975 the sessions took place at Geneva). The holding of such a European security conference was first proposed by the Soviet Union. Every European State with the exception of Albania participated; the United States and Canada were also represented.

The *Helsinki Final Act, 1 August 1975* (p. 463) is not a 'treaty' and was not signed by the participants; the document nevertheless binds all the States represented at the conference. In some respects it came close to fulfilling the functions of the non-existent peace treaty between the Allies and Germany after World War Two. Building on the earlier treaties concerning the German question, the Final Act contained a declaration that 'the participating States regard as inviolable all one another's frontiers as well as the frontiers of all States in Europe and therefore they will refrain now and in the future from assaulting these frontiers'. While falling short of Russian demands that the Western powers actually recognize the post-war frontiers in Eastern Europe (thus legitimizing, for example, the Russian seizure of the Baltic states and of East Prussian, Polish, Czechoslovak and Rumanian territory during and after the war), this declaration effectively consecrated the territorial status quo in Europe. The Helsinki Final Act contained a number of further declarations, inserted on Western insistence, which stressed human rights and the principle of non-interference in the internal affairs of other States. These brought little immediate change in the actual behaviour of the Soviet Union and its satellites, but the communist bloc States' acceptance of these principles was nevertheless regarded by some Western observers as a potentially useful lever to secure eventual change in Eastern Europe and the Soviet Union. Of greater immediate significance were the passages in the accord that dealt with 'confidence-building measures and certain aspects of security and disarmament'. These provided for prior notification of major military manoeuvres and movements as well as exchanges of military observers.

The Helsinki Final Act marked what in retrospect appears to have been the climax of the process of détente. Thereafter, although East–West negotiations continued, a slow souring of the atmosphere gradually became discernible.

The SALT I agreement was succeeded by intensive Soviet–American talks designed to replace the 'interim' accord with a permanent agreement. At a meeting at Vladivostok in November 1974, President Ford and Mr Brezhnev agreed that the negotiations should continue on the basis of each side being permitted a maximum of 2,400 delivery vehicles of which a maximum of 1,320 would be permitted to carry MIRVs. But attempts during the next few years to translate this outline into a detailed agreement were bedevilled by political and technical difficulties. By the time the five-year time limit set by SALT I had expired in 1977, no new agreement had been reached.

Meanwhile superpower relations had taken a turn for the worse with the Soviet decision to terminate its trade agreement with the United States. The reason for this was the American Congress's attempt to attach to the agreement a condition that the Soviet Union pursue a more liberal emigration policy (the 'Jackson–Vanik amendment'). Although the U.S.S.R. permitted Jews (and some others) to emigrate between 1971 and 1979 much more freely than hitherto, it professed to take affront at what it regarded as the U.S. Congress's interference in its internal affairs.

At the same time it was becoming clear that, in spite of the U.S.S.R.'s formal commitment to the human rights provisions of the Helsinki Final Act, no real change in its internal policies (or those of its satellites) would reflect that diplomatic position. The last section of the Helsinki Final Act had provided for follow-up meetings to be attended by all participants to review implementation of the agreement. The first such meeting opened at Belgrade in October 1977. *The concluding document of the Belgrade follow-up meeting was adopted by consensus on 8 March 1977.* It added little to the Helsinki agreement beyond deciding that a further follow-up meeting would take place at Madrid in 1980.

Following the expiration of the five-year period specified in SALT I, both sides agreed to continue to abide by the provisions of SALT I so long as negotiations for SALT II continued. Agreement on the main points at issue was finally reached in early 1979 and the formal signing of the treaty by Carter and Brezhnev took place in a ceremony in Vienna on *18 June 1979.*

The *SALT II treaty* (p. 471) was the most complex arms control agreement ever signed between the U.S.S.R. and the U.S.A. Its main purpose was to set limits on the number of nuclear-armed missiles to be deployed by each side. The agreed limit for each side of all I.C.B.M. (intercontinental ballistic missile) launchers, S.L.B.M. (submarine-launched ballistic missile) launchers, heavy bombers, and A.S.B.M.s (air-to-surface ballistic missiles) was 2,400 (to be reduced by 1 January 1981 to 2,250). Within that aggregate number each side undertook to adhere to a limit of 1,200 for I.C.B.M., S.L.B.M. and A.S.B.M. missiles equipped with MIRVs (multiple warheads). The number of I.C.B.M.s was limited to 820. The number of warheads on current missile types was limited to the maximum number already flight-tested by 1 May 1979 (ten for I.C.B.M.s, fourteen for S.L.B.M.s). The treaty also placed restrictions on the production and testing of new missiles.

SALT II was to remain in force (upon ratification) until 31 December 1985, unless replaced by a further accord. Brezhnev spoke optimistically in March 1979 about beginning work on a SALT III agreement, once SALT II went into force. But the expectations aroused by the signature of SALT II soon foundered. Opposition in the United States to SALT II (criticized from the right as appeasement) gathered strength after the Soviet invasion of Afghanistan in 1979. The Senate Foreign Relations Committee supported the Administration in urging ratification, but the full Senate never ratified the treaty.

# Treaty between the United States and the Soviet Union on the Limitation of Underground Nuclear Weapon Tests, Moscow, 3 July 1974

The United States of America and the Union of Soviet Socialist Republics, hereinafter referred to as the Parties,

Declaring their intention to achieve at the earliest possible date the cessation of the nuclear arms race and to take effective measures toward reductions in strategic arms, nuclear disarmament, and general and complete disarmament under strict and effective international control,

Recalling the determination expressed by the Parties to the 1963 Treaty Banning Nuclear Weapon Tests in the Atmosphere, in Outer Space and Under Water in its Preamble to seek to achieve the discontinuance of all test explosions of nuclear weapons for all time, and to continue negotiations to this end,

Noting that the adoption of measures for the further limitation of underground nuclear weapon tests would contribute to the achievement of these objectives and would meet the interests of strengthening peace and the further relaxation of international tension,

Reaffirming their adherence to the objectives and principles of the Treaty Banning Nuclear Weapon Tests in the Atmosphere, in Outer Space and Under Water and of the Treaty on the Non-Proliferation of Nuclear Weapons,

Have agreed as follows:

*Article 1.* 1. Each Party undertakes to prohibit, to prevent, and not to carry out any underground nuclear weapon test having a yield exceeding 150 kilotons at any place under its jurisdiction or control, beginning March 31, 1976.

2. Each Party shall limit the number of its underground nuclear weapon tests to a minimum.

3. The Parties shall continue their negotiations with a view toward achieving a solution to the problem of the cessation of all underground nuclear weapon tests.

*Article II.* 1. For the purpose of providing assurance of compliance with the provisions of the Treaty, each Party shall use national technical means of verification at its disposal in a manner consistent with the generally recognized principles of international law.

2. Each Party undertakes not to interfere with the national technical means of verification of the other Party operating in accordance with paragraph 1 of this Article.

3. To promote the objectives and implementation of the provisions of this Treaty the Parties shall, as necessary, consult with each other, make inquiries and furnish information in response to such inquiries.

*Article III.* The provisions of this Treaty do not extend to underground nuclear explosions carried out by the Parties for peaceful purposes. Underground nuclear explosions for peaceful purposes shall be governed by an agreement which is to be negotiated and concluded by the Parties at the earliest possible time.

*Article IV.* This Treaty shall be subject to ratification in accordance with the constitutional procedures of each Party. This Treaty shall enter into force on the day of the exchange of instruments of ratification.

*Article V.* 1. This Treaty shall remain in force for a period of five years. Unless replaced earlier by an agreement in implementation of the objectives specified in paragraph 3 of Article 1 of this Treaty, it shall be extended for successive five-year periods unless either Party notifies the other of its termination no later than six months prior to the expiration of the Treaty. Before the expiration of this period the Parties may, as necessary, hold consultations to consider the situation relevant to the substance of this Treaty and to introduce possible amendments to the text of the Treaty.

2. Each Party shall, in exercising its national sovereignty, have the right to withdraw from this Treaty if it decides that extraordinary events related to the subject matter of this Treaty have jeopardized its supreme interests. It shall give notice of its decision to the other Party six months prior to withdrawal from this Treaty. Such notice shall include a statement of the extraordinary events the notifying Party regards as having jeopardized its supreme interests.

3. This Treaty shall be registered pursuant to Article 102 of the Charter of the United Nations.

Done at Moscow on July 3, 1974, in duplicate, in the English and Russian languages, both texts being equally authentic.

For the United States of America:
The President of the United States of America

For the Union of Soviet Socialist Republics:
General Secretary of the Central Committee of the C.P.S.U.

## Protocol to the Treaty

. . .

1. For the purpose of ensuring verification of compliance with the obligations of the Parties under the Treaty by national technical means, the Parties shall, on the basis of reciprocity, exchange the following data:

(a) The geographic coordinates of the boundaries of each test site and of the boundaries of the geophysically distinct testing areas therein.

(b) Information on the geology of the testing areas of the sites (the rock characteristics of geological formations and the basic physical properties of the rock, i.e. density, seismic velocity, water saturation, porosity and depth of water table).

(c) The geographic coordinates of underground nuclear weapon tests, after they have been conducted.

(d) Yield, date, time, depth and coordinates for two nuclear weapon tests for calibration purposes from each geophysically distinct testing area where underground nuclear weapon tests have been and are to be conducted.

. . .

[This treaty was not ratified by the United States.]

---

# Final Act of the Conference on Security and Cooperation in Europe, Helsinki, 1 August 1975

. . .

## Questions relating to security in Europe

The States participating in the Conference on Security and Cooperation in Europe,

*Reaffirming* their objective of promoting better relations among themselves and ensuring conditions in which their people can live in true and lasting peace free from any threat to or attempt against their security;

*Convinced* of the need to exert efforts to make détente both a continuing and an increasingly viable and comprehensive process, universal in scope, and that the implementation of the results of the Conference on Security and Cooperation in Europe will be a major contribution to this process;

*Considering* that solidarity among

peoples, as well as the common purpose of the participating States in achieving the aims as set forth by the Conference on Security and Cooperation in Europe, should lead to the development of better and closer relations among them in all fields and thus to overcoming the confrontation stemming from the character of their past relations, and to better mutual understanding;

*Mindful* of their common history and recognizing that the existence of elements common to their traditions and values can assist them in developing their relations, and desiring to search, fully taking into account the individuality and diversity of their positions and views, for possibilities of joining their efforts with a view to overcoming distrust and increasing confidence, solving the problems that separate them and cooperating in the interest of mankind;

*Recognizing* the indivisibility of security in Europe as well as their common interest in the development of cooperation throughout Europe and among themselves and expressing their intention to pursue efforts accordingly;

*Recognizing* the close link between peace and security in Europe and in the world as a whole and conscious of the need for each of them to make its contribution to the strengthening of world peace and security and to the promotion of fundamental rights, economic and social progress and well-being for all people;

Have adopted the following:

1. (a) DECLARATION ON PRINCIPLES GUIDING RELATIONS BETWEEN PARTICIPATING STATES.
The participating States,

. . .

*Declare* their determination to respect and put into practice, each of them in its relations with all other participating States, irrespective of their political, economic or social systems as well as of their size, geographical location or level of economic development, the following principles, which are all of primary importance, guiding their mutual relations:

*1. Sovereign equality, respect for the rights inherent in sovereignty*

The participating States will respect each other's sovereign equality and individuality as well as all the rights inherent in and encompassed by its sovereignty, including in particular the right of every State to juridical equality, to territorial integrity and to freedom and political independence. They will also respect each other's right freely to choose and develop its political, social, economic and cultural systems as well as its right to determine its laws and regulations.

Within the framework of international law, all the participating States have equal rights and duties. They will respect each other's right to define and conduct as it wishes its relations with other States in accordance with international law and in the spirit of the present Declaration. They consider that their frontiers can be changed, in accordance with international law, by peaceful means and by agreement. They also have the right to belong or not to belong to international organizations, to be or not to be a party to bilateral or multilateral treaties including the right to be or not to be a party to treaties of alliance; they also have the right to neutrality.

*II. Refraining from the threat or use of force*

The participating States will refrain in their mutual relations, as well as in their international relations in general, from the threat or use of force against the territorial integrity or political independence of any State, or in any other manner inconsistent with the purposes of the United Nations and with the present Declaration. No consideration may be invoked to serve to warrant resort to the threat or use of force in contravention of this principle.

Accordingly, the participating States will refrain from any acts constituting a threat of force or direct or indirect use of force against another participating State. Likewise they will refrain from any manifestation of force for the purpose of inducing another participating State to renounce the full exercise of its sovereign rights. Likewise they will also refrain in their mutual relations from any act of reprisal by force.

No such threat or use of force will be employed as a means of settling disputes, or questions likely to give rise to disputes, between them.

### III. Inviolability of frontiers

The participating States regard as inviolable all one another's frontiers as well as the frontiers of all States in Europe and therefore they will refrain now and in the future from assaulting these frontiers.

Accordingly, they will also refrain from any demand for, or act of, seizure and usurpation of part or all of the territory of any participating State.

### IV. Territorial integrity of States

The participating States will respect the territorial integrity of each of the participating States.

Accordingly, they will refrain from any action inconsistent with the purposes and principles of the Charter of the United Nations against the territorial integrity, political independence or the unity of any participating State, and in particular from any such action constituting a threat or use of force.

The participating States will likewise refrain from making each other's territory the object of military occupation or other direct or indirect measures of force in contravention of international law, or the object of acquisition by means of such measures or the threat of them. No such occupation or acquisition will be recognized as legal.

### V. Peaceful settlement of disputes

The participating States will settle disputes among them by peaceful means in such a manner as not to endanger international peace and security, and justice.

They will endeavour in good faith and a spirit of cooperation to reach a rapid and equitable solution on the basis of international law.

For this purpose they will use such means as negotiation, enquiry, mediation, conciliation, arbitration, judicial settlement or other peaceful means of their own choice including any settlement procedure agreed to in advance of disputes to which they are parties.

In the event of failure to reach a solution by any of the above peaceful means, the parties to a dispute will continue to seek a mutually agreed way to settle the dispute peacefully.

Participating States, parties to a dispute among them, as well as other participating States, will refrain from any action which might aggravate the situation to such a degree as to endanger the maintenance of international peace and security and thereby make a peaceful settlement of the dispute more difficult.

### VI. Non-intervention in internal affairs

The participating States will refrain from any intervention, direct or indirect, individual or collective, in the internal or external affairs falling within the domestic jurisdiction of another participating State, regardless of their mutual relations.

They will accordingly refrain from any form of armed intervention or threat of such intervention against another participating State.

They will likewise in all circumstances refrain from any other act of military or of political, economic or other coercion designed to subordinate to their own interest the exercise by another participating State of the rights inherent in its sovereignty and thus to secure advantages of any kind.

Accordingly, they will, inter alia, refrain from direct or indirect assistance to terrorist activities, or to subversive or other activities directed towards the violent overthrow of the regime of another participating State.

### VII. Respect for human rights and fundamental freedoms, including the freedom of thought, conscience, religion or belief

The participating States will respect

human rights and fundamental freedoms, including the freedom of thought, conscience, religion or belief, for all without distinction as to race, sex, language or religion.

They will promote and encourage the effective exercise of civil, political, economic, social, cultural and other rights and freedoms all of which derive from the inherent dignity of the human person and are essential for his free and full development.

Within this framework the participating States will recognize and respect the freedom of the individual to profess and practise, alone or in community with others, religion or belief acting in accordance with the dictates of his own conscience.

The participating States on whose territory national minorities exist will respect the right of persons belonging to such minorities to equality before the law, will afford them the full opportunity for the actual enjoyment of human rights and fundamental freedoms and will, in this manner, protect their legitimate interests in this sphere.

The participating States recognize the universal significance of human rights and fundamental freedoms, respect for which is an essential factor for the peace, justice and well-being necessary to ensure the development of friendly relations and cooperation among themselves as among all States.

They will constantly respect these rights and freedoms in their mutual relations and will endeavour jointly and separately, including in cooperation with the United Nations, to promote universal and effective respect for them.

They confirm the right of the individual to know and act upon his rights and duties in this field.

In the field of human rights and fundamental freedoms, the participating States will act in conformity with the purposes and principles of the Charter of the United Nations and with the Universal Declaration of Human Rights. They will also fulfil their obligations as set forth in the international declarations and agreements in this field, including inter alia the International Covenants on Human Rights, by which they may be bound.

## VIII. *Equal rights and self-determination of peoples*

The participating States will respect the equal rights of peoples and their right to self-determination, acting at all times in conformity with the purposes and principles of the Charter of the United Nations and with the relevant norms of international law, including those relating to territorial integrity of States.

By virtue of the principle of equal rights and self-determination of peoples, all peoples always have the right, in full freedom, to determine, when and as they wish, their internal and external political status, without external interference, and to pursue as they wish their political, economic, social and cultural development.

The participating States reaffirm the universal significance of respect for and effective exercise of equal rights and self-determination of peoples for the development of friendly relations among themselves as among all States; they also recall the importance of the elimination of any form of violation of this principle.

## IX. *Cooperation among States*

The participating States will develop their cooperation with one another and with all States in all fields in accordance with the purposes and principles of the Charter of the United Nations. In developing their cooperation the participating States will place special emphasis on the fields as set forth within the framework of the Conference on Security and Cooperation in Europe, with each of them making its contribution in conditions of full equality.

They will endeavour, in developing their cooperation as equals, to promote mutual understanding and confidence, friendly and good-neighbourly relations among themselves, international peace, security and justice. They will equally endeavour, in developing their cooperation, to improve the well-being of peoples and contribute to the fulfilment of their aspirations through, inter alia, the benefits resulting from increased mutual knowledge and from progress and achievement in the economic, scientific, technological, social, cultural and humanitarian fields. They will take steps to promote conditions favourable to making these benefits available to all: they will take into account the interest of all in the narrowing of differences in the levels of economic development, and in particular the interest of developing countries throughout the world.

They confirm that governments, institutions, organizations and persons have a relevant and positive role to play in contributing toward the achievement of these aims of their cooperation.

They will strive, in increasing their cooperation as set forth above, to develop closer relations among themselves on an improved and more enduring basis for the benefit of peoples.

## X. Fulfilment in good faith of obligations under international law

The participating States will fulfil in good faith their obligations under international law, both those obligations arising from the generally recognized principles and rules of international law and those obligations arising from treaties or other agreements, in conformity with international law, to which they are parties.

In exercising their sovereign rights, including the right to determine their laws and regulations, they will conform with their legal obligations under international law; they will furthermore pay due regard to and implement the provisions in the Final Act of the Conference on Security and Cooperation in Europe.

The participating States confirm that in the event of a conflict between the obligations of the members of the United Nations under the Charter of the United Nations and their obligations under any treaty or other international agreement, their obligations under the Charter will prevail, in accordance with Article 103 of the Charter of the United Nations.

. . .

## 2. DOCUMENT ON CONFIDENCE-BUILDING MEASURES AND CERTAIN ASPECTS OF SECURITY AND DISARMAMENT

The participating States,
*Desirous* of eliminating the causes of tension that may exist among them and thus of contributing to the strengthening of peace and security in the world;
*Determined* to strengthen confidence among them and thus to contribute to increasing stability and security in Europe;
*Determined* further to refrain in their mutual relations, as well as in their international relations in general, from the threat or use of force against the territorial integrity or political independence of any State, or in any other manner inconsistent with the purposes of the United Nations and with the Declaration on Principles Guiding Relations between Participating States as adopted in this Final Act;
*Recognizing* the need to contribute to reducing the dangers of armed conflict and of misunderstanding or miscalculation of military activities which could give rise to apprehension, particularly in a situation where the participating States lack clear and timely information about the nature of such activities;
*Taking into account* considerations relevant to efforts aimed at lessening tension and promoting disarmament;
*Recognizing* that the exchange of observers by invitation at military manœuvres will help to promote contacts and mutual understanding;
*Having studied* the question of prior notification of major military movements in the context of confidence-building;
*Recognizing* that there are other ways in which individual States can contribute further to their common objectives;
*Convinced* of the political importance of prior notification of major military

manœuvres for the promotion of mutual understanding and the strengthening of confidence, stability and security;

*Accepting* the responsibility of each of them to promote these objectives and to implement this measure, in accordance with the accepted criteria and modalities, as essentials for the realization of these objectives;

*Recognizing* that this measure deriving from political decision rests upon a voluntary basis;

Have adopted the following:

*1. Prior notification of major military manœuvres*

They will notify their major military manœuvres to all other participating States through usual diplomatic channels in accordance with the following provisions:

Notification will be given of major military manœuvres exceeding a total of 25,000 troops, independently or combined with any possible air or naval components (in this context the word 'troops' includes amphibious and airborne troops). In the case of independent manœuvres of amphibious or airborne troops, or of combined manœuvres involving them, these troops will be included in this total. Furthermore, in the case of combined manœuvres which do not reach the above total but which involve land forces together with significant numbers of either amphibious or airborne troops, or both, notification can also be given.

Notification will be given of major military manœuvres which take place on the territory, in Europe, of any participating State as well as, if applicable, in the adjoining sea area and air space.

In the case of a participating State whose territory extends beyond Europe, prior notification need be given only of manœuvres which take place in an area within 250 kilometres from its frontier facing or shared with any other European participating State; the participating State need not, however, give notification in cases in which that area is also contiguous to the participating State's frontier facing or shared with a non-European non-participating State.

Notification will be given 21 days or more in advance of the start of the manœuvre or in the case of a manœuvre arranged at shorter notice at the earliest possible opportunity prior to its starting date.

Notification will contain information of the designation, if any, the general purpose of and the States involved in the manœuvre, the type or types and numerical strength of the forces engaged, the area and estimated time-frame of its conduct. The participating States will also, if possible, provide additional relevant information, particularly that related to the components of the forces engaged and the period of involvement of these forces.

*Prior notification of other military manœuvres.* The participating States recognize that they can contribute further to strengthening confidence and increasing security and stability, and to this end may also notify smaller-scale military manœuvres to other participating States, with special regard for those near the area of such manœuvres.

To the same end, the participating States also recognize that they may notify other military manœuvres conducted by them.

*Exchange of observers.* The participating States will invite other participating States, voluntarily and on a bilateral basis, in a spirit of reciprocity and goodwill towards all participating States, to send observers to attend military manœuvres.

The inviting State will determine in each case the number of observers, the procedures and conditions of their participation, and give other information which it may consider useful. It will provide appropriate facilities and hospitality.

The invitation will be given as far ahead as is conveniently possible through usual diplomatic channels.

*Prior notification of major military movements.* In accordance with the Final Recommendations of the Helsinki Consultations the participating States studied the question of prior notification of major military movements as a measure to strengthen confidence.

Accordingly, the participating States recognize that they may, at their own discretion and with a view to contributing to confidence-building, notify their major military movements.

In the same spirit, further consideration will be given by the States participating in the Conference on Security and Cooperation in Europe to the question of prior notification of major military movements, bearing in mind, in particular, the experience gained by the implementation of the measures which are set forth in this document.

*Other confidence-building measures.* The participating States recognize that there are other means by which their common objectives can be promoted.

In particular, they will, with due regard to reciprocity and with a view to better mutual understanding, promote exchanges by invitation among their military personnel, including visits by military delegations.

In order to make a fuller contribution to their common objective of confidence-building, the participating States, when conducting their military activities in the area covered by the provisions for the prior notification of major military manœuvres, will duly take into account and respect this objective.

They also recognize that the experience gained by the implementation of the provisions set forth above, together with further efforts, could lead to developing and enlarging measures aimed at strengthening confidence.

## II. *Questions relating to disarmament*

The participating States recognize the interest of all of them in efforts aimed at lessening military confrontation and promoting disarmament which are designed to complement political détente in Europe and to strengthen their security. They are convinced of the necessity to take effective measures in these fields which by their scope and by their nature constitute steps towards the ultimate achievement of general and complete disarmament under strict and effective international control, and which should result in strengthening peace and security throughout the world.

. . .

[The next section of the Final Act dealt with economic, scientific, technological and environmental cooperation. This was followed by a section setting out general principles for security and cooperation in the Mediterranean.]

. . .

## COOPERATION IN HUMANITARIAN AND OTHER FIELDS

The participating States,
*Desiring* to contribute to the strengthening of peace and understanding among peoples and to the spiritual enrichment of the human personality without distinction as to race, sex, language or religion,
*Conscious* that increased cultural and educational exchanges, broader dissemination of information, contacts between people, and the solution of humanitarian problems will contribute to the attainment of these aims,
*Determined* therefore to cooperate among themselves, irrespective of their political, economic and social systems, in order to create better conditions in the above fields, to develop and strengthen existing forms of cooperation and to work out new ways and means appropriate to these aims,
*Convinced* that this cooperation should take place in full respect for the principles guiding relations among participating States as set forth in the relevant document,
Have adopted the following:

### 1. *Human Contacts*

The participating States,
*Considering* the development of contacts to be an important element in the streng-

thening of friendly relations and trust among peoples,

*Affirming*, in relation to their present effort to improve conditions in this area, the importance they attach to humanitarian considerations,

*Desiring* in this spirit to develop, with the continuance of détente, further efforts to achieve continuing progress in this field,

*And conscious* that the questions relevant hereto must be settled by the States concerned under mutually acceptable conditions,

*Make it their aim* to facilitate freer movement and contacts, individually and collectively, whether privately or officially, among persons, institutions and organizations of the participating States and to contribute to the solution of the humanitarian problems that arise in that connexion,

*Declare their readiness* to these ends to take measures which they consider appropriate and to conclude agreements or arrangements among themselves, as may be needed, and

*Express their intention* now to proceed to the implementation of the following:

### (a) Contacts and Regular Meetings on the Basis of Family Ties

In order to promote further development of contacts on the basis of family ties the participating States will favourably consider applications for travel with the purpose of allowing persons to enter or leave their territory temporarily, and on a regular basis if desired, in order to visit members of their families.

Applications for temporary visits to meet members of their families will be dealt with without distinction as to the country of origin or destination: existing requirements for travel documents and visas will be applied in this spirit. The preparation and issue of such documents and visas will be effected within reasonable time limits; cases of urgent necessity – such as serious illness or death – will be given priority treatment. They will take such steps as may be necessary to ensure that the fees for official travel documents and visas are acceptable.

They confirm that the presentation of an application concerning contacts on the basis of family ties will not modify the rights and obligations of the applicant or of members of his family.

### (b) Reunification of Families

The participating States will deal in a positive and humanitarian spirit with the applications of persons who wish to be reunited with members of their family, with special attention being given to requests of an urgent character – such as requests submitted by persons who are ill or old.

They will deal with applications in this field as expeditiously as possible.

They will lower where necessary the fees charged in connexion with these applications to ensure that they are at a moderate level.

Applications for the purpose of family reunification which are not granted may be renewed at the appropriate level and will be reconsidered at reasonably short intervals by the authorities of the country of residence or destination, whichever is concerned; under such circumstances fees will be charged only when applications are granted.

Persons whose applications for family reunification are granted may bring with them or ship their household and personal effects; to this end the participating States will use all possibilities provided by existing regulations.

Until members of the same family are reunited meetings and contacts between them may take place in accordance with the modalities for contacts on the basis of family ties.

The participating States will support the efforts of Red Cross and Red Crescent Societies concerned with the problems of family reunification.

They confirm that the presentation of an application concerning family reunification will not modify the rights and obligations of the applicant or of members of his family.

The receiving participating State will take appropriate care with regard to employment for persons from other participating States who take up permanent residence in that State in connexion with family reunification with its citizens and see that they are afforded opportunities equal to those enjoyed by its own citizens for education, medical assistance and social security.

. . .

[Other parts of this section were designed to help resolve problems arising from marriages between citizens of different states, to ease restrictions on travel, and to permit international contacts of 'religious faiths, institutions and organizations'. Succeeding sections dealt with information, cultural cooperation, and educa-tional cooperation and exchanges. The latter section concluded:]

*National minorities or regional cultures.* The participating States, recognizing the contribution that national minorities or regional cultures can make to cooperation among them in various fields of education, intend, when such minorities or cultures exist within their territory, to facilitate this contribution, taking into account the legitimate interests of their members.

[In the last part of the Final Act the participating states declared their 'resolve to continue the multilateral process initiated by the Conference' and undertook to attend further meetings to promote the objectives of the Conference. The first such meeting was to be held at Belgrade in 1977.]

# Treaty between the United States and the Soviet Union on the limitation of strategic offensive arms ('SALT II'), Vienna, 18 June 1979

The United States of America and the Union of Soviet Socialist Republics, here-inafter referred to as the Parties,

Conscious that nuclear war would have devastating consequences for all mankind,

Proceeding from the Basic Principles of Relations Between the United States of America and the Union of Soviet Socialist Republics of May 29, 1972,

Attaching particular significance to the limitation of strategic arms and deter-mined to continue their efforts begun with the Treaty on the Limitation of Anti-Ballistic Missile Systems and the Interim Agreement on Certain Measures with Respect to the Limitation of Strategic Offensive Arms, of May 26, 1972,

Convinced that the additional measures limiting strategic offensive arms provided for in this Treaty will contribute to the improvement of relations between the Parties, help to reduce the risk of out-break of nuclear war and strengthen international peace and security,

Mindful of their obligations under Article VI of the Treaty on the Non-Proliferation of Nuclear Weapons,

Guided by the principle of equality and equal security,

Recognizing that the strengthening of strategic stability meets the interests of the Parties and the interests of interna-tional security,

Reaffirming their desire to take mea-sures for the further limitation and for the further reduction of strategic arms, having in mind the goal of achieving general and complete disarmament,

Declaring their intention to undertake in the near future negotiations further to limit and further to reduce strategic offensive arms,

Have agreed as follows:

*Article I.* Each Party undertakes, in accordance with the provisions of this Treaty, to limit strategic offensive arms quantitatively and qualitatively, to exercise restraint in the development of new types of strategic offensive arms, and to adopt other measures provided for in this Treaty.

*Article II.* For the purposes of this Treaty:

1. Intercontinental ballistic missile (I.C.B.M.) launchers are land-based launchers of ballistic missiles capable of a range in excess of the shortest distance between the northeastern border of the continental part of the territory of the United States of America and the north-western border of the continental part of the territory of the Union of Soviet Socialist Republics, that is, a range in excess of 5,500 kilometers.

2. Submarine-launched ballistic missile (S.L.B.M.) launchers are launchers of ballistic missiles installed on any nuclear-powered submarine or launchers of modern ballistic missiles installed on any submarine, regardless of its type.

3. Heavy bombers are considered to be:

(a) currently, for the United States of America, bombers of the B–52 and B–1 types, and for the Union of Soviet Socialist Republics, bombers of the Tupolev–95 and Myasishchev types;

(b) in the future, types of bombers which can carry out the mission of a heavy bomber in a manner similar or superior to that of bombers listed in subparagraph (a) above;

(c) types of bombers equipped for cruise missiles capable of a range in excess of 600 kilometers; and

(d) types of bombers equipped for A.S.B.M.s.

4. Air-to-surface ballistic missiles (A.S.B.M.s) are any such missiles capable of a range in excess of 600 kilometers and installed in an aircraft or on its external mountings.

5. Launchers of I.C.B.M.s and S.L.B.M.s equipped with multiple independently targetable reentry vehicles (MIRVs) are launchers of the types developed and tested for launching I.C.B.M.s or S.L.B.M.s equipped with MIRVs.

6. A.S.B.M.s equipped with MIRVs are A.S.B.M.s of the types which have been flight-tested with MIRVs.

7. Heavy I.C.B.M.s are I.C.B.M.s which have a launch-weight greater or a throw-weight greater than that of the heaviest, in terms of either launch-weight or throw-weight, respectively, of the light I.C.B.M.s deployed by either Party as of the date of signature of this Treaty.

8. Cruise missiles are unmanned, self-propelled, guided, weapon-delivery vehicles which sustain flight through the use of aerodynamic lift over most of their flight path and which are flight-tested from or deployed on aircraft, that is, air-launched cruise missiles, or such vehicles which are referred to as cruise missiles in subparagraph 1(b) of Article IX.

*Article III.* 1. Upon entry into force of this Treaty, each Party undertakes to limit I.C.B.M. launchers, S.L.B.M. launchers, heavy bombers, and A.S.B.M.s to an aggregate number not to exceed 2,400.

2. Each Party undertakes to limit, from January 1, 1981, strategic offensive arms referred to in paragraph 1 of this Article to an aggregate number not to exceed 2,250, and to initiate reductions of those arms which as of that date would be in excess of this aggregate number.

3. Within the aggregate numbers provided for in paragraphs 1 and 2 of this Article and subject to the provisions of this Treaty, each Party has the right to determine the composition of these aggregates.

4. For each bomber of a type equipped for A.S.B.M.s, the aggregate numbers provided for in paragraphs 1 and 2 of this Article shall include the maximum number of such missiles for which a bomber of that type is equipped for one operational mission.

5. A heavy bomber equipped only for A.S.B.M.s shall not itself be included in the aggregate numbers provided for in paragraphs 1 and 2 of this Article.

6. Reductions of the numbers of strategic offensive arms required to comply with the provisions of paragraphs 1 and 2 of this Article shall be carried out as provided for in Article XI.

*Article IV.* 1. Each Party undertakes not to start construction of additional fixed I.C.B.M. launchers.

2. Each Party undertakes not to relocate fixed I.C.B.M. launchers.

3. Each Party undertakes not to convert launchers of light I.C.B.M.s, or of I.C.B.M.s of older types deployed prior to 1964, into launchers of heavy I.C.B.M.s of types deployed after that time.

4. Each Party undertakes in the process of modernization and replacement of I.C.B.M. silo launchers not to increase the original internal volume of an I.C.B.M. silo launcher by more than thirty-two percent. Within this limit each Party has the right to determine whether such an increase will be made through an increase in the original diameter or in the original depth of an I.C.B.M. silo launcher, or in both of these dimensions.

5. Each Party undertakes:

(a) not to supply I.C.B.M. launcher deployment areas with intercontinental ballistic missiles in excess of a number consistent with normal deployment, maintenance, training, and replacement requirements;

(b) not to provide storage facilities for or to store I.C.B.M.s in excess of normal deployment requirements at launch sites of I.C.B.M. launchers;

(c) not to develop, test, or deploy systems for rapid reload of I.C.B.M. launchers.

6. Subject to the provisions of this Treaty, each Party undertakes not to have under construction at any time strategic offensive arms referred to in paragraph 1 of Article III in excess of numbers consistent with a normal construction schedule.

7. Each Party undertakes not to develop, test, or deploy I.C.B.M.s which have a launch-weight greater or a throw-weight greater than that of the heaviest, in terms of either launch-weight or throw-weight, respectively, of the heavy I.C.B.M.s deployed by either Party as of the date of signature of this Treaty.

8. Each Party undertakes not to convert land-based launchers of ballistic missiles which are not I.C.B.M.s into launchers for launching I.C.B.M.s, and not to test them for this purpose.

9. Each Party undertakes not to flight-test or deploy new types of I.C.B.M.s, that is, types of I.C.B.M.s not flight-tested as of May 1, 1979, except that each Party may flight-test and deploy one new type of light I.C.B.M.

10. Each Party undertakes not to flight-test or deploy I.C.B.M.s of a type flight-tested as of May 1, 1979 with a number of reentry vehicles greater than the maximum number of reentry vehicles with which an I.C.B.M. of that type has been flight-tested as of that date.

11. Each Party undertakes not to flight-test or deploy I.C.B.M.s of the one new type permitted pursuant to paragraph 9 of this Article with a number of reentry vehicles greater than the maximum number of reentry vehicles with which an I.C.B.M. of either Party has been flight-tested as of May 1, 1979, that is, ten.

12. Each Party undertakes not to flight-test or deploy S.L.B.M.s with a number of reentry vehicles greater than the maximum number of reentry vehicles with which an S.L.B.M. of either Party has been flight-tested as of May 1, 1979, that is, fourteen.

13. Each Party undertakes not to flight-test or deploy A.S.B.M.s with a number of reentry vehicles greater than the maximum number of reentry vehicles with which an I.C.B.M. of either Party has been flight-tested as of May 1, 1979, that is, ten.

14. Each Party undertakes not to deploy at any one time on heavy bombers equipped for cruise missiles capable of a

range in excess of 600 kilometers a number of such cruise missiles which exceeds the product of 28 and the number of such heavy bombers.

*Article V.* 1. Within the aggregate numbers provided for in paragraphs 1 and 2 of Article III, each Party undertakes to limit launchers of I.C.B.M.s and S.L.B.M.s equipped with MIRVs, A.S.B.M.s equipped with MIRVs, and heavy bombers equipped for cruise missiles capable of a range in excess of 600 kilometers to an aggregate number not to exceed 1,320.

2. Within the aggregate number provided for in paragraph 1 of this Article, each Party undertakes to limit launchers of I.C.B.M.s and S.L.B.M.s equipped with MIRVs and A.S.B.M.s equipped with MIRVs to an aggregate number not to exceed 1,200.

3. Within the aggregate number provided for in paragraph 2 of this Article, each Party undertakes to limit launchers of I.C.B.M.s equipped with MIRVs to an aggregate number not to exceed 820.

4. For each bomber of a type equipped for A.S.B.M.s equipped with MIRVs, the aggregate numbers provided for in paragraphs 1 and 2 of this Article shall include the maximum number of A.S.B.M.s for which a bomber of that type is equipped for one operational mission.

5. Within the aggregate numbers provided for in paragraphs 1, 2, and 3 of this Article and subject to the provisions of this Treaty, each Party has the right to determine the composition of these aggregates.

*Article VI.* 1. The limitations provided for in this Treaty shall apply to those arms which are:

(a) operational;

(b) in the final stage of construction;

(c) in reserve, in storage, or mothballed;

(d) undergoing overhaul, repair, modernization, or conversion.

2. Those arms in the final stage of construction are:

(a) S.L.B.M. launchers on submarines which have begun sea trials;

(b) A.S.B.M.s after a bomber of a type equipped for such missiles has been brought out of the shop, plant, or other facility where its final assembly or conversion for the purpose of equipping it for such missiles has been performed;

(c) other strategic offensive arms which are finally assembled in a shop, plant, or other facility after they have been brought out of the shop, plant, or other facility where their final assembly has been performed.

3. I.C.B.M. and S.L.B.M. launchers of a type not subject to the limitation provided for in Article V, which undergo conversion into launchers of a type subject to that limitation, shall become subject to that limitation as follows:

(a) fixed I.C.B.M. launchers when work on their conversion reaches the stage which first definitely indicates that they are being so converted;

(b) S.L.B.M. launchers on a submarine when that submarine first goes to sea after their conversion has been performed.

4. A.S.B.M.s on a bomber which undergoes conversion from a bomber of a type equipped for A.S.B.M.s which are not subject to the limitation provided for in Article V into a bomber of a type equipped for A.S.B.M.s which are subject to that limitation shall become subject to that limitation when the bomber is brought out of the shop, plant, or other facility where such conversion has been performed.

5. A heavy bomber of a type not subject to the limitation provided for in paragraph 1 of Article V shall become subject to that limitation when it is brought out of the shop, plant, or other facility where it has been converted into a heavy bomber of a type equipped for cruise missiles capable of a range in excess of 600 kilometers. A bomber of a type not subject to the limitation provided for in paragraph 1 or 2 of Article III shall become subject to that limitation and to the limitation provided for in paragraph 1 of Article V when it is brought out of the shop, plant,

or other facility where it has been converted into a bomber of a type equipped for cruise missiles capable of a range in excess of 600 kilometers.

6. The arms subject to the limitations provided for in this Treaty shall continue to be subject to these limitations until they are dismantled, are destroyed, or otherwise cease to be subject to these limitations under procedures to be agreed upon.

7. In accordance with the provisions of Article XVII, the Parties will agree in the Standing Consultative Commission upon procedures to implement the provisions of this Article.

*Article VII.* 1. The limitations provided for in Article III shall not apply to I.C.B.M. and S.L.B.M. test and training launchers or to space vehicle launchers for exploration and use of outer space. I.C.B.M. and S.L.B.M. test and training launchers are I.C.B.M. and S.L.B.M. launchers used only for testing or training.

2. The Parties agree that:

(a) there shall be no significant increase in the number of I.C.B.M. or S.L.B.M. test and training launchers or in the number of such launchers of heavy I.C.B.M.s;

(b) construction or conversion of I.C.B.M. launchers at test ranges shall be undertaken only for purposes of testing and training;

(c) there shall be no conversion of I.C.B.M. test and training launchers or of space vehicle launchers into I.C.B.M. launchers subject to the limitations provided for in Article III.

*Article VIII.* 1. Each Party undertakes not to flight-test cruise missiles capable of a range in excess of 600 kilometers or A.S.B.M.s from aircraft other than bombers or to convert such aircraft into aircraft equipped for such missiles.

2. Each Party undertakes not to convert aircraft other than bombers into aircraft which can carry out the mission of a heavy bomber as referred to in subparagraph 3(b) of Article II.

*Article IX.* 1. Each Party undertakes not to develop, test, or deploy:

(a) ballistic missiles capable of a range in excess of 600 kilometers for installation on waterborne vehicles other than submarines, or launchers of such missiles;

(b) fixed ballistic or cruise missile launchers for emplacement on the ocean floor, on the seabed, or on the beds of internal waters and inland waters, or in the subsoil thereof, or mobile launchers of such missiles, which move only in contact with the ocean floor, the seabed, or the beds of internal waters and inland waters, or missiles for such launchers;

(c) systems for placing into Earth orbit nuclear weapons or any other kind of weapons of mass destruction, including fractional orbital missiles;

(d) mobile launchers of heavy I.C.B.M.s;

(e) S.L.B.M.s which have a launch-weight greater or a throw-weight greater than that of the heaviest, in terms of either launch-weight or throw-weight, respectively, of the light I.C.B.M.s deployed by either Party as of the date of signature of this Treaty, or launchers of such S.L.B.M.s; or

(f) A.S.B.M.s which have a launch-weight greater or a throw-weight greater than that of the heaviest, in terms of either launch-weight or throw-weight, respectively, of the light I.C.B.M.s deployed by either Party as of the date of signature of this Treaty.

2. Each Party undertakes not to flight-test from aircraft cruise missiles capable of a range in excess of 600 kilometers which are equipped with multiple independently targetable warheads and not to deploy such cruise missiles on aircraft.

*Article X.* 1. Subject to the provisions of this Treaty, modernization and replacement of strategic offensive arms may be carried out.

*Article XI.* 1. Strategic offensive arms which would be in excess of the aggregate numbers provided for in this Treaty as well as strategic offensive arms prohibited by this Treaty shall be dismantled or destroyed under procedures to be agreed upon in the Standing Consultative Commission.

2. Dismantling or destruction of strategic offensive arms which would be in excess of the aggregate number provided for in paragraph 1 of Article III shall begin on the date of the entry into force of this Treaty and shall be completed within the following periods from that date: four months for I.C.B.M. launchers; six months for S.L.B.M. launchers; and three months for heavy bombers.

3. Dismantling or destruction of strategic offensive arms which would be in excess of the aggregate number provided for in paragraph 2 of Article III shall be initiated no later than January 1, 1981, shall be carried out throughout the ensuing twelve-month period, and shall be completed no later than December 31, 1981.

4. Dismantling or destruction of strategic offensive arms prohibited by this Treaty shall be completed within the shortest possible agreed period of time, but not later than six months after the entry into force of this Treaty.

*Article XII.* In order to ensure the viability and effectiveness of this Treaty, each Party undertakes not to circumvent the provisions of this Treaty, through any other State or States, or in any other manner.

*Article XIII.* Each Party undertakes not to assume any international obligations which would conflict with this Treaty.

*Article XIV.* The Parties undertake to begin, promptly after the entry into force of this Treaty, active negotiations with the objective of achieving, as soon as possible, agreement on further measures for the limitation and reduction of strategic arms. It is also the objective of the Parties to conclude well in advance of 1985 an agreement limiting strategic offensive arms to replace this Treaty upon its expiration.

*Article XV.* 1. For the purpose of providing assurance of compliance with the provisions of this Treaty, each Party shall use national technical means of verifica-

tion at its disposal in a manner consistent with generally recognized principles of international law.

2. Each Party undertakes not to interfere with the national technical means of verification of the other Party operating in accordance with paragraph 1 of this Article.

3. Each Party undertakes not to use deliberate concealment measures which impede verification by national technical means of compliance with the provisions of this Treaty. This obligation shall not require changes in current construction, assembly, conversion, or overhaul practices.

*Article XVI.* 1. Each Party undertakes, before conducting each planned I.C.B.M. launch, to notify the other Party well in advance on a case-by-case basis that such a launch will occur, except for single I.C.B.M. launches from test ranges or from I.C.B.M. launcher deployment areas, which are not planned to extend beyond its national territory.

2. The Parties shall agree in the Standing Consultative Commission upon procedures to implement the provisions of this Article.

*Article XVII.* 1. To promote the objectives and implementation of the provisions of this Treaty, the Parties shall use the Standing Consultative Commission established by the Memorandum of Understanding Between the Government of the United States of America and the Government of the Union of Soviet Socialist Republics Regarding the Establishment of a Standing Consultative Commission of December 21, 1972.

2. Within the framework of the Standing Consultative Commission, with respect to this Treaty, the Parties will:

(a) consider questions concerning compliance with the obligations assumed and related situations which may be considered ambiguous;

(b) provide on a voluntary basis such information as either Party considers necessary to assure confidence in compliance with the obligations assumed;

(c) consider questions involving un-intended interference with national technical means of verification, and questions involving unintended impeding of verification by national technical means of compliance with the provisions of this Treaty;

(d) consider possible changes in the strategic situation which have a bearing on the provisions of this Treaty;

(e) agree upon procedures for replacement, conversion, and dismantling or destruction, of strategic offensive arms in cases provided for in the provisions of this Treaty and upon procedures for removal of such arms from the aggregate numbers when they otherwise cease to be subject to the limitations provided for in this Treaty, and at regular sessions of the Standing Consultative Commission, notify each other in accordance with the aforementioned procedures, at least twice annually, of actions completed and those in process;

(f) consider, as appropriate, possible proposals for further increasing the viability of this Treaty, including proposals for amendments in accordance with the provisions of this Treaty;

(g) consider, as appropriate, proposals for further measures limiting strategic offensive arms.

3. In the Standing Consultative Commission the Parties shall maintain by category the agreed data base on the numbers of strategic offensive arms established by the Memorandum of Understanding Between the United States of America and the Union of Soviet Socialist Republics Regarding the Establishment of a Data Base on the Numbers of Strategic Offensive Arms of June 18, 1979.

*Article XVIII.* Each Party may propose amendments to this Treaty. Agreed amendments shall enter into force in accordance with the procedures governing the entry into force of this Treaty.

*Article XIX.* 1. This Treaty shall be subject to ratification in accordance with the constitutional procedures of each Party. This Treaty shall enter into force on the day of the exchange of instruments of ratification and shall remain in force through December 31, 1985, unless replaced earlier by an agreement further limiting strategic offensive arms.

2. This Treaty shall be registered pursuant to Article 102 of the Charter of the United Nations.

3. Each Party shall, in exercising its national sovereignty, have the right to withdraw from this Treaty if it decides that extraordinary events related to the subject matter of this Treaty have jeopardized its supreme interests. It shall give notice of its decision to the other Party six months prior to withdrawal from the Treaty. Such notice shall include a statement of the extraordinary events the notifying Party regards as having jeopardized its supreme interests.

Done at Vienna on June 18, 1979, in two copies, each in the English and Russian languages, both texts being equally authentic.

For the United States of America
JIMMY CARTER
President of the United States of America

For the Union of Soviet Socialist Republics
L. BREZHNEV
General Secretary of the C.P.S.U., Chairman of the Presidium of the Supreme Soviet of the U.S.S.R.

[The treaty was accompanied by a number of 'agreed statements' and 'common understandings'. Among documents accompanying the treaty were the following:]

## Protocol to the Treaty between the United States of America and the Union of Soviet Socialist Republics on the limitation of strategic offensive arms

The United States of America and the Union of Soviet Socialist Republics, hereinafter referred to as the Parties,

Having agreed on limitations on strategic offensive arms in the Treaty,

Have agreed on additional limitations

for the period during which this Protocol remains in force, as follows:

*Article I.* Each Party undertakes not to deploy mobile I.C.B.M. launchers or to flight-test I.C.B.M.s from such launchers.

*Article II.* 1. Each Party undertakes not to deploy cruise missiles capable of a range in excess of 600 kilometers on sea-based launchers or on land-based launchers.

2. Each Party undertakes not to flight-test cruise missiles capable of a range in excess of 600 kilometers which are equipped with multiple independently targetable warheads from sea-based launchers or from land-based launchers.

3. For the purposes of this Protocol, cruise missiles are unmanned, self-propelled, guided, weapon-delivery vehicles which sustain flight through the use of aerodynamic lift over most of their flight path and which are flight-tested from or deployed on sea-based or land-based launchers, that is, sea-launched cruise missiles and ground-launched cruise missiles, respectively.

*Article III.* Each Party undertakes not to flight-test or deploy A.S.B.M.s.

*Article IV.* This Protocol shall be considered an integral part of the Treaty. It shall enter into force on the day of the entry into force of the Treaty and shall remain in force through December 31, 1981, unless replaced earlier by an agreement on further measures limiting strategic offensive arms.

. . .

## Memorandum of Understanding between the United States of America and the Union of Soviet Socialist Republics regarding the establishment of a data base on the numbers of strategic offensive arms

For the purposes of the Treaty Between the United States of America and the Union of Soviet Socialist Republics on the Limitation of Strategic Offensive Arms, the Parties have considered data on numbers of strategic offensive arms and agree that as of November 1, 1978 there existed the following numbers of strategic offensive arms subject to the limitations provided for in the Treaty which is being signed today.

|  | U.S.A. | U.S.S.R. |
|---|---|---|
| Launchers of I.C.B.M.s | 1,054 | 1,398 |
| Fixed launchers of I.C.B.M.s | 1,054 | 1,398 |
| Launchers of I.C.B.M.s equipped with MIRVs | 550 | 576 |
| Launchers of S.L.B.M.s | 656 | 950 |
| Launchers of S.L.B.M.s equipped with MIRVs | 496 | 128 |
| Heavy bombers | 574 | 156 |
| Heavy bombers equipped for cruise missiles capable of a range in excess of 600 kilometers | 0 | 0 |
| Heavy bombers equipped only for A.S.B.M.s | 0 | 0 |
| A.S.B.M.s | 0 | 0 |
| A.S.B.M.s equipped with MIRVs | 0 | 0 |

At the time of entry into force of the Treaty the Parties will update the above agreed data in the categories listed in this Memorandum.

. . .

## Joint statement of principles and basic guidelines for subsequent negotiations on the limitation of strategic arms

The United States of America and the Union of Soviet Socialist Republics, hereinafter referred to as the Parties,

Having concluded the Treaty on the Limitation of Strategic Offensive Arms,

Reaffirming that the strengthening of strategic stability meets the interests of the Parties and the interests of international security,

Convinced that early agreement on the

further limitation and further reduction of strategic arms would serve to strengthen international peace and security and to reduce the risk of outbreak of nuclear war,

Have agreed as follows:

*First.* The Parties will continue to pursue negotiations, in accordance with the principle of equality and equal security, on measures for the further limitation and reduction in the numbers of strategic arms, as well as for their further qualitative limitation.

In furtherance of existing agreements between the Parties on the limitation and reduction of strategic arms, the Parties will continue, for the purposes of reducing and averting the risk of outbreak of nuclear war, to seek measures to strengthen strategic stability by, among other things, limitations on strategic offensive arms most destabilizing to the strategic balance and by measures to reduce and to avert the risk of surprise attack.

*Second.* Further limitations and reductions of strategic arms must be subject to adequate verification by national technical means, using additionally, as appropriate, cooperative measures contributing to the effectiveness of verification by national technical means. The Parties will seek to strengthen verification and to perfect the operation of the Standing Consultative Commission in order to promote assurance of compliance with the obligations assumed by the Parties.

*Third.* The Parties shall pursue in the course of these negotiations, taking into consideration factors that determine the strategic situation, the following objectives:

1. significant and substantial reductions in the numbers of strategic offensive arms;

2. qualitative limitations on strategic offensive arms, including restrictions on the development, testing, and deployment of new types of strategic offensive arms and on the modernization of existing strategic offensive arms;

3. resolution of the issues included in the Protocol to the Treaty Between the United States of America and the Union of Soviet Socialist Republics on the Limita-

tion of Strategic Offensive Arms in the context of the negotiations relating to the implementation of the principles and objectives set out herein.

*Fourth.* The Parties will consider other steps to ensure and enhance strategic stability, to ensure the equality and equal security of the Parties, and to implement the above principles and objectives. Each Party will be free to raise any issue relative to the further limitation of strategic arms. The Parties will also consider further joint measures, as appropriate, to strengthen international peace and security and to reduce the risk of outbreak of nuclear war.

Vienna, June 18, 1979

## Soviet Backfire statement (and U.S. response)

On June 16, 1979, President Brezhnev handed President Carter the following written statement:

'The Soviet side informs the U.S. side that the Soviet "Tu-22M" airplane, called "Backfire" in the U.S.A., is a medium-range bomber, and that it does not intend to give this airplane the capability of operating at intercontinental distances. In this connection, the Soviet side states that it will not increase the radius of action of this airplane in such a way as to enable it to strike targets on the territory of the U.S.A. Nor does it intend to give it such a capability in any other manner, including by in-flight refueling. At the same time, the Soviet side states that it will not increase the production rate of this airplane as compared to the present rate.'

President Brezhnev confirmed that the Soviet Backfire production rate would not exceed 30 per year.

President Carter stated that the United States enters into the SALT II Agreement on the basis of the commitments contained in the Soviet statement and that it considers the carrying out of these commitments to be essential to the obligations assumed under the Treaty.

[The SALT II Agreement was not ratified by the United States.]

## The dwindling of détente, 1980–6

The failure of the United States to ratify the SALT II agreement marked an end to the decade-long period of superpower détente agreements. The invasion of Afghanistan and the Soviet opposition to the Solidarity trade union upsurge in Poland rendered public and Congressional opinion in the United States in the early 1980s much more suspicious of the intentions of the Soviet Union and wary of the alleged advantages of détente. The election of Ronald Reagan to the presidency in November 1980 brought into office the following January an Administration which was much more hard-line in its approach to nearly all aspects of relations with the other superpower.

From November 1980 until September 1983 a second follow-up meeting to the Helsinki conference took place, this time at Madrid. *The concluding document of the Madrid meeting of the Conference on Security and Cooperation in Europe was agreed by the thirty-five participating States on 9 September 1983.* The document recorded that 'different and at times contradictory opinions were expressed as to the degree of implementation of the Final Act reached so far by participating States'. The United States used the conference as a platform from which to castigate the Soviet Union for what the U.S. Secretary of State, George Shultz, termed 'blatant acts of Soviet defiance against the spirit and the letter of the Helsinki accords'.

During President Reagan's first term in office no summit meeting took place with the Soviet leadership and no important agreements were signed between the superpowers. The only significant exception was a *Soviet–American memorandum of understanding on the direct communications link, 17 July 1984,* which provided for an improved technological basis (using artificial satellites) for the 'hot line'. Arms control talks continued at intervals, but without achieving much progress. On the other hand, both superpowers continued to observe the SALT II limitations on a voluntary basis, in spite of the non-ratification of the treaty by the U.S.

With the opening of President Reagan's second term in January 1985, some small signs of an easing of tension appeared. In November 1985 Reagan met the new Soviet leader, Mikhail Gorbachev, at a summit conference in Geneva: a minor agreement on cultural and scientific exchanges resulted, but otherwise nothing was achieved. A further minor agreement between the U.S.A. and the U.S.S.R. concerning nuclear safety was signed on 22 August 1986: this provided for reciprocal on-site inspections of selected atomic research stations. In the following month the atmosphere was improved by an exchange of alleged spies between the two superpowers and by the conclusion of a more substantive accord on European security issues. *The Final Act of the Conference on Confidence- and Security-Building Measures and Disarmament in Europe was agreed at Stockholm and formally dated 19 September 1986* (p. 482). In fact, since agreement on the terms of the Final Act had not been reached by the deadline on 19 September, the conference clock was stopped while delegates consulted with each other and with their Governments. The clock remained stuck at 10.59 p.m. from Friday 19 September until the morning of Monday 22 September (the weekend was called the 'longest day in diplomatic history'). Unlike the earlier Helsinki follow-up meetings in Belgrade and Madrid, the Stockholm meeting did achieve some advances beyond what had been agreed at Helsinki. The Stockholm agreement laid down precise guidelines for the prior notification of military activities in Europe and for the exchange of military observers.

Hopes aroused by these agreements were, however, dimmed by the failure of a second meeting between Reagan and Gorbachev, at Reykjavik in October 1986. Although some progress towards arms accords appeared to have been made, the Soviet sticking-point seemed to be the determination of the United States to continue with research on a space-based anti-missile defence programme (the so-called Strategic Defense Initiative, popularly dubbed 'Star Wars'). Each side charged the other with breaching the 1972 A.B.M. treaty, and the Soviet Union appeared to make any further agreement on arms control conditional on abandonment of 'Star Wars'. President Reagan had already announced in May 1986 that the United States would no longer regard itself as bound by the terms of SALT II in making decisions on strategic weapons. Meanwhile research on S.D.I. went ahead at full speed, and agreements were concluded with Britain, West Germany, Italy, and Israel (as well as an arrangement with Japan) for participation by those countries in the programme. On 28 November 1986, the U.S. announced that it had actually exceeded the SALT II treaty limits. On 5 May 1987 U.S. and Soviet negotiators agreed on a draft accord to establish 'risk reduction centers' to diminish the danger of war arising from 'miscalculation' or 'misunderstanding'. By the summer of 1987 the U.S. and U.S.S.R. appeared to have inched close to an agreement on reducing medium- and short-range nuclear missiles in Europe. Whether all this was 'brinkmanship' heralding a lurch forward to a new series of arms control agreements, or whether it betokened rather the collapse of what remained of the flimsy edifice of détente – this central question remained unanswered in July 1987 (when this book went to press).

# Final Act of the Conference on Confidence- and Security-Building Measures and Disarmament in Europe, Stockholm, 19 September 1986

## I. Prior notification of certain military activities

The participating States will give notification in writing through diplomatic channels in an agreed form of content, to all other participating States 42 days or more in advance of the start of notifiable military activities in the zone of application for C.S.B.M.s [Confidence- and Security-Building Measures].

Notification will be given by the participating State on whose territory the activity in question is planned to take place even if the forces of that State are not engaged in the activity or their strength is below the notifiable level. This will not relieve other participating States of their obligation to give notification, if their involvement in the planned military activity reaches the notifiable level.

Each of the following military activities in the field conducted as a single activity in the zone of application for C.S.B.M.s at or above the levels defined below, will be notified:

The engagement of formations of land forces of the participating States in the same exercise activity conducted under a single operational command independently or in combination with any possible air or naval components.

This military activity will be subject to notification whenever it involves at any time during the activity:

at least 13,000 troops, including support troops, or
● at least 300 battle tanks
● if organized into a divisional structure or at least two brigades/regiments, not necessarily subordinate to the same division.

The participation of air forces of the participating States will be included in the notification if it is foreseen that in the course of the activity 200 or more sorties by aircraft, excluding helicopters, will be flown.

The engagement of military forces either in an amphibious landing or in a parachute assault by airborne forces in the zone of application for C.S.B.M.s.

These military activities will be subject to notification whenever the amphibious landing involves at least 3,000 troops or whenever the parachute drop involves at least 3,000 troops.

The engagement of formations of land forces of the participating States in a transfer from outside the zone of application for C.S.B.M.s to arrival points in the zone, or from inside the zone of application for C.S.B.M.s to points of concentration in the zone, to participate in a notifiable exercise activity or to be concentrated.

The arrival or concentration of these forces will be subject to notification whenever it involves, at any time during the activity:
● at least 13,000 troops, including support troops, or
● at least 300 battle tanks
● if organized into a divisional structure or at least two brigades/regiments, not necessarily subordinate to the same division.

Forces which have been transferred into the zone will be subject to all provisions of agreed C.S.B.M.s when they depart their arrival points to participate in a notifiable exercise activity or to be concentrated within the zone of application for C.S.B.M.s.

Notifiable military activities carried out without advance notice to the troops involved, are exceptions to the requirement for prior notification to be made 42 days in advance.

Notification of such activities, above the agreed thresholds, will be given at the time the troops involved commence such activities.

Notification will be given in writing of each notifiable military activity in the following agreed form:

[A] GENERAL INFORMATION

The designation of the military activity;

The general purpose of the military activity;

The names of the States involved in the military activity;

The level of command, organizing and commanding the military activity;

The start and end dates of the military activity.

[B] INFORMATION ON DIFFERENT TYPES OF NOTIFIABLE MILITARY ACTIVITIES:

The engagement of land forces of the participating States in the same exercise activity conducted under a single operational command independently or in combination with any possible air or naval components:

The total number of troops taking part in the military activity (i.e., ground troops, amphibious troops, airmobile and airborne troops) and the number of troops participating for each State involved, if applicable;

Number and type of divisions participating for each State;

The total number of battle tanks for each State and the total number of anti-tank guided missile launchers mounted on armoured vehicles;

The total number of artillery pieces and multiple rocket launchers (100 mm calibre or above);

The total number of helicopters, by category;

Envisaged number of sorties by aircraft, excluding helicopters;

Purpose of air missions;

Categories of aircraft involved;

The level of command, organizing and commanding the air force participation;

Naval ship-to-shore gunfire;

Indication of other naval ship-to-shore support;

The level of command, organizing and commanding the naval force participation.

The engagement of military forces either in an amphibious landing or in a parachute assault by airborne forces in the zone of application for C.S.B.M.s:

The total number of amphibious troops involved in notifiable amphibious landings, and/or the total number of airborne troops involved in notifiable parachute assaults;

In the case of a notifiable amphibious landing, the point or points of embarkation, if in the zone of application for C.S.B.M.s.

The engagement of formations of land forces of the participating States in a transfer from outside the zone of application for C.S.B.M.s to arrival points in the zone, or from inside the zone of application for C.S.B.M.s to points of concentration in the zone, to participate in a notifiable exercise activity or to be concentrated.

The total number of troops transferred;

Number and type of divisions participating in the transfer;

The total number of battle tanks participating in a notifiable arrival or concentration;

Geographical coordinates for the points of arrival and for the points of concentration.

[C] THE ENVISAGED AREA AND TIMEFRAME OF THE ACTIVITY:

The area of the military activity delimited by geographic features together with geographic coordinates, as appropriate;

The start and end dates of each phase (transfers, deployment, concentration of forces, active exercise phase, recovery phase) of activities in the zone of application for C.S.B.M.s of participating formations, the tactical purpose and corresponding geographical areas (delimited by geographical coordinates) for each phase;

[D] OTHER INFORMATION:

Changes, if any, in relation to information provided in the annual calendar regarding the activity;

Relationship of the activity to other notifiable activities.

## II. Observation of certain military activities

The participating States will invite observers from all other participating States to the following notifiable military activities:

• The engagement of formations of land forces of the participating States in the same exercise activity conducted under a single operational command independently or in combination with any possible air or naval components.

• The engagement of military forces either in an amphibious landing or in a parachute assault by airborne forces in the zone of application for C.S.B.M.s.

• In the case of the engagement of formations of land forces of the participating States in a transfer from outside the zone of application for C.S.B.M.s to arrival points in the zone, or from inside the zone of application for C.S.B.M.s to points of concentration in the zone, to participate in a notifiable exercise activity or to be concentrated, the concentration of these forces. Forces which have been transferred into the zone will be subject to all provisions of agreed confidence- and security-building measures when they depart their arrival points to participate in a notifiable exercise activity or to be concentrated within the zone of application for C.S.B.M.s.

The above-mentioned activities will be subject to observation whenever the number of troops engaged meets or exceeds 17,000 troops, except in the case of either an amphibious landing or a parachute assault by airborne forces, which will be subject to observation whenever the number of troops engaged meets or exceeds 5,000 troops.

The host State will extend the invitations in writing through diplomatic channels to all other participating States at the time of notification. The host State will be the participating State on whose territory the notified activity will take place.

The host State may delegate some of its responsibilities as host to another participating State engaged in the military activity on the territory of the host State. In such cases, the host State will specify the allocation of responsibilities in its invitation to observe the activity.

Each participating State may send up to two observers to the military activity to be observed.

The invited State may decide whether to send military and/or civilian observers, including members of its personnel accredited to the host State. Military observers will, normally, wear their uniforms and insignia while performing their tasks.

Replies to the invitation will be given in writing not later than 21 days after the issue of the invitation.

The participating States accepting an invitation will provide the names and ranks of their observers in their reply to the invitation. If the invitation is not accepted in time, it will be assumed that no observers will be sent.

Together with the invitation the host State will provide a general observation program, including the following information:

• the date, time and place of assembly of observers;

• planned duration of the observation program;

• languages to be used in interpretation and/or translation;

• arrangements for board, lodging and transportation of the observers;

• arrangements for observation equipment which will be issued to the observers by the host State;

• possible authorization by the host State of the use of special equipment that the observers may bring with them;

• arrangements for special clothing to be issued to the observers because of weather or environmental factors.

The observers may make requests with regard to the observation program. The host State will, if possible, accede to them.

The host State will determine a duration of observation which permits the observers to observe a notifiable military activity from the time that agreed... thresholds are met or exceeded until, for the last time during the activity, the... thresholds are no longer met.

The host State will provide the observers with transportation to the area of the notified activity and back. This transportation will be provided from either the capital or another suitable location to be announced in the invitation, so that the observers are in position before the start of the observation program.

The invited State will cover the travel expenses for its observers to the capital, or another suitable location specified in the invitation, of the host State, and back.

The observers will be provided equal treatment and offered equal opportunities to carry out their functions.

The observers will be granted, during their mission, the privileges and immunities accorded to diplomatic agents in the Vienna Convention on Diplomatic Relations.

The host State will not be required to permit observation of restricted locations, installations or defense sites.

In order to allow the observers to confirm that the notified activity is non-threatening in character and that it is carried out in conformity with the appropriate provisions of the notification, the host State will:

• at the commencement of the observation program give a briefing on the purpose, the basic situation, the phases of the activity and possible changes as compared with the notification and provide the observers with a map of the area of the military activity with a scale of 1 to not more than 500,000 and an observation program with a daily schedule as well as a sketch indicating the basic situation;

• provide the observers with appropriate observation equipment; however, the observers will be allowed to use their personal binoculars, which will be subject to examination and approval by the host State;

• in the course of the observation program give the observers daily briefings with the help of maps on the various phases of the military activity and their development and inform the observers about their positions geographically; in the case of a land force activity conducted in combination with air or naval components, briefings will be given by representatives of these forces;

• provide opportunities to observe directly forces of the State/States engaged in the military activity so that the observers get an impression of the flow of the activity; to this end, the observers will be given the opportunity to observe major combat units of the participating formations of a divisional or equivalent level and, whenever possible, to visit some units and communicate with commanders and troops; commanders or other senior personnel of participating formations as well as of the visited units will inform the observers of the mission of their respective units;

• guide the observers in the area of the military activity; the observers will follow the instructions issued by the host State in accordance with the provisions set out in this document;

• provide the observers with appropriate means of transportation in the area of the military activity;

• provide the observers with opportunities for timely communication with their embassies or other official missions and consular posts; the host State is not obligated to cover the communication expenses of the observers;

• provide the observers with appropriate board and lodging in a location suitable for carrying out the observation program and, when necessary, medical care.

The participating States need not invite observers to notifiable military activities which are carried out without advance warning to the troops involved unless these notifiable activities have a duration of more than 72 hours. The continuation of these activities beyond this time will be subject to observation while the agreed thresholds are met or exceeded. The observation program will follow as closely as practically possible all the provisions for observation set out in this document.

## III. Annual calendars

Each participating State will exchange, with all other participating States, an annual calendar of its military activities subject to prior notification, within the zone of application for C.S.B.M.s, forecast for the subsequent calendar year. It will be transmitted every year, in writing, through diplomatic channels, not later than 15 November for the following year.

Each participating State will list the above-mentioned activities chronologically and will provide information on each activity in accordance with the following model:

● type of military activity and its designation;
● general characteristics and purpose of the military activity;
● States involved in the military activity;
● area of the military activity, indicated by appropriate geographic features and/or defined by geographic coordinates;
● planned duration of the military activity and the 14-day period, indicated by dates, within which it is envisaged to start;
● the envisaged total number of troops engaged in the military activity;
● the types of armed forces involved in the military activity;
● the envisaged level of command under which the military activity will take place;
● the number and type of divisions whose participation in the military activity is envisaged;
● any additional information concerning, inter alia, components of forces, which the participating State planning the military activity considers relevant.

Should changes regarding the military activities in the annual calendar prove necessary, they will be communicated to all other participating States no later than in the appropriate notification.

Information on military activities subject to prior notification not included in an annual calendar will be communicated to all participating States as soon as possible, in accordance with the model provided in the annual calendar.

## IV. Constraining provisions

Each participating State will communicate, in writing, to all other participating States, by 15 November each year, information concerning military activities subject to prior notification involving more than 40,000 troops, which it plans to carry out in the second subsequent calendar year. Such communication will include preliminary information on each activity, as to its general purpose, timeframe and duration, area, size and States involved.

Participating States will not carry out military activities subject to prior notification involving more than 75,000 troops, unless they have been the object of communication as defined above. Participating States will not carry out military activities subject to prior notification involving more than 40,000 troops unless they have been included in the annual calendar, not later than 15 November each year.

If military activities subject to prior notification are carried out in addition to those contained in the annual calendar, they should be as few as possible.

## V. Compliance and verification

According to the Madrid Mandate, the confidence- and security-building measures to be agreed upon 'will be provided with adequate forms of verification which correspond to their content'.

The participating States recognize that national technical means can play a role in monitoring compliance with agreed C.S.B.M.s.

In accordance with the provisions contained in this document each participating State has the right to conduct inspections on the territory of any other participating State within the zone of application for C.S.B.M.s.

Any participating State will be allowed to address a request for inspection to another participating State on whose territory, within the zone of application for C.S.B.M.s, compliance with the agreed C.S.B.M.s is in doubt.

No participating State will be obliged to accept, on its territory within the zone of application for C.S.B.M.s, more than three inspections per calendar year.

No participating State will be obliged to accept more than one inspection per calendar year from the same participating State.

An inspection will not be counted if, due to force majeure, it cannot be carried out.

The participating State which requests an inspection will state the reasons for such a request.

The participating State which has received such a request will reply in the affirmative to the request within the agreed period of time, subject to the provisions contained in paragraphs (5 and 6 of this working document).

Any possible dispute as to the validity of the reasons for a request will not prevent or delay the conduct of an inspection.

The participating State which requests an inspection will be permitted to designate for inspection, on the territory of another State within the zone of application for C.S.B.M.s, a specific area. Such an area will be referred to as the 'specified area'. The specified area will comprise terrain where notifiable military activities are conducted or where another participating State believes a notifiable military activity is taking place. The specified area will be defined and limited by the scope and scale of notifiable military activities but will not exceed that required for an army level military activity.

In the specified area the representatives of the inspecting State accompanied by representatives of the receiving State will be permitted access, entry and unobstructed survey, except for areas or sensitive points to which access is normally denied or restricted, military and other defense installations, as well as naval vessels, military vehicles and aircraft. The number and extent of the restricted areas should be as limited as possible. Areas where notifiable military activities can take place will not be declared restricted areas, except for certain permanent or temporary military installations which, in territorial terms, should be as small as possible, and consequently those areas will not be used to prevent inspection of notifiable military activities. Restricted areas will not be employed in a way inconsistent with the agreed provisions on inspection.

Within the specified area, the forces of participating States other than the receiving State will also be subject to the inspection conducted by the inspecting State.

Inspection will be permitted on the ground, from the air, or both.

The representatives of the receiving State will accompany the inspection team, including when it is in land vehicles and on aircraft from the time of their first employment until the time they are no longer in use for the purposes of inspection.

In its request, the inspecting State will notify the receiving State of:

(a) the reasons for the request;

(b) the location of the specified area defined by geographical coordinates;

(c) the preferred point(s) of entry for the inspection team;

(d) mode of transport to and from the point(s) of entry and, if applicable, to and from the specified area;

(e) where in the specified area the inspection will begin;

(f) whether the inspection will be conducted from the ground, from the air, or both simultaneously;

(g) whether aerial inspection will be conducted using an airplane, a helicopter, or both;

(h) whether the inspection team will use land vehicles provided by the receiving State or, if mutually agreed, its own vehicles;

(i) information for the issuance of diplomatic visas to inspectors entering the receiving State.

The reply to the request will be given in the shortest possible period of time, but within not more than 24 hours. Within 36 hours after the issuance of the request, the inspection team will be permitted to enter the territory of the receiving State.

Any request for inspection as well as the reply thereto will be communicated to all participating States without delay.

The receiving State should designate the point(s) of entry as close as possible to the specified area. The receiving State will insure that the inspection team will be able to reach the specified area without delay from the point(s) of entry.

All participating States will facilitate the passage of the inspection teams through their territory.

Within 48 hours after the arrival of the inspection team at the specified area, the inspection will be terminated.

There will be no more than four inspectors in an inspection team. While conducting the inspection the inspection team may divide into two parts.

The inspectors and, if applicable, auxiliary personnel, will be granted during their mission the privileges and immunities in accordance with the Vienna Convention on diplomatic relations.

The receiving State will provide the inspection team with appropriate board and lodging in a location suitable for carrying out the inspection, and, when necessary, medical care; however, this does not exclude the use by the inspection team of its own tents and rations.

The inspection team will have use of its own maps, own photo cameras, own binoculars and own Dictaphones, as well as own aeronautical charts.

The inspection team will have access to appropriate telecommunications equipment of the receiving State, including the opportunity for continuous communica-

tion between the members of an inspection team in an aircraft and those in a land vehicle employed in the inspection.

The inspecting State will specify whether serial inspection will be conducted using an airplane, a helicopter or both. Aircraft for inspection will be chosen by mutual agreement between the inspecting and receiving States. Aircraft will be chosen which provide the inspection team a continuous view of the ground during the inspection.

After the flight plan, specifying, inter alia, the inspection team's choice of flight path, speed and altitude in the specified area, has been filed with the competent air traffic control authority the inspection aircraft will be permitted to enter the specified area without delay. Within the specified area, the inspection team will, at its request, be permitted to deviate from the approved flight plan to make specific observations provided such deviation is consistent with paragraph (12 of this working paper) as well as flight safety and air traffic requirements. Directions to the crew will be given through a representative of the receiving State on board the aircraft involved in the inspection.

One member of the inspection team will be permitted, if such a request is made, at any time to observe data on navigational equipment of the aircraft and to have access to maps and charts used by the flight crew for the purpose of determining the exact location of the aircraft during the inspection flight.

Aerial and ground inspectors may return to the specified area as often as desired within the 48-hour inspection period.

The receiving State will provide for inspection purposes land vehicles with cross country capability. Whenever mutually agreed, taking into account the specific geography relating to the area to be inspected, the inspecting State will be permitted to use its own vehicles.

If land vehicles or aircraft are provided by the inspecting State, there will be one accompanying driver for each land vehicle, or accompanying aircraft crew.

The inspecting State will prepare a report of its inspection and will provide a copy of that report to all participating States without delay.

The inspection expenses will be incurred by the receiving State except when the inspecting State uses its own aircraft and/or land vehicles. The travel expenses to and from the point(s) of entry will be borne by the inspecting State.

Diplomatic channels will be used for communications concerning compliance and verification.

Each participating State will be entitled to obtain timely clarification from any other participating State concerning the application of agreed C.S.B.M.s. Communications in this context will, if appropriate, be transmitted to all other participating States.

The participating States stress that these C.S.B.M.s are designed to reduce the dangers of armed conflict and of misunderstanding or miscalculation of military activities and emphasize that their implementation will contribute to these objectives.

Reaffirming the relevant objectives of the Final Act, the participating States are determined to continue building confidence, to lessen military confrontation and to enhance security for all. They are also determined to achieve progress in disarmament.

The measures adopted in this document are politically binding and will come into force on 1 January 1987.

The Government of Sweden is requested to transmit the present document to the follow-up meeting of the C.S.C.E. in Vienna and to the Secretary-General of the United Nations. The Government of Sweden is also requested to transmit the present document to the Governments of the non-participating Mediterranean States.

The text of this document will be published in each participating State, which will disseminate it and make it known as widely as possible.

The representatives of the participating States express their profound gratitude to the Government and people of Sweden for the excellent arrangements made for the Stockholm Conference and the warm hospitality extended to the delegations which participated in the Conference.

Stockholm, 19 September 1986

## Chairman's statement

It is understood that, taking into account the agreed date of entry into force of the agreed confidence- and security-building measures and the provisions contained in them concerning the time frames of certain advance notifications, and expressing their interest in an early transition to the full implementation of the provisions of this document, the participating States agree to the following:

The annual calendars concerning military activities subject to prior notification and forecast for 1987 will be exchanged not later than 15 December 1986.

Communications, in accordance with agreed provisions, concerning military activities involving more than 40,000 troops planned for the calendar year 1986 will be exchanged by 15 December 1986. Participating States may undertake activities involving more than 75,000 troops during the calendar year 1987 provided that they are included in the annual calendar exchanged by 15 December 1986.

Activities to begin during the first 42 days after 1 January 1987 will be subject to the relevant provisions of the Final Act of the C.S.C.E. [the Conference on Security and Cooperation in Europe, Helsinki 1975, p. 463]. However, the participating States will make every effort to apply to them the provisions of this document to the maximum extent possible.

. . .

## Chairman's statement

It is understood that each participating State can raise any question consistent with the mandate of the Conference on Confidence- and Security-Building Measures and Disarmament in Europe at any stage subsequent to the Vienna C.S.C.E. Follow-Up Meeting.

. . .

# Appendix · Multilateral Treaties on Human Rights and the Environment

Until the late nineteenth century most treaties were bilateral rather than multilateral. The main exceptions were treaties ending wars (such as the Treaty of Paris, ending the Napoleonic wars, signed on 30 May 1814 by Britain, Austria, France, Portugal, Prussia, Russia, Spain, and Sweden), treaties of alliance (such as the Holy Alliance treaty signed by Austria, Prussia and Russia on 14–26 September 1815 – and later by other States) or treaties of guarantee (such as the treaty guaranteeing Belgian independence and neutrality signed by Britain, Austria, France, Prussia, and Russia – as well as Belgium – on 19 April 1839). In the late nineteenth century, however, multilateral treaties, dealing with both political and other subjects, became more common. The twentieth century brought a further increase and the post-war period witnessed a veritable explosion of such treaties. In the period 1946–56 alone, more than 576 multilateral treaties were recorded by the United Nations. Some of the most important of such post-war multilateral treaties (such as the United Nations Charter) are printed in this volume; others (such as the Vienna Convention on the Law of Treaties) have been discussed briefly in the introduction; and others again have been mentioned in the course of this book. There remain, however, many multilateral treaties and agreements which have not been mentioned, since they do not fit conveniently into any of the geographical or thematic categories into which this book is divided; yet these are often of fundamental importance in diplomatic discourse. This appendix therefore outlines some of the most significant of these post-war multilateral treaties – those concerning human rights and the environment.

TREATIES CONCERNING HUMAN RIGHTS

In the area of human rights the fundamental document is the *Universal Declaration of Human Rights, 10 December 1948*. This draws on many sources, containing echoes, for example, of the English Bill of Rights (December 1689), the French Declaration of the Rights of Man and Citizen (26 August 1789), and the American Bill of Rights (15 December 1791). The 1948 declaration was adopted by the United Nations General Assembly as a 'common standard of achievement for all peoples and all nations'. It prohibited slavery and torture, as well as arbitrary arrest, detention, or exile. It affirmed the right to equality before the law, to privacy, to freedom of movement within and beyond the boundaries of each State, to asylum, to a nationality, to property ownership, to freedom of thought, conscience and religion, to freedom of expression, to freedom of assembly and association, to free choice of employment, to equal pay for equal work, to rest and leisure, to an adequate standard of living, to free education (at least at the elementary level), to social security, and to free participation in cultural life. It affirmed that 'everyone has the right to take part in the government of his country, directly or through freely chosen representatives' and that 'the will of the people shall be the basis of the authority of government', this to be 'expressed in periodic and genuine elections which shall be by universal and equal suffrage and shall be held by secret vote'. It declared that everyone was entitled to these rights 'without distinction of any kind, such as race, colour, sex, language, religion, political or other opinion, national or social origin, property, birth or other status'. Article 29 added that, in addition to all these rights, 'everyone has duties to the community in which alone the free and full development of his personality is possible'. A draft article, guaranteeing the right of petition (enshrined in the English Bill of Rights of 1689) was not adopted. A proposal for the inclusion of a reference in the text of the declaration to the rights of minorities was similarly rejected, although a note was attached to the declaration stating that 'the United Nations cannot remain indifferent to the fate [note 'fate' not 'rights'] of minorities'.

The declaration was adopted by the U.N. General Assembly by 48 votes to 0 with 8 abstentions. Unfortunately, both at the time of its adoption and ever since, most of the rights thus proclaimed have been withheld from the overwhelming majority of people on earth.

The abuse of human rights has been particularly blatant in all countries in time of war. In an effort to tame the bestiality of human conflict a number of international agreements have been concluded, constituting a corpus of international laws of war. The earliest of these in modern times was the *Geneva Convention for the Amelioration of the Condition of the Wounded in Armies in the Field, 22 August 1864*. This was followed by other agreements notably the *Declaration of St Petersburg to the Effect of Prohibiting the Use of Certain Projectiles in Wartime, 11 December 1868*; the *Hague Conventions, 29 July 1899 and 18 October 1907*, which banned aerial bombardment, submarine mines and poison gas; and the *Geneva Protocol for the Prohibition of the Use in War of Asphyxiating, Poisonous and Other Gases and of Bacteriological Methods of Warfare, 17 June 1925*. The most optimistic agreement ever signed in this area was the *Treaty Providing for the Renunciation of War as an Instrument of National Policy, 27 August 1928*, also known as the Kellog–Briand Pact (after its originators, the U.S. Secretary of State, Frank B. Kellog, and the French statesman, Aristide Briand). Sixty-five States eventually acceded to this treaty; most of these same countries were belligerents in the Second World War. Two agreements which had some (limited) effects in mitigating the horrors of warfare between 1939 and 1945 were, however, signed in 1929: the *Geneva Convention for the Amelioration of the Condition of the Wounded and Sick in Armies in the Field* and the *Geneva Convention relative to the Treatment of Prisoners of War, both signed on 27 July 1929*.

The unprecedented scale and viciousness of human-inflicted pain, misery and death between 1939 and 1945 evoked a major new attempt to create an internationally agreed framework for what was henceforth known as the law of armed conflicts. Four conventions agreed at Geneva in 1949 sought to create such a framework.

The *Geneva Convention for the Amelioration of the Condition of the Wounded and Sick in Armed Forces in the Field, 12 August 1949*, built on the experience of earlier such agreements since 1864. The convention accorded a recognized status to the International Committee of the Red Cross as an 'impartial humanitarian body'. The *Geneva Convention for the Amelioration of the Condition of Wounded, Sick and Shipwrecked Members of Armed Forces at Sea, 12 August 1949*, attempted to provide for naval forces protection similar to that provided for land armed forces in the first Geneva Convention. The *Geneva Convention Relative to the Treatment of Prisoners of War, 12 August 1949*, laid down conditions for the humane treatment of prisoners who were members of armed forces, militias, and (on certain conditions) 'organized resistance movements', as well as 'inhabitants of a non-occupied territory, who on the approach of the enemy spontaneously take up arms to resist the invading forces'. The *Geneva Convention Relative to the Protection of Civilian Persons in Time of War, 12 August 1949*, prescribed conditions of fair and humane treatment for civilians in war, particularly those in areas of armed conflict or in enemy-occupied territory.

The Geneva Conventions have been augmented by two additional protocols, adopted by a United Nations conference on 8 June 1977. These broadened the definition of 'international armed conflicts' to include 'armed conflicts in which people are fighting against colonial domination and alien occupation and against racist régimes in the exercise of their right of self-determination'. By February 1987 more than a hundred States had signed the Protocols, and more than forty had ratified them. The U.S., France, and Israel, however, were among States which refused to ratify one or both of the Protocols on the ground that the new formulation might give legal protection to terrorists. Another document which aroused Western opposition was U.N. General Assembly Resolution 1653 of 24 November 1961 which declared that 'the use of nuclear weapons is a direct violation of the Charter of the United Nations'. A *Convention on the Prohibition of the Development, Production, and Stockpiling of Bacteriological (Biological) and Toxin Weapons and on their Destruction* was opened for signature on *10 April 1972*. But in spite of the support it received from the two superpowers it was widely believed that they (and perhaps other States) continued with research into biological warfare.

The experience of the Second World War produced several international agreements relating to the apprehension, trial and punishment of persons guilty of committing war crimes. The mass murder of millions of Jews in Europe by the Nazis during the war gave rise in 1944 to the term 'genocide' (coined by a Polish–Jewish lawyer, Raphael Lemkin) to denote massacres of ethnic or other groups. *The Convention on the Prevention and Punishment of the Crime of Genocide* was adopted unanimously by the U.N. General Assembly on *9 December 1948*. The convention defined genocide as 'acts committed with intent to destroy, in whole or in part, a national, ethnical, racial or religious group'. (A proposal for the inclusion of 'political' groups was opposed by the Soviet and other delegates.) The majority of States signed and ninety-seven ratified the convention, but one signatory conspicuously refused for more than three decades to accord it ratification – the United States. President Truman transmitted it to the Senate for approval on 16 June 1949, but it languished in committee for years. From 1967 until 1986 Senator William Proxmire of Wisconsin rose in the Senate every morning that it was in session, without a single exception, and spoke in favour of ratification. He was opposed, however, by several conservative senators as well as by the American Bar Association (which reversed its position only in 1976). The Senate eventually decided to approve ratification (by 83 votes to 11) on 19 February 1986. This approval was, however, subject to a number of reservations. As of May 1987, however, Congress had still not completed the ratification process by enacting the necessary implementing legislation.

Other forms of violence have also been the subject of international agreements since 1945. A *Declaration on the Protection of All Persons from being Subjected to Torture and Other Cruel, Inhuman or Degrading Treatment or Punishment* was adopted by the U.N. General Assembly on *9 December 1975*. An *International Convention against the Taking of Hostages* was adopted by the General Assembly on *17 December 1979* (a few weeks after the seizure of American diplomats in Teheran). But the convention had depressingly little effect.

Social and political changes in the post-war period, including the retreat of the colonial powers and the rise of the feminist movement, produced a refashioning of many existing treaties as well as some wholly new agreements. A *Protocol*, signed at Lake Success, New York on *12 November 1947 amended two earlier conventions* (of 30 September 1921 and 11 October 1933) *concerning the suppression of the traffic in women and children*. A *Convention relating to the Status of Refugees* was signed at Geneva on *28 July 1951*, and augmented by a *Protocol* on *31 January 1967*. A *Supplementary Convention on the Abolition of Slavery, 7 September 1956*, followed many earlier international enactments on the subject, most notably the *Berlin Conference resolutions, 26 February 1885*, the *Brussels Act, 2 July 1890*, the *International Slavery Convention, 25 September 1926*, and an amending *Protocol, 7 December 1953*. An *International Covenant on the Elimination of all Forms of Racial Discrimination* was opened for signature on *7 March 1966*. An *International Covenant on Civil and Political Rights* and another *on Economic, Social and Cultural Rights* were opened for signature at the United Nations on *19 December 1966*. A *Convention on the Elimination of All Forms of Discrimination against Women* was adopted by 130 to 0 (with 10 abstentions – sex of abstaining delegates not recorded) by the U.N. General Assembly on *18 December 1979*.

TREATIES CONCERNING THE ENVIRONMENT

A United Nations Conference on the Human Environment, held at Stockholm in June 1972, and attended by representatives of 114 States, adopted a *Declaration on the Human Environment, 16 June 1972*. Proclaiming that 'man is both creature and moulder of his environment', the declaration enunciated twenty-six principles for the protection of 'the natural resources of the earth, including the air, water, land, flora and fauna and especially representative samples of natural ecosystems'. The document drew attention to the dangers of pollution and called for national and international action to preserve the environment. This declaration represented the culmination of more than a century of environmentalist propaganda – a century during which the pressures of massive population increase, of the growth of cities, of the clearing of forests and jungles, of the development of land, sea, and air communications, and of the expansion of industry had all reached levels which posed serious dangers to the survival not only of vegetable matter and animals but even of man himself.

Until the Second World War there were few international agreements concerning the environment – with the exception of treaties governing the extraction of mineral or other resources (such as coal, oil or fish) and those relating to communications (particularly at sea or through rivers, straits or other waterways). The post-war period produced a large number of agreements for the protection of flora and fauna and for the prevention of pollution. Recent technological developments have added new concerns which have resulted in treaties, most notably those dealing with outer space and with nuclear energy.

Among treaties seeking to protect animals, one of the earliest was the *International Convention for the Regulation of Whaling, 2 December 1946*. This agreement (which followed an earlier one signed in London on 8 June 1937) was concluded in Washington by seventeen States, including all those operating whaling fleets in the Antarctic region. The accord created an International Whaling Commission which limited whaling to certain months of the year and restricted (in some cases prohibited) the killing of certain species of whale. Whaling nevertheless continued and some types of whale came perilously close to extinction. Compliance with the Commission's restrictions, particularly by the whaling fleets of the U.S.S.R. and Japan, was difficult to enforce. (Nor, it must be said, did the whale itself cooperate fully: large numbers committed suicide by beaching themselves and resisting the efforts of dedicated environmentalists to refloat them.) The slogan 'save the whale' became a major element in the environmentalist crusade in the 1970s. By 1987, partly as a consequence of these efforts, and partly because of the serious depletion of whale stocks, compliance with the convention improved.

Disputes over fishing rights in seas produced a number of bilateral agreements in the post-war period (a notable example was the 'cod war' between Britain and Iceland which led to Anglo-Icelandic agreements on

11 March 1961 and 1 June 1976). But such accords were generally more concerned with the commercial sharing out of fishing grounds or catches rather than with protecting marine life for its own sake. The *Convention on Fishing and Conservation of the Living Resources of the High Seas, 29 April 1958* attempted to deal with these problems on an international level. Other multilateral agreements for the protection of flora and fauna include: the *Convention on Wetlands of International Importance Especially as Waterfowl Habitat, 2 February 1971*; the *Convention on Trade in Endangered Species, 3 March 1973*; the *Agreement on the Conservation of Polar Bears, 15 November 1973*, signed at Oslo by Canada, Denmark, Norway, the U.S.S.R. and the U.S.A.; the *Convention on Migratory Species, 23 June 1979*; and the *Final Act of the Conference on Conservation of Antarctic Marine Resources, 20 May 1980* which included a convention on the subject signed at Canberra on the same date.

The prevention of pollution of the sea and of rivers and lakes by industrial effluent or other causes (such as oil tanker spills) was the object of international agreements signed on 12 May 1954 and 11 April 1962 but these were found to be not fully effective. Following large-scale pollution of the British and French coasts by the oil tanker, *Torrey Canyon*, which ran aground off Land's End on 18 March 1967, as well as other such oil tanker spills, a *Tanker Owners Voluntary Agreement concerning Liability for Oil Pollution* (TOVALOP) was signed on *7 January 1969*. This document is of interest as an international agreement concluded not between national Governments but between multinational corporations (the original signatories were the seven major oil companies of the world). The agreement stated that disputes would be 'settled under the rules of conciliation and arbitration of the International Chamber of Commerce'; the 'governing law' was stated to be 'the laws of England'. This voluntary arrangement failed to solve the problem of marine pollution (exacerbated in the late 1960s and early 1970s by the construction of vast supertankers to transport oil, particularly from the Persian Gulf to Europe). A series of international agreements sought to solve this and related difficulties. The *Convention for the Prevention of Marine Pollution by Dumping from Ships and Aircraft* was concluded at Oslo on *15 February 1972*. A *Convention on the Prevention of Marine Pollution by Dumping of Wastes and Other Matter* was concluded on *29 December 1972*. A *Convention for the Prevention of Marine Pollution from Land-Based Sources* followed on *21 February 1974*. Meanwhile an *International Convention on Civil Liability for Oil Pollution Damage*, which was concluded at Brussels on 29 November 1969 but which did not enter into immediate effect, finally entered into force on 19 June 1975. These agreements were in large measure superseded in 1982 by the *Law of the Sea* (see below).

International cooperation in the field of atomic energy was given a symbolic priority by the United Nations General Assembly on *24 January 1946* with the passage of its first resolution. This called for the establishment of an *Atomic Energy Commission* which would supervise all nuclear energy activities throughout the world. The scheme was based on the 'Baruch Plan' (named after its originator, the American financier and statesman, Bernard Baruch) which enjoyed the support of the U.S.A., Britain, and Canada – but not of the U.S.S.R. Although the Commission came formally into being, the opposition of the U.S.S.R. rendered it ineffective and it quickly drifted into abeyance. The attempt to create an international framework of control of all nuclear materials thus failed. It was not until the 1960s that agreements were signed seeking to limit the testing and proliferation of nuclear weapons (see Chapter X) – and in neither sphere were such accords completely effective. The peaceful development of nuclear energy, on the other hand, was eventually provided with a system of international supervision. On *26 October 1956* an international conference at the United Nations headquarters approved the statute of the *International Atomic Energy Agency* which came into existence on 29 July 1957. Most member States of the United Nations became members of the I.A.E.A., whose objects were defined as 'to accelerate and enlarge the contribution of atomic energy to peace, health and prosperity throughout the world' and 'to ensure so far as it is able, that assistance provided by it or at its request or under its supervision or control is not used in such a way as to further any military purpose'. The agency concluded bilateral agreements with a large number of States providing for safeguards to ensure nuclear safety and to prevent the diversion of nuclear materials to non-peaceful uses. An example of such an accord was the *Agreement between the Soviet Union and the International Atomic Energy Agency on the Application of Safeguards in the U.S.S.R.*, signed at Vienna on *21 February 1985*. This document, in which the U.S.S.R. undertook to provide detailed information to the I.A.E.A. in the event of 'any accidental or unmeasured loss that might occur' and to submit to I.A.E.A. inspection of its peaceful nuclear energy plants, acquired a sudden currency in 1986 following the disastrous explosion at a nuclear plant at Chernobyl in the Ukraine; in spite of Western complaints of delay by the U.S.S.R. in providing necessary information, the U.S.S.R. did comply with its agreement with the I.A.E.A.

The first important agreement regulating activity in space was the

*Treaty on Principles Governing the Activities of States in the Exploration and Use of Outer Space, including the Moon and other Celestial Bodies, 27 January 1967*. This declared that 'outer space, including the moon and other celestial bodies, is not subject to national appropriation by claim of sovereignty, by means of use or occupation, or by other means'. The signatories undertook not to place nuclear weapons in orbit round the earth or anywhere else in space. On *22 April 1968* an *Agreement on the Rescue of Astronauts, the Return of Astronauts, and the Return of Objects Launched into Outer Space* was opened for signature at London, Moscow and Washington. A further *Agreement Governing the Activities of States on the Moon and other Celestial Bodies*, which expanded the provisions of the 1967 treaty, was appended to a U.N. General Assembly resolution on *5 December 1979* (without a vote) and opened for signature on 18 December 1979.

The most complex, and in many ways the most important, multilateral treaty concerning the environment to be concluded since the war was the *Law of the Sea Convention*, concluded under United Nations auspices on *10 December 1982*. The negotiations leading up to this agreement occupied nine years, beginning with a conference in December 1973. The treaty, which contains some four hundred articles, attempts to constitute a comprehensive legal régime for almost every aspect of human activity in relation to the sea, i.e. for more than two thirds of the surface of the earth. Among other matters the treaty enacts rules governing territorial waters (extending twelve miles from the coast of a State), free passage of vessels and planes, 'exclusive economic zones' (the exclusive right of each State to fish and other marine life up to 200 miles from its coast), straits, the continental shelf (this vitally important section grants exclusive rights to mineral and other resources in the shelf for 350 miles beyond the coast of each State), environmental protection, and arrangements for deep-sea mining of minerals on the ocean floor.

The Law of the Sea Convention was signed at Montego Bay on 10 December 1982 by representatives of 140 States. By 30 September 1985 a total of 156 signatories had acceded to the treaty, although only 24 (not including any of the great powers) had ratified it. Three major powers refused to sign: Britain, West Germany, and the United States. The European Community did sign, thus committing Britain and West Germany, but the Community's competence extended only to certain parts of the treaty (such as fishing) and not to others (such as deep-sea mining) to which non-signatories within the Community objected. In a statement on 10 March 1983 President Reagan reiterated the American refusal to sign 'because several major problems in the Convention's deep-sea bed mining provisions are contrary to the interests and principles of industrialized nations and would not help attain the aspirations of developing countries'. President Reagan added that the U.S. did accept many other provisions of the treaty and would act in accordance with those. At the same time he announced 'an exclusive economic zone in which the United States will exercise sovereign rights in living and non-living resources within 200 nautical miles of its coast. This will provide United States jurisdiction for mineral resources out to 200 nautical miles that are not on the continental shelf.' A statement issued on 23 April 1983 by the Soviet Government (which had itself abstained in an earlier vote on approval of the draft treaty) complained that the United States was 'showing its disregard for the collective opinion of the overwhelming majority of States' and that the U.S. proclamation of an exclusive zone extending for 200 miles from its coast (i.e. extending in some places *beyond* the continental shelf) was 'no more than an unseemly manoeuvre'. The non-universality of adhesion to the Law of the Sea, and its consequent embroilment in East–West polemics, cast a shadow over the treaty and placed in doubt some aspects of its enforcement. The document nevertheless remained a landmark in the effort to secure a codified international legal order.

# Sources for Treaty Texts

## Key to abbreviations

| | |
|---|---|
| Bevans | *Treaties and Other International Agreements of the United States of America 1776–1949*, compiled by Charles I. Bevans (12 volumes, Washington 1968–74). |
| BFSP | *British and Foreign State Papers* (London). |
| DDR | *Dokumente zur Aussenpolitik der Regierung der Deutschen Demokratischen Republik* (Berlin 1954). |
| ILM | *International Legal Materials*. |
| JNM | *The Arab–Israeli Conflict* edited by John Norton Moore (3 volumes, Princeton, N.J. 1974). |
| UNTS | United Nations Treaty Series (New York 1946–    ). |
| UST | *United States Treaties and Other International Agreements* (Washington D.C.). |

## 1945

Yalta Agreements, 11 February 1945   Bevans 3:1005
Pact of the Arab League, 22 March 1945   UNTS 70:248
Soviet–Yugoslav Alliance, 11 April 1945   BFSP 145:1177
Soviet–Polish Alliance, 21 April 1945   UNTS 12:391
Four-Power Declarations on Germany, 5 June 1945   Bevans 3:1140
United Nations Charter, 26 June 1945   UNTS 1:XVI
Potsdam Conference Protocol, 2 August 1945   Bevans 3:1207
Sino-Soviet Treaty, 14 August 1945   UNTS 10:334
World Bank Articles of Agreement, 27 December 1945   Bevans 3:1390
IMF Articles of Agreement, 27 December 1945   Bevans 3:1351

## 1947

Italian Peace Treaty, 10 February 1947    UNTS 49:3
Treaty of Dunkirk, 4 March 1947    UNTS 9:187
Pact of Rio, 2 September 1947    Bevans 4:559

## 1948

Soviet–Rumanian Alliance, 4 February 1948    UNTS 48:189
Brussels Treaty, 17 March 1948    UNTS 19:51
Soviet–Finnish Treaty, 6 April 1948    UNTS 48:149
OAS Charter, 30 April 1948    UNTS 119:4
Pact of Bogotá, 30 April 1948    UNTS 30:55

## 1949

North Atlantic Treaty, 4 April 1949    UNTS 34:243

## 1950

U.S.–Korea Agreement, 26 January 1950    UNTS 178:102
Sino-Soviet Alliance, 14 February 1950    UNTS 226:12
Tripartite Declaration on Near East, 25 May 1950    JNM 3:574
Poland–G.D.R. Agreement, 6 July 1950    DDR 1:341

## 1951

Paris Treaty establishing E.C.S.C., 18 April 1951    UNTS 261:140
ANZUS Treaty, 1 September 1951    UST (1952) 3:3420
Japanese Peace Treaty, 8 September 1951    UNTS 136:46
U.S.–Japan Security Treaty, 8 September 1951    UST (1952) 3:3329

## 1953

Panmunjom Armistice, 27 July 1953    UST 4:232
Anglo-Libyan Alliance, 29 July 1953    UNTS 186:185
U.S.–Korea Mutual Defense Treaty, 10 October 1953    UNTS 202:1956

## 1954

Geneva Agreements on Indo-China, 21 July 1954    BFSP 161:359;
    Cmd 9239
Balkan Pact, 9 August 1954    UNTS 211:237

SEATO Treaty, 8 September 1954    UNTS 209:28
Pacific Charter, 8 September 1954    UNTS 209:22
Anglo-Egyptian Agreement, 19 October 1954    UNTS 210:24
Agreement Terminating Occupation Régime in West Germany, 23 October 1954    UNTS 331:252
U.S.–China (Taiwan) Treaty, 2 December 1954    UNTS 248:214

## 1955

Baghdad Pact, 24 February 1955    UNTS 233:199
Warsaw Pact, 14 May 1955    UNTS 219:3
Austrian State Treaty, 15 May 1955    UNTS 217:223

## 1957

Treaty of Rome, 25 March 1957    UNTS 295:2

## 1959

U.S.–Iran Agreement, 5 March 1959    UST 10 (part 2):314
Antarctic Treaty, 1 December 1959    UNTS 402:71

## 1960

Stockholm Convention establishing E.F.T.A., 4 January 1960    UNTS 370:3
U.S.–Japan Security Treaty, 19 January 1960    UST 11:1632, 1652, 2160
Cyprus Guarantee Treaty, 16 August 1960    ILM 13:1259
Cyprus–Greece–Turkey Alliance, 16 August 1960    ILM 13:1254

## 1961

Alliance for Progress, 17 August 1961    OAS Official Record, 1961

## 1962

Evian Agreements on Algeria, 18 March 1962    ILM 1:214
Declaration on Neutrality of Laos, 23 July 1962    UST 14:1104

## 1963

OAU Charter, 25 May 1963   UNTS 479:39
'Hot Line' Agreement, 20 June 1963   ILM 2:793
Limited Nuclear Test Ban Treaty, 5 August 1963   UNTS 480:43

## 1964

U.S.S.R.–G.D.R. Alliance, 12 June 1964   ILM 3:754

## 1965

Singapore Independence Agreement, 7 August 1965   ILM 4:928

## 1966

British–Venezuelan Agreement, 17 February 1966   ILM 5:764

## 1967

U.A.R.–Jordan Defence Agreement, 30 May 1967   ILM 6:516

## 1968

Nuclear Non-Proliferation Treaty, 1 July 1968   UST 21:483
Soviet–Czechoslovak Treaty, 16 October 1968   ILM 7:1334

## 1970

Soviet–Czechoslovak Treaty, 6 May 1970   *Pravda*, 7 May 1970
U.S.S.R.–West German Treaty, 12 August 1970   ILM 9:1026
Polish–West German Treaty, 7 December 1970   ILM 10:127

## 1971

Soviet–Egyptian Treaty, 27 May 1971   ILM 10:836
Anglo-Argentine Agreement on Falklands, July–August 1971   UNTS
   825:145
Soviet–Indian Treaty, 9 August 1971   ILM 10:904

Four-Power Agreement on Berlin, 3 September 1971    ILM 10:895
U.S.–U.S.S.R. Agreements to Reduce Risk of Outbreak of Nuclear War, 30 September 1971    ILM 10:1172

## 1972

U.S.–Chinese Joint Communiqué, 28 February 1972    ILM 11:443
U.S.–U.S.S.R. Agreement on Cooperation in Space, 24 May 1972    ILM 11:766
A.B.M. Treaty, 26 May 1972    ILM 11:784
SALT I Agreement, 26 May 1972    ILM 11:791
U.S.–U.S.S.R. Agreement on Basic Principles, 29 May 1972    ILM 11:756
Simla Agreement, 3 July 1972    ILM 11:954
G.D.R.–West German Treaty, 21 December 1972    ILM 12:16

## 1973

Vietnam Peace Agreement, 27 January 1973    ILM 12:48
U.S.–Cuba Hijacking Agreement, 15 February 1973    ILM 12:370
Declaration of International Conference on Vietnam, 2 March 1973    ILM 12:370
West German–Czechoslovak Treaty, 11 December 1973    ILM 13:19

## 1974

Israel–Egypt Disengagement Agreement, 18 January 1974    ILM 13:23
Israel–Syria Disengagement Agreement, 5 June 1974    ILM 13:880
U.S.–Egypt Agreement, 14 June 1974    UNTS 967:137
Treaty Limiting Underground Nuclear Weapons Tests, 3 July 1974    ILM 13:906

## 1975

Iran–Iraq Treaty, 13 June 1975    ILM 14:1133
Helsinki Final Act, 1 August 1975    ILM 14:1293
Israel–Egypt Agreement on Sinai and Suez Canal, 4 September 1975    ILM 14:1450
Declaration of Principles on Western Sahara, 14 November 1975    UNTS 988:257

## 1976

Graeco-Turkish Agreement on Procedures for Negotiation of Aegean Continental Shelf Issue, 11 November 1976   ILM 16:13

## 1977

Panama Canal Treaties, 7 September 1977   ILM 16:1021

## 1978

China–Japan Peace Treaty, 12 August 1978   ILM 17:1054
Camp David Agreements, 17 September 1978   ILM 17:1463
Soviet–Vietnamese Treaty, 3 November 1978   ILM 17:1485
Soviet–Afghan Treaty, 5 December 1978   ILM 19:1

## 1979

Argentina–Chile Agreement on Papal Mediation in Beagle Channel Dispute, 8 January 1979   ILM 18:1
Vietnam–Cambodia Peace Treaty, 18 February 1979   ILM 18:394
Israel–Egypt Peace Treaty, 26 March 1979   ILM 18:362, 530
SALT II Agreement, 18 June 1979   ILM 18:1112
U.S.S.R–South Yemen Treaty, 25 October 1979   ILM 19:644
Zimbabwe (Rhodesia) Independence Agreement, 21 December 1979   ILM 19:387

## 1981

U.S.–Iran Hostage Crisis Settlement, 18–20 January 1981   ILM 20:223
U.S.–Haiti Agreement on Migration, 23 September 1981   ILM 20:1198
U.S.–Israel Memorandum of Understanding on Strategic Cooperation, 30 November 1981   ILM 20:1420
Agreement on Sinai Multinational Force, 3 August 1981   ILM 20:1190

## 1982

South Africa–Swaziland Security Agreement, 12–17 February 1982   ILM 23:286

## 1984

Agreement between Italy and Holy See, 18 February 1984    ILM 24:1589
South Africa–Mozambique Non-Aggression Agreement, 16 March 1984
    ILM 23:282
Argentina–Chile Treaty, 29 November 1984   ILM 24:1
Agreement on Future of Hong Kong, 19 December 1984    ILM 23:1366

## 1985

North Pacific Air Traffic Control Agreement, 29 July 1985    ILM 25:74
Anglo-Irish Agreement on Northern Ireland, 15 November 1985    ILM
    24:1579

## 1986

Stockholm Final Act, 19 September 1986 *New York Times*, 22
    September 1986

# Index

Page references in **bold** lettering refer to the texts of the treaties.